Christine Amann

Gregg Typing/Series Seven

TYPING
COMPLETE COURSE

ALAN C. LLOYD, Ph.D.
Director of Career Advancement, The Olsten Corporation, Westbury, New York

FRED E. WINGER, Ed.D.
Former Professor of Office Administration and Business Education, Oregon State University, Corvallis, Oregon

JACK E. JOHNSON, Ph.D.
Professor, Department of Office Administration/Business Education, East Texas State University, Commerce, Texas

REBECCA A. HALL
Department Chairperson for Business and Office Education, Centerville High School, Centerville, Ohio

PHYLLIS C. MORRISON, Ph.D.
Professor of Business and Business Education, Robert Morris College, Coraopolis, Pennsylvania

JOHN L. ROWE, Ed.D.
Late Chairperson of Business and Vocational Education, University of North Dakota, Grand Forks, North Dakota

GREGG DIVISION/McGRAW-HILL BOOK COMPANY

New York   Atlanta   Dallas   St. Louis   San Francisco   Auckland   Bogotá   Guatemala
Hamburg   Johannesburg   Lisbon   London   Madrid   Mexico   Montreal   New Delhi
Panama   Paris   San Juan   São Paulo   Singapore   Sydney   Tokyo   Toronto

Sponsoring Editors/Joseph Tinervia, Barbara N. Oakley
Editing Supervisors/Matthew Fung, Scott Kurtz, Gloria Schlein
Design Supervisors/Caryl Valerie Spinka, Sheila Granda
Production Supervisors/Frank Bellantoni, Laurence Charnow

Text Designer/Michaelis/Carpelis Design Associates, Inc.
Cover Designer/Studios South
Text Photographs/Corporate Studios Communications, Inc.
Text Illustrators/Helen Miner, Jon Weiman
Technical Studio/Burmar Technical Corp.

The equipment shown in the photographs on pages 3, 65, 128, 189, 251, 306, 362, and 417 was provided through the courtesy of J. P. Egan Co., IBM, The Mead Corporation, Olivetti Corporation, Royal Business Machines, Inc., and SCM Corporation.

Library of Congress Cataloging in Publication Data

Main entry under title:

Typing, complete course.

    Includes index.
    1. Typewriting—Study and teaching (Secondary)—
United States.   I. Lloyd, Alan C.
Z49.T957   652.3   81-17116
ISBN 0-07-038280-8   AACR2

Gregg Typing, Series Seven
Typing, Complete Course

1 2 3 4 5 6 7 8 9 0 JHJH 8 9 8 7 6 5 4 3 2 1

ISBN   0-07-038280-8

PREFACE

Series Seven is an exciting all-new edition of the famous *Gregg Typing* programs. Developed with the needs of students and teachers in mind, *Series Seven* offers all the text and workbook materials needed for a comprehensive, modern typewriting program. It also offers many exciting features that make *Series Seven* an effective instructional system.

PARTS OF THE PROGRAM

Designed to meet the needs of one-semester, one-year, or two-year courses of instruction, *Series Seven* offers a variety of student's textbooks and workbooks, as well as a special Teacher's Edition for each student's text:

Typing 1, General Course. The first-year *Gregg Typing* book offers 150 lessons of instruction. The first 75 lessons (one semester) are devoted to learning the keyboard and typing for personal use.

Typing 2, Advanced Course. The second-year *Gregg Typing* text includes a useful, comprehensive Reference Section for students. It also includes, of course, Lessons 151 through 300 of the *Gregg Typing* program.

Typing, Complete Course. Specially designed for the two-year program of instruction, the *Complete Course* text offers all 300 lessons from *Typing 1* and *Typing 2* in one binding.

Teacher's Editions. The three separate Teacher's Editions—one for each of the student's texts—include all the pages in the corresponding student's texts plus annotations intended only for the teacher. Each Teacher's Edition also includes a separate section of teaching methodology, as well as lesson-by-lesson teaching notes for all the lessons in that text.

Learning Guides and Working Papers. Four workbooks—one for each 75 lessons of instruction—provide not only the stationery and forms needed for all text jobs and in-baskets but also a variety of reinforcement and enrichment exercises correlated to the text copy and to the LABs (Language Arts for Business).

Instructional Recordings. The *Keyboard Presentation Tapes for Gregg Typing* are cassettes correlated to the textbook keyboard lessons in *Typing 1, General Course,* and in *Typing, Complete Course.*

Transparencies and Transparency Masters. These additional teaching tools are available to enhance the classroom presentation.

Resource Manual and Key. A complete key to all text jobs and projects (both in pica and in elite) is given in the *Resource Manual and Key.*

FEATURES OF GREGG TYPING, SERIES SEVEN

The *Series Seven* program incorporates many time-tested features from past editions of *Gregg Typing*; at the same time, it introduces innovative new features that both students and teachers will welcome. For example:

Diagnostic Exercises. Many timings utilize the Pretest/Practice/Posttest routine, which allows each student to diagnose areas in which additional skill development is needed. After taking a Pretest, students practice according to their specific needs (as diagnosed from the Pretest). After the Practice session, students take a Posttest, which enables them to see how the Practice session improved their skill.

Skill-Building Routines. In addition to the Pretest/Practice/Posttest routine, a variety of other skill-building routines are provided in the program. These routines help maintain student interest while developing the basic keyboarding skill.

Clinics. The Clinic that appears every sixth lesson is intended to strengthen skill development. Many of the Clinics use diagnostic routines.

Language Arts for Business (LABs). Concise, easy-to-understand LABs help students to review the basic uses of punctuation, capitalization, and abbreviations and to avoid the most common errors in using plurals, contractions, possessives, and so on. Students reinforce and apply the LAB rules as they type sentences and production assignments.

Cyclical Approach. In *Series Seven*, concepts are taught once and recycled several times, with each cycle building on the previous one and becoming progressively more complex. Each cycle is a "level," equal to half a semester. Thus the full two-year program includes eight levels—four per year.

Competency Checks. At the conclusion of each level of work, a Competency Check provides both the student and the teacher with an opportunity to check the student's level of performance. These Competency Checks may be used as informal or formal evaluations.

Tests. In the *Resource Manual and Key* are eight additional Competency Checks parallel to those in the text. These may be reproduced for classroom use as formal tests.

Information Processing. Word processing and data processing terminology and special applications are integrated into the text. Students, for example, format (and later fill in) form letters, type from simulated dictated copy, and prepare a procedures manual for a word processing center.

Decision-Making Exercises. To simulate real-life business experience, the *Series Seven* program includes many exercises that require students to make realistic "on-the-job" decisions. The complexity of the decisions to be made increases as students progress through the program.

Various Input Modes. Students will format letters, memos, and so on, from various input modes—for example, from unarranged copy, from handwritten copy, from rough draft, and from incomplete information.

The *Series Seven* program greatly reflects the comments, suggestions, and recommendations we received from many teachers, graduate students, and students throughout the country. We sincerely appreciate their contributions to the effectiveness of this publication. We especially thank all the teachers who participated in group sessions to discuss their needs and their students' needs, the teachers who reviewed the manuscripts that were developed as a result of the group sessions, the students who tested all our materials, and of course, the researchers who are continually helping to improve the teaching of typing. All have been instrumental in the development of *Series Seven*.

The Authors

CONTENTS

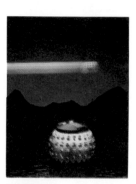

CONTENTS (Continued)

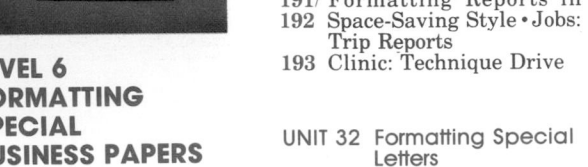

LEVEL 7
TEXT
PROCESSING

GOAL: 48/5'/3e

LEVEL 8
TEXT EDITING

GOAL: 50/5'/3e

SUPPLEMENTARY
MATERIAL

INDEX

INTRODUCTION

The *Series Seven* program has been specially designed to help you develop your typewriting skills through a carefully planned, step-by-step process. To be sure that you understand the terms, the proce-dures, and the directions used throughout this book, as well as the operation of the machine you are using, be sure to read this introduction and refer to it whenever you have any question or problem.

GLOSSARY OF TERMS

The special terms and symbols used throughout this text are very easy to un-derstand. Read the following glossary to be sure you know the meaning of the terms and symbols, and refer to the glossary whenever necessary.

GOAL STATEMENTS

Skill Goal. At the beginning of every unit, a skill goal is given—the goal you are aiming to achieve by the end of that unit. For example, the skill goal *To type 35/5/5e* means "to type 35 words a minute for 5 minutes with 5 or fewer errors."

Production Goal. At the beginning of every lesson, one or more production goals are given for that lesson; for example, "To format a report from handwritten copy." Production goals alert you to the kinds of activities that you will type in each lesson.

FORMATTING INSTRUCTIONS

A number of formatting terms and symbols are used to help you clearly understand the directions for completing each activity in *Series Seven.* The most commonly used terms and symbols and their meanings are given below.

Single spacing (or *double* or *triple spacing*) tells you how to set your typewriter for that particular lesson.

40-, 50-, 60-, or 70-Space line tells you the specific line length to use.

60P/70E indicates a 60-space line for type-writers with pica (P) type, a 70-space line for typewriters with elite (E) type.

5-Space tab tells you precisely where to set your tab stops for a particular lesson—in this case, 5 spaces from the left margin.

Arrows in production work are used as follows:

→ This arrow is used in some tables to show you the vertical center of your work.

↑3 Arrows with numbers tell you how many lines down the next line should be typed—in this case, 3 lines.

Standard format will be stated in the directions for letters, tables, and so on, once you have learned the standard format for these kinds of jobs. To refresh your memory of the standard format, page numbers are often provided; for example, "Standard for-mat (see page 209)."

Body 120 words tells you there are 120 words in the body of a letter. Knowing the approximate length of a letter will help you to adapt the standard format to position the letter on the page. Thus the number of words in the body of the letter is given to help guide you.

Workbook 86 indicates that a form or a letterhead for that specific job is provided in the *Learning Guides and Working Papers* workbook. If no workbook page is cited, then you are to use plain paper.

SKILL-BUILDING ROUTINES

Typewriting is a skill, and a skill is best developed through directed practice. *Series Seven* provides a variety of effective skill-building routines to improve the speed and the accuracy of your typing, including the following:

A variety of **Pretest/Practice/Posttest** routines is offered—all designed to improve either speed or accuracy through a proven, step-by-step procedure. First the *Pretest* (a 2-, 3-, or 5-minute timing) helps you identify your speed or accuracy needs. Having identified your needs, you then do the *Practice* exercises—a variety of intensive improvement drills. After you have completed the *Practice* exercises, you take a *Posttest*. Because the Posttest is identical to the Pretest, the Posttest measures your improvement.

12-Second timings are routines in which you take a series of short timings to boost speed or accuracy.

30-Second timings are slightly longer routines in which you take a series of short timings.

"OK" timings help you build accuracy on alphabetic copy (that is, copy that includes all 26 letters of the alphabet). You take three 30-second timings on the copy to see how many error-free copies you can type.

SCALES AND INDEXES

Series Seven uses a variety of scales and indexes designed to help you (1) measure quickly—with little counting—how many words you have typed, (2) analyze whether you should practice speed drills or accuracy drills, and (3) identify the relative difficulty of the copy you are typing.

Word Count Scales. You get credit for typing a "word" whenever you advance 5 spaces. Thus when you have typed a 60-space line, you have typed 12 words. To save you time, word counts that appear at the right of a timing tell you the cumulative number of words you have typed at the end of each completed line.

The scale shown at the right, for example, is used with timings that have 12 words a line. In production work, the scale at the right also gives you stroking credit for using the tabulator, for centering, and for other nonstroking movements.

	12
	24
	36
	48
	60

To quickly determine the words typed for *in*complete lines, use the scale that appears below each timing:

| 1 | 2 | 3 | 4 | 5 | 6 | 7 | 8 | 9 | 10 | 11 | 12 |

This scale quickly indicates the number of words typed. Just align the last word typed with the number on the scale.

When you take a 3- or 5-minute timing, use the speed markers (the small numbers above the copy) to quickly find your words-a-minute speed.

This special scale appears with 12-Second Timings:

| 25 | 30 | 35 | 40 | 45 | 50 | 55 | 60 |

It converts your typing speed during a 12-second timing into words-a-minute.

Practice Guide. In certain skill-building routines, you will use the following chart to find the drill lines you should type:

Pretest errors	0-1	2-3	4-5	6+
Drill lines	29-33	28-32	27-31	26-30

For example, if you made only 1 error in the Pretest, then the guide directs you to complete "Drill lines 29–33"; if you made 3 errors, you should complete "Drill lines 28–32"; and so on.

Syllabic Intensity (SI) Index. To indicate the relative difficulty of copy, syllabic intensity (SI) is often listed. The SI number is computed by dividing the number of actual words in the copy into the total number of syllables of all words. Thus 1.00 indicates copy that has one syllable per word; 1.50 indicates copy that has an average of one and a half syllables a word; and so on. The higher the number, the more difficult the copy.

LABs

Effective typewriting requires a knowledge of at least the basics of grammar, punctuation, and style. The *Series Seven* program provides Language Arts for Business (LABs) that offer concise, practical reviews and application exercises on punctuation, capitalization, and number use, for example. Thus you may review the most common language arts principles *as you type* sentences and production activities.

Before you start to type, take a few minutes to get to know the names, locations, and uses of the main parts of your typewriter. First, note whether you are using an electric or a manual machine. If you have an electric, decide whether you have a typebar machine similar to the one illustrated below or an element machine similar to the one shown on the next page. Now refer to the proper illustration as you take these steps for learning each machine part listed and described below and on the next page.

1. Read the description of the machine part.

2. Look at the drawing and note the location of the part.

3. Find the part on your machine—but do not operate it until instructed to do so. (The location of some parts varies from one make of machine to another.) If you cannot find a part quickly, ask your teacher or a classmate to help you find it.

BACKSPACE KEY. Moves the carriage or carrier backward one space at a time.

CARRIAGE (typebar only). Movable part of the machine that allows the typewriter to print across the page.

CARRIAGE RELEASE (typebar only). Frees the carriage so you can move it by hand.

CARRIAGE RETURN (typebar only). A lever (manual) or key (electric) used for returning carriage to left margin and advancing the paper for start of next line.

CARRIER (element only). Movable part of the machine that allows the typewriter to print across the page.

CARRIER RETURN (element only). Used for returning carrier to left margin and advancing the paper for start of next line.

ELEMENT (element only). Ball-like device that contains all the letters and symbols.

EXPRESS KEY (found on many element machines). Moves the carrier rapidly to the left without line spacing.

LINE SPACE SELECTOR. Controls space between lines of typing.

MARGIN RELEASE. Temporarily unlocks the margin.

MARGIN SCALE. Guides setting the margins (sometimes called *Carriage-Position Scale*).

MAIN PARTS OF A TYPEBAR MACHINE

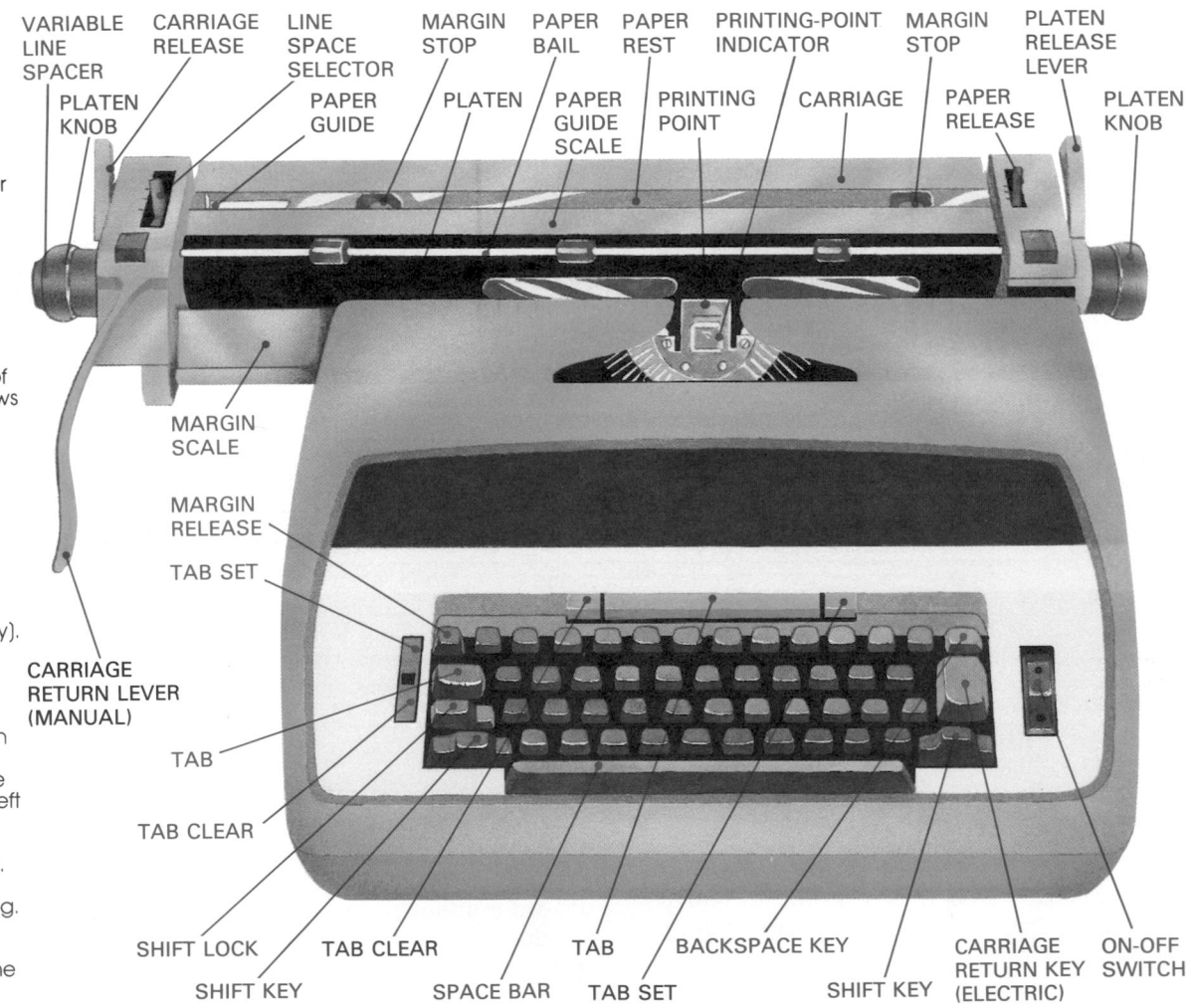

MAIN PARTS OF AN ELEMENT MACHINE

MARGIN STOPS. Key or lever used to block off side margins.

ON-OFF SWITCH (electric only). Controls motor power.

PAPER BAIL. Holds paper against the platen.

PAPER GUIDE. Blade against which paper is placed when paper is inserted.

PAPER RELEASE. Loosens paper for straightening or removing.

PLATEN. Large roller around which paper is rolled.

PLATEN KNOBS. Used to turn paper into the machine.

PLATEN RELEASE LEVER. Allows a temporary change in the line of writing.

PRINTING POINT. The place where the typebar or the element strikes the paper.

PRINTING POINT INDICATOR. Shows the position on the margin scale where the machine is ready to print.

SHIFT KEY. Positions the typebar or the element so that a capital letter can be typed.

SHIFT LOCK KEY. Permits typing a series of all-capital letters.

SPACE BAR. Used for spacing between characters or words.

TAB/TABULATOR. Moves the carriage/carrier freely to preset points.

TAB CLEAR. Used to remove tab stops one at a time.

TAB SET. Positions tab stops.

VARIABLE LINE SPACER. Permanently changes the line of writing.

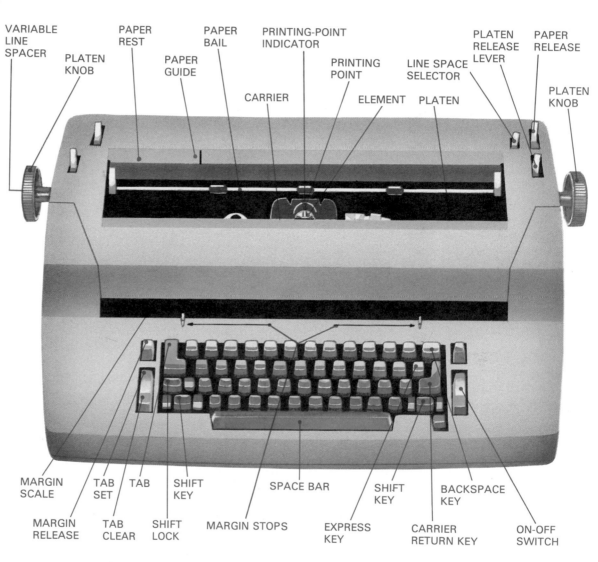

VARIABLE LINE SPACER — PLATEN KNOB — PAPER REST — PAPER GUIDE — PAPER BAIL — CARRIER — PRINTING-POINT INDICATOR — PRINTING POINT — ELEMENT — LINE SPACE SELECTOR — PLATEN — PLATEN RELEASE LEVER — PAPER RELEASE — PLATEN KNOB

MARGIN SCALE — MARGIN RELEASE — TAB SET — TAB CLEAR — TAB — SHIFT KEY — SHIFT LOCK — MARGIN STOPS — SPACE BAR — EXPRESS KEY — SHIFT KEY — CARRIER RETURN KEY — BACKSPACE KEY — ON-OFF SWITCH

GETTING READY TO TYPE

TYPE SIZES

10 pitch--pica
12 pitch--elite

Typewriters are usually equipped with one of two sizes of type: pica or elite.

Pica type (also called *10 pitch*) is larger than elite. Pica prints 10 letters to an inch (25.4 mm). Elite type (called *12 pitch*) prints 12 letters to an inch (25.4 mm).

The width of standard paper is 8 1/2 inches (216 mm), which is equal to 85 spaces of pica type or 102 spaces of elite type. Thus the center of standard paper is 42 on pica machines and 51 on elite machines, usually written 42P/51E.

CENTERING POINT

Three common methods for selecting a centering point are explained below. Each requires you to set the paper guide differently.

1. Set the paper guide at 0 and insert a sheet of paper. If you are using a pica machine, your centering point will be 42. If you are using an elite machine, your centering point will be 51. There-fore, if you use 42P/51E as the centering point, be sure to set your paper guide at 0 before you insert the paper.

2. The second method is to use 50 (or some other common centering point) as the centering point for any machine, pica or elite. Follow these steps to determine where the paper guide belongs:
   a. Pull the paper bail forward or up.
   b. Move the paper guide as far to the left as it can go.
   c. Set the carriage or carrier at 50 (or the centering point of your choice).
   d. Mark the center of the top of a sheet of paper by creasing it.
   e. Insert the creased sheet; hold it in your left hand, place it behind the platen, and draw the paper into the machine by turning the platen knob with your right hand.
   f. Engage the paper release to loosen the paper; then slide the paper left or right until the center crease is at the printing point—the point where the printing occurs. Then return the pa-per release to its original position.
   g. Slide the paper guide to the right until its blade is snugly against the sheet of paper.

   Note on the margin scale exactly where you have set the paper guide. Now you will be able to confirm or correct the position of the paper guide very easily and quickly. Do so each time you begin typing.

3. Another method is to use the center of the platen as the centering point. (The center is usually marked by a small dot on the margin scale.) Depending on the length of the platen, the center may be 55P/66E or 65P/78E. Follow the same steps given in method 2 above to deter-mine where the paper guide belongs.

PAPER GUIDE

PLATEN CENTER

PAPER HANDLING

Practice this routine several times:

1. Confirm the paper guide setting.
2. Pull the paper bail forward or up.
3. With your left hand, place the paper behind the platen and against the paper guide; use your right hand to turn the right platen knob to draw in the paper. Advance the paper until about a third of the front is visible.
4. Check that the paper is straight by aligning the left edges of the front and the back against the paper guide. If they do not align, loosen the paper guide (by engaging the paper release) and straighten it.
5. Place the paper bail back against the paper. Adjust the rollers on the bail so that they are spread evenly across the paper.
6. Turn the right-hand platen knob until only 1/4 inch or so of the paper shows above the bail. Now the paper is in the correct position for the opening drill of each lesson.
7. To remove the paper, draw the bail forward or up. Then engage the paper release (right hand) as you silently draw out the sheet of paper (left hand). Fi-nally, return the paper release to its normal position.

FORMATTING

Formatting a document means arranging it according to a specific set of rules (or, sometimes, according to your own preference). Deciding on margins and line spacings is part of formatting.

MARGIN PLANNING

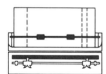

Margins at the left and right sides of a typed page are controlled by margin stops that limit the line of typing. To plan the left and right margin settings:

Left Margin. Subtract half the desired line from the center. For example, for a 40-space line, subtract 20 from the centering point you are using.

Right Margin. Add half the desired line length to the center. Then add 5 extra spaces (an allowance for line-ending adjustments).

Some sample margin settings appear in the next column.

Margin settings using 50 as the center:

Line Length	Pica	Elite
40-space line	30–75	30–75
50-space line	25–80	25–80
60-space line	20–85	20–85

Margin settings using 42P/51E as the center:

Line Length	Pica	Elite
40-space line	22–67	31–76
50-space line	17–72	26–81
60-space line	12–77	21–86

MARGIN SETTING

SPRING SET

HOOK ON

Spring-Set Machines. Some typewriters have a margin set key at each end of the carriage. For the *left margin*: (1) press the left margin set key, (2) move the carriage to the desired scale point, and (3) release the set key. For the *right margin*: (1) press the right margin set key, (2) move the carriage to the desired scale point, and (3) release the set key.

Hand-Set Machines. Many typewriters (including most element machines and most portables) have hand-set levers, not margin set keys. Each lever is moved separately by hand: (1) press down, or push in, the lever, (2) slide the stop right or left to the desired scale point, and (3) release the lever.

Hook-On Machines. Some typewriters have margin set keys on the keyboard. For the *left margin*: (1) move the carriage to the left margin, (2) hook onto the left margin stop by holding down the margin set key, (3) move the carriage to the desired scale point, and (4) release the set key. For the *right margin*: (1) move the carriage to the right margin, (2) hook onto the right margin stop by holding down the set key, (3) move the carriage to the desired point, and (4) release the set key.

LINE SPACING

The blank space between lines is controlled by the line space selector. Set it at *1* for single spacing, which provides no blank space between typed lines, and at *2* for double spacing, which provides 1 blank line between lines. Many machines also have 1½ spacing, 2½ spacing, and/or triple spacing.

Line Space Selector

	Set at 1	Set at 2
	single	double
	single	
	single	double
	single	
	single	double

TYPEWRITING POSTURE

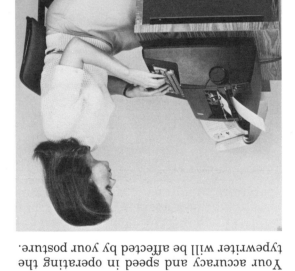

Your accuracy and speed in operating the typewriter will be affected by your posture.

Use appropriate posture from the first day so that you can learn to type well. Sit like the typist in the illustration:

Head erect and facing the book, which is tilted to reduce reflected light on the paper.

Back straight with body leaning forward slightly; shoulders level.

Body a handspan from the machine, centered opposite the J key.

Feet apart, firmly braced on the floor, one foot ahead of the other.

Fingers curved so that only the tips touch the keys.

Palms up slightly, off the front of the machine so that the fingers are free to move as you type.

WORK STATION ARRANGEMENT

Organizing the work station around the typewriter helps you complete your assignments more efficiently. For most typewriters and desk styles, the most efficient way to organize a typewriting work station is to:

1. Place the typewriter near the center of the desk, even with the front of the desk.
2. Place supplies to one side of the typewriter.
3. Place materials to be typed on the opposite side of your supplies.
4. Store away all other items that are not being used.

If you are using a manual typewriter, arrange your work station as shown in the illustration above. Place the materials to be typed to your right, otherwise your vision will be blocked during carriage returns. On electric machines, the return of the carriage or carrier will not block your vision, so you may arrange the materials to be typed at your left or your right, depending on the desk style or whether you are left-handed or right-handed.

EXTRA PAPER

TYPEWRITER

BOOK

SENTENCE COMPOSITION (Continued)

10. What are you going to do when you finish high school?
11. Why do some people dislike going to a dentist?
12. What were some of the hardships faced by the pioneers?
13. What is significant about July 4, 1776?
14. Why do we celebrate Thanksgiving?
15. What is the equator?

PARAGRAPH COMPOSITION

Use a paragraph of at least three complete sentences to answer each of the questions below. Use a clean sheet of paper, start on line 10 from the top, and type on a 50-space line. *Keep your eyes on your copy and concentrate on the words as you type.*

1. Where would you like to spend your next vacation and why?
2. Name your favorite season of the year, and tell why you prefer that time of year.
3. Describe what the world will be like in the year 2050.
4. What career do you want to pursue and why?
5. In what state would you like to live the rest of your life and why?

The typewriter keyboard is now part of many, many different pieces of equipment. In the office, workers at all levels use the keyboard to type letters and memos, to input information into a computer or to retrieve data from the computer, to send electronic communications across the country or around the world, to reproduce copy quickly, and to perform any number of other tasks. In the home, men and women use the keyboard to input and calculate data on "personal" computers or to play electronic games. In schools, students use the keyboard to prepare reports, to solve problems, and to take tests.

Thus the term *keyboarding* is used to describe the process of inputting data by means of a keyboard. Keyboarding is a very valuable skill, and it is the skill you will concentrate on developing in Level 1.

In Level 1 you will . . .

1. Demonstrate which fingers control each key on the keyboard and each part of the typewriter.

2. Condition your fingers to control the keyboard at a useful level of operation.

3. Use your typewriter to produce very short written communications.

LESSON 1

UNIT 1 KEYBOARDING—THE ALPHABET

UNIT GOAL
16 WORDS A MINUTE

GOAL
- To type the home keys, use the space bar, and return the carriage or carrier with eyes on copy.

FORMAT
- Single spacing   40-space line

HOME KEY POSITION

The dark keys shown with white letters in the keyboard chart are the home keys.

Left Hand.   Place your fingertips on the **A S D** and **F** keys.
Right Hand.   Place your fingertips on **J K L** and **;** keys.

Curve your fingers so that only their tips lightly touch the keys. Your fingers are named for the home keys on which they rest: A finger, S finger, D finger, and so on, ending with Sem finger for the little finger on the ; key.

SPACE BAR

You will strike the space bar with the thumb of your writing hand—the right thumb if you are right-handed, the left thumb if you are left-handed. Whichever thumb you use should be poised above the middle of the space bar. The other thumb is not used; hold it close to its adjacent forefinger.

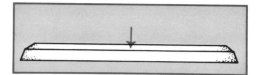

Strike center of space bar with thumb.

Now practice using the space bar with the right or left thumb.

Space once [*tap the space bar once*] . . . twice [*tap the space bar twice*] . . . once . . . once . . . twice . . . once . . . twice . . . once . . . twice . . . twice . . . once . . . once. . . .   **Repeat.**

PHRASE COMPOSITION (Continued)

3. What is the name of your school newspaper or local newspaper?
4. What is your favorite television program?
5. What is your favorite record?
6. Name a book that you enjoyed reading.
7. What city and country would you like to visit?
8. Who is your favorite sports personality?
9. Who is the President of the United States?
10. Name two large cities in the United States.
11. Name two large states in the United States.
12. Name a past president of the United States.
13. Give the last names of two of your teachers.
14. Name two jobs you would enjoy doing.
15. Name two popular soft drinks.

SENTENCE COMPOSITION

Answer each of the following questions by typing a complete sentence of six or more words. (Each sentence must have a subject and a predicate.) Use a clean sheet of paper, start on line 10 from the top, and type on a 50-space line. *Keep your eyes on your copy and concentrate on each sentence as you type.*

Example Question:
When do the leaves start to fall?

Example Response:
In my state, the leaves start to fall in September.

1. What is the most difficult thing about a foreign language?
2. Why do we have taxes?
3. Why do we have insurance?
4. How is typewriting going to help you?
5. What have you learned from any one of your courses in school this year?
6. Why did you enroll in typewriting?
7. What kind of person would you like to have as a friend?
8. What are some of your assets?
9. What is the purpose of a space bar on a typewriter?

(Continued on next page)

CARRIAGE OR CARRIER RETURN

Manual Machine. Place the left forefinger and the next two fingers against the return lever. Flip the lever with a toss of the wrist to return the carriage to the margin, and return the hand to home key position.

Electric Machine. Extend the Sem finger to the adjacent return key. Lightly press the return key causing the carriage or carrier to return automatically, and return the finger to home key position.

Now practice using the carriage or carrier return.

Space once . . . twice . . . once . . . twice. . . . Ready to return [*move hand to return lever or finger to return key*]. Return! [*Return the carriage or carrier.*] . . . Home! [*Place fingers on home keys.*] . . . Repeat.

STROKING PRACTICE

SPACE BAR

Practice the F and J and space strokes shown in the drill below. If you are using a manual machine, experiment to see how hard you must tap the keys to get them to print evenly. Type each line once. After completing a set of lines, return the carriage or carrier twice.

Left forefinger, spacing thumb. fff fff ff ff f f ff ff f f Return.

Right forefinger, spacing thumb. jjj jjj jj jj j j jj jj j j Return twice.

  KEYS

Use forefingers.

1 fff jjj fff jjj fff jjj ff jj ff jj f j Return.
2 fff jjj fff jjj fff jjj ff jj ff jj f j Return twice.

  KEYS

Use second fingers.

3 ddd kkk ddd kkk ddd kkk dd kk dd kk d k
4 ddd kkk ddd kkk ddd kkk dd kk dd kk d k

  KEYS

Use third fingers.

5 sss lll sss lll sss lll ss ll ss ll s l
6 sss lll sss lll sss lll ss ll ss ll s l

  KEYS

Use fourth fingers.

7 aaa ;;; aaa ;;; aaa ;;; aa ;; aa ;; a ;
8 aaa ;;; aaa ;;; aaa ;;; aa ;; aa ;; a ;

NUMBER COMPOSITION

Use *only one number* to answer each of the following questions. Use a clean sheet of paper, start on line 10 from the top, and type on a 50-space line. *Keep your eyes on your copy and concentrate on each answer as you type.*

Example Question:
How many days are there in December?

Example Response:
31

1. How many letters are there in the alphabet?
2. How many states are there in the United States?
3. How many brothers do you have?
4. How many sisters do you have?
5. What is the current year?
6. How old are you?
7. How many different teachers do you have this year?
8. How many months in a year?
9. How many days in a week?
10. How many letters in your first name?
11. How many letters in your last name?
12. How many years have you been going to school?
13. How many movies did you see last month?
14. How many cents in a dollar?
15. How many years in a century?

PHRASE COMPOSITION

Use a phrase of two or three words to respond to each of the following. Use a clean sheet of paper, start on line 10 from the top, and type on a 50-space line. *Keep your eyes on your copy and concentrate on each answer as you type.*

Example Question:
Where would you like to live?

Example Response:
In Colorado

1. What are your school colors?
2. Who is your best friend?

(Continued on next page)

CHECKPOINT

Type each character and space with a quick, sharp stroke.

Type lines 9–10 once. Then repeat lines 3, 5, and 7 or repeat the Checkpoint at a faster rate.

9 ff jj dd kk ss ll aa ;; f j d k s l a ;

10 ff jj dd kk ss ll aa ;; f j d k s l a ;

PRETEST

Type lines 11–12 at least once keeping your eyes on the copy.

11 fad fad ask ask lad lad dad dad sad sad   Return.

12 as; as; fall fall alas alas flask flask   Return twice.

HOME KEY WORD BUILDING

When you have completed a set of lines (13–14, 15–16, and so on), return the carriage or carrier an extra time.

Type lines 13–24 once.

13 fff aaa ddd fad fad aaa sss kkk ask ask

14 fff aaa ddd fad fad aaa sss kkk ask ask

15 aaa lll lll all all sss aaa ddd sad sad

16 aaa lll lll all all sss aaa ddd sad sad

17 lll aaa ddd lad lad aaa ddd ddd add add

18 lll aaa ddd lad lad aaa ddd ddd add add

19 ddd aaa ddd dad dad aaa sss ;;; as; as;

20 ddd aaa ddd dad dad aaa sss ;;; as; as;

21 a al ala alas alas; f fa fal fall falls

22 a al ala alas alas; f fa fal fall falls

23 l la las lass lass; f fl fla flas flask

24 l la las lass lass; f fl fla flas flask

POSTTEST

Type lines 25–26 at leat once keeping your eyes on the copy. Note your improvement.

25 fad fad ask ask lad lad dad dad sad sad

26 as; as; fall fall alas alas flask flask

At the End of a Typewriting Session

Remove paper using paper release.

Center carriage or carrier.

Turn machine off if electric.

Cover machine at end of last period.

COMPOSITION EXERCISES

In this course you learned how to format typewritten letters, reports, and tables. But you also need to acquire the skill of composing copy at the typewriter. Then when you have developed your composition skills, you will be able to create projects in your own words and display each project in one of the various formats you learned in this course.

The following section is designed to strengthen your composition skills. The jobs in this section are arranged from simple to complex, starting with a one-word response and concluding with an entire-paragraph response.

Follow the directions and examples given for each stage of composition as you compose your answers to each of the questions. Single-space each response, but double-space between responses.

ONE-WORD COMPOSITION

Use *only one word* whenever possible to answer each of the following questions. Use a clean sheet of paper, start on line 10 from the top, and type on a 50-space line. *Keep your eyes on your copy and concentrate on each answer as you type.*

Example Question:
What is your favorite color?

Example Response:
Blue

1. What is your favorite sport?

2. What color eyes do you have?

3. What vegetable do you like best?

4. What color is your hair?

5. What is your favorite fruit?

6. What is your favorite class?

7. What is your favorite hobby?

8. What is your favorite make of automobile?

9. What is your favorite season of the year?

10. What is the last name of your favorite actor?

11. What is the last name of your favorite actress?

12. What is your favorite month?

13. What is your favorite day of the week?

14. In what month is your birthday?

15. Name one of the oceans.

LESSON 2

GOAL
- To control H, E, and O keys by touch.

FORMAT
- Single spacing   40-space line

KEYBOARDING REVIEW

Type each line twice.

1 ff jj dd kk ss ll aa ;; f j d k s l a ;

2 asks asks fall fall lads lads lass lass

SPACE BAR

H KEY

Use J finger.

Type each line twice.

3 jjj jhj hhh jjj jhj hhh jjj jhj hhh jhj

4 jhj ash ash jhj had had jhj has has jhj

5 jhj; a lad has; a lass has; add a half;

E KEY

Use D finger.

Type each line twice.

6 ddd ded eee ddd ded eee ddd ded eee ded

7 ded she she ded led led ded he; he; ded

8 ded; he led; she led; he sees; she sees

O KEY

Use L finger.

Type each line twice.

9 lll lol ooo lll lol ooo lll lol ooo lol

10 lol hoe hoe lol ode ode lol foe foe lol

11 lol old ode; oak hoe; sod fed; old foe;

CHECKPOINT

Eyes on copy while typing Checkpoint.

Type lines 12–13 once. Then repeat lines 3, 6, and 9 or repeat the Checkpoint at a faster rate.

12 she sells jade flakes; he sells old oak

13 she sells jade flakes; he sells old oak

PRETEST

Type lines 14–15 at least once keeping your eyes on the copy.

14 half dead hold sash jell look lake seed

15 half dead hold sash jell look lake seed

The conversion to a metric system of measurement in this country is slowly taking place in business and industry; therefore, in the office environment you may need to learn certain style rules for typing. Read each metric rule presented below. For each rule, type the group of four drill lines once. Repeat the lines or take a series of 1-minute timings.

Rule 1. A lowercase letter is used to spell a metric term or abbreviation except for (1) a metric term that begins a sentence, (2) the word *Celsius*, and (3) the abbreviation *L*, for liter or liters.

1   Kilometers, centimeters, and millimeters measure distances.   12
2   The big jar holds exactly 7.1 liters; that can, 9.7 liters.   12
3   The carton of butter we bought yesterday weighed 454 grams.   12
4   The Celsius thermometer read 26 degrees; it was a nice day.   12
  | 1 | 2 | 3 | 4 | 5 | 6 | 7 | 8 | 9 | 10 | 11 | 12

Rule 2. The singular and the plural forms of metric abbreviations are the same.

5   Only 1 L of fluid is left; she already used more than 50 L.   12
6   The box contains 12 g of powder, but you must mix only 1 g.   12
7   Each granule weighs 1 dg (decigram); the jar is over 16 dg.   12
8   One particle is 1 mm long; the others are about 10 mm long.   12
  | 1 | 2 | 3 | 4 | 5 | 6 | 7 | 8 | 9 | 10 | 11 | 12

Rule 3. A blank space is used in place of the comma to separate sets of three digits.

9   In metrics we must type 1,000,000 grams as 1 000 000 grams.   12
10   She obtained these results: 0.293 847 mL and 0.567 340 mL.   12
11   The ship weighed nearly 20 000 kg; the canoe weighed 20 kg.   12
12   The distance from the earth to the moon is over 358 770 km.   12
  | 1 | 2 | 3 | 4 | 5 | 6 | 7 | 8 | 9 | 10 | 11 | 12

Rule 4. A period is not used after a metric abbreviation, except at the end of a sentence.

13   They lost 150 mL, 225 mL, 350 mL, and 425 mL in four weeks.   12
14   One boxer weighed 67 kg; the opponent weighed nearly 69 kg.   12
15   The measurements were off by nearly 5 cm, 14 cm, and 25 cm.   12
16   One of my friends lost 10 kg; the other gained about 12 kg.   12
  | 1 | 2 | 3 | 4 | 5 | 6 | 7 | 8 | 9 | 10 | 11 | 12

Rule 5. Figures (and words) are used with metric terms and abbreviations (unless the reference is obviously general and nontechnical).

17   We drove 500 kilometers today and 400 kilometers yesterday.   12
18   Make a mixture by adding 1.3 g of powder to 1.5 L of water.   12
19   The length of the paper is 215 mm, and the width is 280 mm.   12
20   The specifications require strips exactly 2.5 mm in length.   12
  | 1 | 2 | 3 | 4 | 5 | 6 | 7 | 8 | 9 | 10 | 11 | 12

PRACTICE

When You Repeat a Line

Speed up on the second typing.

Make second typing smoother too.

Leave a blank line after second typing (return carriage or carrier twice).

Type each line twice.

16 half half hall hall hale hale hole hole
17 dead dead deal deal heal heal head head
18 hold hold sold sold fold fold folk folk
19 sash sash dash dash lash lash hash hash
20 jell jell sell sell self self elf; elf;
21 look look hook hook hood hood hoof hoof
22 lake lake fake fake fade fade jade jade
23 seed seed deed deed feed feed heed heed

POSTTEST

Type lines 14–15 at least once keeping your eyes on the copy. Note your improvement.

LESSON 3

GOAL
- To control M, R, and I keys by touch.

FORMAT
- Single spacing   40-space line

KEYBOARDING REVIEW

Type each line twice.

1 asdf jkl; heo; asdf jkl; heo; asdf jkl;
2 fake fake lose lose jade jade held held

M KEY

Use J finger.

Type each line twice.

3 jjj jmj mmm jjj jmj mmm jjj jmj mmm jmj
4 jmj me; me; jmj mom mom jmj ham ham jmj
5 jmj; fold a hem; make a jam; less fame;

JOB 299/300-1 (Continued)

termination. The lessee will be billed for excessive mileage at a rate of *18* cents per mile for each mile driven in excess of the mileage herein allowed. *Executed this 15th day of June 19—.*

_____ _____
Lessor   Lessee

JOB 299/300-2. FORM LETTER

Standard format. Needs editing.

we hope that you are enjoying the new automobile that you purchased from us this year it is always our intention to give our customers the best possible service *paragraph* with this in mind we would like to respectfully remind you that it is time for your 12,000-mile or your annual checkup on the items listed below *paragraph arrange in two columns without headings Column 1* transmission check *Column 2* brake check *Column 1* cooling system check *Column 2* general tuneup *Column 1* oil/lubrication *Column 2* wheel balancing and alignment *Column 1* emission control test *Column 2* catalytic converter test *new paragraph* please give us a call in the next two weeks so that we may help you keep your automobile running in top shape

JOB 299/300-3. COMPOSED LETTER

Select appropriate format. Workbook 779

You have just received a new shipment of the newest compact economy cars—all American-made. You want to promote them to past customers. Compose a form letter promoting the car. Use your own creativity to describe the car, and give reasons why past customers might want to purchase another car at this time. Use the following subject/salutation instead of an inside address: Notice to our special customers. The letter must be in the mail a week from today.

JOB 299/300-4. INVOICE

Standard format. Workbook 781.

To: Ms. Judy Wheeler
      155 North Avenue
      Chicago, IL 60637

For replacement of a transmission with parts costing $225 and labor costing $150. (You should add a 5% sales tax on parts only and total the invoice.)

JOB 299/300-5. INVOICE

Standard format. Workbook 781.

To: Mr. Jeffrey Snyder
485 Walnut Avenue
Cincinnati, OH 45218

For replacing thermostat, $9.00; replacing coolant, $12.00; replacing two hoses, $27.50; and labor, $25.00. (Add 5% sales tax on parts only, and total the invoice.)

JOB 299/300-6. TABLE

Select appropriate format.

This is the work schedule of the service department for the week of May 18, 19—. There are two shifts: 6 a.m. to 2 p.m. and 12 noon to 8 p.m. There are four work stations, which can be labeled "Station 1," "Station 2," and so forth. The schedule begins with Monday and runs through Saturday. The first shift will be Michael Bippus, Wan Chong, Bridget Vagades, and Leslie Trezise assisted by Eric Thomson, Julie Toma, Anthony Viola, and James Tomallo. The second shift will be Jeffrey Myers, Joseph Lavigne, Cynthia Detter, and Jessanne Attalla assisted by Michael Dean, Alison Akers, Cynthia Spoor, and Stacey Vreeland. *Assign stations and assistants alphabetically.*

SPACE BAR

 KEY

Use F finger.

Type each line twice.

6 fff frf rrr fff frf rrr fff frf rrr frf

7 frf for for frf far far frf err err frf

8 frf; from me; for her marks; more jars;

I KEY

Use K finger.

Type each line twice.

9   kkk kik iii kkk kik iii kkk kik iii kik

10 kik lid lid kik dim dim kik rim rim kik

11 kik; dear sir; for his risk; if she is;

CHECKPOINT

Type lines 12–13 once. Then repeat lines 3, 6, and 9 or repeat the Checkpoint at a faster rate.

12 her dark oak desk lid is a joke; he has

13 added a rare look from some old red oak

PRETEST

Type lines 14–15 at least once keeping your eyes on the copy.

14 mare hire elms foal lame dark aide jars

15 mare hire elms foal lame dark aide jars

PRACTICE

Type each line twice.

Eyes on Copy

It will be easier to keep your eyes on the copy if you:

Understand how the line is arranged.

Review the chart for key positions.

Maintain an even pace.

Resist looking up.

16 mare mare mere mere mire mire more more

17 hire hire fire fire dire dire sire sire

18 elms elms alms alms arms arms aims aims

19 foal foal loam loam foam foam roam roam

20 lame lame dame dame fame fame same same

21 dark dark dare dare dale dale sale sale

22 jars jars jams jams jade jade joke joke

POSTTEST

Type lines 14–15 at least once keeping your eyes on the copy. Note your improvement.

JOB 299/300-1. LEASE AGREEMENT

Workbook 775, 777. Standard legal format.

NONMAINTENANCE LEASE AGREEMENT

Monarch Motors, Lessor, who se address is *419 Southdale Drive, Chicago, IL 60637,*

agrees to lease to *Shikir Jadron,* Lessee, whose address is *1549*

Calhoun St., Gary, IN, 46401, and Lessee agrees to lease from lessor,

subject to the terms set from below, the following described motor

vehicle, attachments, and accessories, delivery and acceptance of

which is hereby acknowledged in good order by Lessee, for a term of

12 months, commencing on the date of executive of this lease as

shown below. *19__ Pontiac red Sunbird with automatic Transmission, Tinted glass, and luxury interior Package.*

The Lessee represents that this lease is entered into primarily

for business or commercial use.

The Lessee agrees to pay $ *160*   per month for lease of the

above mentioned vehicle. Total monthly payment will be due on the

15th of each month beginning with *June 15, 19__ .*

The lease grants the Lessee the right to drive this vehicle for

as many as *12,000* miles during the full term of this lease without

incurring a charge for execussive mileage. In the event of premature

lease termination the number of miels that the Lessee will be

entitled to drive without incurring a charge for excessive mileage

is to be determined by prorating the mileage allowed for the full lease

term according to the proportion of the full lease term presented by

the number of months the lease was in effect prior to premature

(Continued on next page)

LESSON 4

GOALS
- To control T, N, and C keys by touch.
- To figure speed using the speed scales.

FORMAT
- Single spacing   40-space line

KEYBOARDING REVIEW

Type each line twice.

1 asdf jkl; heo; mri; asdf jkl; heo; mri;
2 safe safe herd herd joke joke mild mild

SPACE BAR

 KEY

Use F finger.

Type each line twice.

3 fff ftf ttt fff ftf ttt fff ftf ttt ftf
4 ftf kit kit ftf ate ate ftf toe toe ftf
5 ftf; it is the; to the; for the; at it;

N KEY

Use J finger.

Type each line twice.

6 jjj jnj nnn jjj jnj nnn jjj jnj nnn jnj
7 jnj ten ten jnj and and jnj net net jnj
8 jnj; for the; in an effort; of an honor

 KEY

Use D finger.

Type each line twice.

9 ddd dcd ccc ddd dcd ccc ddd dcd ccc dcd
10 dcd can can dcd ace ace dcd arc arc dcd
11 dcd; on a deck; in each car; cannot act

CHECKPOINT

Type lines 12–13 once. Then repeat lines 3, 6, and 9 or repeat the Checkpoint at a faster rate.

12 there is a carton of jade on this dock;
13 mail a file card to the nearest stores;

GOALS
■ To type 50/5'/3e.
■ To demonstrate competency in producing appropriately
formatted communications from unarranged, handwritten,
rough-draft, unedited, and incomplete copy.

FORMAT
■ Single spacing   60-space line   5-space tab

**PREVIEW
PRACTICE**

Type lines 1–3 twice as a preview to the 5-minute timings below.

1 administrative opportunities description processing quality
2 phototypesetting photocomposition variations analyst senior
3 responsibilities punctuation keyboarding formatting grammar

**5-MINUTE
TIMINGS**

Take two 5-minute timings on lines 4–24.

4   Job titles and descriptions for personnel working with   12
5 word processing continue to grow. Several different titles   24
6 show job opportunities depending upon the size of a center.   36
7   One group of titles and descriptions focuses on people   48
8 whose major responsibilities are tied to the keyboarding of   60
9 documents. There are eight categories of personnel listed: 72
10 a word processing trainee who must have entry-level skills;   84
11 a competent word processing operator; a specialist who does   96
12 some formatting variations and understands total operations   108
13 of the center; a phototypesetting specialist who enters the   120
14 special codes for photocomposition systems; a word process-   132
15 ing trainer who controls quality and teaches; a proofreader   144
16 who checks text for spelling, punctuation, grammar, format,   156
17 and content; a word processing supervisor who directs oper-   168
18 ation of a section; and a word processing manager who takes   180
19 responsibility for the operations of the entire center.   191
20   The other group of titles and descriptions encompasses 203
21 mainly administrative positions. Six categories are listed   215
22 for this division: administrative secretary, senior admin-   227
23 istrative secretary, administrative supervisor, administra-   239
24 tive manager, staff analyst, and information manager.   250

| 1 | 2 | 3 | 4 | 5 | 6 | 7 | 8 | 9 | 10 | 11 | 12 | SI 2.05

FIGURING SPEED

Workbook 5.

1. **If you type for 1 minute:** Find out how many "average" words you type in the time allowed. Every 5 strokes (letters and spaces) counts as 1 average word. Thus a 40-stroke line is 8 words long; two such lines, 16 words; and so on.

2. For an incomplete line, use the scale (below line 15 on this page); the number above which you stop is your word count for that incomplete line. **Example:** If you type lines 14 and 15 (see below) and start over, getting as far as the word *sink* in line 14, you have typed 16 + 1 = 17 words.

3. **If you type for more than 1 minute:** To find out your 1-minute rate, you will need to divide the word total by the number of minutes you typed. **Example:** 37 words in 2 minutes would be 37 ÷ 2 = 18½ = 19 wam (words a minute). Count a fraction as a whole word.

4. **If you type for less than 1 minute:** To find out your 1-minute rate, you will have to multiply the total number of words typed because you typed for less than 1 minute. If you type for 30 seconds, you will have to multiply by 2 (2 × 30 = 60 or 1 minute). If you type for 12 seconds, you will have to multiply by 5 (5 × 12 = 60—1 minute). **Example:** 9 words in 30 seconds would be 9 × 2 = 18 wam.

PRETEST

Type lines 14–15 at least once keeping your eyes on the copy.

```
14   sink cane tone then tick jots etch rain
15   sink cane tone then tick jots etch rain
```

PRACTICE

Check Your Posture

Feet—apart, on floor.

Back—erect, leaning forward.

Hands—close together, fingers curved, low.

Eyes—focused on book.

Type each line twice.

```
16   sink sink rink rink link link kink kink
17   cane cane came came cake cake care care
18   tone tone done done lone lone none none
19   then then than than thin thin this this
20   tick tick lick lick sick sick kick kick
21   jots jots lots lots lets lets jets jets
22   held held herd herd hard hard hand hand
23   rain rain raid raid said said sail sail
```

POSTTEST

Type lines 14–15 at least once keeping your eyes on the copy. Note your improvement.

TURNAROUND TIME

The Word Processing Center is operating with five word processing operators and a word processing center supervisor. The center is serving over ~~four hundred~~ 400 authors who have 24-hour access to the dictating facilities.

PRIORITY AND CONFIDENTIAL COMMUNICATIONS

Communications ~~which~~ that are marked priority and/or confidential ordinarily come from the Management Division. The turnaround time for these documents will not exceed 3 hours.

ROUTINE COMMUNICATIONS

Routine correspondence is normally received from the supervisory personnel and makes up the majority of the word processing work load. The turnaround time for these documents will not exceed 5 hours.

LONG DOCUMENTS

Long documents such as procedures manuals and company reports come from all levels of the company. ~~The~~ Such documents usually ~~will~~ require numerous revisions before a final draft is ~~accomplished.~~ completed. Turnaround time cannot be predicted since it depends upon the nature of the document and the number of revisions needed for completion.

This page is placed last because it was not determined where it should go in the manual. You decide where it should go.

[*you decide*] section, corrections and revisions

Responsibility for the accuracy of all documents rests with both the author and the word processing operator.

1. The author will clearly dictate and/or handwrite copy with all relevant information to complete the document.

2. The word processing operator will proofread all material before it is returned to the author. The author, however, should also proofread material when it is returned.

3. When a correction is necessary, note lightly on the copy in pencil any corrections in spelling, typing, punctuation, or content. Minor corrections may not require rerunning the document.

4. Return the original document and the copy on which the corrections are indicated to the word processing center. This is accomplished via the special word processing mail runs or by hand-carrying the document to the word processing center.

5. Do not accept work of inferior quality. Feedback to the supervisor of the word processing center is important and appreciated.

6. Revision of documents will be channeled according to the same priority as the original documents unless otherwise indicated. Thus a routine letter that has been revised will be processed as a routine letter again, a priority letter will be processed again as a priority letter, and so on.

LESSON 5

GOALS
- To control the right shift key, V, and period keys by touch.
- To recognize typographical errors in copy and count them.
- To use the paper bail as an aid for locating copy errors.

FORMAT
- Single spacing   40-space line

KEYBOARDING REVIEW

Type each line twice.

```
1 asdf jkl; jh de lo jm fr ki ft jn dc ;;
2 cash free dine jolt milk iron trim star
```

SPACE BAR

RIGHT SHIFT KEY

Use Sem finger.

Use the right shift key to capitalize letters typed with the left hand. To make the reach easier, curl the second and third fingers of your right hand as you complete the following three-step sequence:

1. **Cap!** Keeping J finger in home position, extend Sem finger to press the right shift key and hold it down firmly.
2. **Strike!** [or the name of the letter to be capitalized]. While the shift is still depressed, use the left hand to strike the letter that is to be capitalized.
3. **Home!** Release the shift key, and return all fingers to home position.

For a capital A, for example, you would think "Cap!" as you press the right shift, "A!" as you strike the letter, and "Home!" as all fingers snap back to home position.

Type each line twice.

```
3 ;;; C;; C;; ;;; S;; S;; ;;; T;; T;; ;;;
4 ;;; Cal Cal ;;; Sam Sam ;;; Ted Ted ;;;
5 ;;; Ada Ada ;;; Rae Rae ;;; Dee Dee ;;;
```

V KEY

Use F finger.

Type each line twice.

```
6 fff fvf vvv fff fvf vvv fff fvf vvv fvf
7 fvf vie vie fvf via via fvf eve eve fvf
8 fvf; via a van; move over; vie for love
```

3. prepare an outline after some experience in some cases a mental run-through of points you wish to cover is the only outline you need you may wish to underline important points in the letter or memo you are answering to or write notes in the margin you may want a detailed outline for the first few tries
4. be concise clear and complete make sure your outline is adequate before you begin dictating break up paragraphs that are too long

REMEMBER GOOD LETTERS JUST DON'T HAPPEN—THEY ARE PLANNED THAT WAY

Workflow section, mailing procedures

1. Pickup and delivery. Pick up and delivery between the center and the various departments occurs every hour on the half hour, beginning at 9:30 a.m. and ending at 3:30 p.m. with the exception of 11:30 a.m. (lunch period). These times are subject to change as more departments begin to use the word processing center. Each department using the center has special input and output bins for routing work to and from the center:

Input: Completed documents are delivered.

Output: Revised or handwritten documents are picked up.

If a document is confidential, place it in an interoffice envelope and seal it with a secure-a-tie. Address the envelope to "Confidential" and place it in the output bin. It will be delivered directly to the "Confidential" word processing specialist. You may also hand-carry your document to the word processing supervisor.

2. Dating of correspondence. Material transcribed after 2:30 p.m. is automatically dated for the next working day, unless the author designates it as a rush or requests a specific date for the document.

3. Priorities. Work is processed in the following order:

a. Rush requests. A rush may be requested through the dictation system or by hand-carrying the document to the word processing center.

b. Corrections and retypes.

c. Routine work. This is processed on a first come, first served basis.

d. Forms.

Remember: Plan ahead to eliminate rushes. Rushes are subject to the approval of the word processing supervisor.

Formatting section, manuscripts and reports

Manuscripts are typed on a 6-inch line. The first page begins 2 inches from the top of the page, and all succeeding pages begin 1 inch from the top of the page. Titles are typed in all capitals, and side headings are typed in all capitals. Both are preceded by a triple space. All pages should have a 1-inch bottom margin. All manuscripts will be double-spaced unless otherwise designated.

 . KEY

Use L finger.

Type each line twice.

9 111 1.1 ... 111 1.1 ... 111 1.1 ... 111

10 1.1 Sr. Sr. 1.1 Fr. Fr. 1.1 Dr. Dr. 1.1

11 vs. ea. Co. Ms. Mr. Mrs. Inc. ctn. std.

PUNCTUATION

Type each line twice.

Space twice after a period at the end of a sentence. Do not space at the end of a line.

12 Roll the dimes. There are five stacks.

13 See Ann at the door. She has the food.

Space once after a period that follows an abbreviation and after a semicolon.

Type each line twice.

14 Dr. S. Romer called; he read the lines.

15 Elm St. is ahead; East Ave. veers left.

CHECKPOINT

Type lines 16–17 once. Then repeat lines 3, 6, and 9 or repeat the Checkpoint at a faster rate.

16 Dr. Sara is on call; she asked Anne for 8

17 five half liters of cold milk in a jar. 16

| 1 | 2 | 3 | 4 | 5 | 6 | 7 | 8

COUNTING ERRORS

Workbook 6.

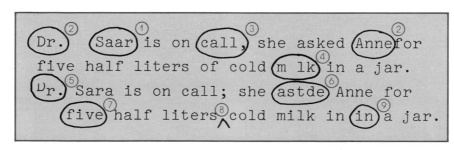

1. Circle any word in which there is an error.

2. Count a word as an error if the spacing after it is incorrect.

3. Count a word as an error if the punctuation after it is incorrect.

4. Count a word as an error if it contains a letter so light that you can't read it.

5. Count a word as an error if it contains a raised capital letter.

6. Count only 1 error against 1 word, no matter how many errors it may contain.

7. Count each failure to follow directions in spacing, indenting, and so on, as an error.

8. Count each word that is omitted as an error.

9. Count each word that is repeated incorrectly as an error.

Formatting section, forms

All forms processed by the center must have been designed with common horizontal and vertical measurements. (The vertical placement must be 1, 1½, 2, 2½, or 3 line spaces.) The horizontal placement must accommodate as many common tab stops as possible. The memo invoice form that follows illustrates all these principles.

OFFICE SYSTEMS, INC.

DATE	[*Current date*]	
TO	Research Division	
FROM	Word Processing Center	
SUBJECT	Procedures Manual	
500	Printed procedures manuals @ $10	5 000 00
500	Special-design covers @ $2	<u>1 000 00</u>
	Total amount due	6 000 00

Dictation section, the system

the following are features of the word processing center's dictating system

1. the dictating equipment is voice activated the tape moves only when you talk no pauses during replay
2. the recorder levels volume automatically alternate shouts and whispers sound essentially the same on replay the equipment also filters out high- and low-frequency background noises outside the normal voice range
3. dictated material is processed on a first-in first-out basis this sequence may be altered to accommodate priorities
4. your current dictation may be played back however to ensure privacy you as well as anyone else are locked out of prior dictation it is impossible for one author to play back anothers dictation
5. when you have access to a recorder you will hear a beep tone when you are in a dictate mode but not talking you will hear a continuous tone
6. if the recorders are busy you will get a regular busy signal hang up don't wait long to try again
7. your communications with the exception of some tabulated materials will come back faster from the word processing center if they are processed through the dictation system specialists can transcribe dictation much faster and more nearly free of errors than they can transcribe handwritten copy

Dictation section, techniques

dictating is a learned skill as in the case of all skills it requires planning practice and careful execution the following four techniques will help you dictate better communications

1. gathering reference material this includes the letter or memo you are answering all necessary names and addresses and any information you may need from files reports and so on
2. establish your purpose decide your objective first load your brain before firing your mouth have clear in your own mind why this dictation is necessary

PROOFREAD USING THE PAPER BAIL

When you proofread copy, you are looking mainly for typographical errors (incorrect characters or spaces). Proofreading your typewritten copy accurately is as important as typing it accurately in the first place. Using your paper bail like a ruler to guide your eyes line by line across the page will help you proofread accurately.

LESSON 6

CLINIC

GOALS
- To analyze key control and complete special drills to strengthen control.
- To type 16 words a minute for 1 minute.

FORMAT
- Single spacing   40-space line

PRETEST

Take two 1-minute timings on lines 1–3 to determine your typing rate. Figure your speed and count your errors.

```
1  keel dose fell seat fool sale veer tone     8
2  fall dear mail reed coil jest dead race    16
3  tee; heal amt. Todd keel dose fell seat    24
   |  1  |  2  |  3  |  4  |  5  |  6  |  7  |  8
```

PRACTICE

Type lines 4–15 four times. Then proofread and circle errors. Repeat words or lines in which you made errors.

If You Omit Spaces, as in the Example Above, Then:

Check that your palms do not touch the machine.

Think "Space" for each space bar stroke.

Type calmly, evenly— not hastily or hurriedly.

Check that thumb is only ¼ inch above space bar.

Workbook 7–10.

```
4   keel keel feel feel heel heel reel reel
5   dose dose nose nose rose rose lose lose
6   fell fell tell tell sell sell jell jell
7   seat seat feat feat heat heat meat meat

8   fool fool food food mood mood hood hood
9   sale sale male male tale tale dale dale
10  veer veer jeer jeer seer seer deer deer
11  tone tone done done lone lone cone cone

12  fall fall mall mall tall tall hall hall
13  dear dear hear hear fear fear near near
14  mail mail sail sail jail jail rail rail
15  reed reed need need deed deed heed heed
```

(Continued on next page)

Formatting section, letters

Formatting section, letters

All routine letters will be typed on a 6-inch line with the date displayed at the center of the writing line, 15 lines down from the top of the page. Inside address will be placed 5 lines below the dateline and against the left margin. All paragraphs of letters will be blocked and single-spaced with double spacing between paragraphs. All closing lines begin at the center, and all other notations (reference initials, enclosures, postscripts, etc.) will be typed below the typed name, against the left margin. Note the following example:

Ms. Marilyn Spangenberg, 1536 Princewood Court, Cincinnati, OH 45223, Dear Ms. Spangenberg: Your request for additional information concerning the new data processing laboratory has been referred to our district manager. There are four different systems that our company can offer, and an analysis of your school's needs will have to be conducted before any recommendations can be made.

You can expect to hear from Mr. Thomason within the next two to three weeks. In the meantime, I have enclosed a description of each system. Sincerely, Mark A. Johnson, Marketing Representative, Enclosure

Formatting section, tables and charts

Only routine tabulated data should be dictated. It is strongly recommended that long and detailed tabulated information be sent to the center in handwritten drafts.

All tabulated data will be typed as designated by the author. Please be specific with your directions concerning the formatting. Examples of a ruled table and a leadered table follow:

Word Processing Center Input

Type of Document	Turnaround Time
Priority/Confidential	3 hours
Routine Correspondence	5 hours
Long Documents	Varies *

*Depends upon number of revisions required.

Word Processing Center Personnel

Supervisor	Shannon Murphy
CRT Operator	Lori Otten
CRT Operator	Janet Copenhefer
CRT Operator	Lloyd James
CRT Operator	Lisa Shepherd
CRT Operator	Albert Daniels

PRACTICE (Continued)

Type lines 16–23 four times. Then proofread and circle errors. Repeat words or lines in which you made errors.

16 coil coil soil soil toil toil foil foil
17 jest jest vest vest nest nest rest rest
18 dead dead head head lead lead read read
19 race race lace lace face face mace mace

20 tee; tee; teen teen seen seen see; see;
21 heal heal veal veal meal meal real real
22 amt. amt. dis. dis. std. std. ins. ins.
23 Todd Todd Sara Sara Vera Vera Cass Cass

POSTTEST

Take two 1-minute timings on lines 1–3. Figure your speed and count your errors. Note your improvement.

LESSON 7

UNIT 2 KEYBOARDING—THE ALPHABET

GOAL
- To control W, comma, and G keys by touch.

FORMAT
- Single spacing   40-space line

* 20 words a minute for 2 minutes with 4 errors or less.

KEYBOARDING REVIEW

Type each line twice.

1 jest fail sake not; mist card Rev. chin
2 Rick loves that fame; Val did not join.

 W KEY

Use S finger.

Type each line twice.

3 sss sws www sss sws www sss sws www sws
4 sws hew hew sws own own sws war war sws
5 sws; white swans swim; sow winter wheat

, KEY

Use K finger.
Space once after a comma.

Type each line twice.

6 kkk k,k ,,, kkk k,k ,,, kkk k,k ,,, k,k
7 k,k it, it, k,k an, an, k,k or, or, k,k
8 k,k; if it is, as soon as, two or three

Workflow section, organizational chart

Arrange a full-page display of the information flow for the center from this handwritten draft.

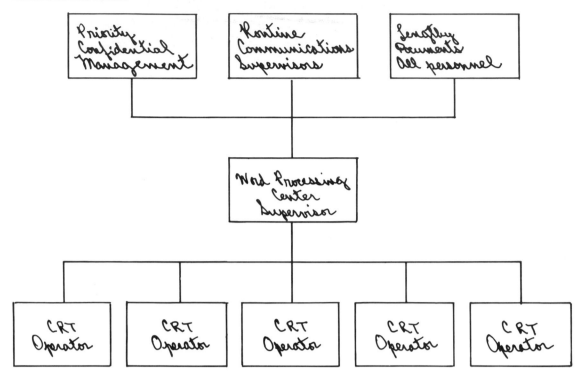

Formatting section, envelopes for routine correspondence

Window envelopes are used for ~~the majority of~~ all direct correspondence leaving the center. This procedures is used for several reasons:

1. Elimination of typing time.
2. Elimination of possible typing errors on envelopes ⊙
3. Elimination of a matching problem of envelopes and correspondence ⊙

The typing of the inside address is set up to allow the complete address to show through the window of the envelope.

¶ A window envelope will accompany all direct correspondence unless the word processing supervisor is directed otherwise by the author.

¶ No ¶ Whenever a window envelope is too small to accommodate the correspondence, the word processing supervisor will instruct the operator to type the address on a gum label. The gum label can then be placed on a larger envelope ⊙

SPACE BAR

G KEY

Use F finger.

Type each line twice.

9 fff fgf ggg fff fgf ggg fff fgf ggg fgf
10 fgf egg egg fgf leg leg fgf get get fgf
11 fgf; give a dog, saw a log, sing a song

CHECKPOINT

Type lines 12–14 once. Then repeat lines 3, 6, and 9 or take two 2-minute timings on the Checkpoint.

12 While we watched, the first team jogged 8
13 to the front of the field. The win was 16
14 two in a row; the team likes victories. 24
   | 1 | 2 | 3 | 4 | 5 | 6 | 7 | 8

PRETEST

Take two 1-minute timings on line 15, and determine your speed by using the faster rate.

15 king scow well gown elk, crew mow, sag,
   | 1 | 2 | 3 | 4 | 5 | 6 | 7 | 8

PRACTICE

Type each line twice.

16 king king sing sing wing wing ring ring
17 scow scow stow stow show show snow snow
18 well well welt welt went went west west
19 gown gown town town tows tows toes toes

20 elk, elk, ilk, ilk, irk, irk, ink, ink,
21 crew crew grew grew grow grow glow glow
22 mow, mow, how, how, hot, hot, not, not,
23 sag, sag, wag, wag, rag, rag, gag, gag,

POSTTEST

Take two 1-minute timings on line 15, and determine your speed by using the faster rate. Note your improvement.

Cover Page
The key elements of a word processing operation are people, procedures, and equipment. Design a cover using these terms as well as the name of the center.

Table of Contents
Prepare a table of contents that will make it easy to find information in the procedures manual.

Workflow section, data input

Work is received in the word processing center in the following ways:

1. Via the telephone. Dictating into one of the dictating systems (available to the authors 24 hours a day, 7 days a week).

2. Via Form 6700. Request for form (repeat or model) letter. Mailed to the center through the special word processing mail runs.

3. Via Form 6800. Request for word processing service. Mailed to the center through the special word processing mail runs. This form must accompany all work sent to the center except for form letters, corrections, and retypes.

4. Corrections and retypes. Mailed to the center through the special word processing mail runs.

Dictation section, guidelines for dictation

1. identify yourself by name division and group
2. state what you are dictating letter memo report rough draft form
3. spell out names and addresses use phonetic alphabet for initials spell out numbers that might be confusing (for example fifty and fifteen)
4. use the proper method of dictating an address
5. indicate the end of the subject line
6. use the proper method for capitalization
7. indicate end of sentence punctuation only
8. say "operator" before giving special instructions
9. spell out all mechanical instructions—paragraphs to be indented beyond the regular margins quotes to be given special margin treatment columns of figures and charts (give headings that go across paper then all data in each column (under each heading) across like it will be typed) entries to be numbered and typed under one another and titles to be underlined
10. spell out any words that might give trouble
    a. homonyms—accept, except; council, counsel; elicit, illicit
    b. other words that might be misunderstood—fiscal, physical
    c. medical and technical terms—myocardial, infarction
    d. uncommon words—rectify, aforementioned, indebtedness, reiterate
11. maintain voice control
    a. use a relaxed, normal conversational tone
    b. do not go too fast (especially on material that's familiar to you)
    c. avoid mumbling, smoking, chewing gum, fumbling with instruments— moving phone around causes chopping of words
    d. use appropriate inflections and pauses
12. dictate the copies of the letter in the order in which you want them to appear on your document (by rank, alphabetical, by sex, and so on)
13. indicate the end of the document

LESSON 8

KEYBOARDING REVIEW

Type each line twice.

1 wick foal corn them jive logo dim, wags

2 Coco gave me jewels; Frank mailed them.

 KEY

Use F finger.

Type each line twice.

3 fff fbf bbb fff fbf bbb fff fbf bbb fbf

4 fbf bag bag fbf rob rob fbf ebb ebb fbf

5 fbf, a bent bin, a big bag, a back bend

U KEY

Use J finger.

Type each line twice.

6 jjj juj uuu jjj juj uuu jjj juj uuu juj

7 juj jug jug juj flu flu juj urn urn juj

8 juj; jumbo jet, jungle bugs, just a job

LEFT SHIFT KEY

Use A finger.

Use the left shift key to capitalize letters typed with the right hand. To make the reach easier, curl the second and third fingers of your left hand as you complete the following three-step sequence:

1. Cap!   Keeping F finger in home position, extend A finger to press the left shift key and hold it down firmly.

2. Strike!   While the shift key is still depressed, use the right hand to strike the letter that is to be capitalized.

3. Home!   Release the shift key, and return all fingers to home position.

Type each line twice.

9 aaa Jaa Jaa aaa Kaa Kaa aaa Laa Laa aaa

10 aaa Joe Joe aaa Kim Kim aaa Lee Lee aaa

11 Otis Iris Nita Mark Uris Hans Jose Kebo

IN-BASKET K: WORD PROCESSING CENTER

Office Systems, Inc., has operated a word processing center for about six months. During this time various procedures have been set up and tested for effectiveness and efficiency. As an employee of the center, you will now prepare the final draft of a procedures manual that the center has decided to use. Since you are an experienced operator, you have been given some responsibility for the general formatting of the manual. Arrange the material so that it will be a good reference manual.

PRIORITY SHEET AND TIME LOG

Read the entire document before beginning work. The pages are not necessarily in the correct order. You must decide the correct order. Then complete the priority sheet. Be sure to keep an accurate time log as you complete each job. Workbook 769–770.

General Layout

There are 12 pages to the manual as well as a cover page and a table of contents. There are three sections: Workflow, Formatting, and Dictation. The Workflow section has three pages: a one-page organizational chart, a page explaining how to input data, and a page explaining output. The Formatting section has one page each for envelopes, letters, forms, tables, and reports. The Dictation section has a page explaining the system, a page for techniques, and a page for guidelines. You decide the sequence of the various sections. You also decide which section should include the page on corrections and revisions. Below are sample pages from a procedures manual for another company. Use this format or create one of your own. Once you decide on a format, be consistent in using it for all 12 pages.

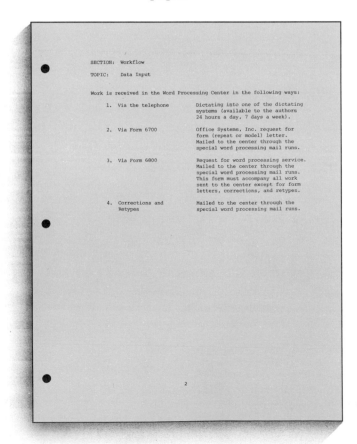

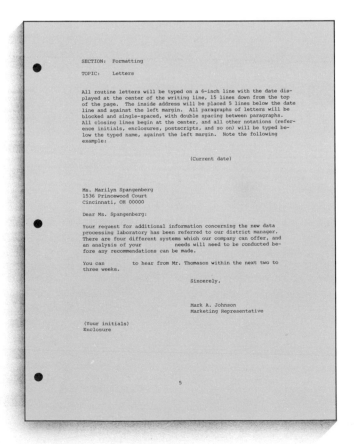

CHECKPOINT

Type lines 12–14 once. Then repeat lines 3, 6, and 9 or take two 2-minute timings on the Checkpoint.

12 Sharing a new car with friends is great 8
13 fun. Just look at that engine; hear it 16
14 hum. Drive with a flair, but use care. 24

| 1 | 2 | 3 | 4 | 5 | 6 | 7 | 8

PRETEST

Take two 1-minute timings on line 15, and determine your speed by using the faster rate.

15 beef junk bout sun, blot vast gist bran

| 1 | 2 | 3 | 4 | 5 | 6 | 7 | 8

PRACTICE

Type each line twice.

Check Your Feet.
They Should Be:

In front of the chair.

Firmly on the floor, square, flat.

Apart, with 6 or 7 inches between the ankles.

One foot a little ahead of the other.

16 beef been bean bead beak beam beat bear
17 junk dunk bunk bulk hulk hunk sunk sulk
18 bout boat boot bolt bold boll doll dole
19 sun, nun, run, bun, gun, gum, hum, sum,
20 blot blob blow blew bled bred brad bran
21 vast vest jest lest best west nest rest
22 gist list mist must gust dust rust just
23 bran brad bred brew brow crow crew craw

POSTTEST

Take two 1-minute timings on line 15, and determine your speed by using the faster rate. Note your improvement.

LESSON 9

GOAL
- To control P, Q, and colon keys by touch.

FORMAT
- Single spacing   40-space line

KEYBOARDING REVIEW

Type each line twice.

1 blue java brag mold silk when face club
2 Cora waved flags, but Jama went hiking.

GOALS
- To type 50/5'/3e.
- To prioritize and determine format for a word processing procedures manual.

FORMAT
- Single spacing 60-space line 5-space tab

KEYBOARDING SKILLS

Type lines 1–4 once. Then capitalize the appropriate words in line 5 as you type it. Repeat lines 1–4, or take a series of 1-minute timings.

Speed
Accuracy
Numbers
Symbols
Capitalization

1 Andy may pay me for the bicycle if he is paid for the work. 12
2 Have you queried Jack Flagg about his experiment with zinc? 12
3 She sold 1,234 in June, 3,456 in July, and 7,890 in August. 12
4 Type 1 + 2 − 3 + 4 − 5 + 6 − 7 + 8 − 9 + 10 − 11 + 12 − 13. 12
5 ms. owens met ken vance at the sheridan hotel in texarkana.

| 1 | 2 | 3 | 4 | 5 | 6 | 7 | 8 | 9 | 10 | 11 | 12

5-MINUTE TIMINGS

Take two 5-minute timings on lines 6–27.

6   If you accept a position as a word processing operator 12
7 in a center or in an office, you can expect input to arrive 24
8 in different ways. Standard transcription of documents and 36
9 correspondence which doesn't need revision usually requires 48
10 more time. Another type of input is correspondence that is 60
11 primarily repetitive in content. Insurance firms and legal 72
12 offices utilize form letters, fill−in forms, and many other 84
13 documents that are repetitive in content. 92

14   Multiple revision documents are those which undergo an 104
15 enormous amount of text editing. Innumerable revisions may 116
16 take place from the time the initial draft is keyed until a 128
17 final draft is keyed. Format and content which receive the 140
18 major changes require more skills in keying. Documents can 152
19 be composed from standard paragraphs stored on diskettes to 164
20 be recalled later. Very few changes are made since each of 176
21 the paragraphs has been heavily edited before. The changes 188
22 which are made are those made to personalize the documents. 200

23   The most difficult keying is that of statistical docu− 212
24 ments and typesetting related skills. Skill in calculating 224
25 the placement and skill in manipulating the data as it goes 236
26 on the screen is needed. Some documents may need more than 248
27 one code. 250

| 1 | 2 | 3 | 4 | 5 | 6 | 7 | 8 | 9 | 10 | 11 | 12   SI 1.71

SPACE BAR

P KEY

Use Sem finger.

Type each line twice.

3 ;;; ;p; ppp ;;; ;p; ppp ;;; ;p; ppp ;p;
4 ;p; pen pen ;p; nap nap ;p; ape ape ;p;
5 ;p; a pen pal, a pale page, a proud pup

Q KEY

Use A finger.

Type each line twice.

6 aaa aqa qqq aaa aqa qqq aaa aqa qqq aqa
7 aqa quo quo aqa que que aqa qui qui aqa
8 aqa quiet quip, quick quote, aqua quilt

: KEY

Use Sem finger and left shift key.
Space twice after a colon.

Type each line twice.

9 ;;; ;:; ::: ;;; ;:; ::: ;;; ;:; ::: ;:;
10 Ms. Lia: Mr. Kwi: Dr. Que: Mrs. Boe:
11 Dear Ms. Jo: Dear Mr. Mai: Dear Jeri:

CHECKPOINT

To figure rate for 1 minute, divide by 2 the total number of words typed for 2 minutes.

Errors, however, are not divided but recorded as a total for the entire timing.

Type lines 12–14 once. Then repeat lines 3, 6, and 9 or take two 2-minute timings on the Checkpoint.

12 TV lets us view the top news as it pops   8
13 up around the globe; an item takes life   16
14 with the clever quip of the journalist.   24
   | 1 | 2 | 3 | 4 | 5 | 6 | 7 | 8

PRETEST

Take two 1-minute timings on line 15, and determine your speed by using the faster rate.

15 pace quit prep quad ping shop quey quod
   | 1 | 2 | 3 | 4 | 5 | 6 | 7 | 8

PRACTICE

Type each line twice.

16 pace pack park part pare page pane pale
17 quit quip quiet quill quick quirk quire

(Continued on next page)

BID FOR REPAIR AND PAINTING OF FENCE

Bid Specifications
To: Mr. James H. Tilton, 900 East
Main Street, Albany, NY 12201.
Date: May 9, 19---.
Description of Job:
Repair three sections of the
Wegerston Garden fence with
penta-treated posts and boards.
The job involves removing the
four old posts and nine old
boards and replacing them
with new posts and boards.
Stain the three new sections of
fencing and the remainder
of the original fencing. The
job includes applying two
coats of stain to the new
fencing and one coat to the
remaining original fencing.
Plants near the fence are
not to be damaged in
any way.

Materials:
The following materials
will be purchased by Handy
& is to be used on the job:

4 penta-treated Wooden full posts @ $4.50 each	$18.00
5 boards, 1" by 5' by 8', free of warping and knots, @ $3.00 each	$15.00
2 gallons of Rustic Valley outside wood stain @ $13.98	$27.96
2 pairs of gloves @ $1.50	$3.00
2 brushes @ $.94	$1.88
1 day rental of posthole diggers	$15.00
1 bag of fencing nails	$1.80
1 tape measure	$2.50
1 kite-string ball	$1.00
Total cost of materials	$86.14
2 Workers @ $4.00 an hour for 8 hours	$_____
Total cost of job	$

TWO INVOICES FOR SMALL JOBS

The first invoice is to Mr. Farwell Paulsen for typing a brochure. He lives at 2980 Martindale Avenue, Albany, NY 12201. Charge him $2.00 a page for 7 pages of statistical manuscript with 1 carbon copy for each page.

The second invoice is to Ms. Hillary Witham of 89 Junipher Street, Albany, NY 12201 for washing windows. Charges are for two 16-oz bottles of solution @ $.89; rental of ladder for 4 hours, $4.00; and 4 hours labor at $4.00 an hour.

THANK-YOU LETTERS TO COMPOSE

Earlier you asked Mrs. Wheeler to be a reference for your new company operation. She agreed to do so and has provided your group with several job leads. Write her a thank-you letter expressing your appreciation for her support of your new venture. Mr. Ryan also agreed to be a reference. As your neighbor and friend, he has also given you three good leads, including the painting of Mr. Barrington's garage—your biggest job so far. Write him a letter of thanks.

**PRACTICE
(Continued)**

18 prep peep jeep weep beep seep step stop
19 quad aqua quack quail quake quart qualm
20 ping pint pins pink pine pike pile pipe
21 shop chop crop prop plop flop slop slow
22 quey ques quest queen quell queue queer
23 quod quot quota quoth quoit quote quori

POSTTEST

Take two 1-minute timings on line 15, and determine your speed by using the faster rate. Note your improvement.

LESSON 10

GOALS
- To control hyphen, Z, and diagonal keys by touch.
- To use correct spacing with the semicolon, colon, period, comma, hyphen, dash, and diagonal.

FORMAT
- Single spacing   40-space line

KEYBOARDING REVIEW

Type each line twice.

1 left best dome quip wave jogs chin bake
2 Meg saved her worn black quilt for Pam.

 KEY

Use Sem finger.
Do not space before or after hyphens.

Type each line twice.

3 ;;; ;p- ;p; --- ;;; ;p- ;-; --- ;p- ;-;
4 ;p- ;-; self-made ;p- ;-; one-third ;-;
5 ;p- ;-; part-time ;p- ;-; one-fifth ;-;

 KEY

Use A finger.

Type each line twice.

6 aaa aza zzz aaa aza zzz aaa aza zzz aza
7 aza zip zip aza zap zap aza zed zed aza
8 aza, to zig, to zag, to zing, to seize,

AGREEMENT FOR PAINTING A GARAGE

This agreement made and concluded this fourth day of May, 19--, by and between Handy 8s and Norwell T. Barrington of 14 West Fifth Street, Albany, NY 12203.

Article 1. Service. Handy 8s agrees to provide not fewer than four painters for a period of 1 week (5 working days) of 8 hours a day, to scrape, sand, and paint the garage of Mr. Barrington of 14 West Fifth Street.

Article 2. Wages. Handy 8s agrees to provide painters at the rate of four dollars ($4) an hour per employee, not to exceed 40 hours per employee, for the length of time it takes to complete the job.

Article 3. Materials. Handy 8s agrees to furnish all the materials and to perform all the work specified in the Bid Specifications prepared by Handy 8s on the fourth day of May, 19--, and appended to and made a part of this agreement.

Article 4. Payment. Mr. Barrington agrees to pay the full amount of the agreement on completion of the job as work done satisfactorily and according to the agreement.

IN WITNESS WHEREOF, the parties hereto have executed this agreement, the fourth day of May, 19--.

_____   _____
For Handy 8s   Norwell T. Barrington

_____   _____
Witness   Witness

LETTER REQUESTING REFERENCE

Your neighbor, Mr. Ryan, of 454 West Lyons Road in Albany, NY 12203, has allowed you to do several odd jobs for him in the past. He also knows your three friends very well. Ask him if you can use his name as a reference in your new business. Choose the letter style; the letter must be clear and courteous.

INVOICE

To: Mrs. Marshall T. Wilshire, 14 Hampton Way, Albany, NY 12203, for 6 hours' labor for cleaning windows and 1 gallon of Eze-Wipe window cleaner.

BID SPECIFICATIONS

To: Mr. Norwell T. Barrington, 14 West Fifth Street, Albany, NY 12203.

Date: May 4, 19--.

Description of Job. Scrape, sand, and paint a one-story frame garage at 14 West Fifth Street, Albany, New York. The job includes complete scraping, sanding, and cleaning of surface before painting, one coat of oil-base primer to be applied to all surfaces including windows and doors, two coats of oil-base regular outside paint to be applied to all surfaces. The windows are to be cleaned upon completion of the painting, and the entire area around the house is to be left as it was before the painting began.

Materials. The following materials will be purchased or rented (if so stated) by the Handy 8s to be used on the job: 6 gallons of white oil-base primer Colonial Mark paint @ $12.95 a gallon to be used on all surfaces; 8 gallons of gray oil-base regular outside Colonial Mark paint @ $12.95 a gallon, to be used on all surfaces; 1 gallon of Colonial Mark paint thinner @ $10.95; 1 roll of 50-foot polyethylene sheeting to protect driveway and shrubbery @ $9.50; 2 roller cover replacements @ $1.98; 1 box of razor blades @ $1.89; 1 gallon of Eze-Wipe window cleaner @ $.98; 24 squares of coarse sandpaper @ $.75; rental of ladders, $30; and rental of electric sanding machine, $50.

Labor. 4 painters, each working 5 days, 8 hours a day, @ $4.00 an hour

Total cost _____

TWO CHECKS

Type one check to Central Paint Supplies for $30 for the rental of ladders on a job that you have already completed. Type a second check to Albany Hardware Supplies for $89.74 for supplies used during the month of April.

KEY

Use Sem finger.

Do not space before or after a diagonal.

Type each line twice.

9 ;;; ;/; /// ;;; ;/; /// ;;; ;/; /// ;/;

10 ;/; his/her ;/; her/him ;/; us them ;/;

11 to/from slow/fast fall/winter Mar./Apr.

CHECKPOINT

Type lines 12–14 once. Then repeat lines 3 and 6 (page 18) and 9 or take two 2-minute timings on the Checkpoint.

12 Our teams would not quit because of the 8

13 size and voice of their pep club crowd. 16

14 Their jumps and tricks brought the win. 24

  | 1 | 2 | 3 | 4 | 5 | 6 | 7 | 8

PUNCTUATION SPACING

Type lines 15–24 once. Note the spacing before and after each punctuation mark.

Space once after a semicolon.

15 The dance looks nice; it shows balance.

16 The skit was tops; it was so organized.

Space twice after a colon.

17 Two courses are open: science and art.

18 Three members went: Ann, Lee, and Joe.

Space twice after a period at the end of a sentence.

19 Send it to me. I can print it so fast.

20 The skirt is plaid. It matches a suit.

Space once after a period used with some initials and titles.

21 Ms. Kebo asked Dr. T. S. Laos to speak.

22 Mr. and Mrs. Lark were honored at noon.

Do not space after a period used with degrees or with letters in a group.

23 She earned her Ph.D. from Oregon State.

24 The U.S.A. and the U.S.S.R. were there.

Type lines 25–32 once. Again, note the spacing before and after each punctuation mark.

Space once after a comma.

25 When Jean called me, I was not at home.

26 Send them red, white, and green copies.

Do not space before or after a hyphen.

27 The up-to-date calendar was so helpful.

28 His mother-in-law is the new president.

Do not space before or after a dash (two hyphens).

29 That machine--the black one--is broken.

30 The office gives good service--on time.

Do not space before or after a diagonal.

31 The fall/winter catalog has new colors.

32 The on/off button is on the right side.

IN-BASKET J: SMALL BUSINESS

You and three of your friends have formed a company called Handy 8s to do odd jobs for summer employment. Your company requires quite a bit of recordkeeping and typing—and you're in charge! Workbook 743 bottom–767.

PRIORITY SHEET AND TIME LOG

Read through the entire in-basket and then complete the priority sheet. Be sure to keep an accurate time log as you complete each job.

LETTER ASKING FOR REFERENCE

mrs. aileen wheeler 87 adams avenue albany ny 12205 dear mrs. wheeler we know that you will be pleased to hear that a group of young people are industrious enough to cooperate in creating summer employment for themselves / harvey schmidt lowell greene rosemary barton and i have formed a partnership to offer our skills in performing various jobs in the community like cutting grass cleaning garages cleaning vacant lots painting and typing / we call ourselves the handy 8s and we hope to provide special services which are not so easily obtainable in our community / since you know all four of us quite well and can attest to our character and our abilities we would like to use your name as a reference for our new business / may we have your permission to do so / please do let us know / sincerely

LETTER TO ANSWER COMPLAINT

Dear Mrs. Witham: We are very sorry that we left ladder marks on your siding when we cleaned your windows last week. If you will show us how you would like the marks removed or covered up, we will be at your house Wednesday morning to complete the job.

We hope that you will accept our apology for any inconvenience that we may have caused you. We are very eager to do quality work, and we would like to repair your siding to your satisfaction. Sincerely,

NEWSPAPER AD

Need an extra hand – or maybe eight?
Call the Handy 8s.
Four reliable students from
Hardin High School would like
summer employment.
Excellent references available.
Call 555-8296 or 555-7291.
Quality guaranteed.
   Cleaning   Painting
   Typing   Mowing

ANSWER TO INQUIRY LETTER

Mr. James H. Tilton
900 East Main Street
Albany, NY *12201*
Dear Mr. Tilton:
Thank you for asking us to submit a bid on the painting of the fence around the *Wegerston* ~~Weagerton~~ Garden Center. We have long admired the beauty of the garden and the special place that it has in our community. ¶ May we meet with you *next* Monday afternoon to discuss the specific requirements necessary to complete the job and the type of materials that you wish used for the job? ¶ Please call *us* ~~me~~ at 555-8296 or 555-7291 after 6:00 p.m. any evening this week.

      Cordially,

      THE HANDY 8s

LESSON 11

GOAL
- To control Y, X, and question mark keys by touch.

FORMAT
- Single spacing   40-space line

KEYBOARDING REVIEW

Type each line twice.

1 deft lack vase more haze wing quip jibe
2 Zipp made quick jet flights over Nawbi.

SPACE BAR

 KEY

Use J finger.

Type each line twice.

3 jjj jyj yyy jjj jyj yyy jjj jyj yyy jyj
4 jyj yip yip jyj aye aye jyj joy joy jyj
5 jyj; yard of yarn, yield a yawn, a Yule

 KEY

Use S finger.

Type each line twice.

6 sss sxs xxx sss sxs xxx sss sxs xxx sxs
7 sxs vex vex sxs mix mix sxs wax wax sxs
8 sxs; next taxi, sixty Texans, lax taxes

 KEY

Use Sem finger and left shift key.
Space twice after a question mark.

Type each line twice.

9   ;;; ;/; ;/? ;?; ;;; ;/; ;/? ;?; ;/; ;?;
10 ;/; ;?; now? now? ;?; how? how? ;?;
11 who? when? where? what? why? next?

CHECKPOINT

Type lines 12–14 once. Then repeat lines 3, 6, and 9 or take two 2-minute timings on the Checkpoint.

12 Grab your camera; fix the lens. Take a   8
13 quick shot. Go to the zoo. Wait for a 16
14 move or a jump. Ready? Get that shot. 24
    | 1 | 2 | 3 | 4 | 5 | 6 | 7 | 8

GOALS
- To type 50/5'/3e.
- To prioritize and format related office communications.

FORMAT
- Single spacing   60-space line   5-space tab

KEYBOARDING SKILLS

Type lines 1–4 once. Then practice using the shift lock while typing the words in all capitals in line 5. Repeat lines 1–4, or take a series of 1-minute timings.

Speed 1   The bush bent in the wind and lost its leaves with a shrug.   12
Accuracy 2   As Elizabeth requested, Jack will pay for fixing my silver.   12
Numbers 3   Five camps are 10, 29, 38, 47, and 56 kilometers from here.   12
Symbols 4   The "home position" on the TEN–KEY is on the 4–5–6 key row.   12
Practice Shifts 5   The popular ADDING–LISTING machine is a TEN–KEY calculator.

  | 1 | 2 | 3 | 4 | 5 | 6 | 7 | 8 | 9 | 10 | 11 | 12

5-MINUTE TIMINGS

Take a 5-minute timing on lines 6–26. Type six times each word on which you made an error, hesitated, or stopped during the 5-minute timing. Then take a 5-minute timing to see how much your skill has improved.

6   Modern offices must operate as communications systems.   12
7   Modern offices must operate as communications systems.   24
8   Modern offices must operate as communications systems.   36
9   Most activities that include personnel, equipment, and pro–   48
10   Most activities that include personnel, equipment, and pro–   60
11   Most activities that include personnel, equipment, and pro–   72
12   cesses are analyzed according to how they affect each other   84
13   cesses are analyzed according to how they affect each other   96
14   cesses are analyzed according to how they affect each other   108
15   in the whole communications operation. Personnel must work   120
16   in the whole communications operation. Personnel must work   132
17   in the whole communications operation. Personnel must work   144
18   in clusters and alone. Equipment is sophisticated and very   156
19   in clusters and alone. Equipment is sophisticated and very   168
20   in clusters and alone. Equipment is sophisticated and very   180
21   capable of adjusting for extra work loads. Procedures lend   192
22   capable of adjusting for extra work loads. Procedures lend   204
23   capable of adjusting for extra work loads. Procedures lend   216
24   support to personnel and equipment to reach common goals.   228
25   support to personnel and equipment to reach common goals.   240
26   support to personnel and equipment to reach common goals.   250

  | 1 | 2 | 3 | 4 | 5 | 6 | 7 | 8 | 9 | 10 | 11 | 12   SI 1.97

Take two 1-minute timings on line 15, and determine your speed by using the faster rate.

15   play zany yoke pays zest yews jazz tax?
    | 1 | 2 | 3 | 4 | 5 | 6 | 7 | 8

PRACTICE

Type each line twice.

To Type Faster
Read copy before typing it.
Aim for smoothness in stroking.

16   play flay clay slay shay stay sway away
17   zany maze daze doze hazy lazy hazy haze
18   yoke yolk your you, year yea, yet, yes?
19   pays nays mays jays hays days cays bays

20   zest sizes oversize full-size half-size
21   yews yaws yams yaps yaks yard yarn yawn
22   jazz nuzzle muzzle puzzle dazzle razzle
23   tax? taxi? text? next? flex? flax?

POSTTEST

Take two 1-minute timings on line 15, and determine your speed by using the faster rate. Note your improvement.

LESSON 12

CLINIC

GOALS
- To strengthen reaches on third, home, and bottom rows.
- To type 20 words a minute for 2 minutes with 4 errors or less.

FORMAT
- Single spacing   40-space line

PRETEST

Take a 1-minute timing on each line.

Third row   1   They will type quiet quips from a page.   8
Home row   2   Jed had asked for the glass in a flash.   8
Bottom row   3   Zach, move that ax back into that cave.   8
             | 1 | 2 | 3 | 4 | 5 | 6 | 7 | 8

PRACTICE

Type lines 4–8 twice. Then proofread and circle errors.

4   rook work lurk dirk kirk keep kelp kilt
5   full foul fowl file fire four fort fore
6   jolt jets joke just jerk jugs jowl jaws
7   tort were quit quip tour prep pour were
8   your type true pert pipe wipe ripe prop

(Continued on next page)

TABLE

Use an attractive, easy-to-read format.

GIVE TO MANAGER BEFORE YOU LEAVE TODAY.

STOCK OWNERSHIP IN SOS, INC.

	DECEMBER 31, 1980		LAST YEAR	
	HOLDERS	PERCENT	HOLDERS	PERCENT
INDIVIDUALS:				
MEN..........................	4,500	25.7	4,950	25.1
WOMEN........................	4,200	24.0	4,600	23.3
JOINT OWNERS.................	5,000	28.6	5,555	28.2
STOCKBROKERS, SECURITY DEALERS...	950	5.4	890	4.5
NOMINEES.....................	350	2.0	530	2.7
FOREIGN HOLDERS..............	400	2.3	600	3.0
INSTITUTIONS AND MUTUAL FUNDS....	1,900	10.9	2,280	11.6
ALL OTHERS...................	200	1.1	310	1.6
TOTALS	17,500	100.0	19,715	100.0

ORGANIZATIONAL CHART

This regional sales office has been given new territories and new personnel. Please make a new chart using the names written in. Type the names in all capitals and their titles in capitals and lowercase.

DO WHEN YOU HAVE TIME

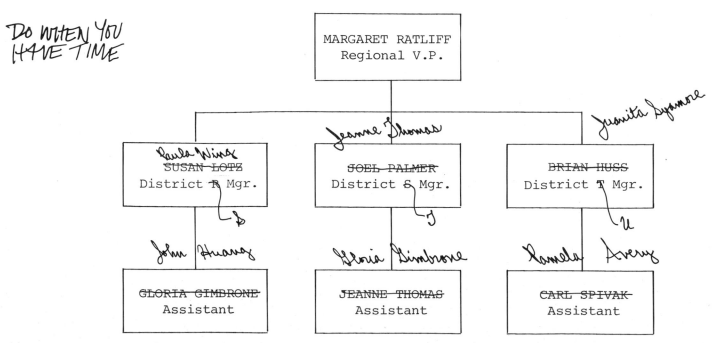

PRACTICE
(Continued)

Check Your Hands

Palms are low but do not touch the machine.

Hands are flat and level across their backs.

The thumb is above the center of the space bar.

Hands are so close you could lock the thumbs.

All fingers are curved so that you type on the tips.

Type lines 9–13 twice. Then proofread and circle errors.

```
 9  wade jade fade fads gads dads lads lass
10  hash mash cash wash rash gash lash dash
11  gall fall hall hale kale sale dale gale
12  skid slid sled fled flag slag shag shad
13  drag lark lake khan fast load glad clad
```

Type lines 14–18 twice. Then proofread and circle errors.

```
14  pan, tan, man, fan, ran, van, ban, can,
15  bend bind mine mice mace calm acme came
16  move cove cave nave vain vein vine vane
17  nabs cabs cubs cobs cons conk cone cane
18  mix, fix, nix, ace, size daze maxe viz.
```

Repeat the group of lines that was the most difficult.

POSTTEST

Take a 1-minute timing on each of lines 1–3. Note your improvement.

2-MINUTE TIMINGS

SI means "syllabic intensity—the average number of syllables per word." A paragraph with all one-syllable words would have an SI of 1.00.

Take two 2-minute timings on lines 19–23. Use your paper bail to proofread your copy. Circle your errors and figure your score on each timing.

```
19  By the time you have typed the lines in    8
20  these first twelve lessons, you will be   16
21  able to type faster than you can write.   24
22  Relax.  You can adjust the machine, and   32
23  you can zoom through your work quickly.   40
    | 1 | 2 | 3 | 4 | 5 | 6 | 7 | 8   SI 1.16
```

LESSON 13

UNIT 3 FORMATTING—BASIC TECHNIQUES AND PROCEDURES

UNIT GOAL
24/2'/4e

GOALS
- To use the shift lock to type all capitals.
- To use three tabular keys to set a tab, to clear a tab, and to indent a new paragraph.

FORMAT
- Single spacing   50-space line

KEYBOARDING SKILLS

Type each line twice.

Words

Speed

Accuracy

```
1  aqua wish face join milk cozy play sobs over text
2  The girls may make a profit if they sing for Dot.
3  Just pack my box with five dozen quilts and rugs.
```

TYPE THIS WHEN YOU HAVE THE TIME.

WATCH FOR ERRORS — I MARKED MOST OF THEM.

MAKE A CARBON COPY OF THIS FOR MY FILE.

CONFERENCE REPORT

Over 1,400 exhibits, 95 sessions, a personal computing festival, and A special conference on minicomputers ~~was~~ WERE featured at the national computer conference, December 28-29, at the Anaheim California convention center. THE ~~presentation of the~~ American federation of Information Processing Societies, Inc., had as its theme "New directions for THE new decade." Pam Rizzo of Moorpark College was the program chairperson.

Beginning the first session was Paula Wing, who presented a seminar on "A Pragmatic View of Distributed Processing Systems." IT WAS moderated by Susan Lotz. Full-day seminars included "Performance measurement in systems and programming" by Pam Avery, "Quality control for software" by Mary Monk, "Structuring the Data Base System" by Natalie Caskey, "Software Design Techniques" by Julie Schaefer, "Computer Security" by Lori Robins, AND "Software Tools" by Gloria Gimbrone.

Half-day seminars were conducted by Julie Scheper on "Design by Objectives," Kelly Maxton on "Packaging Your Image for Success," Tammy Colton on "How to Develop a Long-Range Plan," Dixie Wiseman on "Contract Negotiations," and Jeannie Thomas on "An Overview of Distributed Processing."

A complete file of the literature from the conference is available for anyone who is interested in reviewing materials from any of the sessions. Cassette tapes are also available OF ~~from~~ the sessions that I attended.

TITLE THE REPORT FOR ME. TYPE IT IN ALL CAPS AT THE CENTER.

CHECKS

Send two commission checks to the following two salespersons: Sandra J. Henkel for $450 and James L. Hustad for $730.

30-SECOND TIMINGS

How fast can you type with no more than 1 error for 30 seconds? Find out by taking two 30-second timings on lines 4–5 below. Remember to multiply the total words typed by 2 to find your 1-minute rate.

4 When you go for a ride in a car, take a look from 10

5 the window and view the sights as you move along. 20
   | 1 | 2 | 3 | 4 | 5 | 6 | 7 | 8 | 9 | 10

ACCURACY

Accuracy lines should be typed as a paragraph.

Type lines 6–10 twice.

6 aaa aye aaa air aaa ail aaa aim aaa aria aaa alma

7 eee elf eee ewe eee eye eee end eee even eee earn

8 iii six iii did iii win iii fin iii city iii give

9 ooo oak ooo sod ooo own ooo ore ooo oboe ooo oleo

10 uuu sub uuu cub uuu rub uuu cup uuu sure uuu much

SPEED

Speed lines should be typed individually.

Type each line twice.

11 isle fuel flay gown keys then she for and the own

12 fish sign form wish duck they eye icy dig sow bug

13 pale idle gush slay torn roam sue hay sob man oak

14 goal bush firm chap lake city pay wit fur irk urn

15 lead coal pane risk half kept has lot yam cut fix

TAB STOPS

A formatting technique.

To make the carriage or carrier skip to a selected point, set a tab stop at that point and use the tab key.

1. Eliminate any stop that may be in the way. Press the all-clear key if your machine has one; or move the carriage or carrier to the right margin, and then hold down the tab clear key as you return the carriage or carrier.

2. Set the tab stop by moving the carriage or carrier to the point where you want it and pressing the tab set key.

3. Test the setting. Bring the carriage or carrier back to the left margin, and then press the tabulator key or bar—hold it down firmly until the carriage or carrier stops moving. It should stop where you set the tab stop.

Practice: Set a tab stop 5 spaces in from the left margin, and type *The* indented on three lines.

　　→ 5
　　　The
　　　The
　　　The

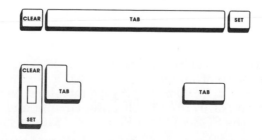

You are a secretary for the regional sales office for SOS, Inc., an information processing equipment distributor. Your boss is Margaret Ratliff, Vice President for Marketing. Ms. Ratliff has left the office for one week with directions for you to complete the following jobs. *Remember to prioritize your work before you begin.* Record documents in the order in which you complete them. Record the amount of time you used to complete each job. Workbook 737–743 top.

PRIORITY SHEET AND TIME LOG

Read through the entire in-basket, and then complete the priority sheet. Be sure to keep an accurate time log as you complete each job.

FORM LETTER

Plain paper.

GET THIS TO THE GRAPHIC ARTS DEPARTMENT BY NOON TOMORROW.

I would like to take this opportunity to invite you to the Westboro Regional Center Open House, which will be held on Wednesday, January 28, 19—. The hours will be 3 p.m. to 8 p.m. This event will be a gala new product introduction featuring many exciting innovations!

Every 15 minutes there will be a miniseminar on one of several topics of interest such as the Model SOS-90, the SOS-12 Pocket Computer, and the SOS-80 Word Processor. Refreshments will be served, and for each attendee there will be a coupon worth $20 toward any of our educational classes.

You will have the opportunity to meet with all our trained sales personnel as well as with other company representatives. This promises to be the most fascinating event in our area for some time to come. If you will be able to attend, please mail the enclosed postal card today. Please feel free to invite any of your colleagues who would enjoy this experience. Best regards,

POSTAL CARD

Yes! I will attend the Westboro Regional Center Open House on January 28, 19--. I will bring _____ guests with me.

Name _____ Company/School _____

IMMEDIATELY! EDIT THIS CAREFULLY.

DICTATED MEMO

to all sales personnel from margaret ratliff vice president for sales subject open house the letters for the open house will be mailed next week to all sales prospects in the westboro area please check the computer printout in the next two days and let my secretary know if you have additional prospects this open house is going to be an excellent opportunity for us to show our new products and familiarize clients with our complete line of services please review your sales

INVOICES

Send two invoices. (1) To Info Systems, 9025 South Broadway, Westboro, NJ 07701, for 3 boxes of minidiskettes @ $90 a box, 6 dozen polyfilm ribbons @ $29.95 a dozen. (2) To Montgomery County Joint Vocational School, 191 Hoke Road, Westboro NJ 07701, for cleaning circuits and repairing the alternating component on the SOS-80 Word Processor—$45 for labor and $15 for the part.

INDENTING FOR PARAGRAPHS
A formatting technique.

When a paragraph is indented, as it is below, the indention is 5 spaces. Each indention counts as 5 strokes (1 word), the same as 5 space bar strokes would count. Use the tab to indent line 16 in the paragraph below.

2-MINUTE TIMINGS

Take two 2-minute timings on lines 16–20. Use your paper bail to proofread your copy. Circle your errors and figure your score on each timing. Format: Double spacing.

16   To watch the squirrel is a good lesson, some   10
17   say. It takes some time to zip from limb to limb   20
18   and fix a place to put the food it hopes to save.   30
19   It makes the time to join a friend and bring some   40
20   happiness.   42
     | 1 | 2 | 3 | 4 | 5 | 6 | 7 | 8 | 9 | 10   SI 1.09

TYPING ALL-CAPITAL LETTERS

A formatting technique.

1. Press the shift lock. It is above one or both of the shift keys.
2. Type the words that are to be in all capitals.
3. Release the shift lock by touching the opposite shift key. (**Caution:** Release the lock before typing a stroke that, like a hyphen, cannot be typed as a capital.)

Practice: Type each line twice.

21   I need ONE MORE letter to FINISH the word puzzle.
22   Our team is FIRST-RATE. We WON the CHAMPIONSHIP.
23   MARILEE and KIPP and BO were selected as LEADERS.

LESSON 14

GOALS
- To use the backspace key to center items horizontally.
- To center items horizontally (across) on a page.

FORMAT
- Single spacing   50-space line

KEYBOARDING SKILLS

Type each line twice.

Words   1   know deck file pogo jobs quey mare vote oxen hazy
Speed   2   This girl is to go to the field to work for them.
Accuracy 3   Packy quietly boxed these frozen jams with vigor.

LESSONS 287—289

UNIT 47 IN-BASKETS

GOALS
- To type 50/5'/3e.
- To prioritize and format related office communications.

FORMAT
- Single spacing   60-space line   5-space tab

KEYBOARDING SKILLS

Type lines 1–4 once. Then practice your space-bar technique on line 5. Repeat lines 1–4, or take a series of 1-minute timings.

Speed 1 Their firm is paid to paint half the signs for those towns. 12
Accuracy 2 Francis and Max proved quite lucky with the big jazz bands. 12
Numbers 3 Type 1 and 2 and 3 and 4 and 5 and 6 and 7 and 8, 9, or 10. 12
Symbols 4 The runners were numbered "10," "29," "38," "47," and "56." 12
Space Bar 5 Write again . . . and again . . . and again . . . and stop.

| 1 | 2 | 3 | 4 | 5 | 6 | 7 | 8 | 9 | 10 | 11 | 12

5-MINUTE TIMINGS

Take two 5-minute timings on lines 6–27.

6   It is amazing what major breakthroughs word processing 12
7 enjoys. Software has been developed to permit operators to 24
8 input text in over 15 different languages without knowledge 36
9 of the language that is input. Two disks hold the required 48
10 software that enables the units to use two languages at the 60
11 same time. An operator types copy from foreign manuscript, 72
12 inserting proper accent marks. The table disk converts the 84
13 keystrokes on the keyboard to the designated characters for 96
14 the particular language on the display screen; and with the 108
15 proper printwheel inserted, it coordinates the keyboard and 120
16 the rotary printer. The message disk converts these system 132
17 messages to each language. 137

18   The entire procedure for adapting a word processor for 49
19 another language can be quickly done. The machine operator 61
20 accomplishes this with a few keystrokes by transferring the 173
21 tables of the desired language from one disk to another one 185
22 while the word processor automatically adapts to the desig– 197
23 nated language. The word processor is actually communicat– 209
24 ing in more than one language at a time. A German operator 221
25 can, for example, key and print letters in French; however, 233
26 the machine will display the message in German to allow the 245
27 operator to proofread it. 250

| 1 | 2 | 3 | 4 | 5 | 6 | 7 | 8 | 9 | 10 | 11 | 12   SI 1.70

Take two 30-second timings on lines 4–5, or type each line twice.

4 Can you think of all the things that you would do 10

5 if you could do just as you wanted to for a week? 20

| 1 | 2 | 3 | 4 | 5 | 6 | 7 | 8 | 9 | 10

ACCURACY

Type lines 6–10 twice.

6 see butt happy errors flivver carriage occasional

7 off poll dizzy middle blabber possible bookkeeper

8 zoo buff radii sizzle powwows followed additional

9 inn ebbs gummy bottle accused slowness beginnings

10 Hannah took a dotted swiss dress to the Mall Inn.

SPEED

Type each line twice.

11 formal prisms blend panel busy chap cut ham is it

12 social glands visit field torn sign rid air to do

13 eighty blames audit forms half fuel apt owl of an

14 profit island slept right tidy cork fix hem am so

15 The theme for the eighth panel is When to Fix It.

FORMATTING: HORIZONTAL CENTERING

Workbook 15–16.

To center horizontally:

1. Set the carriage or carrier at the center.

2. Find the backspace key (upper left or right corner of the keyboard).

3. Say the strokes (including spaces) in pairs to yourself, depressing the backspace key once after you say each pair. If you have an odd letter left over after calling off all pairs, do *not* backspace for it.

Example: Center these ⏑⏑⏑⏑⏑⏑ to center ⏑⏑⏑⏑

4. Type the material. It should appear in the middle of the paper.

Practice: Type each of the following two drills. Use half sheets of paper. Format: Begin on line 14; double-space.

```
        ↓
        |
  Center these

 lines by using

the backspace key.
```

```
        ↓
        |
   It is easy

  to center

by backspacing.
```

JOB 14-1. CENTERING

Format the names by centering on a full sheet of paper. Double-space. Begin on line 15. Leave 5 blank lines between each group of names.

Les Boland	Marijane Landon	Stepha Mark
Bill Colburn	Anna Lee Lipton	Steve Fabr
Stan Orlen	Patsy Clark	Hester V. Starfire
Jerry Longaman	Robin Salmon	Stella Jo Garman
Fran Mortimer	Noel Wilson	Lawrence Oren

CLINIC

GOAL
- To review contractions, possessives, spelling, and subject-verb agreement while typing sentences.

FORMAT
- Single spacing   60-space line

LAB REVIEW   Workbook 735–736.

Type lines 1–5 once, forming contractions wherever appropriate.

1   We do not want them to feel that they will have to support it.
2   He would not go if he did not feel that it is a very good job.
3   Have not you seen the ad in the paper for someone who will go?
4   I would like them to know that we will be glad to offer our help.
5   Can not you arrange your schedule so that they will come today?

Type lines 6–20 once, choosing the correct word in parentheses.

6   The (Smith's/Smiths') house is new, but the (Joneses'/Jones') home is antique.
7   The (child's/childs') toy was displayed in the (childrens'/children's) department.
8   His (boss's/bosses') office was different from their (boss's/bosses') offices.
9   We appreciate (them/their) being quiet during the (childrens'/children's) play.
10   (Us/Our) working overtime made (them/their) supervising so much easier.
11   (Them/Their) singing so loudly contrasted with (us/our) singing softly.
12   (Pam and Julie's/Pam's and Julie's) assignments were completed by the deadline.
13   (Shannon's and Jerry's/Shannon and Jerry's) duet was better than James and Larry's.
14   They (don't/doesn't) like their data processor, but he (do/does) like his.
15   The program (is/are) interesting; other programs (is/are) not as good.
16   The table (is/are) walnut, but the chairs (is/are) a variety of maple.
17   The books displayed on the shelf (is/are) the last ones ordered.
18   The members of the board (was/were) asked to attend this meeting.
19   Joel, Fred, or Lynn (want/wants) to attend the in-service program.
20   Joel, Fred, and Lynn (want/wants) to attend an in-service program.

Type lines 21–26 once, correcting any misspelled words.

21   I sincerly beleive that they can except the agrement.
22   The new primium notis was enclosed in a seperate enveelope.
23   Which destribution precedure will the new comitee follow?
24   She will recieve the compleat anual busines report today.
25   Do you know weather the matarial will be availible on time?
26   I have a reciept for an item that appears on the statment.

PROOFREAD   Edit your copy as your teacher reads the answers. Retype any lines that you typed incorrectly the first time.

LESSON 15

KEYBOARDING SKILLS

Type each line twice.

Words   1 both cram dyed life give junk quip owes axle size

Speed   2 Six or eight pens go to the man with the oak cot.

Accuracy 3 Quickly box five dozen afghans for W. M. Jeptham.

FORMATTING: BLOCK CENTERING

To center a group of lines (not each line separately), use the following block-centering procedure:

1. Pick the longest line in the group.
2. Backspace to center that line.
3. Set the left margin stop.
4. Begin all lines at the left margin.

Practice: Block-center each of these drills, leaving 5 lines between exercises. Begin on line 26 and double-space.

```
Centering a block
of lines is called
block centering.



LEARNING TO CENTER ITEMS
A Report by
[Your Name]
```

JOB 15-1. BLOCK CENTERING

Format the three groups of names by block centering each group. Use a full sheet of paper. Double-space. Begin on line 15. Leave 5 blank lines between each group.

Mehra Golshan	Jill Poeppelmeier	Kim Kaufenberg
Amy Tidovsky	Mike Goeke	Shakira Jadross
Steve Burton	Melody Luoma	Jenny Chojnacki
Jeff Maresca	Kevin Negilski	Ed Byrum
Jane Williamson	Lisa Serafin	Donita Steger

30-SECOND TIMINGS

Take two 30-second timings on lines 4–5, or type each line twice.

4 When you join your school pep club, you will find   10

5 all kinds of jobs that you can do to gain spirit.   20

| 1 | 2 | 3 | 4 | 5 | 6 | 7 | 8 | 9 | 10

12-SECOND TIMINGS

Type each line four times, or take four 12-second timings on each line. For each timing, type with no error.

```
5  We do not know yet all that we would like to know about it.   12
6  He could go if he wanted to, but he wished to stay at home.   12
7  I can drive the new car to the field and meet their flight.   12
                                         25   30   35   40   45   50   55   60
```

GROUP HOSPITAL INSURANCE FORMS

Insurance forms are prepared by medical typists and sent to insurance companies for charges incurred by policyholders or by members of their families.

GROUP HOSPITAL INSURANCE FORM

To Trail Ridge Clinic Hospital. This certifies that Betty O'Brien is insured for the following Group Hospital Benefits (in behalf of his or her dependent Self (Name) ---- (Relationship)) By Colorado Security Insurance Company (Name of Insurer)

BENEFITS FOR MATERNITY CASES

HOSPITAL ROOM AND BOARD (INCLUDING GENERAL NURSING SERVICE) AND OTHER HOSPITAL SERVICES . . . ACTUAL CHARGES UP TO $ ______

OR

1. HOSPITAL ROOM AND BOARD (INCLUDING GENERAL NURSING SERVICES) $______ FOR EACH DAY OF HOSPITALIZATION UP TO ______ DAYS
2. OTHER HOSPITAL CHARGES FOR HOSPITAL CARE AND TREATMENT (EXCLUDING CHARGES FOR NURSES' AND PHYSICIANS' SERVICES AND TAKE-HOME DRUGS) $______

BENEFITS FOR OTHER THAN MATERNITY CASES

A. HOSPITAL ROOM AND BOARD (INCLUDING GENERAL NURSING SERVICES) ACTUAL HOSPITAL CHARGES UP TO $ 90.00 FOR EACH DAY OF HOSPITALIZATION UP TO 90 DAYS.

B. OTHER HOSPITAL CHARGES FOR HOSPITAL CARE AND TREATMENT (EXCLUDING CHARGES FOR NURSES' AND PHYSICIANS' SERVICES AND TAKE-HOME DRUGS) $ No limit

GROUP POLICYHOLDER: Adams Department Store — ADDRESS: 1496 Broadway Street, Denver, CO 80203 — PHONE: 555-0214

BY (Name and Title): ---- — ABOVE CERTIFICATION VALID FOR ONLY SEVEN DAYS FROM THIS DATE (Exception—Maternity Cases) — DATE: ----

HOSPITAL COMPLETE FOLLOWING AND FURNISH COPY TO: Adams Department Store — ADDRESS: See above

NAME OF PATIENT	AGE	DATE ADMITTED	TIME ADMITTED	DATE DISCHARGED	TIME DISCHARGED
Betty O'Brien	60	6/12/--	2:30 PM	6/30/--	11:15 AM

DIAGNOSIS FROM RECORDS (If Injury, Give Date and Place of Accident): Cerebrovascular spasm and generalized arteriosclerosis

OPERATIONS OR OBSTETRICAL PROCEDURES PERFORMED (Nature and Date): None

HOSPITAL CHARGES (Complete This Section or Attach Copy of Itemized Bill Showing Information Below)

ROOM AND BOARD			
☐ WARD	DAYS AT $	TOTAL	$
☒ SEMIPRIVATE	18 DAYS AT $ 75.00	TOTAL	$1,350.00
☐ PRIVATE	DAYS AT $	TOTAL	$
☐ OTHERS			$

OTHER CHARGES	
OPERATING OR DELIVERY ROOM	
ANESTHESIA	
X-RAY	50.00
LABORATORY	
EKG BMR	35.00
PHYSICAL THERAPY	
AMBULANCE	
MEDICAL AND SURGICAL SUPPLIES	
PHARMACY (Except Take-Home Drugs)	75.50
INHALATION THERAPY	
INTRAVENOUS SOLUTIONS	
Television	36.00
TOTAL	$1,546.50

TOTAL CHARGES $1,546.50

Patient Credit $ 36.00

$ ______

Balance Due $1,510.50

HOSPITAL: Trail Ridge Clinic — ADDRESS: 83 Skyline Drive, Denver, CO 80215

TAKEN FROM RECORDS ON (Current date) 19-- — SIGNED BY

AUTHORIZATION TO RELEASE INFORMATION: I hereby authorize the above-named hospital to release the information requested on this form.

Date ______, 19____ Signed ______ Patient (Parent if a Minor)

AUTHORIZATION TO PAY INSURANCE BENEFITS: I hereby authorize payment directly to the above-named hospital of the Group Hospital Benefits herein specified and otherwise payable to me but not to exceed the hospital's regular charges for this period of hospitalization. I understand I am financially responsible to the hospital for charges not covered by this authorization.

Date ______. 19____ Signed ______ (Insured)

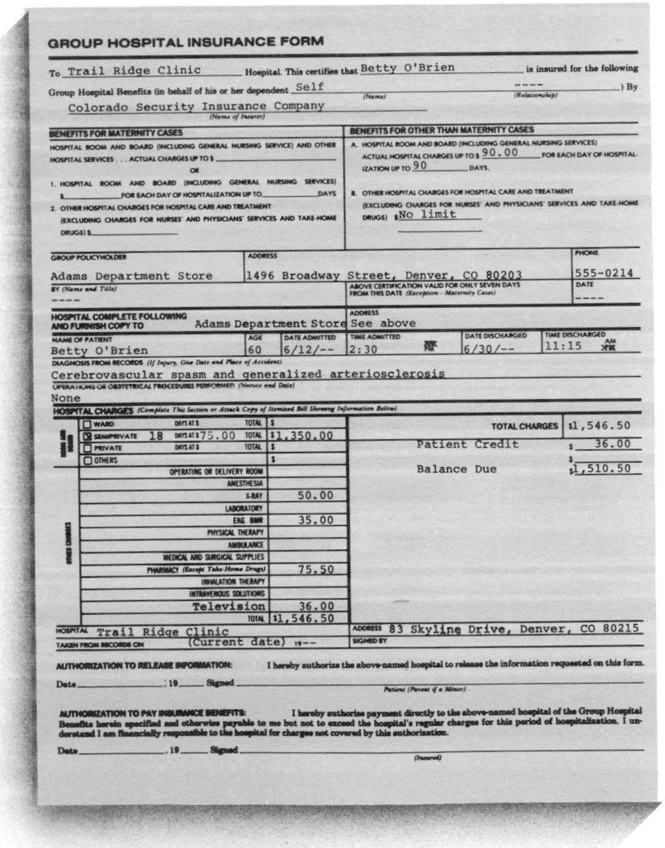

JOBS 285-1 TO 285-3. GROUP HOSPITAL INSURANCE FORMS

Using the data provided for the three patients listed below, complete a form for each patient. Use the illustration on the left as a guide. Workbook 729–733.

Dennis Dieterlie's son, Joe, who is 9 years old, fell off the swing at school on May 10 and was admitted to Trail Ridge Clinic, Inc., Denver, CO, at 11 a.m. Joe broke his left ankle. Mr. Dieterlie's insurance provides coverage of $85 a day for 70 days. He works at Mountain Electric on 3894 Aspen Lane in Denver, CO 80204. Joe was discharged on May 11 with charges of $90 for a semiprivate room, $100 for surgical costs, and $75 for lab costs.

Paula Ruppert, who is 40, was in an automobile accident on May 12 and was admitted to the clinic at 8:45 p.m. with facial lacerations. Insurance provides for $85 a day for 70 days. She works as a counselor at Denver High School on 2625 Main Street in Denver, CO 80208. Paula was discharged on May 13 with charges of $90 for a semiprivate room; $100 for the doctor's fee, and $40 for medical and surgical supplies.

Yolanda Padilla, who is 18, was burned while grilling meat on May 15 and was admitted to the clinic at 7:30 p.m. Insurance provides $95 a day for 60 days. She is a housewife, and her husband, John, works at the Giant Warehouse at 75 Hoke Road, Denver, CO 80207. Jeannie was discharged on May 17 with charges of $125 a day for a private room and $200 for medical and surgical supplies. The doctor's fee was $100.

ACCURACY

Type lines 6–10 twice.

6   on ear kin vat yip acre pill race upon face phony
7   we imp vex hip tag pink case limp zest lion cedar
8   in arc pin age you date jump were honk ease hilly
9   be joy tax oil fad noun tact yolk gear mink verse
10 After Kip agreed, John gave my dad a faster kiln.

SPEED

Type each line twice.

11 find this that who his and why him my be if do no
12 when wish like but out may for she me or am in to
13 them look they our the her got how by us it so up
14 what mine type now can fun put set of at on as go
15 She is to be there at a time when he can see her.

2-MINUTE TIMINGS

Take two 2-minute timings on lines 16–20. Use your paper bail to proofread your copy. Circle your errors and figure your score on each timing.

16   Watch the river move across the plain and on   10
17 to the bluff beyond. It has a tale to tell about   20
18 the ones who have gone this way. The men and the   30
19 women were not unique. They just had the zeal to   40
20 take the extra risk.   44
    | 1 | 2 | 3 | 4 | 5 | 6 | 7 | 8 | 9 | 10   SI 1.16

LESSON 16

GOALS
- To count vertical lines on a page.
- To center items vertically (up and down) on a page.

FORMAT
- Single spacing   50-space line   5-space tab and center tab

KEYBOARDING SKILLS

Type each line twice.

Words   1 away vice jeep high kiln form ribs exit zero quid
Speed   2 Jan works for us but may wish to work for Pamela.
Accuracy   3 Six jet-black vans quietly zip through wet farms.

REQUESTS FOR MEDICARE PAYMENT

This form was designed by the Social Security Administration so that doctors and patients can receive reimbursement for services covered by Medicare.

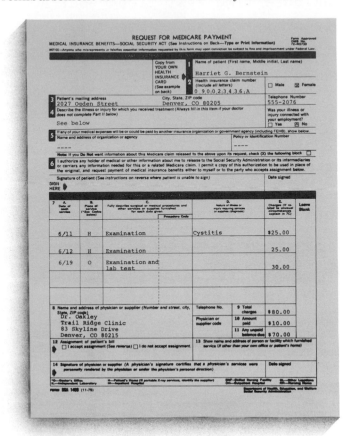

JOBS 284-1 TO 284-3. REQUESTS FOR MEDICARE PAYMENT

Using the data provided for the three patients listed below, complete a form for each patient. Use the illustration on the left as a guide. Workbook 721–725.

Don Erisman, 78 Canyon Rd., Denver 80237, Medicare claim number 072-34-9873A, received special diet for diabetes mellitus on June 3, 19--. The doctor's charge was $65. The patient paid $5, and the unpaid balance is $60. The physician is Dr. Martino [*clinic address: Trail Ridge Clinic, 83 Skyline Drive, Denver, CO 80215*].

Linda Wick, Apartment 4, 31 Rawlins Rd., Denver 80219, Medicare claim number 839-29-72859B, received treatment for pneumonia from June 1 through June 14, 19--. The doctor's charge was $450. The patient paid $25, and the unpaid balance is $425. The physician is Dr. Oakley [*use clinic address*].

Donna Courtney, 45 Sunshine Court, Denver 80212, Medicare claim number 084-94-8293B, received treatment for arthritis on May 4, 19--. The doctor's charge was $73, and the patient paid $5. The unpaid balance is $68. The physician is Dr. Ulrich [*use clinic address*].

LESSON 285

GOALS
- To correct errors in subject-verb agreement while typing sentences.
- To type group hospital insurance forms.

FORMAT
- Single spacing   60-space line

LAB 34

SUBJECT-VERB AGREEMENT

Workbook 727–728.

Type lines 1–4 once, correcting verbs to ensure subject-verb agreement. Edit your copy as your teacher reads the answers. Then retype lines 1–4 from your edited copy.

1 Mr. Zimbalist and Ms. Vickers is excited about your ideas.
2 The owners of that company is eager to purchase this land.
3 Madeline has not yet returned from her vacation in Jamaica.
4 Jenora and Alice has quite large land holdings in Memphis.

30-SECOND TIMINGS

Take two 30-second timings on lines 4–5, or type each line twice.

4 When you take the time to show that you are kind, 10

5 the smile on the face of a child is a joy to see. 20

| 1 | 2 | 3 | 4 | 5 | 6 | 7 | 8 | 9 | 10

ACCURACY

Type lines 6–10 twice.

6 tr tram true trek tray trip trim trap trust tribe

7 as last cast fast wasp mast ease vast tease aspen

8 re care real tore pore sore wore lore flare chore

9 op drop stop flop crop open rope hope scope slope

10 ew brew flew crew stew drew chew grew strew shrew

SPEED

Type each line twice.

11 ful grateful faithful careful fateful tactful ful

12 est greatest interest nearest biggest longest est

13 ing thinking swimming sailing sending writing ing

14 ble portable probable taxable capable visible ble

15 ure fixtures features mixture futures torture ure

2-MINUTE TIMINGS

Take two 2-minute timings on lines 16–20. Use your paper bail to proofread your copy. Circle your errors and figure your score on each timing.

16   There is no equal to the flavor of ice cream 10

17 on hot, humid days. Choices of all types are out 20

18 to engage the eye, and the snappy clerks will fix 30

19 just the mix and size to suit you best. A cup or 40

20 a cone will be fine. 44

| 1 | 2 | 3 | 4 | 5 | 6 | 7 | 8 | 9 | 10   SI 1.13

MEASURING FOR VERTICAL SPACING

Most typewriters space 6 lines to an inch. Standard typing paper is 11 inches long, so there are 11 × 6 = 66 lines on a full page or 33 lines on a half page. Some special and imported typewriters space 5¼ lines to an inch, giving 57 lines on a full page and 28 lines on a half page. A4 metric paper is slightly longer—70 lines to the page.

Practice: (1) Insert a sheet of paper, and count the single-spaced lines. (2)

Type the word *single* on six consecutive lines; then measure the lines with a ruler to see how much space they occupy.

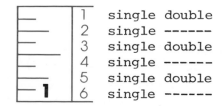

	1	single double
	2	single ------
	3	single double
	4	single ------
	5	single double
1	6	single ------

LESSON 284

GOALS
- To identify subject-verb agreement while typing sentences.
- To type 50/5'/3e.
- To type requests for Medicare payments.

FORMAT
- Single spacing 60-space line 5-space tab

LAB 34

Type lines 1–4 once. Then repeat lines 1–4 or take a series of 1-minute timings. Identify the subjects and verbs as you type.

SUBJECT-VERB AGREEMENT

1 Victor Mazurki has six copies of the required instructions. 12
2 Both managers have assistants to help them to analyze data. 12
3 I am sure that Gary Jeffers will be there for the luncheon. 12
4 Bryant and Darlene are now at a data processing convention. 12
    | 1 | 2 | 3 | 4 | 5 | 6 | 7 | 8 | 9 | 10 | 11 | 12

5-MINUTE TIMINGS

Take a 5-minute timing on lines 5–25. Type six times each word on which you made an error, hesitated, or stopped during the 5-minute timing. Then take a 5-minute timing to see how much your skill has improved.

5   Thousands of documents are handled daily through banks 12
6   Thousands of documents are handled daily through banks 24
7   Thousands of documents are handled daily through banks 36
8 of data linked to hospitals and clinics. Personnel keep an 48
9 of data linked to hospitals and clinics. Personnel keep an 60
10 of data linked to hospitals and clinics. Personnel keep an 72
11 inventory of patient diagnoses on hand and of data that are 84
12 inventory of patient diagnoses on hand and of data that are 96
13 inventory of patient diagnoses on hand and of data that are 108
14 needed. Forms are utilized whenever possible to save time. 120
15 needed. Forms are utilized whenever possible to save time. 132
16 needed. Forms are utilized whenever possible to save time. 144
17 While current patient information is being processed, other 156
18 While current patient information is being processed, other 168
19 While current patient information is being processed, other 180
20 patient information is being adjusted electronically. Data 192
21 patient information is being adjusted electronically. Data 204
22 patient information is being adjusted electronically. Data 216
23 is merged quickly and exactly for individual treatment. 227
24 is merged quickly and exactly for individual treatment. 238
25 is merged quickly and exactly for individual treatment. 250
    | 1 | 2 | 3 | 4 | 5 | 6 | 7 | 8 | 9 | 10 | 11 | 12 SI 1.89

FORMATTING: VERTICAL CENTERING

Workbook 17–18.

To place copy in the vertical center of a page, follow these steps:

1. Count the lines (including blanks) that the copy will occupy when typed.

2. Subtract that number from the available number of lines on your paper.

3. Divide the difference by 2 to find the number of the line on which you should begin typing (drop any fraction).

Example: To center five double-spaced lines on a half page, you need 9 lines for copy (5 typed, 4 blank); 33 − 9 = 24, and 24 ÷ 2 = 12. Begin typing on line 12.

Practice: Block-center these lines vertically on a half sheet of paper. Use double spacing.

```
To count double-spaced

lines that you want to

center vertically, you

must count every typed

line and all the blank

lines in between.
```

Check: When finished typing, fold paper from top to bottom. The crease should be in the center, close to the point indicated by the arrow.

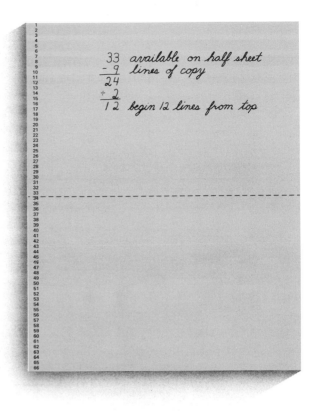

33 available on half sheet
− 9 lines of copy
24
÷ 2
12 begin 12 lines from top

JOB 16-1. ADVERTISEMENT

Format: Center vertically and horizontally on a half sheet of paper. Double-space.

FREE GERBILS
One Month Old
→ Both Males and Females
See Sara Viator
Journalism Room

JOB 16-2. ADVERTISEMENT

Format: Block-center horizontally; center vertically on a half sheet of paper. Double-space.

LOST
Junior Class Ring
Sparkle-Blue Set
→ Initials MCP
See Marla Padraka
Room South A

Her brother-in-law has written a first-class mystery novel. 12 60
10 Shawn is a well-qualified candidate for the director's job. 24 72
11 The question-and-answer period on Tuesday was very popular. 36 84
12 We purchased several 3- by 4-meter rugs for our main house. 48 96

| 1 | 2 | 3 | 4 | 5 | 6 | 7 | 8 | 9 | 10 | 11 | 12

PRACTICE

In which Pretest did you make more errors? If in lines 5–8, type lines 13–16 four times and lines 17–20 two times. If in lines 9–12, reverse the procedure.

13 (0) (1) (2) (3) (4) (5) (6) (7) (8) (9) (10) (11) (12) (13)
14 (and) (for) (the) (cot) (let) (sit) (tie) (tow) (jam) (ham)
15 (for it is) (and it is) (is it for) (is it the) (let it be)
16 (how it is) (if it was) (can it be) (it is one) (yes or no)

17 question-and-answer black-out snow-covered ice-clad up-down
18 wind-swept antique-like small-sized for-against well-marked
19 well-qualified paper-and-pencil up-to-date on-off down-hill
20 mothers-in-law fathers-in-law sisters-in-law brother-in-law

POSTTEST

Repeat the Pretest.

OUTPATIENT RECORD

A record of patients treated at the clinic but not required to stay overnight is kept on a card. Each subsequent visit is also recorded.

JOBS 283-1 AND 283-2. OUTPATIENT RECORDS

Using the data for the two patients listed below, complete a form for each patient.
Use the illustrations as a guide. Workbook 719–720.

Marie Belpalsi; Phone 555-6403; Age 36; Birthdate 2/8/48. Lives at 45 Evergreen, Denver, CO 80204, and is a nurse. Personal History: Patient is a healthy female. Present Illness: Lacerated left thumb from broken test tube in lab at Trail Ridge Clinic, on May 19. Physical Examination: Patient showed a wound about 2 inches long and almost ¼ inch deep. Wound was disinfected, sutured, and bandaged. Dr. Chuang.

Fred Caton; Phone 555-9385; Age 30; Birthdate 2/9/52. Lives at Route 1, Fort Collins, CO 80521, and is a flagman. Personal History: Patient is a healthy male. Present Illness: Snakebite on left ankle occurred on Trail Ridge Road on afternoon of May 19. Physical Examination: Patient showed a bite about ¼ inch deep. Venom was extracted from wound and injection was given immediately to counteract poison. Wound was bandaged. Dr. Ulrich.

LESSON 17

KEYBOARDING SKILLS

Type each line twice.

Words   1 fact bits girl with joke moon pulp quiz void exit
Speed   2 The eighty bushels of corn may be profit for Len.
Accuracy 3 Juarez vowed maximum support to buoy his legions.

30-SECOND TIMINGS

Take two 30-second timings on lines 4–5, or type each line twice.

4 Just how much more time do you think it took them 10
5 to write all these drills that fill up this book? 20
  | 1 | 2 | 3 | 4 | 5 | 6 | 7 | 8 | 9 | 10

ACCURACY

Type lines 6–10 twice.

6 er mere error infer steer power finer tower newer
7 sa said sacks sails safes sakes sandy saves sages
8 ui suit ruins fruit guide fluid juice suite squid
9 io ions lions trios adios scion idiom idiot axiom
10 we were weeps wears welds weans weeds swept weave

SPEED

Type each line twice.

11 ity activity priority charity ability quality ity
12 ial official material cordial special initial ial
13 ify simplify identify specify clarify qualify ify
14 ion deletion relation section mention lesions ion
15 age coverage mortgage average postage package age

2-MINUTE TIMINGS

Take two 2-minute timings on lines 16–20. Use your paper bail to proofread your copy. Circle your errors and figure your score on each timing. Format: Double spacing.

16   The old man who walks in the park always has 10
17 a big smile on his face. He talks to each person 20
18 who comes his way. He gives aid in his quiet way 30
19 and is excited when he makes a new friend. He is 40
20 amazed at those who join him there. 47
  | 1 | 2 | 3 | 4 | 5 | 6 | 7 | 8 | 9 | 10 SI 1.12

Andrew Anspach, Evergreen Drive, Denver, CO 80204. Phone 555-6921. Age 18; Birthdate 6/25/64. Birthplace: Greeley, CO. S.S. No. 384-22-8493. Occupation: Student. Notify Gene Anspach in case of emergency. Father is Gene Anspach; Birthplace is Dayton, Ohio. Mother is Linda Anspach; Birthplace is Lubbock, Texas. Local Blue Cross and Blue Shield Plan and no other insurance; Group No. is 094-9473; Contract No. is B87983; Effective Date is 4/8/65. Admitted 7/14/— at 1:30 p.m. Provisional diagnosis is broken right leg and so is final diagnosis. No surgery required. Doctor is Dr. Ulrich; Attending is Kevin Lia, M.D.

Jane Michener, North Trail, Fort Collins, CO 80522. Phone 555-8392. Age 35; Birthdate 9/18/47. Birthplace: Fort Collins, CO. S.S. No. 382-59-4792. Occupation: Secretary at Colorado State, Fort Collins. Notify husband, Paul Michener, in case of emergency at same address and phone number. Local Blue Cross and Blue Shield Plan and no other insurance; Group No. is 184-8392; Contract No. is B89043; Effective Date is 4/15/65. Admitted 8/3/— at 4:30 p.m. Provisional diagnosis is snake bite and so is final diagnosis. Surgery required to remove venom. Doctor is Dr. Martino; Attending is Kevin Lia, M.D.

LESSON 283

GOALS
- To recognize subject-verb agreement while typing sentences.
- To type outpatient records.

FORMAT
- Single spacing   60-space line

LAB 34

Type lines 1–4 once. Then repeat lines 1–4 or take a series of 1-minute timings. Note subject-verb agreement as you type (the verbs are underscored).

SUBJECT-VERB AGREEMENT

(Sing.) 1 Alex <u>does</u> his work very well, according to Frank Zimbulski.   12
(Pl.) 2 Alex and James <u>do</u> their work very well, according to Frank.   12
(Sing.) 3 She <u>is</u> quite interested in learning to operate the machine.   12
(Pl.) 4 They <u>are</u> quite interested in learning to operate a machine.   12

| 1 | 2 | 3 | 4 | 5 | 6 | 7 | 8 | 9 | 10 | 11 | 12

The verbs *to be*, *to do*, and *to have* need special attention because these irregular verbs are very commonly used. Note how these verbs agree with pronouns and with singular or plural nouns:

Singular	Be	Do	Have	Plural	Be	Do	Have
I	am	do	have	we			
you	are	do	have	you	are	do	have
he				they			
she	is	does	has	the clerks			
it							
the clerk							

PRETEST

Take a 2-minute Pretest on lines 5–8; then take a 2-minute Pretest on lines 9–12 on page 450. Circle and total your errors on each Pretest.

5 All classes meet two days a week (Tuesdays and Wednesdays).   12   60
6 At the time of the merger (1980), they needed more support.   24   72
7 Send the following: (1) sweater, (2) pants, and (3) socks.   36   84
8 Your paper needs several revisions (see attached comments).   48   96

| 1 | 2 | 3 | 4 | 5 | 6 | 7 | 8 | 9 | 10 | 11 | 12

FORMATTING: SPREAD CENTERING

To give added emphasis to a display line, spread it by leaving 1 space between letters and 3 spaces between words, like this:

T H I S   I S   S P R E A D I N G

To center a spread line, be sure to include all the spaces as you say the pairs for backspacing, like "T-space, H-space, I-space, S-space, space-space, I-space," and so on. **Practice:** Center the spread line above. Then center and spread this line: SPREAD WORDS FOR EMPHASIS.

FORMATTING ANNOUNCEMENTS

Announcements of meetings are usually displayed and are typed on either a full sheet or a half sheet of paper. To format an announcement:

1. Center the announcement vertically.

2. Center each line horizontally.

3. Use a variety of display techniques—some lines typed in capital letters and lowercase letters, some lines typed in all-capital letters, some lines spread-centered.

JOB 17-1. ANNOUNCEMENT
Standard format. Full sheet of paper. Double spacing. Spread line 5.

ANNOUNCEMENT

of the

NORTHWEST CANOE TRIP

on the

R O G U E   R I V E R

During the

First Week of July

JOB 17-2. ANNOUNCEMENT
Standard format. Full sheet of paper. Double spacing. Spread line 6.

*The
Morgantown Chapter
of the
FUTURE TEACHERS CLUB
Will Meet With
D R .   C A L   S K I P P E R
in Room S
Wednesday at Three*

LESSON 18

CLINIC

GOAL
- To refine techniques for spacing, shifting, returning, tabulating, and keeping eyes on copy while typing.

FORMAT
- Single spacing   50-space line

SPACE BAR

Type each line twice.

1 ask met paw fix vib yam fog dim aye con sake even
2 jet war hot kin vet zip quo bat ace eke long oxen
3 As you know, a doe hides low before the big snow.
4 As they sat on a mat, a pup and a cat had a spat.

SHIFT LOCK

Type each line twice.

5 The SOPHOMORES were glad about having a SNOW DAY.
6 It was a DIESEL, and it was BLUE-GREEN, not GRAY.
7 She will be in the ELEVENTH grade, not the TENTH.

(Continued on next page)

Take two 30-second timings on lines 6–8, or type the paragraph twice.

```
 6  The sudden revocation of these policies has upset our plans   12
 7  for developing that part of our program.  We must negotiate   24
 8  a new contract or seek some good alternative consideration.    36
    |  1  |  2  |  3  |  4  |  5  |  6  |  7  |  8  |  9  |  10  |  11  |  12
```

ADMISSION RECORDS

An admission record is typed by the receptionist at the time a patient is admitted to a clinic.

JOBS 282-1 TO 282-3. ADMISSION RECORDS

Using the data for the three patients provided below and on page 449, complete a form for each patient. Use the illustrations as a guide. Workbook 713–718.

Belinda Elliott, Route 4, Denver, CO 80208. Phone 555-7384. Age 12; Birthdate 2/11/70. Birthplace: Tucson, Arizona. S.S. No. 425-16-7839. Occupation: Student. Notify Betty Elliott in case of emergency. Mother is Betty Elliott; Birthplace is Tucson, Arizona. Father is deceased. Local Blue Cross and Blue Shield Plan and no other insurance; Group No. is 080-9785; Contract No. is B086374; Effective Date is 5/8/80. Admitted 7/12/— at 2:15 p.m. Provisional diagnosis is emergency appendectomy; Final diagnosis is the same and so is operation. Doctor is Dr. Chuang; Attending is Kevin Lia, M.D.

SHIFT LOCK (Continued)

8 We may choose either a TOY POODLE or a CHIHUAHUA.

9 They typed TURF instead of SURF on my manuscript.

CARRIAGE OR CARRIER RETURN

Type each line once. Return the carriage or carrier after each name.

10M Brett Caryn Robin Susie Bruce Alyn Bess Drew Beth
11M Debra Rhett Terry Carla Edwin Ezra Dale Fran Erik
12M Alexa Cyril Roxie Duane Sammy Greg Fred Evie Stan

10E Helen Julie Kathy Laura Paula Hans Olga Uris Jill
11E Nancy Henry Mella Helga Porgy Jack Lisa Joni Yeta
12E Perry Mehra Jenny Price Kevin Noel Lynn Jeff Kara

TABULATOR

Set four tabs—one every 10 spaces. Type each line once; tab between words.

13 Please   tab   across   the   page.
14 It   is   so   much   faster.
15 The   spaces go   this   way.
16 Do   you   like   typing this?
17 Can   you   tab   better now?

EYES ON COPY

Fill in the missing vowels as you type each line once.

18 Wh-n y-- try t- f-ll -n th- bl-nks -s y-- typ- -n
19 th- l-n-s, y-- w-ll n--d t- st-dy th- p-tt-rns -f
20 --ch -f th- w-rds. D-d y-- s-- th-t -ll -f th--r
21 v-w-ls -r- m-ss-ng? Y-- c-n f-g-r- --t --ch -ne.
22 J-st k--p y--r -y-s -n th- c-py -s y-- typ- th-m.

LESSON 19

UNIT 4 KEYBOARDING—THE NUMBERS

UNIT GOAL 25/2'/4e

GOALS
- To control 1, 2, and 3 keys.
- To format enumerations.

FORMAT
- Single spacing   50-space line   4-space tab

KEYBOARDING SKILLS

Type each line twice.

Words   1 maze elks corn idea flex give shot jobs quip whey
Speed   2 If the men do the audit work by six, they may go.
Accuracy 3 The clown from Quebec completely dazzled the man.

PRACTICE

In the chart below, find the number of errors you made on the Pretest on page 446. Then type each of the designated drill lines four times.

Pretest errors	0–1	2–3	4–5	6+
Drill lines	30–32	29–31	28–30	27–29

```
27  international technology originally computer airline ticket
28  comprehensive management associated property options agents
29  experimenting businesses collection pleasure examine assist

30  the and with that lack small lists banks agent which estate
31  use for data main very local would every store quick obtain
32  are can them lost want items where their costs files access
```

POSTTEST

Repeat the Pretest on page 446 to see how much your skill has improved.

JOB 281-1. PRESCRIPTION LABELS

Standard format. Workbook 711. Worklog: Workbook 707 bottom.

Prescription No. 170954 from Dr. Chuang. Take 1 tablet before meals and at bedtime. For Niko Hagoshima.

Prescription No. 170955 from Dr. Mason. Take 2 tablets every six hours until all tablets are gone. Not refillable. For Sheri Daniels.

Prescription No. 170956 from Dr. Ulrich. Take ½ teaspoon every four hours until all taken. Two refills. For Matthias Lorenz-Meyer.

Prescription No. 170957 from Dr. Ganz. Take 1 teaspoon every four hours. For Renay Penn.

Prescription No. 170958 from Dr. Smith. Take 1 tablet each morning. Refillable. For Jessica Johnson.

Prescription No. 170959 from Dr. Vito. Take 1 teaspoon before bedtime. For Jed Harkinson.

Prescription No. 170960 from Dr. Martino. Take 2 teaspoons every twelve hours. Refillable. For Juanita Valentino.

Prescription No. 170961 from Dr. Oakley. Take 2 tablets every three hours until all tablets have been taken. For Fredrick Hausen.

Prescription No. 170962 from Dr. Alberts. Take 1 tablet every four hours. Refillable. For Leonard Bassett.

Prescription No. 170963 from Dr. Jenkins. Take ½ teaspoon every four hours. For Kim Shih.

LESSON 282

GOAL
- To type admission records.

FORMAT
- Single spacing 60-space line

KEYBOARDING SKILLS

Type lines 1–4 once. Then spell out the numbers in line 5 as you type it. Repeat lines 1–4, or take a series of 1-minute timings.

Speed
1 She is busy with the work but is to go to town for the pen. 12

Accuracy
2 Wolf gave Jake an extra dozen quarts, but he can't pay him. 12

Numbers
3 Tammy read pages 10 through 29, 38 through 47, and page 56. 12

Symbols
4 Add 1 + 2 + 3 + 4 + 5 + 6 + 7 + 8 + 9 + 10 + 11 + 12 + 130. 12

Number Usage
5 Walt needs 3 typists and 8 editors on duty at 5.

```
  |  1  |  2  |  3  |  4  |  5  |  6  |  7  |  8  |  9  |  10  |  11  |  12
```

To Practice Top Row Reaches

Type each reach slowly to feel the distance and direction of the reach.

Then type it again more smoothly.

Remember to anchor the home row fingers.

SPACE BAR

 KEY

Use small l for 1 if you do not have a 1 key.

Use A finger on 1 if you do have a 1 key.

Type each line twice.

4 aqa aql ala lll l,lll ll,lll l.ll ll.ll and ll/ll

5 ll arms, ll areas, ll adages, ll animals, or l.ll

6 My ll aides can type lll pages within ll minutes.

 KEY

Use S finger.

Type each line twice.

7 sws sw2 s2s 222 2,222 22,222 2.22 22.22 and 22/22

8 22 sips, 22 sites, 22 swings, 22 signals, or 2.22

9 I saw 21 ads in Column 2 of 212 papers on July 1.

 KEY

Use D finger.

Type each line twice.

10 ded de3 d3d 333 3.333 33.333 3.33 33.33 and 33/33

11 33 dots, 33 dimes, 33 dishes, 33 daisies, or 3.33

12 She asked 231 persons 132 questions in 123 hours.

CHECKPOINT

Type lines 13–15 once. Then repeat lines 4, 7, and 10 or take two 1-minute timings on the Checkpoint.

13 At least 23 of the 32 sketches were made by 12 of   10

14 the artists for the show on March 11, 12, and 13.   20

15 We need 2 or 3 more sketches for the 3 p.m. show.   30

| 1 | 2 | 3 | 4 | 5 | 6 | 7 | 8 | 9 | 10

2-MINUTE TIMINGS

Take two 2-minute timings on lines 16–20. Format: Double spacing, 5-space tab.

16   To see the artists paint is a joy. The zeal   10

17 with which they work to have the exact tints show   20

18 up on the pad is fun to watch. As they glide the   30

19 new brush quickly across the pad, the bright hues   40

20 take form and bring smiles to our faces.   48

| 1 | 2 | 3 | 4 | 5 | 6 | 7 | 8 | 9 | 10   SI 1.10

LESSON 281

GOALS
- To correct errors in subject-verb agreement while typing sentences.
- To type 50/5′/3e.
- To type prescription labels.

FORMAT
- Single spacing   60-space line   5-space tab

LAB 33

SUBJECT-VERB AGREEMENT

Workbook 709–710.

Type lines 1–4 once, correcting verbs to ensure subject-verb agreement. Edit your copy as your teacher reads the answers. Then retype lines 1–4 from your edited copy.

1 Federal law prohibit discrimination because of age or sex.
2 Many employees complains about these six billing procedures.
3 Only Joanne like the new offices better than the old ones.
4 Liza and Al Aqualina gives superb talks on money management.

PRETEST

Take a 5-minute Pretest on lines 5–26. Then circle and count your errors. Use the chart on page 447 to determine which lines to type for practice.

5   With the growth of information and the technology that   12
6   permits management of it, data banks are cropping up every—   24
7   where. Data banks are comprehensive collections of data in   36
8   library form. Data is stored so that it can be accessed by   48
9   quick, efficient use of computer terminals.   57
10   Numerous businesses have acquired access to data banks   69
11 and use them as the main service components of their opera—   81
12 tions. Airline ticket agents make reservations by consult—   93
13 ing a computer data bank for obtaining flight times, ticket   105
14 costs, passenger lists, and seating options. A terminal is   117
15 accessed to get the information the agent needs, and reser—   129
16 vations are confirmed or adjusted.   136
17   Real estate listing used to be very laborious, and the   148
18 sale of property could be lost because of lack of knowledge   160
19 of certain opportunities. Multiple listings allow an agent   172
20 to examine national and international offerings through the   184
21 data banks, which store most real estate that is available.   196
22   Data banks were originally associated with large files   208
23 of information containing millions of citations. Now small   220
24 communities are experimenting with smaller banks of data to   232
25 aid local businesses and citizens who want special informa—   244
26 tion for work or for pleasure.   250

   | 1 | 2 | 3 | 4 | 5 | 6 | 7 | 8 | 9 | 10 | 11 | 12   SI 1.77

FORMATTING ENUMERATIONS

Some jobs have arrows and numbers to help you space vertically. For example, ↓3 means "go down 3 lines." (Leave 2 lines blank, and type on the third line.)

An enumeration is a series of numbered or lettered words, phrases, or sentences. Enumerations are centered vertically and block-centered horizontally. They may be double-spaced, or each lettered item may be single-spaced with a blank line between items. Titles, if used, are typed in all-capital letters and centered over the enumeration. Two blank lines separate the title from the enumeration.

JOB 19-1. ENUMERATION
Standard format. Double spacing. Full sheet of paper.

TYPING AN ENUMERATION ↓3

A. An enumeration can be a set of steps or a series of numbered or lettered words or statements.

B. It is set up so that the numbers or letters stand by themselves in the margin.

C. Each number or letter is followed by a period, and the period is followed by two spaces.

D. All lines that do not start with a number or a letter are tabbed in four spaces.

E. This job uses letters to separate the items because you have not learned all the numbers.

JOB 19-2. ENUMERATION
Retype Job 19-1. Standard format. Single spacing. Half sheet of paper.

LESSON 20

GOALS
- To control 4, 5, and 6 keys.
- To format enumerations.

FORMAT
- Single spacing   50-space line

KEYBOARDING SKILLS

Type each line twice.

Speed   1 The goal of the firm is to fix the antique autos.

Accuracy   2 Lazy Jacques picked two boxes of oranges with me.

Numbers   3 The answer is 33 when you add 12 and 21 together.

LESSON 280 CLINIC

GOAL
- To use intensive drill to improve basic skills.

FORMAT
- Single spacing   60-space line

PRETEST 1

Take two 2-minute timings on lines 1–4. Proofread both, and note the more accurate of the two scores.

```
1        Each anthill will have capacity for a full family even   12
2   though it looks like only a pile of loose dirt.  It carries   24
3   a group of rooms and tunnels at several levels.  Each queen   36
4   soon produces a brood of willing workers to carry out soil.   48
    |  1  |  2  |  3  |  4  |  5  |  6  |  7  |  8  |  9  |  10 |  11 |  12
```

PRACTICE 1

Type lines 5–10 five times. Repeat individual lines for speed gain if you had two or fewer errors on Pretest 1; otherwise repeat each block of lines for accuracy gain.

```
5   allowing tunnels common supply annual bluff cooks full feel
6   attitude connect allied affair school malls books week toll
7   attorney billing lesson appeal affect tolls carry seem door

8   dropping connect choose proofs canned heels polls cool seem
9   commutes calling button billed chills affix calls been nook
10  applying channel collar called cannot bells apply book ball
```

POSTTEST 1

Take two 2-minute timings on lines 1–4. Proofread and note your improvement.

PRETEST 2

Take two 2-minute timings on lines 11–14. Proofread both, and note the more accurate of the two scores.

```
11       Did you ever think of the phenomenon that normally the   12
12  fish is a truly active animal?  Some fish do the minimum of   24
13  swimming, but this group is small; the busy fish abide in a   36
14  hungry bowl, and any fish that slows down is soon devoured.   48
    |  1  |  2  |  3  |  4  |  5  |  6  |  7  |  8  |  9  |  10 |  11 |  12
```

PRACTICE 2

Type lines 15–20 five times. Repeat individual lines for speed gain if you had two or fewer errors on Pretest 2; otherwise repeat each block of lines for accuracy gain.

```
15  visitor neither bushel handle world moths then with got for
16  trouble visible signal mighty amend turns rich body but aid
17  profits supreme repair social signs abide fish town icy ham

18  perhaps signals normal owners fancy eight busy such aid the
19  channel further bought entire ought giant down work did and
20  neither visible social repair eight turns then fish but got
```

POSTTEST 2

Take two 2-minute timings on lines 11–14. Proofread and note your improvement.

 KEY

Use F finger.

Type each line twice.

4 frf fr4 f4f 444 4,444 44,444 4.44 44.44 and 44/44
5 44 foes, 44 films, 44 flukes, 44 folders, or 4.44
6 Show No. 4 is for May 1, 2, 3, 4, 12, 14, and 23.

 KEY

Use F finger.

Type each line twice.

7 ftf ft5 f5f 555 5,555 55,555 5.55 55.55 and 55/55
8 55 fins, 55 facts, 55 fields, 55 futures, or 5.55
9 There are 24 errors on 1,253 of the 4,135 sheets.

 KEY

Use J finger.

Type each line twice.

10 jyj jy6 j6j 666 6,666 66,666 6.66 66.66 and 66/66
11 66 jaws, 66 jokes, 66 judges, 66 jackets, or 6.66
12 Items 43, 45, and 61 are due by October 25 or 26.

CHECKPOINT

Type lines 13–15 once. Then repeat lines 4, 7, and 10 or take two 1-minute timings on the Checkpoint.

13 As you edit page 26, check line 14 to see that it   10
14 has exactly 35 spaces in it. Lines 12 and 14 are   20
15 both to be 35 spaces--space 36 is for the return.   30
    | 1 | 2 | 3 | 4 | 5 | 6 | 7 | 8 | 9 | 10

2-MINUTE TIMINGS

Take two 2-minute timings on lines 16–20. Format: Double spacing, 5-space tab.

16   When you check your typed words, you need to   10
17 examine them for thoughts as well as for how they   20
18 look. The paper bail will help you to check. It   30
19 quickly guides your eyes across the maze of lines   40
20 and helps you pick out errors with ease.   48
    | 1 | 2 | 3 | 4 | 5 | 6 | 7 | 8 | 9 | 10   SI 1.17

FORMATTING A CHART

An organizational chart is a common form. To format:

1. Make all boxes the same size: For length, add 2 spaces to the longest line of type. For depth, add 2 blank lines to the copy that has the most lines of type. Thus the boxes in Job 279-1 are 18 spaces wide (2 spaces wider than "Thomas A. Easton") and 4 lines deep (2 lines for typed copy and 2 lines for blanks).

2. For vertical placement, count lines as you would for ruled tables. In Job 279-1 the page is turned lengthwise and the copy requires 12 lines. Thus 51 − 12 = 39, and 39 ÷ 2 = 19.5; begin on line 19.

3. For horizontal placement, decide how many boxes will be placed side by side, and multiply by the length of each box. In Job 279-1, 3 boxes × 18 spaces/box = 54 spaces, plus 6 spaces between boxes gives a total of 66 spaces. Backspace 33 spaces (half of 66) from the center of page.

Type underscores the correct length for the top and bottom of each box and for the horizontal connecting line. Type colons for, or pen in, the vertical lines.

JOB 279-1. CHART

Full page, sideways. Note the penned-in spacing directions as you format this organizational chart.

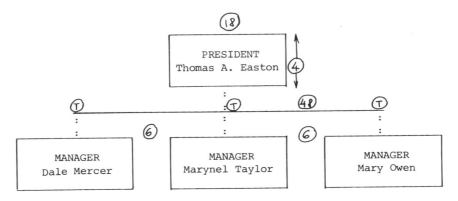

JOB 279-2. CHART

Standard format.

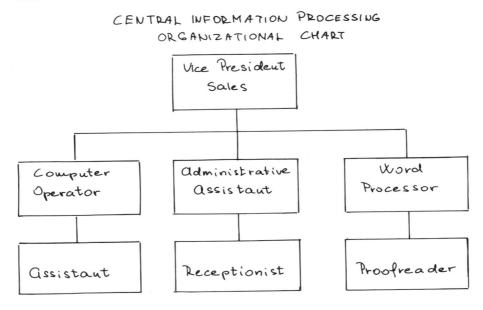

JOB 279-3. CHART

Design an organizational chart headed by Ann Williams, Regional Manager. Reporting to Ms. Williams are three district managers, Joan V. Prescott, Edward J. Riley, and Jacob Hirschen, each of whom has, respectively, one field manager: Andrew Carson, Donna P. Merrill, and Owen C. Taylor. Standard format.

Read the jobs on this page to review the steps for horizontal and vertical centering.

JOB 20-1. ENUMERATION
Standard format. Type line for line. Double spacing.

VERTICAL CENTERING ↓3

1. Count the number of lines needed.
2. Subtract needed lines from the number available on the paper.
3. Divide the difference by 2 to find line on which to start.
4. If a fraction is left, drop it.
5. Check center by folding the paper from top to bottom.

JOB 20-2. ENUMERATION
Standard format. Type line for line. Double spacing.

HORIZONTAL CENTERING ↓3

1. Determine the paper center.
2. Set the carriage or carrier at the center of the paper.
3. Locate the backspace key.
4. Backspace once for every two spaces/characters in the line to be centered.
5. Type the lines.
6. Check center by folding the paper from left to right.

LESSON 21

GOALS
- To control 7, 8, and 9 keys.
- To format poems.

FORMAT
- Single spacing   50-space line

KEYBOARDING SKILLS

Type each line twice.

Speed 1 By the time the dial turns, it may be time to go.
Accuracy 2 Six bright families quickly plowed the vineyards.
Numbers 3 Lines 13, 24, and 56 were right; line 65 was not.

 KEY

Use J finger.

Type each line twice.

4 juj ju7 j7j 777 7,777 77,777 7.77 77.77 and 77/77
5 77 jets, 77 jumps, 77 jokers, 77 joggers, or 7.77
6 We sang 34 songs for 7,657 people at 12 concerts.

JOB 278-1. TWO-PAGE RULED TABLE

Standard format. Underscore the braced heading.

STOCK DISTRIBUTION   OFFICE SYSTEMS, INC.

	January 1, 1960		January 1, 1970		January 1, 1980		Last Year	
	Holders	Percent	Holders	Percent	Holders	Percent	Holders	Percent
Individuals:								
Joint Owners	3,600	30.0	4,200	26.1	4,500	24.4	4,950	23.5
Men	3,850	32.1	4,400	27.4	5,000	27.1	5,550	26.3
Women	2,600	21.7	3,500	21.9	4,200	22.8	4,600	21.8
Stockbrokers	1,000	8.4	1,650	10.3	1,900	10.3	2,280	10.8
Nominees	120	1.0	200	1.3	400	2.2	600	2.8
Foreign Holders	280	2.3	300	1.9	350	1.9	530	2.5
Institutions	400	3.3	1,000	6.2	1,100	5.9	1,260	6.0
Mutual Funds	100	0.8	650	4.0	800	4.3	1,020	4.8
All others	50	0.4	150	0.9	200	1.1	310	1.5
Totals	12,000	100.0	16,050	100.0	18,450	100.0	21,100	100.0

LESSON 279

GOALS
- To correct errors in subject-verb agreement while typing sentences.
- To format and type organizational charts.

FORMAT
- Single spacing   60-space line

LAB 33

SUBJECT-VERB AGREEMENT

Type lines 1–4 once, correcting verbs to ensure subject-verb agreement. Edit your copy as your teacher reads the answers. Then retype lines 1–4 from your edited copy.

1 Kay want several dozen more boxes to store all your files.
2 They needs Joseph's approval before they order this machine.
3 Helene signs all purchase requisitions as soon as possible.
4 The managers buys all their supplies from Craig & Craig Inc.

"OK" TIMINGS

Type as many 30-second "OK" (errorless) timings as possible out of three attempts on lines 5–7. Then repeat the effort on lines 8–10.

5 Junior executives request broad help from weekly magazines. 12
6 Junior executives for the biweekly magazine requested help. 24
7 Junior executives requested help for the biweekly magazine. 36
8 Jack was dazzled by a requisition for moving the top boxes. 12
9 Jack typed white requisitions for moving large-sized boxes. 24
10 Jack typed requisitions for white moving boxes (long size). 36

| 1 | 2 | 3 | 4 | 5 | 6 | 7 | 8 | 9 | 10 | 11 | 12

SPACE BAR

8 KEY

Use K finger.

Type each line twice.

7 kik ki8 k8k 888 8,888 88,888 8.88 88.88 and 88/88
8 88 kegs, 88 kilns, 88 knocks, 88 kickers, or 8.88
9 At 27 she has 18 titles in 36 of the 45 contests.

9 KEY

Use L finger.

Type each line twice.

10 lol lo9 l9l 999 9,999 99,999 9.99 99.99 and 99/99
11 99 laps, 99 loops, 99 lilies, 99 lifters, or 9.99
12 Do pages 19, 29, 39, 49, 59, 69, 79, 89, and 119.

CHECKPOINT

Type lines 13–15 once. Then repeat lines 4 (page 36), 7, and 10 or take two 1-minute timings on the Checkpoint.

13 Plant the red bulbs in beds 2, 4, 6, and 8. Then   10
14 plant the yellow bulbs in beds 1, 3, 5, 7, and 9.   20
15 Plant the white bulbs in 3, 5, and 7 for balance.   30
    | 1 | 2 | 3 | 4 | 5 | 6 | 7 | 8 | 9 | 10

2-MINUTE TIMINGS

Take two 2-minute timings on lines 16–20. Format: Double spacing, 5-space tab.

16   The green tree in the corner of our yard has   10
17 grown just a little bit every year. It gives the   20
18 squirrel next door a place to make a home, and it   30
19 offers shade for our big, old, lazy dog. The big   40
20 tree has something to share with us all.   48
    | 1 | 2 | 3 | 4 | 5 | 6 | 7 | 8 | 9 | 10   SI 1.14

FORMATTING POEMS

Use the following steps when you are formatting a poem (see next page):

1. Set the left margin by centering the longest line (block-center).
2. Determine where you will type the first line (vertical centering).
3. Begin each line with a capital let-ter.
4. Show the scheme of the poem by indenting every other line 5 spaces.
5. Single-space stanzas; double-space between stanzas.

LESSON 278

GOALS
- To identify subject-verb agreement while typing sentences.
- To type 50/5'/3e.
- To type a two-page ruled table.

FORMAT
- Single spacing   60-space line   5-space tab and other tabs as needed

LAB 33

SUBJECT-VERB AGREEMENT

Type lines 1–4 once. Then repeat lines 1–4 or take a series of 1-minute timings.

```
1  Six buyers plan to distribute dozens of catalogs next week.   12
2  One buyer plans to distribute dozens of catalogs next week.   12
3  Bob orders jade rings from Algonquin Jewelers in Tennessee.   12
4  They order jade rings from Algonquin Jewelers in Tennessee.   12
   |  1  |  2  |  3  |  4  |  5  |  6  |  7  |  8  |  9  | 10  | 11  | 12
```

1- AND 5-MINUTE TIMINGS

Take two 1-minute timings on each paragraph. Then take one 5-minute timing on the entire selection. Use single spacing for the 1-minute timings and double spacing for the 5-minute timing.

5   Information processing popularity continues to explode as the service   15
6   businesses continue to grow. At the present time, law offices, insurance   30
7   companies, hospitals, and some sales offices are using terminals to   43
8   boost their productivity rates.   50

9   Legal offices produce dozens of lengthy agreements and wills in a   14
10   very short time. These documents will sometimes show great simi-   27
11   larities in their contents. Thus previously keyed documents can be   40
12   edited for other situations and save much time.   50

13   Insurance companies send innumerable communications to clients   14
14   concerning their policies. The repetitiveness that insurance companies   28
15   encounter as they correspond with their clients makes them important   42
16   candidates for word processing equipment.   50

17   A sales office that operates in the home office or any branch office   15
18   benefits from having terminals at each office for personnel to com-   28
19   municate with each other quickly. They can tabulate sales projections   42
20   and communicate the data via terminals.   50

21   Hospitals constantly need to update patient records to diagnose   14
22   illnesses and save lives. Communicating terminals increase the   27
23   efficiency of their operation tremendously. A form is processed quickly,   41
24   and a patient is treated in much less time.   50

```
   |  1  |  2  |  3  |  4  |  5  |  6  |  7  |  8  |  9  | 10  | 11  | 12  | 13  | 14   SI 1.92
```

JOB 21-1. POEM

Standard format. Center author's name 2 lines below the title.

RULES $\downarrow_2$

By Darrell Tedrick $\downarrow_3$

```
     Rules for the classroom,
          And rules for the hall.
     Rules for the lunchroom,
          And rules for the wall.

     There are rules for our talking,
          And rules to make us blink.
     There are rules for our listening,
          But do rules help us think?
```

JOB 21-2. POEM

Standard format. Type author's name starting at the center, 2 lines below the poem.

HOMEWORK $\downarrow_3$

```
     Thirteen pages in a night,
          So much homework is a fright.
     Dates and math and all that stuff,
          That much homework is too rough.

     I wrote and typed throughout the night,
          And do not yet have this thing right.
     I have never had a job so tough,
          This time I have really had enough.
                    ↓2
                    By Leigh Robbins
```

LESSON 22

GOALS
- To control 0, ½, and ¼ keys.
- To select an appropriate format for a document.
- To arrange a document in the selected format.

FORMAT
- Single spacing   50-space line

KEYBOARDING SKILLS

Type each line twice.

Speed   1   The ducks may be the first to go to the big lake.

Accuracy   2   Twelve zebras quickly jumped high over ten foxes.

Numbers   3   Type 1 or 2 or 3 and 4 or 5 or 6 and 7 or 8 or 9.

 KEY

Use Sem finger.

Type each line twice.

4   ;p; ;p0 ;0; 000 2,000 30,000 4.00 50.00 and 11:00

5   600 parts, 700 planks, 800 parades, 900 particles

6   Our classes are set for 2:00 and 7:00 on Mondays.

Subjects and verbs must agree. When the subject is the pronoun *he, she,* or *it* or a singular noun, the present-tense verb must end in *s*—for example, *he types, she runs*. For all other pronouns (*I, you, we, they*) and for all plural nouns, the present-tense verb does not end in *s*.

Singular

I ⎱ type
you ⎰ run

he ⎫
she ⎬ types
it ⎭ runs
the clerk

Plural

we ⎫
you ⎬ type
they ⎭ run
the clerks

30-SECOND TIMINGS

Take two 30-second timings on lines 5–7, or type the paragraph twice.

```
5  I recommend moving the conference from the hotel to the new   12
6  motor court at the edge of the town.  The place has two big    24
7  rooms for meetings and a restaurant with excellent service.    36
   | 1 | 2 | 3 | 4 | 5 | 6 | 7 | 8 | 9 | 10 | 11 | 12
```

JOB 277-1. TABLE WITH BRACED HEADING

Standard format. Full page. Arrange branches in alphabetic order.

ANALYSIS OF FIRST QUARTER SALES

Branch	Type of Product		Total
	Computers	Word Processors	
Boston	186	58	244
Houston	843	429	1,272
Milwaukee	1,107	967	2,074
Seattle	639	240	879
Oklahoma City	908	624	1,532
San Francisco	927	597	1,524
St. Louis	584	342	926
Detroit	736	517	1,253

JOB 277-2. TABLE WITH BRACED HEADINGS

Standard format. Turn page sideways.

FIRST QUARTER COMPARISON
Budgeted and Actual Sales

Branch	January		February		March	
	Budgeted	Actual	Budgeted	Actual	Budgeted	Actual
Boston	$25,000	$24,500	$25,000	$25,500	$15,000	$17,500
Detroit	35,000	36,000	40,000	38,500	26,500	25,950
Houston	90,000	95,000	95,000	90,000	39,000	39,500
Milwaukee	45,000	50,000	50,000	50,000	94,000	92,250
Oklahoma City	70,000	68,500	70,000	69,500	50,000	49,800
San Francisco	50,000	35,000	40,000	38,250	71,000	70,250
St. Louis	20,000	18,600	18,000	19,675	19,500	20,500
Seattle						
Totals	$335,000	$327,000	$338,000	$331,425	$315,000	$315,750

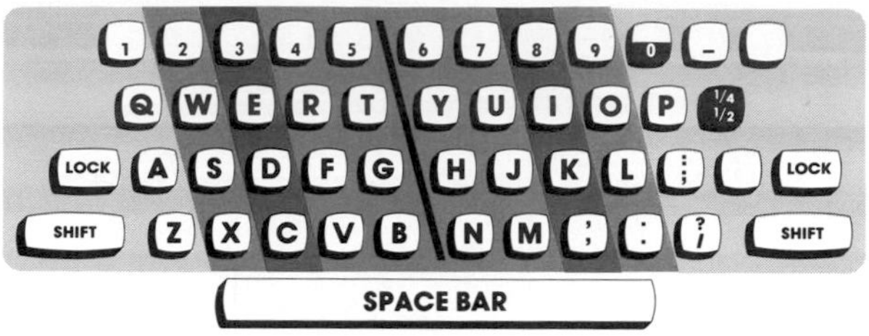

½ KEY

Use Sem finger.

Type each line twice.

7 ;p; ;p½ ;½; ½½½ 1½ 2½ 3½ 4½ 5½ 6½ 7½ 8½ 9½ or 10½

8 Is my size 7½, or did he say 6½? Maybe it is 8½?

9 Mark the boxes: 10½ or 29½ or 38½ or 47½ or 56½.

¼ KEY

Shift of ½.

Type each line twice.

10 ;p; ;p¼ ;¼; ¼¼¼ 1¼ 2¼ 3¼ 4¼ 5¼ 6¼ 7¼ 8¼ 9¼ or 10¼

11 I think it is 3¼, or is it 4¼? I think it is 5¼.

12 Label each box: 10¼ or 29¼ or 38¼ or 47¼ or 56¼.

CHECKPOINT

Type lines 13–15 once. Then repeat lines 4 (page 38), 7, and 10 or take two 1-minute timings on the Checkpoint.

13 If you like to work with fractions, try adding up   10

14 these: 10½, 29¼, 38½, 47¼, and 56½. If you find   20

15 the answer to be 182, you are absolutely correct.   30

| 1 | 2 | 3 | 4 | 5 | 6 | 7 | 8 | 9 | 10

2-MINUTE TIMINGS

Take two 2-minute timings on lines 16–20. Format: Double spacing, 5-space tab.

16   Getting up in the morning is quite a job for   10

17 me. I grab my yellow jacket and go for the bus--   20

18 just in time to miss it. Five more minutes would   30

19 have done it. Next time I will not doze so long.   40

20 I can still make it. Maybe I will beat the bell.   50

| 1 | 2 | 3 | 4 | 5 | 6 | 7 | 8 | 9 | 10   SI 1.13

SELECTING AN APPROPRIATE FORMAT FOR A DOCUMENT

Selecting a format is partly a matter of learning formatting guidelines and partly a matter of using your own good judgment. You have just practiced typing a series of jobs in which you used several formatting guidelines:

1. Typing in all capitals (p. 23).

2. Indenting for paragraphs (p. 24).

3. Centering horizontally (p. 25).

4. Centering vertically (p. 29).

5. Spread centering (p. 31).

6. Typing enumerations (p. 34).

7. Spacing for titles/subtitles (pp. 34 and 38).

JOB 276-1.
BOXED TABLE
Standard format.
Full page.

ANALYSIS OF MARCH SALES
Based on April 1 Figures

Branch	Budget	Actual	Percent
Boston*	$ 15,000	$ 17,500	116.7
Detroit	26,500	25,950	97.9
Houston	39,000	39,500	101.3
Milwaukee	94,000	92,250	98.1
Oklahoma City	50,000	49,800	99.6
San Francisco	71,000	70,250	98.9
Seattle	19,500	20,500	105.1
Totals	$315,000	$315,750	102.5

* New Branch added March 15 when St. Louis was dropped.

JOB 276-2.
BOXED TABLE
Standard format.
Full page.

ANALYSIS OF FIRST QUARTER SALES
January 1 to March 31, 19—
By Branch Districts

Branch	January	February	March	Total
Boston*	—	—	$ 17,500	$ 17,500
Detroit	$ 24,500	$25,500	25,950	75,950
Houston	36,000	38,500	39,500	114,000
Milwaukee	95,000	90,000	92,250	277,250
Oklahoma City	50,000	50,000	49,800	149,800
San Francisco	68,500	69,500	70,250	208,250
St. Louis	35,000	38,250	—	73,250
Seattle	18,000	19,675	20,500	58,175
Totals	$ 327,000	$331,425	$ 315,750	$974,175

* New branch added March 15 when St. Louis was dropped.

LESSON 277

GOALS
- To recognize subject-verb agreement while typing sentences.
- To type tables with braced headings.

FORMAT
- Single spacing   60-space line   Tabs as needed

LAB 33

Type lines 1–4 once. Then repeat lines 1–4 or take a series of 1-minute timings. Note subject-verb agreement as you type each line (verbs are underscored).

SUBJECT-VERB
AGREEMENT

(Sing.) 1 Only Laura DePasquale <u>knows</u> the combination to these safes. 12
(Pl.) 2 Most employees <u>want</u> us to close this store earlier than 10. 12
(Sing.) 3 Joe Nizer <u>begins</u> his six-week vacation on December 1 or 12. 12
(Pl.) 4 All our sales representatives <u>talk</u> with customers each day. 12

| 1 | 2 | 3 | 4 | 5 | 6 | 7 | 8 | 9 | 10 | 11 | 12

JOB 22-1. DISPLAY

Format: You decide (1) single-, double-, or triple-space lines; (2) spread-center a word or a line; (3) use all caps or both uppercase and lowercase letters; (4) center each line or block-center.

Bake Sale
Monday, October 24, 19--
Main lobby
11 a.m. until 1 p.m.
Sponsored by
The Language Club
Have dessert with us

JOB 22-2. DISPLAY

Format: You decide (1) single-, double-, or triple-space lines; (2) spread-center a word or a line; (3) use all caps or both uppercase and lowercase letters; (4) center each line or block-center.

You are cordially invited
to attend the annual
Winter Breakfast
for the
Student Council
Wednesday, December 13, 19--
8 to 10 a.m.
West Dining Hall
R.S.V.P. 555-7462

LESSON 23

GOALS
- To construct fractions not on keyboard.
- To type mixed numbers with constructed fractions.
- To format recipes.

FORMAT
- Single spacing   50-space line

KEYBOARDING SKILLS

Type each line twice.

Speed
1 She paid for a title to the island with the oaks.

Accuracy
2 Jack amazed Rex by pointing quickly to five haws.

Numbers
3 Type these: $10\frac{1}{2}$ and $29\frac{1}{4}$ and $38\frac{1}{2}$ and $47\frac{1}{4}$ and $56\frac{1}{2}$.

CONSTRUCTING FRACTIONS

To construct a fraction, use the diagonal key.

Type each line twice.

4 1/3, 3/4, 4/8, 5/10, 6/12, 7/14, 9/18, and 24/48.
5 Now add 1/4, 4/8, 1/2, and 6/8.   The answer is 2.
6 Other fractions are 4/10, 13/78, 9/25, and 11/60.

TYPING MIXED NUMBERS

Mixed numbers are whole numbers with fractions. Space between the number and a constructed fraction (9 3/16). Do not space between the number and a keyboard fraction (9½).

Type each line twice.

7 Type: 7 3/4, 8 9/12, 5 1/2, 34 6/9, and 85 3/10.
8 His Maltese weighs $13\frac{1}{2}$ lb; my terrier weighs $15\frac{1}{4}$.
9 My room is 12 2/3 feet wide and 14 1/2 feet long.
10 This jar is 12 1/2 oz, but the other is 7 1/8 oz.
11 Melody worked 6 1/4 days in 3 of her 3 1/5 weeks.
12 There are $5\frac{1}{4}$ weeks left to my $2\frac{1}{2}$-year assignment.

LESSON 276

GOAL
- To type boxed tables from handwritten copy.

FORMAT
- Single spacing 60-space line 5-space tab and other tabs as needed

KEYBOARDING SKILLS

Type lines 1–4 once. Then spell out the numbers in line 5 as you type it. Repeat lines 1–4, or take a series of 1-minute timings.

Speed 1 I am to go to work for the audit firm by the eighth of May. 12

Accuracy 2 Seizing the wax buffers, Jensen quickly removed a big spot. 12

Numbers 3 They had rooms 10 and 28. We had rooms 39, 47, and 56 too. 12

Symbols 4 The room went from 10^0 to 28^0 to 39^0 to 47^0 to 56^0 Celsius. 12

Number Usage 5 Please send us 6 clerks, 4 typists, and 1 secretary.

| 1 | 2 | 3 | 4 | 5 | 6 | 7 | 8 | 9 | 10 | 11 | 12

PREVIEW PRACTICE

Type lines 6 and 7 as a preview to the 3-minute timings below.

Accuracy 6 varying magnetic document graduated processing requirements

Speed 7 proportional durability particular directly ribbons various

3-MINUTE TIMINGS

Take two 3-minute timings on lines 8–20. Proofread using the paper bail.

8 Word processing supplies come in all sizes and shapes. 12

9 You begin with magnetic media for document storage, ribbons 24

10 for hard-copy output, and print elements also for hard-copy 36

11 output. Each of the various types of magnetic media allows 48

12 storage for a particular length document, with special disk 60

13 requirements for revision, at a specific cost by page. The 72

14 variety of ribbons provides document output in several hues 84

15 and in graduated types of image quality, each directly pro- 96

16 portional to page sizes and price. Print elements are also 108

17 available in a range of font styles, in varying degrees for 120

18 quality, durability, and price. Because supplies should be 132

19 adjusted to text length and size, text processing should be 144

20 decided before buying supplies. 150

| 1 | 2 | 3 | 4 | 5 | 6 | 7 | 8 | 9 | 10 | 11 | 12   SI 1.75

Type either lines 13–15 or 13a–15a, depending on which applies. Then repeat each line two more times or take two 1-minute timings on the Checkpoint.

Fractions on keyboard.

13 Store No. 13 will stock sizes 5¼ through 9½. The 10

14 annual sale is April 7 until April 20. A display 20

15 of 48 spring styles will be set up in 16 windows. 30

Fractions not on keyboard.

13a Store No. 3 will stock sizes 5 1/4 to 9 1/2. The 10

14a annual sale is April 7 until April 20. A display 20

15a of 48 spring styles will be set up in 16 windows. 30

| 1 | 2 | 3 | 4 | 5 | 6 | 7 | 8 | 9 | 10

2-MINUTE TIMINGS

Take two 2-minute timings on lines 16–20. Format: Double spacing, 5-space tab.

16   When you work with people every day, you get 10

17 to know what it is that they like best. You also 20

18 find out quickly what makes them frown. A little 30

19 extra effort in a dozen small ways will make your 40

20 office a pleasant place in which to do your work. 50

| 1 | 2 | 3 | 4 | 5 | 6 | 7 | 8 | 9 | 10   SI 1.20

FORMATTING RECIPES

A recipe consists of (1) a list of ingredients and (2) the directions for mixing the ingredients. To format a recipe, center the title in all-capital letters. Block-center the list of ingredients. Type the directions on a 40-space line. The recipe should be centered vertically. Leave 2 blank lines after the title and 1 blank line between the ingredients and the directions.

Note: To make numbers align at the right, set a tab for the longest number, and indent the shorter ones. If an ingredient takes more than one line, align the second line with the words on the first line.

JOB 23-1. RECIPE
Standard format. Half sheet of paper.

CHEESE WAFERS
↓3

1/2 cup butter
  1 cup grated Swiss cheese
3/4 cup flour
1/2 teaspoon salt
1/2 teaspoon dry mustard
1/8 teaspoon pepper
↓2

Blend ingredients in a bowl. Drop by teaspoonfuls, 2 inches apart, onto ungreased baking sheet. Bake at 350 degrees for 14 to 20 minutes. Cool and store in a tight container. Yield: 30.

JOB 23-2. RECIPE
Standard format. Half sheet of paper.

MERINGUE COOKIES

2 egg whites
1/8 teaspoon cream of tartar
  1 teaspoon vanilla
1/2 cup sugar
  1 cup chopped nuts or
    chocolate bits

Beat egg whites and cream of tartar until peaks form. Add remaining ingredients. Mix thoroughly, and drop by teaspoonfuls onto greased baking pan. Bake 30 minutes at 300 degrees. Cool. Yield: 40.

JOB 275-1.
RULED TABLE
Standard format.
Full page. Work log:
Workbook 707 top.

ANALYSIS OF FOURTH QUARTER SALES

October 1 to December 31, 19--

Branch	Budget	Actual	Percent
Detroit	$ 75,000	$ 80,000	106.7
Houston	100,000	124,500	124.5
Milwaukee	250,000	245,500	98.2
Oklahoma City	130,500	130,000	99.6
San Francisco	280,900	290,100	103.3
St. Louis	150,000	140,500	93.7
Seattle	50,000	67,500	135.0
Totals	$1,036,400	$1,078,100	104.0

JOB 275-2.
RULED TABLE
Standard format.
Full page.

ANALYSIS OF JANUARY SALES

Based on March 1 Figures

Branch	Budget	Actual	Percent
Detroit	$ 25,000	$ 24,500	98.0
Houston	35,000	36,000	102.9
Milwaukee	90,000	95,000	105.6
Oklahoma City	45,000	50,000	111.1
San Francisco	70,000	68,500	97.9
St. Louis	50,000	35,000	70.0
Seattle	20,000	18,000	90.0
Totals	$335,000	$327,000	97.6

JOB 275-3.
RULED TABLE
Standard format.
Full page.

ANALYSIS OF FEBRUARY SALES

Based on March 1 Figures

Branch	Budget	Actual	Percent
Detroit	$ 25,000	$ 25,500	102.0
Houston	40,000	38,500	96.3
Milwaukee	95,000	90,000	94.7
Oklahoma City	50,000	50,000	100.0
San Francisco	70,000	69,500	99.3
St. Louis	40,000	38,250	95.6
Seattle	18,000	19,675	109.3
Totals	$338,000	$331,425	98.1

LESSON 24

CLINIC

GOALS
- To review number-key controls.
- To build skill in typing numbers by touch.

FORMAT
- Single spacing   50-space line

PRETEST

Take two 2-minute timings on lines 1–5. Proofread your copy and circle your errors.

```
1  0101 0202 0303 0404 0505 0606 0707 0808 0909 1010    10
2  1111 1212 1313 1414 1515 1616 1717 1818 1919 2020    20
3  2121 2222 2323 2424 2525 2626 2727 2828 2929 3030    30
4  3131 3232 3333 3434 3535 3636 3737 3838 3939 4040    40
5  4141 4242 4343 4444 4545 4646 4747 4848 4949 5050    50
   |  1  |  2  |  3  |  4  |  5  |  6  |  7  |  8  |  9  | 10
```

PRACTICE

Type lines 6–10 four times. Proofread your copy and circle your errors.

```
6   1 aql aql aql 1 11 111 11 1 11 111 11 1 11 111 11
7   0 ;p0 ;p0 ;p0 0 10 100 10 0 01 001 01 0 10 100 10
8   2 sw2 sw2 sw2 2 20 220 20 2 02 022 02 0 20 220 20
9   9 lo9 lo9 lo9 9 93 939 93 9 39 399 09 9 39 999 90
10  3 de3 de3 de3 3 33 332 38 3 38 383 03 3 38 323 30
```

Type lines 11–15 four times. Proofread your copy and circle your errors.

```
11  8 ki8 ki8 ki8 8 82 882 80 8 28 288 08 8 82 882 80
12  4 fr4 fr4 fr4 4 43 432 42 4 44 489 04 4 44 474 40
13  7 ju7 ju7 ju7 7 78 747 47 7 74 787 07 7 74 747 70
14  5 ft5 ft5 ft5 5 54 535 25 5 75 557 05 5 55 535 50
15  6 ju6 ju6 ju6 6 67 686 65 6 56 667 07 6 56 656 60
```

Type lines 16–20 four times. Proofread your copy and circle your errors.

```
16  we 23 24 25 we 23 24 25 - up 70 71 72 up 70 71 72
17  re 43 44 45 re 43 44 45 - or 94 95 96 or 94 95 96
18  ow 92 93 94 ow 92 93 94 - it 85 86 87 it 85 86 87
19  ie 83 84 85 ie 83 84 85 - ru 47 48 49 ru 47 48 49
20  qu 17 18 19 qu 17 18 19 - ye 63 64 65 ye 63 64 65
```

POSTTEST

Take two 2-minute timings on lines 1–5. Proofread your copy and circle your errors. Note your improvement.

POSTTEST 1

Take two 2-minute timings on lines 1–4 on page 436. Proofread and note your improvement.

PRETEST 2

Take two 2-minute timings on lines 11–14. Proofread both, and note the more accurate of the two scores.

11 She informs me that the boy was running by the office door. 12
12 Just for the fun of it, I gave my aunts one cent for lunch. 24
13 We have to admit that the stones somehow broke the windows. 36
14 Tod doubts the main brakes have a chance of working anyhow. 48

| 1 | 2 | 3 | 4 | 5 | 6 | 7 | 8 | 9 | 10 | 11 | 12

PRACTICE 2

Type lines 15–20 five times. Repeat individual lines for speed gain if you had two or fewer errors on Pretest 2; otherwise repeat each block of lines for accuracy gain.

15 windows somehow timely office print night tiny pain act nor
16 unknown tactful prompt stones round smoke skin main sun any
17 orchard shelves lesson motive hints exact room noon mob run
18 primary running expand having lunch knife inch aunt ice cry
19 leading mounted chance driven bench count gave from win beg
20 informs helping anyhow brakes doubt admit have cent fun one

POSTTEST 2

Take two 2-minute timings on lines 11–14. Proofread and note your improvement.

UNIT 45 PROCESSING TABULATED INFORMATION

UNIT GOAL
50/5'/3e

GOALS
- To correct 12 commonly misspelled words while typing sentences.
- To type ruled tables.

FORMAT
- Single spacing   60-space line   Tabs as needed

LAB 32

Type lines 1–4 once, correcting the spelling of any misspelled words. Edit your copy as your teacher reads the answers. Then retype lines 1–4 from your edited copy.

SPELLING

Workbook 705–706.

1 He needs separat proceedures for handling premeums quickly.
2 Six custemers would not except our annaul interest charges.
3 I don't know wether Jan Zbar will recieve her notise soon.
4 The originle agrement does not include disteribution costs.

12-SECOND TIMINGS

Type each line four times, or take four 12-second timings on each line. For each timing, type with no error.

5 He said that they will rule that page with four long lines. 12
6 They will note this thin line when they look over this job. 12
7 They must have good jobs with very good pay; they told her. 12

25   30   35   40   45   50   55   60

GOAL
- To control #, $, %, and & keys by touch.

FORMAT
- Single spacing   50-space line

KEYBOARDING SKILLS

Type each line twice.

Speed   1 This title to the island is the first to be kept.

Accuracy 2 A quick tally shows that taxi drivers whiz along.

Numbers   3 Al jumped over Nos. 10, 29, 38, 47, and 56 today.

KEY

Shift of 3. Use D finger.

Do not space between the number and the #.

Type each line twice.

4 ded de3 d3d d3#d d#d d#d #3 #33 #333 d#d d3d #333

5 Catalog #56 weighs 38#, and Catalog #2947 is 10#.

6 My favorite ones are #10, #29, #38, #47, and #56.

$ KEY

Shift of 4. Use F finger.

Do not space between the $ and the number.

Type each line twice.

7 frf fr4 f4f f4$f f$f f$f $4 $44 $444 f$f f4f $444

8 The latest rates are $10, $29, $38, $47, and $56.

9 Who bought a $56 suit at the Fashionette for $38?

CHECKPOINT

The symbol # before a number means "number"; # after a number means "pounds."

Type lines 10–13 once. Then repeat lines 4–9 or take two 1-minute timings on the Checkpoint.

10 Item #1029 lists at $38.50 but will be reduced in   10

11 June to $34.50. Item #847, which weighs 56#, can   20

12 be bought for $74. Items #1029, #3847, and #5665   30

13 will all sell for $2 in June and $3.95 in August.   40

| 1 | 2 | 3 | 4 | 5 | 6 | 7 | 8 | 9 | 10

JOB 273-2. FORM LETTER WITH INSERTS
Standard format.

[Allow room for inside address, salutation, and insertions in the body.] This letter is to advise you that we are canceling your *[insert type of]* coverage as of *[insert date and hour]*.

This notice is in line with the "Conditions" of the policy. Your policy now covers bodily injury liability, property damage liability, medical payments, and protection against uninsured motorists within the limits shown on your policy.

Our action was influenced by information in a consumer report, made at our request, by our company representative. Very truly yours,

JOB 273-3. FORM LETTER WITH INSERTS
Standard format.

[Allow room for inside address and salutation and insertions in the body.] When your homeowners'

insurance policy is due for renewal on *[date]*, the billing system will be changed for handling your policy.

Due to a change in Americana's billing procedures, your bill will be sent to Americana's home office in Atlanta instead of to our branch office at *[fill in branch address—leave room for street and city]*.

If you have any questions, please call us at *[fill in branch number—leave enough room for area code and number]*. Sincerely,

JOB 273-4. FORM LETTER
Retype Job 273-2 using the following information for the fill-ins. Standard format. Workbook 701–702.

Mr. Dan Wilson, 15 South Broadway, Center Junction, Iowa 52212, Limited Collision Policy, 10 days from *today's date*, at 12:01 a.m. CST.

LESSON 274

CLINIC

GOALS
- To use intensive drill to improve basic skills.

FORMAT
- Single spacing   60-space line

PRETEST 1

Take two 2-minute timings on lines 1–4. Proofread both, and note the more accurate of the two scores.

```
1  Frank knows about the campus campaign to back a labor vote.   12
2  Carol gave six tubs of shrubs to enable the band to travel.   24
3  Scott and Elmer called the track coaches about those races.   36
4  Benjamin will carry about nine heavy loads to the big barn.   48
   |  1  |  2  |  3  |  4  |  5  |  6  |  7  |  8  |  9  |  10  |  11  |  12
```

PRACTICE 1

Type lines 5–10 five times. Repeat individual lines for speed gain if you had two or fewer errors on Pretest 1; otherwise repeat each block of lines for accuracy gain.

```
5   bay mad tax map tab mar van nab car ink can jam bat jab man
6   baby mast vary mall sack pack care jack bank hymn tack jobs
7   enemy vault blame clams mulch bands truck track bulbs nails
8   cab mob bag mix vat men bin lob act inn bar nob may bad vim
9   back maze bake navy calm mast many came zany cage bend mint
10  meant coach manly basic naval cable lemon canal money candy
```

 % KEY

Shift of 5. Use F finger.

The % symbol is used only in statistical information. Do not space between the number and the %.

Type each line twice.

14 f5f f5% f%f f5f f5% f%f 5% 55% 15% 25% 25.5% 5.5%

15 The return rates are 10%, 29%, 38%, 47%, and 56%.

16 Annette scored 92%, Joe made 83%, and Ed had 74%.

 & KEY

Shift of 7. Use J finger.

Space once before and after an ampersand (&) used between words and numbers. Do not space when used between initials.

Type each line twice.

17 j7j j7& j&j j7j j7& j&j 7 & 8 & 9 & 10 & 11 & 121

18 Jean made profits of 10% & 29% & 38% & 47% & 56%.

19 Joan worked at H&S Company and then Rex & Penrod.

CHECKPOINT

Type lines 20–23 once. Then repeat lines 14–19 or take two 1-minute timings on the Checkpoint.

20 The rates given by L&S Loan Company are 18% for a   10
21 short term and 15% for a long term.   P&W Loan Co.   20
22 offered 17% for short term and 14% for long term.   30
23 Dawes & Kipp have the best deal with 13% and 16%.   40
    | 1 | 2 | 3 | 4 | 5 | 6 | 7 | 8 | 9 | 10

3-MINUTE TIMINGS

Using Speed Markers

The numbers in this timing are speed markers. *At the end of the timing, the number you reach will tell you your WAM speed, because the total words have already been divided by 3. For example, if you end the timing on the last letter of* which *on line 31, you typed 26 WAM.*

Take two 3-minute timings on lines 24–32. Format: Double spacing, 5-space tab.

24   I would really like to join a club at school   10

25 this year.   There are so many from which to pick.   20

26 I just cannot make up my mind.   There is the Swim   30

27 Club and the Ski Club; I could try out for a play   40

28 or try chess.   Debate has quite a record for hard   50

29 work, and the jazz band should be an exciting new   60

30 venture too.   Now which one shall I choose?   Will   70

31 my friends want to help?   Tell me which club will   80

32 be the best for me?   84
    | 1 | 2 | 3 | 4 | 5 | 6 | 7 | 8 | 9 | 10   SI 1.09

GOALS
- To correct 12 commonly misspelled words while typing sentences.
- To type 49/5'/3e.
- To type form letters allowing space for personalized inserts.

FORMAT
- Single spacing   60-space line   5-space tab

LAB 32

SPELLING

Type lines 1–4 once, correcting the spelling of any misspelled words. Edit your copy as your teacher reads the answers. Then retype lines 1–4 from your edited copy.

1 Whethor Kent Lazarus will acept the orriginal is debatable.
2 John F. Quinn will recieve six seperate agreemants to sign.
3 Send each custamer a nottice regarding the premuim increase.
4 The new precedure for the annul destribution is not clear.

5-MINUTE TIMINGS

Take two 5-minute timings on lines 5–15. Type the paragraph twice in five minutes to reach the goal of 49 words a minute.

```
5        Word processors come in many sizes.  One of them looks      12  135
6    like a regular electric typewriter--but it's not.  Technol-     24  147
7    ogy has developed a piece of equipment to fill the gap made     36  159
8    between standard electric typewriters and the sophisticated     48  171
9    text-editing typewriters.  An electronic typewriter is more     60  183
10   efficient to operate than any electric typewriter.  It lets     72  195
11   the operator eliminate keystrokes with recalled characters,     84  207
12   words, lines, or paragraphs which are frequently used by an     96  219
13   operator or business.  Margins and tabs can be adjusted for    108  231
14   later recall as well.  Frequently repeated addresses can be    120  243
15   recalled also.                                                 123  246
     |  1  |  2  |  3  |  4  |  5  |  6  |  7  |  8  |  9  | 10  | 11  | 12   SI 1.86
```

JOB 273-1. FORM LETTER WITH INSERTS
Standard format.

[*Allow room for inside address, salutation, and insertions in the body.*] In approximately   days, a renewal billing will be mailed for this policy. This is the anniversary of the Good Student Discount. For you to retain this discount, we will require a new Good Student Certificate Form GU-6866A.

If the new certificate is not received prior to   , you will be billed without the Good Student Discount, and you will not be eligible for the discount until the next renewal date.

This is the only notification that you will receive regarding this discount. Sincerely,

GOAL
■ To control), (, ', and " keys.

FORMAT
■ Single spacing   50-space line

KEYBOARDING SKILLS

Type each line twice.

Speed   1   If Helen owns this land, she may wish to sell it.

Accuracy   2   Zeke was quite vexed about the joke made by Carl.

Numbers   3   Write dates as April 5, 1983 or 4/5/83 or 4-5-83.

Symbols   4   When J&R orders it at a 3.6% discount, #1 is $29.

) KEY

Shift of 0 (zero). Use Sem finger.

Space once after a closing parenthesis; do not space before it.

5   ;p; ;p) ;); ;); 10) 29) 38) 47) 56) ½) ½) ;p; ;);

6   We included 1) skis, 2) coats, 3) hats, 4) boots.

7   My rates are 1) 5%, 2) 7%, 3) 9%, 4) 16%, 5) 18%.

(KEY

Shift of 9. Use L finger.

Space once before an opening parenthesis; do not space after it.

8   lol lo(l(l l(l (10) (29) (38) (47) (56) (½) (1¼)

9   My speech (it is not too long) will cover skiing.

10   Your car (the convertible) is our favorite color.

CHECKPOINT

Type lines 11–14 once. Then repeat lines 5–10 or take two 1-minute timings on the Checkpoint.

11   When typing a symbol, follow the steps: (1) cap,   10

12   (2) strike, and (3) home. They help you feel the   20

13   motions of (1) cap, (2) strike, and (3) home in a   30

14   smooth rhythm--(1) cap, (2) strike, and (3) home.   40

    | 1 | 2 | 3 | 4 | 5 | 6 | 7 | 8 | 9 | 10

 ' KEY

Shift of 8.
Use K finger.

Or next to ; key.
Use Sem finger.

Do not space before or after an apostrophe.

15M   kik ki' ki' It's Mia's job to get Lynn's lessons.

15E   ;'; ;'; ''' It's Mia's job to get Lynn's lessons.

16   Wasn't Paul going? Isn't Jim here? Help us now.

17   We're so happy. Aren't you pleased? It's not I.

Type each line four times, or take four 12-second timings on each line. For each timing, type with no error.

```
 5  Jane will sell four lots when they find the cash they need.  12
 6  They will sell him some more lots when they need more cash.  12
 7  Jane will give them back the money they gave her last week.  12
```

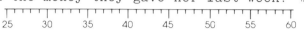

```
25    30    35    40    45    50    55    60
```

LETTERS FROM FORM PARAGRAPHS

Some word processing centers have a bank of form letters such as the ones you typed in Lesson 271. Other centers build a bank of paragraphs that can be used interchangeably to develop different letters—for examples see the following paragraphs. Read each paragraph carefully for content. Note that the first ones (PC01–PC03) are *introductory* paragraphs, the next ones (PC11–PC14) are *middle* paragraphs, and the last ones (PC21–PC24) are *closing* paragraphs.

JOBS 272-1 TO 272-4. LETTERS FROM FORM PARAGRAPHS

Standard format. Compose four letters using the paragraphs below. Workbook 693–700.

The first letter is to Ms. Jennifer Shapiro, 22 Peachtree, Atlanta, Georgia 30303. She is a new college graduate.

The second letter goes to Mr. and Mrs. Geoffrey Lippman, 38 Meadow Grove, Atlanta, Georgia 30315. They have a new baby girl.

The third letter goes to John Allen, a business executive who is new in Atlanta. His address is 10 Parkview Place, Atlanta, GA 30337.

The last letter goes to Ms. Sherri J. Atworst, Apartment K, Willow Court, Atlanta, GA 30329. She is new to the community also, but don't make her letter exactly like the one to Mr. Allen. Each letter must sound as if it were written especially for each client.

PC01. Congratulations on the arrival of your new baby! We'd like you to accept our gift along with the others you have received for the new arrival.

PC02. Congratulations on your graduation from college! We know that you are anxious to begin your career, and we would like you to accept a gift from us along with the others you have received.

PC03. Welcome to Atlanta! We hope that you will learn to love the charm of the city as we do. Please accept our gift as a welcome to our city.

PC11. We offer this gift to acquaint you with the services that Americana has to offer. We offer insurance plans for life, health, home, and auto. Our company is a family company which has been in business for 40 years.

PC12. We offer you this gift to acquaint you with the special services that we have to offer new families in our community. Thousands of new parents are choosing our plan.

PC13. We offer you this gift to acquaint you with information about a plan that enables you to wrap up your family's insurance protection in one convenient, low-cost plan.

PC14. We offer you this gift to acquaint you with the special services that we have to offer young adults in regard to health and life insurance coverage.

PC21. For information about our insurance coverage, just mail the postpaid card. No signature is required, and there is no obligation whatsoever.

PC22. In the next few days, I will call to arrange a brief appointment at your convenience. I know you will find the services we have to offer well worth the few minutes we will need to discuss them.

PC23. In the next few days, I will call to arrange a mutually convenient appointment. I know that you will find this service well worth the small amount of time it requires.

PC24. May I call on you within the next few days to explain to you our special coverage? I know that the time you spend will be well worth it.

CONSTRUCT AN EXCLAMATION POINT

If your machine has no exclamation point, you may construct one: (1) strike the period, (2) backspace, and (3) strike the apostrophe. Type each line once.

18 That song must have taken many months to compose!

19 My, how well she plays! She's a superb musician!

20 His accompaniment is superb! He's a new pianist!

" KEY

Shift of 2. Use S finger.

Or shift of ' key. Use Sem finger.

Type each line twice.

21M sws sw" sw" "Here," she cried. "I am over here."

21E ;"; ;"; """ "Here," she cried. "I am over here."

22 The signal is "blue" for up and "green" for down.

QUOTATION MARKS

Workbook 23–24.

Quotation marks are used in pairs. Often the second quotation mark is used with another punctuation mark, as shown below.

Follow these rules when using quotation marks with other punctuation:

1. Place commas and periods *before* the second quotation mark (see A and B).

2. Place colons and semicolons *after* the second quotation mark (see C and D).

3. Place question marks and exclamation marks before the second quotation mark *only if* the entire quotation is a question or an exclamation (see E). In all other cases, place the question mark or exclamation mark *after* the second quotation mark (see F and G).

Practice: Type lines 23–27 once.

23 "Good morning,"Ⓐ said Joe. "Come in."Ⓑ

24 I did as he "offered"Ⓒ: I went in. He

25 said that I seemed "excited"Ⓓ; he listened.

26 "What's your news?"Ⓔ he asked. "Tell me!"Ⓔ

27 Did he already "know"Ⓕ? I think he "guessed"!Ⓖ

CHECKPOINT

Type lines 28–31 once. Then repeat lines 16–17 (page 45) and 22 or take two 1-minute timings on the Checkpoint.

28 It's not very often that we hear the words "thank   10

29 you" or "please." Is it that we don't "care" and   20

30 "feel," or is it that we just don't "think" to be   30

31 courteous? We all "know" that we "ought" to try.   40

   | 1 | 2 | 3 | 4 | 5 | 6 | 7 | 8 | 9 | 10

JOB 271-1. FORM LETTER
Standard format.

In approximately 40 ~~30~~ days, a renewal billing will be mailed for this policy. This
is the anniversary of the "good student
discount." For you to retain this discount, we will require a new "good student"
certificate, form GU-6866A. ¶If the new
certificate is not recieved prior to the
billing of this policy, it will be billed
without the "good student discount," and you
will not be eligible for the discount
until the next renewal date. ¶This is the
only notification that you will receive
regarding this discount. Sincerely,

JOB 271-2. FORM LETTER
Standard format.

As of the renewal date of your homeowners'
insurance policy, the filling system will
be changed. ¶Due to ~~the~~ a change in Americana's billing procedure, your bill ~~will~~ will
be sent to Americana's home office in

Atlanta instead of ~~from~~ to our office. The
payment can be sent in directly to the
home office in the envelope it provides,
or it can be made here at our office. ¶If
you have any questions about this new
billing, please feel free to call us.
¶Thank you!

JOB 271-3. FORM LETTER
Standard format.

This letter is to advice you that we are
canceling the above coverages as of the
date and the hour indicated. ¶This notice
is in line with the "conditions" of the
policy. Your policy now covers bodily
injury liability, property damage liability, medical payments, and protection
against uninsured motorists within the
limits shown in your policy. ¶If a company
name and address is shown below, our action was influenced by information in a
consumer report, made at ~~the~~ our request, by
that company. Very truly yours,

LESSON 272

GOALS
- To identify the correct spelling of 12 commonly misspelled words while typing sentences.
- To combine designated paragraphs into acceptable letters.

FORMAT
- Single spacing   60-space line

LAB 32

SPELLING

Type lines 1–4 once. Then repeat lines 1–4 or take a series of 1-minute timings.

1 Did Burton and Jeffrey quickly accept the original premium? 12
2 The new procedure is to send a separate notice to each one. 12
3 An annual distribution of catalogs to customers is planned. 12
4 Do you know whether Frank Zora will receive six agreements? 12

| 1 | 2 | 3 | 4 | 5 | 6 | 7 | 8 | 9 | 10 | 11 | 12

LESSON 27

GOAL
- To control __, *, ¢, and @ keys.

FORMAT
- Single spacing   50-space line

KEYBOARDING SKILLS

Type each line twice.

Speed 1 It is the duty of six girls to cut down that oak.
Accuracy 2 Joel quickly fixed five zippers while she waited.
Numbers 3 Now read this new order: 10, 29, 38, 47, and 56.
Symbols 4 It's not "up" but "down." She saw him (Joel) go.

 KEY

Shift of 6.
Use J finger.
Or shift of -
(hyphen).
Use Sem finger.
Workbook 25–26.

To underscore a word or a group of words: (1) type the word or words, (2) backspace to the first letter of the word or words to be underscored, (3) depress the shift lock, and (4) strike the underscore key repeatedly until all the words have been underscored. **Note:** Do *not* underscore the punctua-

tion or the space following an under-scored word or phrase. (**Exception:** If the punctuation is part of a title—as in Oklahoma!—then the punctua-tion *is* underscored.) *Do* underscore the punctuation or the space *within* a group of words to be underscored. See, for example, lines 6 and 7 below.

On some typewriters, the underscore key may operate continuously, like the space bar. Make sure you stop in time.

Type each line twice.

5M ju6 ju_ j_j j_j Mary did say she would not drive.
5E ;p_ ;p_ ;_; ;_; Mary did say she would not drive.
6 It is not, Linda claims, very, very well written.
7 Sara read her class the book Alice in Wonderland.

KEY

Shift of - (hyphen).
Use Sem finger.
Or shift of 8.
Use K finger.
*Do not space between the word and the *.*

Type each line twice.

8M ;p_ ;p* ;*; ;*; A style manual* is of great help.
8E ki8 ki* k*k k*k A style manual* is of great help.
9 Rules in the reference book* help solve problems.
10 He recommends this manual* for grammar and style.

CHECKPOINT

In figuring speed, count underscored words triple.

Type lines 11–14 once. Then repeat lines 6–7 and 9–10 or take two 1-minute timings on the Checkpoint.

11 A reference manual* is valuable for all of us who 10
12 write letters, memos, and reports. A manual will 20
13 help to solve problems in using who and whom, for 33
14 example, and in using punctuation marks properly. 43
      | 1 | 2 | 3 | 4 | 5 | 6 | 7 | 8 | 9 | 10

Take a 5-minute Pretest on lines 5–25. Then circle and count your errors. Use the chart below to determine which lines to type for practice.

```
 5        Electronic mail is defined as the delivery of messages    12
 6   electronically.  There are numerous differences among audio     24
 7   and hard-copy delivery systems, but there are more similar-     36
 8   ities than differences.  Therefore, many market analyses do     48
 9   include the telephone and other audio communication devices     60
10   in the category of electronic mail.                             67
11        The telephone is used in business situations as a gen-     79
12   eral message delivery system, as a sales tool, as an order-     91
13   entry device, and as an administrative message system.  One    103
14   limitation is that there is no hard copy, or any other form    115
15   of visual record, available.  When the telephone is used in    127
16   the transmission of long messages, the possibility of error    139
17   increases greatly with the length of the message.              149
18        The demand for electronic mail message systems and the    161
19   services which accompany them continues to increase.  Major    173
20   components of these systems are facsimile equipment, commu-    185
21   nicating word processors, and telex service.  Other message    197
22   services are continuing to grow as the communication demand    209
23   moves ahead and as technology provides more efficient tools    221
24   to implement faster communication flow.  As quick decisions    233
25   are demanded, even quicker communications must be realized.    245
     |  1  |  2  |  3  |  4  |  5  |  6  |  7  |  8  |  9  |  10  |  11  |  12   SI 1.92
```

In the chart below, find the number of errors you made on the Pretest. Then type each of the designated drill lines four times.

Pretest errors	0–1	2–3	4+
Drill lines	28–31	27–30	26–29

```
26   administrative substantially components accompany situation
27   communications differences, technology telephone electronic
28   continuing facsimile efficient analyses inquiry visual mail
29   hard copy other ahead device record system services quicker
30   many more used them word grow long audio telex order demand
31   for the and are any move sale flow tool that form must even
```

Repeat the Pretest above to see how much your skill has improved.

 ¢ KEY

Next to ; key.
Use Sem finger.

Or shift of 6.
Use J finger.

Do not space between the number and the symbol.

Type each line twice.

15M ; ; ; ;¢; ; ; ; ;¢; Is it 10¢, 29¢, 38¢, 47¢, or 56¢?

15E jy6 jy¢ j¢j j¢j Is it 10¢, 29¢, 38¢, 47¢, or 56¢?

16 Lisa has too many for 67¢ and not enough for 20¢.

17 The sales taxes total 56¢, 47¢, 38¢, 29¢, and 1¢.

 @ KEY

Shift of ¢ key.
Use Sem finger.

Or shift of 2.
Use S finger.

Space once before and after an @.

Type each line twice.

18M ;¢; ;¢@ ;@; ;@; She wants 21 @ 11¢, not 11 @ 21¢.

18E sw2 sw@ s@s s@s She wants 21 @ 11¢, not 11 @ 21¢.

19 Pat and Ted sold them for 20 @ 14¢, not 14 @ 20¢.

20 How much are 10 apples @ 12¢ and 14 lemons @ 10¢?

CHECKPOINT

Type lines 21–24 once. Then repeat lines 16–17 and 19–20 or take two 1-minute timings on the Checkpoint.

21 The following increases were noted: cereal, 10¢;   10

22 milk, 29¢; bread, 38¢; sugar, 47¢; and beef, 56¢.   20

23 A dozen apples @ 15¢ each is also a big increase,   30

24 but buying oranges @ 20¢ is an even larger total.   40

| 1 | 2 | 3 | 4 | 5 | 6 | 7 | 8 | 9 | 10

3-MINUTE TIMINGS

Take two 3-minute timings on lines 25–33. Use the speed markers to figure your speed. Format: Double spacing, 5-space tab.

25   When you want to mail a letter or a package,   10

26 you have a choice as to the way you want it sent.   20

27 If you want a package to be sent very fast, place   30

28 it in Express Mail. If you are not in a rush for   40

29 it to be sent, you can send it third class. Most   50

30 letters are mailed first class, but they just may   60

31 go quicker by special delivery. The size and the   70

32 weight may mean that you must change the way that   80

33 an item may be sent.   84

| 1 | 2 | 3 | 4 | 5 | 6 | 7 | 8 | 9 | 10   SI 1.12

JOB 270-4. FORM LETTER

Standard format. Prepare a carbon copy. Workbook 691–692.

May I introduce you to a savings plan that thousands of other promising young adults have found attractive?

At your age the plan is available at modest cost and can guarantee that you will be able to obtain life insurance later when your needs and ability to pay increase. It may also have tax and other advantages.

The idea can be explained in just 15 minutes. I shall give you a call soon to arrange a convenient appointment. Cordially,

JOB 270-5. ADDRESSING FORM LETTERS

Send four of the form letters you prepared to the following people. Use the originals you typed.

Dr. and Mrs. James Hough, Chatham Apartments, 669 Abercorn, Savannah, GA 31401, letter 270-1.

Mrs. Edward Wade, 155 Forest Avenue, NE, Albany, GA 31703, letter 270-2.

Mr. Todd Ruppert, Armstrong College, 11935 Abercorn, Savannah, GA 31406, letter 270-3.

Ms. Elizabeth Tincher, Coronado Apartments, 317 23d Avenue, Columbus, GA 31903, letter 270-4.

LESSON 271

GOALS
- To recognize the correct spelling of 12 commonly misspelled words while typing sentences.
- To type 49/5'/3e.
- To type form letters from rough-draft copy.

FORMAT
- Single spacing 60-space line 5-space tab

LAB 32

Type lines 1–4 once. Then repeat lines 1–4 or take a series of 1-minute timings. Note the spelling of the underscored words as you type.

SPELLING

1 Six <u>distribution</u> centers offer <u>customers</u> <u>annual</u> incentives.   12
2 Jo Adzick doesn't know <u>whether</u> they'll <u>accept</u> my <u>agreement</u>.   12
3 Barbara already mailed the <u>original</u> <u>notice</u> for the <u>premium</u>.   12
4 Did Leon Quimby <u>receive</u> a <u>separate</u> <u>notice</u> on the <u>procedure</u>?   12

| 1 | 2 | 3 | 4 | 5 | 6 | 7 | 8 | 9 | 10 | 11 | 12

LESSON 28

GOALS
- To control !, +, and = keys.
- To construct special symbols.

FORMAT
- Single spacing   50-space line

KEYBOARDING SKILLS

Speed
Accuracy
Numbers
Symbols

Type each line twice.

1 The firm that they own may make a big profit now.
2 Her job was to pack a dozen equal boxes by night.
3 Mark will order 10, 29, 38, 47, and 56 varieties.
4 The book* is on sale at P&H (2 copies @ $3 each).

 KEY

Shift of 1.
Use A finger.

Or next to P.
Use Sem finger.

Or construct. (See page 46.)

Type each line twice.

5M aql aq! a!a a!a Watch! Watch them! Watch those!
5E ;;; ;!; ;;; ;!; Watch! Watch them! Watch those!
6 Look! Look there! Look there! Look everywhere!
7 She paced: Five! Four! Three! Two! One! Go!
8 Look at the sky! You can see it from here! Wow!

KEYS

+ is shift of =

Next to hyphen.
Use Sem finger.

Or next to P.
Use Sem finger.

Type each line twice.

9 ;=; === ;=; === = A = 40, B = 35, C = 25, D = 20.
10 ;+; +++ ;+; +++ 0 + 10 + 29 + 38 + 47 + 56 = 100.
11 Yes, 3 + 3 = 6 and 9 + 9 = 18; but 3 + 18 = what?

CHECKPOINT

Space once before and after the + and the =.

Type lines 12–15 once. Then repeat lines 6–11 or take two 1-minute timings on the Checkpoint.

12 If 2 + 2 = 4 and 7 + 7 = 14, how much is 14 + 14? 10
13 Watch the ball go! It's a home run for the team! 20
14 If 4 + 6 = 10 and 6 + 4 = 10, what will 5 + 5 be? 30
15 Watch the beautiful eagle! It's building a nest! 40
      | 1 | 2 | 3 | 4 | 5 | 6 | 7 | 8 | 9 | 10

Take two 30-second timings on lines 6–8, or type the paragraph twice.

6 If that job is really the one you prefer, then you would be 12
7 wise to take some steps to get it. To wait for somebody to 24
8 approach you about the job might leave you waiting forever. 36
   | 1 | 2 | 3 | 4 | 5 | 6 | 7 | 8 | 9 | 10 | 11 | 12

JOB 270-1. FORM LETTER
Standard format. Prepare a carbon copy. Workbook 685–686.

An investment in four years of college may cost anywhere from $10,000 to $30,000 or more. For most parents, even the lower figure is a problem.

Americana has some ideas that have provided solutions for a great number of parents. I would like to share these ideas with you.

At the same time, I'd like to give you, with my compliments, a current copy of "College Costs". This booklet contains information about tuition, fees, and room and board for just about every college in the country.

May I call to arrange a brief talk with you? I know you'll find the few minutes well spent. Cordially yours,

JOB 270-2. FORM LETTER
Standard format. Prepare a carbon copy. Workbook 687–688.

Your birthday is an important insurance date. On that day, any additional life insurance you might need will cost more than it does today.

That fact alone is not a reason for you to buy new insurance, but it is a good reason to review your present insurance. Not only does your own life situation change from year to year, but life insurance plans and benefits change and improve from year to year too.

In the next few days, I shall call to arrange a brief appointment. I know you will find it well worth the few minutes we shall need to review your program.
Cordially yours,

JOB 270-3. FORM LETTER
Standard format. Prepare a carbon copy. Workbook 689–690.

Congratulations on the good news I've just heard about you. Naturally, this will affect your financial plans for the future. I would like to suggest an idea that might be valuable to you.

In the next few days, I will call to arrange an appointment. I know you will find this idea worth a few minutes of your time. Cordially,

PHRASES Practice lines 16–18 to build speed on familiar phrases.

```
16  by me, by it, by him, by her, by our, by the way,
17  or if, or so, or the, or our, or his, or her way,
18  in my, in it, in for, in our, in the, in the way,
```

CONSTRUCTED CHARACTERS Every typist should know how to construct these special symbols, which are needed from time to time. Using the procedures given in Column 3, practice constructing each of the characters listed in Column 1. Then type only Column 2 centered on a full page and double-spaced.

Column 1	Column 2	Column 3
19. Cents	He charges 2¢	Small letter C, intersected by diagonal.
20. Star	☆ ☆ ☆ ☆ ☆	Capital A, typed over small letter V.
21. Caret	They try/hard ^{so}	Underscore and diagonal; word centered above diagonal.
22. Brackets	He /Johnston/	Diagonals, with underscores facing inside.
23. Roman numerals	Chapter XVIII	Capitals of I, V, X, L, C, D, and M.
24. Pounds sterling	£8 is English	Capital L, typed over small letter F.
25. Degrees	32°F (or 0°C)	Small letter O, raised slightly (turn cylinder by hand).
26. Military zero	Leave at Ø1ØØ	The number 0, intersected by a diagonal.
27. Times, by	What is 4 x 5	Expressed by the small letter X.
28. Divided by	120 ÷ 10 = 12	Colon, intersected by hyphen.
29. Equals	11 x 11 = 121	Two hyphens, one below the other (turn cylinder by hand).
30. Plus	87 + 18 = 105	Hyphen, intersected by diagonal or apostrophe.
31. Minus	140 – 56 = 84	Expressed by a single hyphen; space before and after.
32. Superscript	$8^2 + 6^2 = 10^2$	Type number or letter above line (turn cylinder by hand).
33. Subscript	H_2O is water.	Type number or letter below line (turn cylinder by hand).
34. Square root	$\overline{\sqrt{90000}}$ is 300	Small V, off-positioned to meet diagonal, followed by underscores typed on line above.
35. Divide into	45)9045 = 201	Right parenthesis and underscores.
36. Feet and inches	Mary is 5' 2"	For feet, apostrophe; for inches, quotation mark.
37. Minutes, seconds	Time: 3' 15"	For minutes, apostrophe; for seconds, quotation mark.
38. Ellipsis	He . . . also He I	Three periods, spaced apart (but four periods if there is a sentence ending within the omitted material).
39. Section	§20. Symbols	Capital S, intersected by a raised capital S.
40. Paragraph	¶21. Symbols	Capital P, intersected by the small letter L.
41. Ratio	1:4::2:X = 8.	Use one or two colons, as appropriate.
42. Bar graph line	mmmmmmmmmmmmmm	Small M, W, O, or X, typed in a solid row.

JOB 269-1. FORM LETTER
Standard format. Work log: Workbook 659 bottom.

As an Americana Insurance Company policy   8
owner, you are entitled to periodic review of   17
your life and health insurance programs.   26

Such things as beneficiary designations, use   36
of dividends, social security benefits, and other   46
matters need periodic checking. You will find   55
it worth your while to take a few minutes for   64
this service.   67

I shall give you a call in the near future to   78
arrange an appointment at your convenience.   87
Cordially yours,   92

JOB 269-2. FORM LETTER
Standard format.

As an Americana Insurance policy owner,   8
you are eligible to receive, free and without   17
obligation, the benefits of our Futures Plan-   26
ning Service.   29

Futures Planning Service is a financial ser-   39
vice. It can actually increase the value of your   49
present life insurance without any further   58
expense to you. By means of a simple analysis,   67
your present financial situation and future   76
financial needs and assets are clearly shown.   85

The service can give you a complete under-   95
standing of your social security benefits and   104
how they relate to your life insurance program.   114

You will know exactly where you stand in   122
terms of family security and retirement in-   131
come.   132

I shall call within a few days to find the   142
most convenient time to provide this service.   151
Sincerely,   155

JOB 269-3. FORM LETTER
Block format.

Subject: Futures Planning Conference   8
Futures Planning is a service that almost   17
invariably increases the value of a person's   26
present insurance. It starts with a conference   36
based on two premises: 40
   1. No effort will be made to sell anything   51
     during that conference.   59
   2. You will not be contacted again unless   68
     you request it.   73
These two premises set the stage for a fair,   83
relaxed discussion.   88

The service can give you a complete under-   97
standing of your social security and other   106
benefits and how they relate to your life in-   116
surance program. You'll know exactly where   123
you stand in terms of family security and   132
retirement income.   136

I shall call you within a few days to arrange   146
an appointment. Cordially yours,   154

LESSON 270

GOAL
- To type form letters from handwritten copy.

FORMAT
- Single spacing   60-space line

KEYBOARDING SKILLS

Type lines 1–4 once. Then punctuate line 5 as you type it. Repeat lines 1–4, or take a series of 1-minute timings.

Speed	1	She got the land and the eighty oaks, but Bob got the lake. 12
Accuracy	2	I was quickly penalized five or six times by the big major. 12
Numbers	3	Ship 1 or 2 or 3 or 4 or 5 or 6 or 7 or 8 or 9 or 10 or 11. 12
Symbols	4	Use a diagonal (/) when typing 1/10, 2/9, 3/8, 4/7, or 5/6. 12
Punctuation	5	Yes the boss Ms Kahl gave the order to the salesperson

     | 1 | 2 | 3 | 4 | 5 | 6 | 7 | 8 | 9 | 10 | 11 | 12

LESSON 29

GOALS
- To review the symbol-key controls.
- To format two items that use symbols.

FORMAT
- Single spacing   50-space line

KEYBOARDING SKILLS

Type each line twice.

Speed 1 She may wish to amend the form when she signs it.

Accuracy 2 Jackey's vague quip amazed and vexed her brother.

Numbers 3 Your fingers can now find 10, 29, 38, 47, and 56.

Symbols 4 Do 10 + 29 + 38 + 47 + 56 = 180? Yes! It's 180.

REVIEW

Type each line twice.

( ) 5 He listed items (10), (29), (38), (47), and (56).

+ 6 Millie counted 10 + 29 + 38 + 47 + 56 to get 180.

= 7 Grades: 10 = D, 29 = C, 38 = B, 47 = A, 56 = A+.

$ 8 My special rates are $10, $29, $38, $47, and $56.

¢ 9 I collected 10¢, 29¢, 38¢, 47¢, and 56¢ for them.

@ 10 They saw 12 pears @ $1.28 and 12 bananas @ $1.39.

CHECKPOINT

Type lines 11–12 once. Then repeat any of lines 5 –10 that contain symbols you need practice in or take two 1-minute timings on the Checkpoint.

11 Anna, did you know that (9 + 9)(8 + 8) = 18 × 16? 10

12 Buy 8 @ 75¢ and 26 @ 25¢; total (plus 4%) is $13. 20
    | 1 | 2 | 3 | 4 | 5 | 6 | 7 | 8 | 9 | 10

REVIEW

An asterisk (*) follows a punctuation mark.

Type each line twice.

13 Carpet remnants were #10, #29, #38, #47, and #56.

% 14 New rates: 1% to 10%, 29% to 38%, or 47% to 56%.

! 15 Shout! Up! No! Down! There! Yes! Here! Oh!

: 16 Times listed: 10:29, 11:38, 2:47, 1:56, or 2:01.

& 17 Pair them as follows: 10 & 29, 38 & 47, 56 & 29.

* 18 Note the following: 10,* 29,* 38,* 47,* and 56.*

" 19 "Isn't it fine!" she exclaimed. "Look at it go!"

' 20 It's not that he won't speak; it's that he can't.

_ 21 Please send <u>Return of Lassie</u> or <u>Call of the Wild</u>.

LESSON 269

UNIT 44 PROCESSING CORRESPONDENCE

GOALS
- To correct 12 commonly misspelled words while typing sentences.
- To type form letters.

FORMAT
- Single spacing   60-space line

LAB 31

Type lines 1–4 once, correcting the spelling of any misspelled words. Edit your copy as your teacher reads the answers. Then retype lines 1–4 from your edited copy.

SPELLING

Workbook 683–684.

1 I sincereley think Gus will quickly compleat these reciepts.
2 Sixty comittee members read there statment with intrest.
3 I beleive Jack put the materiel in the envelop, Ms. Fazio.
4 Helen Daley's busness is now availible for sale, isn't it?

PRETEST

Take a 2-minute Pretest on lines 5–8; then take a 2-minute Pretest on lines 9–12. Circle and total your errors on each timing.

Quotation marks

5 The so-called "expert" on finance is our manager, Mr. Lang. 12
6 Ellen gave a firm "no" when asked if she planned to retire. 24
7 Read the third chapter, "Planning," when you have time, Al. 36
8 Rejecting the offer was, as he pointed out, "discourteous." 48

Dashes

9 Ann's word processor--the CRT--is easy to learn to operate. 12
10 I ordered a new word processor--a special standalone model. 24
11 Making major changes--text editing--is very quick on a CRT. 36
12 Please format this copy--a rough draft--for me before noon. 48

    | 1 | 2 | 3 | 4 | 5 | 6 | 7 | 8 | 9 | 10 | 11 | 12

PRACTICE

In which Pretest did you make more errors? If in lines 5–8, type lines 13–16 below four times and lines 17–20 two times. If in lines 9–12, reverse the procedure.

13 "the" "hay" "and" "men" "for" "pan" "but" "own" "fix" "may"
14 "mat" "vat" "ham" "pat" "tab" "van" "war" "add" "bag" "cab"
15 "palm" "past" "load" "leap" "name" "mark" "hot" "sea" "fad"
16 "loan" "feel" "bale" "dart" "gaze" "bake" "pal" "act" "cat"

17 the--now--for--and--for--but--may--too--was--had--its--will
18 text--very--easy--word--part--name--gaze--jump--time--vines
19 major--order--makes--blind--learn--asked--drive--such--call
20 check--lives--finds--while--yours--dates--keyed--week--when

POSTTEST

Repeat the Pretest.

TYPING FORM LETTERS

As a correspondence secretary, you are to key form letters into a CPU (Central Processing Unit). They will be recalled later. No dates, addresses, or salutations are keyed at this time; allow space for them.

CHECKPOINT

Type lines 22–24 once. Then repeat any of lines 13–21 (page 51) that contain symbols you need to practice or take two 1-minute timings on the Checkpoint.

22 Their #7 and #4 sizes are 30% to 40% higher here. 10

23 K&D arrived at 1:30. L&W came later on at 2:45.* 20

24 "It's Oklahoma!" Jean said. "Let's buy tickets!" 30

| 1 | 2 | 3 | 4 | 5 | 6 | 7 | 8 | 9 | 10

3-MINUTE TIMINGS

Take two 3-minute timings on lines 25–33. Format: Double spacing, 5-space tab.

25   A jigsaw puzzle is such fun. To fit all the 10

26 shapes is a game. At first it is a game of hues, 20

27 and then it is a game of sizes, and at the last a 30

28 game of fits. Each piece looks as though it will 40

29 fit, but just one piece will do so. You can push 50

30 and squeeze all day, but only the right shape and 60

31 proper size will drop into place. Many pieces do 70

32 look equal to the holes, but only the exact match 80

33 fits in the puzzle. 84

| 1 | 2 | 3 | 4 | 5 | 6 | 7 | 8 | 9 | 10   SI 1.13

JOB 29-1. ANNOUNCEMENT
Standard format. Double spacing. Half sheet of paper.

SWIM & SKI CLUB

Fall Roundups

from

1:30 to 4:30

Saturday, October 25, 19--

Fees: $75 each semester

JOB 29-2. ENUMERATION
Standard format. Double spacing. Full sheet of paper.

SENIOR READING LIST

1. Ivanhoe
2. The Seekers
3. The Third Wave
4. A Walk Across America
5. Blind Ambition*
6. Gone With the Wind
7. Roots
8. Holocaust
9. The Immigrants

*Optional

LESSON 268

CLINIC

GOALS
- To build competency on selected keyboard motions and reaches.

FORMAT
- Single spacing   60-space line

PRETEST 1

Take two 2-minute timings on lines 1–4. Proofread both, and note the more accurate of the two scores.

```
1  Mark ought to clear enough money from our pipes to go home.   12
2  Carl bought a sixty-pound crate of cotton from that farmer.   24
3  Leonard wrote to you last month about coming to our picnic.   36
4  I doubt Ruth won a hat as one of the prizes at the meeting.   48
   |  1  |  2  |  3  |  4  |  5  |  6  |  7  |  8  |  9  |  10  |  11  |  12
```

PRACTICE 1

Type lines 5–10 five times. Repeat individual lines for speed gain if you had two or fewer errors on Pretest 1; otherwise repeat each block of lines for accuracy gain.

```
5   you won pin out add sad are fly one hat mar ate coy mat lye
6   toys adds tone clad spur flag come glad song size pure road
7   wrong adapt woman flags doubt touch roads ought prize spurs

8   the jab rat you rot yes red ore vat her nor hat big lit aft
9   long hats pure jets gone navy club part bond jack flue puff
10  ghost earth ready virus think teach spunk vague yearn yacht
```

POSTTEST 1

Take two 2-minute timings on lines 1–4. Proofread and note your improvement.

PRETEST 2

Take two 2-minute timings on lines 11–14. Proofread both, and note the more accurate of the two scores.

```
11  The river runs in every season but not once has ice formed.   12
12  The women were given a refund and made a fortune in prizes.   24
13  It is much too soon to detect minor defects in the new car.   36
14  Now is the moment to save and protect our younger citizens.   48
    |  1  |  2  |  3  |  4  |  5  |  6  |  7  |  8  |  9  |  10  |  11  |  12
```

PRACTICE 2

Type lines 15–20 five times. Repeat individual lines for speed gain if you had two or fewer errors on Pretest 2; otherwise repeat each block of lines for accuracy gain.

```
15  joining matched utmost saying zones place unit text act run
16  protect routine season invest women river pins mill inn nor
17  utilize younger paying refund serve thing army live won bid

18  fortune exposed making prompt using prize done none ton gun
19  correct defects gained detect minor night save much now son
20  appoint citizen finish import aimed catch once soon fun ice
```

POSTTEST 2

Take two 2-minute timings on lines 11–14. Proofread and note your improvement.

LESSON 30

GOAL
- To build keyboarding speed using 12-second timings, 30-second timings, and preview practice.
- To type 28/3'/5e.

FORMAT
- Single spacing   50-space line

PRETEST

Use the 3-minute timings from Lesson 29 (page 52) as a Pretest. Take two 3-minute timings, and determine your speed by using the faster rate.

12-SECOND TIMINGS

How fast can you type without error for 12 seconds? Find out by taking four 12-second timings on each of lines 1–3. Your speed is the number on the scale over which you stop.

1 It is time to work on my speed with fewer errors.   10

2 This is the day that you will make a better rate.   10

3 Just let your hands move over the keys with ease.   10

25   30   35   40   45   50

30-SECOND TIMINGS

Take two 30-second timings on lines 4–6, or type each line twice.

4 When you can practice each day for a few minutes,   10

5 you will see how much more you can type. It is a   20

6 matter of knowing the reach for each of the keys.   30

| 1 | 2 | 3 | 4 | 5 | 6 | 7 | 8 | 9 | 10

PREVIEW PRACTICE

Preview words provide a chance to prevent errors and to increase speed. The words come from the timing and are grouped into drills. Type each line twice.

Accuracy   7 lucky exam, quite course shadow students semester

Speed   8 just were term have done hold lone all the end of

3-MINUTE TIMINGS

Take two 3-minute timings on lines 9–17. Format: Double spacing, 5-space tab.

9. 　　　　The end of a semester would be just great if   10

10 it were not for the tests. It is a joy to finish   20

11 the term, to have the course done, to have a hold   30

12 on things we have mastered, etc. The lone shadow   40

13 is the course exam. But, on the other hand, some   50

14 students like tests; they see tests as the chance   60

15 to prove how much they have learned. Things that   70

16 are a puzzle to most of us are quite clear to all   80

17 those lucky persons.   84

| 1 | 2 | 3 | 4 | 5 | 6 | 7 | 8 | 9 | 10   SI 1.13

LESSON 267

GOALS
- To correct 12 commonly misspelled words while typing sentences.
- To adapt and type a property deed.

FORMAT
- Single spacing   60-space line

LAB 31

SPELLING

Type lines 1–4 once, correcting the spelling of any misspelled words. Edit your copy as your teacher reads the answers. Then retype lines 1–4 from your edited copy.

1 A comittee reviewed all statments with compleet intrest.
2 There receit for the busyness materiel is in the envalope.
3 Alex sincerly questions the legality of these zoning laws.
4 If you beleeve that a good apartment is availible, rent it.

12-SECOND TIMINGS

Type each line four times, or take four 12-second timings on each line. For each timing, type with no error.

5 There are many types of legal forms that you can use today. 12
6 Some kinds are printed and others are typed on legal paper. 12
7 Set margins a space or two inside the rules on legal paper. 12

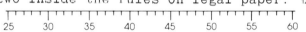

25   30   35   40   45   50   55   60

"OK" TIMINGS

Type as many 30-second "OK" (errorless) timings as possible out of three attempts on lines 8–10. Then repeat the effort on lines 11–13.

8   Maizie quickly paid Joan for the five new taxis she bought. 12
9   Jack's man found exactly a quarter in the woven zipper bag. 24
10 Weekly magazines request help by and for junior executives. 36

11 Ziggy jumped up and quickly paid Bertha for five new taxis. 12
12 Why did Max become eloquent over a zany gift like jodhpurs? 24
13 My folks proved his expert eloquence was just a big hazard. 36

| 1 | 2 | 3 | 4 | 5 | 6 | 7 | 8 | 9 | 10 | 11 | 12

JOB 267-1. PROPERTY DEED

Standard format. Workbook 679, 681.

Prepare a second deed for property to be transferred from the Williamsons to Carolyn and Jerry Basford of Paintsville, Kentucky. Use lot number 27 in the same area and record book for the county. Date this deed June 29, 19—.

GOALS
- To correct errors using a variety of techniques.
- To format notes.

FORMAT
- Single spacing   60-space line

KEYBOARDING SKILLS

Type each line twice.

Speed   1   On the shelf he may find the map for the lake and the land.

Accuracy   2   Sew the azure badge on my velvet jacket before the banquet.

Numbers   3   Type 1 or 2 or 3 or 4 or 5 or 6 or 7 or 8 or 9 or 10 or 11.

Symbols   4   Pay 80% of $2.59 for #7 ledgers at Owens & Barnes Supplies.

PREVIEW PRACTICE

Type each line twice.

Accuracy   5   text dizzy covers neatly errors liquid corrects typewriter.

Speed   6   nice look will when page from take hole your have that sign

3-MINUTE TIMINGS

Take two 3-minute timings on lines 7–14. Use the speed markers to figure your speed. Format: Double spacing, 5-space tab.

```
                    1              2              3              4
 7        When you correct an error that you have typed, you are    12
              5              6              7              8
 8   to do it as neatly as you can.  A smear or a hole in a page    24
              9             10             11            12
 9   is a sign that you do not take pride in the text that comes    36
             13             14             15            16
10   from your typewriter.  If you make a page dizzy with liquid    48
             17             18             19            20
11   corrections, the page will not look nice at all.  That tape    60
             21             22             23            24
12   which covers is fine, but you must be sure that you are not    72
             25             26             27            28
13   able to see where you used it.  Chalk will do on some jobs,    84
             29             30
14   but it will rub off with time.                                90
     | 1 | 2 | 3 | 4 | 5 | 6 | 7 | 8 | 9 | 10 | 11 | 12    SI 1.11
```

CORRECTING ERRORS

Errors may be corrected in a number of ways: erasing, using correction tape to cover up or lift off, or using a correction fluid to cover errors.

To erase errors:

1. Turn the paper so that the error will be at the top of the cylinder.
2. Using the margin release, move the carriage or carrier as far left or right as possible (to keep eraser grit out of the operating parts of the machine).
3. Press the paper tightly against cylinder with fingertips.
4. With a typewriting eraser, erase each letter to be deleted; use light up-and-down strokes.
5. Turn the paper back to writing line.
6. Insert the correction.

Practice

Type this: There are four rules to remember. Try to learn then today.

Correct it to: There are five rules to remember. Try to learn them today.

JOB 266-1. PROPERTY DEED
Standard format. Workbook 675, 677.

PROPERTY DEED   8

Know all men by these presents: that *Frank E. Williamson and*   19

Reva F. Williamson of Floyd County, Kentucky, in consideration   34

of one dollar *$1.00* and other valuable consideration to them in hand 48

paid by *Wallace R. Herald and William G. Herald,* whose address is   61

Route 3, Wheelright, Kentucky, do hereby grant, bargain, sell,   74

and convey to the said *Wallace R. Herald and William G. Herald*   86

their heirs and assigns forever, the following described real   99

estate, (1) situated in the Township of *Wheelright,* County of *Floyd* 112

and State of Kentucky, and being Lot numbered twenty-three *23* of   126

Second Addition to Clintwood Subdivision, Section Two *27,* Town Two,   139

Page 42 of the Plat Records of Floyd County, Kentucky. The said   152

Frank E. Williamson and Reva F. Williamson do hereby covenant and war- 166

rant that the title so conveyed is clear, free, and un~~im~~^{en}cumbered, 179

and that they will defend the same against all lawful claims of   192

all persons whomsoever.   197

     In witness whereof, the said *Frank E. Williamson* and   208

Reva F. Williamson have hereunto set their hands this *twenty-fifth* day 223

of *June* in the year A.D. nineteen hundred and (*fill in year*).   233

Signed and acknowledged in the presence of us: 243

_____   _____   257

_____   _____   271

State of Kentucky, County of *Floyd:* On this *twenty-fifth* day of   284

June, 19--, before me a notary public and for said County,   296

personally came *Frank E. Williamson* and *Reva F. Williamson* the grantors in 311

the foregoing deed, and acknowledge signing thereof to be their   324

voluntary act and deed. Witnesseth my official signature and   336

seal on the day last above mentioned.   344

_____   _____   358

        Notary   Attorney   367

FORMATTING NOTES

Informal notes are short and therefore are usually typed on a half sheet of paper. To format informal notes:

1. Use a 60-space line.
2. Begin date at the center on line 7.
3. Leave 4 blank lines between date and salutation.
4. Type salutation at the left margin.

5. Leave 1 blank line between salutation and body (the message).
6. Indent paragraphs 5 spaces from the left margin.
7. Single-space each paragraph, but double-space between paragraphs.
8. Type the closing a double space below the body, beginning at the center.

JOBS 31-1 AND 31-2. INFORMAL NOTE

Type the note below and check it for format. Correct all errors. Then retype the note; address it to someone in your class. Standard format.

Date   November 18, 19--
                                                        ↓5

Salutation   Dear Club Member:
                                    ↓2
Body   We have planned a special program on diving techniques for
our next Swimming Club meeting. Lisa Cammero, last year's city
diving champion, will demonstrate proper diving for all of us. ↓2

        The meeting will be held at the Civic Center in the pool
area at 7 p.m., Wednesday, November 29. You won't need a pass
to enter. We have made special arrangements for everyone to
swim free for this meeting. ↓2

Closing   Bring your suit and join us.

Signature   *Gloria*

LESSON 32

GOALS
- To correct errors by squeezing and spreading characters and spaces.
- To type notes.

FORMAT
- Single spacing   60-space line

KEYBOARDING SKILLS   Type lines 1–4 on page 54 twice each.

CORRECTING ERRORS   Workbook 29–30.

Problem: In making a correction, how can you squeeze in an extra letter?
Answer: Move the word a half space to the *left* so that only a half space precedes and follows it.

To do this, you must keep the carriage or carrier from spacing normally. You can use one of three ways to control the carriage or carrier movement: (1) press your fingertips against the end of the platen or carrier, (2)

LESSON 266

GOALS
- To identify the correct spelling of 12 commonly misspelled words while typing sentences.
- To type 49/5'/3e.
- To type a property deed.

FORMAT
- Single spacing 60-space line 5-space tab

LAB 31

Type lines 1–4 once. Then repeat lines 1–4 or take a series of 1-minute timings. Note the spelling of the underscored words as you type.

SPELLING

1 I quickly sent them a <u>receipt</u> for <u>their</u> <u>envelopes</u>, Kenneth. 12
2 Yes, the <u>committee</u> submitted six <u>complete</u> <u>business</u> reports. 12
3 I <u>sincerely</u> <u>believe</u> that my <u>materials</u> will <u>interest</u> Jo Zak. 12
4 If a <u>statement</u> is <u>available</u>, Gloria will send it to Andrew. 12
  | 1 | 2 | 3 | 4 | 5 | 6 | 7 | 8 | 9 | 10 | 11 | 12

1- AND 5-MINUTE TIMINGS

Take two 1-minute timings on each paragraph. Then take one 5-minute timing on the entire selection. Use single spacing for the 1-minute timings and double spacing for the 5-minute timing.

1'

5 Word processors are making many typewriting tasks much easier 13
6 to complete. Correcting a keyboarding error is very simple. Just 27
7 backspace and key correct characters over the top of incorrect char- 40
8 acters. The changes now appear on the page. 49

9 Making major changes in business communications always frus- 13
10 trates even the most proficient typist. Words or lines left out mean 27
11 retyping the complete document. Even a small error that was 39
12 undetected earlier may mean retyping a whole page. 49

13 Major changes on the CRT screen are called editing. A text may 14
14 need different margins, different line spacing, or different positioning 28
15 of characters, lines, and paragraphs. Word processors allow quick, 42
16 easy movement within any document. 49

17 Combining data from two or more sources into one document is 14
18 called merging. Individual addresses can be easily added to form 27
19 letters. Form letters can be personalized by merging key phrases into 41
20 open spaces in the letters using a code. 49

21 When documents will be used again--even with changes--they can 14
22 be stored on magnetic tape or diskettes. Rekeying isn't necessary. 28
23 Documents can be reprinted as they are or they can be edited to 40
24 incorporate whatever changes that you need. 49
  | 1 | 2 | 3 | 4 | 5 | 6 | 7 | 8 | 9 | 10 | 11 | 12 | 13 | 14   SI 1.73

depress the halfspace key if your machine has one, or (3) partly depress the backspace key.

By squeezing   a   You say that you will help us.   You say that you will work.

   b   You   that you will help us.   You   that you will work.

Practice: Type lines a and b *exactly* as shown; then insert *said* in each of the two blank areas in line b.

Problem: How do you spread a word so that it will occupy an extra space?
Answer: Move the word a half space to the *right* so that 1½ spaces precede and follow it. This requires your controlling the carriage or carrier just as you did in the preceding exercise.

Practice: Type lines c and d *exactly* as shown; then insert *say* in each of the two blank areas in line d.

By spreading   c   You said that you will help.   You said that you will do it.

   d   You   that you will help.   You   that you will do it.

PREVIEW PRACTICE

Type each line twice.

Accuracy   5   for amazed friend special whether hobbies thoughts choosing

Speed   6   also joke gift your will when what that how you may has the

3-MINUTE TIMINGS

Take two 3-minute timings on lines 7–14. Format: Double spacing, 5-space tab.

7   When you select a gift for a friend, how do you decide   12

8   what it will be? You will be amazed at the hours which you   24

9   spend choosing the exact gift. You may choose a gift to be   36

10   worn, or you may choose a gift to be read. The gift may be   48

11   a joke which brings a smile. You could also note whether a   60

12   friend is active or quiet, and you could check hobbies that   72

13   your friend has. The gift will convey the special thoughts   84

14   that you have for your friend.   90

| 1 | 2 | 3 | 4 | 5 | 6 | 7 | 8 | 9 | 10 | 11 | 12 | SI 1.13

JOBS 32-1 AND 32-2. INFORMAL NOTE

Type the note below and check the format. Correct all errors. Then retype the note; address it to someone in your class. Standard format.

December 5, 19--

Dear Fred

    Several of us are planning a trip for spring break. We want to come to the beach. Our break falls the last week in March this year. Is this the same week that you will have off? We hope that we can get together with you if it is.

    Would you recommend some motels where you think that we might stay for the week? We need to make our plane reservations before Christmas, and we would like to make our motel plans at the same time.

       See you soon

       Rick

LESSON 265

GOALS
- To recognize the correct spelling of 12 commonly misspelled words while typing sentences.
- To format and type a reciprocal will.

FORMAT
- Single spacing   60-space line

LAB 31

Type lines 1–4 once. Then repeat lines 1–4 or take a series of 1-minute timings. Note the spelling of the underscored words as you type.

SPELLING

1 All _available_ bank _statements_ were sent to _their_ _committee_.   12
2 Please quiz John about the _business_ _envelopes_ and _receipts_.   12
3 I _sincerely_ _believe_ that Karl can explain all the _material_.   12
4 Gus, _complete_ the withdrawal form and compute the _interest_.   12

    | 1 | 2 | 3 | 4 | 5 | 6 | 7 | 8 | 9 | 10 | 11 | 12

30-SECOND TIMINGS

Take two 30-second timings on lines 5–7, or type the paragraph twice.

5 Our school day ends at three. I hope that they will take a   12
6 plane that will get here at four or five. If they do, then   24
7 I can drive the new car to the field and meet their flight.   36

    | 1 | 2 | 3 | 4 | 5 | 6 | 7 | 8 | 9 | 10 | 11 | 12

FORMATTING RECIPROCAL DOCUMENTS

In law offices many documents such as wills and powers of attorney are prepared simultaneously for both husband and wife. If the clauses in the documents are identical except for the reversal of the names, they are called _reciprocal_ documents.

When typing a reciprocal document, you must remember to change all the names, pronouns, and other identifying nouns. For example, in the will for Job 264-1 on pages 421–422, the testator (maker) of the will is Earl Sizemore. He has named his wife, Barbara Sizemore, as executrix. In a reciprocal will, Barbara Sizemore is the testatrix, and she will name her husband, Earl Sizemore, as the executor.

JOB 265-1. WILL
Standard format. Workbook 671, 673.

Type a reciprocal will for Barbara Sizemore. Make appropriate changes in names. Her will is made out to Earl Sizemore, and he is the executor if living. Her daughter is the executrix if he is not living.

LESSON 33

GOAL
▪ To use the bell to make line-ending decisions.

FORMAT
▪ Single spacing 60-space line

KEYBOARDING SKILLS

Type each line twice.

Speed 1 Dick may wish to type the forms with the aid of some codes.
Accuracy 2 My lazy, gray dog curled up very quietly and went to sleep.
Numbers 3 Kay had to try 546 samples before she found any of No. 329.
Symbols 4 He read "How to Type" in Max's August issue of Office News.

PREVIEW PRACTICE

Type each line twice.

Accuracy 5 new jazz music sounds country classical different depending
Speed 6 like tune have fast slow beat show rock mind much tale rich

3-MINUTE TIMINGS

Take two 3-minute timings on lines 7–14. Format: Double spacing, 5-space tab.

```
                 1              2              3              4
7         Which kind of music do you like best?  A jazz tune can   12
           5              6              7              8
8  have a fast or a slow beat, depending on the mood the tunes    24
           9             10             11             12
9  are meant to show.  Rock music has a different beat and can    36
          13             14             15             16
10 bring a new set of moods to mind.  Much of folk music has a    48
          17             18             19             20
11 tale of joy or grief as its text.  Country tunes are like a    60
          21             22             23             24
12 folk tune, but they are a blend of other types.  Music that    72
          25             26             27             28
13 is classical has rich tones of quiet or blaring sound.  The    84
          29             30
14 choice is as wide as you wish.                                 90
   |  1  |  2  |  3  |  4  |  5  |  6  |  7  |  8  |  9  |  10  |  11  |  12   SI 1.14
```

RIGHT MARGIN BELL Workbook 31.

To help make the right margin even, a bell rings when the carriage or carrier approaches the margin. Depending on the machine, the bell may ring as few as 8 or as many as 15 spaces before the margin. (Check *your* machine. How many spaces before the margin does it ring?)

Assume that your machine will ring 8 spaces before the right margin. Assume, too, that you have set your right margin at 85 (80 plus 5 spaces). The bell will ring when you reach 77. When the bell rings, you must decide how best to end the line closest to 80—preferably without dividing words. Here are some typical line-ending decisions:

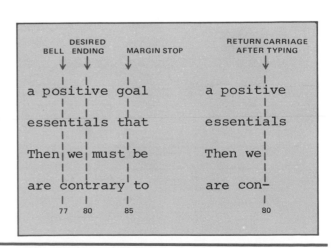

estate, succession and other taxes of similar nature levied or imposed by reason of my death, together with interest and penalties thereon, if any, regardless of against whom the same may be assessed, shall be paid by my Executor from the residue of my estate, and my Executor shall not request or obtain reimbursement or contribution from any person.

ITEM II: I give, bequeath, and devise all my property, real, personal, and mixed, of every kind and description, wheresoever situated, which I may own or have the right to dispose of at the time of my death, to my beloved wife, Barbara Sizemore.

ITEM III: I make, nominate, and appoint my wife, Barbara Sizemore, to be the Executrix of my estate if she is living at the time of my death. In the event that said wife is not living or for any reason is unable to serve, then I make, nominate, and appoint my daughter, Aleen, to be the Executrix.

In Witness WHEREOF I have hereunto set my hand at Lebanon, Tennessee, this fourteenth day of April, 19—.

_____

SUBSCRIBED, Sealed, Published, and Declared by the Testator, Earl Sizemore, on the date above written, as and for his Last Will and Testament in the presence of each of us, who, at his request, in his presence and in the presence of each other, have hereunto subscribed our names as witnesses.

_____ residing at _____
                                    _____
_____ residing at _____
                                    _____
_____ residing at _____
                                    _____

MAKING LINE-ENDING DECISIONS BY USING RIGHT MARGIN BELL

¶ means start a new paragraph.

JOB 33-1. INFORMAL NOTE

Note: Do not divide a word at the end of any line. Standard format.

[*Current date*] / Dear [*Use a friend's name*] / How do you like the way this note looks? I'm typing it in my typing class. We are practicing listening for the bell at the end of a line. We must type the note without dividing words. ¶Our teacher says that we will learn how to type reports soon. Then I can type all my papers for my English class. / Until next time, / [*Sign your name*]

JOB 33-2. INFORMAL NOTE

Retype Job 33-1 using a 50-space line. Do not divide words.

JOB 33-3. INFORMAL NOTE

Retype Job 33-1 using a 40-space line. Do not divide words.

LESSON 34

GOALS
- To align typed words on a page.
- To align words on a printed postal card.

FORMAT
- Single spacing   60-space line

KEYBOARDING SKILLS

Type lines 1–4 on page 57 twice each.

PREVIEW PRACTICE

Type each line twice.

Accuracy
Speed

5 quite other means nicely change around expanding attractive
6 page make from just such that they some type both line them

3-MINUTE TIMINGS

Take two 3-minute timings on lines 7–14. Format: Double spacing, 5-space tab.

7   To format words on a page means to make them look just   12
8 as attractive as you can. It also means that you plan them   24
9 in such a way that they are easily read. One way to change   36
10 a format of a page is to type some parts in all caps and to   48
11 type other parts in both caps and lowercase. Expanding the   60
12 letters in a line or two makes them stand out from the maze   72
13 of words quite nicely. The use of a box around word groups   84
14 makes it simple to read a page.   90

| 1 | 2 | 3 | 4 | 5 | 6 | 7 | 8 | 9 | 10 | 11 | 12   SI 1.16

FORMATTING POSTAL CARD MESSAGES

Workbook 32.

Postal cards are often used to send very short impersonal messages. To format a postal card:

1. Set margins for a 45-space line.
2. Type the date on line 3, beginning at the center.
3. Type the salutation on line 5.
4. Begin the message on line 7.
5. Single-space paragraphs; double-space between paragraphs.
6. Type the sender's name a double space below the message, at the center.
7. Begin all lines except date and sender's name at the left margin.

Type lines 6 and 7 twice as a preview to the 3-minute timings below.

Accuracy

6   processors standalones requirement information manipulating

Speed

7   conjunction businesses terminals connected diskettes figure

3-MINUTE TIMINGS

Take two 3-minute timings on lines 8–20.

```
            1              2                3              4
8       There are numerous varieties of word processors on the      12
            5              6                7              8
9    market.  Some have screens and are called CRTs.  Others are     24
            9              10               11             12
10   blind processors, which do not have screens; operators must     36
            13             14               15             16
11   key documents without viewing what they're recording on the    48
            17             18               19             20
12   diskettes or magnetic tape.  Some are standalones because a     60
            21             22               23             24
13   central processing unit is not connected to them.  Some are     72
            25             26               27             28
14   connected to CPUs and operate in conjunction with terminals     84
            29             30
15   handling similar or different text.                             91
            31             32               33             34
16      Combining the newest types of word processors and data      103
            35             36               37             38
17   processors has helped businesses realize the requirement of     115
            39             40               41             42
18   heavy paper flow.  Businesses can merge information in word     127
            43             44               45             46
19   and figure forms by manipulating and changing formats elec-    139
            47             48               49
20   tronically to speed up information flow.                        147
```

| 1 | 2 | 3 | 4 | 5 | 6 | 7 | 8 | 9 | 10 | 11 | 12 | SI 1.74

JOB 264-1. WILL

Standard format. Workbook 667, 669.

Last Will and Testament

I, EARL SIZEMORE, of 1729 Marlborough Court, Lebanon, Tennessee, being of full age, sound mind and memory, and under no restraint, do make, publish, and declare this to be my Last Will and Testament, hereby revoking and making null and void any and all last wills and testaments and any codicils thereto by me heretofore made.

ITEM I: I direct that my legal debts, including the expense of my last illness and funeral, be first paid out of my estate as soon as practicable after the time of my decease. I further direct that all my inheritance,

(Continued on next page)

Form Messages. Sometimes postal cards are used to send out standardized "form" messages. A reminder for a dental appointment (like the one shown below) is an example. When you type a form message, (1) do not fill in the date, (2) type only the word *Dear,* and (3) leave space for any information to be filled in later.

JOB 34-1. POSTAL CARD FORM MESSAGES

Prepare four form messages on postal cards. Do not type the words shown in color. Use Workbook 33. Save your work for use in Job 34-2.

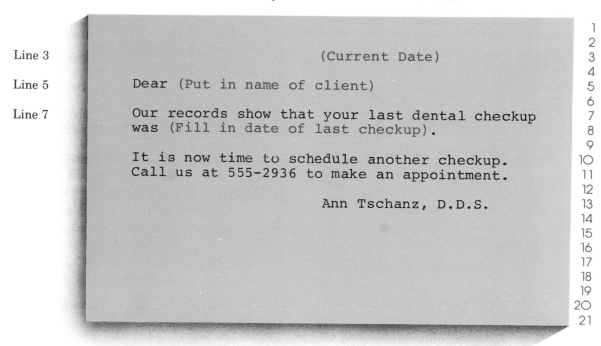

Line 3   (Current Date)

Line 5   Dear (Put in name of client)

Line 7   Our records show that your last dental checkup
was (Fill in date of last checkup).

It is now time to schedule another checkup.
Call us at 555-2936 to make an appointment.

                 Ann Tschanz, D.D.S.

1 2 3 4 5 6 7 8 9 10 11 12 13 14 15 16 17 18 19 20 21

ALIGNING

1. Locate exactly the printing point between the aligning scales.

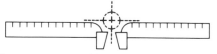

2. Insert paper. Shift it until the end of the printing is exactly in the printing point.

Name:

3. Strike the space bar three times. Type the insertion.

Name: Pat Elkins

Practice 1. At four different places on a sheet of paper, type the printed guide words illustrated here. Use double spacing. Remove the paper, insert it, then fill in the requested data—yours, not the data used in the illustration.

Practice 2. Repeat Practice 1 on the other side of the paper.

Date:	October 3, 19--
Name:	Pat Elkins
Grade:	10
Age:	16
City:	Topeka
State:	Kansas

JOB 34-2. FILL-IN POSTAL CARD MESSAGES

Send cards to the people listed at the right using the cards you prepared in Job 34-1. Be sure to align the fill-ins. Addresses do not have to be typed because printed labels will be used.

Kathleen Davis—last checkup June 13
Oliver Treadway—last checkup June 15
Margaret Tolley—last checkup May 3
Jose Martino—last checkup May 15

FORMATTING COURT HEADINGS

Some legal documents are papers used in court. These documents need a court heading in addition to the title of the document. Format court headings as follows:

1. Center the name of the court in all-capital letters on line 13.
2. Display the title of the court action. See the illustration at the right for one such display.
3. Type the number of the court action in the right half of the page, on the middle line of the displayed court action title.
4. Begin the title of the document a triple space below the court action title.

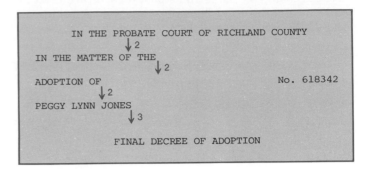

IN THE PROBATE COURT OF RICHLAND COUNTY
↓2
IN THE MATTER OF THE
↓2
ADOPTION OF ↓2   No. 618342
PEGGY LYNN JONES
↓3

FINAL DECREE OF ADOPTION

JOB 263-2. FINAL DECREE OF ADOPTION

Standard legal format. Workbook 665.

IN THE PROBATE COURT OF RICHLAND COUNTY	23
IN THE MATTER OF THE	27
ADOPTION OF No. 618342	34
PEGGY LYNN JONES	37

FINAL DECREE OF ADOPTION 56

This day, this cause came on for a full 67 hearing before the Court upon the petition of 76 John Jones and Linda Jones, and the proceed- 85 ings had thereafter for the adoption of Peggy 94 Lynn, who prior to the interlocutory decree 103 herein was known as Infant Girl Johnson, and 112 who was born on April 12, 19—, at Mansfield, 121 Ohio. 123

It appearing to the Court that more than 132 six months have expired from the date on 140 which the Court entered the interlocutory 148 decree of adoption herein, and that said inter- 158 locutory decree has not been revoked, and it 167 further appearing that the next friend here- 176 tofore appointed by the Court has submitted 185 to the Court a further report of their findings 194 relative to the suitability of this adoption, the 204 Court therefore finds that adoption will be to 213 the best interests of said child. 220

It is therefore ordered and adjudged by the 230 Court that a final decree of adoption be and is 239 hereby entered in this adoption and that hence- 249 forth said child shall have the status of an 258 adopted child of said petitioners. 265

_____ 274
                 Judge 282

Approved: 285

_____ 292

F. J. Stockwell 297
Attorney for Petitioners 304

LESSON 264

GOAL
- To type a will from handwritten copy.

FORMAT
- Single spacing   60-space line   5-space tab

KEYBOARDING SKILLS

Type lines 1–4 once. Then punctuate line 5 as you type it. Repeat lines 1–4, or take a series of 1-minute timings.

Speed	1	We had a chance to try on the suits before he had to leave.	12
Accuracy	2	Pat quickly froze the gold mixtures in five old brown jars.	12
Numbers	3	Just order 1 or 2 or 3 or 4 or 5 or 6 or 7 or 8 or 9 or 10.	12
Symbols	4	Report Friday on Sections (10), (29), (38), (47), and (56).	12
Punctuation	5	Ann our manager ordered paper erasers carbons and rulers	

| 1 | 2 | 3 | 4 | 5 | 6 | 7 | 8 | 9 | 10 | 11 | 12

LESSON 35

GOALS
- To type words on ruled lines.
- To type words on a lined, fill-in postal card.

FORMAT
- Single spacing   60-space line   5-space tab

KEYBOARDING SKILLS

Type each line twice.

Speed
Accuracy
Numbers
Symbols

1 Alene's neighbor owns six or eight antique autos right now.
2 Five lizards very quickly jumped into the box on the table.
3 we 23 up 70 to 59 or 94 it 85 yi 68 et 35 op 90 ur 74 re 43
4 File cards (unlined) will be purchased 100 @ 59¢ at school.

PREVIEW PRACTICE

Type each line twice.

Accuracy
Speed

5 who senior others flowers citizen service students projects
6 their time work with some done take read like and the to by

3-MINUTE TIMINGS

Take two 3-minute timings on lines 7–14. Format: Double spacing, 5-space tab.

```
                  1              2              3              4
7        Many students give hours of their time to work for the    12
              5              6              7              8
8    service projects in their towns.  Some jobs are done with a    24
              9             10             11            12
9    group, while some are not.  Students work with kids at some    36
             13             14             15            16
10   parks, and they work with kids who are ill.  They take food    48
             17             18             19            20
11   to senior citizens and read to those who are blind.  Bright    60
             21             22             23            24
12   flowers and green trees are planted, and trash is picked up    72
             25             26             27            28
13   by some students.  These nice young people like helping out    84
             29             30
14   others in many different ways.                                 90
     |  1  |  2  |  3  |  4  |  5  |  6  |  7  |  8  |  9  |  10  |  11  |  12    SI 1.20
```

TYPING ON RULED LINES

1. Preliminary step: On a blank sheet, type your name and underscore it. Note (a) exactly where the underscore touches or almost touches the aligning scale and (b) exactly how much room is between the letters and line.

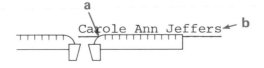

2. Now insert the paper with the ruled lines, and adjust it so that one of

the ruled lines is in the position of an underscore.

The ruled line should look like this:

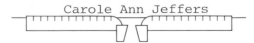

3. Type what is to be on the line.

Practice: At various places and angles on a page, type underscore lines 30 spaces long. Remove the paper. Reinsert it. Type your name on each line.

As you learned in the Projects, some word processing centers measure an operator's work by the number of correct lines he or she can produce in a given amount of time. In Level 8 you should log *all* your production work according to the number of lines you can produce in a given amount of time. Use the logs on Workbook page 659 top.

**FORMATTING
REVIEW**

*Legal
Documents:*

1. *Set margins 2 spaces inside ruled lines on legal paper.*

2. *Type title on line 13.*

3. *Type page number 6 lines from the bottom—Page 1 of 3, and so on.*

4. *Begin continuation pages on line 10.*

JOB 263-1. INTERLOCUTORY AGREEMENT
Standard legal format. Workbook 661, 663.

THAT WHEREAS Buckeye Children's Agency is a corporation organized 30
for the care of children, and 36

WHEREAS, Buckeye Children's Agency has on occasions children placed 51
with it for the purpose of adoption, and 59

WHEREAS John Jones and Linda Jones are desirous of having placed with 74
them a child for adoption, 79

BE IT THEREFORE agreed by and between said parties as follows: that 94
in consideration of Buckeye Children's Agency's placing with them Infant Girl 110
Johnson to be known as Peggy Lynn, a child to which Buckeye Children's 124
Agency has for the purpose of adoption, 132

John Jones and Linda Jones hereby agree to accept said child, to maintain 148
and support it, to assume all responsibility for said child from the time it is 164
placed in their possession; that they will obtain the services of an attorney and 180
prepare and file a petition for the adoption of said child with Richland County 196
Probate Court within 30 days after written approval for adoption has been 211
given by the physician of their choice. 219

SAID John Jones and Linda Jones further say that in accepting said child, 235
it is their intent within a time specified herein, to make application to the 250
Richland County Probate Court for the purpose of adoption of said child. 265

SAID John Jones and Linda Jones further agree to pay the placement fee 280
in full at the time the medical approval of the aforesaid child is filed with 296
Buckeye Children's Agency. 302

IN WITNESS WHEREOF, said parties have hereunto set their hands and 316
seal this tenth day of May, 19—. 323

_____ 332

John Jones 343

_____ 353

Linda Jones 364

WITNESSETH THAT the above-mentioned parties appeared before me 378
this tenth day of May, 19—, and acknowledged the signing of the foregoing 393
instrument to be their voluntary act and deed. 402

IN TESTIMONY WHEREOF, I have hereunto set my hand and seal on the 417
day and year last aforesaid. 423

_____ 432

Jane Casady, Notary Public 452

FORMATTING FILL-INS ON RULED LINES

Because postal card messages are often used as reply cards, they may have ruled lines to show where information should be filled in. Short fill-ins are usually centered:

1. Insert and adjust the card so that the ruled line is in the position of the underscore.
2. Position the printing point at the beginning of the ruled line.
3. Space across the line, counting the spaces.
4. Then count the spaces of the copy to be typed on the line.

5. Subtract the spaces to be typed (Step 4) from the spaces available (Step 3).
6. Divide the difference by 2; drop any fraction. Indent that number of spaces to reach the starting point (for the fill-in).

Long fill-ins may follow a colon or be typed from margin to margin:

1. Begin two spaces after a colon. **or:**
2. Set your left margin at the beginning of the rule and your right margin at the end of the rule. Type from margin to margin; do not type beyond the edges of the ruled line.

Reservations for the January 15 Annual Sports
Banquet are now being taken. If you plan to
attend, please list the names of the members
of your group and return the card with $5.50
for each person. Deadline: December 1, 19--

Name of coach   Joe Witzman

Sport   Cross country

Members of group: Rick Sizemore, Jason

Underleider, Jayne Bishop, Sally Jones,

Bernie Beyler

JOB 35-1. RULED FILL-INS ON REPLY CARDS

Use the information below to complete the reply cards. Standard format.   Workbook 35.

1. *Coach,* John Lantz, *Sport,* football, *Players,* Bill Jones, Ed Lukins, Joe Eads, Paul Johns, Ted Ley.
2. *Coach,* Mary Allen, *Sport,* volleyball, *Players,* Anne Reed, Kathy Nickel, Pam Rizzo, Lori Robins, Tammy Colton.
3. *Coach,* Chris Spangs, *Sport,* tennis, *Players,* Don Tia, Patty Kipp, Fred Vines, Willie Parks, Julie Scheper.
4. *Coach,* Fred Caton, *Sport,* baseball, *Players,* Gloria Gimbrone, Kelly Maxton, Pam Avery, Jeff Meyer, David Paxton.

LESSON 36

REVIEW

GOALS
- To type 30/3'/5e.
- To review formatting and operating techniques used for typewriting.
- To demonstrate knowledge of basic terminology and rules for using the typewriter.

FORMAT
- Single spacing   60-space line   5-space tab

PREVIEW PRACTICE

Type each line twice as a preview to the 3-minute timing on page 62.

Accuracy 1 quite errors adjust through learned symbols numbers letters
Speed   2 each have type with page your make soon will that well book

Once information has been keyed onto a word processing machine, the data is stored for future use. Among the timesaving features of word processors is the simplicity with which the operator can edit the text or data stored in the machine. Four text-editing functions of word processors are *inserting* and *deleting* letters, spaces, words, or paragraphs; *moving* a word or a group of words—or a paragraph or a group of paragraphs—within one document or from one document to another document; and *merging* data by taking text from two different documents and combining them into one new document. Amazingly, these text-editing functions can be completed quickly and effectively.

Level 8 will give you practice on text-editing related projects in various business settings, including a law firm, an insurance company, a sales office, and a word processing center.

In Level 8 you will:

1. Demonstrate keyboarding accuracy and speed on straight copy with a goal of 50 words a minute or more for 5 minutes with no more than 3 errors.

2. Correctly proofread copy for errors and edit copy for revision.

3. Apply production skills in keyboarding and formatting copy for four categories of business documents from six input modes in the following settings: law firm (Lessons 263–268); insurance company (Lessons 269–274); sales office (Lessons 275–280); medical clinic (Lessons 281–286); information processing distributorship (In-Basket I); small business (In-Basket J); and word processing center (In-Basket K).

4. Decide about formatting and priority in completing tasks for two in-baskets and a word processing procedures manual.

5. Spell correctly commonly misspelled business words and apply rules for subject-verb agreement in communications.

LESSON 263

UNIT 43 PROCESSING LEGAL DOCUMENTS

UNIT GOAL
49/5'/3e

GOALS
- To format and type legal documents.
- To format and type court headings.

FORMAT
- Single spacing   60-space line   5-space tab

KEYBOARDING SKILLS

Type lines 1–4 once. Then punctuate line 5 as you type it. Repeat lines 1–4, or take a series of 1-minute timings.

Speed	1	As soon as we had tried on the blue suits, we had to leave.	12
Accuracy	2	Brown jars prevented the mixture from freezing too quickly.	12
Numbers	3	No. 101 is 29 mm wide, 38 cm long. It now weighs 47.56 kg.	12
Symbols	4	Add up $1 and $2 and $3 and $4 and $5 and $6 and $7 and $8.	12
Punctuation	5	Martha placed her coat hat scarf and boots in the closet	

| 1 | 2 | 3 | 4 | 5 | 6 | 7 | 8 | 9 | 10 | 11 | 12

12-SECOND TIMINGS

Type each line four times, or take four 12-second timings on each line. For each timing, type with no error.

6 Please stop at the store and pay the man for the new shoes. 12
7 We hope that the eight of them will visit the lake with us. 12
8 Ask her to run over to the bank and ask for some new dimes. 12

25   30   35   40   45   50   55   60

Take two 3-minute timings on lines 3–10. Format: Double spacing.

```
3       You have almost completed the first level of the book.        12
4    You have learned how to type letters, numbers, and symbols.      24
5    With these, you have learned to format words on a page, and      36
6    you have learned how to adjust your machine and correct any      48
7    errors that you make.  The skill with which you type is now      60
8    growing with each day.  Soon you will learn to compose your      72
9    own words as you type.  You will zip through a page and fix      84
10   errors quite well in seconds.                                    90
     |  1  |  2  |  3  |  4  |  5  |  6  |  7  |  8  |  9  |  10  |  11  |  12     SI 1.20
```

TECHNICAL QUESTIONS

Type one- or two-word answers to the following 15 questions.

1. If you type 60 words in 2 minutes, what is your speed for 1 minute?

2. If you type 15 words in ½ minute, what is your speed for 1 minute?

3. How many times do you strike the hyphen key to make a dash?

4. How many spaces follow a period at the end of a sentence?

5. How many spaces follow a period in the initials of a person's name?

6. How many blank lines separate single-spaced paragraphs?

7. What does the term *keyboarding* mean?

8. How many times do you backspace to center a line with 15 strokes?

9. How many spaces are there between letters when a title is expanded?

10. To center a 15-line, single-spaced display on a half page, on what line would you begin?

11. An all-cap title is separated from the body of an item by how many blank lines?

12. If a subtitle follows an all-cap title, the two are separated by how many blank lines?

13. How many spaces follow a period in an enumeration?

14. What does the term *formatting* mean?

15. Most typewriters have how many vertical lines to an inch?

JOB 36-1. ENUMERATION
Standard format.

> Participating 4-H Clubs
> For the year 19--
> 1. Bell Brook
> 2. Camden
> 3. Clearcreek Local
> 4. Edgarsville
> 5. Farmington
> 6. Mohawk Valley
> 7. Seven Mile
> 8. Spring Valley

JOB 36-2. INFORMAL NOTE
Standard format.

> (Date)
> Dear Sally and Joe
> Our 4-H Club judging will take place the last Friday in July at the Allen County Fairgrounds.
> We would like to have you come to see our projects. Ann has an especially well-fed steer, and I am going to compete in the advanced bake-off.
> See you at the fair!
> Ed

LEVEL 8

TEXT EDITING

JOB 36-3. DISPLAY

Format: You decide. Use a full sheet of paper.

Program for Judging
4-H Club Projects
Hereford steers at 9:00
Angus steers at 9:30
Shorthorn steers at 10:00
Open class at 10:30
Showmanship at 11:00
Lunch break
Beginner's bake-off at 1:00
Advanced bake-off at 2:00
Beginning sewing projects at 3:00
Complete outfit projects at 3:30
Booth displays at 4:00

JOB 36-4. POSTAL CARD MESSAGE WITH LINED FILL-INS

Type the card shown below. Type a second card for Ann Kelly, who is participating in the Angus steer competition. She has been in 4-H for 6 years and is 17 years old. She belongs to the same club as Ed does, and she has the same advisers. Standard format. Workbook 37.

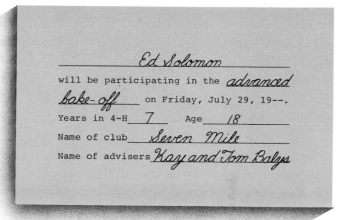

LESSON 37

COMPETENCY CHECK

GOALS
- To type 30/3'/5e.
- To demonstrate competency in basic operating techniques of the typewriter.
- To demonstrate competency in basic formatting procedures on the typewriter.

FORMAT
- Single spacing   60-space line   5-space tab

PREVIEW PRACTICE

Type each line twice as a preview to the 3-minute timing below.

Accuracy 1 to school active realize express campaign question politics
Speed   2 part they read will know what hand type more want join that

3-MINUTE TIMINGS

Take two 3-minute timings on lines 3–10. Format: Double spacing, 5-space tab.

```
 3        High school students can be an active part of politics     12
 4   if they choose.  They can keep up with the news for the day     24
 5   and know what issues are at hand.  They can type letters to     36
 6   be put in papers to question and express points of view for    48
 7   the public to read.  If they choose to be more active, then    60
 8   they may want to join a campaign team and work for a person    72
 9   who seeks an office.  All students realize that their votes    84
10   will also be the way to speak.                                 90
     |  1  |  2  |  3  |  4  |  5  |  6  |  7  |  8  |  9  |  10  |  11  |  12      SI 1.20
```

JOB 262-1. DICTATED FORM LETTER WITH CARBON COPY

Standard format. Workbook 655–656.

dear colleagues a special workshop is being offered to office workers of our company the first weekend in april office politics and human relations is the topic five guest speakers have been invited to share thier expertise with you the program will begin on friday evening at 7:00 at the helena hotel with a keynote adress by margo joplinski following her speech a wine and cheese party is planed in the ivory room saturdays program is a full one with four speakers conducting sessions during the day lunch will be served by the hotel and is included in the cost of the workshop which is only $58 wont you join us at the helena on april 4–5 for an exciting and challenging workshop cordially farla marscalco program chairperson

JOB 262-2. PARTIAL DRAFT OF A SPEECH

Standard format. Plain paper.

Work Space	6

If I were to say to you that your job space is just one space in a much larger area called your life space, what would your reaction be? If you were to draw a line horizontally across the page and then divide that line into various segments, each segment—not necessarily the same size—would be considered a space, and the entire line would be your life space.

When you began your life, the first space became childhood. It may have been a happy, fun-filled childhood, or it may have been one clouded with many hardships and much unhappiness. Nevertheless, it exists as part of your life. What you have done since that time has been affected by what happened during your childhood segment.

Other segments to follow might be called teenage, young adult, adult, middle age, senior citizen, and others. The point at which the work space enters the life space has been

18 / 26 / 36 / 45 / 55 / 64 / 72 / 81 / 90 / 99 / 109 / 117 / 126 / 135 / 144 / 149 / 158 / 168 / 177 / 185

different for each one of us. It is these differences which make work space perception very different for each of us. This is where human relations becomes a part of work space. It is our human relations with ourselves, with each other, and with the world around us that makes our work space become a worthwhile and fulfilling space in our life space.

195 / 204 / 213 / 223 / 232 / 240 / 248 / 256

JOB 262-3. LEADERED PROGRAM WITH COUPON

Standard format. Plain paper.

Weekend Workshop
Office Politics and Human Relations
Friday, April 4, 19—
and
Saturday, April 5, 19—
at Helena Hotel, 713 Locust
Creek Drive   7:00 p.m.
Friday
7:00 – 8:30   Ms. Margo Joplinski
8:30 – ??   Wine and cheese party
Saturday
8:30 – 9:00   Coffee
9:00 – 10:30   James T. Lenrow
10:30 – 12:00   Jayne Abernathy
12:00 – 1:30   Luncheon
                   (included in registration)
1:30 – 3:00   Lawrence M. Turton
3:00 – 4:30   J. J. Brunston

I plan to attend the weekend workshop, Office Politics and Human Relations. Enclosed is my $300.
Name _____ Position _____
Company _____
Address _____
City _____ State ___ ZIP _____

You have just taken a job as a faculty assistant during your study hall. You are working for Jane Bowman, who is head of the Speech Department at Clover Hill High School. She is getting ready for a regional speech tournament to be held at Clover Hill. Your job is to help her with all of the paperwork for the tournament.

JOB 37-1. ENUMERATION

Prepare a list of the participating schools that will be involved in the tournament. Put them in alphabetic order. Standard format.

Participating Schools
Speech Tournament
December 23, 19--
1. *Wayne Township High School*
2. *Martinsburg High School*
3. *Clover Hill High School*
4. *Yorktown Career Center*
5. *Crockett High School*
6. *Addams High School*
7. *St. Joseph's High School*
8. *Lee Joint Vocational School*

JOB 37-2. DISPLAY

Format: You decide (see page 39).

PROGRAM
Fifth Annual
Regional Speech Tournament
Clover Hill High School
Saturday, December 23, 19--
Extemp I, 9:00, Room 102
Extemp II, 9:00, Room 104
Prepared Speech I, 10:30, Room 106
Prepared Speech II, 10:30, Room 108
Lunch, 12:00, West Commons
Debate I, 1:00, Room 102
Debate II, 1:00, Room 104
Closing Assembly, 2:30, Auditorium

JOB 37-3. INFORMAL NOTE

Standard format.

(Date)
Dear Mr. Salvato:
Thank you for approving the schedule for the regional speech tournament at Clover Hill High School. It is an honor for us to host the tournament, and your support of it will make it the best tournament ever. Lisa Comerchero will contact you next week to explain the closing assembly. We appreciate your volunteering to make the opening introductions.

[Leave room for Ms. Bowman to sign her name.]

JOB 37-4. POSTAL CARD MESSAGE WITH RULED FILL-INS

Complete one postal card as shown below. Then complete one card for each of the other seven schools listed in Job 36-1; for these cards, fill in only the school name, not the sponsor name or the number of participants. Standard format. Workbook 39, 41.

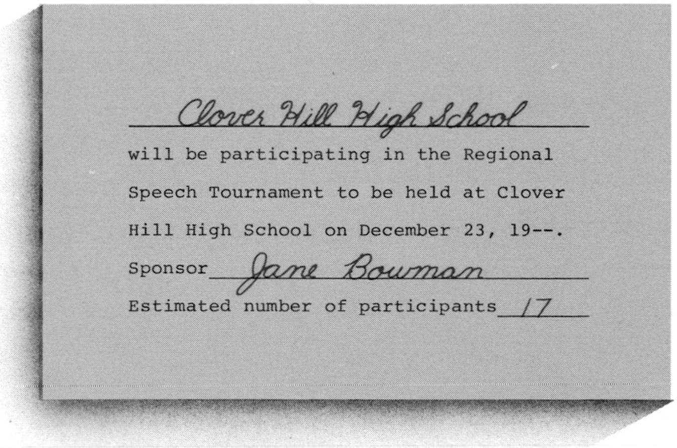

Clover Hill High School
will be participating in the Regional Speech Tournament to be held at Clover Hill High School on December 23, 19--.
Sponsor *Jane Bowman*
Estimated number of participants *17*

LESSON 262

GOALS
- To type 48/5'/3e.
- To demonstrate competency in producing appropriately formatted communications from unarranged, handwritten, and unedited copy.

FORMAT
- Single spacing   60-space line   5-space tab

PREVIEW PRACTICE

Type lines 1 and 2 twice as a preview to the 5-minute timings below.

Accuracy
Speed

1 message accuracy satellite attitudes transmitted assignment
2 cooperatively attractively pleasantly dependably completely

5-MINUTE TIMINGS

Take two 5-minute timings on lines 3–23.

3   Succeeding on the job always has at least two aspects.   12
4 You must be able to perform any task required of you with a   24
5 degree of accuracy and speed. You must be able to complete   36
6 a task pleasantly, cooperatively, and dependably also. The   48
7 blending of both skills and attitudes on the job is often a   60
8 very challenging task for veterans as well as for those who   72
9 are beginners.   75
10   As surveys indicate, however, the human element in all   87
11 work situations is extremely important. The growth of word   99
12 processing centers emphasizes this point. No longer do all   111
13 office workers complete assignments alone. Many tasks need   123
14 to be completed as team efforts, with every person within a   135
15 cluster responsible for a section of the completed job. It   147
16 can be very frustrating when someone fails to cooperate.   158
17   Many persons will be responsible for a completed docu–   170
18 ment in a large company. An author dictates the message to   182
19 a central processing unit; a word processor transcribes the   194
20 message onto a screen and formats it attractively to be put   206
21 on printed paper or to be transmitted via satellite to some   218
22 business located halfway around the globe. Each communica–   230
23 tion is quickly received and the response returned.   240

| 1 | 2 | 3 | 4 | 5 | 6 | 7 | 8 | 9 | 10 | 11 | 12 | SI 1.66

LEVEL 2

FORMATTING FOR PERSONAL USE

BROCHURE

Place the following information on the front cover of the brochure.

THE FRANKLIN AREA HISTORICAL SOCIETY PRESENTS
"A Walk Through the Past"
Sunday, July 9, Through Saturday, July 15

Place the following list on the two inside pages. Divide the list evenly, half on each page. Each item should be numbered so that the numbers can be placed on the map that will be prepared later.

1. Begin at the Harding Museum at 320 Park Avenue. The museum was donated by the late Mrs. William Harding along with the items that are displayed on the first floor of the museum. The rooms on the second floor have pieces donated by members of the Franklin community and surrounding area.

2. Mr. and Mrs. James Roberts, 230 Park Avenue. This home was built in 1891 by David Carpenter. The architecture is Victorian and Queen Anne.

3. Mr. and Mrs. Dan Neal, 221 Elm Street. This home was built in 1906. Mr. and Mrs. Roy Eldridge lived in it for 50 years. Their daughter, Joyce, was married to Clarence Brown (now congressman) in the formal garden at the rear of the home.

4. Mr. and Mrs. Thomas Shera, 303 Elm Street. This home of Queen Anne architecture was built in 1893 by Will Vail, a farmer. He lived in the home for 20 years. Adam Bridge then bought the home. The original structure of the home has never been changed.

5. Mrs. Jesse Adkins, 301 Oxford Road. Built in 1927, this home shows Georgian influence in its architectural design. The home was built by S. S. Tibbals, publisher, and business executive and editor of the *Franklin Chronicle*.

6. Mr. and Mrs. Jack Rhude, 227 Oxford Road. The oldest home in the district is a fine example of Greek architecture and originally included 1,000 acres. It was built in 1847.

7. Mr. and Mrs. Frank Neal, 123 Miami Avenue. This home was built in 1922 on the old Baptist parsonage site by Harry C. Eldridge, founder of the Eldridge Entertainment House. The home was later owned by Paul Logan of Logan-Long Paper Company.

8. Mr. and Mrs. Seth Howard, 117 Miami Avenue. Built in 1890, this example of Queen Anne architecture has Eastern Stick influence. At one time it was sold for as little as $700.

9. Mr. and Mrs. Thomas Burns, 321 Park Avenue. This home was originally located on the Harding Museum plot and was moved to the present location in 1896. It was built in 1882 and is an example of Victorian architecture.

10. Mr. and Mrs. Robert Morton, 103 Miami Avenue. This home was built in 1880 by Derrick B. Anderson, assessor for Franklin Township. The architecture is Italian with Greek Revival influence.

INVITATION
Half sheet of plain paper.

You are cordially invited
to attend the
dedication ceremony
and
walking tour
sponsored by
Franklin Area Historical Society
Sunday, July 9, 19—

MEMBERSHIP CARDS
We just ran out of membership cards. New ones are on order, but they may not arrive in time for the walking tour. Prepare six temporary cards.

is a member in good standing of
THE FRANKLIN AREA HISTORICAL SOCIETY
for the year
19— to 19—

President   Treasurer

School reports, letters, tables, various forms—these are some of the many messages that you will need to type for personal use. To prepare such messages effectively, you must improve your ability to keyboard by touch with speed and accuracy on the alphabet, number, and symbol keys, and you must learn the basics of formatting such messages.

In Level 2, "Formatting for Personal Use," you will:

1. Demonstrate keyboarding accuracy and speed on straight copy with a goal of 35 words a minute or more for 3 minutes with no more than 5 errors.

2. Demonstrate improved skill in the control of the nonprinting parts of the typewriter.

3. Detect, mark with proofreaders' marks, and correct errors in typewritten copy.

4. Use a typewriter to format reports, letters, tables, and forms for personal use.

5. Apply rules for correct use of word division, capitalization, numbers, and punctuation in communications.

LESSON 38

UNIT 7 PREPARING FOR PRODUCTION TYPING

UNIT GOAL 32/3'/5e

GOAL
- To apply some rules of word division.

FORMAT
- Single spacing   60-space line   5-space tab

KEYBOARDING SKILLS

Type lines 1–4 once. Then do what line 5 tells you to do as you type it. Repeat lines 1–4, or take a series of 1-minute timings.

Speed	1 If they handle the work right, the eight may make a profit.	12
Accuracy	2 Our packing the dozen boxes for fresh jam was quite lively.	12
Numbers	3 We counted 38, 47, and 56; they counted 10, 29, 38, and 47.	12
Symbols	4 Mark 38¢, 49¢, and 50¢ after each item shown with a # sign.	12
Technique	5 Return the carriage or carrier after each word as you type.	

| 1 | 2 | 3 | 4 | 5 | 6 | 7 | 8 | 9 | 10 | 11 | 12 |

1- AND 3-MINUTE TIMINGS

Take two 1-minute timings on each paragraph. Then take one 3-minute timing on the entire selection. Use single spacing for the 1-minute timings and double spacing for the 3-minute timing.

6   Have you ever gone to a flea market? At flea markets,   12

7 people try to sell their crafts, junk items, or things they   24

8 no longer can keep or store in an attic.   32

9   Often it happens that one person can use any old thing   12

10 that someone else seems most anxious to get rid of. Such a   24

11 sale makes both buyers and sellers glad.   32

12   Sometimes it amazes people to find that what they hate   12

13 so much, others like. A vase you do not like in your house   24

14 may be quite right in a neighbor's home.   32

| 1 | 2 | 3 | 4 | 5 | 6 | 7 | 8 | 9 | 10 | 11 | 12 | SI 1.23 |

"We're trying to encourage outside fixup," said Brenda Litsch, current president of the area historical society. "The organization wants people to see the possibilities of the homes." Mrs. Litsch lives at 832 Park Avenue and owns two rentals in the district. "Over the past 10 to 20 years many of the houses owned by absentee landlords suffered from neglect, and the area received the stigma of being a slum and high-crime area," she said. Now residents say they have no fear about living in the area.

"We are doing things we never knew we could do," Mrs. Newland said. "We read books and learn how to do them—strip woodwork, strip floors, refinish furniture." "Everything that has to be replaced has to be made special," say many of the residents. "Screen doors just aren't made for such high doorways. Drapes and curtains aren't long enough either."

Not all the houses are in such poor repair. The Cases of 131 Oxford State Road were "lucky." They replaced some of the plumbing and most of the wiring, but otherwise their Colonial Revival home was livable when they moved in four years ago. The house has 12 rooms with nine-feet ceilings. Special features of the house include double glass interior and exterior door and windows and some stained glass in the dining room.

House tours are being arranged for the week of July 9. All the owners of homes in the restoration district who wish to participate will have their homes open for the public to enjoy.

LETTER

Mr. Frank Neal, 123 Miami Avenue, Franklin, OH 45005, Dear Mr. Neal: Thank you very much for the beautiful Victorian chest that you recently donated to the Harding Museum. Mrs. Rousch is especially pleased with the way it blended with her newest arrangement on the second floor.

A plaque is now being engraved and should be in place within the next few weeks. The plaque will have your name and a short history of the Victorian chest.

Please stop in and see our newest display when you have an opportunity. Thank you again for your contribution to the Harding Museum. Cordially, Brenda Litsch, President

LETTER

Mrs. Sally Cheney also donated some china dolls recently. She lives at 307 Park Avenue in Franklin. The dolls are historically significant to our area because they belonged to Juanita Anderson, a well-known music teacher in the area. Please write Mrs. Cheney a thank-you letter similar to the one written to Mr. Neal.

RULES OF WORD DIVISION

When your typewriter bell rings, you must often decide whether you have space to complete a word or whether you should divide it. To divide words, follow the rules given below; other rules will be given in Lesson 39.

1. Divide only between syllables. If you are not sure where a syllable ends, use a dictionary. Never guess—some words are tricky.

   Examples: syl-la-ble   prod-uct   chil-dren   pro-ject (v.)   proj-ect (n.)

2. Do not divide:

   a. A word pronounced as one syllable: *shipped, strength, tire.*
   b. A word of 5 or fewer letters: *about, into.*
   c. Any contraction: *couldn't, can't, o'clock.*
   d. Any abbreviation: *dept., UNICEF, a.m.*

3. Leave a syllable of at least 2 letters on the upper line.

   Line 1: to-   ab-   around   **not** a-
   Line 2: gether   solute   round

4. Carry to the next line a syllable of at least 3 letters (or 2 letters and a punctuation mark that follows the word):

   Line 1: full-   cov-   teacher   **not** teach-
   Line 2: est   er,   er

JOB 38-1. DIVIDING WORDS BY SYLLABLES

Type lines 15–17. Then study each word and draw a vertical line on your paper between syllables if the word may be divided. Check your answers. Then retype lines 15–17 from your edited copy, inserting hyphens at the correct division points.

15   knowledge doesn't children worthwhile tricky; settle profit

16   stop leading steamed mfg. p.m. UNESCO planned signed worthy

17   around, court; mixer, sixty, shouldn't, service area; into.

JOB 38-2. LISTENING FOR THE BELL

Type the paragraph below. Some words will have to be divided at the end of the line, so listen for the bell. If you make the correct line-ending decisions, all lines except for the last will end evenly. Format: Double spacing, 50-space line, 5-space tab.

Do not divide words at end of more than 2 consecutive lines.

18   All of us need to watch our diets to maintain good health. If
19   you do not know much about nutrition, then you should start to
20   learn--now. Eating habits can destroy good health or can help
21   you attain good health, so be sure to eat wholesome food at ev-
22   ery meal. If you would like to read some information on nutri-
23   tion, visit your library or your local bookstore. Also, be sure to
24   learn how vitamin supplements ensure that we receive the mini-
25   mum daily requirements of vitamins and minerals.

IN-BASKET H: HISTORICAL SOCIETY

You have been employed to work in your home for the newly formed Historical Society in your community. The major thrust of the organization presently is to gain publicity for the restoration district recently approved by the federal government. The documents about the dedication and walking tour are the most important. Use letterheads and forms where appropriate. Workbook 641–653.

PRIORITY SHEET AND TIME LOG

Read through the entire in-basket and then complete the priority sheet. Be sure to keep an accurate time log as you complete each job.

DICTATED LETTER

mr and mrs seth adkins 301 oxford road franklin ohio 45005 dear mr and mrs adkins congratulations on having your home placed in the national register of historic homes the franklin area historical society is extremely proud to include your home in its restoration district during the next month our organization will be planning our summer activities the main event will be a tour of the historical homes in the restoration district of course you will want to have your home included in the tour a brochure is being prepared with a brief description of each home in the district and an accompanying historical reference would you please prepare both of these items for us within the next two weeks so that we may properly identify your home in the brochure cordially brenda litsch president

DICTATED LETTER

mrs josephine rousch 319 park avenue franklin ohio 45005 dear josephine i have just returned from the museum and was most impressed with the new display in the harding room you certainly have spent a great deal of time searching for the unusual pieces which are displayed i was especially impressed with the number of victorian pieces of furniture you were able to locate the plaques that you have requested for each of the pieces will take about three weeks to be engraved this will be in plenty of time for our special events this summer i will notify you when the plaques are finished so that you can personally see that they are attached to the proper pieces thank you so much for the marvelous display cordially brenda litsch president

NEWS RELEASE

Get ready for local paper immediately.

RESTORATION DISTRICT TAKES SHAPE

Area residents are quietly admiring their finished and partially finished buildings in preparation for the first annual tour of homes in the newest restoration district in Ohio. Two things sold me on the house, Mrs. Greene said, "the stairway with a winding cherry banister and the arch way door between the dining room and library."

One of the homes on this tour, the Bookwalter–Brewster house at 311 Park Avenue, is considered an outstanding example of French Second Empire style from the 1870s. It was listed in the National Register this spring. Being listed in the National Register puts restrictions on the architectural alterations that can be made to a house, but it also qualified the owner for federal loans and grants.

(Continued on next page)

LESSON 39

GOAL
- To apply additional rules of word division.

FORMAT
- Single spacing   60-space line   5-space tab

KEYBOARDING SKILLS

Type lines 1–4 once. Then do what line 5 tells you to do. Repeat lines 1–4, or take a series of 1-minute timings.

Speed   1 Helen paid the city firm for the land she owns by the lake. 12
Accuracy   2 Quickly fix the seven wires that jeopardized the big camps. 12
Numbers   3 Please vote, when you can, for Laws 10, 29, 38, 47, and 56. 12
Symbols   4 Use these percentages when you write a chart: 38% and 56%. 12
Technique 5 Center your name; then center your teacher's name below yours.
              | 1 | 2 | 3 | 4 | 5 | 6 | 7 | 8 | 9 | 10 | 11 | 12

1- AND 3-MINUTE TIMINGS

Take two 1-minute timings on each paragraph. Then take one 3-minute timing on the entire selection. Use single spacing for the 1-minute timings and double spacing for the 3-minute timing.

```
                 1              2                3              4
 6       Do you want to get better grades in school?  Then here   12
               5              6               7              8
 7  are a few tips you should follow for doing good work in all   24
               9             10
 8  courses, no matter which ones they are.                       32
            11           12                13            14
 9       You should prepare for each class, so that you will be   12
         15             16              17            18
10  able to respond when there is any chance to discuss a major   24
         19           20             21
11  issue or a point made by another student.                    32
              22             23              24             25
12       Discover what all your teachers expect of each student   12
         26              27             28             29
13  in and out of class.  Listen.  Be exact in all answers that  24
            30            31            32
14  you give on a quiz.  Know all the facts.                      32
    |  1  |  2  |  3  |  4  |  5  |  6  |  7  |  8  |  9  |  10  |  11  |  12   SI 1.25
```

MORE RULES OF WORD DIVISION

Workbook 43–44.

Rule	Preferred	Avoid
1. Divide a compound word between the whole words that it contains. Similarly, divide a hyphenated compound word after the hyphen.	business–men under–stand father–in–law clerk–typist	busi–nessmen un–derstand fa–ther–in–law clerk–typ–ist
2. Divide after a one-letter syllable unless it is part of a suffix. Divide between two consecutive, separately pronounced vowels.	sepa–rate simi–lar radi–ation valu–able	sep–arate sim–ilar rad–iation valua–ble
3. When dates, personal names, street names, and long numbers must be broken, do not separate parts that must be read as units. Follow preferred examples.	June 10, / 1982 132 Eastern / Road Ms. Elsie / Berndt 1,583,– / 000,000	May / 21 132 / Eastern Road Mr. / Swenson 2,– / 567

(Continued on next page)

LESSONS 259—261

GOALS
- To type 48/5'/3e.
- To prioritize and format related office communications with speed and accuracy.

FORMAT
- Single spacing   60-space line   5-space tab

KEYBOARDING SKILLS

Type lines 1–4 once. Then do what line 5 tells you to do. Repeat lines 1–4, or take a series of 1-minute timings.

Speed   1 If the eight men do the work right, they may make a profit. 12
Accuracy 2 Jebb gave my excited dog quite a prize for his clever work. 12
Numbers 3 Que Company ordered 10, 29, and 38; we asked for 47 and 56. 12
Symbols 4 Mello (the fluffy one) won't win the prize--she's too slow! 12
Technique 5 Underscore each of the words immediately after you type it.

| 1 | 2 | 3 | 4 | 5 | 6 | 7 | 8 | 9 | 10 | 11 | 12

5-MINUTE TIMINGS

Take a 5-minute timing on lines 6–25. Type six times each word on which you made an error, hesitated, or stopped during the 5-minute timing. Then take a 5-minute timing to see how much your skill has improved.

6   Many persons enjoy keeping accurate historical records 12
7   Many persons enjoy keeping accurate historical records 24
8   Many persons enjoy keeping accurate historical records 36
9   Many persons enjoy keeping accurate historical records 48
10 of homes and communities. The excitement is often enhanced 60
11 of homes and communities. The excitement is often enhanced 72
12 of homes and communities. The excitement is often enhanced 84
13 of homes and communities. The excitement is often enhanced 96
14 through group efforts. Citizens usually pick structures to 108
15 through group efforts. Citizens usually pick structures to 120
16 through group efforts. Citizens usually pick structures to 132
17 through group efforts. Citizens usually pick structures to 144
18 restore and request grants to provide money to return these 156
19 restore and request grants to provide money to return these 168
20 restore and request grants to provide money to return these 180
21 restore and request grants to provide money to return these 192
22 buildings to their original status and keep them that way. 204
23 buildings to their original status and keep them that way. 216
24 buildings to their original status and keep them that way. 228
25 buildings to their original status and keep them that way. 240

| 1 | 2 | 3 | 4 | 5 | 6 | 7 | 8 | 9 | 10 | 11 | 12   SI 1.77

4. Divide after a prefix or before a suffix.

```
super-sonic        su-personic
legal-ize          le-galize
```

5. Avoid dividing the last word on a page.

JOB 39-1. WORD DIVISION PRACTICE

Clear your tabulator; then set tab stops 20 spaces and 40 spaces from the left margin. Type lines 15–19, which show all syllable breaks for the words given. Then retype lines 15–19, showing only the *best* division point for each word.

```
15   sep-a-rate        in-tro-duce       re-ad-just
16   crit-i-cal        grad-u-a-tion     ret-ro-ac-tive
17   time-ta-ble       le-gal-ize        care-less-ness
18   eye-wit-ness      pre-ma-ture       val-u-a-ble
19   reg-u-late        su-per-star       cen-ter-piece
```

JOB 39-2. WORD DIVISION PRACTICE

Using the same margins and tabs as in Job 39-1, type lines 20–23. Then decide on the *best* division point for each word given. **Hint:** Some words or phrases cannot be divided.

```
20   Dr. Hamill        radiation         international
21   1,265,610,000     May 31, 1984      cross-reference
22   masterpiece       $265.22           facilitate
23   September 21      Ms. E. Swenson    23 Mulberry Avenue
```

LESSON 40

GOALS
GOALS
- To recognize how words are capitalized while typing sentences.
- To type from rough draft.

FORMAT
- Single spacing   60-space line   5-space tab

LAB 1

CAPITALIZATION

Type lines 1–4 once. Then repeat lines 1–4 or take a series of 1-minute timings.

```
1   Jane's instructor, Ms. Patterson, teaches in New York City.    12
2   Gerald hopes to travel to Mozambique and Germany next year.    12
3   Dr. Frey, the new museum director, bought a rug in Bangkok.    12
4   Today, Global Airlines travels to most countries in Europe.    12
    |  1  |  2  |  3  |  4  |  5  |  6  |  7  |  8  |  9  |  10  |  11  |  12
```

Capitalize a proper noun (the name of a specific person, place, or thing): *Ms. Patterson, Germany, New York, Kleenex, Spanish.*

Note: Common nouns such as *museum, high school,* and *city* are also capitalized when they are part of proper names: *Carnegie Museum, Patterson High School, New York City.*

Capitalize the first word of a sentence.

Corporations in the city contribute to public museums.

STATEMENT OF OPERATIONS
Mail this with the report.

PRECAST TECHNOLOGY, INC. ⎤ *Center*

Consolidated Statement of Operations

For Quarter Ended March 31, 19--

Summary Items	This Year	Last Year
Net Profit After Taxes	$ 48,247	$ 123,642
Federal and State Income Tax	10,700	128,521
Sales	2,241,507	2,285,474
Resale Material Sales Cost	136,825	153,596
Delivery Sales Cost	137,314	89,542
Installation Sales Cost	392,910	395,923
Net Plant Sales	(1,514,458)	1,646,413
Orders	2,193,966	(2,392,743)
Backlog	932,605	1,042,329
Employees	70	67
Stockholders	127	128
Stock Investment	182,915	183,915
Shares	16,855	16,772
Book Value per Share	22.18	19.42
Net Earnings per Share	2.86	7.52

MEETING AGENDA

Change order of items so that they follow in more logical order.

Agenda
Annual Meeting of the Stockholders
Precast Technology, Inc.
3 p.m., April 23, 19--

1. Report by Charlene Grimes, V.P. in charge of operations, explain new methods of erecting precast.

2. Presentation by James T. Hilgeman about plans for expansion of plant facilities.

3. Report by Richard Wilkins concerning new research in precast surfaces.

4. Report of financial status by Richard Wilkins.

5. Further discussion of plant expansion led by James T. Hilgeman.

6. Election of board of directors.

7. Dinner at the Inn to be served immediately following the meeting.

ACCIDENT REPORT

[*Client*] Juan Dimetro; [*Date reported*] 2/15/—; [*Address*] Apartment A, 54 Main Street, Springfield, OH 45502; [*Phone*] None; [*Explanation of accident*] Juan Dimetro works as an employee on the loading dock for Precast Technology, Inc. On the morning of February 15, 19—, Mr. Dimetro slipped on some ice on the dock and fell between the dock and the trailer, twisting his back as he fell. The client did require a doctor—Dr. Theodore Garland, 14 South Ludlow Street, Springfield, OH 45507 (Phone 555-5038). Mr. Dimetro was taken to Springfield City Hospital at 25 South Ludlow Street. The client is insured with National Cross, 237 Allendale Drive, Columbus, OH 43227. Witnesses to the accident were Richard Sizemore, Barry Coppock, and Michael Smith. Person in charge was Charlene Grimes.

12-SECOND TIMINGS

Type each line four times, or take four 12-second timings on each line. For each timing, type with no more than one error.

```
5  If the order is a big one, we will make a profit this year.   12
6  We will do all we can to help them win the big prize today.   12
7  He cannot go there if he is to come here first for an hour.   12
```

```
   25    30    35    40    45    50    55    60
```

PROOFREADERS' MARKS

Workbook 45–46

When corrections must be made in copy, professional writers, editors, proofreaders, and typists use proofreaders' marks. These symbols are quick and easy to use, and they make typing from a rough draft faster or easier for the typist. Study the proofreaders' marks shown below.

Proofreaders' Mark	Draft	Final Copy	Proofreaders' Mark	Draft	Final Copy
SS Single-space	SS first line / second line	first line second line	/or – Delete and change	paragraph (r)	paragraph
ds Double Space	ds first line / second line	first line second line	⋯ Don't delete	and if it (so)	and so it
⌒ Omit space	to gether	together	/ Lowercase letter (make letter small)	can we go	can we go
# Insert space	It may be	It may not be	≡ Capitalize	Business	business
Move as shown	it is (not)	it is	] Move to right	mrs. Wade	Mrs. Wade
Transpose	(is it) so	it is so	5 Indent 5 spaces	it is so]	it is so
◯ Spell out	the only (1)	the only one	[Move to left	5 Let it be	Let it be
¶ Paragraph	¶ If he is	If he is	∧ Insert punctuation mark	[let us	let us
∧ Insert word	and it (so)	and so it	⊙ Make it a period	style and	style, and
Delete	it may be	it may		other way⊙	other way.

JOB 40-1. PARAGRAPH COPY WITH PROOFREADERS' MARKS

Type a corrected copy of the paragraph below, making all changes indicated by proofreaders' marks. Format: Double spacing, 60-space line, 5-space tab. Half sheet of paper. Center title on line 7.

Cooking Chinese Style

¶ The chinese cook foods so that neither the color nor vitamins are lost

in the pan. So, if you want to cook chinese style make sure that you

cook your vegetables in a Wok (with a touch of oil) rather than a skillet

do not over cook. With Wok the cook can toss food about so that heat

is evenly spread. ¶ The chinese like their vegetables to be crisp

and very fresh. Have you ever tasted foods cooked in a Wok?

JOBS 40-2 AND 40-3. ENUMERATION WITH PROOFREADERS' MARKS

Format: Block-center on a half sheet of paper a corrected copy of the rough draft shown on page 71. Center the copy vertically on the page. Then retype on a full sheet of paper, using double spacing.

LETTER

Signature: Richard Wilkins, President. Send special delivery today.

Mr. Gregg R. Snapp, General Contractor, Box 44, Bowling Green, KY 42101, Dear Mr. Snapp: Your precast has been successfully delivered and was installed without incident at the building site. Your construction chief complimented our erecting crew on the professional job they performed. There is only one problem. We have not received your check in the mail.

Please help us complete the paperwork on this job by mailing us your check as soon as possible. As we are a new business, we do not have an excess in operating capital. We need your prompt payment.

Sincerely,

DICTATED LETTER

Signature: James T. Hilgeman, Vice President for Sales.

mid-atlantic precast concrete company, 9914 elizabeth road waynesboro va 22980 gentlemen thank you for offering to share your display area with us at the national precast convention in minneapolis next month since we are new in the busness we appreciate your thoughtfulness at this time we are manufacturing a limited number of options but by next year we hope to have some additional ones with this in mind i shall be displaying twelve 12″ × 12″ blocks of our product samples we have the display racks to set them upright if you think that you will have room for them i look forward to seeing you in minneapolis sincerly

JOB DESCRIPTION

The Vice President in Charge of Operations needs this immediately.

Position Title: Plant Manager; Department: Operations; Responsible to: Charlene Grimes, V.P. in Charge of Operations; Description of Position:

To manage work load in the plant, report time spent making each piece of precast, to maintain safe working conditions. Duties: 1. Assigns specific work to employees, 2. Costs each piece of work on official report, 3. Reports condition of safety equipment weekly, 4. Reports any accidents on official report, 5. Schedules shipping of precast to erection sites, 6. Inspects quality of each piece of precast before shipment.

MEMO TO EMPLOYEES

[To] All Plant Employees of Precast Technology, Inc.; [From] Charlene Grimes, Vice President in Charge of Operations; [Subject] Plant Safety. Our plant was recently inspected by federal officials, who found violations of some safety codes. Three employees were not wearing hard hats while working in the loading area, and four employees were not wearing safety glasses while operating the high-speed router and sanding equipment. The safety equipment has been provided by the company for your protection. Please use glasses and hard hats while on the job for both your protection and ours.   CG

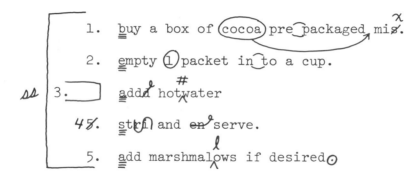

how to make hot cocoa

1. buy a box of (cocoa) pre packaged mix.

2. empty ① packet in to a cup.

ss   3. ☐ add hot water

4 5. stir and en serve.

5. add marshmalows if desired.

LESSON 41

GOALS
- To identify how words are capitalized while typing sentences.
- To use proofreaders' marks in editing copy and to type from rough draft.

FORMAT
- Single spacing   60-space line   5-space tab

LAB 1

CAPITALIZATION

Type lines 1–4 once. Then repeat lines 1–4 or take a series of 1-minute timings.

1 Our supervisor, Mrs. Jezarian, is flying to Iraq next year.   12
2 El Duo Corporation, a Spanish company, does this work best.   12
3 Lincoln Center will feature a hula dance group from Hawaii.   12
4 My French teacher will visit the Grand Canyon during March.   12
   | 1 | 2 | 3 | 4 | 5 | 6 | 7 | 8 | 9 | 10 | 11 | 12

**1- AND
3-MINUTE
TIMINGS**

Take two 1-minute timings on each paragraph. Then take one 3-minute timing on the entire selection. Use single spacing for the 1-minute timings and double spacing for the 3-minute timing.

5   Jazz and blues music have the same roots from the past   12
6   in black gospel singing; slaves had just religion and music   24
7   to escape the hardships of their lives.   32
                                                                   —
8   When days were bad, captives wrote and sang the blues.   12
9   When life was freer, jazz was sung to express joy. Both of   24
10   these are popular with all races today.   32
                                                                   —
11   Whether played and sung by a lone guitarist or done by   12
12   a quintet, the music and the mood are sensed best by people   24
13   if they grasp the meaning of the words.   32
   | 1 | 2 | 3 | 4 | 5 | 6 | 7 | 8 | 9 | 10 | 11 | 12   SI 1.26

PRACTICE

In the chart below, find the number of errors you made on the Pretest. Then type each of the designated drill lines four times.

Pretest errors	0–1	2–3	4+
Drill lines	28–31	27–30	26–29

26 American Baroque Modern Gothic Greece Middle East Taj Mahal
27 architecture magnificent usefulness durability ornate basic
28 sun-dried structures available reinforced skillful textures

29 their color blend often basic goals every world first ideas
30 that have been each were made with them used came more then
31 are one its the and two new now for not era own of to as in

POSTTEST

Repeat the Pretest on page 407 to see how much your skill has improved.

IN-BASKET G: ARCHITECTURE

You are employed as a full-time secretary for an architectural precast concrete firm. The firm has three principals who need paperwork to be completed by you—the Vice President for Sales, the Vice President in Charge of Operations, and the President. Use letterheads and forms where appropriate. Workbook 631 bottom–639.

PRIORITY SHEET AND TIME LOG

Read through the entire in-basket and then complete the priority sheet. Be sure to keep an accurate time log as you complete each job.

REPORT TO STOCKHOLDERS

First Quarter Report Precast Technology Inc.

We I have three pieces of information to share with you for this quarter. ¶1. It has been only an average year so far. Last quarter we told you that we were quite concerned about the business scene for the next two quarters. Our concern was well placed: *We are caught in a squeeze between rising costs and firm resistance to rising costs.* As the enclosed statement shows, the results of that squeeze has been a lower sales volume and therefore, less profit and lower net earnings per share; however, we have turned the corner and expect the rest of the year to be normal, *or even better than normal.*

2. We are planning an expansion of our plant. Our sales staff has been working overtime to secure a wider market, and their work has paid off. New plant plans will be explained at the meeting.

3. New research in the area of precast concrete reveals *promising* possibilities of ~~two~~ three new surfaces. Molds are now being designed to allow us to produce these surfaces.

We ~~I~~ hope that you will be able to attend the annual stockholders' meeting on April 28. ~~I look forward to seeing you there.~~

JOB 41-1. TYPING FROM A HANDWRITTEN DRAFT

Format: Double spacing, 60-space line, 5-space tab. Half sheet of paper. Begin on line 7.

Smoking and Sleeping

¶ Smoking has been linked to many health problems, including lung cancer and heart disease. Now it also appears to cause sleeping problems.

¶ A recent 2-year study in Washington of 100 smokers and non-smokers found that non-smokers fall asleep after an average of 30 minutes, while it takes smokers about 50 to 70 minutes. That's because the nicotine in cigarettes is a stimulant.

JOB 41-2. ROUGH-DRAFT ENUMERATION

Standard format. Half sheet of paper.

do you read bumper stickers?

1. Some ask questions: "Have you Hugged your Child today?"

2. Some give answers: "Don't follow me. I'm lost too."

3. Some are serous: "50 is Thirfty."

4. Some are for small cars: "I'm Pedaling As Fast As I can."

JOB 41-3. ROUGH-DRAFT ENUMERATION

Standard format. Half sheet of paper.

HINTS FOR HELPING THE NEW DRIVER

1. keep in mind that the new driver needs more time to deal with traffic.

2. inform a new driver well in advance of the need to make a turn at a certain corner.

3. give practice driving in the rain.

4. give practice parking the car.

LESSONS 256—258

UNIT 42 IN-BASKETS

GOALS
- To type 48/5'/3e.
- To prioritize and format related office communications with speed and accuracy.

FORMAT
- Single spacing   60-space line   5-space tab and other tabs as needed

KEYBOARDING SKILLS

Type lines 1–4 once. Then use the tabulator as you type line 5. Repeat lines 1–4, or take a series of 1-minue timings.

Speed	1	Janet is busy with the key, so the man is to do the panels.	12
Accuracy	2	Roxie jumped off the van quickly when we saw the big plaza.	12
Numbers	3	They found Invoices 10, 29, 38, 47, and 56 in the corridor.	12
Symbols	4	"Here we are," he said. "We have $30 (in change) to give."	12
Technique	5	Now set the tabs five spaces apart.	

| 1 | 2 | 3 | 4 | 5 | 6 | 7 | 8 | 9 | 10 | 11 | 12

PRETEST

Take a 5-minute Pretest on lines 6–25. Then circle and count your errors. Use the chart on page 408 to determine which lines to type for practice.

6   The history of a people is often traced via structures   12
7   people have made. Architectural history reveals how humans   24
8   have created structures in each period of time blending the   36
9   usefulness, durability, and beauty of each style. Although   48
10   several differences appear for each period of architecture,   60
11   each one displays a distinctive blend of these basic goals.   72
12   Every area of the world offers different materials and   84
13   designs. In the Middle East, structures were first created   96
14   of rushes and sun-dried bricks. Two walls were constructed   108
15   with an arch between them. Eastern architecture used giant   120
16   carvings and created such magnificent structures as the Taj   132
17   Mahal. With classical architecture came the famous columns   144
18   of Greece and those huge arches and vaults of Rome. Design   156
19   became more ornate with Gothic and Baroque styles, and then   168
20   American architecture blended the best to create new ideas.   180
21   Modern architecture now uses reinforced concrete for a   192
22   durable structure and precast concrete for special textures   204
23   or colors not otherwise available. Each new era brings new   216
24   excitement as architects realize the wealth of choices made   228
25   possible from their own skillful researching and designing.   240

| 1 | 2 | 3 | 4 | 5 | 6 | 7 | 8 | 9 | 10 | 11 | 12   SI 1.71

LESSON 42

GOALS
- To capitalize words correctly while typing sentences.
- To type 32/3'/5e.
- To align roman numerals in an outline and to format an outline.

FORMAT
- Single spacing   60-space line   5-space tab

LAB 1

Type lines 1–4 once, providing the missing capitals. Edit your copy as your teacher reads the answers. Then retype lines 1–4 from your edited copy.

CAPITALIZATION

1 Their teacher, ms. quartz, hopes to visit sicily this year.

2 The buhl planetarium in pittsburgh is a great place to see.

3 The president of our company also serves the jacox company.

4 He bought a swiss clock at the st. louis auction last week.

1- AND 3-MINUTE TIMINGS

Take two 1-minute timings on each paragraph. Then take one 3-minute timing on the entire selection. Use single spacing for the 1-minute timings and double spacing for the 3-minute timing.

5 You simply do not go rafting down the quick river that 12

6 flows through the Grand Canyon without skills and plenty of 24

7 help. The many hazards are truly great. 32

8 It's one of the longest waterways in the world, and it 12

9 has rapids that are fearsome to hear. see, and run; but the 24

10 first trip can be filled with excitement. 32

11 The lovely canyon is rocky, thorny, and hot in summer. 12

12 Sometimes it is so windy that the spray and sand hit you in 24

13 the face with a brisk and stinging jolt. 32

| 1 | 2 | 3 | 4 | 5 | 6 | 7 | 8 | 9 | 10 | 11 | 12   SI 1.26

FORMATTING AN OUTLINE

To format an outline of, for example, a term paper, follow these rules:

1. Set your margins so that the outline will be approximately centered horizontally. Or if you wish, use the same margins as those used in your term paper.

2. Type the title on line 13, or center it vertically.

3. Align the periods after the roman numerals, like this:

    I.
    II.
    III.
    IV.

Use the margin release key and backspace from the left margin for roman numerals that take more than one space.

4. Use single spacing, but leave 2 blank lines before and 1 blank line after a line that begins with a Roman numeral.

5. Indent each subdivision 4 more spaces.

    I.##
        A.##
            1.##
                a.##
                    (1)## (etc.)

LETTER

Send a letter to Designers, Inc., in New York and ask them to send their new catalog and price list. Tell them you are especially interested in a new line they are developing for men. Tell them that you are going to be in New York in March and would like to set up an appointment to talk to them about their merchandise. There is no rush for this letter.

LETTER

Send this letter to Ms. Jacqueline Brubaker in Casper, Wyoming 82630. Her street address is 35 West Mountain View.

I have sent your sweater back to the supplier, as you requested. Obviously, there is a flaw in the yarn which caused the sweater to appear pulled. ¶The supplier from whom I purchased the sweater assured me by phone that she will replace your sweater with another one of identical style. Unfortunately, she will not be able to ship it for two weeks. ¶Please let me know when your sweater arrives and whether it is of the style and quality you expected. Sincerely, [*Sign your own name as owner or manager of the Igloo Sportswear Shop.*]

STATEMENTS

Prepare end-of-month statements for the four customers who owe the most. You will have to do the rest later this week.

DICTATED LETTER

Send this letter to Mountain Construction Company, 45 West Broadway, Jackson Hole, Wyoming 83001. It needs to be edited as it is typed.

gentlemen and ladies this leter is to confirm the telephone conversation that we had earlier this week i have decided that i do want to expand the display area of the shop the storage area also needs to be expanded by about ten feet as i look at the volume of business, it appears that sometime during the month of may would be the best time to complete the project most of the skiers will be gone and the summer tourists will have started to come in enclosed is the bid request form which you sent to me it should help in figuring costs of remodeling please let me know if these requests can be completed by the end of may sincerely

INCOME STATEMENT

Complete the figures on the income statement and type it with leaders.

IGLOO SPORTSWEAR
INCOME STATEMENT SUMMARY
FOR MONTH ENDED FEBRUARY 28, 19—

SALE OF GOODS		$21,570
DEDUCT COST OF GOODS SOLD		
GOODS IN SHOP FEB. 1, 19—	$ 9,231.18	
GOODS PURCHASED DURING MONTH	4,507.00	
TOTAL AVAILABLE GOODS FOR SALE	$13,738.18	
GOODS IN SHOP FEB. 28, 19—	9,418.30	
COST OF GOODS SOLD		4,319.88
GROSS PROFIT ON GOODS SOLD		
DEDUCT EXPENSES		
RENT OF SHOP	$400.00	
UTILITIES	180.00	
TOTAL EXPENSES		_____
NET INCOME FOR MONTH OF FEBRUARY		_____

JOB 42-1. OUTLINE

Format the outline shown below. Use a half sheet of paper and single spacing. 50-space line. Set tab stops 4, 8, and 12 spaces from your left margin.

FORMING A BICYCLE TOURING CLUB

Align periods after roman numerals.

I. PLAN A SHORT TRIP.

    A. Take a one—day city tour.
    B. Take a weekend trip.
        1. Go to a state park.
            a. Eat at a country inn.
            b. Camp overnight.
        2. Go to Lake Erie.

Leave 2 blank lines before and 1 blank line after lines that begin with roman numerals.

II. PLAN A LONG TRIP.

    A. Write to other clubs in our country.
    B. Write to clubs in foreign countries.

III. TAKE CLASSES IN BIKE SAFETY.

JOB 42-2. OUTLINE

Standard format. 30-space line. Half sheet of paper.

MAKING FRIENDS
I. Join a Club
A. School Clubs
1. The Business Club
2. Junior Achievement
3. Y-Teens
B. Out-of-School Clubs
II. Get a Pen Pal
III. Take Up a Sport
A. Join a Team
B. Learn a New Sport
1. Tennis
2. Golf
3. Skiing

You may replace tennis, golf, or skiing with your favorite sports.

You have your own specialty shop in Jackson Hole, Wyoming, which you started about six months ago. Your business is growing, and today is especially busy because it's the end of the month and you have a lot of secretarial work to catch up on. You need to prioritize your work before you begin. Use letterheads and forms where appropriate. Workbook 615 bottom–631 top.

PRIORITY SHEET AND TIME LOG
Read through the entire in-basket and then complete the priority sheet. Be sure to keep an accurate time log as you complete each job.

DISPLAY AD
This ad has to be typed and taken to the local newspaper by 2 p.m. today.

```
                SKI EQUIPMENT AND WINTER SPORTSWEAR        IGLOO SPORTSWEAR

                New styles just arrived for
CENTER                  sweaters    suits              BOOTS  SKIS
AND ARRANGE             slacks      blouses            BINDINGS   POLES
BETTER                  jackets     skirts

                Complete line of ski supplies
                For both cross-country and downhill skiing
        Open Monday-Saturday, 10-6               Glenwood & Broadway  St.
```

BID REQUEST
This is the enclosure for the letter to Mountain Construction Company.

Enlarge storage area to 9′ × 12′ size, enlarge display area to 30′ × 30′, install double-insulated front doors for display area, add 6 new counters 4′ high and 12′ long, add shelving in storage area on two ends of room, install additional lighting for display area, and recarpet display area with dark indoor-outdoor carpeting.

ACCOUNTS RECEIVABLE
Type the accounts receivable list for February 28, 19—. List the customers alphabetically and use leaders.

Sandra Henkel owes $120, Lois Shannon owes $240, Janice Hustad owes $98, Donald Erisman owes $155, Carolyn Basford owes $225, Jacqueline Brubaker owes $137, Lawrence Budich owes $79, Jayne Abernathy owes $183, Linda Wick owes $127, Lyn Spangenberg owes $45, Margaret Fulwiler owes $68, and Frederick Caton owes $93. [*Total the amount due.*]

PURCHASE ORDERS
You need additional ski boots: 6 pairs size 10, order number 4389 @ $75 and 6 pairs size 12 with same order number and price. Order from Mott Ski Supplies in Ann Arbor, MI 48104. Purchase Order 231.

You also need to order more designer sweaters from Designers, Inc., at 5527 Lexington Avenue, New York, NY 10037. Order 12 medium size of Group 492 @ $60 and 12 small size of Group 510 @ $68. Add a note to rush the merchandise. Purchase Order 232.

NEWS RELEASE
The local Chamber of Commerce is doing a special on the shops in town for a tourist bulletin to come out this month. The chairperson needs your draft by tomorrow. Compose a couple of paragraphs about the opening of the shop. It specializes in ski equipment plus a complete line of winter sportswear. You started the business to meet the needs of local residents as well as the needs of tourists. Your hours are 10–6, Monday–Saturday, and you are located at Glenwood & Broadway Streets.

LESSON 43

CLINIC

GOALS
- To build typing speed.
- To type 32/3'/5e.

FORMAT
- Single spacing   60-space line   5-space tab

KEYBOARDING SKILLS

Type lines 1–4 once. Then do what line 5 tells you to do. Repeat lines 1–4, or take a series of 1-minute timings.

Speed   1   The eight may make a profit if they handle the forms right.   12
Accuracy   2   Quietly pick up the box with five dozen gum and candy jars.   12
Numbers   3   On May 29 and June 10, I will use 38, 47, and 56 if we can.   12
Symbols   4   Jarris & Sons buys from Wilson & Harris and M&E in Houston.   12
Technique 5   Type line 2; remove your paper; reinsert; align and retype over the original.
           | 1 | 2 | 3 | 4 | 5 | 6 | 7 | 8 | 9 | 10 | 11 | 12

PREVIEW PRACTICE

Type lines 6 and 7 twice as a preview to the Pretest.

Accuracy   6   rapids without waterways longest hazards rafting excitement
Speed   7   windy help trip sand it's jolt with hear down that many hit

PRETEST

Take a 3-minute timing on lines 5–13, page 73.

PRACTICE

Type each line three times, and take a series of 1-minute timings on each line, working to increase your speed.

8   tool well soon keep look fill need less been eggs ebbs burr   12
9   ball miss mill pass good pool feel sees toss seem will book   12
10   wall door hood food ooze buff mitt cuff putt miff mutt full   12

11   Both the men may go to town if he pays them for their fuel.   12
12   She may make the girls do the theme for their eighth panel.   12
13   They paid for the pen and the box, so I paid for the forks.   12
     | 1 | 2 | 3 | 4 | 5 | 6 | 7 | 8 | 9 | 10 | 11 | 12

12-SECOND TIMINGS

Type each line four times, or take four 12-second timings on each line. For each timing, type with no more than one error.

14   Now is the hour to come to the aid of those of us who work.   12
15   She works with them and with the boss in this small office.   12
16   They put a box down the chute and into a van waiting there.   12
                    25   30   35   40   45   50   55   60

30-SECOND TIMINGS

Take two 30-second timings on lines 17–19, or type the paragraph twice.

17   There is no quick way to learn to spell. But if you are an   12
18   expert typist, there is one very good method for you. Just   24
19   teach your fingers to spell as you zip through the lessons.   36
     | 1 | 2 | 3 | 4 | 5 | 6 | 7 | 8 | 9 | 10 | 11 | 12

POSTTEST

Repeat the Pretest twice to see how much your speed has improved.

LESSONS 253—255

GOALS
- To type 48/5'/3e.
- To prioritize and format related office communications with speed and accuracy.

FORMAT
- Single spacing   60-space line   5-space tab and other tabs as needed

KEYBOARDING SKILLS

Type lines 1–4 once. Then use the shift lock for the last word as you type line 5. Repeat lines 1–4, or take a series of 1-minute timings.

Speed   1   She may make the girls do the theme for their eighth panel.   12
Accuracy   2   With all kinds of gripes, Buz rejected every required exam.   12
Numbers   3   Was the number 10, 29, 38, 47, or 56? Can you remember it?   12
Symbols   4   Max & Erma's has a new sign; it's brighter than Al & Joe's.   12
Technique   5   If you type Chicago with the shift lock down, it's CHICAGO.

| 1 | 2 | 3 | 4 | 5 | 6 | 7 | 8 | 9 | 10 | 11 | 12

1- AND 5-MINUTE TIMINGS

Take two 1-minute timings on each paragraph. Then take one 5-minute timing on the entire selection. Use single spacing for the 1-minute timings and double spacing for the 5-minute timing.

         1'

6   Managing a clothing shop in a tourist area requires an   12
7   amazingly high degree of proficiency in business skills. A   24
8   venture into the business means you'll be a salesperson, an   36
9   accountant, and a secretary--and you must try to excel too.   48

10   As a salesperson, you will design exciting displays of   12
11   your merchandise. Assisting customers in purchasing unique   24
12   items as gifts or selecting garments for themselves will be   36
13   your major task. Making decisions will take much time too.   48

14   When you are the accountant, you'll find yourself busy   12
15   with purchasing, pricing, and inventorying. Closing state-   24
16   ments must be prepared regularly, and progress necessitates   36
17   a payroll, but tax reports will be your greatest challenge.   48

18   As secretary, you will prepare all the communications,   12
19   and you will have to type them too. Prioritizing the tasks   24
20   will not be easy either. Now you must meet all the demands   36
21   of being a manager, salesperson, accountant, and secretary.   48

22   Although your life may seem hectic, the opportunity of   12
23   owning your own business makes it worthwhile. Perhaps that   24
24   explains why some businesses survive in spite of high risk.   36
25   Being your own manager and decision maker is very exciting.   48

| 1 | 2 | 3 | 4 | 5 | 6 | 7 | 8 | 9 | 10 | 11 | 12   SI 1.68

GOALS
- To capitalize words correctly while typing sentences.
- To format a one-page report.

FORMAT
- Single spacing   60-space line   5-space tab

LAB 1

Type lines 1–4 once, providing the missing capitals. Edit your copy as your teacher reads the answers. Then retype lines 1–4 from your edited copy.

CAPITALIZATION

1   I hope that ms. sajovic and ms. quinn fly to great britain.

2   We met mr. and mrs. dextor when they visited san francisco.

3   We wrote to the peking art museum about the chinese sketch.

4   A big american flag was flying atop new zenith high school.

12-SECOND TIMINGS

Type each line four times, or take four 12-second timings on each line. For each timing, type with no more than one error.

5   The new moon went over the hills and out of sight too soon.   12
6   We know that he had the spools when he left here about six.   12
7   If the wind hits the leaves, they will come down very soon.   12

        25   30   35   40   45   50   55   60

30-SECOND TIMINGS

Take two 30-second timings on lines 8–10, or type the paragraph twice.

8   On a clear day the view from the top of a tall building can   12
9   be lovely. The azure sky looks so inviting that you expect   24
10   a quiet cloud to be a magic jet plane to fly you to Utopia.   36

    | 1 | 2 | 3 | 4 | 5 | 6 | 7 | 8 | 9 | 10 | 11 | 12

FORMATTING A ONE-PAGE REPORT

Many reports are short enough to fit on one page. To format a one-page report:

1. Set margins for a 60-space line on a pica typewriter (60P) and for a 70-space line on an elite typewriter (70E).

2. Center the title on line 13. Type the title in all-capital letters.

3. Center the subtitle a double space below the title. Use initial caps. The subtitle may further explain the title or may be a *by-line*—the name of the author of the report. Triple-space after typing the subtitle.

4. Double-space the body of the report.

5. Indent paragraphs 5 spaces.

JOB 44-1. ONE-PAGE REPORT

Type the one-page report shown on page 77. Standard format. Workbook 49.

MANUSCRIPT

Type on a 40-space line, single-spaced. The editor needs it by noon today.

```
EDITOR'S CORNER
You've finally made it.   You either have your first job or are looking
for one, or you may be sitting in a dormitory on a campus somewhere
facing your first college exam.   It's a new feeling, one that is chal-
lenging and frustrating at the same time.   DIMES 'N' DOLLARS is
designed to give you suggestions along the way.   The cover story
focuses on the changing economic conditions and the effect on today's
youth.   You'll also read about the ups and downs of 3 young office
workers, some super exercises that you can do to keep in shape, and
what role you can play as a new voter.
The special feature of this issue is about Ms. Alicia Fezer, who has
been a personnel assistant for 2 years.   There's a fun quiz to test
your knowledge of current events too.   We think that you will find
DIMES 'N' DOLLARS interesting and useful reading, and we welcome any
comments or suggestions for future issues.   Let us hear from you.
```

TABLE WITH LEADERS

Set this up as a table of employees and positions. We need it by 10 a.m.

Editor in Chief, Marion Weaver; Assistant Editor, James J. Riley; Art Director, Valerie Randolph; Senior Editors, Robin Byer, Joseph Madison, Lorraine Reade, Darryl Geller; Art Editors, Katharine Vito, Ruth Pavlov, Joan Greif; Research Editor, Bonnie Daignelt; Copy Editor, Susanne Manelli; Production Editor, Paul Covell; Promotion Director, Alta Warner; Business Manager, Paulette Zucker; Advertising Manager, Grigsby Jones; Publisher, Jeanne Ziegler

ADDRESS CARDS

The following names need to be added to the computer list of subscribers. Make address cards for each, and then alphabetize them.

Mr. Jay Yeary, 84A Wildhurst Apartments, Paintsville, KY 41240
Ms. Deanna Zbacnik, 47 Tipperary Court, Nageezi, NM 87037
Mr. George L. Weitkamper, 422 Jewel Lane, Modesto, CA 95352
Mr. Alvin MacGregor, 738 Hawthorne Circle, Skokie, IL 60076
Ms. Marilyn Pearson, 8830 Carberry Drive, Hiko, NV 89017
Ms. Marla Patrick, 975 Wheeling Street, Hogsett, WV 25525
Mrs. Tamara Meulendyke, 4830 Decker Drive, Tivoli, TX 77990

CARE OF YOUR RECORDS ↓ 13

By Jane Baxter ↓ 2

↓ 3

The most important part of taking care of your records is protecting them from dust. What harm will dust do to your records? Dust settles into the record grooves, and when the stylus hits the dust, your records can be hurt in two ways.

First, the stylus will grind dust into the soft vinyl grooves, creating pock marks that will be heard as "clicks and pops" the next time you play the record.

Second, the stylus will pick up the dust as it goes along, which will keep the stylus from tracking clearly or cause it to skid to the end of the record.

The best way of keeping dust off your records is to put a cover on your machine, even when a record is playing. The only time the cover should be off is when you are changing a record.

Never store your records in the plastic wrap that they come sealed in. This material will shrink when it is exposed to heat, which can cause your records to warp during hot weather if they are stored in the wrap.

ONE-PAGE REPORT IN PICA TYPE

REPLY CARDS

Two different reply cards are needed—one for customers who need to renew CURRENT SPORTS and one for potential subscribers of DIMES 'N' DOLLARS. Make the cards 4¼ by 6 inches. Arrange them attractively.

The CURRENT SPORTS card should have this beginning paragraph:

Every week 25,000 people open their mail to CURRENT SPORTS. Each issue is packed with information, insights, and ideas. Renew your subscription now with this card. You'll save over 50% off CURRENT SPORTS' newsstand price of $1.50. Use three lines for name, address, and city/state/ZIP. *Below these double-spaced lines, type* Send me 25, 40, 60, or 104 issues. *Put a small box beside each choice. Below that, also using boxes, type* Payment enclosed *and* Bill me later.

The DIMES 'N' DOLLARS card should have this beginning paragraph:

Save over 15% on a charter subscription to DIMES 'N' DOLLARS. *Below that, and with a box in front of it, type* Starting with the premier issue, please enter a one-year charter subscription to DIMES 'N' DOLLARS for me at the current low price of only $8 (regular rate: $10). *Below that, with another box preceding, type* I prefer two years at $15 for an additional saving. *Below that, with boxes in front, type* Payment enclosed *and* Bill me later. *At the bottom, double-spaced, type a line for name, a line for address, and a line for city/state/ ZIP.*

RULED TABLE

The advertising manager wants this information in table form immediately. The main heading is *Youth, Inc., 2112 Avenue of the Americas, New York, NY 10020.* The column headings are *Size* and *Advertising Rates.* ⅛ page is $200, ¼ page is $300, ½ page is $500, 1 full page is $800, the back cover is $1,000, and 1 column inch is $.75. Put a note at the bottom that it is $100 extra for two-color displays.

LETTER

The cover story for DIMES 'N' DOLLARS was submitted by Calvin Ellston, a professor of economics at Wellston University in Hanover, Indiana. He lives at 1156 College Avenue, Hanover, IN 47243. Please compose a letter to him thanking him for his manuscript. Give him the same information as Ms. Fetzer, but make the following changes: Tell him that his article was selected for the cover story since it best reflects the theme of the magazine. Add that he will receive a $200 check for the article.

TABLE

Type a geographic listing of the names of the new subscribers as well as an alphabetic listing. Add the following names:

Ms. Penny McNab, 68 Elton Street, Eagle, WI 53119; Mr. Sidney Meehan, 385 J-Mar Drive, Franklin, OH 45005; Mrs. Ellen Thompson, Centerburg High School, Brookville, IN 47012. [*Put an asterisk after her name, and make a note at the bottom of the page that it is for 20 copies at school rate.*]

DICTATED LETTER

Type the following letter to Alicia Fetzer, 1783 Berwyn Avenue, Chicago, IL 60640. The letter is unedited— watch for spelling and punctuation!

thank you very much for submiting your article on job interviews to our editor dimes n dollars is a new publication and will be circulating its first issue next month your article is exactly what we were looking for to complete the section on employment since you have been working in personal for sometime i am sure that our subscribers are going to be interested in reading your excellant suggestions as soon as this issue is printed you will recieve advanced copies and a check for $100 thank you for your contribution to our new magazine sincerly james t. riley

JOB 44-2. ONE-PAGE REPORT

Type the report shown below. Standard format (see page 76).

WHAT MESSAGE ARE YOU SENDING?
By [*Your name*]

Without your saying a word, your posture and your walk might tell people what is on your mind. Although your walking style may not tell the whole story, it can send a message about your moods. Check the way you walk.

When you walk at a slow pace, with your head down and hands in your pockets, you tell others that you want to be alone. If your shoulders are drooped, your head is downcast, and your gait is a kind of shuffle, you are telling others that you feel sad. But when you walk at a brisk pace, hold your head up, look relaxed, swing your arms, and use your entire body, you express a sense of openness to everyone.

LESSON 45

GOALS
- To format a one-page report with side headings.

FORMAT
- Single spacing   60-space line   5-space tab

KEYBOARDING SKILLS

Type lines 1–4 once. Then do what line 5 tells you to do. Repeat lines 1–4, or take a series of 1-minute timings.

Speed   1   Then the boys moved with their friends to the right corner.   12
Accuracy   2   Jack Dorp and Vera Lopez quietly bought six new farm tools.   12
Numbers   3   The May 3 group included 38 men, 47 women, and 56 children.   12
Symbols   4   Contracts were sent to L&R and to T&W but not to Rod & Loo.   12
Technique 5   As you retype line 4, underscore all proper nouns in it.

| 1 | 2 | 3 | 4 | 5 | 6 | 7 | 8 | 9 | 10 | 11 | 12 |

3-MINUTE TIMINGS

Take a 3-minute timing on lines 6–13. Type six times each word on which you made an error, hesitated, or stopped during the 3-minute timing. Then take a 3-minute timing to see how much your skill has improved.

6   Strong legs, quick reflexes, and great team spirit are   12
7   what it takes to play the really fast game of soccer. Both   24
8   men and women can play, since skill--not size--is required.   36
9   Long the most widely played sport in Europe, soccer in this   48
10   country is all the rage. It is beloved in other countries,   60
11   too, such as Brazil and Japan. Many high schools that have   72
12   had football as a major team sport have dropped the game in   84
13   favor of soccer, since players are less likely to get hurt.   96

| 1 | 2 | 3 | 4 | 5 | 6 | 7 | 8 | 9 | 10 | 11 | 12 | SI 1.26

FORMATTING SIDE HEADINGS IN REPORTS

Side headings divide reports into sections. To format side headings:
1. Type the side headings in all-capital letters.
2. Triple-space (leaving 2 lines blank) before a side heading.
3. Double-space after a side heading.

JOB 45-1. REPORT WITH SIDE HEADINGS

Type the report shown on page 79. Standard format.

PRACTICE

In the chart below, find the number of errors you made on the Pretest. Then type each of the designated drill lines four times.

Pretest errors	0–1	2–3	4+
Drill lines	27–30	26–29	25–28

25 experiencing interpreting influencing advertising marketing
26 entertaining informative information magazines gather sizes
27 publishers eventually illiteracy explosion potential glance

28 enter areas about range began could print voice early reach
29 take they just from work most sign with over more goal sold
30 any and the are for was ago for out new can and the for are

POSTTEST

Repeat the Pretest on page 400 to see how much your skill has improved.

IN-BASKET E: PUBLISHING

You are a typist for a publisher of magazines. They have two magazines on the market and are preparing to begin publication of a third. It is your job to type the following communications. Use letterheads and forms where appropriate. Workbook 605–615 top.

PRIORITY SHEET AND TIME LOG
Read through the entire in-basket and then complete the priority sheet. Be sure to keep an accurate time log as you complete each job.

FORM LETTER
Set up a copy of this form letter on plain paper. Remember to leave room for the date, inside address, and salutation.

Welcome to the world of DIMES 'N' DOLLARS. We are sure that you are going to be pleased with every issue of our young adult consumer magazine. Designed especially for persons who are beginning their first job or going on to college, DIMES 'N' DOLLARS is written by young adults between the ages of 18 and 25 who will assist you in finding an apartment, purchasing an automobile, and planning a budget. In addition, DIMES 'N' DOLLARS will inform you about the latest fashions for the working set and offer special seasonal pointers.

Your first issue of DIMES 'N' DOLLARS should arrive within the next two weeks. We know that you're going to enjoy all the advantages DIMES 'N' DOLLARS will bring you. Cordially, Paulette Zucker, Business Manager

FORM LETTER
Several subscribers of CURRENT SPORTS have not renewed their subscriptions. Set up this letter on plain paper for these customers.

CURRENT SPORTS is written for people who have a deep interest in the sports world—people like *you*. That's why we're sending you a *free copy* of this month's issue. ¶When you read and enjoy our clear, concise articles, you will want to join the 250,000 other readers who now enjoy CURRENT SPORTS every month. When you decide that you want CURRENT SPORTS—and you will—simply fill out the enclosed card and return it to us. We will then send you CURRENT SPORTS every month, so that you can continue to enjoy the lively features on your favorite sports personalities and sports teams. ¶Cordially, Paulette Zucker, Business Manager PS: You are still eligible for the multiyear savings options shown on the enclosed card. Won't you put your card in the mail today?

HANDLING AND STORING YOUR RECORDS $\downarrow$ 13

$\downarrow$ 2

By Gordon MacIntosh $\downarrow$ 3

Taking good care of your records is very important to good sound. Here are some basic things you should do to make sure that your records keep their clear tone. $\downarrow$ 3

CARE IN HANDLING $\downarrow$ 2

Hold your records at the edges with two hands or balanced with your thumb at the outer edge and the tips of your fingers on the center label. Don't touch the playing surface of the record. Your fingers leave skin oils and moisture that act as glue for the dust that settles there.

CARE IN STORING

After each time you play one of your records, put it back in its inner sleeve and then in its jacket. Store your records upright, away from heat and the direct rays of the sun.

Before playing a record, sweep the dust away with a velour pad that comes in the form of a wooden block with a handle. Use the pad with a wiping and lifting motion. However, the best record-care product will not do much good for your records if you use it only twice a year.

ONE-PAGE REPORT WITH SIDE HEADINGS

LESSONS 250—252

GOALS
- To use possessive forms correctly while typing sentences.
- To type 48/5'/3e.
- To prioritize and format related office communications with speed and accuracy.

FORMAT
- Single spacing   60-space line   5-space tab and other tabs as needed

LAB 30

POSSESSIVES BEFORE GERUNDS; JOINT AND SEPARATE OWNERSHIP

Workbook 603–604.

Type lines 1–4 once, providing the correct possessive form for each line. Edit your copy as your teacher reads the answers. Then retype lines 1–4 from your edited copy.

1 You taking these contracts to Mr. Provenzano will help me.
2 Everyone was surprised to hear about Sy quitting his job.
3 Have you seen Kyle and Andrew's new home on Axelrod Avenue?
4 No, Kyle and Andrew's jobs do not require much commuting.

PRETEST

Take a 5-minute Pretest on lines 5–24. Then circle and count your errors. Use the chart on page 401 to determine which lines to type for practice.

5   Enter any bookstore and take a glance at the magazines   12
6   on display. They are published in all sizes and shapes and   24
7   in just about any language. The topics range from a formal   36
8   literary work to the most trivial aspects of modern living.   48
9   Magazines are just another sign of the gigantic information   60
10 explosion the world is experiencing as technology advances.   72
11   The real magazine explosion was seen over a century or   84
12 more ago. The spread of education became important, and an   96
13 even more important goal was the reduction of illiteracy in   108
14 the country. People began to gather in large cities, where   120
15 magazines could be sold more easily. Printing presses were   132
16 improved; they could print faster and with greater quality.   144
17   Throughout their existence, magazines have served as a   156
18 voice in the influencing of culture and the interpreting of   168
19 society. Early magazines printed special literary works of   180
20 their time, and eventually some ladies' journals and sports   192
21 magazines were added. Modern editors and publishers branch   204
22 out to reach as many new marketing areas as they can. They   216
23 flood potential customers with requests for the purchase of   228
24 magazines which promise to be entertaining and informative.   240

| 1 | 2 | 3 | 4 | 5 | 6 | 7 | 8 | 9 | 10 | 11 | 12   SI 1.69

JOB 45-2. REPORT WITH SIDE HEADINGS

Retype Job 44-2, page 78, inserting side headings as follows: Before the first paragraph, YOUR WALKING STYLE; before the second paragraph, WHAT OTHERS SEE. Standard format.

LESSON 46

GOALS
- To recognize how words are capitalized while typing sentences.
- To produce a one-page report with side and paragraph headings.

FORMAT
- Single spacing   60-space line   5-space tab

LAB 2

CAPITALIZATION

Type lines 1–4 once. Then repeat lines 1–4 or take a series of 1-minute timings.

1 North Dakota and South Dakota are states north of Nebraska. 12
2 Just five bankers went to the West to tour Northern Realty. 12
3 Jo Proxmire is moving from West Virginia to the West Coast. 12
4 Go quickly to 1700 East Graham, on the south side of Azusa. 12
    | 1 | 2 | 3 | 4 | 5 | 6 | 7 | 8 | 9 | 10 | 11 | 12

Capitalize *north, south, east,* and *west* when they refer to definite regions, are part of a proper noun, or are within an address.

  in the West   West Company   610 West Carson Street

Do not capitalize *north, south, east,* and *west* when they merely indicate direction or general location.

  Drive *west* on Hatteras Street.
  We live in the *south* part of Italy.

12-SECOND TIMINGS

Type each line four times, or take four 12-second timings on each line. For each timing, type with no more than one error.

5 Once the boy began to laugh, all of us began to laugh also. 12
6 Where in the world can we find an island on which to relax? 12
7 Now is the time for all of us to rush and join a good team. 12
                              25   30   35   40   45   50   55   60

30-SECOND TIMINGS

Take two 30-second timings on lines 8–10, or type the paragraph twice.

8 All of us need to relax our minds each day. You may not be 12
9 able to use a technique such as yoga, but you can realize a 24
10 true inner peace by thinking about happy days in your life. 36
    | 1 | 2 | 3 | 4 | 5 | 6 | 7 | 8 | 9 | 10 | 11 | 12

FORMATTING PARAGRAPH HEADINGS IN REPORTS

Paragraph headings further subdivide a report. To format paragraph headings:

1. Type paragraph headings at the beginning of a paragraph in *initial* caps; that is, capitalize the first letter of each important word.

2. Underscore paragraph headings.

3. Follow paragraph headings by a period and 2 spaces.

PRACTICE 1

In which lines did you make more errors? If in lines 1–4, type lines 9–12 four times and lines 13–16 twice. If in lines 5–8, reverse the procedure.

Commas

9 maps, girl, make, firm, kept, busy, half, snap, held, when,
10 pens, turn, odor, worn, name, they, pays, them, kept, such,
11 have, paid, wish, form, land, lake, duty, down, oaks, gown,
12 held, busy, with, envy, they, kept, snap, form, sign, town,

Semicolons

13 down; jamb; wish; name; them; hard; such; paid; form; make;
14 city; paid; fish; maps; they; land; also; kept; coal; lame;
15 ivory; slept; panel; girls; turns; fight; melt; idle; slay;
16 field; audit; firms; signs; voted; prize; they; them; time;

POSTTEST 1

Repeat Pretest 1 on page 398, score your work, and note your improvement.

PRETEST 2

Take a 2-minute timing on lines 17–20; then take a 2-minute timing on lines 21–24 and compare your scores.

Apostrophes

17 It's their turn to cut the neighbor's field of corn or hay.   12
18 Lena's firm may make a big profit with the auditor's forms.   24
19 Bob's profit with the corn may go to aid the widow's girls.   36
20 My town's citizens voted not to approve the firm's invoice.   48
                                                                  —
Colons

21 Here is my problem: I must complete the project by June 1.   12
22 They visited these cities: Des Plains, Chicago, and Wayne.   24
23 Remember: Always wear your safety mask in this laboratory.   36
24 The committee nominated two people: Mona Webb and Hal Loo.   48
   | 1 | 2 | 3 | 4 | 5 | 6 | 7 | 8 | 9 | 10 | 11 | 12

PRACTICE 2

In which lines did you make more errors? If in lines 17–20, type lines 25–28 four times and lines 29–32 twice. If in lines 21–24, reverse the procedure.

Apostrophes

25 visitor's problem's title's panel's widow's lemon's giant's
26 auditor's memento's shelf's ivory's field's audit's whale's
27 antique's element's graph's proof's juror's badge's right's
28 speaker's luggage's wagon's habit's zebra's grape's stage's

Colons

29 signal: island: chapel: handle: formal: height: than:
30 drinks: scores: ethics: tables: candid: thanks: tank:
31 basics: habits: enable: inland: vacant: topics: that:
32 almost: employ: events: mother: intent: source: cope:

POSTTEST 2

Repeat Pretest 2, score your work, and note your improvement.

PHRASE PRACTICE

Type lines 33–40 twice. Then repeat twice more those lines in which you made more errors.

With punctuation marks

33 to snap, to turn, to name, to wish, to them, to dot, to it,
34 to make, to melt, to slay, to town, to tidy, to end, to go,
35 for half; for duty; for envy; for maps; for work; for time;
36 for them; for land; for oaks; for pens; for fish; for them;

37 from the visitor's, from the problem's, from the memento's,
38 from the auditor's, from the speaker's, from the antique's,
39 with the token: with the badge: with the tank: with aid:
40 with the wagon: with the juror: with the corn: with the:

JOBS 46-1 AND 46-2. REPORT WITH SIDE AND PARAGRAPH HEADINGS

Type the one-page report with side and paragraph headings as shown below. Standard format. Then retype the report using single spacing.

About Apples

PICKING APPLES

If you live near apple-growing farms, you can get the very freshest fruit, along with some fresh air and exercise, by going to a pick-your-own orchard. These fruit farms often post signs on roads or run ads in local papers. Call in advance to see if you need to bring baskets and to check on the kinds of apples they grow.

RATING APPLES

Big apples may look solid, but often they are mealy and mushy inside. Small- or medium-sized fruit may taste better. Here are some names of apples and their features to help you get the right kind of apple for your needs.

Northern Spy. This kind of apple is somewhat tart and is best for baking because it holds its shape well when cooked.

Cortland. This apple is somewhat tart, too, but it has a nice crunch. It is best for salads because it won't discolor as fast as some others.

Red and Golden Delicious. Both kinds are good to eat; both kinds are sweet and juicy.

Remember that paragraph headings are typed in capital and lowercase letters at the beginning of a paragraph, underscored, and followed by a period and 2 spaces.

LESSON 47

GOALS
- To identify how words are capitalized while typing sentences.
- To produce from rough-draft copy a one-page report with run-in references.

FORMAT
- Single spacing   60-space line   5-space tab

LAB 2

CAPITALIZATION

Type lines 1–4 once. Then repeat lines 1–4 or take a series of 1-minute timings.

1 On Saturday, he will zip to South Carolina for an election.   12

2 Back East in my home town of Quincy, Maine, we like to ski.   12

3 When we visit Mississippi, we enjoy our long journey South.   12

4 I live at 16 East Sixth Avenue, but I will soon move North.   12

| 1 | 2 | 3 | 4 | 5 | 6 | 7 | 8 | 9 | 10 | 11 | 12

CREATING FORMS (Continued)

3. Use at least one and a half spacing if the form will be filled out in handwriting.

4. Make sure ruled lines are long enough for the information that is to be filled in.

5. Center column headings over the columns, if used. Make sure the column is wide enough for the column heading.

6. Vertical rules may be typed or penned in. If penned in, be sure to use a ruler.

JOBS 248-1 AND 248-2. FORMS

Prepare two forms from the copy shown. Use a half sheet of paper for each. Arrange attractively on the page.

WEEKLY RUNNING LOG

	Date	Course	Distance	Time	Comments
M					
T					
W					
T					
F					
S					
S					

INDIVIDUAL PROGRESS CHART
Type of Membership_____   Name_____Phone_____
Is spouse a member?_____   Address_____
Date Enrolled_____   _____Age_____

LESSON 249

CLINIC

GOALS
- To improve technique in typing commas, semicolons, apostrophes, and colons.

FORMAT
- Single spacing   60-space line

PRETEST 1

Take a 2-minute Pretest on lines 1–4; then take a 2-minute timing on lines 5–8 and compare your scores.

Commas
1 They paid the city, town, and county for the right to fish. 12
2 They may make a big profit with the corn, hay, and turkeys. 24
3 Janice may own title to the land, lake, and island by June. 36
4 I think we should have meat, potatoes, and milk for dinner. 48

Semicolons
5 The secretary got the audit form; the city auditor sent it. 12
6 Their big problems may end; their firm is busy with panels. 24
7 Robert pays for the land work; they pay for the audit work. 36
8 It is now time for us to go; it is not time for them to go. 48

| 1 | 2 | 3 | 4 | 5 | 6 | 7 | 8 | 9 | 10 | 11 | 12

12-SECOND TIMINGS

Type each line four times, or take four 12-second timings on each line. For each timing, type with no more than one error.

5 When you turn the pages in the book, do not make any sound.   12
6 The sail of the boat caught the wind, and we scooted north.   12
7 The skies were gray; then the rain became a heavy downpour.   12

        25   30   35   40   45   50   55   60

30-SECOND TIMINGS

Take two 30-second timings on lines 8–10, or type the paragraph twice.

8 As a cause of hearing loss, nothing exceeds the damage that   12
9 is done by loud noises. If you work quite near a very loud   24
10 machines, you may perhaps become dizzy or injure your ears.   36

    | 1 | 2 | 3 | 4 | 5 | 6 | 7 | 8 | 9 | 10 | 11 | 12

FORMATTING RUN-IN REFERENCES

When you are writing a report in which you refer to or quote an idea, fact, or statement of someone else, you should give your readers the source of this information. In this way, you give credit to the original author. You also aid your readers, who may want to find additional information on the subject about which you are writing.

In this lesson you will practice using run-in references in a report. Format a book reference as follows: Author, book title, publisher, place of publication, year of publication, page number (if reference is being made to a specific page).

(Note the underscored book title.)

(John Speer, Airplanes, McGraw–Hill Book Company, New York, 1981, p. 10.)

Format a reference to a magazine article as follows: Author [*if known*], "article title," name of magazine, date, page number. (Note the quotation marks for the article title and the underscored magazine title.)

(Beth Zeiman, "The Friendly Skies," Time, September 4, 1981, p. 88.)

JOB 47-1. REPORT WITH RUN-IN REFERENCES

Type the following one-page report with run-in references. Standard format.

A HISTORY OF PARACHUTING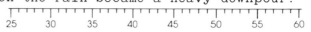
by Grace ackerman #

There are clues that many years ago the chinese tried to invent a

sort of "roof tent" for jumping. But the parachute as we know it

was not made until the 1700's. (Ted Terrance, A History of Flying

Glenmore Press, New York, 1980, p. 104.) Balloonists worked to

build a type of parachute because they needed a safe way to land if the

balloon burst.

(Continued on next page)

JOB 247-1. INVOICE

Standard format. Workbook 599.

Bill and ship to Fran Jenkins, treasurer, Cynthiana 4-H Club, Route 3, Cynthiana, KY 41031; 1 evening rental of the swimming pool, $50; 1 attendant on duty, $15. [You figure the total.]

JOB 247-2. PURCHASE ORDER

Standard format. Workbook 599.

No. 7786: Spangenberg Electric Company, 35 North Main Street, Lexington, KY 40507; 80 4-foot Dual tube ceiling fixtures, [Catalog] CF 42, [Unit] $15; 160 4-foot Dual tube fluorescent lights, [Catalog] DT 4, [Unit] $1.50. [You figure the extensions and the total cost.]

JOB 247-3. PURCHASE REQUISITION

Standard format. Workbook 601.

Meadowgrove Health Spa needs two additional electric rollers and three additional belt machines.

The requisition is to Main Office Health Spa, and it is from the Meadowgrove Health Spa. The request is being made by Melody Byrnes. Use the current date for the request, and date it a week later for the date wanted. The reason for the request is expanded enrollment. Suggested supplier is Lexington Sports Supply, 314 Willoughby Street, Lexington, KY 40505.

JOB 247-4. REQUEST FOR QUOTATION

Standard format. Workbook 601.

Meadowgrove Health Spa is considering purchasing additional health exercise equipment from Lexington Sports Supply: 1 Roman chair, 1 multiple leg lift, and 2 twisters. Use current date with required delivery two weeks later. Reply to the attention of Melody Byrnes, Purchasing Manager.

LESSON 248

GOALS
- To use possessive forms correctly while typing sentences.
- To type 47/5'/3e.
- To create, format, and type forms.

FORMAT
- Single spacing   60-space line   Tabs as needed

LAB 30

POSSESSIVES BEFORE GERUNDS; JOINT AND SEPARATE OWNERSHIP

Type lines 1–4 once, providing the correct possessive form for each line. Edit your copy as your teacher reads the answers. Then retype lines 1–4 from your edited copy.

1 Him helping us on these New Zealand exports is appreciated.

2 Jim reviewing the receipts helped prevent several errors.

3 Ms. Klinger liked George and Warren's speeches yesterday.

4 Yes, Laura and Betty's consulting firm is here in the city.

5-MINUTE TIMINGS

Take a 5-minute timing on lines 5–24, page 391. Type six times each word on which you made an error, hesitated, or stopped during the 5-minute timing. Then take a 5-minute timing to see how much your skill has improved.

CREATING FORMS

Often a company needs a new form. It is typed, and then it is duplicated or sent to a printer.

To format a form:

1. Decide whether the form is to be filled out in handwriting or is to be typed.
2. Use at least double spacing if the form will be filled in on the typewriter.

(Continued on next page)

JOB 47-1 (Continued)

invention #

    In france a man by the name of garnerin made the first drop in

a cone-shaped parachute. (Scot Webber, "Sky Diving," <u>Sports Today</u>,

May, 1981, p. 154.) He made many jumps but got airsick because of

the wobbly ride down. Then, a friend told him to cut a hole in the

top of the chute, allowing air to flow though. This cone shape with

a hole in the top is still used today.

<u>modern uses</u>

    With the use of airplanes in world war I, we were able to drop

supplies by para chute to our forces deep in hostile lands. the parachute

pack has saved the lives of ~~lots of~~ many pilots. Today there are ~~lots~~ all kinds of

people who enjoy the sport of sky diving.

JOB 47-2. REPORT WITH RUN-IN REFERENCES

Retype Job 47-1. Insert a run-in reference after the first sentence in the third paragraph, as follows:

> (Sarah Rosenblatt, <u>Heroes of World War I</u>, Victor Ludwig and Company, Boston, 1978, p. 271.)

LESSON 48

GOALS
- To capitalize words correctly while typing sentences.
- To type 32/3'/5e.
- To produce a one-page report with an enumeration and run-in references.

FORMAT
- Single spacing   60-space line   5-space tab

LAB 2

Type lines 1–4 once, providing the missing capitals. Edit your copy as your teacher reads the answers. Then retype lines 1–4 from your edited copy.

CAPITALIZATION

1 Jean Azar moved from the northeast in april or may of 1980.

2 During the Civil War, the north attacked southern shipping.

3 Our south side high school is two miles south of knoxville.

4 The northern and southern railroad travels north to quebec.

JOB 246-2. NEWS RELEASE

Standard format. Workbook 597.

Release: Immediately 2
From: Carol Mack, 7
Regional Manager 12

SPECIAL
~~OLYMPICS~~ SPONSORED BY HEALTH SPA 39

5LEXINGTON, KY., APR. 1--The ~~Eighth~~ *Ninth* an- 50

nual Track and Field Special Olympics 57

program will be held Wednesday, April 65

15, from 9 a.m. to 9 p.m. at the Lex- 72

ington Fairgrounds. Mentally handi- 79

capped individuals ⑧ years of age or 87

older are eligible to partcipate in ~~t~~ 95

the events, which will include the 50- 102

meter dash, 200-meter run, 400-meter 110

relay, *400-meter dash,* 1-mile run, long jump, ~~high~~ 120

~~jump,~~ and softball throw. 125

Created by the Joseph P. Kennedy 132
which sponsors the program internationally,
Jr. Foundation, Special Olympics is 145
locally
sponsored by Meadowgrove Health Spa 157

and the Lexington Public Schools. An 164
international
program of sports training, physical 174

fitness, and athletic competition, 181

Special Olympics accommodates competi- 189

tors of all ability levels by assign- 196

ing them to "competition divisions" 203

based on age and performance. Meadow- 223

grove Health Spa and the Lexington 230

public schools have sponsored the 237

Special Olympics program since 1973. 245

(END) *Division winners may advance* 246
to the International Games.

LESSON 247

GOALS
- To identify how possessive forms are used before gerunds and how possessive forms show joint or separate ownership while typing sentences.
- To type forms requiring carbon copies.

FORMAT
- Single spacing   60-space line

LAB 30

POSSESSIVES BEFORE GERUNDS; JOINT AND SEPARATE OWNERSHIP

Type lines 1–4 once. Then repeat lines 1–4 or take a series of 1-minute timings.

1 Zachary and Vera's mother is a well-respected tax attorney. 12
2 Karl's and Al's offices are just down the hall to the left. 12
3 All of us welcomed Helen's figuring out the expense budget. 12
4 Evelyn knows about his wanting to work on the Denk account. 12
   | 1 | 2 | 3 | 4 | 5 | 6 | 7 | 8 | 9 | 10 | 11 | 12

12-SECOND TIMINGS

Type each line four times, or take four 12-second timings on each line. For each timing, type with no error.

5 Gary won five more prizes but quickly junked the xylophone. 12
6 As Elizabeth requested, Jack will pay for fixing my silver. 12
7 Jack found the gravel camp six below zero quite a few days. 12

25   30   35   40   45   50   55   60

Take a 3-minute Pretest on lines 5–12. Then circle and count your errors. Use the chart below to determine which lines to type for practice.

```
            1                    2                    3                    4
 5        Outer space is an exciting new place about which we do        12
        5                6                7                8
 6   not know very much.  Science has tried to guess some of the        24
            9                10               11               12
 7   answers to the questions, but we need more facts.  We have,        36
            13               14               15               16
 8   of course, done amazing feats in space, such as land on the        48
            17               18               19               20
 9   moon and shake hands during a walk in space among the stars        60
            21               22               23               24
10   and planets; but there are vast areas still to be explored.        73
            25               26               27               28
11   Do you think that you would like to take a fun journey into        84
            29               30               31               32
12   outer space?  Would you be afraid to encounter the unknown?        96
     |  1  |  2  |  3  |  4  |  5  |  6  |  7  |  8  |  9  |  10  |  11  |  12     SI 1.26
```

PRACTICE

In the chart below, find the number of errors you made on the Pretest. Then type each of the following designated drill lines four times.

Pretest errors	0–1	2–3	4–5	6+
Drill lines	16–20	15–19	14–18	13–17

Accuracy

```
13   walk feats areas space tried place amazing unknown exciting
14   land shake among outer hands facts answers science explored
15   not stars guess about would course afraid journey encounter
16   be you has there hands which think during planets questions
```

Speed

```
17   know very much into new the but and you fun not is an we do
18   some need more like have done such that moon vast take area
19   space tried facts feats areas land know much into are be to
20   hands outer place would shake walk more some like has if so
```

POSTTEST

Repeat the Pretest to see how much your skill has improved.

FORMATTING REFERENCES

Two References in a Row. When a reference notation in a report refers to a book or magazine article that is the same as the one immediately preceding, you may shorten it by using the abbreviation *Ibid.* (meaning "in the same place"). Add a page number if the page is different.

    Ibid., p. 63.

Two References in the Same Work. When a reference notation in a report refers to a book or magazine article fully identified in an earlier reference—but not the one immediately preceding—it may be shortened as follows: Author's surname, page number.

    Speer, p. 11.

Formatting Enumerations in a Report. When an enumeration appears in a report, indent the enumerated items 5 spaces on both sides. If the items take more than 1 line, single-space each item and double-space between items.

JOB 48-1. REPORT WITH ENUMERATION AND RUN-IN REFERENCES

Type the report shown on page 85, providing the needed capitalization. Edit your copy as your teacher reads the correct capitalization. Standard format.

PRACTICE

In which Pretest did you make more errors? If in lines 5–8, type lines 13–16 six times and lines 17–20 three times. If in lines 9–12, reverse the procedure.

Periods	13	theme.	world.	visit.	usual.	theme.	rush.	pale.	goal.
	14	black.	chair.	audit.	dozen.	eight.	form.	name.	gown.
	15	table.	bored.	claim.	nurse.	seven.	gull.	give.	gave.
	16	basic.	finds.	giant.	third.	drill.	play.	step.	ride.
Question Marks	17	doors?	panel?	angle?	dials?	claim?	push?	rich?	rush?
	18	score?	hopes?	rifle?	onion?	shell?	coin?	burn?	worn?
	19	forms?	giant?	ivory?	fight?	milky?	blue?	noun?	clue?
	20	nylon?	garbs?	shake?	towns?	pupil?	hymn?	torn?	honk?

POSTTEST

Repeat the Pretests.

FORMATTING NEWS RELEASES

Companies often use news releases when they are releasing a new product or introducing a new service. News releases should contain the following information: Who? What? Why? Where? When? and How?

News releases may be typed on a printed form or on plain paper. To format a news release:

1. Type the heading fill-ins aligned with the guide words on a printed form (A), or type the data starting on line 9, aligned at the center tab stop on plain paper (B).
2. Center the title in all-capital letters (C). Leave 3 blank lines before and 2 blank lines after the title.
3. Type a date line: city, abbreviated date, and a dash before the first sentence (D). Include the state (E) only if the city is not well known or could be confused with a city in another state.
4. Set margins for 60P/70E. Double-space and indent paragraphs 5 spaces.
5. Type (END) at the end of the release.

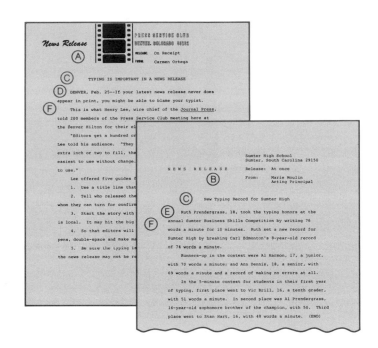

JOB 246-1. NEWS RELEASE

Standard format. Workbook 595.

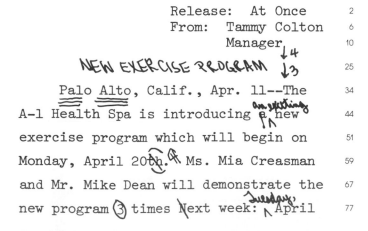

Release: At Once	2
From: Tammy Colton	6
Manager	10

NEW EXERCISE PROGRAM   25

Palo Alto, Calif., Apr. 11--The   34
A-1 Health Spa is introducing *an exciting* new   44
exercise program which will begin on   51
Monday, April 20th. Ms. Mia Creasman   59
and Mr. Mike Dean will demonstrate the   67
new program 3 times Next week: *Tuesday,* April   77

18; April 19; and April 20 *especially designed for weight reduction*   87
No ¶ Each demonstration will begin at   102
10 a.m. and will last about 1 hour.   110
Persons interested in   116
attending one of Ms. Creasman and Mr.   123
Dean's sessions should call the spa at   131
555-4729 by noon on *Monday,* April 17.   139
Additional programs in exercise   146
are also offered at A-1 Health Spa.   153
Brochures on the entire offerings are   161
available on request. (END)   167

PASTA

By joyce pavavatti

*How well can you
apply the rules of
capitalization?*

WHO FIRST MADE PASTA?

You may think that pasta came from italy, but it has for many,
many years been part of the diet of the people of china. (Alfonse
Conti, <u>Great Foods</u>, Howe House, new york, 1979, p. 144.) Some sources
say that the chinese first made pasta and that marco polo found it
in china and brought it back to rome. Other sources say this is not so
because pasta was referred to in old roman writings. (Ibid., p. 145.)

IS PASTA GOOD FOOD?

Pasta is easy to digest and low in fat. Although it is also low
in protein, the meat or cheese served with noodles and other types of
pasta raises the protein content and food value of the dish. (Ruth
Roth, "Cut Your Food Bill," <u>Foods Today</u>, june 1981, p. 14.)

When you buy your pasta at the store, be sure the product is made
from semolina, which holds its shape well during cooking.

For best results, keep in mind these pointers:

*Indent enumerations
5 spaces on each
side. Single-space
turnovers.*

1. don't rinse cooked pasta unless it will be used in a
    salad.

2. Don't overcook pasta; test it often to be sure it is
    tender but firm.

3. Serve it at once. (conti, p. 267.)

**ONE-PAGE REPORT WITH ENUMERATION AND RUN-IN REFERENCES
(ELITE TYPE)**

JOB 245-2. FORM

Fill in membership cards. Workbook 593–594.

Membership cards need to be typed for Pamela Avery, Margaret Ratliff, Julie Sheper, and Julie Schaefer. All enrolled 4/15/—; their membership expires a year later. All membership cards were issued by Sarah on 4/15/—.

Additional membership cards need to be typed for Joseph Attala, Brian O'Leary, Harvey Montgomery, and Geoffrey Collins. Enrollment date is 4/18/—. These four memberships were issued by Elliot and expire in one year.

LESSON
246

GOALS
- To recognize how possessive forms are used before gerunds and how possessive forms show joint or separate ownership while typing sentences.
- To improve technique in typing end-of-sentence punctuation marks.
- To format and type a news release.

FORMAT
- Single spacing   60-space line

LAB 30

Type lines 1–4 once. Then repeat lines 1–4 or take a series of 1-minute timings.

(Noun) 1 Justin appreciated Ken's meeting us in Kalamazoo yesterday. 12
(Pronoun) 2 Your checking the six questionnaires helped all of us, Sam. 12
(Joint) 3 Kevin and Alice's boss is away on vacation for three weeks. 12
(Separate) 4 Paul's and John's homes are one block away from each other. 12

| 1 | 2 | 3 | 4 | 5 | 6 | 7 | 8 | 9 | 10 | 11 | 12

POSSESSIVES BEFORE GERUNDS; JOINT AND SEPARATE OWNERSHIP

Use a possessive before a gerund (an *ing* verbal used as a noun):

Did you know about *his* taking a leave of absence? (**Not**: him taking)
I heard about *Eve's* winning the sales contest. (**Not**: Eve winning)

To show *separate* ownership of two nouns, make *each* noun possessive. To show *joint* ownership, make only the *second* noun possessive:

May's and Jane's husbands are teachers. (Separate)
May and Jane's business is very profitable. (Joint)

PRETESTS

Take a 2-minute Pretest on lines 5–8; then take a 2-minute Pretest on lines 9–12. Circle and count your errors on each timing.

Periods 5 Jamie Tymes is very busy. She works for a big health firm. 12
6 Robert paid for the audit and for a map. He paid the city. 24
7 Lois bought a membership. She likes to go to the new spas. 36
8 Ben is at the store. He is paying for groceries they sent. 48

Question Marks 9 Did they blame the cat? Did they blame her for the attack? 12
10 Why did he give away that money? Did he owe it to someone? 24
11 What is the theme? Is it apt to irk the ones on the panel? 36
12 When did the salesperson come? Did she explain the design? 48

| 1 | 2 | 3 | 4 | 5 | 6 | 7 | 8 | 9 | 10 | 11 | 12

CLINIC

GOALS
- To build typing accuracy.
- To type 32/3'/5e.

FORMAT
- Single spacing   60-space line   5-space tab

KEYBOARDING SKILLS

Type lines 1–4 once. Then do what line 5 tells you to do. Repeat lines 1–4, or take a series of 1-minute timings.

Speed	1 She is busy with the work but is to go to town for the pay.	12
Accuracy	2 Wes vexed Jack by quietly helping to farm a dozen zucchini.	12
Numbers	3 Do not take 10, 29, and 38 in place of 47 and 56 right now.	12
Symbols	4 Order #29 is for 38 pounds of #10 nails by the end of June.	12
Technique	5 Type line 3 in all caps; release the shift lock as you type the numbers.	

| 1 | 2 | 3 | 4 | 5 | 6 | 7 | 8 | 9 | 10 | 11 | 12 |

PRETEST

Take a 3-minute timing on lines 5–12, page 84.

PRACTICE

Type lines 8–11 three times. Then type lines 12–15 three times.

6 sws swim swam swell swaps swish sweeps swanky sweats sweets
7 kik skim skid kindly skinny skimpy killer skips skins skimp
8 lol long love loosen clouds sloppy floods loyal along loses
9 ded deer deck dealer seeded headed leaded ceded deeds deuce

10 waw wade wage awake waist waxen awards warden waxers wander
11 lil like lilt milky light slips lilies flight limber slices
12 drd draw drab draft drama drawn drills droopy drives dreads
13 nkn inks pink skunk ankle chunk linked banker tanker dunker

"OK" TIMINGS

This version of a 30-second timing is used to build your accuracy on alphabetic copy. Try to type as many 30-second "OK" (errorless) timings as possible out of three attempts on lines 16–18. Then repeat the effort on lines 19–21.

14	Things seem to happen just right for some people. When the	12
15	good chance comes along to be seized, they are quick to get	24
16	the exact vision of how the lucky moment can work for them.	36
17	Quite by chance you may have seen a person of the other sex	12
18	do a crazy thing. You want to explode in laughter, but you	24
19	just smile. The other person smiles back. You feel great.	36

| 1 | 2 | 3 | 4 | 5 | 6 | 7 | 8 | 9 | 10 | 11 | 12 |

POSTTEST

Repeat the 3-minute timing on page 84 to see how much your skill has improved.

Take two 30-second timings on lines 6–8, or type the paragraph twice.

```
6        Exercise gives your body the zip it needs to adjust to  12
7  a pace required to live in this modern society.  Walking is  24
8  just one way that you are likely to add years to your life.  36
   |  1  |  2  |  3  |  4  |  5  |  6  |  7  |  8  |  9  | 10  | 11  | 12
```

JOB 245-1. FORM
Fill in information. Carbon copy. Workbook 591.

ACCIDENT REPORT

Client _Pam Rizzo_   Date reported _3/12/—_

Address _25 Southview Drive, Apt. 6_   Phone _555-3748_

Explanation of accident _Ms. Rizzo fell and hit her head as she was going from the exercise room to the sauna. Her head hit the side of a bench, causing a laceration on that side of her head. She was not unconscious at any time._

Did client see a doctor? _Yes_   Name _Dr. Frederick Vito_

Address _59 Worthington Circle_   Phone _555-8372_

Was hospitalization required? _No_   How long? _____

Name of hospital _____

Address of hospital _____

Did client have insurance? _Yes_   Name _National Cross_

Address _237 Allendale, Columbus, OH 45321_

Name of attendant on duty at time of accident _James Bassford_

Witnesses to accident _Kelly Maxton, Susan Lotz, and Paula Wing_

Signature of person filing this report _James Bassford_

Hint: Remember that signatures on forms are not typed.

GOALS
- To capitalize words correctly while typing sentences.
- To format a personal-business letter.

FORMAT
- Single spacing   60-space line   5-space tab

LAB 2

CAPITALIZATION

Workbook 53–54.

Type lines 1–4 once, providing the missing capitals. Edit your copy as your teacher reads the answers. Then retype lines 1–4 from your edited copy.

1 I moved to james plaza, which is south of butternut square.

2 The hotel is on north valley drive, just north of oak road.

3 On my birthday we may fly north to vermont for some skiing.

4 We will drive to the west coast next week for a short rest.

12-SECOND TIMINGS

Type each line four times, or take four 12-second timings on each line. For each timing, type with no more than one error.

5 The man and the woman got a day off and got their pay also.   12

6 Did you see that our new red car is in the lot, out of gas?   12

7 It is not at all clear to us why he is to get a part of it.   12

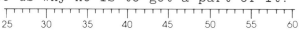

25   30   35   40   45   50   55   60

FORMATTING PERSONAL-BUSINESS LETTERS

A letter from an individual to a department store concerning a personal bill or to a company asking for a job interview is called a *personal-business letter*. A personal-business letter has these standard parts:

Heading. The heading consists of a return address (the writer's address) and the date.

Opening. The opening is the inside address (the address of the person or firm to whom the letter is being sent) and the salutation or greeting.

Body. The message of the letter.

Closing. A complimentary closing, such as *Yours truly* or *Sincerely yours*, and the name of the writer.

To format a personal-business letter:

1. Use standard-size paper (8½ by 11 inches or 216 by 279 mm) or A4 paper (210 by 297 mm, or 8¼ by 11¾ inches).

2. Set margins for a 50-space line (pica) or a 60-space line (elite).

3. Begin the return address on line 13, at the center.

4. Type the date on the line below the return address, aligned with it.

5. Type the inside address 5 lines below the date, at the left margin.

6. Type the salutation, followed by a colon, a double space below the inside address.

7. Begin the message a double space below the salutation. Single-space paragraphs, but double-space between paragraphs. Block paragraphs at the left margin.

8. Type the complimentary closing, followed by a comma, a double space below the body, beginning at the center.

9. Type the writer's name 4 lines below the complimentary closing, beginning at the center. This space is for the writer's signature.

The format described here is the most commonly used letter style and is considered to be the standard format. This style is known as *modified-block style*.

JOBS 50-1 AND 50-2. PERSONAL-BUSINESS LETTER

Type the letter shown on page 88. Standard format. Then retype the letter, using your own address in the return address position, the current date, and your own name as the writer.

PRACTICE

In the chart below, find the number of errors you made on the Pretest. Then type each of the designated drill lines four times.

Pretest errors	0–1	2–3	4+
Drill lines	27–30	26–29	25–28

25 possibilities manipulated development stretching management
26 additional individual conclusion rigorous bicycles numerous
27 worthwhile equipment apparatus available generally exercise

28 some your must body that more warm tone area also just help
29 give then legs back have with room pool spa any one zip add
30 the spa its own you and get may for are but far lie sit can

POSTTEST

Repeat the Pretest on page 391 to see how much your skill has improved.

JOB 244-1. FORM

Fill in application. Workbook 585.

Kip Ungerleider, who lives at 1439 Brookhaven Drive, Lexington, KY 40502, was born June 18, 1945. Social Security Number is 278-45-7849; phone number is 555-3927. She is employed by Joseph P. Robinson, dentist. She was referred by Cara Kalal. She is interested in joining the spa to exercise and to lose weight.

JOB 244-2. FORM

Fill in application. Workbook 587.

The applicant is Belinda Meisenheimer, who lives at Melrose Park Apartments, No. 4B, Lexington, KY 40502. She was born on January 13, 1950,

and her Social Security Number is 354-58-9385. Her phone number is 555-3850. She is employed by Lexington City Schools and was referred by Anne Williamson. She wants to join for exercise and relaxation after work.

JOB 244-3. FORM

Fill in application. Workbook 589.

Jerry Killian lives at 7748 Oakridge Drive, Lexington, KY 40505. He was born on May 7, 1952, and his Social Security Number is 348-87-3415. His phone number is 555-2958, and he is a sales representative for Gregory Publishing Company. He was referred by Tim Ballard. He is interested in joining the spa to lose weight and to get some regular exercise.

LESSON 245

GOALS
- To build competency in typing letters, numbers, and symbols and in using the margin release key to type outside the margin.
- To fill in forms using the typewriter.

FORMAT
- Single spacing   60-space line

KEYBOARDING SKILLS

Type lines 1–4 once. Then, as you type line 5, do what line 5 tells you to do. Repeat lines 1–4, or take a series of 1-minute timings.

Speed   1 Now is the time for you to spend more of your day at a spa. 12
Accuracy   2 The very next question emphasized the growing lack of jobs. 12
Numbers   3 Type page 10 or 29, page 38 or 47, and then page 56 or 100. 12
Symbols   4 Invoice #3478 was addressed to Smith & Hart, Inc., for $29. 12
Technique 5 When you want to type outside a margin, depress the release key.

   | 1 | 2 | 3 | 4 | 5 | 6 | 7 | 8 | 9 | 10 | 11 | 12

672 Western Parkway ↓ 13
Park City, UT 84060
April 10, 19-- ↓ 5

Heading
Writer's address
Date

Opening
Name
Inside address
Salutation

Body

Mrs. Violet Logan
LaVista High School
2400 Highland Avenue
Park City, UT 84060 ↓ 2

Dear Mrs. Logan: ↓ 2

Last fall I was a student in an advanced course in typing that you taught at the high school on Monday evenings, starting September 4. I received an "A" grade in the course. ↓ 2

Perhaps you will remember that you helped me get a typing job at the Mesa Clinic in Salt Lake City. I have been working for two months now for Dr. Joel Weiss, and I enjoy my work a great deal. But I find that I need more practice in typing medical terms and filling out forms for patients. ↓ 2

Do you know where I can take a course in typing for medical office workers? I would be grateful if you would send any brochures about such a course to my home. The address is at the top of this letter. ↓ 2

Sincerely yours, ↓ 4

Closing
Complimentary
  closing
Writer's name

Nadine Hooper

PERSONAL-BUSINESS LETTER

UNIT 40 PROCESSING FORMS

UNIT GOAL
47/5'/3e

GOALS
- To select possessives of singular and plural nouns correctly while typing sentences.
- To type 47/5'/3e.
- To type application forms.

FORMAT
- Single spacing   60-space line   5-space tab

LAB 29

POSSESSIVES OF NOUNS

Workbook 583–584.

Type lines 1–4 once, providing the correct possessive form of the noun. Edit your copy as your teacher reads the answers. Then retype lines 1–4 from your edited copy.

1 One (man's/men's) briefcase was quickly found by the night janitor.
2 Six (man's/men's) suits imported from Zurich will again be on sale.
3 One (attorney's/attorneys') salary was reviewed yesterday by Ms. Ritter.
4 Those (attorney's/attorneys') salaries were reviewed yesterday by Diana.

PRETEST

Take a 5-minute Pretest on lines 5–24. Then circle and count your errors.

```
                          1                              2
5       The management of a health spa means handling quite an    12
        3                        4
6  array of equipment.  Every spa boasts about its own special    24
   5                      6                        7
7  apparatus.  Some equipment forces your body in a variety of    36
                      8                    9
8  directions, while other pieces of equipment must be manipu-    48
          10                11
9  lated by different parts of your body.                         56
                    12                    13
10      Almost every spa has numerous bicycles that assist you    68
        14                  15                        16
11  in warmups and toning exercises which precede more rigorous   80
                  17                    18
12  exercises.  Some spas provide belts and rollers to warm up,   92
               19                    20
13  tone up, and generally get started.  An extra area may also   104
      21                  22                        23
14  be provided for just stretching your muscles without having   116
                    24                    25
15  equipment to help you, and spas may provide exercise music.   128
               26                    27                    28
16      Additional equipment is available to give variety when    140
                    29                    30
17  warmups are finished.  A twister reduces a bulky waist, but   152
              31                    32
18  fat legs require pushing weights overhead with your legs as   164
      33                  34                        35
19  you lie on your back or sit.  Pulleys and presses have some   176
                    36                    37
20  possibilities for development and reduction.  An individual   188
            38                    39                        40
21  program can be built especially for anyone.  Of course, the   200
                    41                    42
22  sauna, whirlpool, steam room, and swimming pool attract the   212
              43                    44
23  tired body at the conclusion of rigorous exercise and add a   224
      45                    46                        47
24  zip to the routine, which gives you a worthwhile feeling.     235
   |  1  |  2  |  3  |  4  |  5  |  6  |  7  |  8  |  9  |  10  |  11  |  12   SI 1.66
```

LESSON 51

GOALS
- To type a personal-business letter in correct format.
- To address small envelopes and fold letters to fit small envelopes.

FORMAT
- Single spacing   60-space line   5-space tab

KEYBOARDING SKILLS

Type lines 1–4 once. Then do what line 5 tells you to do. Repeat lines 1–4, or take a series of 1-minute timings.

Speed   1   It is his fault if he does not help us find the six orders.   12
Accuracy   2   Jumping quickly from the taxi, Hazel brushed a woven chair.   12
Numbers   3   Please get some price tags for 10¢, 29¢, 38¢, 47¢, and 56¢.   12
Symbols   4   "Why must I leave?" she asked. "Well," we said, "why not?"   12
Technique   5   Depress the shift lock and type line 4 in all-capital letters.

        | 1 | 2 | 3 | 4 | 5 | 6 | 7 | 8 | 9 | 10 | 11 | 12

1- AND 3-MINUTE TIMINGS

Take two 1-minute timings on each paragraph. Then take one 3-minute timing on the entire selection. Use single spacing for the 1-minute timings and double spacing for the 3-minute timing.

6   The Inca Indians lived hundreds of years ago near what   12
7   is now Peru; they were a great nation well known for unique   24
8   buildings, which can still be seen in jungle ruins.   34

9   The temples that stand can be searched for clues about   12
10   these people and their way of life. Some knowledge exists,   24
11   for we know that they were a people of many skills.   34

12   The Incas still have lots of secrets which are lost in   12
13   the haze of their culture. The best kept secret is why the   24
14   Incas vanished. In time, we may learn the secret.   34

        | 1 | 2 | 3 | 4 | 5 | 6 | 7 | 8 | 9 | 10 | 11 | 12   SI 1.24

JOB 51-1. PERSONAL-BUSINESS LETTER

Standard format. Use your own return address and the current date; use your own name as the writer. Body 127 words.

B&B Agency / 4 Rockefeller Plaza / New York, NY 10020 / Ladies and Gentlemen: / In our class in office practice, our teacher showed your new film, You CAN Succeed. All of us enjoyed it very much. I thought the film was really good for young people who are trying to decide whether they want a career in business. ¶ Our Business Club will hold its state meeting next year. As I am a member of the group that will plan the program, I should like to suggest this film for one of our sessions at the state meeting. ¶ Will you please let me know as soon as possible how much it would cost our organization to rent the film You CAN Succeed for viewing next March. / Yours truly,

LESSON 243

CLINIC

GOAL
▪ To build competency on selected keyboard reaches.

FORMAT
▪ Single spacing   60-space line

PRETEST 1

Take a 30-second timing on each line. Proofread and score each timing.

1 The spider created webs in the corner of the flower garden. 12
2 In her blazer she ran an errand before the volcano erupted. 12
3 The reply was read prior to her resigning the union regime. 12
4 His nephew used a new pewter bowl to hold the boiling stew. 12
  | 1 | 2 | 3 | 4 | 5 | 6 | 7 | 8 | 9 | 10 | 11 | 12

PRACTICE 1

Type lines 5–10 four times. If you averaged two or fewer errors in the Pretest, repeat individual lines; otherwise, repeat each block of lines for accuracy gains.

5 we weaved cobweb sweet mower welds lower weans wept were we
6 ew pewter nephew askew jewel sewer views newer drew stew ew
7 io lotion ration axiom union prior ratio adios zion lion io

8 er blazer errand erupt ergot erode miner truer errs seer er
9 re resign regime reign relax reply resin realm ream read re
10 oi voices avoids point going coins voids toils boil soil oi

POSTTEST 1

Repeat Pretest 1. Proofread and score each timing.

PRETEST 2

Take a 30-second timing on each line. Proofread and score each timing.

11 The soloist sang high treble notes at the opera last night. 12
12 She poured a sample of the savory sauce through this spout. 12
13 The poster on the power pole is flopping in the brisk wind. 12
14 He tried to barter at the mart for a strap for an old cart. 12
  | 1 | 2 | 3 | 4 | 5 | 6 | 7 | 8 | 9 | 10 | 11 | 12

PRACTICE 2

Type lines 15–20 four times. If you averaged two or fewer errors in the Pretest, repeat individual lines; otherwise, repeat each block of lines for accuracy gains.

15 rt assert barter blurt parts dirty carts sorts pert mart rt
16 tr treble trying tract trend triad tress strap tray trek tr
17 op floppy oppose optic opted scope opera opals cope open op

18 as ascend ashore aspen aside toast yeast aster cast fast as
19 sa sample safety salon sappy sauce savor sauna sake said sa
20 po powder poster power spots polyp polar spout poke pole po

POSTTEST 2

Repeat Pretest 2. Proofread and score each timing.

FORMATTING SMALL ENVELOPES (No. 6¾)

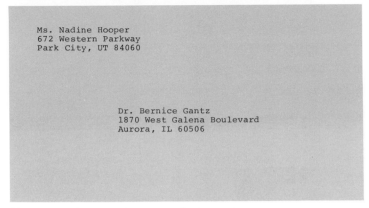

```
Ms. Nadine Hooper
672 Western Parkway
Park City, UT 84060




        Dr. Bernice Gantz
        1870 West Galena Boulevard
        Aurora, IL 60506
```

No. 6¾ (6½ by 3⅝ inches, or 165 by 92 mm)
Metric: No. C7/6 (162 by 81 mm, or 6⅜ by 3⅛ inches)

Envelopes contain two addresses—the mailing address, to which the letter is sent, and the writer's return address.

1. To format a return address, begin on line 3, in 5 spaces from the left edge. Single-space the address.
2. To format the mailing address, begin the addressee's name and address on line 12, at 20 spaces from the left edge of the envelope. Single-space the address.

In all addresses, type the city, state, and ZIP Code on one line. Remember to leave 1 space between the state and the ZIP Code number.

FOLDING LETTERS FOR SMALL ENVELOPES

To fold a letter for a small envelope, bring the bottom edge up to ⅜ inch (10 mm) from the top edge, fold the right-hand third toward the left, fold the left-hand third toward the right. Then insert the last crease into the envelope.

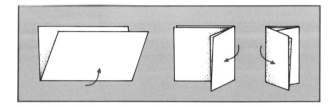

JOB 51-2. ADDRESSING SMALL ENVELOPES

Address three envelopes as follows: (1) as shown in the illustration of the small envelope above, (2) for the letter in Job 51-1, page 89, and (3) for the letter in Job 50-2, pages 87–88. Workbook 55.

LESSON 52

GOALS
- To recognize how numbers are expressed while typing sentences.
- To produce two personal-business letters, with addressed envelopes.

FORMAT
- Single spacing   60-space line   5-space tab

LAB 3

NUMBER STYLE

Type lines 1–4 once. Then repeat lines 1–4 or take a series of 1-minute timings.

```
1  Jack ordered five boxes of pads and eight boxes of pencils.   12
2  This aircraft will hold 152 passengers and 12 crew members.   12
3  Fourteen members of the panel voted in favor of my quizzes.   12
4  The room is precisely 8.5 meters long and 4.57 meters wide.   12
   |  1  |  2  |  3  |  4  |  5  |  6  |  7  |  8  |  9  |  10  |  11  |  12
```

Spell out numbers from *1* through *10*; use figures for numbers above *10*. (**Exception:** Spell out any number that begins a sentence.)

Only *three* offices have been painted.
Send *12* brochures and *75* order forms to Ms. Ames.
Fifteen applicants were interviewed today.

In technical copy and for emphasis, use figures for numbers: *4 p.m., 3 liters, 2.5 miles, 7 spaces, 12 lines, page 9, $8.*

JOB 242-1. INCOME STATEMENT
Standard format with leaders.

Central City Cleaners

INCOME STATEMENT

For the Year Ended December 31, 19--

REVENUE
    Sales $148,000.00

EXPENSES
    Insurance Expense .... $ 4,000.00
    Repairs Expense 14,000.00
    Salaries Expense 63,000.00
    Supplies Expense .... <u>18,000.00</u>
        Total Expenses ....   <u>99,000.00</u>

NET INCOME BEFORE INCOME TAXES ... $ 49,000.00

PROVISION FOR INCOME TAXES ....   <u>13,230.00</u>

NET INCOME AFTER INCOME TAXES ....   <u>$ 35,770.00</u>

DISTRIBUTION OF NET INCOME
    Melody J. Barnheiser $17,885.00
    Martin W. Barnheiser .... <u>17,885.00</u>
NET INCOME ALLOCATED ....   <u>$ </u>

JOB 242-2. BALANCE SHEET
Standard format with leaders.

Central City Cleaners

BALANCE SHEET

For the Year Ended December 31, 19--

ASSETS
    Cash $14,000.00
    Accounts Receivable 400.00
    Equipment 12,100.00
    Machinery 65,000.00
    Supplies .... <u>100.00</u>
        Total Assets ....   <u>$ </u>

LIABILITIES
    Loans Payable .... $ 5,000.00
    Income Taxes Payable .... <u>3,230.00</u>
        Total Liabilities .... $ 8,230.00

PARTNERS' EQUITY
    Melody J. Barnheiser, Capital ... $41,685.00
    Martin W. Barnheiser, Capital ... <u>41,685.00</u>
        Total Partners' Equity $83,370.00
        Total Liabilities and
               Partners' Equity ...   <u>$ </u>

Take two 30-second timings on lines 5–7, or type the paragraph twice.

5 If there is a blaze in a home near us, we can be so excited 12

6 that we want to dash to see it.   So many observers may come 24

7 that they quite often jeopardize the work of fire fighters. 36

| 1 | 2 | 3 | 4 | 5 | 6 | 7 | 8 | 9 | 10 | 11 | 12

JOB 52-1. PERSONAL-BUSINESS LETTER

Standard format. Address an envelope. Envelope: Workbook 57. Body 132 words.

Notice that the number 5 has been circled—the proofreaders' mark for spelling out a numeral.

62 Hadley Avenue / Dayton, OH 45419 / October 19, 19— / LaViva Foods, Inc. / 1200 East Brady Street / Erie, PA 16505 / Ladies and Gentlemen: / Yesterday I bought ⑤ LaViva frozen pizzas for a party I had last night. Although I baked the pizzas as directed, the crust was tough, and the sauce was so bitter that we could not eat them. I had to throw them out. ¶ Today I took my receipt to the Fair Price market where I bought the pizzas. The manager gave me a refund; then he asked me to write to you because he thought that you should know about this problem. ¶ I hope that you will check this matter so that your food products will always be up to your usual high standards. The code number on the boxes was CX-463. / Yours truly, / Peggy Hamner

JOB 52-2. PERSONAL-BUSINESS LETTER

Standard format. Use your own return address and the current date; use your name as the writer. Address an envelope. Envelope: Workbook 57. Body 122 words.

Mr. Edward L. Brown, Manager / The Skyline Motel / Mercer, PA 16137 / Dear Mr. Brown: / Last week my two friends and I stayed at your motel for a weekend of skiing in the area. As members of the Skyline Ski Club and guests at your motel, we were to be given free ski-tow passes. ¶ When I got home, however, I checked the bill dated _____ [*fill in last Sunday's date*] and discovered that we were charged $36 for the use of the ski tow. Since we are all members of the Skyline Ski Club, we should not have been charged for the use of these facilities. ¶ I would appreciate your taking the time to correct our bill and send me a check for the sum of $36, the amount of the overcharge. My address is at the top of this letter. / Sincerely,

LESSON 242

GOALS
■ To select possessives of singular and plural nouns correctly while typing sentences.
■ To type an income statement and a balance sheet.

FORMAT
■ Single spacing   60-space line   Tabs as needed

LAB 29

POSSESSIVES OF NOUNS

Type lines 1–4 once, providing the correct possessive form of the noun. Edit your copy as your teacher reads the answers. Then retype lines 1–4 from your edited copy.

1 All (client's/clients') orders deserve special treatment, Diaz claims.

2 Any (client's/clients') order gets quick treatment from Maxine Hubert.

3 One (partner's/partners') share in the firm is small, according to Jed.

4 Both (partner's/partners') shares equal less than half the total stock.

30-SECOND TIMINGS

Take two 30-second timings on lines 5–7, or type the paragraph twice.

5   In 1980 there were 45 centers located within 150 miles   12

6 of one another. Of these centers, 23 were designed to work   24

7 at least 6 days a week. Others operated during all 7 days.   36
   | 1 | 2 | 3 | 4 | 5 | 6 | 7 | 8 | 9 | 10 | 11 | 12

"OK" TIMINGS

Type as many 30-second "OK" (errorless) timings as possible out of three attempts on lines 8–10. Then repeat the effort on lines 11–13.

8 Jasper quietly viewed the fox, zebra, kangaroo, and camels.   12

9 The six zebras very quickly jumped out of the winter glaze.   24

10 He quickly trained a dozen brown foxes to jump over a gate.   36

11 Six jumbo elephants quickly moved the wagon from the blaze.   12

12 Jack quietly gave some dog owners most of his prize boxers.   24

13 Bo ran quickly from the zone when dogs jumped over an exit.   36
    | 1 | 2 | 3 | 4 | 5 | 6 | 7 | 8 | 9 | 10 | 11 | 12

LESSON 53

GOALS
- To identify how numbers are expressed while typing sentences.
- To format two business letters.

FORMAT
- Single spacing   60-space line   5-space tab

LAB 3

NUMBER STYLE

Type lines 1–4 once. Then repeat lines 1–4 or take a series of 1-minute timings.

1 Eighty-eight students will tour Europe for five long weeks. 12
2 Just mix 12.5 grams of powder in 10.5 liters of the liquid. 12
3 I will purchase 13 pairs of socks, 15 blazers, and 22 ties. 12
4 Yes, 14 students from my college are among the 77 scholars. 12
  | 1 | 2 | 3 | 4 | 5 | 6 | 7 | 8 | 9 | 10 | 11 | 12

12-SECOND TIMINGS

Type each line four times, or take four 12-second timings on each line. For each timing, type with no more than one error.

5 Most of the good guys in the movie were wearing white hats. 12
6 Her jolly friends have been glad that she has done so well. 12
7 He has found that a bit of music is a help when he studies. 12

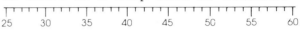

25   30   35   40   45   50   55   60

FORMATTING BUSINESS LETTERS

Workbook 59–60.

A business letter represents a company, not an individual, and is therefore typed on printed letterhead—official company stationery on which are printed the company's name, address, and telephone number.

The parts of the business letter—heading, opening, body, closing—are similar to the parts of the personal-business letter. However, there are some differences.

1. Most of the heading information is already included in the letterhead; only the date must be added.

2. In a business letter the closing includes not only the writer's name but also his or her title. (Together the name and title lines are called the *writer's identification*.)

3. The closing in a business letter includes the typist's initials (see page 93).

To format a business letter: (1) Type the date on line 15, beginning at the center. (2) Type the writer's title on the line below the writer's name, aligned with it. (3) Type the initials of the typist at the left margin, a double space below the writer's title. Type the initials without periods in either lowercase letters or in all-capital letters.

This format is most commonly used in business and is considered to be the standard format. It is known as *modified-block style*.

JOB 53-1. BUSINESS LETTER

Type the letter on page 93.   Standard format.   Workbook 61, 63–64. Body 178 words.

JOB 53-2. BUSINESS LETTER

Standard format. Workbook 65–66. Body 111 words.

Remember

Titles of books and magazines are underscored with an unbroken line.

[*Today's date*] / Ms. Jane Petit / 462 West Omaha Avenue / Akron, OH 44301 / Dear Ms. Petit: / Thank you for your letter telling us how much you enjoyed the story that appeared in the June issue of Young Views about new careers in the health field. / We are sending you the booklet you asked for, Your Future as a Health Worker. There is, of course, no charge for the booklet. / We hope that you will continue to follow your plans to train for a job in the health professions. If we can be of any further service to you, please write to us or call our toll-free number: (800) 555-6000. / Very truly yours, / Henry J. Templer / Editor in Chief [*Your initials*]

JOB 241-1. BALANCE SHEET

Standard format. Fill in missing figures.

Schroeder and Van Tine

BALANCE SHEET

For the Year Ended December 31, 19--

A S S E T S

In very detailed balance sheets, major entries are spread centered.

Current Assets

Cash	$ 7,000.00	
Petty Cash	15.00	
Exchange Fund	25.00	
Notes Receivable	4,000.00	
Interest Receivable	160.00	
Accounts Receivable (Less Allowance for Bad Debts)	5,489.00	
Merchandise Inventory	34,000.00	
Prepaid Insurance	800.00	
Total Current Assets		$

Fixed Assets

You will know that your figures are correct if your Total Assets line is the same as your Total Liabilities and Partners' Equity line. The same totals show that the balance sheet "balances."

Land	6,000.00	
Building (Less Accumulated Depreciation)	14,600.00	
Delivery Equipment (Less Accumulated Depreciation)	3,690.00	
Office Equipment (Less Accumulated Depreciation)	4,749.00	
Total Fixed Assets		
Total Assets		$

L I A B I L I T I E S

Current Liabilities

Notes Payable	$ 2,600.00	
Interest Payable	150.00	
Accounts Payable	7,000.00	
Salaries Payable	290.00	
Employees' Withholding Taxes Payable	300.00	
FICA Taxes Payable	200.00	
Sales Taxes Payable	400.00	
Total Current Liabilities		$

Long-Term Liabilities

Mortgage Payable		12,000.00
Total Liabilities		$

P A R T N E R S '   E Q U I T Y

George S. Schroeder, Capital	$28,794.00	
James Van Tine, Capital	28,794.00	
Total Partners' Equity		
Total Liabilities and Partners' Equity		$

LaVIVA FOODS, Inc.

1200 East Brady Street
Erie, Pennsylvania 16505
814–555–7000

↓ 15

July 14, 19--

↓ 5

Ms. Peggy Hamner
62 Hadley Avenue
Dayton, OH 45419

↓ 2

Dear Ms. Hamner:

↓ 2

We are very sorry to learn that you could not eat the
four LaViva frozen pizzas you bought at your local
store last week. Thank you for writing to us about
this matter. We want all our customers to be pleased
with our products.

↓ 2

When our pizzas leave our plant, they are fresh, with
all the flavor frozen in; but sometimes the shipper
or the grocer does not put the pizzas in the freezer
right away. The food begins to defrost, and when at
last the pizzas are put in the freezer case, they
have lost their true flavor. There is nothing we can
do about this.

↓ 2

We want to give you a gift for trying to help us. If
you will take this letter to your Fair Price store,
your grocer will give you free $10 worth of LaViva
frozen foods of your choice. We hope that you will
enjoy these great foods and that you will continue to
buy our pizzas.

↓ 2

Sincerely yours,

↓ 4

Closing
Writer's name
  and job title

Dominic Sparanta
Vice President

↓ 2

km

BUSINESS LETTER, STANDARD FORMAT

LESSON 241

GOALS
- To identify possessives of singular and plural nouns while typing sentences.
- To type 47/5'/3e.
- To type a balance sheet supplying missing figures.

FORMAT
- Single spacing   60-space line   5-space tab and other tabs as needed

LAB 29

POSSESSIVES OF NOUNS

Type lines 1–4 once. Then repeat lines 1–4 or take a series of 1-minute timings.

1 Her boss's answer was different from their bosses' answers. 12
2 This clerk's records are neater than other clerks' records. 12
3 One child requested six toys in that children's department. 12
4 The Rizzo's van left already, but the Joneses' van has not. 12
   | 1 | 2 | 3 | 4 | 5 | 6 | 7 | 8 | 9 | 10 | 11 | 12

1- AND 5-MINUTE TIMINGS

Take two 1-minute timings on each paragraph. Then take one 5-minute timing on the entire selection. Use single spacing for the 1-minute timings and double-spacing for the 5-minute timing.

1'

5   If a firm contracts with a data control center to pre- 12
6 pare its records, the center will handle at least four main 24
7 financial documents--balance sheets, income statements, and 36
8 schedules of accounts receivable and accounts payable. 47
9   The relationship between what a business owns and what 12
10 it owes is revealed on a balance sheet. It, too, is needed 24
11 each month, quarter, and year. The balance sheet expresses 36
12 how a company's assets and liabilities are distributed. 47
13   An income statement contains the income and expenses a 12
14 company has for a month, a quarter, or a year. Summarizing 24
15 these two categories in one report allows a firm to analyze 36
16 the vital relationship between its income and expenses. 47
17   Businesses must keep a close record of their customers 12
18 and their creditors. Customers are referred to as accounts 24
19 receivable, and creditors are called accounts payable. The 36
20 lists are prepared with names, amounts owed, and dates. 47
21   A data control center has the capability to input data 12
22 and readjust data, permitting numerous analyses and compar- 24
23 isons. A firm's future depends upon its ability to analyze 36
24 its statements and make careful long-range predictions. 47
   | 1 | 2 | 3 | 4 | 5 | 6 | 7 | 8 | 9 | 10 | 11 | 12   SI 1.72

LESSON 54

GOALS
- To express numbers correctly while typing sentences.
- To type 34/3'/5e.
- To format business letters with enclosures.
- To address large envelopes and fold letters to fit in large envelopes.

FORMAT
- Single spacing   60-space line   5-space tab

LAB 3

Type lines 1–4 once, correcting any errors in number-style rules. Edit your copy as your teacher reads the answers. Then retype lines 1–4 from your edited copy.

NUMBER STYLE

1 Joann listed 100 items to be discussed in the next meeting.

2 The engineer said that the precise diameter is 1.75 meters.

3 We need 10 samples, but they shipped us only 4 or 5.

4 426 women attended the huge convention.

1- AND 3-MINUTE TIMINGS

Take two 1-minute timings on each paragraph. Then take one 3-minute timing on the entire selection. Use single spacing for the 1-minute timings and double spacing for the 3-minute timing.

```
                 1              2              3              4    1'
5        Health foods may seem ridiculous to some of us; but if   12
              5                6              7              8
6  you enjoy pure and natural foods, you know what a change it     24
              9              10             11
7  makes in your life when you eat all-natural foods.              34
                                                                   —
             12             13             14             15
8        It is a fact that most people who eat health foods all    12
             16             17             18             19
9  the time require less medical care.  If you play a sport or     24
             20             21             22
10  exercise and get plenty of rest, you are sensible.             34
                                                                   —
             23             24             25             26
11        Explore health foods like fruits, fresh produce, nuts,   12
             27             28             29             30
12  grains, and dairy foods; they make up a basic diet that all    24
             31             32             33             34
13  need to preserve their strength for zestful lives.             34
   |  1  |  2  |  3  |  4  |  5  |  6  |  7  |  8  |  9  |  10  |  11  |  12   SI 1.26
```

FORMATTING ENCLOSURE NOTATIONS

Whenever an item is sent within a letter, the word *Enclosure* is typed below the reference initials. The enclosure notation reminds the sender to include the item, tells the receiver to look for the item, and serves as a record on the file copy. For more than one item, type *2 Enclosures, 3 Enclosures,* and so on.

```
                              John Harman Jones
                              President


TCW
3 Enclosures
```

JOB 240-1. COMPARATIVE INCOME STATEMENT
Standard format. Turn lengthwise.

Martin and Bellingham, Inc.

COMPARATIVE INCOME STATEMENT ~~SUMMARY~~ AND MAY 31,

~~For the Month Ended~~ April 30, 19—

	APRIL 30	MAY 31
SALES	$48,431	$59,651
COST OF GOODS SOLD		
Merchandise Inventory, April 1 .... $16,401		$16,512
Merchandise Purchases 35,208		33,147
Total Available for Sale $51,609		$49,659
Merchandise Inventory, April 30 ... 16,512		14,185
Cost of Merchandise Sold	35,097	35,474
GROSS PROFIT ON SALES	$13,334	$24,177
EXPENSES		
Depreciation of Equipment .... $ 400		$ 400
Utilities Expense 361		450
Rent Expense 2,500		2,500
Sales Expense 4,341		4,518
Total Expenses	7,602	7,868
NET INCOME BEFORE TAXES	$ 5,732	$16,309

JOB 240-2. COMPARATIVE INCOME STATEMENT
Standard format. Turn lengthwise. Add figures for May, indicated in the column on the left, and make appropriate changes in the headings.

Data for May

Sales: $26,943.35

Inventory, May 1:
$12,613.50

Inventory Purchases:
$18,732.90

Inventory, May 31:
$19,290.60

Depreciation: $1,000

Utilities: $481.30

Rent: $2,500

Sales: $5,109.20

Note: You will have to calculate the missing figures from the data given you.

Schroeder and Van Tine

INCOME STATEMENT

For the Month Ended April 30, 19—

SALES		$29,453.28
COST OF MERCHANDISE		
Inventory, April 1	$15,267.00	
Inventory Purchases	8,476.50	
Total Available	$23,743.50	
Inventory, April 30	12,613.50	
Cost of Merchandise Sold ...		11,130.00
GROSS PROFIT ON SALES		$18,323.28
EXPENSES		
Depreciation of Equipment	$ 1,000.00	
Utilities Expense	520.43	
Rent Expense	2,500.00	
Sales Expense	5,436.84	
Total Expenses		9,457.27
NET INCOME BEFORE TAXES		$ 8,866.01

JOB 54-1. BUSINESS LETTER

Standard format. Prepare the small addressed envelope that is to be enclosed.
Workbook 67–68. Body 94 words.

(Today's date) Mr. Rudolph Martino / 412 Ash Street / Terre Haute, IN 47804 / Dear Mr. Martino:

We are pleased that you plan to enter our pizza bake-off contest and test your skills in making pizza. ¶ The first round of the bake-off will be on Sunday, May 10, at 1 p.m. at the Erie Home Show. You must be 18 years old or under to enter, and we ask that you bring all your own supplies. Twenty-six persons have already entered. ¶ If you will need a hotel room in Erie, please use the enclosed envelope to send me your reservation request. Good luck next Sunday. / Sincerely yours, / Alfred J. Leary, Director of Public Relations / Enclosure

Workbook 69–70.

FORMATTING LARGE ENVELOPES (NO. 10)

To format a large envelope:

1. (*a*) Type a return address. Begin on line 3, 5 spaces from the left edge. Single-space the address. **Or:** (*b*) If the envelope already has a printed return address, type the sender's name on the line above the address. Block the name if the address is blocked; center the name if the address is centered.

2. Begin the mailing address on line 14, 40 spaces from the left edge. Single-space the address, and remember to leave only 1 space between the state and the ZIP Code.

FORMATTING SPECIAL ENVELOPE DIRECTIONS

To format special directions:

1. Type an on-arrival direction (such as *Personal* or *Confidential*) on line 9, aligned at left with the return address. Use capital and small letters, and underscore the direction.

2. Type a mailing direction (such as *Special Delivery* or *Registered*) on line 9, ending about 5 spaces from the right edge of the envelope. Use all-capital letters. Do not underscore.

Nathan Parks

THOMPSON & EVANS

LAWYERS BUILDING
PITTSBURGH, P.A. 15219

<u>Confidential</u>

SPECIAL DELIVERY

Ms. Linda T. Humphries
5650 Southeast Fremont Street
Atlanta, GA 30315

No. 10 (9½ by 4⅛ inches, or 241 by 105 mm)
Metric: No. DL (220 by 110 mm, or 8⅝ by 4⅜ inches)

JOB 239-2. BANK RECONCILIATION STATEMENT
Standard format with leaders.

```
Bank Statement Balance, May 31                    $2,961.17
    Deposit in Transit, May 29      $461.20
    Deposit in Transit, May 30       390.16          851.36
              Subtotal                             $3,812.53
    Outstanding Check  # 382      $  29.17
    Outstanding Check  # 383         36.45
    Outstanding Check  # 385        806.14          871.76
              Adjusted Bank Balance               $2,940.77


Checkbook Balance, May 31                         $2,948.72
    Bank Service Charge           $   2.00
    Stop Payment Charge               5.00
    Error in Arithmetic                .95            7.95
              Adjusted Checkbook Balance          $2,940.77
```

LESSON 240

GOALS
- To recognize possessives of singular and plural nouns while typing sentences.
- To format and type comparative income statements.

FORMAT
- Single spacing   60-space line   Tabs as needed

LAB 29

Type lines 1–4 once. Then repeat lines 1–4 or take a series of 1-minute timings.

POSSESSIVES OF NOUNS

(Sing.) 1 The manager's reply was extremely helpful to Jackie Quimby.   12
(Pl.)   2 The managers' replies were very helpful to Fred and Maxine.   12
(Sing.) 3 A new employee's chart must be sent to a dozen departments.   12
(Pl.)   4 New employees' charts must be duplicated by your secretary.   12
           | 1 | 2 | 3 | 4 | 5 | 6 | 7 | 8 | 9 | 10 | 11 | 12

Plural nouns that end in *s* show ownership by adding an apostrophe: both *sisters'* husbands, those *managers'* offices, two *secretaries'* desks. Singular nouns—and plural nouns that do *not* end in *s*—show ownership by adding an apostrophe plus *s*: my *sister's* job, a *manager's* office, one *secretary's* desk; both *women's* preferences, the *children's* schools.

FORMATTING COMPARATIVE INCOME STATEMENTS

A comparative income statement allows a company to "compare" the income summary of one quarter with another, one month with another, and so on.
   To format a comparative income statement:

1. Use standard format for financial statements.
2. Center a braced heading over the appropriate columns.
3. Type an underscore below the braced heading the full width of the columns being braced.

JOB 54-2. ADDRESSING LARGE ENVELOPES

Address three envelopes, using the copy given in (1) the illustration at the bottom of page 95, (2) the letter in Job 54-1 on the top of page 95, and (3) the letter in Job 53-1 on pages 92–93. Workbook 71, 73.

FOLDING A BUSINESS LETTER

To fold a letter for a large envelope, (1) fold up the bottom third of the paper, (2) fold the top third over the bottom third, and (3) insert the letter into the envelope, with the last crease going first.

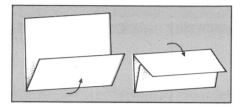

LESSON 55

CLINIC

GOALS
- To build typing speed.
- To type 34/3′/5e.

FORMAT
- Single spacing   60-space line   5-space tab

KEYBOARDING SKILLS

Type lines 1–4 once. Then do what line 5 tells you to do. Repeat lines 1–4, or take a series of 1-minute timings.

Speed	1	Kay got the forms for the firm and may also work with them.	12
Accuracy	2	Six jumbo elephants quickly moved the wagon from the blaze.	12
Numbers	3	You can take the 1:38 bus, the 4:56 bus, or the 8:47 train.	12
Symbols	4	Grant & Harris developed the Kenyan, Smith & Blake project.	12
Technique	5	Retype line 3. Underscore only the figures—not the words.	

| 1 | 2 | 3 | 4 | 5 | 6 | 7 | 8 | 9 | 10 | 11 | 12 |

PRETEST

Take a 3-minute timing on lines 6–14.

6   A batik is a dyed cloth that has hot wax painted on it   12

7   to form a design. The artist melts wax, tints it different   24

8   colors, paints a design, and then dyes each cloth.   34

9   But some artists paint the cloth with clear wax. Then   12

10   the batik is dyed again and again, using many colors. Just   24

11   the part not coated with that wax is then colored.   34

12   The second method requires more work on the part of an   12

13   artist, but the colors in the finished batik will have more   24

14   zest and look brighter to those who see the cloth.   34

| 1 | 2 | 3 | 4 | 5 | 6 | 7 | 8 | 9 | 10 | 11 | 12 | SI 1.26

Take two 3-minute timings on lines 8–20. Circle your errors.

```
                1               2               3               4
 8      Businesses are finding that the management of the many   12
           5             6               7             8
 9  records they have to keep is sometimes best performed by an   24
               9               10              11              12
10  automated data control center.  Data can be communicated by   36
           13              14              15              16
11  a terminal from an individual's business to a center across   48
           17              18              19              20
12  town or across the country.  It's amazing how efficiently a   60
           21
13  center can operate.                                           64
               22              23              24              25
14      Both financial records and correspondence are recorded   76
           26              27              28              29
15  for a firm to replay, edit, or merge.  A center offers many   88
           30              31              32              33
16  ways of storage and retrieval with such exactness that will  100
           34              35              36              37
17  justify its existence for many large firms.  Companies that  112
           38              39              40              41
18  require that data be compared and analyzed are impressed by  124
           42              43              44              45
19  the labor saved when different kinds of data can be merged,  136
           46              47
20  printed, and distributed.                                    141
    |  1  |  2  |  3  |  4  |  5  |  6  |  7  |  8  |  9  |  10  |  11  |  12    SI 1.69
```

JOB 239-1. BANK RECONCILIATION STATEMENT

Standard format for financial statements.

Martin and Bellingham, Inc.
Bank Reconciliation Statement
Month Ended May 31, 19—

Bank Statement Balance, May 31....		$1,624.88
Deposit in Transit, May 29		763.18
Subtotal		$2,388.06
Outstanding Check #52 ...	$ 24.09	
Outstanding Check #53 ...	423.76	447.85
Adjusted ~~Corrected~~ Bank Balance		$1,940.21
Checkbook Balance, May 31		$1,942.21
Bank Service Charge		2.00
Adjusted Checkbook Balance		$1,940.21

PRACTICE	Practice the words in the Pretest on which you made errors or slowed down. Type each word at least three times.
30-SECOND TIMINGS	Take three 30-second timings on each paragraph on page 96. Try to increase your speed each time.
1-MINUTE TIMINGS	Take two 1-minute timings on each paragraph on page 96. Try to maintain your 30-second speed.
POSTTEST	Repeat the Pretest on page 96 twice to see how much your skill has improved.

LESSON 56

UNIT 10 FORMATTING TABLES

GOALS
- To express numbers correctly while typing sentences.
- To format 2-column tables and 3-column tables.

FORMAT
- Single spacing   60-space line   Tabs as needed

LAB 3	Type lines 1–4 once, correcting any errors in number-style rules. Edit your copy as your teacher reads the answers. Then retype lines 1–4 from your edited copy.

NUMBER STYLE

1 Over 250 people attended the party for Jacqueline and Gary.

2 90 pens were left on the desk for their art instructor.

3 About 5 or 6 members of the club attended the meeting.

4 6 students helped the 120 senior citizens plan that tour.

30-SECOND TIMINGS

Take two 30-second timings on lines 5–7, or type the paragraph twice.

5 All of us must make decisions every day. Some of these are   12

6 quite routine, but others can be of major importance. Good   24

7 citizens work at always making logical and exact decisions.   36

| 1 | 2 | 3 | 4 | 5 | 6 | 7 | 8 | 9 | 10 | 11 | 12

FORMATTING TABLES

A table lists data in columns and rows. For quick understanding and easy reference, most tables are worded concisely.

A table can be included as part of a letter, memo, or report, or it can be displayed on a separate sheet of paper.

When a table is typed on a separate sheet of paper, it is centered horizontally and vertically. Standard formatting instructions apply. Use double spacing unless directed to do otherwise.

To format the body of a table horizontally, follow these steps:

1. Clear the margins and tabs on the machine.

2. Identify a "key line." Find the longest entry in each column and add 6 spaces between the columns, as shown below and on page 98:

```
To Kill a Mockingbird       Shakespeare
              123456
```

(**Note:** Six spaces are standard, but you may use any number of spaces that will make the table attractive and easy to read.)

(*Continued on next page*)

JOB 238-2. RULED TABLE

Using the information in the computer printout that is illustrated, prepare a three-column ruled table. Standard format. Arrange last names first.

```
ACCOUNTS RECEIVABLE     MAY 1 19--      MARTIN AND BELLINGHAM INC
BRECHAK        BARRY      9310 WEST SECOND ST              300
CHUANG         LEAH       257 NORTH OLMSTED AVE            450
GADBOIS        DEBORAH    4608 CENTRAL PKWY                325
HARAKAY        ALLISON    4983 MAIN ST                     250
KELLY          HOWARD     793 SOUTHERN BLVD                150
PADAVANIJI     PHATAMA    ROUTE 7 BOX 34                   350
STABLEIN       ROBERT     893 SOUTH PADDINGSTON AVE        200
TICKNOR        STEPHEN    87 WINDING WAY                  1000
VAGEDES        BRIDGET    79 SOUTH RIVERSIDE DR APT 25      50
```

JOB 238-3. RULED TABLE

Using the information in the computer printout that is illustrated, prepare a ruled table. Standard format. Arrange alphabetically.

```
ACCOUNTS PAYABLE    MAY 1 19--       MARTIN AND BELLINGHAM INC
FIRST NATIONAL BANK       68 MARTINDALE SQ              4000
FIRST CITY LOAN           70 MARTINDALE SQ              2000
KOCOL AND KREUTZ          14 SOUTH MAIN ST              1000
VREELAND AND ZUMMO        487 CENTRAL BLVD               280
CENTRAL SUPPLY            87 NORTH LUDLOW AVE            200
GABRIEL AND LAVIGNE       89 NORTH MAIN ST               140
ATTALLA CLEANING INC      45 EAST MIDDLEBORNE AVE         50
SCHUH OFFICE SUPPLIES     135 EAST DIXIE ST               25
```

LESSON 239

GOAL
- To format and type leadered tables from handwritten data.

FORMAT
- Single spacing   60-space line   Tabs as needed

KEYBOARDING SKILLS

Type lines 1–4 once. Then practice using the apostrophe in line 5. Repeat lines 1–4, or take a series of 1-minute timings.

Speed
1 They may end the big fight by the lake by the usual signal. 12

Accuracy
2 Fred amazed Pat by how quickly he waxed a single jumbo van. 12

Numbers
3 The dates to remember are 1910, 1928, 1939, 1947, and 1956. 12

Symbols
4 Two hyphens typed without spaces--like this--make the dash. 12

Punctuation
5 it's they're weren't you'll Mary's Joneses' writers' lion's

| 1 | 2 | 3 | 4 | 5 | 6 | 7 | 8 | 9 | 10 | 11 | 12

PREVIEW PRACTICE

Type lines 6 and 7 twice as a preview to the 3-minute timings on page 383.

Accuracy
6 compared analyzed terminal retrieval automated communicated

Speed
7 ways they many when firm that have best data both with such

3. From the center of the page, back-space-center the key line and set the left margin stop at the point to which you backspaced.

4. Space across the paper to the start of the next column (the width of column 1 plus 6 spaces) and set a tab stop. No matter how many columns there are in the table, use the margin stop for the first column and a tab stop for each additional column.

5. When you type a table, use your tabulator to move from column to column as you type each line.

JOB 56-1. TWO-COLUMN TABLE
Format a copy of the table shown below. Standard format. Half sheet of paper.

Title

CLASSICS FOR TEENAGERS

Body with two columns

Animal Farm	Orwell
Frankenstein	Shelley
Lord of the Flies	Golding
Moby Dick	Melville
Romeo and Juliet	Shakespeare
To Kill a Mockingbird	Lee

Column width is determined by longest item in a column.

Key line

To Kill a Mockingbird   Shakespeare
123456

JOB 56-2. TWO-COLUMN TABLE
Standard format. Half sheet of paper.

GIRLS' LACROSSE RECORDS

Goals in a game	Chris Chester
Goals in a season	Charlene Hvorecky
Goals by a freshman	Lynn Armstrong
Goals by a sophomore	Barb McCoy
Goals by a junior	Karen Schultz
Goals by a senior	Lee Van Ban
Assists in a game	Chris Chester
Assists in a season	Gwen Chan

JOB 56-3. THREE-COLUMN TABLE
Standard format. Half sheet of paper.

HOME TEAMS IN VARIOUS STATES

Georgia	Atlanta	Falcons
Maryland	Baltimore	Colts
Illinois	Chicago	Bears
Missouri	Kansas City	Chiefs
Missouri	St. Louis	Cardinals
Washington	Seattle	Seahawks

GOALS
- To select the correct contraction or possessive pronoun while typing sentences.
- To format and type tables from computer printouts.

FORMAT
- Single spacing   60-space line   Tabs as needed

LAB 28

Type lines 1–4 once, providing the appropriate answers. Edit your copy as your teacher reads the answers. Then retype lines 1–4 from your edited copy.

CONTRACTIONS AND POSSESSIVE PRONOUNS

Workbook 581–582.

1 (Its/It's) an excellent choice because (its/it's) price has just fallen.

2 (Your/You're) responsible for handling (your/you're) dozen accounts, Myrna.

3 (Their/They're) quick decision surprised us, but (their/they're) right to go.

4 (Their/They're) agent, Jack Waverly, said that (their/they're) eager to sell.

12-SECOND TIMINGS

Type each line four times, or take four 12-second timings on each line. For each timing, type with no error.

5 Max worked quietly, alphabetizing the cards for vital jobs. 12
6 Beckwith just managed to verify his extremely popular quiz. 12
7 To jeopardize and hit six of the brigade, we moved quickly. 12

```
    25    30    35    40    45    50    55    60
```

FORMATTING FROM COMPUTER PRINTOUTS

Computer printouts appear in all-capital letters with abbreviations and no punctuation. Numbers often align at the left.

To format information from computer printouts:

1. Use initial caps for words.

2. If names are to be arranged with the last name first, separate last names from first names by a comma.

3. Do not abbreviate unless told to do so.

4. Align numbers on the right, and insert commas in numbers of 1,000 or more.

JOB 238-1. OPEN TABLE

Using the information in the computer printout that is illustrated, prepare a two-column open table. Standard format. Arrange last names first.

PROSPECTIVE CUSTOMER LIST FOR MARTIN AND BELLINGHAM INC			
BIPPUS	MICHAEL	TRITCH	CHRISTOPHER
CHONG	WAN	TRUSCELLI	ANTHONY
MILLER	LAURA	TURTON	MATTHEW
REILING	ELIZABETH	TYRA	MELISSA
SWIFT	DANIEL	VANDERPOOL	CHERYL
SWIGART	CHRISTOPHER	VIOLA	ANTHONY
THOMSON	ERIC	WILLIAMSON	SUSAN
TOMA	JULIA	WILSON	MARGUERITA
TOMALLO	JAMES	WYCOFF	PHILLIP
TOMLINSON	DONNA	YAUGER	PRISCILLA

LESSON 57

GOALS
- To format subtitles and to align numbers and decimals in tables.

FORMAT
- Single spacing   60-space line   Tabs as needed

KEYBOARDING SKILLS

Type lines 1–4 once. Then do what line 5 tells you to do. Repeat lines 1–4, or take a series of 1-minute timings.

Speed   1   If they give him a good price, he might take a lot of them.   12
Accuracy   2   Jeff quickly amazed the audience by giving six new reports.   12
Numbers   3   The years to remember are 1910, 1929, 1938, 1947, and 1956.   12
Symbols   4   Please find #2938, #4756, #1029, #1038, and #1947 for them.   12
Technique 5   Retype line 3. Underscore each of the years.

| 1 | 2 | 3 | 4 | 5 | 6 | 7 | 8 | 9 | 10 | 11 | 12

PRETEST

Take a 3-minute Pretest on lines 6–14. Then circle and count your errors. Use the chart below to determine which lines to type for practice.

6   High tech is the name given to a basic and useful type   12
7   of design that is changing the concept of modern living and   24
8   things we use daily. It has long enjoyed a quiet appeal in   36
9   places like stores and restaurants, but now it is coming to   48
10   be used in homes. High tech designs are not expensive, and   60
11   they are built to last. They come in a wide range of zany,   72
12   bright colors; things such as water pipes, tire rubber, and   34
13   window glass are often used with style in high tech designs   96
14   and are fun to own and use.   102

| 1 | 2 | 3 | 4 | 5 | 6 | 7 | 8 | 9 | 10 | 11 | 12   SI 1.26

PRACTICE

In the chart below, find the number of errors you made on the Pretest. Then type each of the designated drill lines four times.

Pretest errors	0–1	2–3	4–5	6+
Drill lines	18–22	17–21	16–20	15–19

Accuracy   15   own basic quiet stores design concept expensive restaurants
           16   built style pipes range bright rubber window appeal designs
           17   use and are they tech living modern useful designs changing
           18   now but used come water things colors coming places enjoyed

Speed   19   glass daily wide zany such tire come like home with has not
           20   homes given high tech name type long used they last now are
           21   appeal living useful given basic things daily long type use
           22   colors bright stores water pipes style glass range zany are

POSTTEST

Repeat the Pretest to see how much your skill has improved.

LESSON 237

CLINIC

GOALS
- To build competency on selected keyboard reaches.

FORMAT
- Single spacing   60-space line

PRETEST 1

Take a 30-second timing on each line. Proofread and score each timing.

```
1   Now is the moment to save and protect our younger citizens.   12
2   The river runs in all seasons, and not once has ice formed.   12
3   The women were given a refund and made a fortune in prizes.   12
4   It is much too soon to detect minor defects in the new car.   12
    |  1  |  2  |  3  |  4  |  5  |  6  |  7  |  8  |  9  |  10  |  11  |  12
```

PRACTICE 1

Type lines 5–10 four times. If you averaged two or fewer errors in the Pretest, repeat individual lines; otherwise, repeat each block of lines for accuracy gains.

```
5    routine utilize paying refund serve thing army live bid won
6    younger protect season invest women river pins mill inn nor
7    matched joining utmost saying zones place unit text run act

8    defects correct gained import aimed catch once soon fun ice
9    exposed appoint gained detect minor night save much now won
10   citizen fortune making prompt using prize done none ton gun
```

POSTTEST 1

Repeat Pretest 1. Score your work and note your improvement.

PRETEST 2

Take a 30-second timing on each line. Proofread and score each timing.

```
11   We have to admit that the stones somehow broke the windows.   12
12   Tod doubts the main brakes have a chance of working anyhow.   12
13   She informs me that the mob was running to the office room.   12
14   Just for the fun of it, I gave my uncle one cent for lunch.   12
     |  1  |  2  |  3  |  4  |  5  |  6  |  7  |  8  |  9  |  10  |  11  |  12
```

PRACTICE 2

Type lines 15–20 four times. If you averaged two or fewer errors in the Pretest, repeat individual lines; otherwise, repeat each block of lines for accuracy gains.

```
15   somehow windows office timely might print pain tiny act nor
16   tactful unknown stones prompt smoke round main skin any sun
17   shelves orchard motive lesson exact hints noon room run mob

18   running primary having expand knife lunch inch line cry ice
19   mounted leading driven chance count bench gave from beg win
20   helping informs anyhow brakes admit doubt cent have one fun
```

POSTTEST 2

Repeat Pretest 2. Score your work and note your improvement.

FORMATTING SUBTITLES IN TABLES

Workbook 77.

Subtitles in tables are formatted the same way as subtitles in other documents: (1) Center the subtitles. (2) Double-space before and triple-space after them. (3) Use initial caps.

NUMBERS IN COLUMNS

Align numbers. Numbers are aligned at the right. If a column of numbers contains items with decimals or amounts of money with decimals, as shown at the right, the decimals should be aligned.

Key line. Use the longest item in the column—just as you would if the column contained words. If the column contains a dollar sign, be sure to include it in the key line.

Margin and Tabs. Since spacing forward and backward will be needed to align the number items at the right, set the margin or tab stops for the digit that requires the least forward and backward spacing (note where the margin and the tabs were set for the illustration at the right).

```
        HEMP'S DEPARTMENT STORE
                                    ↓2
            Fall Clearance Sale
                                    ↓3

    564      Silk Ties          $10.62
     19      Belts                1.43
      5      Wool Sweaters       19.95
   1500      Pairs Socks           .75
    M        T                    T
```

JOB 57-1. THREE-COLUMN TABLE WITH SUBTITLE AND NUMBERS

Type the copy in the column to the right. Standard format (see pages 97 and 98). Double spacing. Half sheet of paper.

ASTRO CONSTRUCTION
Number of Employees on June 30

Warehouse	Lima, OH	116
Plant	Denver, CO	1,235
Office	New York, NY	954
Branch	Seattle, WA	28
Branch	Chicago, IL	39
Branch	Atlanta, GA	9
Branch	Dallas, TX	11

JOB 57-2. THREE-COLUMN TABLE WITH SUBTITLE AND NUMBERS

Standard format. Double spacing. Half sheet of paper.

The Great Race
Kilometers Completed by City Business Club Members

G. Craig	Beaver High	12.6
W. Kahn	Denby High	10.5
L. Mervis	Lincoln High	8.0
R. Bennett	Oliver High	7.2
S. Bellini	Gladstone High	6.1
A. Deuer	Kenton High	5.7

LESSON 236

GOALS
- To select the correct contraction or possessive pronoun while typing sentences.
- To type 46/5'/3e.
- To create final drafts of letters that are unarranged and incomplete in their present form.

FORMAT
- Single spacing   60-space line   5-space tab

LAB 28

Type lines 1–4 once, providing the appropriate answers. Edit your copy as your teacher reads the answers. Then retype lines 1–4 from your edited copy.

CONTRACTIONS AND POSSESSIVE PRONOUNS

1 (Whose/Who's) fixtures are these, and (whose/who's) going to ship them all?

2 When (your/you're) ready, quickly send (your/you're) order to Kaye Juarez.

3 (Their/They're) ready, but (their/they're) supervisor is not here yet.

4 (Its/It's) exciting to have our firm enjoying (its/it's) best year ever.

5-MINUTE TIMINGS

Take a 5-minute timing of lines 6–25 on page 374. Type six times each word on which you made an error, hesitated, or stopped during the 5-minute timing. Then take a 5-minute timing to see how much your skill has improved.

JOB 236-1. LETTER
Standard format. Workbook 575–576 top.

I need to send four letters to members of the staff. I'll give you the main parts of the message, but please word each letter just a little differently. I would not want the staff to compare letters and find the same message in all four letters.

The first letter goes to David L. Martin. He lives here in Indianapolis at 593 North Street, 46227. Please make one carbon of the letter, and address envelopes for all the letters.

Dear Mr. Martin: Congratulations on your recent appointment as chairperson of the Indianapolis campaign. It must be a great satisfaction to you to know that other members of your group respect you so much. I am sure that the campaign will be very successful under your leadership. I should like to invite you and your wife to an informal social gathering at my home at seven o'clock on April 4. I hope that you will be able to join us. Very cordially yours, Tony A. Makato.

JOBS 236-2 TO 236-4. LETTERS TO BE COMPLETED
Standard format. Workbook 575–578.

There are three other members of the staff who must receive letters. Ms. Molly Alsop lives at 56 Ninth Street, 46204. She will be the assistant to the chairperson for this campaign. She has served on campaign committees for several years and is always responsible for seeing that large numbers of volunteers help with last-minute tasks for the campaign.

Mrs. Andrea Kilran will be the treasurer for the campaign. Her address is 67 Valleyview Drive, 46227. She was very efficient in her work as treasurer for the past two campaigns.

Mr. Richard Callahan, 462 Northern Avenue, 46208, is the new secretary and has worked on just one campaign before. He has been active in supporting local candidates and has become interested in being part of this national campaign. Invite his wife also.

Please sign these letters for me, and get them in today's mail. I want them to have plenty of notice about this social gathering. Thanks.

LESSON 58

GOALS
- To recognize how numbers are expressed while typing sentences.
- To format tables with blocked column headings.

FORMAT
- Single spacing   60-space line   Tabs as needed

LAB 4

Type lines 1–4 once. Then repeat lines 1–4 or take a series of 1-minute timings.

NUMBER STYLE

1 They have fine new offices at 171 Seventh Avenue in Queens.   12
2 The Orin Building is located at 56th Street and West Fifth.   12
3 They built a new zoo at 462 Sixth Avenue--or is it Seventh?   12
4 Our jet departs at 11:45 a.m. and arrives 30 minutes later.   12
| 1 | 2 | 3 | 4 | 5 | 6 | 7 | 8 | 9 | 10 | 11 | 12

Spell out street names from *first* through *tenth*; use figures for street names above *tenth*. Also use figures for all house numbers except *one*: *One Third Avenue, 12 West 22 Street, 7 Fifth Avenue.*

Use figures to express most periods of time: *45 minutes, 10:15 a.m., 7 o'clock, 30 days.* Use figures for dates: *May 9, 1989.*

12-SECOND TIMINGS

Type each line four times, or take four 12-second timings on each line. For each timing, type with no more than one error.

5 See if this paper will fit in the slot near the right wall.   12
6 We hope to get a big order from one of the firms near here.   12
7 Sue did her best to get a pup that we can keep in the yard.   12

25   30   35   40   45   50   55   60

FORMATTING BLOCKED COLUMN HEADINGS

Column headings in tables clarify the data in each column and eliminate unnecessary words. In draft copies and in informal correspondence, column headings may be blocked.

To format blocked column headings:
1. Begin the column heading at the left edge of the column (at the margin or tab stop).
2. Type the column heading in initial caps and underscore it.
3. Triple-space before and double-space after a column heading.

MEMBERSHIP NOMINEES
↓2

Report of the
Membership Committee
↓3

Juniors   Seniors
↓2

Sally Hollins   Richard Belemy
Max Schroeder   Alice Bickmore

JOB 58-1. TWO-COLUMN TABLE WITH BLOCKED COLUMN HEADINGS

Type the copy in the column to the right. Standard format. Half sheet of paper.

JOB 58-2. THREE-COLUMN TABLE WITH BLOCKED COLUMN HEADINGS

Retype Job 58-1 adding the name of the country as column 1. Use the column heading *Country*. Standard format. Half sheet of paper.

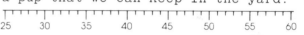

International TRAVELERS' FORECAST
Today's Projected Whether Conditions

City	Forecast
Amsterdam	Cloudy
Frankfurt	rain
Peking	Fair
London	Heavy Fog
Mexico City	hazy
Tel Aviv	Clear

LESSON 235

GOALS
- To identify, while typing sentences, the difference between contractions and possessive pronouns that sound alike.
- To create final drafts of dictated letters.

FORMAT
- Single spacing   60-space line

LAB 28

CONTRACTIONS AND POSSESSIVE PRONOUNS

Type lines 1–4 once. Then repeat lines 1–4 or take a series of 1-minute timings.

1 You're well prepared to give all your six speeches, Alonzo. 12
2 Their letters must be signed first because they're waiting. 12
3 Its quiet movement is a sign that it's operating very well. 12
4 Do you know who's riding in whose jeep for the noon parade? 12
| 1 | 2 | 3 | 4 | 5 | 6 | 7 | 8 | 9 | 10 | 11 | 12

12-SECOND TIMINGS

Type each line four times, or take four 12-second timings on each line. For each timing, type with no error.

5 She counted one, two, three, four, five, six, seven, eight. 12
6 Her speech was very good; she will do well in the election. 12
7 I read all of the issues when I voted; some were very long. 12

JOB 235-1. DICTATED LETTER
Standard format. Workbook 569–570.

ms nadine bergman 757 newscastle drive akron ohio 44313 dear nadine thank you for designing the letterhead for our regional campaign both the artwork and the slogan are most appropriate for our candidate i am mailing you under seperate cover our ideas for the billboards please feel free to modify them in any way that you wish if you can possible do it we would like to have the artwork to give to the printer by next month please let me know whether you can met that deadline cordially tony a makato

JOB 235-2. DICTATED LETTER
Standard format. Workbook 571–572.

mr duke bellas 1044 state street marysville ohio 43040 dear duke thank you for agreeing to prepare the copy for the special brochure highlighting the political history of our candidate my secretary will send you a number of photographs which you may want to include in the brochure our budget will allow us to have two 8½ by 11 pages printed on both sides thus making four pages in all the printer has set a deadline of the first of the month for all copy would you please let my secretary know this week whether you will be able to meet such a deadline thanks again for volunteering your time toward the campaign sincerely tony a makato

JOB 235-3. DICTATED LETTER
Standard format. Workbook 573–574.

doctor aileen madison 5649 centennial drive reynoldsburg ohio 43068 dear aileen i recieved your script for the three-minute television spots we have planned for next month they are extremely creative and do an excellant job of highlighting the good points about our candidate the film is being shot this week and should be ready for editing by next monday would you please check your schedule to see if you could come to indianapolis on monday to assist us with this operation the photographer has agreed to take a number of poses for each portion of the script to allow us a number of alternatives when we edit and combine the two please call my secretary and let her know if you will be able to help with the editing best wishes tony a makato

Paper turned lengthwise has the following dimensions: Width, 110 pica spaces or 132 elite spaces. Depth, 51 lines.

JOB 58-3. FOUR-COLUMN TABLE WITH BLOCKED COLUMN HEADINGS

Standard format. Full sheet of paper turned lengthwise.

PORTLAND TOWN HALL
Winter Program of Events

Date	Topic	Speaker	Location
January 15	Books	L. T. Borman	Downtown YMCA
January 29	Music	Sandra Cotts	East End Library
February 12	Real Estate	Fred T. Hamma	South High School
February 26	Theater	Betty Jean Bay	College Club
March 10	Business	Stuart Green	Civic Hall

LESSON 59

GOALS
- To identify how numbers are expressed while typing sentences.
- To format tables with short centered column headings.

FORMAT
- Single spacing   60-space line   Tabs as needed

LAB 4

NUMBER STYLE

Type lines 1–4 once. Then repeat lines 1–4 or take a series of 1-minute timings.

```
1  My jet should depart at 10:47 a.m. and arrive at 12:34 p.m.   12
2  Eighty-six people will attend the workshops in New Zealand.   12
3  Meet Bart at 12 o'clock on 142d Street near Seventh Avenue.   12
4  Amy lives quietly on Third Avenue, but she prefers Seventh.   12
   |  1  |  2  |  3  |  4  |  5  |  6  |  7  |  8  |  9  |  10  |  11  |  12
```

30-SECOND TIMINGS

Take two 30-second timings on lines 5–7, or type the paragraph twice.

```
5  Success is very much needed by all in the learning process.   12
6  The exercises that the students type must not cause them to   24
7  just quit working; students need their work recognized too.   36
   |  1  |  2  |  3  |  4  |  5  |  6  |  7  |  8  |  9  |  10  |  11  |  12
```

FORMATTING SHORT CENTERED COLUMN HEADINGS

When a column heading is shorter than the longest line in a column, the heading should be centered over the column. Follow these formatting directions:

1. Subtract the number of spaces in the column head from the number of spaces in the longest line in the column.
2. Divide the answer by 2 (drop any fraction) and indent the column head that many spaces.

```
            Date

    September 12
    September 30
    October 10
```

In the column above, the heading is 4 spaces long; the longest line is 12. Thus 12 − 4 = 8 and 8 ÷ 2 = 4. Indent the head 4 spaces from the start of the column.

JOB 234-1. LETTER

Standard format. Workbook 563–564.

Mr. Fred Flanagan, 11134 Mill Road,   15
Cincinnati, OH ~~45506~~ 45240, Dear Mr. Fla^n^gan: 25
As regional campa^i^gn chairperson for   33
the ~~midest~~ *Midwest*, I have been asked by   40
Mr. Matthews to arrange for his offi-   47
cial candidacy ^to be^ announced in your city.   56
There are a number of strong supporters   64
in Cincinnati, and we feel that any   72
opening remar~k~s would rec^ei^eve strong   79
support and good media coverage. ¶ Would   88
you please check to see ~if~ *whether* the area   95
around the fountain (during lunch time)   105
is available. A larger crowd might be   111
drawn to such a location during that   118
time of day. Please let ~me~ *my* secretary   126
know as soon as possible. ¶ There will   134
be approximately ~forty~ *50* people with the   144
campaign in Cincinnati. We shall need   152
about 34 rooms and a hospitality suite   160
to ac^c^ommodate everyone. I assume that   168
the City Center Motel will ~be the best~ *offer the best accommodations*   176
~location.~ ¶ Thank you for your ~help~ *assistance* in   187
this important part of the campaign.   195
Sincerely, Tony A. Makato, Regional   209
Campaign Chairperson   215

JOB 234-2. LETTER

Standard format. Workbook 565–566.

Ms. Alice Barrington-Barton, 56 Pleas-   16
ant Street, Pittsburgh, PA 15206, Dear   24
~Mr.~ *Ms.* Barrington-Barton: This letter is   33
to confirm our telephone conversation   41
of February 28 concerning the speech   48
Mr. Matthews ^will be making^ ~plans to make~ in your   55
city next month. He plans to open his   63
campaign in Cincinnati on ~Thursday~ *Friday*   70
morning before he speaks in Pittsburgh   78
on Monday afternoon. ¶ He has agreed   86
that while he is in Pittsburgh he will   94
also devote some time to lending sup-   101
port to ~Senator~ *Representative* Romanson. ~He~ *Mr. Romanson* has been   112
a loyal member of the party and has   119
voted for most of the legislation ~for~   126
~which~ *that* Mr. Matthews ~is most concerned.~ *has sponsored.*   133
~He~ ^Mr. Matthews^ will also spend a few days in Ohio   143
supporting Ms. Jacot in her bid for   150
reelection to the house. ¶ ~Their~ *There* will   158
be approximately ~fifty~ *50* persons with   165
the campaign in Pittsburgh. We ~will~ *shall*   172
need about 34 rooms and a hospitality   180
suite to take care of everyone. The   187
selection of hotels is up to you.   194
Sincerely, Tony A. Makato, Regional   209
C^a^mpaign Chairperson   214

JOB 234-3. LETTER

Retype Job 234-2 with two additions. Standard format.
Workbook 567–568.

As the final paragraph in the letter:

Thank you for arranging for Mr. Matthews' speech and visit to Pittsburgh.

As a postscript:

We shall be forwarding a number of brochures to you in a couple of weeks. You may use them before Mr. Matthews' visit.

JOB 59-1. TABLE WITH SHORT CENTERED COLUMN HEADINGS

Standard format. Half sheet of paper.

OAKDALE HIGH SCHOOL
Varsity Field Hockey Schedule

Date	Opponent	Site
September 12	Ellis	Home
September 21	St. Agnes	Away
September 30	Quaker Valley	Home
October 10	Keystone	Home
October 18	Winchester	Away

JOB 59-2. TABLE WITH SHORT CENTERED COLUMN HEADINGS

Standard format. Half sheet of paper.

WINTER TOURNAMENT
Varsity Basketball

Player	Position
B. Ligurski	R. Forward
D. Swenson	L. Forward
C. Brewster	R. Guard
C. Kanter	L. Guard
D. Sirinek	Center

JOB 59-3. TABLE WITH SHORT CENTERED COLUMN HEADINGS

Standard format. Half sheet of paper.

GEMS OF THE WORLD _#
Origin of the most Precious Stones
2—#

Gem	Country
Emerald	Colombia
amethyst	Brazil
Opal	Australia
diamond	South africa
Ruby	Burma

JOB 59-4. TABLE WITH SHORT CENTERED COLUMN HEADINGS

Standard format with 8 spaces between columns. Full sheet of paper.

EXPEDITIONS TO THE NORTH POLE
By ice, air, and sea _#
2—#

Name	Vehicle	Year
Byrd	airplane	1926
Norge	Dirigible	1926
Nautilus	Submarine	1958
Plaisted	Snow mobile	1968
Herbert	Dog sled	1969
Arktika	Icebreaker	1977

LESSON 60

GOALS
- To express numbers correctly while typing sentences.
- To type 34/3'/5e.
- To format tables with long and short centered column headings.

FORMAT
- Single spacing   60-space line   Tabs as needed

LAB 4

NUMBER STYLE

Type lines 1–4 once, correcting any errors in number-style rules. Edit your copy as your teacher reads the answers. Then retype lines 1–4 from your edited copy.

1 His jet from Mexico to Quebec leaves at eight-fifteen p.m. today.

2 You are invited to attend our sorority meeting at two-thirty p.m.

3 7 days ago she bought 2 new skirts and 3 blazers.

4 I walked down 6th Avenue last evening looking for a sale.

JOB 233-3. LETTER
Standard format. Workbook 561–562.

Washington Memorial High School, 1411 — 16	I am looking forward to meeting — 67
Arlington Avenue, Dayton, OH 45402, — 23	you and your team at your annual — 74
Attention: Soccer Coach Dear Sir: — 32	honors assembly in May. A plaque — 81
Congratulations to you and your team — 41	will be given to your school in — 87
on a fine season. Your contribution — 48	your honor. Cordially, Sarah Jacot, — 100
to the growth of soccer in our state — 55	Representative, Third District — 109
is most appreciated. — 60	Copy to Dan Davidson, Superintendent — 117

LESSON 234

GOALS
- To recognize, while typing sentences, the difference between contractions and possessive pronouns that sound alike.
- To type letters from rough drafts.

FORMAT
- Single spacing   60-space line   5-space tab

LAB 28

CONTRACTIONS AND POSSESSIVE PRONOUNS

Type lines 1–4 once. Then repeat lines 1–4 or take a series of 1-minute timings.

```
1  You're working quickly with James to complete your reports.   12
2  They're planning to itemize all taxes before their meeting.    12
3  It's good to see that the firm is improving its poor image.    12
4  Tony and I will decide who's going to present whose awards.     12
   |  1  |  2  |  3  |  4  |  5  |  6  |  7  |  8  |  9  |  10  |  11  |  12
```

Contractions such as *it's, they're,* and *you're* sound like the possessive pronouns *its, their,* and *your*. To avoid mistakes, say "it is" whenever you see *it's*; say "they are" whenever you see *they're*; and so on. By doing so, you will always know if the contraction is correct.

I know *you're* pleased with *your* results. ("You are pleased." Okay. "You are results." Not okay, so *your results* is correct.)

30-SECOND TIMINGS

Take two 30-second timings on lines 5–7, or type the paragraph twice.

```
5      Please send seven boxes of election fliers to my south    12
6  precinct as quickly as you can.  We just realized that they   24
7  were going to run out.  Thank you for helping me with this.    36
   |  1  |  2  |  3  |  4  |  5  |  6  |  7  |  8  |  9  |  10  |  11  |  12
```

PRETEST

Take a 3-minute Pretest on lines 5–13. Then circle and count your errors. Use the chart below to determine which lines to type for practice.

5　　　　Antiques are old items that have become valued objects　12

6　with the passing of time. Rugs, lamps, chairs, silverware,　24

7　and objects of art are bought and sold at auctions and by a　36

8　number of great experts around the world. Antiques are big　48

9　business, and each year some items become the rage with all　60

10　those who like to collect. Prices zip up and down with the　72

11　demand, but antiques can be a good way to invest some money　84

12　that you plan to save. Just be sure not to toss out an old　96

13　piece that may be worth money.　102

| 1 | 2 | 3 | 4 | 5 | 6 | 7 | 8 | 9 | 10 | 11 | 12　SI 1.28

PRACTICE

In the chart below, find the number of errors you made on the Pretest. Then type each of the designated drill lines four times.

Pretest errors	0–1	2–3	4–5	6+
Drill lines	17–21	16–20	15–19	14–18

Accuracy

14　become objects private antiques passing business silverware
15　demand valued chairs bought number around experts business,
16　rage just rugs that have money those world collect auctions
17　with sold lamps items invest prices become objects antiques

Speed

18　prices some down with good save zip who all big are art old
19　collect money items that like each year out not may you way
20　become items those plan toss save time some sure and are up
21　valued invest shops just each sure sold that with can of be

POSTTEST

Repeat the Pretest to see how much your skill has improved.

FORMATTING LONG CENTERED COLUMN HEADINGS

Workbook 78.

When a column heading is longer than any item in the column, the column is centered under the heading. To format the column under the heading:

1. Subtract the number of spaces in the longest line in the column from the number of spaces in the heading.
2. Divide that answer by 2 (drop any fraction), and indent the column that number of spaces. In the example, 23 − 13 = 10 and 10 ÷ 2 = 5. Indent the column 5 spaces.

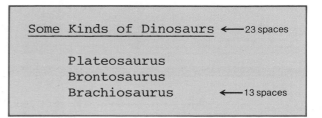

Note: When the column heading is longer than the column, regard the heading as part of the key line.

PRACTICE

In the chart below, find the number of errors you made on the Pretest. Then type each of the designated drill lines four times.

Pretest errors	0–1	2–3	4+
Drill lines	28–31	27–30	26–29

26 participation nominations commercials campaigning caucusing
27 convention difference informally officials selection always
28 television elections selecting delegates exposures citizens

29 media quite their worth every first these state while heavy
30 will lead both such days were this lost made mass when into
31 for was not the our out and led has one are who pay but now

POSTTEST

Repeat the Pretest on page 374 to see how much your skill has improved.

JOB 233-1. LETTER
Standard format. Workbook 557–558.

Jane Addams High School, 45 Meadow- — 15
grove, Delaware, OH 43015 — 20
Attention: OEA Advisors Ladies — 28
and Gentlemen: It is with a — 34
great deal of pleasure that I — 40
congratulate you on the fine — 46
contribution that you and your — 52
chapter of OEA students have — 58
made to the Special Olympics — 64
this year. — 66

Over 25,000 clubs all over the — 74
United States worked together to — 80
make the year a success for — 86
numerous young students. I am — 92
grateful for your efforts in this — 99
worthwhile program. — 104

Because you are one of twelve — 111
chapters in the country who — 116
contributed over $3,000 toward — 123
the program this year, we are — 129
honoring you with a special — 134
plaque, which should arrive — 140
within the next two weeks. We — 146
hope that your chapter will dis- — 152
play it proudly. Best wishes, — 161
Sarah Jacot, Representative, — 171
Third District — 177

JOB 233-2. LETTER
Standard format. Workbook 559–560.

Miss Marie Gabbard, 98 Nutmeg Place, — 15
Urbana, OH 43078, Dear Marie: — 23
Subject: Air Force Academy — 29
Appointment I shall be very — 36
happy to recommend you for — 41
an appointment to the Air Force — 48
Academy for next fall. Your fine — 55
academic standing and your numerous — 62
recommendations from your high school — 69
teachers and principal make you — 76
an excellent candidate. — 81

Your participation in debate at the — 89
national level and your extensive — 96
leadership skills demonstrated in your — 104
community place you among the best — 111
qualified for the work required at the — 118
academy. — 120

I shall contact you by phone as — 128
soon as the official announcements — 135
have been made. Sincerely, Sarah — 148
Jacot, Representative, Third District — 159

JOB 60-1. TABLE WITH LONG CENTERED COLUMN HEADINGS
Standard format. Half sheet of paper.

DINOSAURS

A Parade Through Time

Some Kinds of Dinosaurs	Millions of Years Ago
Plateosaurus	225
Brontosaurus	185
Brachiosaurus	170
Tyrannosaurus Rex	136

JOB 60-2. TABLE WITH LONG CENTERED COLUMN HEADINGS
Standard format. Half sheet of paper.

YEARBOOK ADVERTISERS

Signed Contracts for This Year

Business or Company Name	Local Mailing Address
American Plumbing	120 Second Avenue
Haroldson Printing	15 Third Avenue
Modern Furniture	Fifth and Main
Shaeffer Real Estate	23 Tenth Street
Wagner Equipment	500 Fourth Avenue

JOB 60-3. TABLE WITH CENTERED COLUMN HEADINGS
Standard format. Half sheet of paper.

PARIS

Places of Interest	Location
Eiffel Tower	Avenue de la Bourdonnais
Palais du Louvre	Quai du Louvre
Notre Dame	Ile de la Cité
Arc de Triomphe	Avenue des Champs Elysées

LESSON 233

GOALS
- To type 46/5'/3e.
- To type letters from handwritten copy.

FORMAT
- Single spacing   60-space line

KEYBOARDING SKILLS

Type lines 1–4 once. Then use the shift lock on the words in all-capital letters as you type line 5. Repeat lines 1–4, or take a series of 1-minute timings.

1 Their firm is paid to paint half the signs for those towns. 12
2 Francis and Max proved quite lucky with the big jazz bands. 12
3 The prefix 123 replaces 789, so my new listing is 123-0564. 12
4 The Myer & Lippet Co. is selling "special" T-shirts for us. 12
5 Is ACME-APEX the brand of that company, or is it APEX-ACME?

| 1 | 2 | 3 | 4 | 5 | 6 | 7 | 8 | 9 | 10 | 11 | 12

PRETEST

Take a 5-minute Pretest on lines 6–25. Then circle and count your errors. Use the chart on page 375 to determine which lines to type for practice.

6   Although heavy campaigning for a number of months will 12
7 lead up to a national convention for both parties, such was 24
8 not always the practice in earlier days of elections in our 36
9 country. At first, candidates were selected by members for 48
10 their party in Congress. Selecting candidates by this pro- 60
11 cess is called the caucus method. Caucusing lost out after 72
12 a while, and nominations were made informally in mass meet- 84
13 ings by state officials. These meetings led to the present 96
14 practice of conventions. 101

15   When the national conventions began, they brought more 113
16 national participation into the selection process, and when 125
17 the first television cameras came in 1948, the exposure was 137
18 even greater than before. It has been judged that 68 to 70 149
19 million people watched the 1952 conventions. Today, almost 161
20 every American citizen has watched at least one convention. 173

21   The expenses for a national convention are quite high. 185
22 Citizens who are delegates find that their participation is 197
23 worth whatever it'll cost to go. The parties don't pay for 209
24 television time. Sponsors pay for the commercials, and the 221
25 difference is paid for by the media itself. 230

| 1 | 2 | 3 | 4 | 5 | 6 | 7 | 8 | 9 | 10 | 11 | 12   SI 1.66

LESSON 61

GOALS
- To type 34/3'/5e.
- To review the number keys.

FORMAT
- Single spacing   60-space line   5-space tab

KEYBOARDING SKILLS

Type lines 1–4 once. Then do what line 5 tells you to do. Repeat lines 1–4, or take a series of 1-minute timings.

Speed	1	The man is to go to town and then make six panels for them.	12
Accuracy	2	My fine black ax just zipped through the wood quite evenly.	12
Numbers	3	The 29 boys and 38 girls ate 47 pies and 56 pancakes today.	12
Symbols	4	These forms cost 10¢, 29¢, and 38¢ each, depending on size.	12
Technique	5	Type line 3; then underscore the words and not the numbers.

| 1 | 2 | 3 | 4 | 5 | 6 | 7 | 8 | 9 | 10 | 11 | 12 |

3-MINUTE TIMINGS

Repeat the Pretest/Practice/Posttest routine on page 104.

NUMBERS

Type lines 23–32 four times.

```
23  woe 293 yer 634 tot 595 pet 035 tip 580 owe 923 pow 092 092

24  tip 580 yip 680 row 492 tow 592 yow 693 tie 583 tee 533 533

25  wet 235 pie 083 rip 480 pit 085 rut 475 pop 090 too 599 599

26  were 2343 your 3974 tire 5843 pour 0974 weep 2330 pity 0856

27  wire 2843 pout 9075 toot 5995 peep 0330 type 5603 pyre 0643

28  wore 2943 yore 6943 tour 5974 pore 0943 writ 2485 peer 0334

29  wipe 3802 poor 0994 tout 5975 poet 0935 riot 4895 putt 0755

30  root 4995 trey 5436 yoyo 6969 ewer 3234 yipe 6803 rout 4975

31  troop 54990 trout 54975 tutor 57594 puppy 07006 putty 07556

32  write 24853 witty 28556 wiper 28034 rotor 49594 route 40753
```

LESSON 62

UNIT GOAL 35/3'/5e

GOALS
- To express numbers correctly while typing sentences.
- To format memorandums on plain paper and on forms.

FORMAT
- Single spacing   60-space line   5-space tab

LAB 4

NUMBER STYLE

Workbook 81–82.

Type lines 1–4 once, correcting any errors in number-style rules. Edit your copy as your teacher reads the answers. Retype lines 1–4 from your edited copy.

1 Should Jack go to 6th Street or to 8th Avenue for fun?

2 They live near 16th Street; she lives closer to twenty-third Street.

3 Their plane stopped for forty-five minutes in Iraq around 6:30 a.m.

4 18 zealots have studied four years for the bar exams.

PRETEST

Take a 2-minute Pretest on lines 5–8; then take a 2-minute Pretest on lines 9–12. Circle and count your errors on each timing.

```
 5  Cecile just decided to deduct the old music from her taxes.   12
 6  Ola just loves to ski or swim on holidays in the mountains.   24
 7  Dee declined the grant because she received free schooling.   36
 8  The dents in the desk were made by the students in science.   48

 9  William plans to apply for a legal hearing in a few months.  12
10  Jill tried to climb the cliff seven times before making it.  24
11  Howard will send his books before going to military school.  36
12  Dru drove a car over a drastic course that was quite hilly.  48
    |  1  |  2  |  3  |  4  |  5  |  6  |  7  |  8  |  9  | 10  | 11  | 12
```

PRACTICE

In which Pretest did you make more errors? If in lines 5–8, type lines 13–16 six times and lines 17–20 three times. If in lines 9–12, reverse the procedure.

```
13  sw  swing  sweet  swell  switch  swivel  swollen  sweater  swimming
14  ki  kinds  kings  kinks  kindly  killed  kindest  kitchen  kindness
15  ce  cease  cedar  ceded  center  cement  certify  certain  ceilings
16  lo  loans  local  locks  losses  lovely  located  locally  location

17  aw  award  awful  awake  awhile  awaken  awfully  awkward  awarding
18  hi  hilly  hinge  hints  hinges  higher  highway  himself  highways
19  fe  fears  feels  fewer  fences  feeler  fearing  fencing  feelings
20  li  limit  lists  lives  lining  limits  listing  linings  lifetime
```

POSTTEST

Repeat the Pretest.

JOB 232-1. LETTER
Block format. Workbook 553–554.

Mr. Alfred DeMonaco, 44 Circle Avenue, Lansing, MI 48901, Dear Mr. DeMonaco: I have rearranged my schedule so that I can arrive in Detroit and Buffalo next week. I am sending you my flight numbers so that you can meet me in Detroit and continue with me to Buffalo. ¶I will arrive in Detroit at 9:45 Wednesday morning on United 847 and stay at the motel with you on Wednesday and Thursday evenings. We will leave Detroit on United 582 at 10:15 on Friday morning and arrive in Buffalo an hour later. I will plan to stay with you through the weekend, returning to Indianapolis on Monday evening. ¶Please let me know whether this schedule will coincide with your schedule and whether you will be able to make reservations on the same flight to Buffalo. Cordially, Tony A. Makato, Regional Campaign Chairperson

JOB 232-2. LETTER
Block format. Workbook 555–556.

Ms. Jeanette Williams, 483 West Broad Street, Columbus, OH 43215, Dear Ms. Williams: I have rearranged my schedule so that I can spend half a day with you on Tuesday, March 22. I will be en route to Detroit to meet with Al DeMonaco and can stop long enough for us to plan the campaign for Ohio. ¶I will arrive on American 574 at approximately 2:10 on Tuesday afternoon, and I have arranged to stay at the airport motel so that I can leave immediately on Wednesday morning for Detroit. ¶Please bring your lists of workers with you so that we can organize our efforts. I have two special brochures that I hope will be of assistance to you. One explains the telephone campaign, and the other offers suggestions for dinners and receptions. ¶I look forward to working with you in March. Best wishes, Tony A. Makato, Regional Campaign Chairperson

Take two 1-minute timings on each paragraph. Then take one 3-minute timing on the entire selection. Use single spacing for the 1-minute timings and double spacing for the 3-minute timing.

1'

5   Quilts, or padded covers used on top of beds as lovely   12

6   spreads or just bedding, have a long history. Quilting has   24

7   been done worldwide and has been considered as an art.   35

8   A large part of the social life of our rural folks was   12

9   built around a group party, like a quilting bee. The women   24

10   in a village often met and made many new, warm quilts.   35

11   Quilts that were made of strips of cloth of all colors   12

12   and of crooked shapes were called crazy quilts. These were   24

13   a part of the exciting days of our early Western life.   35

| 1 | 2 | 3 | 4 | 5 | 6 | 7 | 8 | 9 | 10 | 11 | 12 | SI 1.27

FORMATTING MEMOS

Workbook 83.

Memorandums, or memos, are messages written among people in the same organization or business. Less formal than letters, memos have no salutations and no complimentary closings; and they may be typed on half sheets or full sheets, depending on the length. Memos are used so often that most companies use standard memo forms on which the guide words *To, From, Subject,* and *Date* are printed. (The company name and other information may also be printed on the form.) However, memos can also be typed on plain paper. Look at the illustrations on page 108 as you read the formatting directions below.

To format a memo on plain paper:

1. Set margins for 50P/60E.
2. Type the word *Memorandum* in all-capital letters, centered on line 7.
3. Triple-space after *Memorandum.* Type the guide words (*Date:, To:, From:, Subject:*) double-spaced at the left margin in all-capital letters.

4. Type the words that follow the guide words 10 spaces from the margin (2 spaces after *Subject:*).
5. Triple-space after the heading to the body of the memo. Single-space the body; double-space between paragraphs.
6. Type the writer's initials a double space below the body, beginning at the center.
7. Type any notation as in letters (a double space below the writer's initials, typed at the left margin).

To format a memo on a printed form:

1. Set the left margin stop 2 spaces after the longest guide word, and fill in the heading information.
2. Set the right margin stop so that the right margin is approximately the same number of spaces as the left margin.
3. Align the writer's initials with the date.

PRACTICE 1

Type lines 5–10 four times. If you averaged two or fewer errors in Pretest 1 on page 371, repeat individual lines for speed; otherwise, repeat each block of lines for accuracy gains.

5 cymbals evening before played amber night more very may not
6 musical directs corner bright boxes crane turn near bet any
7 waltzes nearing climbs umpire moves lines prom raze tax nor

8 minutes victims zenith mostly broom venom numb vine vat now
9 invites credits crafty notion money mixes cede mice con bow
10 mixture innings victor blazes exert crumb oxen note mit cry

POSTTEST 1

Repeat Pretest 1 on page 371. Score your work, and note your improvement.

PRETEST 2

Take a 30-second timing on each line. Proofread and score each timing.

11 Someone must review the mistake to perfect the main device. 12
12 It was wrong to think that the closing balances were fixed. 12
13 Why not join the best debate teams and have fun as you win? 12
14 Our members were trying their best, but they could not win. 12
    | 1 | 2 | 3 | 4 | 5 | 6 | 7 | 8 | 9 | 10 | 11 | 12

PRACTICE 2

Type lines 15–20 four times. If you averaged two or fewer errors in Pretest 2, repeat individual lines for speed; otherwise, repeat each block of lines for accuracy gains.

15 extreme furnace extent member kinds movie from text mix ton
16 perfect someone paints reveal pound river main over bed gun
17 reviews mistake trying verify think wrong very acre pin act

18 created drawing ignore levels doubt fixed join best won not
19 balance closing atomic device copes above much have ice any
20 country animals debate coding among brown twin save son fun

POSTTEST 2

Repeat Pretest 2. Score your work, and note your improvement.

LESSON 232

UNIT 38 PROCESSING CORRESPONDENCE

UNIT GOAL
46/5'/3e

GOALS
- To form contractions correctly while typing sentences.
- To type letters from unarranged copy.

FORMAT
- Single spacing   60-space line

LAB 27

CONTRACTIONS

Workbook 551.

Type lines 1–4 once, providing appropriate contractions for the underscored words. Edit your copy as your teacher reads the answers. Then retype lines 1–4 from your edited copy.

1 Terri Saxon said that <u>she is</u> going to promote her assistant.
2 Judd Bertram <u>will not</u> be able to attend tomorrow's conference.
3 <u>They will</u> need two dozen more copies, according to Ms. Klein.
4 <u>I would</u> prefer having you and her quickly review these figures.

JOB 62-1. MEMORANDUM

Standard format. Half sheet of plain paper.

TITLE
all caps, centered on line 7.

GUIDE WORDS
in all caps; tab 10 for copy that follows.

BODY
50P/60E, single spacing.

WRITER'S INITIALS
Align at center.

MEMORANDUM ↓7
↓3

DATE: January 4, 19--

TO: Sue Booth, President, South Side High Business Club

FROM: Tom Dunn, President, Green High Business Club

SUBJECT: Joint Meeting ↓3

I have enclosed a copy of the rough draft of the program for the next joint meeting of our clubs, which we discussed on the telephone last week. Notice, Sue, that I have moved the date from February 10 to March 6 because of a conflict with a basketball game at our school. ↓2

Please talk over the events planned with your officers and make any changes you like. Then call me at the school before the end of the week so that I can get my members working on the details. ↓2

                    TD ↓2

Enclosure

JOB 62-2. MEMORANDUM ON A PRINTED FORM

Workbook 85.

PRINTED GUIDE WORDS
Aligned at the bottom, 2 spaces after the colons.

WRITER'S INITIALS
Aligned with date.

TYPIST'S INITIALS

MEMORANDUM

TO: Pat Smith   DATE: May 1, 19--

FROM: George Zonn, Vice President

SUBJECT: Tour of the Building

Lehigh Valley High School will be sending us 15 students for a tour of the building on Thursday, May 10. This program is one of many that we do each year for the young people at the high school. Ms. Hansen, head of the office program at Lehigh Valley, always looks forward to our helping her give her students a look at the real office.

The students will be with us from 9 a.m. to 12 noon. Would you come to my office at 9 a.m. on Thursday, May 10, to assist me in forming small groups and conducting the building tour?

                    GZ

DM

JOB 230-1. DICTATED REPORT IN MEMO FORMAT
Workbook 547.

to the secretary of the interior from senator marilyn heuser about my trip to see the results of the snow mountain volcanic explosion

the cloud of ash cleared for a few hours during the days when i visited the area where snow mountain exploded it's very humbling to gaze at the sight of a once beautiful countryside and see only ash-covered ground and miles of devastated land which once held dense forests of trees one of the photographers in the area describes the event as the transformation of an area from a postcard-symmetrical cone 9,677 feet high to an ugly flattop 1,300 feet lower geologists say the blast had 500 times the punch of the bomb which hit hiroshima some actual statistics which i've been able to secure note that the eruption blew down 150 square miles of timber worth about $200 million, caused an estimated $222 million in damage to wheat, alfalfa, and other crops, and created a 20-mile-long logjam along the snow mountain river and blocked shipping in both washington and oregon a number of residents and visitors who were in the area when the eruption occurred are still being interviewed by the media and by my staff as the threat of more eruptions hangs over the area, it is very difficult for residents to calm down and regain composure the official reports from the geologists and photographers are still being compiled as more and more evidence is gathered, i shall keep you apprised of the situation

JOB 230-2. DICTATED REPORT IN MEMO FORMAT
Workbook 549.

to the president of the united states from representative john glengale concerning the aftermath of the zenith tornado i've just returned from a trip to the southern part of my state and want to report to you some of the sights which i witnessed while there the once-populated city is now completely flattened except for a few concrete structures which amazingly withstood the high winds more than a thousand people have lost their homes and almost every business there has been destroyed both the red cross and the numerous insurance companies have moved in to try to bring comfort to the residents but it's very difficult to do so at present the governor had visited the sight the day before i arrived and there is no doubt in either of our minds that federal funds must be used to help restore this community to some kind of normalcy as quickly as possible i'm sure that a visit from you at this time would be greatly appreciated arrangements will be coordinated with your office to make the visit as worthwhile as possible your immediate attention to this disaster site will be very much appreciated

LESSON 231

CLINIC

GOAL
- To build competency on selected keyboard reaches.

FORMAT
- Single spacing   60-space line

PRETEST 1   Take a 30-second timing on each line. Proofread and score each timing.

```
1   I may not buy any more amber boxes before Craig moves home.   12
2   It may be my turn to direct more waltz music on prom night.   12
3   May played on cymbals for the evening musical in September.   12
4   The crane moved very near the north corner of the building.   12
    |  1  |  2  |  3  |  4  |  5  |  6  |  7  |  8  |  9  | 10  | 11  | 12
```

LESSON 63

GOALS
- To format memorandums.

FORMAT
- Single spacing   60-space line   5-space tab

KEYBOARDING SKILLS

Type lines 1–4 once. Then do what line 5 tells you to do. Repeat lines 1–4, or take a series of 1-minute timings.

Speed   1 All of us are glad that the six of you came over to see us.   12
Accuracy   2 Paul reviewed the subject before giving Max and Kay a quiz.   12
Numbers   3 Sean sold several thousands of #380, #477, #566, and #2910.   12
Symbols   4 Try to locate reports #10, #29, #38, #47, and #56 for them.   12
Technique 5 Retype line 1, capitalizing the first letter of every word.

| 1 | 2 | 3 | 4 | 5 | 6 | 7 | 8 | 9 | 10 | 11 | 12

12-SECOND TIMINGS

Type each line four times, or take four 12-second timings on each line. For each timing, type with no more than one error.

6 When will that bookstore have more copies of the blue book?   12
7 They will move home from the city when they need more cash.   12
8 How soon can you help them get some cash to move back here?   12

25   30   35   40   45   50   55   60

JOBS 63-1 AND 63-2. MEMORANDUMS FROM SCRIPT

Standard format. Type two copies: one on plain paper, the other on a printed form. Workbook 87 top.

Memorandum / Date: (Today's) / To: Jo Anne Jones, Group Leader / FROM: Ruth Lee, Chairperson / SUBJECT: Fund Drive for Children's Home ¶ Thank you for your excellent report, Jo Anne. You, Sybil, and Dick did a great job! ¶ It is good to know that all the classes supported the drive and that we went over our goal of $300. ¶ Don't forget to take the money to the Children's Home before Saturday. Last year we missed the deadline, so our school did not get any credit for our hard work. [We must not let that happen this year.] ¶ If I can be of assistance to you in any way, please let me know. / RL

JOBS 63-3 AND 63-4. MEMORANDUM

Standard format. Type two copies of the memo on page 110: one copy on plain paper; the other, on a printed form. Workbook 87 bottom.

JOB 229-1. (Continued)

PROGRAM

Thursday, March 9

Opening Session, 7 p.m., Grand Ballroom, Speaker: Dr. Barry Brechak, Topic: "World Marketing in the 1980s"

Friday, March 10

Session 1, 9:30 a.m., Suite A, Speaker: Joe La-Vigne, Topic: "The Effects of Grain Embargoes on Domestic Pricing"

Session 2, 11 a.m., Suite C, Speaker: Phatama Shih, Topic: "The Growing Market of Software Products"

Luncheon, 12:30 p.m., Grand Ballroom, Speaker: Alison Aker, Station WTWC

Session 3, 2 p.m., Suite C, Speaker: Noriko Hagashima, Topic: "The World Car Concept in Transition"

Session 4, 3:30 p.m., Suite A, Speaker: Leah Chuang, Topic: "Trends in the Telecommunications and Computer World"

Dinner and Entertainment, 7 p.m., Grand Ballroom, Speaker: Jeffrey Meyer, Topic: "Trends in Language Requirements for Marketing Positions"

Use the copy below for the cover.

National Conference / World Marketing Trends / March 9–10 / Waldorf-Astoria Hotel / New York City

LESSON 230

GOALS
- To form contractions correctly while typing sentences.
- To type reports in memo format.

FORMAT
- Single spacing   60-space line   5-space tab

LAB 27

CONTRACTIONS

Type lines 1–4 once, providing appropriate contractions for the underscored words. Edit your copy as your teacher reads the answers. Then retype lines 1–4 from your edited copy.

1 Al Juarez <u>does not</u> believe that Ken will deliver it on time.

2 When do you think <u>we will</u> be told about that proposed merger?

3 <u>What is</u> the quickest way to order more of this great polish?

4 <u>I have</u> received only five or six suggestions from Mr. Truman.

"OK" TIMINGS

Type as many 30-second "OK" (errorless) timings as possible out of three attempts on lines 5–7. Then repeat the effort on lines 8–10.

5 I quickly explained that few big jobs involve many hazards.   12
6 The very next question emphasizes the growing lack of jobs.   24
7 We acquire jerky habits from having typed exercises lazily.   36

8 Vick did put a dozen jugs from Iraq on the big waxy tables.   12
9 Ms. Black requested sixty jeeps for moving the prizes away.   24
10 Six or seven flashing new jet planes quickly zoomed by him.   36

| 1 | 2 | 3 | 4 | 5 | 6 | 7 | 8 | 9 | 10 | 11 | 12

Much of the material in this level might normally be transcribed from shorthand notes or a machine transcriber, but it will be presented here in typed unarranged copy and will be labeled "Dictated Letter," "Dictated Report," and so on. You will have to supply capitalization, punctuation, and paragraphing. You will also have to check spelling; many words sound alike but are spelled differently.

DATE: (Today's)

TO: Ray Falk, Order Clerk

FROM: kay Bright, Sales

SUBJECT: Order No. 264-1002

¶ a few weeks ago we placed an order for a slide projector for use in our classes, which we hold here in the building during the year. the order was approved, but we have not received the goods. ¶ We are really anxious about this order because a speaker who will be here in 2 weeks wants to use a slide projector. Will you please check on this order for me and let me know when the equipment will be sent to us? ¶ If delivery can not be made by next monday, we will need to rent a projector. I would appreciate your prompt attention to this matter. / kb

LESSON 64

GOALS
- To recognize how commas are used in a series while typing sentences.
- To format ruled forms.

FORMAT
- Single spacing   60-space line   5-space tab

LAB 5

COMMAS IN SERIES

Type lines 1–4 twice. Then take a series of 1-minute timings on each line.

1 The tools, parts, and tires were in the drive near the car. 12
2 I bought a new sweater, a winter jacket, and quilted boots. 12
3 The fruit rolls, pies, cakes, and donuts are most tempting. 12
4 Fritz and Helen joined John, Sally, and Maline in the park. 12
    | 1 | 2 | 3 | 4 | 5 | 6 | 7 | 8 | 9 | 10 | 11 | 12

In a series of three or more numbers, phrases, or clauses, use a comma after each item in the series except the last.

Numbers: This model costs $12, $15, or $18.
Words: Abco manufactures nuts, bolts, and locks.
Phrases: We went into the plane, onto the runway, and into the air.
Clauses: Mel cooked the food, Janice made the salad, and Bob made the dessert.

30-SECOND TIMINGS

Take two 30-second timings on lines 5–7, or type the paragraph twice.

5 To be an expert in typing, you need to spend quite a lot of 12
6 time on drill work, which at times can be a big job, unless 24
7 the teacher recognizes the need for variety in each lesson. 36
    | 1 | 2 | 3 | 4 | 5 | 6 | 7 | 8 | 9 | 10 | 11 | 12

**1- AND
5-MINUTE
TIMINGS
(Continued)**

5   Have you ever wondered just how someone is able to get   12

6 an idea proposed in Congress? Only someone who is a member   24

7 of the legislature can propose a bill. The bill can origi-   36

8 nate anywhere, but a legislator must sponsor it.   46

9   Once it is introduced by a legislator, a bill receives   12

10 a number. The bill is routed to a committee. While in the   24

11 committee, the bill can be killed, amended, or rewritten in   36

12 a special way. Legislators may request hearings.   46

13   If a bill survives the committee, it will be routed to   12

14 the Rules Committee before its scrutinization on the floor.   24

15 Some bills are approved by the House faster than others. A   36

16 bill may also be amended or returned to committee.   46

17   After a bill survives the House, it is referred to the   12

18 Senate in a similar manner. Both houses of the legislature   24

19 must finally approve exact versions of a bill. Approval of   36

20 a bill allows its assignment to a different level.   46

21   Presidential consideration of a bill means it has been   12

22 through both houses and can be signed by the President. It   24

23 may become law even without the President's signature after   36

24 a certain number of days pass without a decision.   46

| 1 | 2 | 3 | 4 | 5 | 6 | 7 | 8 | 9 | 10 | 11 | 12   SI 1.59

**FORMATTING
BROCHURES**

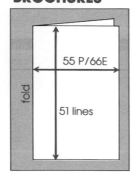

55 P/66E

fold

51 lines

A brochure is a small pamphlet or booklet and is often used to display a program.

To format a four-page brochure:

1. Fold a standard-sized sheet of paper in half from top to bottom.
2. Turn the paper so that the fold is at the left. The measurement of each "page" is 55P/66E wide and 51 lines deep.
3. Display the title in any display format on the front cover.
4. Divide the copy as evenly as possible, and display it on the two inside pages. (Leave the back cover blank unless the copy is too long to fit on two pages.)

JOB 229-1. FOUR-PAGE BROCHURE
Using the copy on page 370, prepare the two inside pages of a brochure. Use any display style, such as spread centering, block centering, underscoring, all-capital letters, leaders.

FORMATTING FORMS

Well-designed forms are set up so that data can be typed using standard vertical spacing and common tabs for horizontal spacing. However, when there is not enough space on a line, you will have to squeeze in the information in the space available.

To format ruled forms:

1. Look at the form before typing it to see where common tabs can be set.
2. Check the information to be placed on each line to see if you have enough space or if you will have to type the information on two lines.
3. Make sure the ruled line is in the position of the underscore and is straight.

MEMBERSHIP APPLICATION
The Business Club

Name Mary Wong   Grade 10

Address 308 Parker Drive, Pittsburgh, PA 15216   Phone 555-5327

Homeroom teacher   Mr. Henderson   Unit South

Business subjects taken Typewriting, general business

Other school activities Gymnastics Club, Drama Club

Why do you want to be a member of The Business Club? I hope to become a secretary, and I want to belong to an organization related to my future career.

When is the best time to contact you for an interview? My study hall is during the second period, or I can be available after school any day except Monday or Friday.

REQUEST FOR TRANSPORTATION

Requesting school Washburn High School   Date of event November 24, 19--

Destination First National State Bank of Connecticut
             6072 North Broadway, Bridgeport, CT

Purpose of trip Observe banking jobs   School group Office procedures class

Number of students 28   Leaving time 1:15 p.m.

Pickup location High school parking lot   Returning time 3:30 p.m.

Signature of Teacher   Signature of Principal

November 1, 19--
Date of Request   Approval of Transportation Officer

Bus assigned   Driver assigned

JOB 64-1. MEMBERSHIP APPLICATION
Workbook 89 top.

Jerry Killian is a junior who lives at 12 Oak Drive, Pittsburgh, PA 15214. His phone number is 555-8937. His homeroom teacher is Ms. Taylor, and the homeroom is in the East Unit. He has taken Accounting and Business Law and is a member of the band and golf team. He wants to be in The Business Club to learn more about accounting and computer sciences. His study hall is fourth period, and he can be interviewed at that time.

JOB 64-2. MEMBERSHIP APPLICATION
Workbook 89 bottom.

Marianne Weatherby is a sophomore who lives at 3492 Southwind Drive, Nashville, TN 37217. Her phone number is 555-7739. Her homeroom teacher is Mr. Johnson, and her homeroom is in the West Unit. She has taken Shorthand, Typewriting, and Word Processing and is a member of the girls' basketball team and the symphonic choir. She also works part-time as a gas station attendant. She wants to join The Business Club because she is interested in meeting other students who are going to major in business in college. She doesn't have any study halls but can stay after school on Tuesdays for an interview.

JOB 64-3. REQUEST FOR TRANSPORTATION
Workbook 91 top.

The Mitchell High School Business Club is requesting a bus for 25 students to attend a word processing installation located in the Americana Insurance Company at 12 East First Street in Mitchell. The trip is scheduled for November 9. The bus should pick up the students at the main entrance to the high school at 8:30 a.m. and will return to school at 1 p.m. The purpose of the trip is to see how a word processing center operates. The date of the request is October 20. (Signatures should not be typed.)

JOB 64-4. REQUEST FOR TRANSPORTATION
Workbook 91 bottom.

The Winchester Career Center Business Club is requesting a bus for 32 students to attend regional skills contests located at Montgomery County Joint Vocational School on Hathaway Road. The contests are scheduled for December 5. The bus should pick up the students at the south entrance at 9:30 a.m. and will return to school at 5:30 p.m. The purpose of the trip is to allow students to participate in regional skills competition. The date of the request is November 10.

JOB 228-1. (Continued)

The lobbyist knows the power of the media. He ^or she^ knows how to get a   382

feature story printed or a special telecast made in ^a^ timely manner.   396

¶ Getting to know other lobbyists opens the way to many kinds of   410

negotiating. Perhaps one lobbyist may be able to cooperate with   423

another in applying pressure for each other's points of view in   436

separate activities.   440

HOW ARE LOBBYISTS CONTROLLED?   446

Although there is a law requiring registration of all persons and   460

organizations who attempt to influence legislation and requiring   473

that financial records be kept by these persons and groups, the   486

opposition is the most active control in keeping lobbyists honest.   500

~~They~~ ^Lobbyists^ act as a system of checks and balances in watching one another   514

operate. Many times legislation ~~have~~ ^has^ been proposed ^to control lobbying^, but it always   532

fails because there are no powerful lobbyists around to help push   545

the legislation through the congress. Thus lobbyists operate with ^very^   559

few ^legislative^ guides in print.   566

LESSON 229

GOALS
- To identify contractions while typing sentences.
- To type 46/5'/3e.
- To format and type a brochure.

FORMAT
- Single spacing   60-space line   5-space tab

LAB 27

Type lines 1–4 once. Then repeat lines 1–4 or take a series of 1-minute timings.

CONTRACTIONS

1 It doesn't seem possible that Joe Rexon is ready to retire.   12
2 Here's the quickest way to go to my warehouse in Kalamazoo.   12
3 What's the reason for sending all your cartons to Veronica?   12
4 It wouldn't be fair to let your customers pay for shipping.   12

| 1 | 2 | 3 | 4 | 5 | 6 | 7 | 8 | 9 | 10 | 11 | 12

1- AND 5-MINUTE TIMINGS

Take two 1-minute timings of each paragraph on page 369. Then take one 5-minute timing on the entire selection. Use single spacing for the 1-minute timings and double spacing for the 5-minute timing.

LESSON 65

GOALS
- To identify how commas are used in series while typing sentences.
- To format display forms.

FORMAT
- Single spacing   60-space line   5-space tab

LAB 5
COMMAS IN SERIES

Type lines 1–4 twice. Then repeat lines 1–4 or take a series of 1-minute timings.

```
1  We packed our clothes, food, and a tent in the large trunk.   12
2  Joyce wrote about cities, tall buildings, and busy offices.   12
3  I very much like to play tennis, racquetball, and baseball.   12
4  We lost 38 balls, 29 bats, and 10 helmets with our luggage.   12
   |  1  |  2  |  3  |  4  |  5  |  6  |  7  |  8  |  9  | 10  | 11  | 12
```

12-SECOND TIMINGS

Type each line four times, or take four 12-second timings on each line. For each timing, type with no more than one error.

```
5  The one problem is that he might not wish to take the work.   12
6  We know that they can do this work as well as we can do it.   12
7  Why did Joe and the dog not see you at the end of the path?   12
             25    30    35    40    45    50    55    60
```

30-SECOND TIMINGS

Take two 30-second timings on lines 8–10, or type the paragraph twice.

```
8   A big study which explores the question of trust shows that    12
9   people who trust others are very happy folks; they can zero    24
10  in on thoughts that keep them well adjusted and well liked.    36
    |  1  |  2  |  3  |  4  |  5  |  6  |  7  |  8  |  9  | 10  | 11  | 12
```

FORMATTING DISPLAY FORMS

Forms such as certificates and membership cards look best when the names are centered on the lines provided. Either all capitals or capital and lowercase letters can be used. Spread centering can be used also. Signatures are not typed.

JOB 65-1. CERTIFICATES

Type four certificates for students who participated in regional contests for The Ohio Business Education Association. All certificates should be dated December 10, 19—. Format: Center items on the lines. Workbook 93, 95.

Geoffrey Collins placed first in Region III in Advanced Data Processing; Colleen Kennedy placed second in Region III in Advanced Information Communications; Jim Hustad placed first in Region III in Beginning Accounting; and Allison Akers placed third in Beginning Stenography.

JOB 65-2. MEMBERSHIP CARDS

Prepare two cards for the applicants in Jobs 64-1 and 64-2. When typing the school year, use the current year for September to June. Format: Center items on the lines. Workbook 97 top.

A contraction is a shortened form of a phrase in which an apostrophe indicates omitted letters.

we have	we've	who will	who'll	I am	I'm
are not	aren't	I have	I've	he is	he's
they are	they're	do not	don't	you would	you'd

30-SECOND TIMINGS

Take two 30-second timings on lines 5–7, or type the paragraph twice.

5   You can be a part of the work of our nation in so many 12

6 ways. If you write a letter to a senator, vote on Election 24

7 Day, or just keep up on the news, you are a part of it all. 36

| 1 | 2 | 3 | 4 | 5 | 6 | 7 | 8 | 9 | 10 | 11 | 12 |

JOB 228-1. ROUGH DRAFT OF A SPEECH
Standard format.

WHAT _IS_ A LOBBYIST?   LOBBYISTS   6

Although there was a time when a lobbyist was thought of as an unscrupulous person who dealt with dishonest legislators. 10

There are many kinds of *pressure* groups operating within the political 25

arena. Those persons who are employed *by* the *pressure* groups to speak for them 41

in an official capacity are known as lobbyists. Since the early 54

lobbyists conducted their operations in the lobby or main corridor 67

of government buildings, the practice was called "lobbying." There 105

are many businesses that now consider the employment of lobbyists 118

as part of their regular staffing. *Since* ~~As~~ most government officials 132

rely on their help in the handling of legislative issues, lobbyists 146

continue to gain ~~have gained~~ respect in political circles. 155

WHAT DOES A LOBBYIST DO? 160

The role of a lobbyist covers a variety of areas. *It is the job of* The lobbyist 177

~~should~~ *to* become friendly with persons who make the laws, *with* persons who 191

control the media, and with other persons who are also lobbyists for 205

other points of view. A lobbyist may get to know a number of 218

representatives and senators who are influential in the congress and 232

who are *especially* ~~particularly~~ involved in a particular kind of legislation 245

that affects the *pressure* group of the industry that he *or she* represents. Getting 262

to know lobbyists informally may be very *advantageous* ~~good~~ in formal occasions 277

later. One example of using informal contacts may be in regard to 290

the appointment of persons to chair special committees. The 303

media--newspapers, *magazines, radio,* and television--play an important part in influenc- 321

ing the operation *of the government.* A lobbyist learns to know how each type of media 338

operates, who the important media *personalities* are, and how they operate. Once 354

something is printed or said, it's extremely hard to retract it. 368

(Continued on next page)

LESSON 66

GOALS
- To use commas in series correctly while typing sentences.
- To type 35/3'/5e.
- To format and produce three invoices.

FORMAT
- Single spacing   60-space line   5-space tab

LAB 5

Type lines 1–4 once, providing the missing commas. Edit your copy as your teacher reads the answers. Then retype lines 1–4 from your edited copy.

COMMAS IN SERIES

1 The children played with the blocks trucks and tricycles.

2 Mr. Velez typed his quizzes tests and exams on Wednesday.

3 Jo fixed the brakes checked the oil and added antifreeze.

4 Can they make some fudge taffy popcorn and candy apples?

1- AND 3-MINUTE TIMINGS

Take two 1-minute timings on each paragraph. Then take one 3-minute timing on the entire selection. Use single spacing for the 1-minute timings and double-spacing for the 3-minute timing.

5   The energy from coal can do lots of jobs for us. Coal   12

6 gives power for machines and heat for our homes. Coal also   24

7 helps scientists to make things that better our lives.   35

8   Today plastics, many drugs, and types of food dyes are   12

9 made from coal. With a possible fuel shortage now, a large   24

10 effort will be made to make coal fill this urgent need.   35

11   We realize that our search for fuels will make a drain   12

12 on our natural resources. So we must be on guard and watch   24

13 that we do not let greedy folks exploit our quantities.   35

| 1 | 2 | 3 | 4 | 5 | 6 | 7 | 8 | 9 | 10 | 11 | 12 | SI 1.29

FORMATTING INVOICES   Workbook 84.

Invoices vary in size, length, and complexity, but all have the same general format, as shown on page 114. A printed invoice form includes the company name and its return address, the guide words *To:* and *Date:*, and the word *Invoice.* For ease in typing invoices, the column areas are ruled.

To format invoices:

Heading. Begin typing the name and the date 2 spaces after the guide words. Align the typed words with the bottom of the guide words.

Quantity, Unit Price, and Amount Columns. The entries in these columns should be centered visually within each ruled area. Type an underscore under the last entry in the Amount column. The underscore should be as long as the longest entry. **Remember:** Columns of numbers align at the right. Set margin or tab stops for the length of the entry most frequently used, and backspace or space in for other entries.

Description Column. Set a tab 2 spaces to the right of the vertical rule. Double-space between entries. Single-space turnovers when an entry is more than one line. Indent turnovers 3 spaces.

Total Amount Due Line. Type the words *Total amount due* in the Description column, approximately aligned with the *D* in the word *Description.* Type the numbers in the Amount column.

(Continued on next page)

JOB 226/7-4. (Continued)

6. Works with other special- 173
ists to complete production 179
deadlines. 181
7. Reports all required main- 188
tenance of terminal to super- 194
visor. 195
8. Participates in weekly in- 201
service program. 205
9. Performs other duties as 211
designated by supervisor. 216

JOB 226/7-5. JOB DESCRIPTION
Standard format.

Job Description 9
Position Title: Word Processing 19
Supervisor 21
Department: Word Processing Center 30
Responsible to: Office Personnel 38
Director 40
Description of Position: Must 47
be able to work well with 52
people in a time-pressured 57
situation. Must be able to 63
direct regular in-service 68

programs for subordinates. Must 75
possess excellent knowledge 80
of English and formatting skills. 87
Duties: 90
1. Receives, codes, sorts, and 97
routes incoming documents. 103
2. Keeps weekly log of center 110
production. 113
3. Keeps up-to-date coding 119
file for all documents pro- 125
duced in the center. 130
4. Routes all completed documents 138
to authors. 141
5. Communicates with authors 148
concerning efficiency of 153
operation of the center. 159
6. Conducts daily "spot checks" of 166
documents being produced in 171
the center. 175
7. Conducts weekly in-service 181
programs for specialists and 187
authors. 189
8. Authorizes maintenance of 195
equipment in center. 199
9. Performs other duties as 205
designated by office per- 210
sonnel director. 213

GOALS
- To recognize contractions while typing sentences.
- To type from a rough draft of a speech.

FORMAT
- Single spacing   60-space line   5-space tab

LAB 27

CONTRACTIONS

Type lines 1–4 once. Then repeat lines 1–4 or take a series of 1-minute timings.

1 Let's quickly get a dozen people together at the local gym. 12
2 I'm sure that they won't miss your excellent speeches, Don. 12
3 Did you know that she'll be the first woman president here? 12
4 Jan isn't a member of the class, but she's very well known. 12

| 1 | 2 | 3 | 4 | 5 | 6 | 7 | 8 | 9 | 10 | 11 | 12

Spacing. Begin the body of the invoice a double space below the horizontal rule. Single-space each entry; double-space between entries, including the Total amount due line.

Note: Dollar signs are not needed in the Unit Price or Amount columns because only dollar amounts are listed there.

JOB 66-1. INVOICE

Type a copy of the invoice shown below. Standard format. Workbook 97 bottom.

SWISSVALE HIGH BUSINESS CLUB
1036 HIGHLAND AVENUE
SWISSVALE, PA 13821

TO: Ms. Marion Mertz
Music Department

DATE: June 11, 19--

INVOICE

QUANTITY	DESCRIPTION	UNIT PRICE	AMOUNT
300	2-page concert programs	.06	18.00
2	Offset masters	1.10	2.20
800	1-page handouts	.03	24.00
1	Stencil	.75	.75
40	Invitations	.08	3.20
	Total amount due		48.15

FORMATTING QUANTITY COLUMNS WITH WORDS

Sometimes the Quantity column contains words as well as numbers. (See examples at the right.) The numbers must align at the right just as they would in a plain number column. The entire entry (both number and word) should be visually centered in the Quantity column. Use the longest number and the longest word.

QUANTITY	DESCRIPTION
3 boxes	Paper clips
1 pkg.	Carbon paper
125	Envelopes

JOB 66-2. INVOICE

Standard format. Workbook 99 top.

[*Today's date*]
TO: Dr. James Fetter, Principal
     Swissvale High School
     1036 Highland Avenue
     Swissvale, PA 13821

500	Parents' Night programs @ .05	25.00
500	Course information sheets @ .03	15.00
3	Offset masters @ 1.10	3.30
2	jars Colored ink @ 4.75	9.50
5	boxes Gold stars (for programs) @ 1.04	5.20
	Total amount due	58.00

legislature cannot afford to give the automo- 193
bile industry as much time as it is suggesting 202
it needs. 205

The public does not want to give up any of 214
its conveniences either. Doing so would mean 223
performing a few more tasks manually. In 232
our society, which has witnessed many tech- 240
nological advances, manual operation of any- 249

thing is considered very unreasonable and 257
very inconvenient. It would mean putting 265
"we" ahead of "me" in order to make progress. 274

FORMATTING JOB DESCRIPTIONS

To format a job description, follow these steps:

1. Type the title on line 13 in all-capital letters.

2. Set margins for a 60P/70E line.

3. Align words in the heading 2 spaces after the colon following the longest guide word. Double-space between items in the heading.

4. Single-space the position description; double-space before and after it.

5. Follow standard format for the enumeration of the duties.

JOB 226/7-3. LONG REPORT

Space-saving format. Combine Jobs 226/7-1 and 226/7-2. Make the main title "Both Sides of the Energy Debate"; use the two original titles as side headings.

```
                         JOB DESCRIPTION

Position Title:  Word Processing Specialist

Department:      Administrative Support, Word Processing Services

Responsible to:  Office Personnel Director

Description of Position:  To offer word processing services to ten
legislative principals of the federal government in a shared communica-
tions atmosphere.

Duties:

1.  Receives, codes, sorts, and routes incoming documents.

2.  Keyboards all communications into terminals and stores them in the
    CPU.
```

JOB 226/7-4. JOB DESCRIPTION

Standard format.

Job Description 9
Position Title: Word Processing Specialist 21
Department: Word Processing Center 30
Responsible to: Word Processing Supervisor 41
Description of Position: Must possess excellent 53
keyboarding, formatting, editing, and 61
transcription skills, and be able to work 69
in a team situation with eight other 76
specialists. 79
Duties: 82

1. Keyboards all communications on terminal 92
and stores them in CPU. 97

2. Performs editing functions for documents 107
called up from CPU for revision. 115

3. Proofreads and edits all copy for typo- 124
graphical, formatting, spelling, grammatical, 134
and content errors. 138

4. Prints out final draft of documents and 148
routes them to supervisor. 154

5. Keeps daily log of number of lines keyed 164
on terminal. 166

(Continued on next page)

FORMATTING ADJUSTMENTS TO INVOICES

Adjustments such as delivery charges, sales taxes, and discounts are typed before *Total amount due* and aligned with it, as shown at the right. First type *Amount due* (a subtotal) a double space below the last entry. Then type the adjustment line (or lines) single-spaced below *Amount due*, with a rule under the last adjustment line.

Double-space and then type *Total amount due.*

```
Amount due              343.35
Sales tax 6%             20.60
Delivery charges         15.00

Total amount due        378.95
```

JOB 66-3. INVOICE
Standard format. Use today's date. Workbook 99 bottom.

To: Scott Klein, Treasurer, The Business Club
Swissvale High School
1036 Highland Avenue
Swissvale, PA 13821

45 cans	Coke, ginger ale, and orange soda @ .30	13.50
6 dozen	Cookies @ .99	5.94
3 dozen	Cupcakes @ 1.89	5.67
5 bags	Potato chips @ .98	4.90
61	Ice cream bars @ .40	24.40
	Amount due	54.41
	Sales tax 6%	3.26
	Total amount due	57.67

LESSON 67

GOALS
- To type 35/3'/5e.
- To practice typing symbols.

FORMAT
- Single spacing   60-space line   5-space tab

KEYBOARDING SKILLS

Type lines 1–4 once. Then practice smooth shift-key control by capitalizing the proper nouns in line 5. Repeat lines 1–4, or take a series of 1-minute timings.

Speed	1	He may wish to pay them if and when they go to town for us.	12
Accuracy	2	Bernard won five major prizes equal to your six big checks.	12
Numbers	3	Please order 10 cakes, 29 pies, and 38 quarts of ice cream.	12
Symbols	4	Jo may write to Dop & Co., Smith & Sons, and Howe & Blaker.	12
Technique	5	Lyle Jinx Lisa Dora Lulu Mina Jack Boyd Nate Hank Jane Saul	12

| 1 | 2 | 3 | 4 | 5 | 6 | 7 | 8 | 9 | 10 | 11 | 12

Take two 3-minute timings on lines 11–22.

```
            1                 2                 3              4
11      Businesses and individuals can write letters to people    12
            5                 6                 7              8
12   in Washington.  There are several persons to whom you might   24
            9                10                11             12
13   send a letter.  You could write to the President, to a sen—   36
           13                14                15             16
14   ator, or to a representative.  Each person who is chosen to   48
           17                18                19             20
15   go to Washington takes a staff along who can answer most of   60
           21                22                23             24
16   the mail citizens send.  Using the mail is one way that the   72
           25                26                27             28
17   legislators continually keep in touch with what is going on   84
           29                30                31
18   in their individual congressional districts.                 93
           32                33                34             35
19      People send inquiries on many subjects.  They may want    105
           36                37                38             39
20   to express a positive feeling, or they may want to complain   117
           40                41                42             43
21   about taxes, pollution, or foreign policy.  Some letters do   129
           44                45                46
22   influence how lawmakers make their decisions.                138

   |  1  |  2  |  3  |  4  |  5  |  6  |  7  |  8  |  9  |  10  |  11  |  12     SI 1.61
```

JOB 226/7-1. ONE-PAGE REPORT
Standard format.

REDUCE ENERGY PRESSURES   14

A review of energy options has not produced   26
any politically acceptable alternatives for cut-   37
ting the uses of energy. This means that we   44
must continue to seek new ways to replace the   54
oil imports. Although Congress does not favor   63
the import fee, it may be the only alternative   72
left once other avenues have been explored.   81

Several alternatives have been expressed by   91
other members of Congress. The first of these   101
is to remove the price controls from gasoline   110
and allow the oil companies to operate under   119
a situation of decontrol for a while. A second   128
alternative which has been discussed before is   138
that we give serious consideration to reducing   147
the import of foreign oil. We are continuing   156
to reduce our consumption each year. This   165
reduction may allow us to eliminate the need   174
for any import of oil in the future.   182

It has been noted with some optimism that   191
new sources of energy are now being discovered   200
along the East Coast of our country. Addi-   209
tional funds to encourage more exploration at   218
this level will need to be given important time   228
in the next session of Congress. One or two   237
large finds along the coast would certainly   246
relieve the pressure on the domestic scene.   254
With the growing pressures on the American   263
economy, it is indeed a risky move to consider   273
adding to the burden of the consumers.   280

JOB 226/7-2. ONE-PAGE REPORT
Standard format.

RESPONSIBILITY MUST BE ASSUMED   18

Although the topic of an energy crisis has   30
been before the public for a number of years,   39
the American people still do not want to accept   49
the fact that there is a crisis. Different reasons   59
for not wanting to take on the responsibility   68
for dealing with a crisis are given by different   78
segments of the population.   84

The oil producers, of course, always favor   93
full decontrol so that there would be no limit   103
to what the domestic businesses and OPEC   111
could demand for oil. They would like to have   120
full rein to determine what costs are necessary   130
in order to operate at an acceptable margin of   140
profit.   142

The automobile industry wants more and   150
more time to make the changes in technology   159
and marketing necessary to allow them to   167
keep a profitable business going. Although   176
many of their arguments make sense, the   184

(Continued on next page)

SYMBOL PRACTICE

Type each line twice, or take a series of 1-minute timings on lines 6–12.

6 John claims Order #38 is for 38#, but Order #38 is for 29#.   12

7 Yes, Jo, it is better to buy 20 @ 15¢ than to buy 10 @ 21¢.   12

8 The box is (1) big, (2) wrapped, and (3) too heavy to lift.   12

9 He said, "Pay the $56 or I'll call the state police today."   12

10 Give Lake & Dun 10%, B&G 12%, Mann & Scot 11%, and T&L 13%.   12

11 Type an asterisk (*) next to the most important references.   12

12 As an example, please write 29 + 38 = 67 on the chalkboard.   12

13 If you must drive to Ohio, then be sure to use a seat belt.   12
    | 1 | 2 | 3 | 4 | 5 | 6 | 7 | 8 | 9 | 10 | 11 | 12

12-SECOND TIMINGS

Type each line four times, or take four 12-second timings on each line. For each timing, type with no more than one error.

14 We would prefer to take a lot of quizzes, not one big exam.   12
15 A small tug pushed the liner into the quay and to the pier.   12
16 If you put the sodas in the fridge, they will soon be cold.   12
    25   30   35   40   45   50   55   60

PREVIEW PRACTICE

Type lines 17 and 18 twice as a preview to the 1- and 3-minute timings below.

Accuracy

17 bolts wrought machines products nonsteel tranquil civilized

Speed

18 could about write least build books paper long iron ore new

1- AND 3-MINUTE TIMINGS

Take two 1-minute timings on each paragraph. Then take two 3-minute timings on the entire selection. Use single spacing for the 1-minute timings and double spacing for the 3-minute timings.   1'

19   Iron and steel are the most useful and least expensive   12

20 metals we have. Iron ore is needed to make steel, which in   24

21 turn is used to make things from bolts to battleships.   35

22   Iron is not new to a civilized world; wrought iron was   12

23 used by people long before they could read and write. Some   24

24 nations have failed because they lacked iron and steel.   35

25   Steel is used to build the machines which produce just   12

26 about all the nonsteel products needed for a tranquil life,   24

27 such as plastic, paper, fibers, books, cans, and jars.   35
    | 1 | 2 | 3 | 4 | 5 | 6 | 7 | 8 | 9 | 10 | 11 | 12   SI 1.29

Text processing, a commonly used business term, refers to formatting information that has been input (*a*) from handwritten, typed rough draft, or typed unarranged copy; (*b*) from shorthand notes; or (*c*) from material dictated on a recording machine.

Specifically, in Level 7 you will:

1. Demonstrate keyboarding accuracy and speed on straight copy with a goal of 48 words a minute or more for 5 minutes with no more than 3 errors.

2. Correctly proofread copy for errors and edit copy for revision.

3. Apply production skills in keyboarding and formatting copy for four categories of business documents from six input modes in the following settings: federal government (Lessons 226–230); political campaign (Lessons 232–237); data control center (Lessons 238–243); health spa (Lessons 244–249); publishing (In-Basket E); speciality shop (In-Basket F); architecture (In-Basket G); and historical society (In-Basket H).

4. Decide about formatting and priority in completing tasks for four in-baskets.

5. Apply rules for correct use of contractions and possessives in communications.

LESSONS 226/ 227

UNIT 37 PROCESSING REPORTS

UNIT GOAL
46/5'/3e

GOALS
- To type three business reports.
- To format and type a job description.

FORMAT
- Single spacing   60-space line   5-space tab

KEYBOARDING SKILLS

Type lines 1–4 once. In line 5, backspace and underscore the titles shown in italics. Repeat lines 1–4, or take a series of 1-minute timings.

Speed	1	It is the time for all of us to take the time to save more. 12
Accuracy	2	The Zanzibar Express was jolting us four but moved quickly. 12
Numbers	3	Would you like to see 10, 29, 38, 47, or 56 new characters? 12
Symbols	4	Adam (my colleague) paid $6.95 a ream for 20# tinted paper. 12
Technique	5	Please make plans to peruse *Future Shock* or *The Third Wave*.

| 1 | 2 | 3 | 4 | 5 | 6 | 7 | 8 | 9 | 10 | 11 | 12

12-SECOND TIMINGS

Type each line four times, or take four 12-second timings on each line. For each timing, type without error.

6 When will she be able to amend the bill that she supported? 12
7 He sent a letter about an issue to two members of Congress. 12
8 When you take a tour, you may see the new Congress at work. 12

25   30   35   40   45   50   55   60

PREVIEW PRACTICE

Type lines 9 and 10 twice as a preview to the 3-minute timings on page 364.

Accuracy 9 inquiries Washington continually individuals representative
Speed 10 keep with mail send most whom what want make some each many

LESSON 68

GOALS
- To use commas in series correctly while typing sentences.
- To format long reports.

FORMAT
- Single spacing   60-space line   5-space tab

LAB 5

COMMAS IN SERIES

Workbook 103–104.

Type lines 1–4, providing the missing commas. Edit your copy as your teacher reads the answers. Then retype lines 1–4 from your edited copy.

1 I hope to go through Germany Holland and Italy next year.

2 Their figures for January are $125.50 $162.19 and $14.24.

3 Look up these numbers: 263-12 410-79 244-83 and 766-42.

4 Harold Betty Alice and Sam have worked on these quizzes.

SKILL DEVELOPMENT DRILL

Type each line twice.

Speed

5 Did she pay the neighbor to fix the oaken box for the coal?

6 I am to go to work for the audit firm by the eighth of May.

Accuracy

7 Jeff amazed the audience by quickly giving six new reports.

8 Five bright boys could work extra now to pass a major quiz.

Numbers

9 She sold 1,234 in June, 3,456 in July, and 7,890 in August.

10 The winning bulletins were numbered 56, 47, 38, 29, and 10.

Symbols

The symbol " also means "inches."

11 The five maple boards measured 10", 29", 38", 47", and 56".

12 I bought 10 shares @ 29, 38 shares @ 47, and 56 shares @ 1.

FORMATTING LONG REPORTS

A *long report* is one that takes more than one page. Long reports usually contain side headings and/or paragraph headings.

The first page of a long report is formatted in the same manner as a one-page report: (1) the title is typed on line 13; (2) margins are set for a 60-space pica or a 70-space elite line; and (3) the body of the report is double-spaced. The bottom margin for any full page should contain a minimum of 6 blank lines or a maximum of 9 blank lines.

To format continuation pages in a long report:

1. Type the page number (the word *page* is unnecessary) on line 7 at the right margin. (Do not type a page number on the first page.)

2. Begin the text of the report on line 10, a triple space below the page number.

↓ 7
2

↓ 3

BOTTOM MARGINS

The bottom margin on each page should be a minimum of 6

or a maximum of 9 lines deep. On standard paper with 66 lines,

JOB 68-1. LONG REPORT
Standard format.

LONG REPORTS

A Report for Typing 1

by (Your name)

¶A long report is one that takes more than ① page. To prepare long reports that ~~is~~ are consistent and attractively arranged, follow the guidelines given in ~~the~~ this paper.

GENERAL RULES

A long # report is typed on a line of 60 pica or 70 elite spaces, with the body ~~single~~ double-spaced. The Main headings--title, subtitle (optional), and author's name--~~are~~ is centered. Side headings are typed at the le~~f~~ft margin in all caps, preceded by 2 blank lines.

HEADINGS AND TOP # MARGINS

First Page. The main heading of two or three double-spaced lines as shown above begins on Line 13, leaving a top margin of 12 blank lines. ~~It~~ The main heading is followed by 2 blank lines. This page is counted, but no page number is typed on ~~it~~ page 1.

Other Pages. The heading of ~~all~~ each other page consists of the page number. (The word Page is not necessary.) The page number is backspaced from the right margin on line 7, leaving 6 lines in the ~~top~~ margin. The page number is followed by 2 blank lines, so that the # body of the report will always resume on line 10 on each continuation page.

Start page 2 here. → BOTTOM MARGINS

The bottom margin on each page should be a minimum of 6 or a maximum of 9 lines. On standard paper with 66 lines, the last line of typing should appear on line 57, 57 8, 59, or 60. if it is necessary to break a paragraph, at least ~~two~~ 2 lines should be typed on the first page and 2 lines on the following page.

JOB 224/5-4. RECEIPTS

Prepare receipts for the following people for deposits they made on scheduled vacation trips. Workbook 523.

1. Mr. and Mrs. Paul Ficorilli, P.O. Box 9652, Baltimore, MD 21237, $200, Hawaii

2. Mrs. G. E. Thayer, 158 De Sabla Drive, Hillsborough, CA 94010. $375. Paris-Rome.

3. Ms. Marion Jefferson, 12507 Southeast River Drive, Portland, OR 97222, $150, California.

4. Professor Dudley Moore, 3606 Arsenal, St. Louis, MO 63148, $500, Orient.

JOB 224/5-5. BULLETIN

Format attractively for posting on a bulletin board at a travel agency.

Baggage Checklist

1. Pack your belongings in a sturdy bag. Molded luggage is best for checked baggage.

2. lock your baggage.

4. Be a smart packer. Pack heavy items at the bottom and back of your bag. put all breakables and items that could leak into plastic bags.

3. put your name on the outside and inside of your baggage. Every piece of your baggage, whether it is carried on or checked, should have your name, address and phone number on the outside and inside.

4. Know the carrier guidelines. On domestic flights you are allowed 3 pieces of luggage. international free baggage allowances vary according to air line destination.

6. Pack for your destination. Be prepared for rain and cold.

7. Carry items of high value with you. Never pack cameras, jewelry, money, or important papers.

8. Get to the check-in counter at least thirty minutes before a domestic flight and sixty minutes before an international flight.

9. Use special containers for special baggage, such as golf clubs, skis, or valet bags.

10. Be sure to keep a checklist of all your luggage items, plus a description of your bags--just in case something does go astray.

JOB 224/5-6. ADDRESSING FORM LETTERS AND ENVELOPES

Use the rent-a-car form letters you prepared. Address them to the persons for whom you prepared receipts. Address envelopes.

To avoid typing in the bottom margin, use ~~any~~ one of these ~~procedures:~~

1. Count the lines, stop on line 57, 58, 59, or 60.

2. Before inserting the paper, draw a very light pencil line at the right edge about 2 inches from the bottom as a caution signal; Erase it when you finish and remove the page.

3. On a separate sheet, draw heavy lines to show where the margins should be. Put this visual guide under the ~~page~~ paper on which you type; the lines will show through to help you maintain correct margins on every page of the report.

LESSONS 69/70

GOALS
- To recognize how commas are used after introductory clauses while typing sentences.
- To format text references and footnotes.

FORMAT
- Single spacing   60-space line   5-space tab

LAB 6

Type lines 1–4 once. Then repeat lines 1–4 or take a series of 1-minute timings.

INTRODUCTORY
IF, AS, **AND**
WHEN
CLAUSES

1 If Barte Gomez calls while we are out, just take a message.   12
2 As David quickly noticed, your extra hours are paid double.   12
3 When Yvette explained zero budgeting, she did so very well.   12
4 Although Jack left quickly, he missed the bus to Kalamazoo.   12

Use a comma after an introductory clause that begins with *if, as, when, although, since, because,* or a similar conjunction. Note the examples in lines 1–7.

12-SECOND
TIMINGS

Type each line four times, or take four 12-second timings on each line. For each timing, type with no more than one error.

5 As we started to dance, the lights were quickly turned off.   12
6 When the moon came up, the lake was a huge sheet of silver.   12
7 When it began to rain, they had to call a halt to the game.   12

25   30   35   40   45   50   55   60

JOB 224/5-1. LETTER WITH RULED TABLE

Standard format. Workbook 513–514. Body 168 words (plus 20 words for table).

Ms. Debbie Schwartz, 1100 Oceana Drive, Aurora, OH 44202, Dear Debbie: I am delighted that you thought of writing to Worldwide Travel Agency to help you with some of the travel questions you and your classmates are discussing in your course entitled World Affairs. It is important for everyone to know about the subject of travel expenses and how to go about finding economical ways to visit other countries.

You particularly asked me to identify the high-cost foreign cities; that is, the places in the world that are expensive to live in. Our latest source of information from the United Nations reports the following statistics. The index is based on a comparison with the costs of living in New York City, which is rated 100.

Add title High-cost-of-living cities

Country	City	Index
Japan	Tokyo	199
Switzerland	Geneva	163
Belgium	Brussels	150
Denmark	Copenhagen	146
Netherlands	The Hague	143
Austria	Vienna	138
France	Paris	136

I hope that this information is complete and pertinent to your course work. Please do not hesitate to call Worldwide Travel whenever we can be of service to you. Sincerely, Holly Allen-Sloan, Manager

JOB 224/5-2. BOXED TABLE

Arrange the table in the letter to Ms. Schwartz on a full sheet of paper. Put cities in the first column and countries in the second column. Arrange the table body alphabetically by city. Use 8 spaces between columns.

JOB 224/5-3. FORM LETTER

Block format. Make three carbon copies.
Workbook 515–522. Body 142 words.

Dear Traveler: Now you can afford to fly to any major American city and rent a car—for less money than you would anticipate paying for such convenience.

BEST Rent-A-Car offers you late-model subcompacts at the economy fare of only $29 a week, or $9.95 a day. Our customer service representatives are at major airports to assist you with every detail, including maps and directions. You get more vehicles to choose from, more people to assist you, and more special services to speed you on your way.

There are minimum day and advance reservation requirements; and if you use one of our many designated locations, there is no drop-off charge. With some rent-a-car companies, you are charged as much as $100 for drop-off privileges between certain locations. Call BEST at 800-555-3300. Or call your travel consultant. Sincerely, Carrie Mitchel Best, Vice President

Take a 3-minute Pretest on lines 8–16. Then circle and count your errors. Use the chart below to determine which lines to type for practice.

```
                    1                    2                3                  4
8        Every day the sun sends out to Earth quiet jet streams      12
              5                    6                 7              8
9    of sunlight, which are a new and vital source of energy.  A    24
              9                 10                11             12
10   nation like ours could adequately fill its needs for energy    36
              13                 14                15              16
11   sources if the rays of the sun could be kept and stored, as    48
              17                 18                19            20
12   in a tank.  Solar energy could be used to heat homes and to    60
              21                 22                23            24
13   run engines, but more research must be done to find ways to    72
              25                 26                27            28
14   store the excess heat from the sun.  We all must constantly    84
              29                 30                31            32
15   work to save fuel; if we rely on the sun rather than oil or    96
              33                 34                35
16   coal, the possibility of a shortage is zero.                   105
     |  1  |  2  |  3  |  4  |  5  |  6  |  7  |  8  |  9  |  10  |  11  |  12     SI 1.30
```

PRACTICE

In the chart below, find the number of errors you made on the Pretest. Then type each of the designated drill lines four times.

Pretest errors	0–1	2–3	4–5	6–7
Drill lines	20–24	19–23	18–22	17–21

Accuracy

```
17   quiet could stored energy source research sunlight shortage
18   be zero earth rather nation excess sources engines research
19   we sun solar store vital every could constantly possibility
20   or jet homes needs which energy engines research adequately
```

Speed

```
21   used done heat ways fill than fuel save for run day out sun
22   rays kept find coal tank rely more ours jet its oil ray all
23   excess rather quiet store tank zero but sun and new are the
24   sources heat must from ways done used like ours jet for out
```

POSTTEST

Repeat the Pretest to see how much your skill has improved.

FORMATTING TEXT REFERENCES

In Lesson 47, you formatted reports with run-in references, which indicate to the reader the source of the statement cited. Run-in references were formatted in parentheses within the body of the report.

Another way to format references is to place the notes at the bottom (or the "foot") of the same page on which they occur. References formatted in this way are called footnotes.

To indicate the presence of a reference in the body of the report, type a superscript (raised) number immediately following the appropriate word, phrase, or sentence.

Practice typing a superscript number; use the example below. To type the raised number, turn the cylinder back slightly with one hand and type the number with the other.

```
     John Henry Abbott wrote the book.[1]  He frequently re-
ferred to the writings of Samuel Brooks Newhouse.[2]
```

LESSONS 224/ 225

COMPETENCY CHECK

GOALS
- To type 45/5'/4e.
- To demonstrate competency in formatting and producing a variety of correctly typed documents from numerous sources.

FORMAT
- Single spacing   60-space line   5-space tab and other tabs as needed

PREVIEW PRACTICE

Accuracy
Speed

Type lines 1 and 2 twice as a preview to the 5-minute timings below.

1 degree career readily cluster average elsewhere competently
2 work type paid make it's this with then but pay if do so or

5-MINUTE TIMINGS

Take two 5-minute timings on lines 3–21. Circle your errors on both timings.

3   The degree of skill required of a word processing typ—   12
4 ist depends on whether you work in a standalone, a cluster,   24
5 or a center. In all three types you are really expected to   36
6 complete numerous kinds of operations, but it is clear that   48
7 the standalone demands the broadest experience, the cluster   60
8 next, and the center least. In other words, a beginner can   72
9 be employed readily in a center but possibly not elsewhere.   84
10   Pay scales are not standardized, but you will probably   96
11 be paid according to the operations you can demonstrate. A   08
12 standalone operator earns more, in most offices, because he   120
13 or she should be able to do more jobs that make the machine   132
14 prove it is cost effective and as productive as advertised.   144
15   If there's something to be acquired from these remarks   156
16 about word processing, it's probably this: A little knowl—   168
17 edge and a little experience are not enough. If you intend   180
18 to pursue a career using this new technology, learn to type   192
19 with above—average speed and accuracy. Then master all the   204
20 operations that your word processing machine is designed to   216
21 do so that you are able to work competently.   225

| 1 | 2 | 3 | 4 | 5 | 6 | 7 | 8 | 9 | 10 | 11 | 12   SI 1.59

FORMATTING FOOTNOTES

To format footnotes:

1. Plan ahead to determine the number of lines you must "save" at the bottom of the page. As you type each superscript in the text, estimate the number of lines for that footnote, and mark lightly with a pencil the point at which you should stop typing the text.

2. Single-space after the last line of text, and type an underscore (20P or 24E strokes) beginning at the left margin. This line separates the footnotes from the text.

3. Double-space, indent 5 spaces, and type the footnote number (use a superscript) and the reference. Use single spacing for any continuation lines needed, and begin them at the left margin, as shown in the illustration below.

4. Double-space between footnotes.

5. Always format footnotes at the bottom of the page—even on the last page of a report that may have only a few lines of text. The bottom margin below the footnote should be a minimum of 6 lines or a maximum of 9 lines.

Note that April 1981 *(rather than* April, 1981,*) is the modern style for month/year dates. Also note that* p. *indicates one page;* pp., *more than one page.*

		Bottom lines
52	the year 1871.[1] This unique invention was not accepted until	15
53		14
54	the turn of the century, when Bobbsfield moved to England.[2]	13
55		12
56	_____	11
57	[1]Barbara Anne Hemsley, "The Distant Land," The National	10
58	Outlook, April 1981, pp. 215-216.	9
59		8
60	[2]Ibid., p. 217.	7
61		6
62		5
63		4
64		3
65		2
66		1

JOB 69/70-1. LONG REPORT WITH FOOTNOTES

Standard format. Change the run-in references to footnotes; use superscripts in the text.

THE HISTORY OF THE OLYMPICS
By Susan Lum Lin

Why did the Olympic Games begin? Why did they die after more than a thousand years of pomp and glory? And what forces caused them to begin again more than a thousand years later in a world that was not the same as the world in which they began?

THE LEGEND

Before you can answer these questions, you must know some facts about the history of the Olympic Games. In 490 B.C., the city-state of Athens sent a force of 9,000 to meet a great Persian army of 90,000.

On the plain of Marathon, where the armies clashed, the Greeks attacked, broke the foe, and won the day. ("The History of the Olympic Games," History of Sports, Randall Books, Chicago, 1982, p. 116.) As the Persians ran for their ships, the leader of the Greeks called for the great runner Pheidippides to carry the word to Athens, where the people longed for news of the battle.

Athens lay 40 kilometers, about 25 miles, south of Marathon. Pheidippides, who had fought in the war, put down his shield and began to run. He had to run uphill and over rough land, but he did not stop. Three hours later he reached

NEWSPAPER ARTICLE

Ms. Allen-Sloan wants you to prepare a correct copy for publication in the *Cleveland News*, Sunday edition, July 29. Standard format.

(Title) Jamaica *PUT MANAGER'S NAME AND AGENCY AS BYLINE.*

Jamaica is an island in the Caribbean, rich in beauty and culture. it has a long history that dates before the days of explorers. Its many different peoples are testimony to it's varied past, and they live in harmony under ~~under~~ a government that maintains friendly con- *ALMOST* tact with all nations on earth.

Tourists love jamaica for its beautiful white-sand beaches and crystal-clear waters, the lush jungles that dot the hillsides, and the exciting night life that features steel-drum bands and reggae music.

The food of Jamica is healthy and natural because most of it *STAPLES* comes from the island. Fresh sea food and delicious fruits are important that the natives cook in a variety of dishes.

HOTELS
Visitors to the island may stay in the big on the beaches, rent homes, or camp out in the country side. The unique aspects of Jamaica is that it is an entire country, not just a resort; so vacationing there becomes a total experience.

ARTICLE MUST BE AT NEWSPAPER OFFICE THREE DAYS BEFORE PUBLICATION.

NO #

Relaxing as a visit may be, it is also educational. The daily life of Jamaicans goes on undisturbed by tourists, and this gives visitors a chance to observe a different culture first hand. Although Jamaica is close to florida, it is far enough away to provide visitors with the feeling of being in a strange land!

FORM LETTER

Standard format. Edit the copy as you type it.

variety is the spice of life! whether you'd like exploring americas favorite resort destenations or cruising the blue caribbean...its up to you. this year, the chamber of commerce has arranged not one, but two greast vacations. you have a choice of:

americas own san francisco, hawaii, and las vegas

or

a caribbean cruise aboard the ss princess grace

we would like to point that the price of each trip (including round-trip jet transportation accommodations all transfers baggage handling plus most taxes and tips) is only $690 less than you would pay to plan the trip yourself. besides, if you traveled on your own you would miss out on the convience and companion ship you'll get when traveling with members of the chamber.

all the excellent features of these too outstanding vacations are discribed in detail in the enclosed brosures. look them over and then join the chanber for a vacation to remember. sincerely, holly allen-sloan.

Athens, where a huge crowd waited. Pheidippides staggered toward the people and spoke these words: "Rejoice--we have won!" (Ibid., p. 119.) Then he fell to the ground and died.

ANCIENT OLYMPIC GAMES

The events of the Olympic Games in ancient Greece centered on the skills that were needed to stay alive; that is, good health and fitness. The athletes were not paid, so they had to pay for all their own expenses. The only prizes were wreaths of olive leaves. Later, though, prizes of money were given, and these prizes caused cheating to become common. (Harold Mark Kokoris, The Greeks, Spartan Press, New York, 1978, p. 79.)

MODERN OLYMPIC GAMES

From the fall of Rome until the late 1800s, nations were so busy fighting wars that they did not compete in sports. When the Olympics were started again in Athens in 1896 be-fore 50,000 people, 12 countries played in the games. Track and field races were the main events, and the United States won first place in nine events. (Deborah and Grace Brumley, "A Man of Peace," Digest of History, April 1980, p. 31.)

Today athletes can score better than ever. They can study their form on slow-motion films. The surface on the track has been improved to give the runners better footing. Rules have changed--starting blocks can be used to give track stars that extra push, and springy poles help high jumpers soar much higher than jumpers in the early 1900s. (Kokoris, The Greeks, p. 88.)

In the Olympic Games, young men and women from many nations meet and compete. In this way, it is hoped that they will build friendships with people around the world so that the Olympics will lead the nations of the world to peace rather than to war.

LESSON 71

GOAL
- To format bibliographies, cover sheets, and endnotes.

FORMAT
- Single spacing   60-space line   5-space tab

KEYBOARDING SKILLS

Type lines 1–4 once. Then do what line 5 tells you to do. Repeat lines 1–4, or take a series of 1-minute timings.

Speed	1	When Lana and Nancy go to town, they may visit Ken and Pam.	12
Accuracy	2	Ask Jack Sworcz if he can quickly fix five machines for us.	12
Numbers	3	Betty ordered 10, 29, 38, 47, and 56 cartons, respectively.	12
Symbols	4	For $9 more (plus tax) she can get 32% more grain--only $9!	12
Technique	5	Retype line 3, underscoring each of the five numbers in the sentence.	

| 1 | 2 | 3 | 4 | 5 | 6 | 7 | 8 | 9 | 10 | 11 | 12 |

30-SECOND TIMINGS

Take two 30-second timings on lines 6–8, or type each line twice.

6	Six big Kansas jewelers have imported quartz for my clocks.	12
7	Alex A. Bishop may want foreign jade and zinc very quickly.	24
8	Six lively clowns quietly joked Fred about his dog, Grumpy.	36

| 1 | 2 | 3 | 4 | 5 | 6 | 7 | 8 | 9 | 10 | 11 | 12 |

DAY	DATE	TIME	EVENT
MONDAY	8/9	8:00 a.m.	TORONTO TO OTTAWA
		1:30 p.m.	TOUR OTTAWA
			VICTORIA PLAZA
TUESDAY	8/10	8:30 a.m.	OTTAWA TO QUEBEC CITY
			CHELSEA HOTEL
WEDNESDAY	8/11	9:00 a.m.	TOUR CITY; VISIT
			ST. ANNE-DE-BEAUPRE
			CHELSEA HOTEL
THURSDAY	8/12	8:00 a.m.	QUEBEC CITY TO MONTREAL
		2:00 p.m.	TOUR THE CITY
			ROYAL HOTEL
FRIDAY	8/13	8:30 a.m.	MONTREAL TO GANANOQUE
		10:30 a.m.	CRUISE THROUGH ISLANDS
		4:15 p.m.	BUS TO KINGSTON
			KINGSTON INN
SATURDAY	8/14	8:30 a.m.	TOUR FORT HENRY
		2:00 p.m.	BUS TO NIAGARA FALLS
			HAMILTON HOUSE
SUNDAY	8/15	9:00 a.m.	TOUR THE FALLS
		5:00 p.m.	BUS TO CLEVELAND

NEWSPAPER ADVERTISEMENT

Format attractively on a half sheet of paper. Final copy should be about 5 by 3 inches in size.

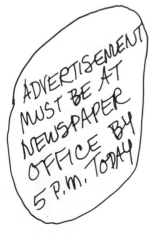

ADVERTISEMENT MUST BE AT NEWSPAPER OFFICE BY 5 P.M. TODAY

LAS VEGAS—Group or Individual Tours

5 days, 4 nights

Price includes round-trip nonstop airfare, shows, top hotels, transportation to/from airport, baggage handling, some meals. From $405 and up per person with double occupancy.

Worldwide Travel Agency.

Phone 555-8900.

Act now!

Space is limited.

FORMATTING ENDNOTES

Endnotes are references gathered in a separate section at the end of a report. They are used instead of footnotes. To format endnotes:

1. Center the heading *Notes* in all-capital letters on line 13. Use a full sheet of paper.

2. Triple-space below the heading to begin typing the first note.

3. Use the same margins for the notes as used in the report.

4. Indent each note 5 spaces, and type the reference number followed by a period, 2 spaces, and the reference. (Do not use a superscript.)

5. Single-space notes that take more than one line, and begin contin-

uation lines at the left margin, as shown in the illustration.

6. Double-space between notes, to leave 1 blank line between them.

7. Number endnotes the same way you number the pages of a long report.

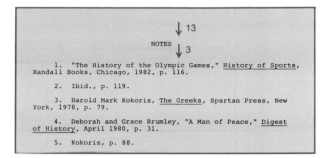

JOB 71-1. ENDNOTES

Prepare endnotes for the report on the Olympics. Use the run-in references in Job 69/70-1 on pages 121–122 as the copy for the endnotes. Standard format.

FORMATTING A BIBLIOGRAPHY

A bibliography is an alphabetic listing of all the books and articles consulted by the writer, including all references cited in footnotes.

To format a bibliography:

1. Center the heading BIBLIOGRAPHY on a fresh sheet of paper, beginning on line 13.

2. Triple-space after the heading before typing the first entry in the bibliography.

3. Use the same margins as used in the report or term paper. Begin each entry at the left margin, and

indent any continuation lines 5 or 10 spaces.

4. Use single spacing for any continuation lines, but double-space between entries.

5. Do not number the entries.

6. List the entries in alphabetic order by the authors' *last* names. For an entry that has no author, alphabetize by the title of the article or book. (See below.)

7. Use six hyphens to avoid repeating an author's name after his or her first listing. (See below.)

When author is not known, put the book or article in alphabetic order by title. (Disregard the words The, A, *and* An.)

```
                              ↓ 13
                    BIBLIOGRAPHY
                              ↓ 3

Brumley, Deborah and Grace, "A Man of Peace," Digest of History,
     April 1980.

Drebrelis, Nichola, "In Search of Ancient Gods," Modern Science
     Today, November 1980.

"The History of the Olympic Games," History of Sports, Randall
     Books, Chicago, 1982.

Kokoris, Harold Mark, The Greeks, Spartan Press, New York, 1978.

------, The Beginning of the Olympics, Dunne Publishing Company,
     Los Angeles, 1982.
```

You are working for Worldwide Travel Agency located at 1200 East Sixth Street, Cleveland, OH 44114. The owner-manager is Ms. Holly Allen-Sloan. Today is July 25, 19—. Use letterheads and forms where appropriate. Workbook 510 bottom–512.

PRIORITY SHEET AND TIME LOG

Read through the entire in-basket, and then complete the priority sheet. Keep an accurate time log as you complete each job.

PROGRAM BULLETIN

Format an attractive bulletin to advertise the agency's fall travelogue series. The agency sponsors the series of programs to promote travel and to advertise its services.

TRAVELOGUE SERIES, FALL 19—, Sponsored by Worldwide Travel Agency

Thursday, September 18
 Exploring Norway—Jonathan Forshee
 The travelogue takes viewers to Norway's famous fjords; to Bergen, Norway's second largest city, which gives the appearance of a quaint eleventh-century Viking seaport, to the ski and resort countryside of rural Norway, and to Oslo, the capital city and chief seaport.

Thursday, October 23
 Alaska Adventure—Betty Ebbert
 Magnificent coverage of the wonders to be found along the great north highways which lead to the innermost points of northern Canada and Alaska. Popular spots, as well as those seldom visited by tourists, are covered. Daring closeups of wildlife, trips to exciting fishing streams, and mountain climbing are featured.

Tuesday, November 11
 Bermuda, Isle of Rest—Thomas O'Reilly
 In Bermuda, viewers will visit the U.S. Naval Base, tour the Cathedral, explore for sunken treasure, and learn of the island's role in our War of Independence.

Tickets are free at Worldwide Travel Agency. Programs will be held at the Downtown Chamber of Commerce Building, Century III Shopping Mall, Cleveland, OH 44114, at 10 a.m. and again at 7:30 p.m.

ITINERARY

Standard format.

ITINERARY FOR MR. AND MRS. GRAY

DAY	DATE	TIME	EVENT
SUNDAY	8/8	8:00 a.m.	BUS FROM CLEVELAND TO TORONTO
		2.00 p.m.	TOUR TORONTO FRIARS' INN

(Continued on next page)

FORMATTING A COVER PAGE

A cover page contains the title of the report, the name of the writer, the course title, the teacher's name for whom the report was prepared, and the date.

To format a cover page:

1. Center the report title and the writer's name in the upper 33 lines of the page.

2. Center the course title, the teacher's name, and the date in the lower 33 lines of the page.

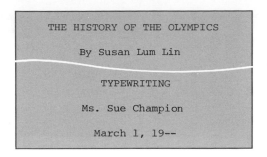

```
THE HISTORY OF THE OLYMPICS

   By Susan Lum Lin



    TYPEWRITING

  Ms. Sue Champion

   March 1, 19--
```

JOB 71-2. BIBLIOGRAPHY AND COVER PAGE

Make a copy of the bibliography illustrated on page 123. Then prepare a cover page for a report entitled *The History of the Olympics*. Use your name as author and use *Typewriting* as the course title; use your teacher's name and today's date. Standard format.

LESSON 72

GOALS
- To identify how commas are used after introductory clauses while typing sentences.
- To type 35/3'/5e.
- To format a bound report.

FORMAT
- Single spacing   60-space line   5-space tab

LAB 6

INTRODUCTORY *IF, AS,* AND *WHEN* CLAUSES

Type lines 1–4 twice. Then take a series of 1-minute timings on each line.

```
1  When the jury was dismissed, everyone decided to celebrate.   12
2  As we walked along quickly, we spoke of their organization.   12
3  If I have time later this week, I'll check into the matter.   12
4  When you finish, let me know if the lock needs to be fixed.   12
   |  1  |  2  |  3  |  4  |  5  |  6  |  7  |  8  |  9  | 10  | 11  | 12
```

3-MINUTE TIMINGS

Take two 3-minute timings on lines 5–13.

```
              1              2              3              4
5        Streets are as old as cities or towns, and some of the   12
              5              6              7              8
6  oldest, like the Appian Way in Rome, are still in use.  The   24
              9             10             11             12
7  whole growth of most towns followed the path where the road   36
             13             14             15             16
8  was first made; so while the buildings in town changed, the   48
             17             18             19             20
9  road remained just about the same.  Quite often one can get   60
             21             22             23             24
10 a history of a city by exploring the names of some streets,   72
             25             26             27             28
11 which were often named after local events or amazing people   84
             29             30             31             32
12 of great deeds.  Are there any such streets in your city or   96
             33             34             35
13 in your community that refer to famous citizens?            105
   |  1  |  2  |  3  |  4  |  5  |  6  |  7  |  8  |  9  | 10  | 11  | 12   SI 1.30
```

GOALS
- To type 45/5'/4e.
- To complete one in-basket in acceptable format and within a reasonable period of time.

FORMAT
- Single spacing   60-space line   5-space tab and other tabs as needed

KEYBOARDING SKILLS

Type lines 1–4 once. Then practice using your shift key by typing line 5—do not use your shift lock. Repeat lines 1–4, or take a series of 1-minute timings.

Speed	1	He and I did work the eighth problem also, and it is right. 12
Accuracy	2	Jacqueline was very glad because her film took sixth prize. 12
Numbers	3	The winning bulletins were numbered 10, 29, 38, 47, and 56. 12
Symbols	4	The asterisk, *, is used to indicate a footnote* reference. 12
Technique	5	Three CPAs with IBM used to work for RCA, ABC, and NBC too.

| 1 | 2 | 3 | 4 | 5 | 6 | 7 | 8 | 9 | 10 | 11 | 12 |

1- AND 5-MINUTE TIMINGS

Take two 1-minute timings on each paragraph. Then take one 5-minute timing on the entire selection. Use single spacing for the 1-minute timings and double spacing for the 5-minute timing.

1'

6   Backpacking through Europe is an economical as well as   12
7   an exciting way to see many countries. In summer, students   24
8   and young working people who have saved their money for the   36
9   experience roam about Europe in this manner.   45

10   The inconveniences that a wealthier tourist pays money   12
11   to shun are what makes backpacking fun, cheap, and so often   24
12   more valuable. These travelers simply carry all their gear   36
13   on their backs; getting around is quite easy.   45

14   Many backpackers travel by train because Europe has an   12
15   efficient rail system, and long-distance travel is not very   24
16   costly. Others prefer hitchhiking or renting a car. Youth   36
17   hostels or local homes provide sleeping rooms.   45

18   Food prices can be kept to a minimum by buying cheese,   12
19   juices, bread, and other basics in the markets. Fast foods   24
20   are offered by sidewalk cafes and restaurants. Many areas,   36
21   though, support cafeterias just for students.   45

22   Since backpackers travel like ordinary people, they do   12
23   come in contact with many kinds of citizens. They can make   24
24   many lasting friendships through shared experiences--a real   36
25   souvenir of a truly great trek through Europe.   45

| 1 | 2 | 3 | 4 | 5 | 6 | 7 | 8 | 9 | 10 | 11 | 12 | SI 1.63

FORMATTING BOUND REPORTS

If a report is so thick or important that it needs a protective binder, the margins and tab stops should be moved 3 spaces to the right to provide space at the left for three-hole punching and notebook binding.

JOB 72-1. BOUND REPORT

Retype Job 69/70-1 on pages 121–122. Do not include footnotes in the report, but do type run-in references. Standard format.

LESSONS 73/74

REVIEW

GOALS
- To type sentences that use commas correctly following introductory clauses.
- To review formatting of personal-business letters, tables, memos, and reports.

FORMAT
- Single spacing   60-space line   5-space tab

LAB 6

Type lines 1–4 once, providing the missing commas. Edit your copy as your teacher reads the answers. Then retype lines 1–4 from your edited copy.

INTRODUCTORY IF, AS, AND WHEN CLAUSES

1 When it got very windy Joe had to call a halt to the game.   12
2 When you type a report be very sure that you erase neatly.   12
3 If I do not return in six hours please call my Azusa home.   12
4 As Pat started the car I realized that it was quite noisy.   12

Workbook 105–106.

PRACTICE

Type lines 5–12 on page 117 twice each.

3-MINUTE TIMINGS

Take two 3-minute timings on lines 7–15 on page 124.

TECHNICAL QUESTIONS

Type short answers to the following 15 questions:

1. What is the difference between a personal-business letter and a business letter.

2. On what line do you type the date in a business letter?

3. What is a salutation?

4. What items appear in the closing of a personal-business letter?

5. What is an enclosure?

6. What is a long report?

7. On what line should the page number of a report be typed?

8. What is a footnote?

9. How is a footnote separated from the body of a report?

10. How should you display the title of a table?

11. How should you display column heads?

12. What is the standard spacing between columns in tables?

13. What is an invoice?

14. Where do you type the words *Total amount due*?

15. On which side (left or right) should a column of numbers align?

DISPLAY NOTICE

Use an attractive format for the safety instructions below, which will be posted at The Cycle Shop for the information of customers who are thinking about buying new bicycles.

PROTECT YOUR bicycle

- Lock your bicycle every time you must leave it unattended. Don't make the mistake of leaving it unlocked or unattended for "just a minute."

- When you are not riding your bicycle, put it away in a locked room, garage, or basement. Don't leave your bicycle in a driveway or front yard where it can be seen.

- Always use a quality lock and case hardened chain (or high-quality cable) to lock your new bicycle. Avoid locks that can be easily broken and chains and cables that are light and readily cut with wire cutters.

- Record the serial number of your bicycle in a safe place and keep it with your permanent records. If possible, register your bicycle with your local police department.

- If your family has a homeowner's insurance, check to see if the policy covers bicycles.

- When you lock your bicycle, be sure to put the chain through both wheels, the frame, and the rack or other stationary object to which you are securing it.

INVOICES

The Cycle Shop marks up the prices in the Sumoto catalog 15 percent for selling to its customers. Prepare invoices for the customers shown below, using marked-up prices. Standard format.

G. T. Miller, 1643 Warren Avenue, Houston, TX 77049. Invoice No. 351. Purchased one each of items 10, 11, 13. Sales tax, 6%.

Cyrus von der Byl, 171 Canton Court, Houston, TX 77045. Invoice No. 352. Purchased one each of items 1, 2, 3, and 9. Sales tax, 6%.

COMPOSE A LETTER

Compose a letter to Dallas International Classics, P.O. Box 165, Dallas, TX 75221. Indicate that you want to stock some T-shirts for the Dallas Super Motorcross. Inquire as to the prices, sizes, colors, and shipping arrangements, since you would like the shirts at least one week before the event. You select the format.

JOB 73/74-1. LONG REPORT

Standard format with side headings. Type run-in references as footnotes. Convert to capitals and insert commas as needed.

GOLD / By [*Your name*]

¶ What is it that gives gold its value? The only real value is that people want it! People everywhere in the world love gold. They trust it. It will not rust or rot. You can hide it--it is better than money. ¶ The first gold money was issued by the lydians in the sixth century B.C. (Charles Grunfeld, <u>The History of Money</u>, Able Press, New York, 1981, p. 65.) Soon the greeks began minting money in the shape of gold disks. Later, the romans notched the edge of each coin as a way to stop the practice of shaving off thin slices of gold. Although our coins today are not made of gold they are still notched in that way. ¶ Every country has had gold in its history. egypt ¶ Early egyptians linked gold to the sun--to life. The burial place of king tut was all of beaten gold. india ¶ In india every bride who has money wears gold trinkets in some form. She will never wear all that again; she will keep it as insurance against bad times. south africa ¶ Two-thirds of the world's production of gold is done here. The people of africa believe that the sight of gold keeps one in touch with powerful spirits. south america ¶ The spanish came here for spices and gold. When they saw the indians wearing gold they forgot about the spices and took all the gold home to spain. united states ¶ The main use of gold in this country is for jewelry. About half our gold reserve is stored in fort knox. The value of this gold is over $11 billion. (Ibid., p. 204.)

JOB 73/74-2. MEMORANDUM

Standard format. Workbook 107 top.

DATE: [*Today's date*] / TO: Sue Booth, President / Business Club, South Side High School / FROM: Tom Dunn, President, Business Club, Swissvale High School / SUBJECT: Joint Meeting.

¶ Sarah Klein and I will drive to South Side High on Wednesday, March 6, to greet you and show your drivers how to get to our school. We will be in your school parking lot at 2 p.m. to lead the way to Swissvale. ¶ If any of your members need a ride, we'll be happy to take three or four in our lead car. ¶ All of us are looking forward to March 6! / TD

JOB 73/74-3. TABLE

Standard format. Double spacing. Half sheet of paper.

Candidates for Club Officers
The Business Club

Office	Candidate	Grade
President	Alice Ann Blake	12
President	Charles B. Kaminsky	12
Secretary	Nancy Epstein	10
Secretary	Ted Woodward	11
Treasurer	Paul Montalvo	12
Treasurer	Virginia A. Petri	11

JOB 73/74-4. PERSONAL-BUSINESS LETTER

Standard format. Envelope: Workbook 107 bottom. Body 109 words.

[*Use your own address and today's date*] / Ms. Brenda Chan, Program Director / Keynote Studios / 50 Rockefeller Plaza / New York, NY 10020 / Dear Ms. Chan: I should like to add my cheers to those you must be receiving for your very fine "Stars of the Silver Screen" series of shows. They are wonderful. ¶ Is it possible to attend a broadcast? I plan to be in New York City on December 12 with three friends. The four of us would very much like to see the show while it is being taped or broadcast. We should be most grateful to you if we could obtain tickets. ¶ I hope that I may hear from you and learn that you can let us have four tickets for December 12. They would make our visit to New York complete. / Yours truly, / [*Your name*]

RECEIPTS

Type receipts for the four customers who gave you cash for the tickets they ordered. They are waiting for the receipts. (The Cycle Shop does not charge for handling the ticket orders.) Standard format.

LETTER

Block format.

Sumoto Corporation, 7800 Grand Avenue, San Diego, CA 92101 Gentlemen and Ladies: Subject: Malfunctions in Model ST-520, During the past two or three months we have had many owner complaints about a breakdown of their Sumoto Super-Twin Motorcycles, Model ST-520 ¶As you know, the points and condenser on the left side of the engine attach around the end of the crankshaft. After 2,000 miles of travel the oil seal breaks down, letting oil into the points and condenser. As a result, the engine loses ignition. ¶We feel that all your Model ST-520s need an improved seal, and we suggest a recall. Your authorized dealers need something to restore the public's confidence in Sumoto. Sincerely, Harry DiSalenti.

ORDER FORMS

Complete four fill-in order forms for tickets for customers who plan to attend the Super Motorcross in Dallas on April 30, 19—. Tickets are scarce, so there is a need to process the orders immediately.

Ticket Prices

Covered box seats: $20
Open box seats: $18
Bleachers: $15
Upper bleachers: $12
No reserved seats.

1. Louise Koegler, 1640 Jancey, Houston, TX 77051: 6 tickets @ $18.
2. Jerome Liskowitz, 117 Braddock Road, Houston, TX 77046: 2 tickets @ $20 and 3 @ $15.
3. Norman Stumpf, 104 Church Avenue, Houston, TX 77037: 7 tickets @ $20.
4. Nancy and Harry DiSalenti, The Cycle Shop, 8 tickets @ $18 and 8 @ $12.

GOALS
- To demonstrate competency by typing 35/3'/5e.
- To demonstrate competency by formatting and correctly typing a personal business letter, a memo, and a table.

FORMAT
- Single spacing   60-space line   5-space tab

PREVIEW PRACTICE

Type lines 1–2 twice as a preview to the 3-minute timings below.

Accuracy   1 art are barns signs noted cheap their native living rotting
Speed   2 examples antiques products through country symbol today era

3-MINUTE TIMINGS

Take two 3-minute timings on lines 3–11.

```
 3     Have you ever driven through the country and noted the    12
 4  number of barns painted with the same sign, all selling the  24
 5  same product?  At the time farmers found it a cheap way for   36
 6  them to have their barns painted.  Makers of products found   48
 7  this to be an amazing idea to push their goods.  Today many   60
 8  of the barn signs are thought to be good examples of living   72
 9  native art.  They are a symbol of an era, and like antiques   84
10  and old things, some are being preserved; but most of these  96
11  barns are just rotting away or falling down.                 105
    |  1  |  2  |  3  |  4  |  5  |  6  |  7  |  8  |  9  |  10  |  11  |  12   SI 1.30
```

JOB 75-1. PERSONAL BUSINESS LETTER
Standard format. Envelope: Workbook 109 top. Body 128 words.

Ms. Ruth E. Gillis, Travel Agent / Western Worlds Agency / 294 Highland Parkway / Buffalo, NY 14223 / Dear Ms. Gillis: / Three of my friends and I want to spend one or two weeks of our next summer vacation at a dude ranch. We have heard from others that dude ranches can be great fun, and we would very much like to learn more about them. ¶ Would you please provide us with information on the activities available at dude ranches and, perhaps, some descriptive brochures? In addition, we would also appreciate your telling us the cost for each of us for two double rooms (with baths) and meals for both for a one-week stay and a two-week stay in the month of July. Can travel arrangements be made to and from our city--and if so, what is the cost of a round trip per person? ¶ We will appreciate hearing from you. / Sincerely yours, / [Your name]

JOB 75-2. MEMO
Standard format. Workbook 109 bottom.

[To] Mr. James Fetter, Principal, Swissvale High School / [From] Roberta Weinberg, Secretary of The Business Club / [Subject] Banquet Plans / [Today's date] / I am pleased to give you, as you requested, a progress report on the plans for our February banquet. I am enclosing copies of the last report from our treasurer and of the banquet program. ¶ So far we have sold 110 tickets, including those of the new members we plan to initiate just before the dinner. There will be 12 nonpaying guests at the head table. / RW

JOB 75-3. TABLE
Standard format. Half sheet of paper.

NEW ADVERTISERS FOR THE YEARBOOK
(Students Who Made the Sale)

Advertisers	Student's Name
Bailey Bottling	J. MacGill
Butler Coal Co.	S. Murray
Painters Resort	B. Chalkey
Rubicam Computer	A. Katzman

IN-BASKET C: WORKING FOR A SMALL SHOP

You are working in the office of The Cycle Shop, which is located at 4100 Graham Blvd., Houston, TX 77052. The shop buys and sells bicycles, mopeds, and motorcycles, as well as parts and accessories. The owners are Nancy and Harry DiSalenti. Today is April 2, 19—. Use letterheads and forms where appropriate. Workbook 495–510 top.

PRIORITY SHEET AND TIME LOG

Read through the entire in-basket, and then complete the priority sheet. Be sure to keep an accurate time log as you complete each job.

PURCHASE ORDERS

Prepare purchase orders for parts from the supplier's motorcycle parts list shown below. Standard format.

Sumoto Corporation, 7800 Grand Avenue, San Diego, CA 92101.

No. 1754. Order six each of items 13, 16, 17, and 18 listed below. Calculate the total. Rush order for good customer.

No. 1755. Order six each of items 7, 8, and 9 listed below. Calculate the total. Rush order for good customer.

SUMOTO MOTORCYCLE PARTS

Item	Number	Description	Unit Price
1	070037	Tank, Fuel	$42.50
2	071076	Cap, Fuel Tank	2.25
3	710032	Fitting, Tank	.79
4	070020	Hose, Rubber	1.52
5	070011	Screen	.40
6	071087	Fitting Assembly	2.38
7	710017	Filter, Fuel	1.86
8	071066	Hose, Insulating	1.15
9	071072	Line, Fuel	3.16
10	051147	Carburetor Assembly	18.51
11	710033	Fitting, "T"	1.15
12	021192	Cable, Throttle	5.25
13	091236	Wire Assembly, Choke	7.49
14	051151	Manifold, Air Intake Inner	4.89
15	720005	Screw, Allen	.45
16	720004	Retainer, Cable	6.65
17	720006	Nut, Self-Locking	.38
18	051156	Rod	.73

LEVEL 3

BASIC BUSINESS
FORMATTING

UNIT 36 IN-BASKETS

UNIT GOAL
45/5'/4e

GOAL
■ To complete one in-basket in acceptable format and within a reasonable period of time.

FORMAT
■ Single spacing   60-space line   5-space tab and other tabs as needed

KEYBOARDING SKILLS

Type lines 1–4 once. Then practice using your backspace and underscore keys by typing line 5 twice. Repeat lines 1–4, or take a series of 1-minute timings.

Speed   1 Both the men may go to town if he pays them for their work. 12
Accuracy   2 Five wizards very quickly jumped into the box on the stage. 12
Numbers   3 By May 10, ship 29 seats, 38 stoves, 47 tents, and 56 cots. 12
Symbols   4 Quotation marks (") set off exact words: "Fire!" he cried. 12
Technique   5 The first week of Time, Newsweek, and People has been sent.
            | 1 | 2 | 3 | 4 | 5 | 6 | 7 | 8 | 9 | 10 | 11 | 12

5-MINUTE TIMINGS

Take one 5-minute timing on lines 6–25. Circle your errors, and practice typing the words you typed incorrectly. Then take another 5-minute timing.

6   Motorcycles are the result of our mechanized age, even   12
7   though their basic model has been with us since the bicycle   24
8   was invented. Their design blends the simple basics of the   36
9   bicycle with the advanced technology that is used in autos.   48
10 The result is a lightweight vehicle, inexpensive to operate   60
11 and maintain and great fun to ride.   67
12   Like all good ideas, motorcycles do have some features   79
13 that are bad. They carry only two passengers, and most are   91
14 uncomfortable for long-distance riding. Hauling equipment,   103
15 luggage, or even a bag of groceries home from the store can   115
16 be an impossible task because motorcycles have no trunk. A   127
17 snowstorm or severe rainfall can be a major problem for the   139
18 motorcycle operator: skidding on wet roads.   148
19   Just like automobiles, motorcycles come in many shapes   160
20 and sizes. There are trail bikes for riding off the street   172
21 or for racing on lonely back roads, city bikes, and mopeds,   184
22 which are ideal for running errands. Some motorcycles have   196
23 been customized by their owners, using fancy handlebars and   208
24 painted gas tanks. In the future each of us may use a bike   220
25 to promote energy economy.   225
    | 1 | 2 | 3 | 4 | 5 | 6 | 7 | 8 | 9 | 10 | 11 | 12   SI 1.59

Written business messages are the energy that moves the huge, complicated world of business. Level 3, "Basic Business Formatting," will introduce you to many essential business documents.

In Level 3 you will:

1. Demonstrate keyboarding accuracy and speed on straight copy with a goal of 38 words a minute or more for 5 minutes with no more than 5 errors.

2. Demonstrate production skills on basic formats for reports, tables, letters, and forms.

3. Correctly proofread copy for errors and edit copy for revision.

4. Apply more advanced techniques for formatting four categories of business documents from six input modes.

5. Apply rules for correct use of punctuation in communications.

LESSON 76

UNIT 13 KEYBOARDING SKILLS REVIEW

UNIT GOAL
35/5'/5e

GOALS
- To identify and practice the alphabetic keys on which more drill is needed.
- To build skill on the alphabetic keyboard.

FORMAT
- Single spacing   60-space line   Tabs every 7 spaces

KEYBOARDING SKILLS

Type lines 1–4 once. In line 5, use your tabulator key to advance from one number to the next through the entire line. Repeat lines 1–4, or take a series of 1-minute timings.

Speed 1 She may go to town for a pen, but she must come right back. 12
Accuracy 2 Five or six big jet planes zoomed quickly by the new tower. 12
Numbers 3 If 56 days are left, then 47, 29, 38, and 10 will not work. 12
Symbols 4 With our 4% raise we bought 17 lb of #38 & #29—what a buy! 12
Technique 5 102   293   384   475   561   102   293   384   475
          | 1 | 2 | 3 | 4 | 5 | 6 | 7 | 8 | 9 | 10 | 11 | 12

PRETEST

Type lines 6–9 twice to find out which alphabetic keys are the most difficult for you. Force yourself to type rapidly—push yourself to your fastest rate. Circle each *letter* in which an error is made.

6 We amazed six judges by quietly giving back the four pages.
7 The expert quickly noted five bad jewels among the zircons.
8 Jack will exhibit very quaint games for Buzz's fall parade.
9 The exits were quickly filled by dozens of jumpy villagers.

PRACTICE

Type lines 10–22 once. Then repeat any of the lines that stress the letter errors you circled in the Pretest.

10 A aid apt ate aide aunt aisle B bus bit bad brag burn below
11 C cob cot cut cold crew cabin D dig dry dye dive dirt depth
12 E eye elf end each ease eight F fix fog fun fort foul fifth
13 G gap gun gem grip grow grant H hit hug hay hike hurt hoist

(Continued on next page)

the house. Some dogs are light shedders--wire haired terriers
and poodles, for example. Heavy-sheding breeds include the dalmaian
and german sheperd.

pupies offered for sale or adoption should always be atleast
6 weeks old. A healthy animal will have bright eyes, a glossy coat,
white teeth, and pink gums. Do not consider a puppy that shows any
signs of illness--a runny nose, watery eyes, or fever--or exhibits
temper ament problems, such as snappyness or extreme shyness.

Data for Table	
1 = 15	11 = 60
2 = 24	12 = 64
3 = 28	13 = 68
4 = 32	14 = 72
5 = 36	15 = 76
6 = 40	16 = 80
7 = 44	17 = 84
8 = 48	18 = 88
9 = 52	19 = 92
10 = 56	20 = 96

TABLE

Standard format. Full sheet of paper. Title: HOW OLD IS YOUR DOG? Title of column 1: Age of Dog (Years). Title of column 2: Equivalent Age of Human (Years). A 1-year-old dog is equated with the human equivalent age of 15—shown in the data as 1 = 15. Use the data given in the margin on the left.

MEDICAL CERTIFICATES

Complete two certificates of vaccination for Dr. Ludwig, who has just examined the two dogs described below. Their owners are in the waiting room.

1. Owner: Jennie Pugh; dog, collie with black/white markings, male, four years old, weight 75 lb., named Max. Lives at 42 Glen Arden Drive, Chicago, IL 60610. Vaccination tag #5754. Owner's telephone: 555-8132. Vaccination for distemper and rabies.

2. Owner: Hilda Schiller; dog, German shepherd with brown and gray spots, female, six years old, weight 95 lb., named Minerva. Lives at 517 Amberson Place, Hoffman Estates, IL 60195. Vaccination tag #5755. Owner's telephone: 555-9101. Vaccination for rabies, distemper, and hepatitis.

NEWSLETTER COLUMN

Newsletter goes to press August 11

The column was written by Dr. Ludwig. Edit the copy as you type it. Standard format for enumerations. Full sheet of paper.

QUESTIONS AND ANSWERS

Q. What are the most prevelent allergy problems in cats?

A. cats do not have allergy conditions nearly as frequently as dogs; but when cats do have allergy conditions, they are usually sever. The causes of allergys in cats are not as well defined or understood as in dogs but there is generally a good response to proper treetment.

Q. is flea allergy in cats as sereous as in dogs?

A. yes this can be a sever condition in cats.

Q. Can cats have allergic reactions to foods?

A. food allergys are very hard to identify; consult your veterinarian.

14 I ice ire imp inch itch ideas J joy jog jug joke just judge
15 K keg key kit kite kick knife L lip lie let land lark light
16 M mow map may mend myth minor N new nor nut nose none notch
17 O our own one oath ouch ought P pay peg pen pure prey probe
18 Q que qui quo quip quit quake R rot rob ran ripe rein ridge

19 S sap sob ski silk sang slide T try toy tip take tend there
20 U urn ups use urge used unite V van vie vow view vise vinyl
21 W way who wig wild wine wring X tax fix wax exam apex index
22 Y yes yet yam yard yawn yours Z zig zip zoo zero zany zebra

POSTTEST

Repeat the Pretest to see how much your skill has improved.

1-AND 5-MINUTE TIMINGS

Take two 1-minute timings on each paragraph. Then take one 5-minute timing on the entire selection. Use single spacing for the 1-minute timings and double spacing for the 5-minute timing. 5-space tab.

1'

23   If you have ever had an opportunity to move to another   12
24 city or town, you realize that it might be quite a big job.   24
25 If you are like many others, you might move yourself.   35
                                                                   —
26   The initial thing to do is to lease a truck or trailer   12
27 for loading all your household belongings. Be very certain   24
28 to get a truck or trailer large enough for your needs.   35
                                                                   —
29   Many large boxes and cartons must be packed and sealed   12
30 carefully. Be sure to pack all your belongings tightly for   24
31 the move so that nothing will break inside the boxes.   35
                                                                   —
32   Have some of your friends assist you in carrying heavy   12
33 items such as sofas, beds, desks, and television sets. All   24
34 your larger items should be placed in the truck first.   35
                                                                   —
35   As you cruise down a highway with a load of furniture,   12
36 watch carefully for any sudden stops in the traffic. Drive   24
37 slowly so that you do not damage any of your furniture.   35

| 1 | 2 | 3 | 4 | 5 | 6 | 7 | 8 | 9 | 10 | 11 | 12   SI 1.38

ADDRESSING COUPON LETTERS AND ENVELOPES

Address the four coupon letters to the new members.

COMPOSE A LETTER

Compose a rough draft of a short letter that can be sent to the four new members. Thank them for contributing to the Animal Rescue League and for being concerned about the humane treatment of animals in the city of Chicago. Explain that their names have been placed on the ARL mailing list to receive the monthly League NEWSLETTER. Invite them to an open house at League Headquarters on Sunday, August 20, from 2 to 5 p.m. If they need further information, suggest that they call the League at 555-6452. The executive director of the League will sign the letter. Use plain paper.

FORM LETTER

Format the letter you composed for new members in block format. Use a subject salutation, such as *To All New Members of the Animal Rescue League.* Do not use an inside address. Prepare an original and three copies. Address a large envelope to each new member.

SPEECH

Standard format. Triple-space. Prepare for the League's veterinarian.

WHAT KIND OF DOG DO YOU WANT TO OWN?

If you are thinking of getting a dog, choose one whose disposition, size, and appearance appeal to you. There are three groups of dogs, according to their original uses: (1) sporting dogs, such as setters, spaniels, and hounds, were bred as hunters; (2) working dogs, such as shepherds, collies, and sheep dogs, were used as herders; (3) toy dogs and nonsporting dogs, such as Boston terriers and poodles, were pets and companions. It helps to be able to recognize breed characteristics in order to predict adult size and behavior.

Families with pre-school children ought to look for sturdy, medium-size breeds that have good temperament and can endure rough play. If you live in the city, you might have difficulty providing outdoor space for large sporting dogs and hounds, which need plenty of running room. The dachshund and cocker spaniel, for example, demand less outdoor exercise and adapt better to "city life."

Many dog owners prefer an animal that does not require frequent grooming. Most breeds shed their coats once a year; but with regular brushings excessive loss of fur should not be a problem around

When you can only guess at the ancestry of a puppy!

note: Dr. Ludwig will give this speech tonight at a P.T.A. meeting.

(*Continued on next page*)

LESSON 77

GOALS
- To identify and practice the number keys on which more drill is needed.
- To build skill in typing numbers.

FORMAT
- Single spacing   60-space line   5-space tab

KEYBOARDING SKILLS

Type lines 1–4 once. In line 5, use the shift lock for each word in all-capital letters. Repeat lines 1–4, or take a series of 1-minute timings.

Speed
Accuracy
Numbers
Symbols
Technique

1 All of them might now work to make the new year a good one.   12
2 Vi kept it blazing sixty minutes with a quart jug of cider.   12
3 We saw 10 fish, 29 rabbits, 38 birds, 47 dogs, and 56 cats.   12
4 We paid 12% on a loan of $900; they (Ann and Joe) paid 13%.   12
5 The metals are COPPER and GOLD and IRON and NICKEL and TIN.

| 1 | 2 | 3 | 4 | 5 | 6 | 7 | 8 | 9 | 10 | 11 | 12 |

PRETEST

Take a 2-minute timing on lines 6–8, or type them twice to find out which number keys are the most difficult for you to type. Keep your eyes on the copy as you type. Circle each digit in which an error is made.

6 2981 1073 5764 4711 5092 8920 3589 4056 8362 1594 2036 4637   12
7 5647 1525 8032 1337 6592 4094 6417 8867 5091 7723 8649 6052   24
8 6328 5049 1157 6924 8037 2480 9935 4062 8135 2766 9317 5048   36

| 1 | 2 | 3 | 4 | 5 | 6 | 7 | 8 | 9 | 10 | 11 | 12 |

PRACTICE

Type lines 9–18 once. Then repeat any of the lines that stress the digit errors you circled in the Pretest.

9 We need 1 chair, 1 desk, 11 staplers, 11 pins, and 11 pens.
10 Player No. 22 ran 22 yards; then the score became 22 to 12.
11 Mel's ticket stub is for Seat 3, 13, 31, or 33--not for 43.
12 Through Gate No. 4 came Nos. 4, 14, 41, 44, 54, 48, and 74.
13 The scores were 65 to 55, 57 to 56,. 59 to 55, and 54 to 45.

14 State highways 16, 26, 66, 126, 166, and 186 are now paved.
15 On May 17 send $77 to reserve 17 seats for the June 7 game.
16 On 6/8, 7/8, and 8/8 we sold 8 quarts and 8 pints of pears.
17 They have 9 quarters, 19 dimes, 29 nickels, and 39 pennies.
18 We led by 10 points at 20 to 30 and by 10 more at 20 to 40.

POSTTEST

Repeat the Pretest to see how much your skill has improved.

PREVIEW PRACTICE

Type lines 19 and 20 twice as a preview to the 1- and 5-minute timing routine.

Accuracy

19 any sets heavy slowly realize carrying furniture belongings

Speed

20 have move city town that like many step load your must pack

1- AND 5-MINUTE TIMINGS

Repeat the 1- and 5-minute timing routine on page 130.

You have volunteered to work in the offices of the Animal Rescue League, 6020 Hamilton Avenue, Chicago, IL 60607. Ms. Carolyn A. Heppenstahl is executive director, and Dr. Henrietta Ludwig is staff veterinarian. Today is August 10, 19—. Use letterheads and forms where appropriate. Workbook 473–493.

PRIORITY SHEET AND TIME LOG

Read through the entire in-basket, and then complete the priority sheet. Be sure to keep an accurate time log as you complete each job.

COUPON LETTER

Standard format with indented paragraphs. Prepare three carbon copies for use in addressing coupon letters and envelopes.

All Chicago area residents under the age of 18 years are invited to register their favorite dogs and cats now in the ARL Dog and Cat Show to be held Saturday, September 3, 19—, at 1 p.m. at the League's Rosedale Kennels, 600 Hoffman Lane, Hoffman Estates, IL 60195.

There is no entry fee for the show. Each exhibitor may show one dog or cat. All pets must be leashed and must have received a distemper vaccination within the past year.

You can use the coupon below to register. Please fill it out and return it to the League offices at 6020 Hamilton Avenue, Chicago, IL 60607, by August 30, 19—.

Prizes will be awarded in 11 classes, so indicate on the coupon the class in which you want your pet to compete.

Sincerely, Carolyn A. Heppenstahl, Executive Director

ARL DOG AND CAT SHOW

Name _____ Age _____
Address _____
_____

Pet's Name _____ Dog   Cat   (Please circle one.)

Class in which you wish your pet to be entered (please circle one):

Shaggiest Dog	Best Groomed	Droopiest Ears
Furriest Cat	Smartest	(Dogs Only)
Most Colorful	Prettiest Tail	Longest Whiskers
Most Typical	Saddest Eyes	(Cats Only)
		Friendliest

INDEX CARDS

Format 5 by 3 cards for the new members to the ARL so that their names and addresses can be added to your mailing list. All are Chicago, IL. Standard format.

Ms. Mattie Bradley, 1214 Manor Road, 60110
Mr. Nick Valenti, 215 Lenore Drive, 60002
Mrs. Wilma Volk, 844 McCoy Road, 60208
Mr. and Mrs. Michael Sullivan, 3101 Grand Avenue, 60043

LESSON 78

GOALS
- To recognize how commas are used in compound sentences while typing.
- To identify the symbol keys on which more drill is needed.
- To build skill in typing symbols.

FORMAT
- Single spacing   60-space line   5-space tab

LAB 7

COMMAS IN COMPOUND SENTENCES

Type lines 1–4 once. Then repeat lines 1–4 or take a series of 1-minute timings.

```
1  Sixteen pages were quite torn, and five dozen were missing.  12
2  Just pay the clerk by noon, or you will lose the last seat.  12
3  They will not accept your bid, nor will they allow another.  12
4  You must read a chapter, but you do not have to outline it.  12
   |  1  |  2  |  3  |  4  |  5  |  6  |  7  |  8  |  9  |  10 |  11 |  12
```

An "independent" clause is one that can stand alone as a sentence. Here are two examples: *Larry took the bus. Mary went by plane.* When two independent clauses are joined by the conjunction *and, but, or,* or *nor* into one compound sentence, place a comma before the conjunction:

Larry took the bus, *but* Mary went by plane.

We have an office in New York, *and* we will have one in Boston soon.

PRETEST

Type lines 5–9 twice to find out which symbol keys are the most difficult for you. Force yourself to keep your eyes on the copy, and type rapidly—push yourself to your fastest rate. Circle each symbol in which an error is made.

```
5  We sold 19 quarts @ $2, 17 quarts @ $3, and 16 quarts @ $4.
6  Our #4729 makes 10% profit; #3810 makes 8%; #5638 makes 7%.
7  Clay & Poe and Day & Ames predicted a 75¢ and an 82¢ climb.
8  Computers use asterisks to multiply:  2 * 3 (6); 4 * 2 (8).
9  In math, 6 - 2 = 4 and 9 - 4 = 5; 6 + 2 = 8 and 9 + 4 = 13.
```

PRACTICE

Type lines 10–19 once. Then repeat any of the lines that stress the symbol errors you circled in the Pretest.

```
@   10  They found 10 @ 29, 29 @ 38, 38 @ 47, 47 @ 56, and 56 @ 10.

¢   11  Soda is 56¢, candy is 47¢, gum is 29¢, and peanuts are 10¢.

*   12  Jones,* Hernandez,* Young,* Moletti,* and Gray* won prizes.

#   13  Our new scale shows #56 at 29#, #47 at 38#, and #29 at 10#.

$   14  Our show tickets should cost us $10, $29, $38, $47, or $56.

%   15  Your sales increased 10%, 29%, 38%, 47%, and 56% last year.

&   16  Day & Cole, Yung & Poe, and Lee & Madera are all attorneys.

( )  17  Troy (Ohio), Leon (Iowa), and Lund (Utah) were represented.

-   18  Label the square cartons as 10-29, 38-47, 56-38, and 47-10.

+ =  19  We know that 56 + 47 = 103, 29 + 10 = 39, and 38 + 58 = 96.
```

GOALS
- To type 45/5'/4e.
- To complete one in-basket in acceptable format and within a reasonable period of time.

FORMAT
- Single spacing   60-space line   5-space tab and other tabs as needed

KEYBOARDING SKILLS

Type lines 1–4 once. Then practice using your shift key by inserting capitals as you type line 5. Repeat lines 1–4, or take a series of 1-minute timings.

Speed	1 If they pay me for the emblem, I may make it to the social.	12
Accuracy	2 Jack found exactly a quarter in the man's woven zipper bag.	12
Numbers	3 Alice read pages 10 through 29, 38 through 47, and page 56.	12
Symbols	4 The parentheses, (), are (1) very neat and (2) easily read.	12
Technique	5 mr. edward c. jones joined smith & smythe, inc., last june.	

| 1 | 2 | 3 | 4 | 5 | 6 | 7 | 8 | 9 | 10 | 11 | 12 |

1- AND 5-MINUTE TIMINGS

Take two 1-minute timings on each paragraph. Then take one 5-minute timing on the entire selection. Use single spacing for the 1-minute timings and double spacing for the 5-minute timing.

6   What do the Kentucky Derby, the circus, zoos, and most   12
7 farms throughout this country all have in common? They are   24
8 all places where animals can be found. And where there are   36
9 animals, there is usually a veterinarian near.   45

10   Veterinarians are doctors who are trained to treat and   12
11 prevent diseases in animals. Although they go to different   24
12 medical schools than doctors trained to treat people, their   36
13 course of study and training are much alike.   45

14   Veterinarians are required to do all aspects of animal   12
15 health care, such as giving shots to prevent sickness, fix-   24
16 ing broken bones, helping owners plan a safe and sound type   36
17 of diet, and doing all kinds of major surgery.   45

18   Many veterinarians limit their practice to one kind of   12
19 animal, such as horses. These doctors are highly paid, for   24
20 they may care for priceless race horses. Some doctors work   36
21 with or do special research on wild animals.   45

22   Doctors of veterinary medicine may travel with a rodeo   12
23 or circus, live in the jungle, or treat rare creatures in a   24
24 zoo. Some, however, help farmers with cattle, hogs, and so   36
25 on; but most others help with city-type pets.   45

| 1 | 2 | 3 | 4 | 5 | 6 | 7 | 8 | 9 | 10 | 11 | 12 | SI 1.55

POSTTEST   Repeat the Pretest on page 132 to see how much your skill has improved.

**1- AND
5-MINUTE
TIMINGS**

Take two 1-minute timings on each paragraph. Then take one 5-minute timing on the entire selection. Use single spacing for the 1-minute timings and double spacing for the 5-minute timing.

```
20          Working with plants could be an exciting and fun hobby     12
21    for you.  If you have never waited, with expectation, for a      24
22    tiny sprig to grow into a plant, you have missed a joy.          35
23          Plants make ideal pets for apartment dwellers.  Plants     12
24    do not bark or meow, and the neighbors don't complain about      24
25    being kept awake or about being annoyed by a loud pet.           35
26          If you decide that plant growing will be an acceptable     12
27    hobby for you, you must be sure to purchase plants that you       24
28    know can survive in the environment of your residence.           35
29          Most plants require at least moderate light and warmth     12
30    to live.  Additionally, plants need to be watered, fed, and      24
31    misted on a regular basis so they will grow and thrive.          35
32          If you are like the many others who like their plants,     12
33    your zeal for growing them will increase rapidly.  You will      24
34    undoubtedly be urging your friends to grow plants too.           35
      |  1  |  2  |  3  |  4  |  5  |  6  |  7  |  8  |  9  | 10  | 11  | 12    SI 1.39
```

LESSON 79

GOALS
- To identify how commas are used in compound sentences while typing.
- To build your typing speed on 12-second timings and on 30-second timings.

FORMAT
- Single spacing   60-space line   5-space tab

LAB 7

Type lines 1–4 once. Then repeat lines 1–4 or take a series of 1-minute timings.

**COMMAS IN
COMPOUND
SENTENCES**

```
1   It is too cloudy to fly today, but tomorrow will be better.   12
2   On Tuesday the movie ends, and on Wednesday another begins.   12
3   Alex will take today's quiz, or he may just wait for Paula.   12
4   You should not send a check, nor should you send any money.   12
    |  1  |  2  |  3  |  4  |  5  |  6  |  7  |  8  |  9  | 10  | 11  | 12
```

FORM LETTER

Standard format. Make four carbon copies. Use letterhead for each copy.
Workbook 461–470.

Open House programs have been scheduled by the Chicora National Forest at its Ranger Station at Smithport on Sunday, June 8, from noon to 5 p.m. Rangers will be on hand at the station to explain the YCC program to interested students and their parents, teachers, and counselors.

Since you have been active in supporting the YCC program, I especially want to invite you to attend and hope that you will be able to help us welcome our guests. Sincerely, Albert R. Fruhauf, District Ranger

ADDRESSING FORM LETTERS AND ENVELOPES

Address the five Open House form letters, using the addresses below. Address five envelopes.

1. Mrs. Betty Myer Birson, President, A.A.U.W., P.O. Box 26, Helena, MT 59601.
2. Ms. Madeline B. Kerr, President, Volunteer Fire Fighters, Butte, MT 59701.
3. Mr. Homer Neff, President, P.T.A., Helena Public Schools, Helena, MT 59601.
4. Mr. Stanley T. Scott, President, Chamber of Commerce, Butte, MT 59703.
5. Ms. Shirley A. Weyrauch, President, Civic Association, Helena, MT 59601.

NEWSLETTER

Standard format. Edit the copy as you type it. Needed for Forest Service Newsletter that goes to press on June 5. Must be hand-delivered to local printer the day before.

YCC AT BLUE KNOLL by Tom Yusi, Chicora High School

48 young people will be at work this summer at Game Lands in northern Sheffield county. They are involved in the second year of work with the game commission's in cooperation with the Youth Conservation Corps. Camp at Blue Knoll state park.

Last summer corps. members developed wildlife management plans for both game and nongame species in various areas, constructed a wooden bridge to gain access to a section of Game Lands where they helped plow and plant food plots for wildlife, and also laid out and marked a hikeing and nature trail.

YCC members are paid for their labor, but their is much more to the interprise than providing summer jobs. The corps. aims to make conservation and envirnment science more significant than textbook abstractions by involving YCC members in actual field situations.

YCY participants work in coed crews of six, including a group leader who is usually a college student. Each year a new group of participants is selected from thousandes of applicants. The program sharpens their awareness of environmental concepts.

COVER LETTER

Jerome Moneta, Forest Supervisor, Bitterroot National Forest, Missoula, Montana 59801, wants a copy of the display notice. Make a carbon copy for him and send it with a cover letter. Standard format.

12-SECOND TIMINGS

Type each line four times, or take four 12-second timings on each line. For each timing, type with no more than one error.

5 If the order is a big one, we will make a very good profit. 12
6 They may not go up there if they are to come up here first. 12
7 We will do all that we can to help them win the big prizes. 12

```
          25    30    35    40    45    50    55    60
```

30-SECOND TIMINGS

Take two 30-second timings on lines 8–10, or type the paragraph twice.

8 One thing of which we are quite sure is never to expect our 12
9 speed to jump or zip higher for three minutes before we can 24
10 type with the same degree of skill for about half a minute. 36

```
     |  1  |  2  |  3  |  4  |  5  |  6  |  7  |  8  |  9  |  10  |  11  |  12
```

PREVIEW PRACTICE

Type lines 11 and 12 twice as a preview to the 5-minute timing below.

Accuracy
11 you deck early dozing nothing relaxing afternoon facilities

Speed
12 what like days near your home want just rise they heat bike

1- AND 5-MINUTE TIMINGS

Take two 1-minute timings on each paragraph. Then take one 5-minute timing on the entire selection. Use single spacing for the 1-minute timings and double spacing for the 5-minute timing.

13   What kinds of activities do you like when summer comes 12
14 and brings along those sunny days? The kinds of things you 24
15 can do usually depend on the facilities near your home. 35

16   You may want to spend your days splashing in the water 12
17 or just dozing on the deck if there's a swimming pool near. 24
18 Whenever the temperature rises, just take a quick dip. 35

19   Or perhaps jogging is what you would rather do. A few 12
20 joggers rise early on hot days, and they run before sunrise 24
21 to avoid the heat that will arrive with the afternoon. 35

22   Playing volleyball on a beach, riding a bike through a 12
23 park, relaxing on a sailboat, playing tennis, and reading a 24
24 terrific book are things you might do on a summer day. 35

25   Whatever you choose to do with your summer, though, be 12
26 sure to set aside some time for doing nothing. During this 24
27 time you might plan ahead for next winter's activities. 35

```
     |  1  |  2  |  3  |  4  |  5  |  6  |  7  |  8  |  9  |  10  |  11  |  12        SI 1.39
```

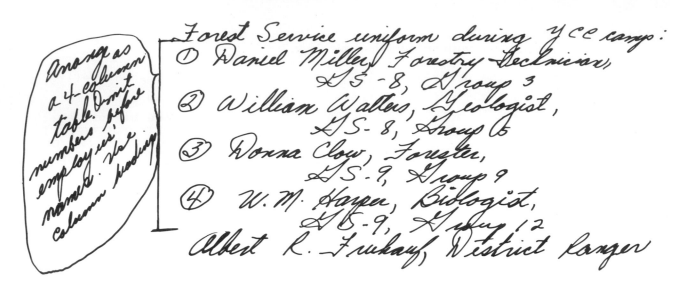

Arrange as a 4-column table. Omit numbers before names. Use employees' names. Use column headings.

Forest Service uniform during YCC camp:
① Daniel Miller, Forestry Technician, GS-8, Group 3
② William Walters, Geologist, GS-8, Group 6
③ Donna Clow, Forester, GS-9, Group 9
④ W. M. Hayes, Biologist, GS-9, Group 12
Albert R. Freihof, District Ranger

DISPLAY NOTICE FOR HIGH SCHOOL BULLETIN BOARDS
Format attractively on a full sheet of paper. Double-space bulletin board display.

The ranger wants to post this at the local high school tomorrow afternoon.

YOU CAN EARN AND LEARN IN THE YOUTH CONSERVATION CORPS THIS SUMMER IF YOU ACT NOW [*Subtitle*] Only Five Openings Left
The YCC is a program sponsored by the U.S. Department of Agriculture Forestry Service. To qualify, you must: (1) be between the ages of 15 and 18, (2) provide your own transportation to and from the camp, (3) work from 8 a.m. to 4:30 p.m., (4) wear hard hats and gloves on all outdoor jobs. MAJOR WORK: Deer fencing, trail maintenance, stream improvement, and soil stabilization. PAY: Minimum wage for eight weeks. Get an application from your school guidance counselor.

ENUMERATION
Format attractively on a full sheet of paper as a handout for the students in YCC who will report for their first day on June 23.

CHICORA NATIONAL FOREST, [*Subtitle*] Smithport Ranger Station, [*Subtitle*] YCC Work Rules
1. No drugs, narcotics, or alcholic beverages are permitted in government VEHICLES OR the work ~~sights.~~ sites
2. Enrolees will report all accidents, ir regardless of ~~there~~ their seriousness, to their crew leader.
3. No fire arms are permitted in government vehicles or on the work sites
4. All smoking at the work sites will be done at "safe" locations.
⑤ Cigarettes and matches will be crushed "deadout" and mixed with soil—not tossed on the ground.
5⑥. Enrolles are expected to do the jobs ~~there~~ their crew leaders assign them. Crew leaders will rotate assignments so that each enrollee will have variety.
6. Workhours are from 8 AM a.m. to 4:30 PM p.m. with one-half hour for lunch. All enrollees are expected to report to the Forest service ~~ware~~ house on time each morning.
7. Since the ycc program is of such a short duration this summer, all enrollees are expected to attend each day.

LESSON 80

GOALS
- To use commas correctly while typing compound sentences.
- To review the use of and gain proficiency in operating the tab, the shift lock, the space bar, the return, and the backspace key.
- To type at least 35/5'/5e.

FORMAT
- Single spacing   60-space line   Tabs every 9 spaces

LAB 7

Type lines 1–4 once, providing the missing commas. Edit your copy as your teacher reads the answers. Then retype lines 1–4 from your edited copy.

COMMAS IN COMPOUND SENTENCES

1 We will save our money this year and we will go on a trip.
2 You can watch the rabbits but they will run when you move.
3 You should not run away nor must you ever leave your post.
4 You may buy the book now or you may wait until next month.

TECHNIQUE REVIEW

Type lines 5–22 once to determine the two groups that gave you the most difficulty. Then type each difficult group once.

Tabulator Review

5 if   or   up   at   be   an   to
6 one   nor   let   two   six   but   for
7 plus   last   nine   zero   four   five   sums
8 ninth   joker   minor   first   sixth   tenth   fewer

Shift Lock Review

9   On FRIDAY, MARY was in RENO; last MONDAY, she was in MIAMI.
10 We drove to HARBOR-DELANEY, INC., to visit PAUL and JANICE.
11 Is JAMES going to read EXODUS or TOPAZ or QB VII on FRIDAY?
12 Drive the HARBOR, the SAN DIEGO, and the PASADENA freeways.

Space Bar Review

13 The sun was high in the sky, but it was not hot in the car.
14 All of us must see it now if it is to be fun for all of us.
15 A big dog and a tiny cat ran down the road at a rapid pace.
16 If it is to be, then we will not have much to say about it.

Carriage/Carrier Return Review

Return carriage or carrier after each word. Type lines 17E and 18E if you have an electric machine or lines 17M and 18M if you have a manual machine.

17E hairy laugh prowl learn acorn churn cramp camel ivory weigh
17M focus robot slant spend cocoa elbow spent their whale endow

18E yearn cameo panel blink adorn clamp usual lapel mourn repel
18M bigot cubic flair rifle shale sight tight aisle civic giant

Backspace Key Review

Backspace and underscore each underlined word immediately after typing it.

19 ah _am_ an _as_ at _be_ by _do_ go _ha_ he _ho_ if _in_ is _it_ me _no_ so _to_
20 was _one_ the _you_ our _for_ per _off_ put _how_ but _nor_ rib _kit_ day
21 last _week_ what _plan_ that _told_ good _more_ seem _sort_ like _this_
22 audit _signs_ blame _slept_ tithe _shame_ visit _gowns_ title _burns_

*An in-basket is a
group of production
typing jobs related to
a particular work
station.*

You are a member of the Youth Conservation Corps, which is a government-sponsored program for young people in high school who want to work summers in the national forests. You are scheduled to work at the Smithport Ranger Station, Chicora National Forest. Because of your business training, the District Ranger, Albert Fruhauf, has asked you to help in the office. Use letterheads and forms where appropriate. Workbook 457–472.

PRIORITY RECORDING SHEET   Workbook 455–456.

Today is June 2, 19—. You have reported for work at the Ranger Station. In your in-basket are the jobs shown on pages 344–346. Before starting to type, you should read through all the jobs to be done and decide which ones (1) are RUSH, to be done immediately; (2) are to be done promptly; or (3) may be completed when time permits. Using a priority recording sheet, list next to each job the priority that you think it should be given.

WORK LOG

Ranger Fruhauf has asked you to keep a work log of the various jobs as you complete them. The log contains a place for you to write in the time started, the time completed, the total minutes taken to complete the job, and the number of lines typed. Many businesses use work logs to evaluate an employee's productivity (the quantity of work produced) and to allocate costs.

GOVERNMENT MEMO WITH TABLE

*Government memos
use this order in the
heading: (1) Reply
to, (2) Subject, and
(3) To. The date is
backspaced from the
right margin on the
same line as Reply
to.*

Standard format. This document should be done within the first or second day of the next month.

[*Reply to*] 7120 Fleet Equipment, [*Subject*] Mileage and Gasoline Use, [*To*] Forest Supervisor

The following shows our vehicle and gasoline use for the YCC recruitment program for the months of March, April, and May:

Vehicle	Mileage	Gasoline (gallons)
YCC Rental	482	17
Privately Owned Vehicles	1,322	84
Forest Service Vehicle	8,383	552
Total	10,187	653

[*Signed*] Albert R. Fruhauf, District Ranger

MEMO WITH TABLE FROM HANDWRITTEN COPY

*Mail to the Forest
Supervisor is picked
up by interoffice
delivery.*

Format as a four-column table the names, job titles, government service classifications, and YCC group assignments for the four employees listed. Standard format. Body 50 words.

[Reply to:] 6150 Uniforms   [Date:]

[Subject:] Designation of Positions
         Requiring a Uniform

[To:] Forest Supervisor

The following employee positions fall into the "other" category for designation for wearing the

(Continued on next page)

Type lines 23 and 24 twice as a preview to the 5-minute timing below.

Accuracy
Speed

23 day your begin merely outside exercise squirrels beginnings
24 door open sign will just very even some seem then they into

**1- AND
5-MINUTE
TIMINGS**

Take two 1-minute timings on each paragraph. Then take one 5-minute timing on the entire selection. Use single spacing for the 1-minute timings and double spacing for the 5-minute timing.

25 The wonders of nature are waiting for you just outside   12
26 your door. The next time you wake up, just open your door,   24
27 and immediately dozens of morning signs will greet you.   35

28 Among the signs of the morning are the rising sun, the   12
29 setting moon, the dimming light of giant stars, the shining   24
30 dew of evening dampness, and the beginning of the day.   35

31 If you are watching and are very quiet, you might even   12
32 see some of nature's creatures begin to prepare for the day   24
33 to come. Rabbits, squirrels, and birds are just awake.   35

34 Listen to the quiet that seems to be all around you in   12
35 these early moments of the day. Listen just a little more,   24
36 and you can distinguish the sounds of nature awakening.   35

37 Rabbits hop through the grass taking their early morn—   12
38 ing exercise; squirrels scamper about looking for food; and   24
39 all the songbirds, young and old alike, start to chirp.   35

| 1 | 2 | 3 | 4 | 5 | 6 | 7 | 8 | 9 | 10 | 11 | 12   SI 1.39

LESSON 81

CLINIC

GOALS
- To review production techniques.
- To practice drills designed to strengthen production techniques.

FORMAT
- Single spacing   60-space line

**KEYBOARDING
SKILLS**

Type lines 1–4 once. Then, as you type line 5, do what line 5 tells you to do. Repeat lines 1–4, or take a series of 1-minute timings.

Speed   1 It is the right time for us to go to the fair and have fun.   12
Accuracy   2 Even Jacques may gaze up to find six crows in the blue sky.   12
Numbers   3 Lee waited 10 days, 29 days, 38 days, 47 days, and 56 days.   12
Symbols   4 Joyce* and David* invested $6.80 for 2 boards @ $3.40 each.   12
Technique 5 Your carriage/carrier will lock before finishing this line;
           use the margin release.

| 1 | 2 | 3 | 4 | 5 | 6 | 7 | 8 | 9 | 10 | 11 | 12

GOAL
- To type 45/5'/4e.
- To complete one in-basket in acceptable format and within a reasonable period of time.

FORMAT
- Single spacing   60-space line   5-space tab and other tabs as needed

KEYBOARDING SKILLS

Type lines 1–4 once. Then practice using your space bar by typing line 5. Repeat lines 1–4, or take a series of 1-minute timings.

Speed
Accuracy
Numbers
Symbols
Technique

1 Sue is to pay the man to fix the bicycle for the six girls. 12
2 Squad sixteen was puzzled by the vigor of the major attack. 12
3 The 10 men lived 29 days at 3847 North Buff Street for $56. 12
4 These test scores ranged from 10% to 56%; my score was 47%. 12
5 Then . . . . Well, I tried . . . and tried . . . and I won.

| 1 | 2 | 3 | 4 | 5 | 6 | 7 | 8 | 9 | 10 | 11 | 12

5-MINUTE TIMINGS

Take two 5-minute timings on lines 6–26. Circle your errors on both timings.

6   Would you like to spend a summer working in one of our   12
7 national parks? The National Park Service, one division of   24
8 the Department of the Interior, maintains a full-time staff   36
9 of workers at every park throughout the country; also, when   48
10 the number of visitors increases in summer, extra employees 60
11 are required to help keep the parks beautiful and safe from 72
12 vandals.   74
13   National parks are owned by the people of America, and   86
14 they are preserves for wildlife and timber. They are cared 98
15 for by our government to make sure parks stay protected and 110
16 guarded resources. Rangers check forest fires, analyze the 122
17 weather conditions, and keep close tabs on the wild animals 134
18 to make certain they're not hunted, diseased, or injured in 146
19 any way. Rangers also make sure that hiking tourists don't 158
20 get lost in the wilderness or hurt climbing mountains. The 170
21 summer employees are expected to assist the rangers as they 182
22 perform these numerous duties.   188
23   Many parks have campgrounds so visitors can spend time   200
24 out of doors, because hotels and motels and restaurants are 212
25 not allowed in most parks. Next summer, see Yellowstone or 224
26 Zion.   225

| 1 | 2 | 3 | 4 | 5 | 6 | 7 | 8 | 9 | 10 | 11 | 12   SI 1.55

PRINT ALIGNMENT REVIEW

Before doing Exercises 1, 2, and 3, review page 59.

Exercise 1. At various places and angles on a page, type three underscore lines 30 spaces long. Remove your paper. Reinsert it. Type your name on each line, blocking the first letter you type with the first underscore in the line.

Exercise 2. Type your first name on a page and then remove the paper. Reinsert the paper, align your first name with the aligning scale, and type your middle name. Once again remove the paper. Reinsert the paper, align your first two names with the aligning scale, and type your last name. Note whether the names have been aligned correctly.

Exercise 3. Type an underscore line 20 spaces long. Remove your paper. Reinsert the paper; then continue the underscore for another 20 spaces. Check to see how straight your underscore is.

ERASER CORRECTIONS REVIEW

Before typing and correcting the lines in Exercise 4, review page 54.

Exercise 4. Type the even-numbered lines (6, 8, 10); then correct these lines so that they look like the odd-numbered lines (7, 9, 11).

```
 6  The teacher said their are four exercises do type by seven.
 7  The teacher said there are four exercises to type by seven.
 8  Please place that vase on the cabinet; than close the door.
 9  Please place that vase in the cabinet; then close the door.
10  The flower grow rapidly in the warm son and gentle breezes.
11  The flower grew rapidly in the warm sun and gentle breezes.
```

SPREADING CORRECTIONS REVIEW

Before typing and correcting the lines in Exercise 5, review page 56 for spreading a correction.

Exercise 5. Type the even-numbered lines. Then type the odd-numbered lines, leaving the exact number of blank spaces shown. Type the words listed in the margin into the blank spaces by spreading.

```
              12  We will go too the fair.  Four children went too the movie.
Insert to.    13  We will go     the fair.  Four children went     the movie.
              14  Please stay bye the car.  We shall walk bye the wide river.
Insert by.    15  Please stay     the car.  We shall walk     the wide river.
              16  We want to sell that product.  They will buy that red sofa.
Insert the.   17  We want to sell      product.  .They will buy      red sofa.
```

SQUEEZING CORRECTIONS REVIEW

Before typing and correcting the lines in Exercise 6, review page 55 for squeezing a correction.

Exercise 6. Type the even-numbered lines. Then type the odd-numbered lines, leaving the exact number of blank spaces shown. Type the words listed in the margin into the blank spaces by squeezing.

```
              18  The to of them may drive.  Would you to want to ride along?
Insert two.   19  The    of them may drive.  Would you    want to ride along?
              20  We want to buy two books.  Do they want to buy two pencils?
Insert four.  21  We want to buy     books.  Do they want to buy     pencils?
              22  They want to sell the product.  They will buy the red sofa.
Insert that.  23  They want to sell     product.  They will buy     red sofa.
```

LESSON 211

GOALS
- To form plurals of nouns correctly while typing sentences.
- To review and apply LAB rules of Levels 5 and 6.

FORMAT
- Single spacing   60-space line

LAB 26

PLURALS

Workbook 453–454.

Type lines 1–4 once, making plurals of the underscored words as you type each line. Edit your copy as your teacher reads each answer. Then retype lines 1–4 from your edited copy.

1 Two district attorney quietly talked with the free agent.
2 Those secretary--Liz, Jan, and Alex--work on annuity.
3 All editor in chief must post jobs on the bulletin board.
4 Send five dictionary to the copywriters in these territory.

LAB REVIEW

Colons

Type lines 5–7, inserting colons wherever needed.

5 I want to do the following eat pizza, go hiking, and run.
6 Check these the carburetor, headlights, brakes, and fuel.
7 We went to check the house roof, stairs, door, and walls.

Hyphens

Type lines 8–10, inserting needed hyphens in compound nouns and adjectives.

8 Please proofread Mr. Burt's report before our get together.
9 She works as a clerk typist in the vice president's office.
10 The old fashioned house had an awe inspiring view, I think.

Dashes

Type lines 11–13, inserting dashes wherever needed.

11 We need time not money to bring about a change of orders.
12 The man to whom I wrote Mr. Gordon, I think will be here.
13 Her methods not her manners are what worry your managers.

Abbreviations

Type lines 14–16, making the correct abbreviations of the underscored words.

14 Our flight will arrive at 1:30 ante merediem and leave at
    12:30 post merediem.
15 Doctor Hammer went to visit Mister Ellsworth Wienstein yesterday.
16 After leaving the United States of America, he flew to
    Colombia that evening.

Plurals

Type lines 17–19, making plurals of the underscored words.

17 The man worked every day in order to get the child ready.
18 Their attorney investigated the case for us for two years.
19 The father-in-law worked all day on the tax for Russell.

PROOFREADING

Edit your copy as your teacher reads the answers. Retype any lines in which you made an error.

UNIT 14 BASIC FORMATTING REVIEW

GOALS
- To use commas correctly while typing compound sentences.
- To review use of the tabulator.
- To review horizontal/vertical centering.
- To review display typing.

FORMAT
- Single spacing   60-space line   5-space tab

LAB 7

Type lines 1–4 once, providing the missing commas. Edit your copy as your teacher reads the answers. Then retype lines 1–4 from your edited copy.

COMMAS IN COMPOUND SENTENCES

1 Jan plays on the tennis team but Ed is on the track squad.
2 The semester is now here but no one is quite ready for it.
3 Geese fly north in the spring and they wing south in fall.
4 Mt. Pleasant is in Texas but it is also found in Michigan.

PRETEST

Take a 5-minute Pretest on lines 5–19. Then circle and count your errors. Use the chart below to determine which lines to type for practice.

5   To some, living in an apartment is enjoyable. At some   12
6   time in your life, it is quite possible that you might live   24
7   in an apartment complex before deciding to buy a home.   35
8   When residing in an apartment complex, you do not have   47
9   to mow lawns, paint a house, or edge the grass next to your   59
10   sidewalk. An apartment manager is supposed to do this.   70
11   Very often an apartment is close to the business area,   82
12   and you will find that your commuting time to work is quite   94
13   minimal. You could take a bus and get to work quickly.   105
14   You will find it easy to make friends in an apartment,   117
15   since so many different people live next door or very close   129
16   to your place. You may find this to be very enjoyable.   140
17   Most apartments can be found with the latest in modern   152
18   appliances, they are carpeted, and they offer a wide choice   164
19   of dazzling features like pools and new tennis courts.   175
    | 1 | 2 | 3 | 4 | 5 | 6 | 7 | 8 | 9 | 10 | 11 | 12   SI 1.39

PRACTICE

In the chart below, find the number of errors you made on the Pretest. Then type each of the designated drill lines on page 139 four times.

Pretest errors	0–1	2–3	4–5	6+
Drill lines	23–27	22–26	21–25	20–24

FORMATTING VOUCHER CHECKS

A voucher check is a check with a tear-off stub. The stub includes the payee's name and address and can therefore be inserted in a window envelope to save typing time. The stub also includes an explanation of the payment—very helpful to the payee. And a copy of the stub serves as a file copy for the sender's records.

To format a voucher check:

1. Check half: Standard format for checks.
2. Stub half:
   a. Type the reason for the check, aligned with the amount, 3 lines below the top of the stub.
   b. Type the name and address 1 double space below the top of the address box, 2 spaces in from the left edge of the box.

PROFESSIONAL TRAVEL SERVICE
1600 Broad Street, Chicago, Illinois 60608

2 - 523
710

May 10, 19-- No. 396

PAY
TO THE
ORDER OF T & G Printing------------------------------ $60.50

Sixty and 50/100-- DOLLARS

Reliable Bank of Chicago
212 South State Street
Chicago, IL 60604

Memo

Sylvia Wong
AUTHORIZED SIGNATURE

⑆0710⑈0523⑆ ⑈324⑈9846307⑈

DETACH AND RETAIN THIS STATEMENT • The attached check is in payment of items described below. If not correct, notify us promptly.

In settlement of your statement of April 1, 19--.

T & G Printing
403 Wacker Drive, S.
Chicago, IL 60607

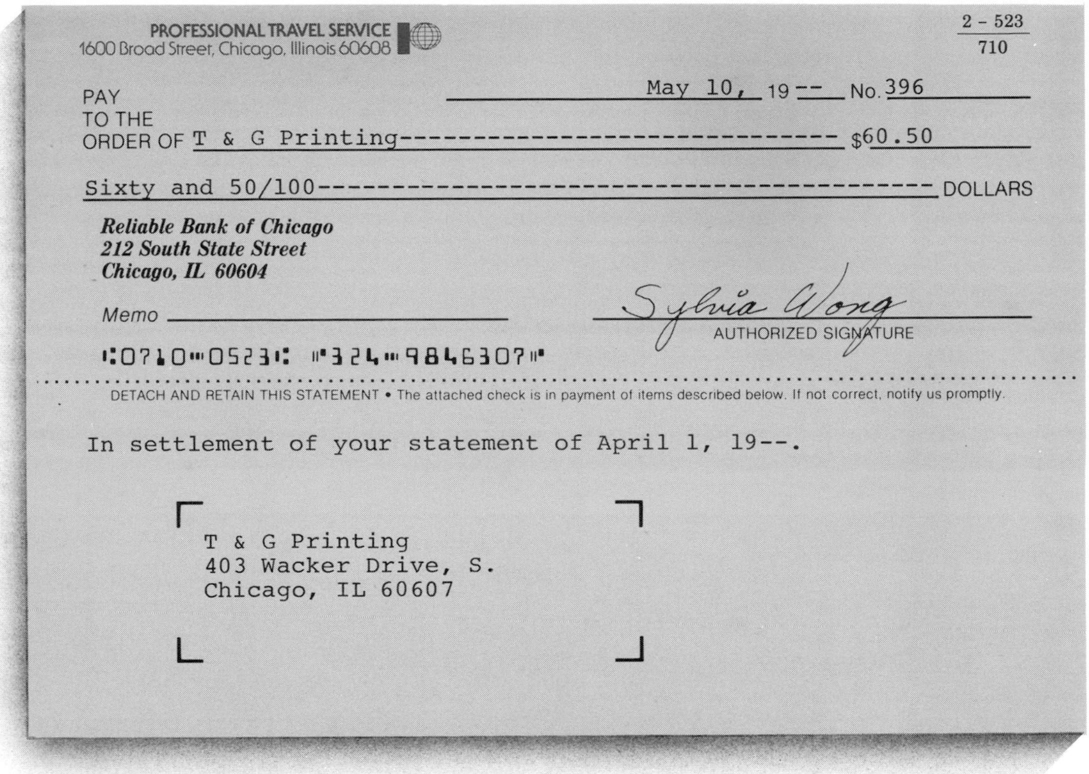

JOB 210-1. VOUCHER CHECK FROM INCOMPLETE COPY

Format the voucher check shown above. Workbook 449 top.

JOB 210-2. VOUCHER CHECK

Format a voucher check from the information given below. Workbook 449 bottom.

> Ms. Michelle Bamonte, 401 Waterman Street, Providence, RI 02910, gets a refund for a deposit she made on a trip with Professional Travel Service, 1600 Broad Street, Chicago, IL 60607. Check No. 467 for $200.00.

JOBS 210-3 AND 210-4. VOUCHER CHECKS

Prepare voucher checks in payment of the statements you typed in Jobs 208/9-5 and 208/9-6, page 339. Standard format. Workbook 451.

Accuracy	20	can time some living features dazzling possible responsible
	21	fun life your friends sidewalk residing enjoyable apartment
	22	you live that quickly business managers deciding appliances
	23	mow edge have minimal carpeted families different commuting
Speed	24	before offers quite might lawns paint areas works wide will
	25	within courts house grass times close edges lives lawn home
	26	latest tennis could since block place areas yours edge mows
	27	modern choice found pools offer court often likes easy very

POSTTEST

Repeat the Pretest on page 138 to see how much your skill has improved.

TABULATOR REVIEW

Review use of the tabulator on page 23. Then set tab stops at 10, 20, 30, 40, and 50 spaces from the left margin, and type by touch the following columns.

123	890	456	724	680
13	570	98	321	76
102	93	847	56	639

PRODUCTION WORD COUNT

The production word count (PWC) is used in production work to give you words-a-minute credit for operations such as using the tabulator, underscoring, and depressing the tab. In the practice exercises below, the PWC allows you additional credit for centering each line, for using the tabulator key, and for underscoring.

The production word count assumes that you have set all necessary margins and tab stops, and that your typewriter is in position to perform the first operation. In the example below, your carriage or carrier would be positioned at the center point, ready to backspace for the title.

CENTERING REVIEW

Practice 1. Review horizontal centering (page 25), vertical centering (page 29), and spread centering (page 31). Then center the display on the right. Add double spacing and use a full sheet of paper.

Practice 2. Repeat Practice 1 on a half sheet, using single spacing.

B U L L E T I N ↓3	9
	11
Homecoming Pep Rally	24
for St. James High School	41
Will Be Held On	51
WEDNESDAY, OCTOBER 1	64
at the School Gym	81

LESSON 83

GOALS
- To review report typing.
- To type a two-page report.

FORMAT
- Single spacing   60-space line   5-space and center tabs

KEYBOARDING SKILLS

Type lines 1–4 once. In line 5, use the shift lock for each word in all-capital letters. Repeat lines 1–4, or take a series of 1-minute timings.

Speed	1	They may take the bus for the day if it is not out of town.	12
Accuracy	2	By quietly giving back six tops, we amazed the four judges.	12
Numbers	3	Oh, 56 and 47 add up to 103; but 29 and 10 do not equal 38.	12
Symbols	4	Vi sold 2 @ $9 (6% profit), and Ed sold 3 @ $8 (5% profit).	12
Technique	5	The dates were MARCH 1, APRIL 2, MAY 3, JUNE 4, and JULY 5.

| 1 | 2 | 3 | 4 | 5 | 6 | 7 | 8 | 9 | 10 | 11 | 12 |

LESSON 210

GOALS
- To identify plural forms of nouns while typing sentences.
- To type 44/5'/4e.
- To format and type voucher checks.

FORMAT
- Single spacing   60-space line   5-space tab

LAB 26

PLURALS

Type lines 1–4 twice. Then repeat lines 1–4 or take a series of 1-minute timings.

```
1   Peter Zak wrote essays on the subject for my English class.   12
2   The armies of the nine nations have signed a unique treaty.   12
3   The mothers-in-law in our neighborhood have a weekly class.   12
4   Several companies have tried to have the taxes lowered now.   12
    | 1 | 2 | 3 | 4 | 5 | 6 | 7 | 8 | 9 | 10 | 11 | 12
```

30-SECOND TIMINGS

Take two 30-second timings on lines 5–7, or type the paragraph twice.

```
5   Recently, people in the business of marketing goods came up   12
6   with the crazy idea of putting names of famous designers on   24
7   things they wanted to sell, and the idea was a real winner.   36
    | 1 | 2 | 3 | 4 | 5 | 6 | 7 | 8 | 9 | 10 | 11 | 12
```

5-MINUTE TIMINGS

Take two 5-minute timings on lines 8–26. Circle your errors on both timings.

```
8        When shopping, in this country we generally accept the    12
9    price tag on merchandise as being the final price the store   24
10   will consider.  If we want the item, we pay the amount that   36
11   is asked.  In some countries, however, prices may fluctuate   48
12   from moment to moment, depending on the purchaser's ability   60
13   to bargain.  Then it becomes a matter of both the buyer and   72
14   the seller reaching a satisfactory price.                    80
15        A simple example of this process awaits the tourist in   92
16   Bangkok who visits the floating market at Damnoen Saduak, a  104
17   charming place of quaint beauty.  Located outside the city,  116
18   this stilt village resembles a boardwalk-like structure, or  128
19   suspended streets, or open-air shops built above the water.  140
20        Cruising to the center of the village, your canoe will  152
21   make a stop where you can disembark and wander through many  164
22   shops lining the boardwalk.  There's a friendly atmosphere,  176
23   with a tremendous selection of unique and prized handcrafts  188
24   made in Thailand.  Prices, of course, depend upon how adept  200
25   you are at bargaining.  Haggling is just a well-established  212
26   way to conduct their everyday business.                     220
     | 1 | 2 | 3 | 4 | 5 | 6 | 7 | 8 | 9 | 10 | 11 | 12   SI 1.60
```

FORMATTING REVIEW

Before you type Job 83-1, review the typing of reports. Specifically, review standard format (page 117), side headings (page 77), paragraph headings (page 80), footnotes (page 121), continuation pages (page 117), and enumerations in reports (page 84). Workbook 133.

Practice 1. Practice the start of a report: type in.

proper position on a page the heading lines and the first paragraph of the report shown below.

Practice 2. Practice the typing of footnotes: type the last paragraph (on page 141) and the footnote. Begin typing on line 30. Remember to place the footnote at the *bottom* of the page on which it is referenced.

JOB 83-1. LONG REPORT

Double spacing, 5-space tab. Workbook 136.

HOW TO TYPE A REPORT	12
A Review of Some Basic Guidelines	34
Prepared by Jane T. Sloan ↓3	51
When you are typing a paper for final copy, you should be sure	68
that it is of the highest quality and that your best efforts have	81
been put into the project. If your report is going to be dupli-	94
cated, you must use a high-quality paper. This report will present	108
the steps you must follow when typing a paper. ↓3	117
SELECTION OF A TYPEWRITER	124
Either a pica or an elite typewriter may be used when typing a	138
report. Whatever the choice, you must be sure that the element or	151
the keys are clean and that they provide a good impression. The	164
platen and bail rollers must also be free of grease, carbon, and	177
dirt. ↓3	179
SELECTION OF SUPPLIES	185
Ribbon. A good ribbon should be used when typing reports.	201
"Use a black ribbon so that the copy will be clear and permanent."[1]	216
A carbon ribbon will give the best results, but cloth ribbons may	229
also be used. A good cloth ribbon should give you a dark, even	242
print.	244
Paper. "Only good-quality bond paper should be used when typ-	259
ing your report."[2] Many believe that 20-pound paper should be used	273
for typing originals and that 16-pound paper should be used if car-	286
bons are typed. The rag content of the paper should be 50 percent.	300

Watching for bottom margin? Remember that a footnote must go on the same page as the reference to it.

Separation line is 20P/24E long. Single-space before and double-space after typing it.

_____

[1]William A. Sabin, <u>The Gregg Reference Manual</u>, 5th ed., Gregg Division, McGraw-Hill Book Company, New York, 1977, p. 271.   +27

[2]Ibid.   +5

(Continued on next page)

FORMATTING REVIEW

Statement of Account

A statement of account itemizes all the transactions completed during the month or other billing period. It tells (1) how much was due at the start of the period, (2) what orders were delivered, by invoice number, (3) what payments were received, and (4) current balance due.

Top: Align fill-ins with guide words. Bottom: (1) Begin a double space below the horizontal rule. (2) Center the number columns. (3) Begin the Reference column 2 spaces after the vertical rule.

JOB 208/9-3. STATEMENT OF ACCOUNT

Standard format. Workbook 445 top.

(Date) May 1, 19— (With) Professional Travel Service, 1600 Broad Street, Chicago, IL 60607

4/1	Brought Forward	0.00
4/12	Invoice T-2939	16.75
4/14	Invoice T-3008	133.00
4/20	Payment on Account	100.00
4/23	Invoice T-4071	10.75

JOB 208/9-4. STATEMENT OF ACCOUNT

Standard format. Type the invoices in the Charges column and add the amount to the balance. Type the payments in the Credits column and subtract the amount from the Balance. Workbook 445 bottom.

(Date) October 1, 19—
(With) Hampshire House
181 Andrews Boulevard
Joliet, IL 60436

9/1	Brought Forward	00.00
9/4	Invoice G-6107	195.50
9/7	Invoice G-71523	422.60
9/24	Payment	500.00
9/30	Invoice G-11044	125.00

JOB 208/9-5. STATEMENT OF ACCOUNT

Standard format. Compute the balances. Hold this job for use in Lesson 210. Workbook 447 top.

(Date) November 1, 19—
(With) Parkway Plaza
3202 Parkway Drive
Peoria, IL 61603

10/1	Brought Forward	120.00
10/3	Invoice XS-43017	56.50
10/12	Payment	75.00
10/22	Invoice XS-57129	164.23

JOB 208/9-6. STATEMENT OF ACCOUNT

Standard format. Compute the balances. Hold this job for use in Lesson 210. Workbook 447 bottom.

(Date) December 1, 19—
(With) The Carriage Inn
676 State Street
Chicago, IL 60606

11/1	Brought Forward	115.85
11/10	Payment	115.85
11/20	Invoice TB-7401-P	176.50
11/24	Invoice TB-7420-P	218.75
11/30	Payment	100.00

Carbon Paper. Many types of carbon paper——thick, colored,   315
soft——may be bought in different sizes and for almost any price   330
you are willing to pay.   335

When you are ready to start typing your report, be certain   348
that the carbon pack (the carbon paper and the paper on which your   362
originals and copies will be typed) is inserted into the machine   375
correctly. To do this, you must: 382

   1.   Check to be sure that the printed side of the letterhead   395
      and the dull side of the carbon sheets are facing you.   407

   2.   Be sure that the pack is straight in the machine.   419

   3.   Operate the paper release to release the tension on the   432
      papers.[3]   437

                                                  +7

[3]Ibid., p. 230.   +6

LESSON 84

GOALS
- To type sentences that use the rule for commas between adjectives.
- To review letter typing.

FORMAT
- Single spacing   60-space line   5-space tab

LAB 8

COMMAS BETWEEN ADJECTIVES

Type lines 1–4 once. Then repeat lines 1–4 or take a series of 1-minute timings.

1 The tall, silent stranger ran quickly down the narrow walk.   12
2 Members of the strong, silent majority seldom speak loudly.   12
3 Diaz is a member of our unbeatable, hard-working judo team.   12
4 Inside Franklin's loose, ill-fitting vest were six tickets.   12

  | 1 | 2 | 3 | 4 | 5 | 6 | 7 | 8 | 9 | 10 | 11 | 12

Adjectives describe or modify nouns. Note the adjectives in italics:

brief speeches   *interesting* speeches   *brief, interesting* speeches
effective ideas   *unique* ideas   *effective, unique* ideas

When two or more adjectives describe the *same* noun, place a comma between the adjectives. In all other cases, use no comma. To determine whether the adjectives do describe the same noun, use the following test:

Janice gave a *factual, detailed* account. (Say "An account that was factual AND detailed." Does it make sense? Yes, proving that each adjective describes *account* and that the comma is needed.)

She distributed a *new summer* schedule. (Say "A schedule that is new AND summer." Does it make sense? No, proving that each adjective does not describe the noun *schedule*. No comma is needed.)

5-MINUTE TIMING

Repeat the Pretest, Practice, Posttest routine on pages 334 and 335.

FORMATTING QUESTIONNAIRES

Questionnaires may be formatted in several ways, depending upon the type of questions you have and how simple you want the form to appear. For example, you can use any of the following styles for displaying short responses:

yes   A ruled line   Ⓧ   A circle

☒   A box   (Yes)   Ask the respondent
No   to circle a word

Use typed lines or open spaces for long responses.

JOB 208/9-1. QUESTIONNAIRE

Select the most appropriate style or styles and format the questionnaire for Western Paradise Resort. Full sheet of paper. Allow space for comments or suggestions at the end of the questionnaire. Try not to crowd the questions.

DID YOU ENJOY YOUR STAY WITH US?

We hope that you enjoyed your visit with us and that you found our services and facilities to your liking. Before you leave, however, we would appreciate your giving us your opinion by completing this questionnaire of the various aspects of our service. so that we can continue to offer our guests the best possible vacation package of it's kind in the country circle your answers:

1. What facilities did you use during your visit? Swimming pool Tennis courts Golf course Sauna Riding academy Bowling alleys Paddle ball courts Health club (Shuffleboard)

2. What organized sports did you participate in? Baseball Volleyball Tennis tournament Golf Tournament Mountain climbing

3. What organized social activities did you participate in? Square dancing Disco dancing contest Waltz contest Wine and cheese party Bingo Bridge Las Vegas night Indian arts festival Rodeo

4. How would you rate our food? Excellent Good Poor

5. How would you rate our house keeping? Excellent Good Poor

6. How would you rate your service? Excellent Good Poor

7. How would you rate your total experience? Excellent Good Poor

JOB 208/9-2. QUESTIONNAIRE FROM ROUGH-DRAFT COPY

Format Job 208/9-1 on an 8 by 5 card. Use both sides.

Take a 5-minute timing on lines 5–19. Type six times each word on which you made an error, hesitated, or stopped during the 5-minute timing. Then take a 5-minute timing to see how much your skill has improved.

```
5        Travel can provide you with exciting, fun experiences.    12
6    The skills you might gain from travel can make you a better   24
7    person when at work, at school, at home, or at leisure.       35
8        While at work, you will come into contact with men and    47
9    women from every walk of life.  The various people that you  59
10   meet in traveling will prepare you for your employment.       70
11       When you travel, you may sometimes find yourself among    82
12   people who do not speak the same language as you.  The tact   94
13   this situation demands may be very useful at home too.       105
14       At school you can share many of your travels with your   117
15   classmates and teachers.  You might tell them all about the  129
16   colorful, historical sites that you were able to visit.      140
17       It might be that the quality of your leisure time will   152
18   improve.  Just think of the dozens of new, unique dances or  164
19   other pastimes you can teach your friends and family.        175
     |  1  |  2  |  3  |  4  |  5  |  6  |  7  |  8  |  9  |  10  |  11  |  12   SI 1.39
```

**FORMATTING
REVIEW**

Review the typing of business letters on pages 92–93 before completing Job 84-1. Workbook 142.

JOB 84-1. LETTER

Standard format. Workbook 137, 139–140. Body 91 words.

[*Today's date*] / Mr. David R. Stone / 1738 (13) Cecil Avenue / San Jose, CA 95128 / Dear Mr. (22) Stone: (24)

You have always been a preferred customer (34) of ours, and we have appreciated your contin- (43) uous, faithful trust in our line of products. (52) You have made it a habit to pay your credit (61) card purchases on time, and this practice has (70) built for you a fine credit rating. (78)

It has come to my attention, though, that (87) you have not used our credit card for the past (97) 12 months. Have we done something to cause (106) you to stop buying our products? If our prompt, (115) reliable service has failed you, please let us (125) know. / Yours, / Ms. Elaine Burrow / (137) Customer Service / [*Your initials*] (143)

JOB 206/7-7. CALL REPORT

Workbook 443. If necessary, use the reverse side for remarks.

[*Date*] January 31, 19—; [*Company*] International Metals Company; [*Place*] Pittsburgh, PA; [*Persons interviewed*] Charlie Van Dorne, Manager, Administrative Services; Scott Roberts, Systems Analyst; Shawn Schwartz, Sales Coordinator; [*Remarks*] Van Dorne was delighted with our computers and is interested in leasing our DX-5500 system. I think they really need our DX-8500, so I suggested that our general sales manager and I call again within a few days so that we can be sure they get the computer that's best for them.

LESSONS 208/209

GOALS
- To recognize plural forms of nouns while typing sentences.
- To format and type two questionnaires.
- To format and type four statements of account.

FORMAT
- Single spacing   60-space line   5-space tab and other tabs as needed

LAB 26

Type lines 1–4 once. Then repeat lines 1–4 or take a series of 1-minute timings. As you type each line, note the noun plurals.

PLURALS

1 Persons in local governments serve the cities and counties. 12
2 Her brothers-in-law went to the studio to quietly do a job. 12
3 The ladies work as volunteers at the exits at the city zoo. 12
4 Dr. Perry's attorneys are working on the case for Mrs. Lee. 12

| 1 | 2 | 3 | 4 | 5 | 6 | 7 | 8 | 9 | 10 | 11 | 12

When a singular noun ends in *y* preceded by a consonant, the plural is formed by changing the *y* to *i* and adding *es* to the singular.

company, companies   authority, authorities

But when a singular noun ends in *y* preceded by a vowel, the plural is formed by adding *s* to the singular.

attorney, attorneys

The plurals of compound nouns spelled with a hyphen or as two words are formed by making the chief element of the compound plural.

brother-in-law, brothers-in-law
account receivable, accounts receivable

12-SECOND TIMINGS

Type each line four times, or take four 12-second timings on each line. For each timing, type without error.

5 When they do the work, try to make the goal right for them. 12
6 Both the city and firm own half the lake and half the land. 12
7 If they do make it to the lake, I may wish to pay for them. 12

25   30   35   40   45   50   55   60

LESSON 85

GOALS
- To type sentences that reinforce the rule for commas between adjectives.
- To review typing two-, three-, and four-column tables.

FORMAT
- Single spacing   60-space line   Tabs at center and as needed

LAB 8

Type lines 1–4 once. Then repeat lines 1–4 or take a series of 1-minute timings.

COMMAS BETWEEN ADJECTIVES

1 A dozen anxious, excited scouts began their overnight trip.   12
2 Last night four neighbors bought Joan a healthy, happy pup.   12
3 The scarecrow is wearing a long, loose coat and a silk hat.   12
4 The salesperson who waits on me is the quiet, helpful type.   12
   | 1 | 2 | 3 | 4 | 5 | 6 | 7 | 8 | 9 | 10 | 11 | 12

FORMATTING REVIEW

Review the typing of tables on pages 97 and 100 before completing Jobs 85-1 and 85-2. Review the typing of tables with column heads on pages 102 and 104 before completing Job 85-3 (below) and Job 85-4 (on page 144).

JOB 85-1. TWO-COLUMN TABLE
Standard format (see pages 97 and 100). Double-space, full sheet of paper.

KVIX CONTEST WINNERS

Week of April 10–14

Monday	Sarah Wheeling
Tuesday	Donald Riley
Wednesday	Edward Bowman
Thursday	Janice Barnes
Friday	Sharon Larson

JOB 85-2. THREE-COLUMN TABLE
Standard format. Double-space, full sheet of paper.

BUSINESS EMPLOYEES
(Texas Branch Offices)

Accountants	Austin	28
Clerks	Austin	42
Clerks	Tyler	26
Secretaries	Dallas	37
Stenographers	El Paso	41
Typists	Houston	50
Typists	San Antonio	42

JOB 85-3. THREE-COLUMN TABLE
Standard format. Single-space, full sheet of paper.

DISTANCES BETWEEN U.S. CITIES

Expressed in Kilometers

West Coast	East Coast	Distance
Seattle	Boston	4,896
Portland	Baltimore	4,481
San Francisco	Philadelphia	4,753
Los Angeles	Washington, D.C.	4,312

JOBS 206/7-1 TO 206/7-4. EXPENSE REPORT FORMS

Standard format (see page 335). Figure totals. Date each form the day after the last date of the trip. Workbook 439, 441.

Robert Carberry, 3900 Fourth Street, Macon, GA 31204. March 2: Airfare to/from Charleston, SC, $87.21; Limousine from airport, $3.75; Convention registration fee, $15.00; Hotel Pecan, including porter's tip, $57.50; Meals, including banquet, $25.00. March 3: Transportation to Charleston airport, $3.75.

Y. K. Pao, 214 Summitt Road, Atlanta, GA 30301. March 7: Luncheon at La Normande Restaurant for customers—Dr. Albert T. Karr (research specialist) and Dr. Greta Speer-Hagen (Dr. Karr's associate), both of I. T. Fragen, Inc., Federal Republic of Germany; and two staff members—$69.50.

Lucille Sanchez, 14 Washington Road, Atlanta, GA 30301. March 14: Limousine to airport, $4.50; Airfare to/from New York, $198.81; Transportation from airport to Rockefeller Center (taxi), $13.00; Dinner, Hotel Ingram, $9.75; Hotel Ingram, $68.35. March 15: Meals, $11.50; Transportation from Rockefeller Center (taxi), $13.00; Limousine from Atlanta airport, $4.50.

Robert Carberry, 3900 Fourth Street, Macon, GA 31204. March 18: Bus to/from Atlanta for GCA meeting, $27.18; Registration fee (including lunch), $25.

FORMATTING CALL REPORTS

When a sales person for a company makes a call on a customer for the purpose of making a sale, a call report is prepared. These forms may be arranged in a variety of ways. Standard formatting rules apply.

CALL REPORT

Date: July 15, 19--

Company: Majestic Instruments

Address: Chicago, IL

Person(s) Interviewed:

William Wise, Director of Purchasing

Emily Heidenkamp, Assistant Director

Sales Representative: G. N. Katzameyer

Remarks: They are interested in our Model ST-4000, but they want to shop around. I'll follow up on this lead.

JOB 206/7-5. CALL REPORT

Workbook 443. If necessary, use reverse side for remarks.

[Date] January 5, 19—; [Company] Bitterman Tool, Inc.; [Place] Cleveland, OH; [Person(s) interviewed] Frank M. Hicks, Vice President; [Sales representative] Anthony Santangelo; [Remarks] We discussed the recent shipment to their Longo Point plant, a shipment they claim was out of specification. The steel pipe was cut too long by $2\frac{1}{2}$ inches. They had to cut the pipe at a cost of $782 and are requesting that we reimburse them. The pipe was shipped according to their order. Since they are good customers, I recommend that we split the cost of cutting the pipe.

JOB 206/7-6. CALL REPORT

Workbook 443. If necessary, use the reverse side for remarks.

[Date] January 6, 19—; [Company] International Metals Company; [Place] Pittsburgh, PA; [Persons interviewed] Rupert Holmgrem, Sales Manager, and Shawn Schwartz, Sales Coordinator; [Sales representative] Victoria Abbett; [Remarks] Systems analyst Scott Roberts joined us for a portion of the discussion. He was very interested; but he needs the approval of his boss, Charlie Van Dorne. Roberts wants me to call again in two weeks when his boss is back from Japan.

JOB 85-4. FOUR-COLUMN TABLE

Standard format. Double-space, full sheet of paper.

NATIONAL LEAGUE PENNANT WINNERS

Highest Won/Lost Percentages

Year	Club	Manager	Percentage
1880	Chicago	Anson	.798
1876	Chicago	Spalding	.788
1885	Chicago	Anson	.777
1906	Chicago	Chance	.763
1884	Providence	Bancroft	.750

LESSON 86

GOALS
- To apply the rule for commas between adjectives.
- To type at least 35/5'/5e.
- To review forms typing.

FORMAT
- Single spacing   60-space line   5-space tab

LAB 8

Type lines 1–4 once, providing the missing commas. Edit your copy as your teacher reads the answers. Then retype lines 1–4 from your edited copy.

COMMAS BETWEEN ADJECTIVES

1 It's dangerous to drive quickly on a wet slippery highway.
2 Soft soothing music plays in most restaurants and offices.
3 Six of us in Jan's building heard the loud strident voice.
4 A hazy summer morning often becomes a hot humid afternoon.

PRETEST

Take a 5-minute Pretest on lines 13–27 on page 145. Circle and count your errors. Use the chart below to find the number of errors you made on the Pretest. Then type each of the designated drill lines four times. Take a 5-minute Posttest on lines 13–27 on page 145 to see how much your skill has improved.

Pretest errors	0–1	2–3	4–5	6+
Drill lines	8–12	7–11	6–10	5–9

PRACTICE

Accuracy

5 would great quickly outside exercise dangerous registration
6 adapt papers puppies Bernard purchase residence housebroken
7 breed enough decide provide assuming life-style combination
8 begin before terrier raising apartment determine protection

Speed

9 praised raising course happy zesty both upon want sure just
10 command expect check train vital hard line part can fun and
11 healthy animal large taken ample work will your may not are
12 respond proper plenty times dogs even must what too its all

In the chart below, find the number of errors you made on the Pretest. Then type each of the designated drill lines four times.

Pretest errors	0–1	2–3	4–5	6+
Drill lines	28–32	27–31	26–30	25–29

Accuracy

25 budget through involved permanent assortment transportation
26 out years windows cluster increasing undeterred spectacular
27 are gave traveler tourists Antarctica businesses remarkably
28 result hazards pleasure unreachable restaurants accommodate

Speed

29 people hotels plane when they trip high also and the one to
30 benefit prices though market their sold some all how led of
31 quality flights world spite visit most this end for ago jet
32 permanent agencies example it's seem with just many even an

POSTTEST

Repeat the Pretest on page 334 to see how much your skill has improved.

FORMATTING EXPENSE REPORTS

To be reimbursed for business expenses such as travel and entertainment expenses, workers must fill out detailed expense reports. For each expense, the report shows the date, the reason, and the actual amount of the cost. The report provides space for the payee's signature and an approval signature.

To format an expense report, follow standard format for business forms. **Note:** If the Amount column contains a vertical rule separating dollars and cents, align the numbers 1 space from the rule.

Pay to Mary Beth Keith _____ Date March 11, 19--
   Claimant to insert name

Address 219 Dellafield Avenue, Brockton, MA 02402 _____
   Claimant to insert address

MONTH	DAY	ITEMS OF EXPENDITURE	DOLLARS	CENTS
3	10	Transportation to Boston airport	17	50
		Plane fare to Washington--round trip	167	00
		Transportation to FBI Building	11	75
		Luncheon ticket	10	00
		Transportation to Washington airport	11	75
		Transportation from Boston airport	17	50
		Total	235	50

Approved:

Signature of Claimant *Mary Beth Keith*   *L. P. Dempster*

Raising dogs can be [1] a combination of [2] both fun and hard 12
work. Before [3] you even begin, you have [4] to decide what breed 24
will [5] best adapt to your life-[6]style and your residence. [7] 35
If you need a dog [8] to protect your house, a [9] terrier may 47
not provide [10] sufficient protection. If [11] you are in an apart- 59
ment, [12] a St. Bernard would [13] certainly be just too large. [14] 70
If you have decided [15] upon the dog you want, [16] be sure you 82
check its [17] registration papers. Then, [18] assuming that you now 94
purchase [19] the puppy, you can [20] expect to need to train it. [21] 105
Of course, you know [22] that most puppies have [23] to be taken 117
outside quite [24] frequently before they [25] are housebroken. They 129
must [26] be praised quickly when [27] they respond to a command. [28] 140
Ample care, plenty [29] of good exercise, a solid [30] diet, and 152
loads of love [31] are all vital in the [32] raising of an animal. A 164
zesty [33] puppy should grow up to [34] be a healthy, happy dog. [35] 175
| 1 | 2 | 3 | 4 | 5 | 6 | 7 | 8 | 9 | 10 | 11 | 12 SI 1.38

POSTTEST Repeat the Pretest to see how much your skill has improved.

FORMATTING REVIEW Before you type Jobs 86-1 and 86-2, review the typing of forms. Specifically, review alignment with guide words (page 59), memos on printed forms (page 107), and invoices on printed forms (pages 113–115).

JOB 86-1. INTEROFFICE MEMO ON A FORM

Standard format. Single-space. Workbook 143 top.

[*Today's date*] / [*To:*] James Bloom / District V Manager / [*From:*] 11
Ruth Lopez / Area Manager / [*Subject:*] Waterwheel Replacements 23
We have had to place your order for 12 dozen #4216 waterwheel 37
sprinklers on back order. Your order will not be processed for at least 52
another two weeks. 56
The whole district has suffered a long, hot drought that has caused 70
a drain on our supplies of those water sprinklers. The cooler weather 85
we are to have next week should bring you some relief until your 98
order can be filled. 102
RL 105
[*Your initials*] 108

LESSONS 206/207

GOALS
- To form plurals of nouns correctly while typing sentences.
- To format and type four expense reports and three call reports.

FORMAT
- Single spacing   60-space line   5-space tab and other tabs as needed

LAB 25

Type lines 1–4 once, making plurals of the underscored words. Edit your copy as your teacher reads the answers. Then retype lines 1–4 from your edited copy.

PLURALS

1   The <u>child</u> working at the <u>computer</u> can check it quickly.
2   The <u>girl</u> went jogging in the <u>field</u> to see the old <u>house</u>.
3   After the <u>accountant</u> checked, the <u>clerk</u> left for the day.
4   The <u>woman</u> drove to the big <u>office</u> next to the lazy <u>river</u>.

PRETEST

Take a 5-minute Pretest on lines 5–24. Then circle and count your errors. Use the chart on page 335 to determine which lines to type for practice.

5   When people travel, they seldom consider just how many   12
6   different businesses are involved in making their journey a   24
7   success. Several modes of transportation, hotels, resorts,   36
8   and restaurants all benefit; and each of these services for   48
9   the traveler adds mainly to the quality and, in the end, to   60
10   the pleasure of the trip.   66
11   Most travel agencies offer a range of prices to accom—   77
12   modate almost any travel budget. They also try to offer an   89
13   assortment of pleasant places to visit. Some tourists seem   101
14   undeterred today by distance or high costs. For example, a   113
15   ship to Antarctica is always sold out, even though it's one   125
16   of the most unreachable places in the world--and one of the   137
17   coldest. And as a result of this increasing tourism, there   149
18   are plans for permanent clusters of tourists' cabins there,   161
19   complete with an airstrip.   166
20   Several years ago the demand to see Antarctica quickly   178
21   and cheaply led to charter-jet flights from New Zealand. A   190
22   flight gave tourists, gawking through windows of the plane,   202
23   a panorama of spectacular scenery. Remarkably, this market   214
24   soared, in spite of hazards.   220

| 1 | 2 | 3 | 4 | 5 | 6 | 7 | 8 | 9 | 10 | 11 | 12   SI 1.60

JOB 86-2. INVOICE ON A FORM
Standard format. Workbook 143 bottom.

[*Today's date*] / Ramirez Home Improvements Inc. / 2320 Merrell Road
/ Dallas, TX 75229

11	Workbenches, Model 9109	69.00	759.00
26	20′ Aluminum drain gutters	27.36	711.36
4	Sure-Right 6″ electric saws, Model R78	47.00	188.00
8	6′ Steel storage cabinets	27.69	221.52
	Amount due		1,879.88
	Delivery charges		37.28
	Total amount due		1,917.16

LESSON
87

CLINIC

GOALS
- To improve accuracy on "OK" timings.
- To type 35/5′/5e.

FORMAT
- Single spacing   60-space line   5-space tab

KEYBOARDING SKILLS

Type lines 1–4 once. Then type line 5 using your return key or lever after each word. Repeat lines 1–4, or take a series of 1-minute timings.

Speed	1 Their big problem is half their profit is spent for enamel.	12
Accuracy	2 Have my six dozen quails joined two big flocks of sparrows?	12
Numbers	3 Shirley got Nos. 10 and 29; Chapin got Nos. 38, 47, and 56.	12
Symbols	4 Fox & Day ordered 25# of cheese (mellow) @ $3.09 per pound.	12
Technique	5 You should always operate the return key or lever by touch.	

| 1 | 2 | 3 | 4 | 5 | 6 | 7 | 8 | 9 | 10 | 11 | 12

12-SECOND TIMINGS

Type each line four times, or take four 12-second timings on each line. For each timing, type with no more than one error.

6 It seemed to me that the birds got silent long before dark. 12

7 She put a stamp on it before she dropped it in the mailbox. 12

8 Six of us pitched in to give the car a push along the road. 12

25   30   35   40   45   50   55   60

"OK" TIMINGS

This version of a 30-second timing is used to build your accuracy on alphabetic copy. Try to type as many 30-second "OK" (errorless) timings as possible out of three attempts on lines 9–11. Then repeat the attempt on lines 12–14, page 147.

9 Five or six big jet planes zoomed quickly by the new tower. 12

10 Jars prevented the brown mixture from freezing too quickly. 24

11 Hal was quick to give us extra pizza and juice for my boss. 36

PRETEST 1

Take two 2-minute timings on lines 6–9. Circle your errors.

6 Phyllis Hinkimin wore a kinky kimono of nylon on Look Hill. 12
7 A pupil in hilly Joplin sold Lou that oil monopoly in June. 24
8 A plump puppy limped in as Johnny looked at the oily pools. 36
9 My polo pony looked jolly as Phillip pulled him in my pool. 48
   | 1 | 2 | 3 | 4 | 5 | 6 | 7 | 8 | 9 | 10 | 11 | 12

PRACTICE 1

Practice lines 10–15 four times.

10 hip ill joy kin lip mop nip oil pin you hop imp lop mum nun
11 kink lily milk nook only pill upon yolk honk join limp mill
12 imply kinky onion hominy kimono limply pinion unhook minion

13 ohm ply hum ink mom non pop hun inn nil pun him pip pup Lon
14 noon oily pink hook kiln lion mink noun plum polk loop jump
15 phony nylon pupil phylon unholy pompom uphill poplin pippin

POSTTEST 1

Repeat the Pretest to see how much your skill has improved.

PRETEST 2

Take two 2-minute timings on lines 16–19. Circle your errors.

16 Adam Fallan, an Anzac man, can scan a ban as calmly as Sam. 12
17 Jack slams a handball hard, and Alan lacks a hard backhand. 24
18 Ben commonly banks a maximum sum of money in his zinc mine. 36
19 Zoe expects to watch a mammoth zebra at the zoo next month. 48
   | 1 | 2 | 3 | 4 | 5 | 6 | 7 | 8 | 9 | 10 | 11 | 12

PRACTICE 2

Practice lines 20–24 four times.

20 next elms name exam ribs fear zeal acts vent zero been mine
21 index zebra exact human, puzzle dozen, pompom mummy, critic
22 numb zinc buzz bomb back comb comma maxim venom annex axiom
23 black balsa blank class lacks small balls calls basal chalk
24 Ezra Saxon said the old lax law on pizzas was quite quaint.

POSTTEST 2

Repeat the Pretest to see how much your skill has improved.

3-MINUTE TIMING

Take one 3-minute timing on lines 5–16 on page 325.

12   Jane gave my excited boy quite a prize for his clever work.

13   I was quickly penalized five or six times by Major Higgins. 24

14   The very next question emphasized the growing lack of jobs. 36

| 1 | 2 | 3 | 4 | 5 | 6 | 7 | 8 | 9 | 10 | 11 | 12

PRETEST

Take a 5-minute Pretest on lines 15–29. Then circle and count your errors. Use the chart below to determine which lines to type for practice.

15   Every once in a while you may come across a typewriter 12

16 with something very unique about it; the thing might simply 24

17 be a tray for a pencil or eraser, or just an extra key. 35

18   Or perhaps you might find a machine with small numbers 47

19 in the place of the symbols on the upper row; these are for 59

20 footnote annotations, for citations in the text, etc. 70

21   You might even find a machine that has a light instead 82

22 of a bell to signal the approach to the margin; the machine 94

23 is intended for somebody who's deaf or hard of hearing. 105

24   In a hospital you might find a typewriter mounted on a 117

25 special contraption that holds the keyboard where a patient 129

26 flat on his or her back is able to manipulate the keys. 140

27   But the most dazzling and unique of the surprise items 152

28 is the discovery that you have keys with accent marks——just 164

29 the thing for a project in typing in a foreign language. 175

| 1 | 2 | 3 | 4 | 5 | 6 | 7 | 8 | 9 | 10 | 11 | 12 SI 1.40

For Extra Speed

Tab-indent quickly, smoothly.

Return carriage or carrier quickly.

Release shift key instantly.

Get off space bar in a flash.

Keep eyes on copy so that you never lose your place.

PRACTICE

In the chart below, find the number of errors you made on the Pretest. Then type each of the designated drill lines four times.

Pretest errors	0–1	2–3	4–5	6+
Drill lines	33–37	32–36	31–35	30–34

Accuracy

30 every patient symbols foreign somebody discovery typewriter

31 thing instead eraser, example citation manipulate something

32 extra accents numbers machine language dazzling annotations

33 upper intends hearing project keyboard surprise contraption

Speed

34 might place these text, come back very just you may see the

35 who's light mount holds with tiny row; text are for the one

36 where would items marks even find that bell who can say you

37 bells trays notes while deaf able keys flat see and use key

POSTTEST

Repeat the Pretest to see how much your skill has improved.

JOB 204-1. TWO-PAGE RULED TABLE
Standard format with triple spacing.

Two dots in a table tell readers information is not available or does not apply. Align the X in other columns with the first dot.

AIRLINES SERVING PRINCIPAL

AIRLINE	FRANCE	GERMANY	U.S.S.R.	CHINA
ATLAS AIR	X	X	X	..
GLOBAL AIR	X	X	..	X
PANOWAY AIR	..	..	..	..
WORLDWIDE AIR	X	X	X	X
ZENITH AIR	..	..	..	X

TRAFFIC CENTERS IN THE WORLD

JAPAN	HAWAII	BRAZIL	MEXICO	CANADA	ENGLAND
..	..	X	..	..	..
X	X	..	..	X	X
..	X	X	X	X	..
X	X	..	X	X	X
X	X	..	X	X	..

LESSON 205

CLINIC

GOAL
- To build competency on selected keyboard reaches.

FORMAT
- Single spacing   60-space line   3 tabs, each 15 spaces apart

KEYBOARDING SKILLS

Type lines 1–4 once. Then practice using your tab key by typing line 5 twice. Repeat lines 1–4, or take a series of 1-minute timings.

Speed	1	The profit she got for the corn and hay may make them rich. 12
Accuracy	2	Jack quietly moved up front and seized the big ball of wax. 12
Numbers	3	By May 10, ship 29 seats, 38 stoves, 47 tents, and 56 cots. 12
Symbols	4	Visitors may park in locations #10, #29, #38, #47, and #56. 12
Technique	5	Abcdefg Hijklmn Opqrstu Vwxyz

| 1 | 2 | 3 | 4 | 5 | 6 | 7 | 8 | 9 | 10 | 11 | 12

GOALS
- To use commas correctly to separate adjectives while typing sentences.
- To improve accuracy on 30-second timings.
- To format minutes of a meeting.

FORMAT
- Single spacing   60-space line   5-space tab

LAB 8

COMMAS BETWEEN ADJECTIVES

Workbook 145–146.

Type lines 1–4 once, providing the missing commas. Edit your copy as your teacher reads the answers. Then retype lines 1–4 from your edited copy.

1 They will have to clean that dusty neglected cellar today.
2 Cool cloudy mornings often turn into beautiful afternoons.
3 That massive well-crafted desk weighs at least 500 pounds.
4 All students are released early on cold windy winter days.

30-SECOND TIMINGS

Take two 30-second timings on lines 5–7, or type each line twice.

5 Six jumbo elephants quickly moved the wagon from the blaze.   12
6 Jack found the gravel camp six below zero quite a few days.   24
7 Jo saw six big packs of cards and seized them very quickly.   36

1-AND 5-MINUTE TIMINGS

Take two 1-minute timings on each paragraph. Then take one 5-minute timing on the entire selection. Use single spacing for the 1-minute timings and double spacing for the 5-minute timing.

1'

8 We have heard in recent years that our nation needs to conserve its   15
9 energy. This is going to be quite a task, and all of us must contribute   29
10 in whatever ways possible to this task.   37

11 For energy conservation to work, please realize we are requiring   14
12 sacrifices. We may not be able to keep our homes as warm in the   27
13 winters or as cool in the summers as we have done.   37

14 Putting better insulation in our houses will also help in the   13
15 conservation program. By doing so, we let less heat escape through   27
16 the walls and ceilings. Yes, this will help a lot.   37

17 To help save energy, we should also turn off all those extra lights   15
18 in our homes while the rooms are not occupied. Over a period of   27
19 months, this effort will conserve a lot of fuel.   37

20 We might also save energy by car pooling when going to work. By   14
21 pooling, we will use only a fourth as much gas if just four of us ride   28
22 together in the morning to our various jobs.   37

| 1 | 2 | 3 | 4 | 5 | 6 | 7 | 8 | 9 | 10 | 11 | 12 | 13 | 14   SI 1.37

LESSON 204

GOALS
- To form plurals of nouns correctly while typing sentences.
- To format and type a two-page ruled table.

FORMAT
- Single spacing   60-space line   Tabs as needed

LAB 25

PLURALS

Type lines 1–4 once, making plurals of the underscored words. Edit your copy as your teacher reads the answers. Then retype lines 1–4 from your edited copy.

1 The <u>employee</u> moved the <u>desk</u>, <u>typewriter</u>, and huge <u>box</u>.

2 Jo took the <u>mix</u> from the <u>bag</u> located near the <u>terminal</u>.

3 The <u>charge</u> listed on the <u>invoice</u> cannot be quoted to him.

4 The <u>bus</u> left the depot at noon, followed by Zelda's <u>van</u> .

"OK" TIMINGS

Type as many 30-second "OK" (errorless) timings as possible out of three attempts on lines 5–7. Then repeat the effort on lines 8–10.

5 We acquire jerky habits from having typed exercises lazily.   12
6 Jumping quickly from the taxi, Hazel brushed a woven chair.   24
7 Max worked quietly, alphabetizing the census of vital jobs.   36

8 Why did Professor Block give you a quiz on the major texts?   12
9 Seizing the wax buffers, Jensen quickly removed a big spot.   24
10 The jewelers quickly made up five boxes in the right sizes.   36

| 1 | 2 | 3 | 4 | 5 | 6 | 7 | 8 | 9 | 10 | 11 | 12

FORMATTING TWO-PAGE TABLES

A table too wide to fit on one page must be split as follows:

1. Type half on one page and half on a second page; then tape both pages together. Carefully position the table so that the two halves will line up.
2. Type ruled lines as close to the center edges of the paper as possible.
3. Use no more than 2 spaces to separate words in the title.
4. Split the table and title as close to the middle as possible, but make the break between columns.

To format the left-hand page:

1. Backspace half the title from the right edge of the paper.
2. Backspace the key line from the right edge of the paper; set the margin and tab stops.
3. Type rules from the left margin to the right edge of the paper.

To format the right-hand page:

1. Begin the title as close to the left edge as possible. Make sure at least 1 space (no more than 2 spaces)

separates it from the end of the title on the left-hand page.

2. Reset the tab stops and the left margin.
3. Type rules from the left edge of the paper to the end of the table.
4. Begin the first column entry as close to the left edge as possible.

Left-hand page   Right-hand page

FORMATTING MINUTES OF A MEETING

Minutes of a meeting are usually saved in a three-ring binder. To format minutes:

1. Set margins for a bound report (60P/70E, shifted 3 spaces to the right).
2. Use a top margin of 6 blank lines.
3. Type the title on line 7 of page 1. Type page numbers on line 7 of additional pages.
4. Single-space.
5. Type side headings in all-capital letters. Double-space before and after side headings.
6. Begin closing lines at the center, a double space below the text. Leave 3 blank lines for the signature.

JOB 88-1. MINUTES OF A MEETING

Standard format. 5-space and center tabs.

New Products Committee

MINUTES OF THE MARCH MEETING

[Today's date]

ATTENDANCE

The March meeting of the New Products committee was held in the Board-room of Sutton Publishing Company. Ms. Mae Lopez, Marketing Director, presided at the meeting. The following were present at the meeting. *stet*

Mr. Frank Swan
Mr. Wayne Hall
Ms. Donna Schultz
Ms. Cathy Cooper
Dr. A. R. Bloome
Mrs. Anne Krouse
Mr. E. G. Moore
Ms. Jan Bennett
Mr. Paul E. Scott
Ms. Mae Lopez

arrange alphabetically in two columns

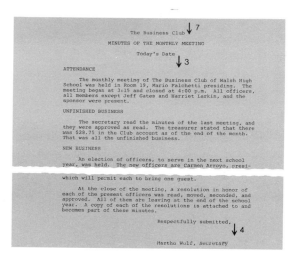

UNFINISHED BUSINESS

The secretary read the minutes of the February meeting, and they were approved as read.

Ms. Moore reported on the progress of the new text on auto repair. Contracts for the text were drawn up and sent to the authors on March 1. First drafts of the text material are to be completed one year from the date of the contract.

New Business

Ms. Schultz suggested that the information processing texts be revised one year earlier than planned because of the rapid changes that have taken place in this area in the past 2 years. A committee was formed to study these changes and to come up with a recommendation at next month's meeting. Ms. Schultz will chair this committee.

Respectfully submitted,

Claire T. Stark, Secretary

LESSON 203

GOALS
- To identify the plural forms of nouns while typing sentences.
- To type 12 file cards and 1 boxed table from incomplete copy.

FORMAT
- Single spacing   60-space line   Tabs as needed

LAB 25

PLURALS

Type lines 1–4 once. Then repeat lines 1–4 or take a series of 1-minute timings.

```
1  Several businesses stay open late; thus Janice may be late.  12
2  Seventy typists and programmers attend college every night.  12
3  The dentist checked the teeth of ten children in West Farm.  12
4  Alice heard the buzzes of the saws and quickly rushed home.  12
   |  1  |  2  |  3  |  4  |  5  |  6  |  7  |  8  |  9  |  10  |  11  |  12
```

5-MINUTE TIMING

Take a 5-minute timing on lines 7–26 on page 322.

JOB 203-1. FILE CARDS

Format a 5 by 3 index card for each foreign embassy listed below. Type the address first, as shown at the right. Workbook 433, 435, 437.

```
4
 → 1732 Massachusetts Avenue, N.W.  ↓2

      Chile
```

Austria—2343 Massachusetts Ave. N.W.
Canada—1746 Massachusetts Ave. N.W.
Chile—1732 Massachusetts Ave. N.W.
Greece—2221 Massachusetts Ave. N.W.
India—2107 Massachusetts Ave. N.W.
Ireland—2234 Massachusetts Ave. N.W.
Japan—2520 Massachusetts Ave. N.W.
Korea—2370 Massachusetts Ave. N.W.
Pakistan—2315 Massachusetts Ave. N.W.
Tunisia—2408 Massachusetts Ave. N.W.
Venezuela—2445 Massachusetts Ave. N.W.
Zambia—2419 Massachusetts Ave. N.W.

JOB 203-2. BOXED TABLE WITH BRACED HEADINGS

Arrange the cards in two piles: place even numbers in one pile and odd numbers in the second pile. Arrange each pile numerically from lowest to highest. Using the cards as your source document, format a four-column boxed table with braced headings on a half sheet of paper. The braced headings should be *Even-Numbered Addresses* and *Odd-Numbered Addresses*. Column headings are *Country* in columns 1 and 3, and *Address* in columns 2 and 4. Title: SELECTED FOREIGN EMBASSIES, WASHINGTON, D.C. Subtitle: 1732–2520 Massachusetts Avenue, N.W.

LESSON 89

GOAL
- To format magazine articles.

FORMAT
- Single spacing   60-space line   5-space and center tabs

KEYBOARDING SKILLS

Type lines 1–5 once. In line 5, use your tabulator key to advance from one word to the next through the entire line. Repeat lines 1–4, or take a series of 1-minute timings.

Speed   1 They both wish to visit Japan and Turkey if they go by air. 12
Accuracy   2 Zachery joked about a group of wax squid from the carnival. 12
Numbers   3 In Chapter 10, we saw that 47 times 56 was less than 2,938. 12
Symbols   4 Please order 480# of #5 grade @ $17.69 before September 23. 12
Technique   5 by   do   go   hi   ha   ho   ma   me   no   pa   so   to
               | 1 | 2 | 3 | 4 | 5 | 6 | 7 | 8 | 9 | 10 | 11 | 12

FORMATTING MAGAZINE ARTICLES
Workbook 147–148.

To format an article you wish to submit to a magazine for publication:

1. Use double spacing and standard 8½- by 11-inch (or metric A4) paper.

2. Use the top margins used in other reports—begin the title on line 13; begin page numbers (beginning with page 2) on line 7.

3. Under the by-line, indicate the line length used and number of lines in the article. (You will have to insert the number of lines after you have finished typing the article.)

4. Use a line length equal to the average line in the magazine (type 10 lines and average them); do not exceed that line by more than 2 spaces.

5. Follow the magazine's display style for headings and spacing.

6. Bottom margins should contain from 6 to 9 blank lines.

7. Except for page 1, type the writer's name before the page number, separating the two items with a diagonal—For example: Perez / 5

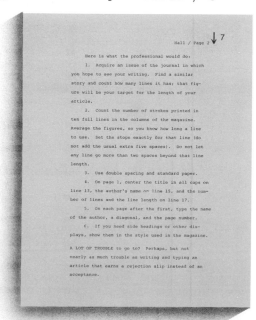

JOB 202-1. RULED TABLE
Standard format with leaders. Half sheet of paper. 10 spaces between columns.

Contico Corporation

Foreign Investment	Market Value
Australia	9,255,190
Belgium	3,425,293
France	13,261,141
Hong Kong	5,383,260
Japan	65,891,889
Netherlands	4,248,516
Spain	3,238,357
Switzerland	11,130,281

Please add:
United Kingdom
30,486,355

JOB 202-2. INCOME STATEMENT SUMMARY
Standard format. Full sheet of paper. 70-space line.

HONG KONG IMPORTERS, LTD.

Income Statement Summary (Worksheet)
For the Month/Quarter Ended March 31, 19--

SALE OF GOODS $17,250.71

DEDUCT COST OF GOODS SOLD

    Goods in shop March 1, 19-- $4,231.18

    Goods purchased during Month 2,507.00

    Total Available goods for sale $6,738.18

    Goods in Shop March 31, 19--   2,476.18

        Cost of Goods sold 4,262.00

GROSS PROFIT ON GOODS SOLD .... $ 5,988.71

DEDUCT EXPENSES
    Employee wages $1,400.00
    Rent of Shop Space 350.00
    Heating, Electricity, Phone 272.88
    Maintenance and Cleaning 98.17
        Total expenses 2,121.05

NET INCOME FOR MONTH OF March 19-- $ 3,867.66

JOB 89-1. MAGAZINE ARTICLE
Standard format.

CREATURES FROM "DOWN UNDER"   16

By Sharon T. Cole   29

(*lines of spaces*)

The most curious creature that   38
lives on the other side of our globe is   46
none other than the kangaroo. Kanga-   53
roos are well known for their sturdy,   61
powerful hind legs and for their se-   68
cluded pouches in which they carry   75
their young. This report will reveal   83
some of the important facts about this   91
"rabbit-like" mammal.   95

PHYSICAL CHARACTERISTICS   102

Kangaroos have either gray or red   110
fur, stand close to 7 feet (2 meters)   117
tall when full grown, and weigh close   125
to 200 pounds (40 kilograms). They   132
travel by jumping on their powerful   139
hind legs, sometimes leaping at the   147
rate of nearly 30 miles (48 kilometers)   155
per hour for short distances. *Their tails*   163
act as levers when they are running   170
at a fast pace and as stools on which   178
they may rest when they are stand-   185
ing still.   187

FAMILY LIFE   192

The male kangaroo accepts no re-   199
sponsibility for the newborn kangaroo.   207
It is the mother's responsibility to   214
feed and shelter the baby. The kanga-   222
roo's family life appears to be rather   230
casual, and there are seldom any long-   237
term commitments to any one group.   245
Kangaroos live 7 years, with a few of   252
them surviving until they are 20 years   260
old. *The greatest enemy of the kangaroo*   268
is drought, but some of the species are   276
killed by hunters and wild dogs.   283

CLOSING REMARKS   288

Kangaroos live both in tropical   296
forests and on the plains. They have   303
very sharp teeth that enable them to   311
eat the grasses much closer to the   318
ground than most other mammals can eat.   326
For this reason, they are a nuisance   333
to stock raisers because they eat the   341
grass that is needed for the raising of   349
livestock such as sheep and cattle.   356

JOB 89-2. MINUTES OF A MEETING
Standard format. 5-space and center tabs.

Staff Retreat Committee   14
MINUTES OF THE MARCH MEETING   32
[*Today's Date*]   45

ATTENDANCE   49

The March meeting of the Staff Retreat   58
Committee was held in the office of Mr. Doyle,   68
who presided at the meeting. The session   76
began at three o'clock and adjourned at five.   85
All members were present except Jean Crews   94
and John Mott.   97

UNFINISHED BUSINESS   103

The secretary read the minutes of the De-   112
cember meeting, and they were approved as   121
read.   122

Ms. Sanchez reported on the staff retreat   132
held last March at Clear Lake. Then it was   140
suggested that we return to Clear Lake for   149
next year's meeting.   153

NEW BUSINESS   158

Mr. Doyle then suggested a need for a theme   168
for this year's staff retreat meeting to be held   178
in June. A committee was organized to study   187
this problem and come up with a suitable   195
theme by next month's meeting. Ruth White   203
will chair this committee.   209

Respectfully submitted,   215

James Moore, Secretary   222

JOB 200/1-5. BOXED TABLE WITH BRACED HEADING
Standard format. Retype Job 200/1-4 on a full sheet of paper turned lengthwise;
use double spacing.

LESSON 202

GOALS
- To recognize plural forms of nouns while typing sentences.
- To type a ruled table and an income statement summary
from a rough draft.

FORMAT
- Single spacing   60-space line   Tabs as needed

LAB 25

Type lines 1–4 once. Then repeat lines 1–4 or take a series of 1-minute timings.
As you type each line, note the noun plurals.

PLURALS

1 The businesses and churches in our town are assisting Jack. 12
2 Thursday the new bands will perform in two quaint villages. 12
3 The boys and girls of the community like puzzles and flags. 12
4 For many years our taxes have been increased by our county. 12
| 1 | 2 | 3 | 4 | 5 | 6 | 7 | 8 | 9 | 10 | 11 | 12

Plurals are regularly formed by adding *s* to the singular form.

    bank, banks   worker, workers   typist, typists   dish, dishes   jazz, jazzes

However, when the singular ends in *s, x, ch, sh,* or *z,* the plural is formed by
adding *es* to the singular.

    business, businesses   tax, taxes   inch, inches

The plurals of some nouns are formed in irregular ways.

    woman, women   child, children   tooth, teeth

**12-SECOND
TIMINGS**

Type each line four times, or take four 12-second timings on each line. For each
timing, type with no error.

5 When did he go to the city and pay them for the world maps? 12
6 They may make a big profit if they work with the field men. 12
7 The man is to go to town and then make six benches for her. 12
25   30   35   40   45   50   55   60

**30-SECOND
TIMINGS**

Take two 30-second timings on lines 8–10, or type the paragraph twice.

8 The actual art of raising and producing foods is one of the 12
9 most significant jobs in the world. If we have no food, we 24
10 would have no use for the many other things we enjoy today. 36
| 1 | 2 | 3 | 4 | 5 | 6 | 7 | 8 | 9 | 10 | 11 | 12

LESSON 90

GOALS
- To recognize when commas are used after introductory words and phrases while typing sentences.
- To format resolutions.

FORMAT
- Single spacing   60-space line   Tabs: 5, 10, center

LAB 9

Type lines 1–4 once. Then repeat lines 1–4, or take a series of 1-minute timings.

COMMAS AFTER INTRODUCTORY WORDS AND PHRASES

1 In case of fire, quickly close the door and leave the room. 12
2 In the meantime, I will wait to hear from you on this plan. 12
3 First, read all the materials you can find on this subject. 12
4 During Zeb's absence, you must attend six meetings for him. 12

| 1 | 2 | 3 | 4 | 5 | 6 | 7 | 8 | 9 | 10 | 11 | 12

Place a comma after introductory words and phrases such as *first, in my opinion, for example,* and so on.

Yes, she decided to cancel her order. (Word.)
Waiting for the next flight, Fred reviewed his speech. (Phrase.)
In answer to the many requests, we prepared a brochure. (Phrase.)

PRETEST

Take a 5-minute Pretest on lines 5–20. Then circle and count your errors. Use the chart on page 153 to determine which lines to type for practice.

5 The skill of proofreading is one of the most critical, 12
6 yet one of the most ignored, skills a person can have. All 24
7 of us have chances to write a few letters. In addition, we 36
8 sometimes must prepare term papers and do projects for some 48
9 classes. If we find that we must write or type a paper, we 60
10 have to be able to find and correct every one of our errors 72
11 if our work is to create the impact we want. 81
12 We must all try quite hard to improve our proofreading 93
13 skill. Before taking a page out of the typewriter, we must 105
14 proofread it. After a page has been typed, we must read it 117
15 word by word, phrase by phrase, and line by line. Then, we 129
16 look closely for spelling, capitalization, or typographical 141
17 errors. Next, the page has to be read sentence by sentence 153
18 in order to find punctuation and grammar mistakes. Lastly, 165
19 a page is read paragraph by paragraph to be sure all errors 177
20 have been erased completely and retyped. 185

| 1 | 2 | 3 | 4 | 5 | 6 | 7 | 8 | 9 | 10 | 11 | 12   SI 1.36

JOB 200/1-3. BOXED TABLE
Standard format. Full sheet of paper.

Large Passenger Liners*

Name of Ship	Flag	Maximum Number of Passengers
Queen Elizabeth 2	British	1,815
Canberra	British	1,800
Oriana	British	1,800
Oceanic	Panamanian	1,034
Festivale	Panamanian	1,400
Rotterdam	Dutch	1,050
Italia	Panamanian	2,258
Britanis	Greek	1,600
Eugenia	Italian	1,637

*Arranged according to the size of the ship.

JOB 200/1-4. BOXED TABLE WITH BRACED HEADING
Standard format. Full sheet of paper.

Dollar signs are not repeated in a column; percent signs are repeated if the word percent is not used in the title or column heading.

International Oil
Current Recommendations

Company	Net Earnings Per Share			Percent Yield
	Last Year	This Year	Next Year*	
Axion Corp.	$4.13	$4.50	$5.25	0.3
Global Corp.	2.25	2.85	3.15	2.7
Motoron Corp.	2.37	3.61	4.20	2.5
Royal Petroleum	9.38	11.07	12.12	1.4
Sestor, Inc.	3.37	3.65	4.05	1.8
Textrono, Inc.	6.15	6.70	7.20	2.6
United Int'l	2.37	3.28	4.10	0.6

*Anticipated

PRACTICE

In the chart below, find the number of errors you made on the Pretest on page 152. Then type each of the designated drill lines four times.

Pretest errors	0–1	2–3	4–5	6+
Drill lines	24–28	23–27	22–26	21–25

Accuracy

21 some term every skills improve addition paragraph proofread
22 yet must ignored sentence spelling sometimes capitalization
23 have write paper errors chances retyped grammar punctuation
24 the most prepare projects mistakes completely typographical

Speed

25 classes closely person skills every able find want work all
26 lastly, correct create papers after hard page been word has
27 improve letters impact errors quite line look next read and
28 closely erased lastly phrase before find sure have been our

POSTTEST

Repeat the Pretest on page 152 to see how much your skill has improved.

FORMATTING RESOLUTIONS

A resolution is a formal statement of opinion or fact presented to an organized group. Study the illustration and follow these steps when formatting a resolution:

1. Use a 50-space line and double spacing on a full sheet of paper.
2. Spread-center the title *RESOLUTION* on line 13.
3. Indent each paragraph 10 spaces, and type the first word in each paragraph in all-capital letters.
4. Center the recipient's name a triple space under the resolution.

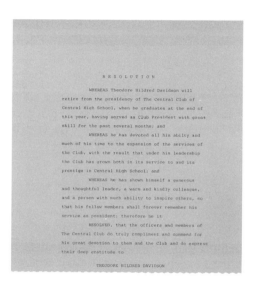

JOB 90-1. RESOLUTION
Standard format. Plain paper.

```
              R E S O L U T I O N                              12

         WHEREAS Philip Andrew Johnson will retire from the presi- 26
dency of The Students' Club of Maple High School, when he graduates 40
at the end of this year, having served as President with great    52
skill for the past nine months; and                               60
         WHEREAS he has devoted all of his abilities and much of  72
his time to the expansion of the services of the Club, with the re- 86
sult that under his leadership the Club has grown both in its ser- 99
vice to and its prestige in Maple High School; therefore be it   112
         RESOLVED, that the officers and members of The Students' 124
Club do commend him for his great devotion to them and do express 137
their deep gratitude to                                          142
                        ↓3
         PHILIP ANDREW JOHNSON                                   159
```

JOB 200/1-1. BOXED TABLE WITH FOOTNOTE

Standard format (see page 292). Full sheet of paper. 8 spaces between columns.

MOST POPULOUS CITIES

City	Population (Estimated)	Year*
Shanghai	10,000,000	1976
Tokyo	8,656,520	1975
Mexico City	8,591,750	1975
Cairo	8,500,000	1975
Moscow	8,011,000	1979
Peking	7,570,000	1970
Seoul	7,500,000	1977

*More recent figures are not available.

FORMATTING TABLES WITH BRACED HEADINGS

A "braced" heading is one that centers over (or *embraces*) two or more columns, such as the heading *Passengers (000)* in Job 200/1-2 below. To format braced headings:

1. Begin by typing the column headings below the braced heading. Leave room for the braced heading.

2. Count the number of spaces in the braced heading. In Job 200/1-2, the heading is 16 spaces.

3. Count the number of spaces in the longest items in the columns to be braced—remember to include the spaces between columns. In Job 200/1-2, the number of spaces is 20 (*20,568* + 6 spaces + *Domestic*).

4. Subtract the number of spaces determined in Step 2 from those in Step 3; divide the difference by 2; drop any fraction. (20 − 16 = 4 ÷ 2 = 2).

5. Roll the paper back and indent the braced heading the number of spaces you determined in Step 4.

6. Begin the underscore a double space below the braced heading, 3 spaces to the left of the beginning of the left column.

Note: Column headings align at the bottom.

JOB 200/1-2. BOXED TABLE WITH BRACED HEADING

Standard format. Full sheet of paper.

In tables, long words may be contracted: Int'l for International, for example. Because all the figures for passengers are in the millions (for example, London 20,568,000), the final three digits are shown in the heading to save column space.

ESTIMATED PASSENGER TRAFFIC AT WORLD AIRPORTS

Airport	City	Passengers (000)	
		Int'l	Domestic
Heathrow	London	20,568	2,822
J. F. Kennedy	New York	11,490	11,056
Frankfurt-Main	Frankfurt	9,634	4,329
Schiphol	Amsterdam	8,444	147
DeGaulle	Paris	7,550	853
Orly	Paris	7,543	5,017
Kastrup	Copenhagen	6,795	1,680

JOB 90-2. RESOLUTION

Standard format. Plain paper.

R E S O L U T I O N   WHEREAS Joyce 12
Renee Boynton is retiring from her position as 21
Chairperson of this board, having served it 30
and her associates for more than ten years; 39
and 40

WHEREAS she has devoted all of her skill 49
to the development of this board and the 57
growth of this firm, its products, and its staff, 67

to the end that today this firm is the most 76
successful in its field; and 82

WHEREAS she has given encouragement 90
to all those who worked with her during her 99
tenure on this board; therefore be it 106

RESOLVED, that the officers and mem- 114
bers of this board do, for her devotion to them 124
and for her loyalty, commend 130

JOYCE RENEE BOYNTON 145

LESSON 91

GOALS
- To identify when commas are used after introductory words and phrases while typing sentences.
- To format tables in reports.

FORMAT
- Single spacing 60-space line 10-space and center tabs

LAB 9

COMMAS AFTER INTRODUCTORY WORDS AND PHRASES

Type lines 1–4 once. Then repeat lines 1–4 or take a series of 1-minute timings.

1 On Friday evening, Joan Kim will go to the Noxzema Company. 12
2 During the spring, Veronica Buckley plans to visit Denmark. 12
3 No, Harris Quentin will not attend next Thursday's seminar. 12
4 At our next committee meeting, Ms. Rudi will discuss taxes. 12
   | 1 | 2 | 3 | 4 | 5 | 6 | 7 | 8 | 9 | 10 | 11 | 12

"OK" TIMINGS

Type as many 30-second "OK" (errorless) timings as possible out of three attempts on lines 5–7. Then repeat the attempt on lines 8–10.

5 Holly acquired a prize for jumping over five feet backward. 12
6 Judy gave a quick jump as the zebra and lynx wildly fought. 24
7 Jacqueline was glad her family took five or six big prizes. 36

8 Max had a zest for quiet living and placed work before joy. 12
9 Zeke quietly placed five new jumping beans in the gray box. 24
10 Ken promptly requested five dozen jugs of wax for the club. 36
   | 1 | 2 | 3 | 4 | 5 | 6 | 7 | 8 | 9 | 10 | 11 | 12

FORMATTING TABLES IN REPORTS

Workbook 149–150.

When a report contains a great deal of statistical information, it is often easier to understand the information if it is arranged as a table. To format tables in reports:

1. Triple-space before and after the table.
2. Center a table number (if used) a double space above the table title.
3. a. Indent the table at least 5 spaces from either margin if possible.
   b. Do not extend the table beyond the line length in the report.
   c. Select intercolumnar spaces that will limit the table width.
4. Single-space the body of the table.

PRACTICE Type lines 20–24 five times.

```
20  ion nation motion station portion rations position donation
21  oin points joints coining appoint joining pointing adjoined
22  min mining minute minting minimum mineral trimming minerals
23  imp import impose imposes imports impress imposing imported
24  ill chills drills fulfill willing billing goodwill waybills
```

POSTTEST Repeat the Pretest on page 324 to see how much your skill has improved.

LESSONS 200/201

UNIT 33 FORMATTING SPECIAL TABLES

UNIT GOAL
44/5'/4e

GOALS
- To use all-capital abbreviations correctly while typing sentences.
- To type 44/3'/3e.
- To type two boxed tables; to format and type three boxed tables with braced headings.

FORMAT
- Single spacing   60-space line   Tabs as needed

LAB 24

ALL-CAPITAL ABBREVIATIONS

Workbook 431–432.

Type lines 1–4 once, providing the standard abbreviations for the underscored words. Edit your copy as your teacher reads the answers. Then retype lines 1–4 from your edited copy.

1 <u>Texas National Airlines</u> flies into <u>John F. Kennedy</u> Airport at
    12:30 p.m. on Thursdays only.
2 After her visit to the <u>Union of Soviet Socialist Republics</u>, Jan
    will get to the <u>United States of America</u>.
3 Bredel sponsors a quiz program on the <u>American Broadcasting
    Company</u> network each day.
4 Zora will earn her <u>master of arts</u> degree in English this fall,
    right?

3-MINUTE TIMINGS

Take two 3-minute timings. Circle your errors.

```
              1              2              3              4
5       For students who can speak a foreign language, there's    12
            5              6              7              8
6   an amazing job market today.  Numbers of major companies in   24
            9              10             11             12
7   other countries have been buying control of or investing in   36
            13             14             15             16
8   American businesses.  Their demand for workers with foreign   48
            17             18             19             20
9   language skills can already be seen in the increased number   60
            21             22             23
10  of want ads for experts with language skills.                 69
            24             25             26             27
11      The fact that so many Americans cannot speak, read, or    81
            28             29             30             31
12  write another language is very tragic because the countries   93
            32             33             34             35
13  of the world today are closely linked.  International trade   105
            36             37             38             39
14  is vital to business and government, and young people can't   117
            40             41             42             43
15  afford to be unequipped to meet the challenge of the future   129
            44
16  that is theirs.                                               132
    |  1  |  2  |  3  |  4  |  5  |  6  |  7  |  8  |  9  |  10 |  11 |  12    SI 1.57
```

JOB 91-1. TWO-PAGE REPORT WITH A TABLE

Double spacing. 5-space tab.

Dodge Skating Rink

By Chris Lee

The young people of Dodge have to drive to other towns for something to do. It is quite evident that the town needs to do something to attract people, rather than drive them away.

THE PROBLEM

The problem is to find out if the people of Dodge would support a skating rink. Four typing students were among the thirty students at Central High School who were asked to take part in a study to find out if a skating rink could survive as a major entertainment center for the people of Dodge. The four typing students typed the study that consisted of responses from 100 people chosen at random.

FINDINGS

The average age of those questioned was 18. Of those who took part in the study, 57 were female and 43 were male. Ninety percent felt Dodge entertainment could be better.

When asked if they knew how to skate, 79 knew how, and only 21 did not know how. Of those who did not know how to skate, 16 expressed an interest in learning how to skate.

Ninety percent believed that the rink should have game machines and pool tables. Another finding was that 89 percent believed there should be specific times for certain age groups to skate. Finally, the study revealed that most people wanted a variety of music played while they skated. Table 1, below, shows that 50 percent of the people wanted a variety of music played. The next most popular type of music was disco, with 22 percent preferring this type. The remaining 28 percent was divided among country and western, rock, and punk.

Table 1
Music Preferences

Type of Music	Percent
Variety	50
Disco	22
Country and western	12
Rock	10
Punk	6

RECOMMENDATIONS

Based upon the findings of this study, the city of Dodge should consider the construction of a skating rink for its residents.

LESSON 92

GOALS
- To use commas after introductory words and phrases while typing sentences.
- To type at least 37/5'/5e.
- To format an itinerary.

FORMAT
- Single spacing   60-space line   5-space tab

LAB 9

COMMAS AFTER INTRODUCTORY WORDS AND PHRASES

Type lines 1–4 once, providing the missing commas. Edit your copy as your teacher reads the answers. Then retype lines 1–4 from your edited copy.

1 In order to get there quickly Joan must leave immediately.
2 On the first day of each month call Ezra for my inventory.
3 Eventually computers will probably take over the business.
4 Actually David will not be able to fix these until Friday.

JOB 197/8-4. LETTER WITH ATTENTION LINE AND POSTSCRIPT

Retype Job 197/8-3. Standard format with indented paragraphs. Add the postscript shown in the next column as the last item in the letter. Workbook 429–430.

PS: I am nominating Fire Fighter Cunningham for our community's Outstanding Citizen Award.

LESSON 199

CLINIC

GOALS
- To build competency on selected keyboard reaches.
- To type 43/2'/2e.

FORMAT
- Single spacing   60-space line   5-space tab

KEYBOARDING SKILLS

Type lines 1–4 once. Then practice using your shift key by typing line 5 twice. Repeat lines 1–4, or take a series of 1-minute timings.

Speed	1	When did he go to the city and pay them for the world maps?	12
Accuracy	2	The wizard's dogs quickly jumped over one pyramid of boxes.	12
Numbers	3	I checked lockers 10, 29, 38, 47, and 56, but not 65 or 74.	12
Symbols	4	Look! What a fantastic sight! The fireworks are terrific!	12
Technique	5	Ruth Mary Zora Paul Rick Kate Dora Jean M.D. B.C. N.Y. N.J.	

| 1 | 2 | 3 | 4 | 5 | 6 | 7 | 8 | 9 | 10 | 11 | 12

PRETEST

Take two 2-minute timings on lines 6–9. Circle your errors.

```
6  I was confident that all packages were delivered with care.  12
7  Eleven local farmers departed during the first of the week.  24
8  The judge gave us the rules to use for the sporting events.  36
9  The guide lowered the ropes to those standing on the ledge.  48
   |  1  |  2  |  3  |  4  |  5  |  6  |  7  |  8  |  9  |  10  |  11  |  12
```

PRACTICE

Type lines 10–15 five times.

```
10  president confident packages handled license grade deck who
11  departure operators surgical secured quarter spray farm how
12  early farms cloth lower guide fixed parts moved seals typed

13  sense rules plant ready means grass judge legal local extra
14  show past lost ours send sole does gets idea lift hose feed
15  bed eat get kit par tag use hot way fat lie red sea dry are
```

POSTTEST

Repeat the Pretest to see how your skill has improved.

PRETEST

Take two 2-minute timings on lines 16–19. Circle your errors.

```
16      Did you ever think of the phenomenon that normally the  12
17  fish is a truly active animal?  Some fish do the minimum of  24
18  swimming, but the group is small; the busy fish abides in a  36
19  bowl, and the hungry fish that slows down is soon devoured.  48
    |  1  |  2  |  3  |  4  |  5  |  6  |  7  |  8  |  9  |  10  |  11  |  12
```

FORMATTING AN ITINERARY

An itinerary is an outline of the details of a planned trip. It includes departure and arrival times, meeting times, flight plans, and other essential information. To format an itinerary on plain paper:

1. Set your margins for a 60P/70E line.
2. Set 5-space and 30-space tabs.
3. Type the itinerary heading as follows:
   a. Type *ITINERARY* centered on line 13.
   b. Double-space, and then type the name of the person for whom the itinerary is prepared at the left margin.
   c. On the same line as the person's name, type the date on which the trip will begin. Backspace this date from the right margin.
   d. Double-space, and then center the names of the city(ies) to be visited; begin with the departure city. Use a dash (two hyphens) to separate the city names.
4. Double-space after the heading information, and begin typing the day-to-day schedule. Beginning at the left margin, type the day, month, and date of departure.
5. Double-space. Indent all time and reminder notes 5 spaces from the left margin. Whenever time zones are changed, specify the time zone after each time.
6. Indent 30 spaces to type the description information for each notation in the left column. Indent any turnover lines 2 spaces from the 30-space tab.
7. Underscore departure and arrival cities and the word *Accommodations*.
8. For itineraries longer than 1 page, leave a bottom margin of 6 to 9 lines. Type page numbers on all pages except the first, beginning on line 7 at the right margin.

JOB 92-1. ITINERARY
Standard format.

<pre>
                          ITINERARY

   M. J. Donaldson   December 10, 19--
                                       c
                    (Memphis--San Francisₒ)

   Sunday, December 10
         9:35 a.m., CST   Depart Memphis, Memphis Municipal Airport,
                                     United Air Lines Coach (Y) one stop
                                     Flight 433, Boeing 727, lunch served.

         1:02 p.m., PST   Arrive San Francisco, San Francisco
                                     International Airport.

                                  Accommodations: Mark Hopkins hotel,
                                    ①Nob Hill.
         5:30 p.m., PST   Depart hotel for Chinatown visit.
   Monday, December 11
         all day
         Reminder   Convention at Mark Hopkins Hotel.

                                  Call Pat Wolton to confirm dinner arrange-
                                    ments for tomorrow.
                                           Mark
   Tuesday, December 12
         9 a.m.-5 p.m.   Convention at Hopkins Hotel.
         7 p.m.   Dinner with Pat Wolton.
   Wednesday, December 13
         10:30 a.m., PST   Depart hotel for airport. San Francisco
                 noon
         12 p.m., PST   Depart San Francisco International Airport,
                                     United Air Lines Coach (Y) two stops
                                     Flight 700, Boeing 727, lunch served.

         7:15 p.m., CST   Arrive Memphis, Memphis Municipal Airport.
</pre>

FORMATTING COVER LETTERS

When a long document, report, or résumé has been prepared for submission to others, a cover letter is attached to explain the purpose of the document. Any letter style may be used.

JOB 197/8-1. COVER LETTER WITH SUBJECT LINE

Block format. Insert the years where instructed to do so. Workbook 423–424. Body 82 words (plus 20 words for subject line).

[To] The Honorable John Boyle Haseleu, Govenor of Ohio, Columbus, OH 43216, Dear Governor Haseleu: Subject: Annual Report—State Human Services Council

As head of the State Human Services Council, I am happy to submit to you our annual report, as required by law under section 3 of the Comprehensive Employment and training Act. This report covers the period from July 1 (last year's date), to June 20, (this year's date). It contains a state wide review of the success of the HHS pro gram and an appendix which gives a summary of expendtures, training, word assignments, and enrollees characteristics for each of the 28 prime sponsors in the state. Sincerely, Shirley Rush, Chairperson

JOB 197/8-2. COVER LETTER WITH SUBJECT LINE

Standard format. Insert the year where instructed to do so. Workbook 425–426. Body 95 words (plus 20 words for subject line).

The Honorable Thomas S. Farro, Governor of Michigan, Lansing, MI 48924, Dear Governor Farro: Subject: Annual Report—Commission on the Status of Women

The Commission on the Status of Women is pleased to sub mit its Annual report for the year (current year). The commission carried out it's charge to be a strong vote for the rights of woman in the state" though the program designed to correct in equities and to provide women with in formation to assist them in attaining equal right and equal opportunity. We are proud of the work that has has been accomplished this year in the fields of credit, education, employment, criminal justice, and legislation. We look forward to further progress and accomplishment in the year a head. Sincerely yours, Alda S. Wexler, Executive Director

JOB 197/8-3. LETTER WITH ATTENTION LINE

Standard format. Workbook 427–428. Body 135 words (plus 20 words for attention line).

Volunteer Fire Fighters of Summittville, P.O. Box 10, Summittville, PA 16238, Attention: Fire Chief Rudy Pedder, Dear Friends:

I am writing to thank all of the volunteer fire fighters in our company who assisted Troopers Woolworth, Hachmeister, Heimer, and Eaton last evening in our search for little Suzie bathurst. Because of your immediate response to our call for help, we were able to find the child before dark. I especially want to commend Fire fighter cunningham who volunteered to be lowered in to the old Pitville min e shaft to look for Suzie. Although he risked his life, he accepted the assignment with courage; and when his efforts failed to find zuzie, he continued with us to search the area. the citizens of summittville are fortunate to have a group of volunteers who work closely with the State Police in any emergeny in order to protect the lives of the people in this country. Sincerely, Captain Carl McKune, Station Commander

LESSON 93

CLINIC

GOALS
- To strengthen accuracy by practicing alphabetic drills.
- To type 37/5'/5e.

FORMAT
- Single spacing   60-space line   Tabs every 5 spaces

KEYBOARDING SKILLS

Type lines 1–4 once. In line 5, use your tabulator key to advance from one word to the next through the entire line. Repeat lines 1–4, or take a series of 1-minute timings.

Speed	1	When I visit the island, I may go down to the lake to fish. 12
Accuracy	2	Quietly, six zebras jumped back over the eight brown rafts. 12
Numbers	3	Diane should not take 10, 29, and 38 in place of 47 and 56. 12
Symbols	4	On 10/29 he (Bart) paid $87, which is 36% less than I paid. 12
Technique	5	as at if be or an up to in ad is it

| 1 | 2 | 3 | 4 | 5 | 6 | 7 | 8 | 9 | 10 | 11 | 12 |

PRETEST

Take a 5-minute Pretest on lines 5–20 on page 152. Circle your errors, and use the Practice lines below and on page 158 to improve your skill. Use double spacing.

PRACTICE

Type lines 6–31 below and on page 158. Then repeat any of the lines that stress the letter errors you circled in the Pretest. Use single spacing.

A	6	Apt ale arch ache arena alibi acquit abound achieve absolve
B	7	Bag bid busy baby bacon basis behave basket bandage brought
C	8	Cup can cost core candy cargo cement center caption cabinet
D	9	Dig did dawn dive drive doubt design digest dentist default
E	10	End eye each edge eight earth enrage extend enforce engrave
F	11	Fly fin fret form fixed float forest formal fragile fortune
G	12	Get gem gift gaze giant going gadget govern garbage gesture
H	13	Hay hen howl huge house horse handle hanger honesty horizon
I	14	Ill ice itch inch index input insure intact impulse iceberg
J	15	Job jar just jinx joker jumpy jigsaw jingle journey jewelry
K	16	Kid key knit knot knock knife kitten kidney kingdom kitchen
L	17	Let lye land lane latch lance ladies length lantern lasting
M	18	Map mud mail make mouth mound marvel magnet martial machine
N	19	New nap name nail niece night nickel nephew neglect neither
O	20	Out old ouch oath onion other object oblige ostrich oatmeal
P	21	Pay par plot plug prowl print pantry pastel poultry prairie
Q	22	Qt. quo quiz quit quest quick quaver queasy qualify quarter
R	23	Rot rub raid raft ridge right raging random reverse romance
S	24	Say sea self sold smack snake scarce scheme shingle shorten
T	25	Tub tip tent team trash tempt tendon temper trouble textile
U	26	Use urn used urge usher until uproar unkind upright unlatch
V	27	Vat van view vote vocal virus victim virtue varsity vehicle
W	28	Won why wish went while where wrench weight without whistle

(Continued on next page)

GOALS
- To identify all-capital abbreviations while typing sentences.
- To type 43/5'/4e.
- To format cover letters; to type two cover letters with a subject line and two letters with an attention line.

FORMAT
- Single spacing   60-space line   5-space tab

LAB 24

ALL-CAPITAL ABBREVIATIONS

Type lines 1–4 once. Then repeat lines 1–4 or take a series of 1-minute timings.

1 In the fall Ms. Polinski will visit the U.S.S.R. and Japan.   12
2 I wrote R.S.V.P. on the invitations to the wedding banquet.   12
3 My address is P.O. Box 165--not 156, as shown on this form.   12
4 Zoe has accepted a position with the CIA for work overseas.   12

| 1 | 2 | 3 | 4 | 5 | 6 | 7 | 8 | 9 | 10 | 11 | 12

PREVIEW PRACTICE
Accuracy
Speed

Type lines 5 and 6 twice as a preview to the 5-minute timing below.

5 fact test only year state detente testees foreign determine
6 choice civics third their high know half when they vote how

1- AND 5-MINUTE TIMINGS

Take two 1-minute timings on each paragraph. Then take one 5-minute timing on the entire selection. Use single spacing for the 1-minute timings and double spacing for the 5-minute timing.

7   Last year a group of high school students participated in a citizenship   15
8   test conducted to determine how much young people know about our   28
9   system of government and about how to split their ballot when they   42
10 vote.   43

11   The results of the test were shocking. Only one-third of the students   15
12 participating in the program recognized the fact that a voter could   29
13 split his or her party choice. The majority were ignorant of politics.   43

14   Barely half of the students in the survey knew that we base the   14
15 number of representatives on population and that a state has only   27
16 two U.S. senators. Many students believed a member of the House   40
17 was appointed.   43

18   On the questions relating to foreign policy, the tests revealed that   15
19 the students were equally uninformed. Around half the testees did   28
20 not know what NATO is; only a few knew the meaning of the word   41
21 "detente."   43

22   The failing marks of these future voters were not much of a surprise   15
23 to high school teachers because students show scant interest in history,   29
24 civics, or political science; so they do not learn about government.   43

| 1 | 2 | 3 | 4 | 5 | 6 | 7 | 8 | 9 | 10 | 11 | 12 | 13 | 14   SI 1.54

```
X   29  Mix wax jinx apex fixed extra reflex expend excited x-rayed
Y   30  Yes you yard your yeast yield yonder yearly yardage younger
Z   31  Zip zig zone zinc zesty zebra zenith zodiac zoology zealous
```

POSTTEST   Repeat the Pretest on page 152 to see how much your skill has improved.

LESSON 94

UNIT 16 FORMATTING TABLES

UNIT GOAL
37/5'/5e

GOALS
- To use commas after introductory words and phrases while typing sentences.
- To type ruled tables.

FORMAT
- Single-spacing   60-space line   5-space tab and as needed

LAB 9

COMMAS AFTER INTRODUCTORY WORDS AND PHRASES

Workbook 151–152.

Type lines 1–4 once, providing the missing commas. Edit your copy as your teacher reads the answers. Then retype lines 1–4 from your edited copy.

```
1  Speaking rapidly Kent explained the reasons for the delay.
2  In any event Ms. Smithe should finish before the deadline.
3  During the question-and-answer period Jan was outstanding.
4  In the first place Ms. Maizley is not a computer operator.
```

1-AND 5-MINUTE TIMINGS

Take two 1-minute timings on each paragraph. Then take one 5-minute timing on the entire selection. Use single spacing for the 1-minute timings and double spacing for the 5-minute timing.

```
                     1                        2            1'
5       Old furniture can look as good as new again.  A marred   12
          3                     4
6  chair or table can become a thing of beauty and a source of   24
     5                   6                        7
7  pride to you with a little bit of concentrated effort.        35

                                 8                   9
8       To begin, you must carefully and thoroughly remove the   12
               10                    11
9  old finish.  To do this, just apply a thick coat of a paint   24
    12                    13                    14
10 or varnish remover.  Then scrub it away with steel wool.      35

                           15                   16
11      Next, it's important to sand the furniture, being sure   12
              17                    18
12 to eliminate any rough spots.  At the same time, you should   24
    19                   20                      21
13 repair any cuts or scratches that have damaged the wood.      35

                           22                       23
14      Once you have completed these steps, you can restain a   12
            24                     25
15 piece of furniture.  The stain should dry quickly, and then   24
    26                    27                     28
16 you can apply the first coat of varnish to the article.       35

                         29                       30
17      Finally, you should smooth the article with new pieces   12
             31                    32
18 of steel wool to remove any rough areas that have appeared,   24
    33                     34              35
19 apply a second coat of varnish, and gaze at your work.        35
   |  1  |  2  |  3  |  4  |  5  |  6  |  7  |  8  |  9  | 10  | 11  | 12   SI 1.35
```

engineer for the 500-home complex, is seeking sewage and access rights through the adjacent Sandy Creek Trailer Park. Residents oppose this.

 a. Report from Mary Ann Snell, speaking for the Sandy Creek Trailer Park residents.

 b. Report from Morris Knapp, attorney for the State Land Use Commission.

 c. Report from Wade Cook, in charge of the site for the Department of Environmental Resources.

Please come prepared to discuss these crucial issues.

 Alice Beck Hoffstat, Chairperson
 Land Use Commission

JOB 196-2. LETTER

Block format. Add a salutation. Workbook 421–422.
Body 65 words (plus 20 words for subject line).

Mr. Chester Hartzell, RD1,   13
St. Augustine, FL 32084,   18
Subject: Town Meeting.   24
I will be holding a town   35
meeting in Interlachen   40
on Thursday, January 15,   45
from 6:30 to 7:30 p.m. in   50
the Council Chambers of   55
the Interlachen   58
Municipal Building.   62
I hope that you and   66

members of your family   70
can attend. Thomas Jefferson   77
said that the basis of   82
our government is the   86
opinion of the people,   91
and that's why I'll   95
be in Interlachen — to   99
get your opinions and   104
to answer your questions.   109
Sincerely yours, Sylvia Nyhart,   119
United States Senator.   125

FORMATTING RULED TABLES

Workbook 153–154.

To format ruled tables, such as the one illustrated at the right, follow these guidelines:

1. Center the table horizontally and vertically.

2. Using your key line, set your left margin. Then space across for the key line as you set your tabs. This will help you determine how wide to type the ruled lines in the table.

3. Type the ruled lines (the underscores) the exact length of the key line. Single-space before each ruled line, and double-space after each ruled line.

4. End the table with a single ruled line, typed the length of the key line.

Practice: Type the table below on a full sheet of paper. Use double spacing. The table should occupy 16 lines.

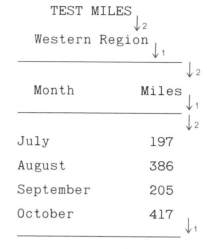

```
          TEST MILES
                        ↓2
          Western Region
                            ↓1
    _____
                              ↓2

      Month          Miles
                            ↓1
    _____
                              ↓2

      July            197

      August          386

      September       205

      October         417
                            ↓1
    _____
```

```
September123456Miles
```

FORMATTING COLUMNS WITH WORDS AND NUMBERS

You have previously learned that words align on the left and numbers align on the right. Sometimes columns contain a mixture of both words *and* numbers.

To format a column of words and numbers, align all entries at the left, as if they were all words.

JOB 94-1. THREE-COLUMN RULED TABLE

Standard format. Double-space on a full sheet of paper.

SPORTS CAR EXHIBITS
(Final Entries)

Car	Model	Country
Corvette	Convertible	United States
Datsun	280ZX	Japan
Ferrari	410	Italy
Jaguar	E-Type	Great Britain
Porsche	911	West Germany

Type each line four times, or take four 12-second timings on each line. For each timing, type with no error.

5 They may end the big fight by the lake by the usual signal. 12
6 Their men wish to blame us for most of their big work jams. 12
7 She is busy with the work but is to go to town for the pen. 12

                    25   30   35   40   45   50   55   60

Type as many 30-second "OK" (errorless) timings as possible out of three attempts on lines 8–10. Then repeat the effort on lines 11–13.

8   Jack found the gravel camp six below zero quite a few days. 12
9   Jacqueline was vexed by the folks who got that prize money. 24
10 Rex amazed Jack by pointing quickly to five of the answers. 36

11 He quickly trained a dozen brown foxes to jump over a gate. 12
12 As Elizabeth requested, Jack will pay for fixing my silver. 24
13 For her quick-dial game, Beverly just won your extra prize. 36

    | 1 | 2 | 3 | 4 | 5 | 6 | 7 | 8 | 9 | 10 | 11 | 12

Take one 5-minute timing on page 316.

JOB 196-1. LETTER WITH AGENDA

Block format. (Add a salutation.) Arrange the agenda attractively within the body of the letter. One carbon copy. Workbook 419–420. Body 122 words (plus 20 words for subject line).

Mr. and Mrs. Ben Azzara, Jr., 425 Avalon Drive, Beckley, WV 25801, [Subject:] Land Use Commission Meeting

The next meeting of the Land Use Commission will be held on Tuesday, April 4, at 7:30 p.m. in the YMCA. Your attendance at this meeting is very important because we have two controversial issues on the agenda:

1. Lodge Valley Mall. Frank Yeo, developer of the $12 million shopping mall, is seeking changes in three building codes.

2. Terrace Heights Home Site. Dagman Swenson, chief

LESSON 95

GOAL
- To format and type two-line column headings in tables.

FORMAT
- Single spacing   60-space line   Tabs at center and as needed

KEYBOARDING SKILLS

Type lines 1–4 once. In line 5, use the shift lock for each word in all-capital letters. Repeat lines 1–4, or take a series of 1-minute timings.

Speed	1	Rush him eight bushels of corn, but make him sign for them.	12
Accuracy	2	Park my gray, bronze jet and quickly wax it for five hours.	12
Numbers	3	Our bills for the week came to $10, $29, $38, $47, and $56.	12
Symbols	4	Listen! I did <u>not</u> say 12 was 1/4 of 60. Did <u>you</u> say that?	14
Technique	5	Go to ADAMS, not to WHITMAN or LANKIN or EDMORE or LANGDON.	

| 1 | 2 | 3 | 4 | 5 | 6 | 7 | 8 | 9 | 10 | 11 | 12

FORMATTING TWO-LINE COLUMN HEADINGS

When a column heading is much longer than any item in the column, the column heading is typed on two lines. To format two-line column headings:

1. Align one-line column headings with the second line of two-line column headings.

2. Center each line. Subtract (a) the number of characters in the shorter line from (b) the number of characters in the longer line.

3. Divide that answer by 2 (drop any fraction), and indent the shorter line by that number of spaces. In the example, 9 − 5 = 4, and 4 ÷ 2 = 2. Indent the shorter line 2 spaces, as in this example:

$$\text{Suggested} \leftarrow 9$$
$$\text{Price} \quad \leftarrow 5$$

4. Underscore the words in each line in open tables; do not underscore in ruled tables.

Practice: Center each of the following two-line column headings:

Number of Units	Daily Expenses	Unit Price

JOB 95-1. THREE-COLUMN TABLE
Standard format. Double-space on a full sheet of paper.

BASKETBALL SCORES

December Games

Home Team's Score	Visitor's Score	Difference
68	66	+ 2
72	81	− 9
59	52	+ 7
65	66	− 1
77	58	+19

JOB 95-2. THREE-COLUMN TABLE
Standard format. Double-space on a full sheet of paper.

SCHEDULE OF SUMMER SEMINARS

Topic	Date	Expected Attendance
Time Management	July 6-9	15
Interview Techniques	July 20-23	19
Decision Making	August 2-5	16
Financial Planning	August 9-11	15
Accounting Principles	August 16-18	12

JOB 194/5-3. COUPON LETTER

Standard format with indented paragraphs. Make five carbon copies for use in Job 194/5-4. Workbook 407–418. Body 72 words.

Locations and descriptions of 153 soil groups 10
in the state are available in the "Land Re- 19
sources Map" published by the state of Penn- 28
sylvania and the faculty in the Department of 37
Science at State College. 42

The map presents land resources in a graphic 53
form. It brings together factors of soil depth, 63
drainage, and yearly moisture. 69

Copies may be ordered for $3.25 from the 80
Department of Land Resources, P.O. Box 5000, 89
Harrisburg, PA 17126. Sincerely yours, Frank 106
J. Silverman, Ph.D., Director of Land Re- 116
sources 119

— 131

Date, Land Resources Map, Department of 149
Land Resources, Box 5000, Harrisburg, PA 157
17126 158

Please send me _____ Land Resources Map(s). 169
My check for $_____ is enclosed. 176

JOB 194/5-4. ADDRESSING COUPON LETTERS AND ENVELOPES

Address the six coupon letters prepared in Job 194/5-3 to the persons listed below. Capitalize as needed. Address six envelopes for the letters. Standard format.

1. mrs. stephen c. mullen, p.o. box 221, ligonier, pa 15658

2. ms. rosemary magagnotti, 16 perry square, erie, pa 16501

3. mr. aldo mc adoo, 110 linden street, scranton, pa 18503

4. miss maude shreckengost, 9456 beacon avenue, philadelphia, pa 19106

5. mr. russell zacherl, 1677 beaver grade road, crafton, pa 15205

6. mrs. glenda johnston, p.o. box 62, portland mills, pa 15850

LESSON 196

GOALS
- To recognize all-capital abbreviations while typing sentences.
- To type two letters in block format.

FORMAT
- Single spacing   60-space line   5-space tab

LAB 24

ALL-CAPITAL ABBREVIATIONS

Type lines 1–4 once. Then repeat lines 1–4 or take a series of 1-minute timings.

1 The FBI will investigate the journals for the UAW members. 12
2 Many students will come to the U.S.A. in the coming years. 12
3 The text centers around a happening in Iraq about 300 B.C. 12
4 Patrick Gazer earned his M.A. degree in English from Yale. 12

| 1 | 2 | 3 | 4 | 5 | 6 | 7 | 8 | 9 | 10 | 11 | 12

Many organizations are commonly identified by all-capital abbreviations without periods:

FBI   CBS   UN   UNESCO   UAW   IBM   RCA

Other all-capital abbreviations do use periods:

U.S.   U.S.A.   U.S.S.R.   M.D.   M.B.A.   R.S.V.P.   P.O.

JOB 95-3. THREE-COLUMN UNARRANGED TABLE

Standard format. Double-space on a full sheet of paper. Add horizontal rules.

[*Title*] DEGREE ABBREVIATIONS

[*Subtitle*] Selected From <u>American Universities and Colleges</u>

[*Column headings*] Abbreviation, Title, Classification

[*Line 1*] D.D., Doctor of Divinity, Honorary

[*Line 2*] D.P.A., Doctor of Public Administration, Earned and Honorary

[*Line 3*] D.Sc., Doctor of Science, Earned and Honorary

[*Line 4*] LL.D., Doctor of Laws, Usually Honorary

[*Line 5*] Pharm. D., Doctor of Pharmacy, Earned and Honorary

LESSON 96

GOALS
- To recognize how commas set off nonessential elements while typing sentences.
- To format and to type tables with leaders.

FORMAT
- Single spacing   60-space line   5-space tab

LAB 10

COMMAS FOR NONESSENTIAL ELEMENTS

Type lines 1–4 once. Then repeat lines 1–4 or take a series of 1-minute timings.

1 It is, however, going to be quite late when we finish here. 12

2 You will, nonetheless, be required to stay until we fix it. 12

3 Joan, too, will represent our school in the skills contest. 12

4 Zach will, in the meantime, be our candidate for secretary. 12

  | 1 | 2 | 3 | 4 | 5 | 6 | 7 | 8 | 9 | 10 | 11 | 12

Words, phrases, or clauses that are not essential to the meaning of a sentence are set off by commas. Names in direct address are also considered nonessential. Use two commas to set off nonessential elements within a sentence. Use one comma if a nonessential element appears at the end or at the beginning of a sentence.

We are planning, *as you know,* to reject their offer.
A quantity discount is available, *of course.*
Lisa requested, *moreover,* that the catalog be reprinted.
You will receive a copy, *Mr. James,* with your next invoice. (Direct address.)

5-MINUTE TIMINGS

Take a 5-minute timing on lines 5–22 on page 162, typing each new line three times (omit the blank lines—they are there to help you keep your eyes on the copy). Type six times each word on which you made an error, hesitated, or stopped during the 5-minute timing. Then take a 5-minute timing to see how much your skill has improved.

October 10, 19--   3

No inside address; subject/ salutation covers all addressees.

To All NAM Members   11
Who Plan to Attend the   16
Chicago Convention: 20

This letter is to remind you that only paid-up Association   33
members will be admitted to the convention sessions we will 45
hold in November at the Drake Hotel in Chicago. Membership 57
dues can, of course, be paid at the registration desk upon   69
arrival at the convention, but the charge there will be $25 81
more per individual than dues paid in advance. So we urge   92
you to remit your dues in advance.   100

You may use the coupon below. Just fill it in, attach your 113
check for $75, and mail them in the enclosed envelope to our 125

Informal complimentary closing.

offices in Washington. Your membership card will be sent   136
immediately.   139

                    See you at the convention!   146

Initials may be on same line as signer's identification to allow for tear-off.

ts   Beverly T. Prescott   154
Enclosure   Executive Director   161
—   173
                    Date_____   181

National Association of Mayors   189
P.O. Box 2173   191
Washington, DC 20013   196

Enclosed is my check for $75 in payment of my Association dues. 210

_____   _____   223
Name   Mayor of   227

_____   240
Address   City   State   ZIP   248

Extra space between every set of three lines is for ease of reading only—do not space extra at these points in the timing.

```
 5        My gardening talents, as they have guessed, are almost  12
 6        My gardening talents, as they have guessed, are almost  24
 7        My gardening talents, as they have guessed, are almost  36
 8    infamous.  There seems to exist a basic mystique around how  48
 9    infamous.  There seems to exist a basic mystique around how  60
10    infamous.  There seems to exist a basic mystique around how  72

11    to keep gardens growing, and I have never, or almost never,  84
12    to keep gardens growing, and I have never, or almost never,  96
13    to keep gardens growing, and I have never, or almost never, 108

14    been able to do it well.  Zillions of persons, both men and 120
15    been able to do it well.  Zillions of persons, both men and 132
16    been able to do it well.  Zillions of persons, both men and 144

17    women, do gardens.  They have a skill I just am not able to 156
18    women, do gardens.  They have a skill I just am not able to 168
19    women, do gardens.  They have a skill I just am not able to 180

20    master.                                                     182

21    master.                                                     184

22    master.                                                     185
      |  1  |  2  |  3  |  4  |  5  |  6  |  7  |  8  |  9  | 10  | 11  | 12    SI 1.39
```

FORMATTING TABLES WITH LEADERS
Workbook 155.

Leaders are rows of periods that lead the reader from one column to the next. Leaders are especially helpful in financial statements, tables of contents, programs, and menus.

To format leadered tables:

1. Set the left margin and tab stops for the table.
2. Find the point on the scale where the final period on each line of leaders will be typed. The final period should be 1 blank space before the item in the second column.
3. Type the first item in the first line, space once, and type the line of periods. Remember to stop 1 space before the item in the second column.
4. Repeat step 3 for each item.

Practice: Type the table below, following the instructions for formatting tables with leaders. Use single spacing and a 40-space line to center the table on a half sheet of paper.

TABLE OF CONTENTS

How to Type With Carbons 139

How to Make Erasures 140

How to Crowd Letters 140

How to Center Horizontally 141

How to Type a Proxy 158

How to Type Minutes 185

PRACTICE

In the chart below, find the number of errors you made on the Pretest. Then type each of the designated drill lines four times.

Pretest errors	0–1	2–3	4–5	6+
Drill lines	28–32	27–31	26–30	25–29

Accuracy

25 monies issues before approved designed decisions television
26 stand elected contracts important assortment responsibility
27 get unique variety building recognize government businesses
28 wants subjects testimony justified responsible implications

Speed

29 permission through quite each must can do by it if an so is
30 officials difficult issue role even much all day yet run up
31 members funding city make help wide both work road vote for
32 ordinary giving comes from have many they such them who and

POSTTEST

Repeat the Pretest on page 316 to see how much your skill has improved.

FORMATTING COUPON LETTERS

Sometimes business letters are formatted so that there is room at the bottom for a tear-off coupon for the convenience of the person receiving the letter to respond to some request.
 To format a coupon letter:

1. Use any letter style, but set margins for a long letter—60P/70E.
2. Separate the coupon from the letter by a line of spaced underscores or hyphens. Single-space before the line; double-space after it.

3. Reference initials and enclosure notations, if used, may be raised up to align with the last line of the writer's identification.
4. Use double spacing between lines of underscores to allow room for the insertions.

Note: Coupon letters are form letters, so they often contain a "subject/salutation" instead of an inside address and salutation.

JOB 194/5-1. COUPON LETTER
Type the coupon letter on page 318. Standard format. Make one carbon copy. Workbook 403–404. Body 124 words.

JOB 194/5-2. COUPON LETTER
Block format. Personalize the letter by using an inside address and salutation. Workbook 405–406. Body 124 words.

Mr. C. W. Cyphert, 214 Seminole Street, Brad- 17
ford, PA 16701, Dear Mr. Cyphert: 25
In answer to numerous requests, we can now 34
supply a selection of PENN NEWS covers in 43
a size and format suitable for framing. A set 52
of four covers, all by famous artists, now is 61
available. ¶ These are full-color prints, en- 71
larged to 9″ by 12″ on heavy, coated paper, 80
without the magazine logo or overprinting. 89
The set includes the Philadelphia harbor from 98
the April issue, Salmon Creek from the July 107
issue, Gettysburg from the September issue, 115
and Amish farms from the December issue. 124
These prints are not available in stores. ¶ The 134
price is $3 per set, delivered. Clip the coupon 144
below, fill it in, and attach your check. Make 154
your check or money order payable to the 162
Pennsylvania State Commission. Order your 170
set today. Sincerely yours, Harvey Laird, 183
Executive Director 187

– 201

(Date) _____ 210

Pennsylvania State Commission 217
P.O. Box 1011 220
Harrisburg, PA 17120 224

Enclosed is a check for $____ for ____ set(s) 234
of the four covers of PENN NEWS. 240

Please send to _____ 253
     Name 255
_____ 264
     Address 266
_____ 276
City   State   ZIP 284

JOB 96-1. TWO-COLUMN TABLE WITH LEADERS

Standard format. Double-space on a half sheet of paper. 45-space line.

SCHOOL LUNCH ENTREES

Greenville High School

Monday .... Turkey with dressing
Tuesday .... *Hot beef sandwich*
Wednesday .... Tacos and beans
Thursday ...... *Barbeque with chips*
Friday .... *Tuna casserole*

JOB 96-2. TWO-COLUMN TABLE WITH LEADERS AND RULES

Standard format. Single-space on a half sheet of paper. 35-space line.

E X O D U S

Table of Contents

Chapter	Page
Jordan Beyond	1
This Land Is Mine	197
A Eye for a Eye	321
Awake in glory	714
With Wings as Eagles	579

LESSON 97

GOALS
- To identify how commas set off nonessential elements while typing sentences.
- To improve accuracy on "OK" timings.
- To format and to type financial statements.

FORMAT
- Single spacing   60-space line   Tab at center

LAB 10

Type lines 1–4 once. Then repeat lines 1–4, or take a series of 1-minute timings.

COMMAS FOR NONESSENTIAL ELEMENTS

1 Please let us know, Dr. Lu, if there is anything we can do. 12
2 That would be an excellent time, therefore, for the picnic. 12
3 You should be aware of all of the qualifications, Ms. Lund. 12
4 Dr. James V. Zak will, as usual, act as committee chairman. 12

| 1 | 2 | 3 | 4 | 5 | 6 | 7 | 8 | 9 | 10 | 11 | 12

"OK" TIMINGS

Type as many 30-second "OK" (errorless) timings as possible out of three attempts on lines 5–7. Then repeat the attempt on lines 8–10.

5 Jack quietly gave some dog owners most of his prize boxers. 12
6 Roxie picked off the amazing yellow jonquils by the cavern. 24
7 Kay bought five or six cans to award as equal major prizes. 36

8 Vicky placed a dozen jugs from Iraq on the waxed tabletops. 12
9 Paul reviewed the subject before giving Max and Kay a quiz. 24
10 With all kinds of gripes, Buz rejected every required exam. 36

| 1 | 2 | 3 | 4 | 5 | 6 | 7 | 8 | 9 | 10 | 11 | 12

LESSONS 194/195

GOALS
- To use abbreviations correctly while typing sentences.
- To format and type three coupon letters and to address six form coupon letters and envelopes.

FORMAT
- Single spacing   60-space line   5-space tab and other tabs as needed

LAB 23

ABBREVIATIONS

Type lines 1–4 once, providing standard abbreviations for the underscored words. Edit your copy as your teacher reads the answers. Then retype lines 1–4 from your edited copy.

1   <u>Doctor</u> Jennie Felix works at the new Mercy Hospital in Dayton.

2   I sent a memo to George Van Sickle, <u>Senior</u>, about the problem.

3   Isabel's class meets at 11:30 <u>ante meridiem</u> on Mondays and Tuesdays.

4   Zuppello Electronics, <u>Incorporated</u>, built a factory in New Zealand.

PRETEST

Take a 5-minute Pretest on lines 5–24. Then circle and count your errors. Use the chart on page 317 to determine which lines to type for practice.

```
                    1                          2
5        All city councils play an important role in each local      12
              3                    4
6   government they serve.  They are elected officials who must       24
        5                    6                            7
7   make the day-to-day decisions that run a city.  A very wide       36
                  8                          9
8   assortment of issues comes before the council, and it's the      48
            10                        11                      12
9   responsibility of all members to recognize the implications      60
                          13
10  of their stands on the issues.                                    66
                  14                        15
11       Every time a new building is designed for the city, it      78
              16                    17                      18
12  must be approved by the city council.  Local monies must be      90
                          19                        20
13  allocated through the council, and projects needing funding     102
                  21                    22
14  from the city must be justified by experts giving testimony     114
            23                    24                      25
15  before the council.  Contracts to businesses who do work in     126
                          26                        27
16  the city, such as road building, are awarded by the vote of     138
              28                        29                    30
17  city council members.  Even a cable television company must     150
                  31                          32
18  get the permission of the council if it wants to operate in     162
19  the city.                                                        164
              33                        34                    35
20       City council members must be quite well informed about     176
                      36                          37
21  a variety of subjects, both ordinary and unique.  They have     188
              38                        39                    40
22  many advisors who help them stay up to date.  Yet it can be     200
                          41                        42
23  difficult for people to be responsible for so much.  Who is     212
                  43
24  on your council?                                                 215
    |  1  |  2  |  3  |  4  |  5  |  6  |  7  |  8  |  9  |  10  |  11  |  12    SI 1.58
```

FORMATTING FINANCIAL STATEMENTS

Workbook 156.

Periodic financial statements help businesses to analyze cash flow, profit and loss, and other important financial information. Among the monthly, quarterly, or yearly statements that are commonly used in business are the balance sheet and the income statement.

Because it is important to compare current financial statements with past statements, they should be formatted consistently.

To format financial statements:

1. Vertically center the statement. Use single spacing (but if the statement is to be displayed on a separate page, use double spacing).

2. Set margins to an assigned line length (usually 60, 65, or 70 spaces).

3. Position money columns only 2 spaces apart (not 6) for easiest reading. Set tabs for the money columns by backspacing from the desired line-ending point.

4. Type major entries in all-capital letters. Double-space before major entries.

5. Capitalize the first letter of each major word in subentries.

6. Use leaders to carry the eye from the first column to the second column.

7. Indent subentries 5 spaces from the left margin.

8. Indent Total lines 5 spaces from the beginning of the line above.

9. Type a single rule to separate groups of numbers that must be added or subtracted.

10. Type a double rule to indicate totals. Use the platen release lever as you turn up the paper for the second line. (The platen release lever allows you to temporarily change the line of writing.)

JOB 97-1. FINANCIAL STATEMENTS: THE BALANCE SHEET

Standard format. 65-space line.

```
                      The Foundation Club

                        BALANCE SHEET

                For the Year Ending June 30, 19--↓3
```

Major entry—all caps.

Subentry—initial caps; indent 5 spaces.

Total line—initial caps; indent 10 spaces.

```
ASSETS
     Supplies on Hand ........................ $231.60
     Cash in Bank ............................  478.59
     Accounts Receivable .....................  166.42
          Total Assets .....................         $876.61↓2

LIABILITIES
     Accounts Payable ........................ $265.98
     Refunds on Memberships ..................   75.00
          Total Liabilities ..................       $340.98↓2

EQUITY
     Capital ................................. $415.75
     Profit from Club Activities ............  119.88
          Total Equity .......................        535.63
          Total Liabilities and Equity ..     $876.61
```

Grand total—indent 15 spaces.

LESSON 193

CLINIC

GOALS
- To type copy that reinforces skill in using the space bar, tabulator, shift key, and margin release.
- To type 43/5'/4e.

FORMAT
- Single-spacing   60-space line   Tabs as needed

KEYBOARDING SKILLS

Type lines 1–4 once. Then practice using your space bar as you type line 5. Repeat lines 1–4, or take a series of 1-minute timings.

Speed	1	The man got a snap of an authentic whale by the big island. 12
Accuracy	2	Six jumbo elephants quickly moved the wagon from the blaze. 12
Numbers	3	He has 10 or 29. She has 38 or 47. I have 10 or maybe 56. 12
Symbols	4	Do you know whether the B/L (bill of lading) has been sent? 12
Technique	5	a b c d e f g h i j k l m n o p q r s t u v w x y z . , / ?

| 1 | 2 | 3 | 4 | 5 | 6 | 7 | 8 | 9 | 10 | 11 | 12

PRETEST

Type lines 6–11 twice to find out which techniques are the most difficult for you. To force the use of the margin-release key at the end of each line, set margins (**M**) for a 60-space line exactly (do not add 5). Keep your eyes on the copy.   ↓

Reset M

6   We are fortunate today that Beth Mason, the famous inventor
7 of ERASE–EZ paper, is scheduled to speak at our fall conference.
8   Welcome, Dr. Mason, to Washington, D.C., our great capital!
9   We all hope Dr. Mason will tell us how she created ERASE–EZ
10 and what it will do to make our typing jobs easier--yes, easier.
11   Ladies and Gentlemen, Dr. Beth Mason, and her new ERASE–EZ.

PRACTICE

Set a tab (**T**) every tenth space; then type lines 12–14 twice, tabbing and backspacing to make each column of decimals align at the decimal, as shown here.

	M	**T**	**T**	**T**	**T**	**T**
12	1	101.0	20.2	101.1	10.0	0.6
13	2	20.1	101.18	2.0	2.21	22.22
14	3	3.6	30.2	203.19	334.0	1.31

Shift Key

Type lines 15–17 twice.

15 A An Ann B Bo Bob C Ca Cal D Da Dan E Ev Eve F Fa Fay G Gus
16 H Ha Hal I Id Ida J Ji Jim K Ka Kay L Li Liz M Ma Mat N Ned
17 O Ol Oli P Pa Pat R Ra Rae S Sa Sam T Te Ted V Va Val W Wes

Margin Release

Set margins for an exact 55-space line. Then type lines 18–21 twice.   ↓

Reset M

18   I hope to get on the bus by two o'clock. If I miss my
19 ride, I must take the next bus. It may not be here by two,
20 and that means that I will have to take my car for the day.
21 Do you think we shall find a place to leave my car in town?

POSTTEST

Repeat the Pretest to see how much your skill has improved.

TIMINGS

Take two 5-minute timings on page 313.

JOB 97-2. FINANCIAL STATEMENTS: THE INCOME STATEMENT

Standard format. 60-space line.

```
                     Baker and Brown Inc.
                                         ↓2
                   SUMMARY INCOME STATEMENT
                                              ↓2
                 For the Month Ended June 30, 19--
                                                    ↓3

SALES ...................................            $38,564.39
                                         ↓2
COST OF GOODS SOLD
     Beginning Inventory ..............$26,378.00
     Inventory Purchases ..............  9,587.60
     Total Available ..................$35,965.60
     Ending Inventory .................. 23,724.60
     Cost of Goods Sold ...............              12,241.00
                                         ↓2
GROSS PROFIT ON SALES .................              $26,323.39
                                         ↓2
EXPENSES
     Selling Expense ..................$ 6,536.96
     Rent Expense .....................  3,699.50
     Heat and Light ...................    731.54
     Depreciation of Equipment ........  2,250.50
     Total Expenses ...................              13,218.50
                                         ↓2
NET INCOME BEFORE TAXES ...............              $13,104.89
```

LESSON 98

GOALS
- To use commas to set off nonessential elements while typing sentences.
- To type at least 37/5'/5e.
- To type tables with leaders and rules.

FORMAT
- Single spacing   60-space line   5-space tab and as needed

LAB 10

COMMAS FOR NONESSENTIAL ELEMENTS

Type lines 1–4 once, providing the missing commas. Edit your copy as your teacher reads the answers. Then retype lines 1–4 from your edited copy.

1 Aquivane Industries in my opinion should handle this job.

2 All of us must of course submit our responses by June 30.

3 If those projects are late though Gus must pay a penalty.

4 When you arrive in Oxnard Mrs. Luzinski we will meet you.

5-MINUTE TIMINGS

Take a 5-minute timing on lines 5–22 on page 166. Type six times each word on which you made an error, hesitated, or stopped during the 5-minute timing. Then take a 5-minute timing to see how much your skill has improved.

REPORT OF TOUR OF SWITZERLAND
Mayor Richard Ginallo, Yorke, ME
October 24-30, 19--

Purpose. I was one of 23 mayors of third-
class cities in the United States who were
seleced by the State department to spend
one week in Switzer land studying that
country government, factories, and business. Switzerland was chosen because
it's not large, has no unemployment, and
is govern by a body of representtives
from each of it's 25 cantons.

Switzerland depends no imports to feed
it's pypulation, which is about 6,000,000
million people These people are a mixture of langage and culture, which breaks
down some what like this:

Language	Percent of Population
German	69
French	19
Italian	10
Rumanish	0.9

Constitutional safe guards prevent any one
person, group or canton from becoming too
powerful. The Swiss president serves a
one-year term and may not immediately succeed him self or herself. By living small
but thinking big Switzerland has forged a
people of many tongues and diverse cul-
tures into one nation; and from Switzerland's lesson, there is much we can learn.

Geneva. Our first stop was Geneva, head
quarters fo 51 internation bodies, including the International Cross. We visited
the archives of the Central Training
Agency where more than 15 million names
are cross-filled on 45 million cards.
During world war II, the ICRC kept track
of captives, making contact with next of
kin. These cards were color-coded--pink
for Germans, white for Americans, and
blue for British.

Crafts workers began building clocks
and watches in Geneva more than 400 year
ago. Many of Switzerland's 515 watch-
assembling plants are small and scattered.
To maintain consistenly high standards,
they still do a lot of the most exacting
work by hand. Even on on small assembly

Today they produce almost half the world's watches - 67 million a year.

lines there is no compromis with pre-
cision.

Baden. In Baden, a few miles northest of
Zurich, large industries flourish and are
dramatic proof that Swiss industry also
thinks big. At Lyck, Inc., we watched
spirals of steel spin off a huge lathe-
like machine, operated by a master machin-
est with 27 years experience. He earns
20,000 francs a year, the equivelent of
$4,600, which is excellent pay by Swiss
standards.

Basel. The Next to machinery, the most
important export is chemicals. The hub
of this industry Basel. Since the early
1900 the industry has branched in all
types of chemical products--dyes, drugs,
pesticides, plastics, inks, and rare
metals. During the 1930 Switzerland began
making vitmins and today is the world's it
largest producer.

Zurich. In Zurich, Switzerland's biggest
city, we visited the headquarter of one
of the country oldest and largest banks,
the Swiss credit bank. In the foreign exchange section teletypes clattered, while
a dozen buyers with direct lines to
London, rome, and New York bargained for
blocks of sterling, lira, and dollar
currencies. Bank employees are allowed
by law to reveal information about depbt
itors. The name of a numbered-acount
depositor is known only to 2 or 3 of the
bank's top officials.

St. Moritz. This city industry is recre-
ation--plush hotels bobsled and toboggan
runs, ski jumps, and facilities for the
whole gamut of snow-and-ice spoots--a
winner among the world's winter resorts.

Appenzell. One of the last areas in
Switzerland where most people still work
the land, this this valley is green and
fruit ful. In the winter, families work
at small embroidery factory in town.

Conclusion. This trip was a great privi-
leage, and I learned many things we can
incorporate in our developmental plan for
Yorke.

5	Yesterday, my puppy took me along on a walk. First, I	12
6	Yesterday, my puppy took me along on a walk. First, I	24
7	Yesterday, my puppy took me along on a walk. First, I	36
8	started walking slowly, but she quickly seized command. We	48
9	started walking slowly, but she quickly seized command. We	60
10	started walking slowly, but she quickly seized command. We	72
11	began the walk, of course, in normal fashion; but just as I	84
12	began the walk, of course, in normal fashion; but just as I	96
13	began the walk, of course, in normal fashion; but just as I	108
14	approached the end of the sidewalk, she tugged, tore loose,	120
15	approached the end of the sidewalk, she tugged, tore loose,	132
16	approached the end of the sidewalk, she tugged, tore loose,	144
17	and zipped across the driveway excitedly. Then, I followed	156
18	and zipped across the driveway excitedly. Then, I followed	168
19	and zipped across the driveway excitedly. Then, I followed	180
20	behind.	182
21	behind.	184
22	behind.	185

| 1 | 2 | 3 | 4 | 5 | 6 | 7 | 8 | 9 | 10 | 11 | 12   SI 1.40

JOB 98-1. RULED TABLE WITH LEADERS

Standard format. Double-space on a full sheet of paper.
10 spaces between columns, with leaders.

CONVERSION CHART

From Standard to Metric Measurements

To change	To	Multiply by
Feet	Meters	.3048
Gallons	Liters	3.7853
Inches	Centimeters	2.5400
Miles	Kilometers	1.6093

JOB 98-2. FIVE-COLUMN UNARRANGED TABLE

Double-space on a full sheet of paper. Add horizontal
rules. Type numbers in Area column in numeric order,
with *Area 1* first. Compute averages that are missing.
Standard format.

[*Title*] QUARTERLY REPORT OF SALES
[*Subtitle*] April Through June
[*Column headings*] Area, April, May, June,
Average

[*Body of table*] Area	April	May	June	Average
3	$10	$47	$57	$38
4	38	23	41	
2	74	65	83	
1	33	82	65	
5	40	44	63	49

LESSONS 191/192

GOALS
- To identify abbreviations while typing sentences.
- To type 43/5'/4e.
- To format and type a report in space-saving style.

FORMAT
- Single spacing   60-space line   5-space tab and other tabs as needed

---

LAB 23

ABBREVIATIONS

Type lines 1–4 once. Then repeat lines 1–4 or take a series of 1-minute timings.

1 The order was sent to Frances Weiler-Zeeb, Ph.D., in April.   12
2 Please let me know if Beman Company, Inc., can do this job.   12
3 They met for dinner at 6:30 p.m. and got home about 10 p.m.   12
4 Mrs. Exeter will check the manuscript for Dr. Vera Nuquist.   12
   | 1 | 2 | 3 | 4 | 5 | 6 | 7 | 8 | 9 | 10 | 11 | 12

5-MINUTE TIMINGS

Take two 5-minute timings on lines 5–21. Circle your errors on both timings.

5   One of the many unique elements of a democracy is that everyone   14
6   of legal age has the right to vote. Voting should be taken very   27
7   seriously because it is a responsibility. It is apparent that a govern-   41
8   ment will not be representative if people do not take an active part   57
9   in choosing the people to represent them. It is easy to criticize our   69
10 leaders, but a part of the blame rests with those citizens who do not   83
11 care enough for our country to vote.   90
12   Voting is done at many levels of government. Federal, state, county,   105
13 and city elections must be planned for every year to choose officials   119
14 whose terms have ended. Primaries are held in the spring to narrow   133
15 the number of persons running. Although the year a president is   146
16 chosen can create a lot of excitement, people should be interested and   160
17 vote for their choice at each election.   168
18   A good voter should pay careful attention to the major issues and   182
19 the candidates. Newspapers, public debates, and interviews are good   196
20 sources of information. Choose the one who shares your views and is   210
21 qualified to do the job.   215
    | 1 | 2 | 3 | 4 | 5 | 6 | 7 | 8 | 9 | 10 | 11 | 12 | 13 | 14   SI 1.52

FORMATTING REPORTS IN SPACE-SAVING STYLE

The space-saving style may be used when the report is long and the originator wants as few pages as possible. To format in space-saving style:

1. Margins: 65P/75E.
2. Begin the title on line 10.

3. Single-space; double-space between paragraphs.
4. Double-space before and single-space after side headings if they are used. Or, use paragraph headings instead of side headings.
5. If your typewriter is equipped with vertical half spacing, use ½ blank line wherever you would normally use 1 blank line.

JOB 191/2-1. TRIP REPORT

Type the report on page 314. Space-saving format with paragraph headings.

JOB 191/2-2. SIDE-BOUND TRIP REPORT

Retype Job 191/2-1. Standard report format with side headings.

LESSON 99

CLINIC

GOALS
- To improve your typing skills on the Selective Practice routine.
- To type 37/2'/2e.

FORMAT
- Single spacing   60-space line   5-space tab

KEYBOARDING SKILLS

Type lines 1–4 once. Do what line 5 tells you to do. Repeat lines 1–4, or take a series of 1-minute timings.

Speed   1   Ms. Lela Dow owns a pair of authentic ivory and clay bowls.   12
Accuracy   2   Next month Phil may just quit work and buy five cozy games.   12
Numbers   3   Marathon Runners #10, 29, and 56 were all tied at 38:56:00.   12
Symbols   4   In Cruz's new book, A NEW MATH, does 2 + 2 = 4? Of course!   12
Technique   5   As you type this line, use your return key after each word.

| 1 | 2 | 3 | 4 | 5 | 6 | 7 | 8 | 9 | 10 | 11 | 12

PRETEST

Take a 2-minute Pretest on lines 6–12; then take a 2-minute Pretest on lines 13–19. Circle and count your errors on each Pretest.

Speed

6   It is again that time of the year when skiers hurry to   12
7   get out their boots, jackets, skis, goggles, plus all other   24
8   equipment and charge to those slopes at the first sign of a   36
9   heavy snowfall. When that first ideal snow appears on that   48
10 high slope, it's usually an exciting moment for most skiers   60
11 in this country. Do you think you would like to enjoy this   72
12 same sport?   74

Accuracy

13   Our lungs will not get in shape if we delay starting a   12
14 specific exercise program. The young and old all need lots   24
15 of good exercise. Many who were just lazy now receive lots   36
16 of exercise by running. Like many people, you can run at a   48
17 slow jog along any route, or you can run at a swift pace if   60
18 you want. Much is gained by pursuing a planned program for   72
19 exercising.   74

| 1 | 2 | 3 | 4 | 5 | 6 | 7 | 8 | 9 | 10 | 11 | 12   SI 1.34

PRACTICE

In which Pretest did you make more errors? If in the speed lines (6–12), type the speed lines below six times and the accuracy lines three times. If in the accuracy lines (13–19), reverse the procedure.

Speed

20   altitude calendar amateur clarity badges client awoke delay
21   diligent enlarged drought helpful edited gentle flies heavy
22   jubilant slightly loyalty planted highly likely lucky pearl
23   obsolete thorough statute warmest roamed stolen sedan story
24   delegate surprise student garment farmed joyful style plays

Accuracy

25   check bound burned anyway diploma belongs colorful audience
26   front doubt growth dental foundry century friendly economic
27   loyal hunch lovely inside kitchen healthy mechanic identify
28   twice round walnut shaped specify musical tendency punching
29   slump fifty hyphen cement brought license comedian multiply

POSTTEST

Repeat the Pretest.

FORMATTING REVIEW

Itineraries

1. 60P/70E.
2. Title, name, date, and cities displayed in 3 lines.
3. Day and date underscored at left margin.
4. Times of events indented 5 spaces from left margin.
5. Tab 30 spaces from left margin for details of trip; indent turnover lines 2 spaces.
6. Single-space turnover lines; double-space between entries.

<u>Monday, October 24</u>
 7:10 p.m. Depart Kennedy International Airport
            TNA Flight #455
<u>Tuesday, October 25</u>
 10:15 a.m. Arrive Geneva, Switzerland
            Accommodations: Hotel Geneva
 3:00 p.m. Tour watch factory
<u>Wednesday, October 26</u>
 9:00 a.m. Train to Bern
 1:00 p.m. Visit Castle of Chillon
 5:15 p.m. Bus to Baden
            Accommodations: Schweiz Hotel
<u>Thursday, October 27</u>
 9:30 a.m. Tour Sorrer Electronics
 11:30 a.m. Bus to Basel
            Accommodations: Vanil-Noir Hotel
 2:00 p.m. Tour Rebound Chemicals
<u>Friday, October 28</u>
 4:40 a.m. Train to Zurich
 2:00 p.m. Tour Swiss Credit Bank
 6:20 p.m. Overnight train to St. Moritz
<u>Saturday, October 29</u>
 9:00 a.m. Tour St. Moritz
            Accommodations: Helvetia Inn
 2:44 p.m. Train to Appenzell
<u>Sunday, October 30</u>
 8:51 a.m. Train to Zurich
 3:05 p.m. Depart Zurich TNA Flight #611
 6:05 p.m. Arrive Kennedy International Airport

JOB 190-2. ITINERARY

Retype Job 190-1 as a three-column table. Use these column heads: *Date, Time, Event*. Double-space on a full sheet of paper.

LESSON 100

UNIT GOAL
38 5' 5e

GOALS
- To use commas to set off nonessential elements.
- To format a short letter.

FORMAT
- Single-spacing   60-space line   5-space tab

LAB 10

Type lines 1–4 once, providing the missing commas for each line. Edit your copy as your teacher reads the answers. Then retype lines 1–4 from your edited copy.

COMMAS FOR NONESSENTIAL ELEMENTS

Workbook 157–158.

1   When will you and Janice arrive in Kalamazoo Mrs. Santori?
2   This is as you know your next chance to take this course.
3   We look forward to hearing you speak to our group Dr. Lon.
4   The vice president must consequently be in command today.

PRETEST

Take a 2-minute Pretest on lines 5–13; then take a 2-minute Pretest on lines 14–22. Circle and count your errors on each Pretest.

Speed
5   Do you at times feel like relaxing with an interesting   12
6   book to read? You, too, will soon find much enjoyment from   24
7   the right book; and here are some good hints to be followed   36
8   when choosing the book that is right for you.   45
9   Choose the author you feel will be appealing. Look to   57
10 see what the author has already written: This will usually   69
11 tell you if an author's style and manner of expression seem   81
12 right for you. Did you realize authors have unique writing   93
13 styles?   95

Accuracy
14   You could also decide whether you want to read fiction   12
15 or nonfiction. If you prefer to gain knowledge, nonfiction   24
16 might be the wiser choice. But if you would prefer to gain   36
17 entertainment from most of the books, fiction may be a wise   48
18 pick.   49
19   The length of the book may also be judged. Some read-   61
20 ers like a shorter book so that they may have a wide choice   73
21 of reading materials; others like to settle down for a long   85
22 period of time with a lengthy, interesting novel.   95

| 1 | 2 | 3 | 4 | 5 | 6 | 7 | 8 | 9 | 10 | 11 | 12   SI 1.37

PRACTICE

In which Pretest did you make more errors? If in the speed lines (5–13), type the speed lines below six times and the accuracy lines three times. If in the accuracy lines (14–22), reverse the procedure.

Speed
23 approach attacked applied deepest accord borrow apply bless
24 billiard channels grammar legally dollar follow ditto issue
25 formally helpless payroll settled looked pegged lobby shall
26 neatness suddenly stalled witness settle thrill skill teeth

Accuracy
27 desks candy candid angora charged antique category although
28 labor flush forgot costly fatigue drought happiest entitled
29 quail parks orient length leaflet history packages marketed
30 waist spent system senses tenants quality vitality surgical

POSTTEST

Repeat the Pretest.

LESSON 190

GOALS
- To recognize abbreviations while typing sentences.
- To type two itineraries.

FORMAT
- Single spacing   60-space line   Tabs as needed

LAB 23

Type lines 1–4 once. Then repeat lines 1–4 or take a series of 1-minute timings. As you type each line, note the abbreviations.

ABBREVIATIONS

1 Mr. and Mrs. Davis just left for a cruise around the world. 12
2 Quintex Box Co. is hiring students who can type accurately. 12
3 Alvin Zembling, Jr., is studying economics and world trade. 12
4 Our plane left at 7:10 a.m. and landed in Peru at 6:15 p.m. 12
| 1 | 2 | 3 | 4 | 5 | 6 | 7 | 8 | 9 | 10 | 11 | 12

Abbreviations are very commonly used in technical writing for emphasis and quick comprehension: *g* for *gram* or *grams*, *in* for *inch* or *inches*, and so on. In nontechnical business writing, abbreviations are generally limited to the most commonly used abbreviations, some of which are never spelled out:

Mr.   Mrs.   Ms.   Dr.   Jr.   Sr.   a.m.   p.m.   Inc.   Co.   Ph.D.

Note the use of periods with the above abbreviations. Standard and metric abbreviations for measurements, such as *g, cm, km, in, qt*, and *ft*, however, need no periods.

12-SECOND TIMINGS

Type each line four times, or take four 12-second timings on each line. For each timing, type without error.

5 The men may fix their antique auto and go downtown with it. 12
6 The six girls held a social to pay for a visit to the lake. 12
7 It is the duty of the eight men to cut down the large oaks. 12

25   30   35   40   45   50   55   60

30-SECOND TIMINGS

Take two 30-second timings on lines 8–10, or type the paragraph twice.

8 So, students keyboard with speed and accuracy various kinds 12
9 of business forms because they must be prepared to type all 24
10 these documents: memos, invoices, requisitions, and bills. 36
| 1 | 2 | 3 | 4 | 5 | 6 | 7 | 8 | 9 | 10 | 11 | 12

JOB 190-1. ITINERARY

Type the itinerary shown on page 312. Standard format. Full sheet of paper. Make two carbon copies. Arrange the heading as follows:

```
                        ITINERARY
Mayor Richard Ginallo                    October 24, 19--

             New York--Switzerland
```

LETTER-PLACEMENT GUIDE

Workbook 159–160.

Some employers prefer using a variable placement plan for very short or very long letters. The variables are shown in the chart below.

Words in Body	Line Length	Date Typed on	From Date to Inside Address	Space for Signature
Under 75	40P/60E	Line 15	5–8 lines	3–6 lines
75–225	50P/60E	Line 15	5 lines	3 lines
Over 225	60P/70E	Lines 12–15	4–5 lines	2–3 lines

JOB 100-1. LETTER

Standard format (see page 92). Workbook 161–162. Body 65 words.

[*Today's date*] / Ms. Elvera Carver / 708 Garland Road / Garland, TX   17
75041 / Dear Ms. Carver: 23

    As you requested in our recent conversation, we are sending you   36
more information about opportunities to own and operate your own   49
Campus Bookstore. ¶ The enclosed materials describe some of the   63
many benefits of our franchises. Of course, there are many more. For   77
more information, make an appointment with one of our representa-   90
tives by completing the enclosed card and returning it to us at your   104
convenience. Sincerely yours, / Kenneth J. Mills / Marketing Director   124
/ [*Your initials*] / Enclosures   128

LESSON 101

GOALS
- To format an attention line in a letter.
- To format a subject line in a letter.

FORMAT
- Single spacing   60-space line   Tab at center

KEYBOARDING SKILLS

Type lines 1–4 once. In line 5, backspace and underscore each underlined word immediately after typing it. Repeat lines 1–4, or take a series of 1-minute timings.

Speed   1   The world's fuel problem may also signal a big proxy fight.   12
Accuracy   2   Calm Rex quit many jobs while driving a bus for a park zoo.   12
Numbers   3   They hoped for 3,856. Only 2,947 paid; 10 did not show up.   12
Symbols   4   An asterisk (*) showed the loss to be $7,946.50 as of 12/8.   12
Technique   5   It is not up to us to pay the bill by the time we get home.

| 1 | 2 | 3 | 4 | 5 | 6 | 7 | 8 | 9 | 10 | 11 | 12

FORMATTING AN ATTENTION LINE

Workbook 163–164.

When a letter is addressed directly to a company, an attention line may be used to route it to a particular person or department.

1. Type the attention line in initial caps at the left margin, a double space below the inside address and a double space above the salutation. Use a colon after the word *Attention*.

```
United Charities Campaign
258 North Star Drive
Anchorage, AK 99503

Attention:  Campaign Manager

Ladies and Gentlemen:
```

Agreed to hire a labor negotiator at $55 per 908
hour, plus expenses, to conduct contract talks 918
for the borough with the police, who are mem- 927
bers of the IMAW union. 932

The meeting adjourned at 11:15 p.m. 941

Respectfully submitted, 949

_____

Osvaldo Medici 957
Borough Secretary 962

FORMATTING BUDGET REPORTS

To format a budget report:

1. Use standard format for unbound reports.

2. Arrange financial data as a two column table within the body of a report. Single-space the table.

3. Do not use a by-line. Budget reports are submitted by the person who prepares them. Use a complimentary closing and a writer's identification as in minutes of a meeting.

JOB 188/9-2. BUDGET REPORT

Standard format.

BUDGET REPORT FOR THE YEAR 19— 19
UNITED WAY OF SENECA COUNTY 37

A $400,000 goal has been tentatively set by 48
United Way of Seneca County for this year's 57
fall campaign. It is the highest goal ever 66
established for the countywide fund drive— 74
about 8 percent higher than last year's 82
$371,655 goal. 86

The United Way Budget Committee, chaired 96
by Jo Ann Lance, spent more than two weeks 104
reviewing agency requests before making final 114
recommendations to the Board. Here is the 122
list they drew up: 126

Association for the Blind—$22,524 137
Boy Scouts—$21,386 143
Community Ambulance Service—$15,960 152
Community Services of Seneca County— 160
  $15,307 163
Decision House—$14,416 169
Family Service and Children's Aid Society— 179
  $30,327 181

Freemont YMCA—$40,198 188
Freemont YWCA—$42,231 195
Girl Scouts—$22,371 201
Red Cross of Fremont—$35,008 208
Red Cross of Troy City—$37,530 217
Salvation Army of Seneca County—$43,527 227
United Services Organization—$4,019 236
United Way of Seneca County—$52,177 245
Youth Alternative, Inc.—$3,019 254

Ruby Montgomery, the chairperson of the 19— 267
campaign, said she feels the $400,000 goal is 278
a realistic one to achieve. Recruitment of 285
campaigners is on target, and the campaign 293
cabinet will meet for the first time at 8 p.m. 303
on August 10 to review plans for the total 311
operation. 314

Respectfully submitted, 322

_____

Dan Vogelbacker, Secretary 332
Budget Committee 337

JOB 188/9-3. REPORT TO A COMMITTEE

Standard format.

REPORT TO BOROUGH PLANNING COM- 18
MISSION ON EXIT DEVELOPMENT ON 38
INTERSTATE 80 44

By Paul S. Hardy, Planning Consultant 69

I have done a thorough study of the possi- 80
bility for development of the land near Exit 89
10 of I-80. In my opinion, such a project should 99
be postponed. 102

The development of the land near Exit 10 111
requires the construction of utilities, such as 121
water, sewage, and power lines. Costs for 129
these installations are high. Also, the devel- 139
opment plans have to be approved by state and 148
federal authorities, possibly a lengthy process. 158

While the land near exits may develop over- 168
night, other tracts may never reach the level 177
of growth that is hoped for by local govern- 186
ments, business people, and property owners. 194

2. After an attention line, use the salutation *Gentlemen:*, *Ladies:*, or *Ladies and Gentlemen:*.

3. On the envelope, type and underscore the attention line in capital and small letters on line 9, 5 spaces from the left edge.

JOB 101-1. LETTER

Type a speed draft of the following letter. Copy at your fastest rate without correcting your errors. Use today's date. Use address and attention line in illustration on page 169. Standard format. Workbook 165–166. Body 82 words (plus 20 words for attention line).

Enclosed are the Southeast Region 8

reports for funds raised in the city of 16

Juneau. I am happy to report 22

that this year we improved on 28

our fund-raising program and 34

as a result were able to 39

Note: Because the attention line will add two lines (one typed, one blank), add 20 words to the body count to determine placement.

meet our quota. 42

Our next report is not due 49

until the middle of next month. 55

By that time we should be able to pre- 63

dict how close we will come to our 70

yearly goal. We believe we will be 77

able to exceed our goal by at 83

least $5,000. / Yours truly, / 91

Ann B. Clifton / Juneau 100

Manager /[Your initials]/Enclosures 105

JOB 101-2. LETTER

Use proofreaders' marks to indicate any needed corrections in the draft of Job 101-1. Then retype a corrected copy of the letter. Standard format. Workbook 167–168.

FORMATTING A SUBJECT LINE

A subject line briefly identifies the main topic of a letter. To format a subject line:

1. Type the subject line in initial caps at the left margin between the salutation and the body of the letter, preceded and followed by 1 blank line.

2. Follow the word *Subject* with a colon and 2 spaces.

Note: The subject line, like the attention line, occupies two lines—add 20 words to the body count to determine placement.

Dear Ms. King:

Subject: Battlefield Charity Dance

I am pleased that you thought of our firm in
tion with your charity dance. We have found

JOB 101-3. LETTER

Standard format. Workbook 169–170. Body 53 words (plus 20 words for subject line).

[Today's date] / Ms. Anne B. clifton / 12

Juneau Manager / United Charities 18

Campaign / Juneau, AK 99801 / Dear Mrs. 26
  Ms.

Clifton: / Subject: Juneau Campaign 34

    Thank you for your report on the 42

Alaska fund-raising campaign. We are 51
Juneau   *always*

happy to hear that the campaign is 58

going well so in your region. 64

    The other regions in Anchorage and 69

Fairbanks are also doing quite well; 74
consequently,

and this may be a banner year for our 85

campaign. We all look forward to re- 91

ceiving your report. / Yours truly, / 102
          final

Ralph B. Jones / Alaska Manager / [Your 114

initials]

Sewage System—Council spent a good part of its three-hour meeting discussing the storm and sewage systems in the borough and the ban on new hookups imposed by the state Department of Environmental Resources.

Councilman Thomas Hessburg, referring to the hydrogen sulfide which Corr Refining released into the system recently, said he had been checking ordinances to determine what can be dumped. He found that the fine for offenders was low, ranging from $10 to $100. Hessburg then offered a motion for three amendments to protect the borough:

1. Increase the fine for dumping, with no limit to the amount that can be charged offenders. Charge a million dollars if necessary.

2. Expand the list of substances that are prohibited from being dumped in the lake.

3. Establish a date by which downspouts on all structures must be disconnected from the sanitary sewage system. Hessburg indicated that borough engineer Art Sears said that a rapid 1-inch rainfall would produce over one million gallons of water. This water empties into the street sewers, causing them to overflow.

Hessburg, Olson, and Segel voted for the amendments; Council member Lew Smyth was absent. The motion passed.

Council member Tony Lomassoni cast the only negative vote on the motion to begin work on the amendments—he argued that it would be hard to force people to take out downspouts.

Plant Odor—Lomassoni conveyed eastside residents' complaints about the sewage plant odor. Mr. Strangis, manager at the firm, reported that a new disposal site had been selected, but he did not promise that dumping at a new site would take care of the odor.

Ben Strange, the borough manager, said he had written to three consulting engineers asking for help in solving the problem. He stressed that the borough needs expertise. He pointed out that there was no panic yet. Lomassoni countered that action should be taken because the problem was critical. No action was taken, however.

Sidewalks on Filbert Street—Just before adjournment, Lomassoni said that residents of Filbert Street had received letters from the borough directing them to repair their sidewalks as a result of a program approved by Council last month and that many homeowners could not pay for this work.

Borough manager Ben Strange noted that some persons on Filbert Street might apply for grants through the HUD small-cities program to repair their sidewalks. Since the notification letters set an October 15 deadline for repairs to be made, Lomassoni made a motion that council recall the ordinance for further study. Neither Hessburg nor Segel would provide a second to the motion.

Second Avenue Traffic—Council approved a 90-day parking and traffic change for the intersection of Second Avenue and South Street. The change calls for installing stop signs on South Street, making Second Avenue a through street with the traffic signal flashing yellow, reducing the speed limit from 35 mph to 25 mph on Second Avenue from Main Street to Lang Avenue, and prohibiting parking on Second Avenue.

Other Business—In other business, Council:

Approved advertising of bids for the storm sewer projects on Elm, Cherry, and Birch Streets.

Heard a protest to its parking ban on Lang Avenue near the Third Avenue intersection but decided not to change the present law.

Accepted a bid of $89,800 from M. M. Brock Company of Erie for heating system work in the borough building. Architect Dick Bell said work should begin within 10 days, and bids for general construction and plumbing will be advertised early next week.

Approved a resolution creating a 15-member auxiliary police force, which will be used for traffic control. Members of this force will have no police powers, such as making arrests; and they will not carry guns.

LESSON 102

GOALS
- To recognize how commas are used to set off appositives while typing sentences.
- To format letters in two styles: blocked with indented paragraphs and full-blocked.

FORMAT
- Single spacing   60-space line   5-space and center tabs

LAB 11

COMMAS WITH APPOSITIVES

Type lines 1–4 once. Then repeat lines 1–4, or take a series of 1-minute timings.

```
1  Our educational consultant, Jan Newby, is highly qualified.   12
2  Mr. Williams, our resident expert, was amazed at this idea.   12
3  We have planned to hold the next meeting on Monday, May 27.   12
4  It is best for you, our client, to know everything we know.   12
   |  1  |  2  |  3  |  4  |  5  |  6  |  7  |  8  |  9  |  10  |  11  |  12
```

An appositive is a word or a phrase that further describes or identifies a person or a thing. Use two commas to separate an appositive within a sentence. Use one comma if the appositive begins or ends the sentence.

Mrs. Baker, *the national sales manager,* approved the raises.
(The words *the national sales manager* further identify *Mrs. Baker.*)

This account was handled by a local firm, *Adams & Fells.*

The seminar has been rescheduled for next Monday, *August 12.*

FORMATTING LETTERS WITH INDENTED PARAGRAPHS

The letters that you have typed in this course have all been formatted in *modified-block style,* with the date, complimentary closing, writer's name or name and title indented to the center. A variation of this style is to also indent the first line of each paragraph 5 spaces.

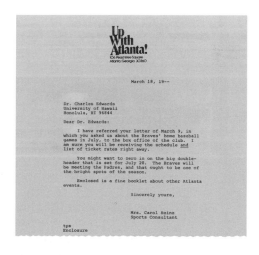

JOB 102-1. LETTER

Standard format with indented paragraphs. Workbook 171–172. Body 90 words.

[*Today's date*] / Dr. Sheng Y. Hwang / 2205   13
Auburn Street / Portland, ME 04105 / Dear   21
Dr. Hwang: 24

    Thank you for your recent request for a copy   35
of a letter written by Dr. E. L. Stewart to   44
Congresswoman Kate Crews.   49

    As chairperson for the committee that used   60
that letter as evidence in the case Bear vs.   69

King, I must inform you that I am not per-   77
mitted to reveal the contents of the letter to   86
you until the case has been closed.   94

    Mr. Lee Hurst, who was also involved in   102
this case, may be able to assist you. He was   111
in close contact with Dr. Stewart on this   119
matter. / Yours truly, / W. L. Safranski /   135
Member of Congress / [*Your initials*]   142

Type lines 8 and 9 twice as a preview to the 3-minute timing below.

Accuracy   8 are major large affect expend street police quality reasons

Speed   9 within local taken today lives sums make easy all and do on

1- AND 3-MINUTE TIMINGS

Take two 1-minute timings on each paragraph. Then take one 3-minute timing on the entire selection. Use single spacing for the 1-minute timings and double spacing for the 3-minute timing.

```
                                                                    1'
10        It is not easy to list all that local governments have   12
11   to do.  The departments of most local agencies include some   24
12   of the following:  police and fire, street repairs, sanita-   36
13   tion, schools, and public health.                             43
                                                                   —
14        Local governments today employ a large number of resi-   12
15   dents.  They also receive and expend major sums of money as   24
16   well as make decisions that affect the lives of all who are   36
17   within the zoned limits of the area.                          43
                                                                   —
18        For these reasons, every person should get to know how   12
19   his or her local government functions and be aware of every   24
20   action that is being taken.  The quality of your local gov-   36
21   ernment depends on your being alert.                          43
   |  1  |  2  |  3  |  4  |  5  |  6  |  7  |  8  |  9  | 10 | 11 | 12   SI 1.52
```

MINUTES OF A MEETING, ALTERNATE FORMAT

1. Headings such as *Attendance, Unfinished Business,* and *New Business* are not used. Other appropriate headings are used.
2. Headings "hang" in the margin. Type headings at the left margin. The copy that follows a heading begins on the same line as the heading. Set a tab 2 spaces after the longest heading. (See the illustration at the right.) Very long headings may be divided on two lines.
3. Do not indent paragraphs. Double-space between paragraphs.
4. All other standard rules apply.

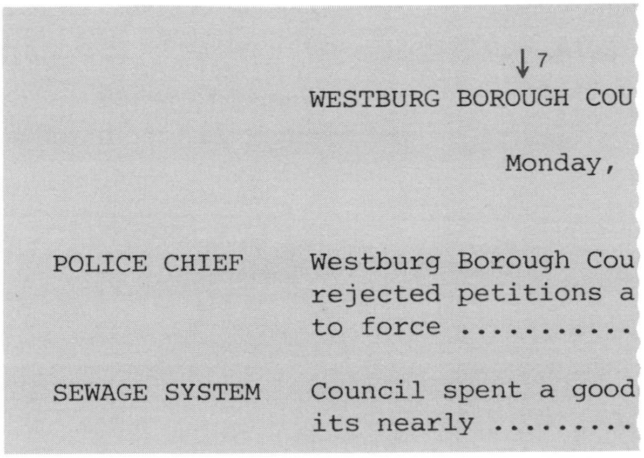

```
                                    ↓ 7
                        WESTBURG BOROUGH COU

                           Monday,


POLICE CHIEF        Westburg Borough Cou
                    rejected petitions a
                    to force ..........

SEWAGE SYSTEM       Council spent a good
                    its nearly .........
```

JOB 188/9-1. MINUTES OF A COUNCIL MEETING

Alternate format, side-bound. Make two carbon copies.

WESTBURG BOROUGH COUNCIL   15
MEETING   19
Monday, June 20, 19—   35

Police Chief—Westburg Borough Council   46
Monday night rejected petitions attempting to   56
force the rehiring of former borough police   64
chief Rex Sill. A brief statement read by   73
Mayor Gail Burns said borough manager Ben   81
Strange had acted within the guidelines of his   91
office to accept Sill's resignation on May 12.   100

FORMATTING LETTERS IN BLOCK STYLE

Another style that is used to format letters is known as the *block style,* where *all* letter parts begin at the left margin. Margins and vertical spacing remain the same.

JOB 102-2. LETTER

Block format. Workbook 173–174. Body 68 words (plus 20 words for subject line).

[*Today's date*] / Mr. Paul Abernathy / Night-	13
light Hotel Inc. / 2670 Blue Bird Drive / Great	22
Neck, NY 11023 / Dear Mr. Abernathy: /	30
Subject: Sales Meeting	36
Last year we had the pleasure of holding our	46
sales meeting at your hotel. Our meeting was	55
a big success; and a large part of our good	64
fortune was due, of course, to the excellent	73
services we received from your hotel.	81

We would like to return	86
to your hotel for our next meet-	93
ing. Would you, therefore, please	100
let me know what your group	105
rates are for this year. / Sincerely /	114
J. J. Reynolds / Program Chairperson /	122
[Your initials]	123

JOB 102-3. LETTER

Block format. Workbook 175–176. Body 78 words.

[*Today's date*] / Mr. Adam T. Weight / 141 Rice	14
Street / LaGrange, TX 38046 / Dear Mr.	22
Weight: / Subject: Luncheon Speaker	30
How delighted I am that you have agreed to	39
speak at our closing luncheon for the Adver-	48
tising Club's annual meeting in Nashville on	57
March 14.	59
As one of the country's foremost authorities	69
on consumerism, you will certainly be able to	78
provide us with important, relevant informa-	88
tion. All of us look forward to hearing you.	96
Your plane tickets and hotel confirmation	105
will be sent to you shortly. The honorarium	114
of $250 will be sent by the end of March.	123
Yours truly, Joan T. Parks	132

LESSON 103

GOALS
- To identify how commas are used to set off appositives while typing sentences.
- To learn how to use carbon packs.
- To format *cc* and *bcc* notations.

FORMAT
- Single spacing   60-space line   5-space and center tabs

LAB 11

COMMAS WITH APPOSITIVES

Type lines 1–4 once. Then repeat lines 1–4 or take a series of 1-minute timings.

1	The book I want, <u>Principles of Management</u>, is out of stock.	22
2	My brother, John Quinn, is a fullback on the football team.	12
3	Your next workshop will be on Valentine's Day, February 14.	12
4	Sue Krzyskowski, our personnel manager, recruits employees.	12

| 1 | 2 | 3 | 4 | 5 | 6 | 7 | 8 | 9 | 10 | 11 | 12

Level 6 provides thorough coverage of the many "special" papers that are required in various business, medical, and government offices.

In Level 6 you will:

1. Demonstrate keyboarding accuracy and speed on straight copy with a goal of 45 words a minute or more for 5 minutes with no more than 4 errors.

2. Correctly proofread copy for errors and edit copy for revision.

3. Apply production skills in keyboarding and formatting copy for four categories of business documents from six input modes in the following settings: local and state government (Lessons 188–199); international trade and travel (Lessons 200–211); Foresty Service—federal government (In-Basket A); veterinary medicine (In-Basket B); vehicle repair and service (In-Basket C); and travel agency (In-Basket D).

4. Decide about formatting and priority in completing tasks for four in-baskets.

5. Apply rules for correct use of abbreviations and plurals in communications.

LESSONS 188/189

UNIT 31 FORMATTING SPECIAL REPORTS

UNIT GOAL
43/5'/4e

GOALS
- To use dashes correctly while typing sentences.
- To format and type minutes of a council meeting, a budget report, and a report to a committee.

FORMAT
- Single spacing   60-space line   5-space tab and other tabs as needed

LAB 22

Type lines 1–4 once, providing the missing dashes. Edit your copy as your teacher reads the answers. Then retype lines 1–4 from your edited copy.

DASHES

Workbook 401–402.

1 I wrote the words Vera wrote the music for several songs.
2 The work needs to be done that means we do the job Monday.
3 Rex is not ready for a promotion he was absent just today.
4 Call Rita Zajac she's with Zuintolla Company and ask her.

30-SECOND TIMINGS

Take four 30-second timings on lines 5–7, or type the paragraph twice.

5 It is a time of change for our local governments. Citizens   12
6 need to be informed if they are to make the right decisions   24
7 about which changes to support and which changes to resist.   36
   | 1 | 2 | 3 | 4 | 5 | 6 | 7 | 8 | 9 | 10 | 11 | 12

FORMATTING A CARBON COPY NOTATION

1. One line below your reference initials (or below the enclosure notation, if there is one), type *cc:*, leave 2 blank spaces, and type the name of the person receiving the copy.

2. Type each additional name on a separate line, aligned with the name on the first line. Do not repeat *cc:* before each name.

```
                              Sincerely yours,



                              Karen Bouchard
                              Director

BPT
Enclosure

cc:  Mr. Crawsen
     Ms. Daniels
```

ASSEMBLING A CARBON PACK

Carbon packs consist of ① the sheet of paper or letterhead on which your original correspondence is to be typed, ② the carbon paper containing the carbon ink that transfers to all sheets but the original, and ③ the onionskin or other thin sheets of paper on which you wish to make carbon copies.

When assembling a carbon pack, make sure the carbon (shiny) side faces the copy paper—not the original.

To insert a carbon pack into your typewriter, you must first straighten the sides and top of the carbon pack so that all edges are even.

After you have straightened the carbon pack, hold it with your left hand with the carbon side (and the copy paper) facing you. Now turn the cylinder smoothly with your right hand. Continue turning the cylinder until you have advanced to the vertical position where you want to start typing.

JOB 103-1. LETTER
Standard format with indented paragraphs (see page 171). Workbook 177–178. Body 76 words.

[Today's date] / Mr. Rick Menlo / Time-   12

keeper watches Co. / 225 Eighth (Ave.) /   19

New York, NY 10027 / Dear Mr. Menlo: 28

     Enclosed is the defective Time-   36

keeper watch to which I referred in my   44

~~recent~~ letter of May 10. We have had   50

this watch in our ~~repair~~ shop on ④ dif-   59

ferent occassions but have been unable   66

to ~~find~~ resolve the problem.   71

     Would you, Mr. menlo, please ask   79

your repair shop to isolate the cause   86

of the problem--a stem/date that does   94

not release. If we cannot correct the   102

defect, we ~~shall~~ will have to give the owner   110

a new watch. / Yours Truly, / Leslie E.   123

Lauson / Manager, Dallas Region / [Your   132

initials] / Enclosure / cc: (Mr) Conrad   136

White   137

LEVEL 6

FORMATTING SPECIAL BUSINESS PAPERS

FORMATTING A BLIND CARBON COPY (*BCC*) NOTATION

When you do not want the addressee to know that a carbon copy is being sent to someone else, use a blind carbon copy (*bcc*) notation on all copies *but not on the original letter*.

To format a *bcc:*

1. Type the *bcc* notation on line 7 at the left margin of the carbon copies.
2. Use the same style for the *bcc* as you would use for a *cc* notation.

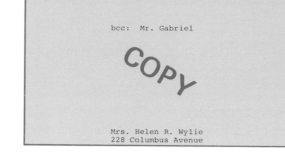

```
bcc:  Mr. Gabriel

COPY

Mrs. Helen R. Wylie
228 Columbus Avenue
```

JOB 103-2. LETTER

Block format (see page 172). Workbook 179–180. Body 65 words.

[*Today's date*] / Mr. Gardner F. West / Ling-	13
Champion Company / 105 Royal Lane / Com-	20
merce, TX 75428 / Dear Mr. West:	28
We will be pleased to welcome your group	37
and take you on a visit of our plant on the	46
date you suggest.	49
If you can, please arrange your arrival for	59
about 9:30 in the morning. We will have our	68
guides waiting for you.	73
The tour takes an hour and a half. It	83
involves walking about two miles—tell your	92
members to wear their walking shoes! / Cor-	101
dially yours, / Elizabeth Hawkins / Guest	112
Receptionist / [*Your initials*]	116

JOB 103-3. LETTER

Standard format with indented paragraphs (see page 171). Workbook 181–182. Body 37 words.

[Today's date] / Ms. Diane Wey /	11
Gross and Crews Inc. / 648	16
South Bridge Way / Brooks,	21
ME 04921 / Dear Ms. Wey:	27
Subject: Analyst Position	33
We wish to acknowledge the	40
letter in which you apply	46
for the post of bank analyst	51
in our Blue Hill office.	57
We enclose an application	64
form that we hope you will	69
fill in and return to us.	75
Sincerely yours, / Gary Holmes /	88
Personnel Director / [Your initials] /	96
bcc: Sam Wade / Enclosure	102

LESSON 104

GOALS
- To use commas to set off appositives while typing sentences.
- To format a postscript notation.
- To type 35/5'/5e.

FORMAT
- Single spacing   60-space line   5-space tab

LAB 11

COMMAS WITH APPOSITIVES

Type lines 1–4 once, providing the missing commas for each line. Edit your copy as your teacher reads the answers. Then retype lines 1–4 from your edited copy.

1. The best runner is Phil Jones a new student at Maxim High.
2. If you have questions, call our service manager Ann Smith.
3. Get in touch with the dean Dr. Leonard for an assignment.
4. Will Liz be available on Tuesday August 21 for a meeting?

25 Call Adam Jones his number is in the book and invite him.
26 Several clerk typists will be needed in our medical center.
27 Janice likes many things perfume clothes and badminton.
28 A well known new author will appear on the late night show.

JOB 187-1. BOXED TABLE

Standard format for a boxed table. Half sheet of paper.

Sales by Region, January – June 19___

Region	Actual Sales *	Budgeted Sales *
Eastern	$121.5	$119.6
Southern	113.6	109.2
Western	97.5	97.0
Mid-Continent	101.9	100.0

In thousands

JOB 187-2. LETTER

Standard format. Center the list attractively within the body of the letter. Workbook 399–400. Body 195 words plus list.

[Today's date] / Ms. Rita DiClemente / Village Tribune / 1624 Aquasco Drive / Owings Mills, MD 21117 / Dear Ms. DiClemente: 29

The present system of filing checks cashed every day, retrieving and placing them in an envelope at the end of the month, and then mailing them to our customers has become so expensive that next month we plan to initiate Free Check Storage Accounts for our commercial customers. 86

With this system we anticipate saving you about 2 cents a check because canceled checks will not be processed numerically and returned to you. Instead, these checks will be stored here at the bank and may be retrieved by you if you find it necessary to produce evidence of payment. 144

If you would like additional information about this new system, we invite you to attend a seminar to learn how you will benefit by this program. Just come to the branch office nearest you on Wednesday [insert date of Wednesday following the date of this letter] at 9 a.m. at one of the following locations: 198

Downtown, Union Bank Building 218
Crafton, Crafton Shopping Plaza 225
Far Hills, Century III Mall 232
Munhall, 3400 Main Street 238
Oakland, Fifth and Oakland 245
Penn Hills, 300 Beaver Drive 251
Stanwix, 6 Gateway Center 258

The meeting will last about an hour, and you will have the opportunity to inspect our storage areas. Do plan to attend. / Sincerely yours, / Zvi Greenman, President 301

JOB 187-3. CHECKS

Standard format. (If necessary, review page 301.) Do not erase on a check. Calculate the total and type the check for the total amount due. You are the person authorized to sign the checks. Use the current date. Workbook 397 bottom.

Your company has redecorated its offices. Write checks to the following for services rendered:

1. [To] Mark Clatterbuck III

Wallpaper	$271.55
Labor	416.50
Paint for ceiling and molding	34.67

2. [To] Laverne's Interiors

Art—paintings and antique clock	$1,780.00
Draperies	791.75
Carpeting	2,352.20
Services—decorator	800.00

Take a 5-minute Pretest on lines 5–20. Circle and count your errors.

When You Type:

Sit all the way back in the chair.

Sit erect, leaning forward slightly.

Set your feet squarely on the floor.

Place your ankles 6 to 8 inches apart.

```
 5        If you attend college upon graduation from high school   12
 6   next year, choose the school you feel will be acceptable to   24
 7   you.  Certain issues must be looked at; and you, the gradu-   36
 8   ating senior, should assess all of them very carefully.  In   48
 9   making a choice, it's essential that you discuss the issues   60
10   with all of your good friends who are attending the schools   72
11   in which you might choose to enroll.  You should also go to   84
12   the college campuses that are of great interest to you.       95
13        While you are in high school is the time to plan for a  107
14   program of study you wish to pursue in college.  Inquire at  119
15   several schools to ascertain whether the college you'd like  131
16   to attend has the precise program of your choice.  You must  143
17   also identify just where you'd like to go to school.  Would  155
18   you prefer staying quite close to home, or would you prefer  167
19   attending college in another state far away from home?  You  179
20   ought to consider your total cost and the school size.       190
     |  1  |  2  |  3  |  4  |  5  |  6  |  7  |  8  |  9  |  10  |  11  |  12  SI 1.38
```

PRACTICE

Type the accuracy lines (21–24) below as a group four times. Type the speed lines (25–28) four times each.

Accuracy

```
21   cliff allow attend allied channel baggage attorney accuracy
22   hills flood enroll collar fulfill drilled colleges carriage
23   proof kitty occupy hidden outdoor illness marriage loudness
24   stuff small tariff rotten warrant spelled withheld socially
```

Speed

```
25   armchair burdened auditor chicken apathy burden burst dough
26   delegate eloquent educate friends fairly height flick lapse
27   latitude neighbor husband network layout sickly mayor rough
28   identify urgently statute without taught waited sorry visit
```

POSTTEST

Repeat the Pretest.

FORMATTING A POSTSCRIPT (*PS:*)

A postscript (*PS:*) is an additional message typed in paragraph form at the end of a letter. To format a postscript:

1. Double-space after the last item in the letter.
2. Type the postscript at the left margin if paragraphs were blocked; indent it if paragraphs were indented.
3. Type *PS:*, leave 2 spaces, and type the message.

```
                              Sincerely your


                         Matthew R. Hal
                         Purchasing Dep

PS:  Please let us know within a week if you
items in stock.
```

LESSON 187

COMPETENCY CHECK

GOALS
- To meet the unit goal of 42/5'/4e.
- To demonstrate competency in advanced formatting of letters, forms, and tables.

FORMAT
- Single spacing   60-space line   5-space tab

PREVIEW PRACTICE

Accuracy
Speed

Type lines 1 and 2 twice as a preview to the 5-minute timings below.

1 starting keyboard calculate developed programmer technology
2 itself growth world their which touch more they into job by

5-MINUTE TIMINGS

Take two 5-minute timings on lines 3–20.

3   Ever since people began to use numbers, they have been   12
4 looking for ways to count and calculate quickly and simply.   24
5 A device such as the abacus, which was invented hundreds of   36
6 years ago, slowly developed into the modern adding machine.   48
7 The rapid growth in business and technology resulted in the   60
8 need for more complex machines--machines that could do more   72
9 than add--a need met by the modern computer.   81
10   Although a machine can easily process large amounts of   93
11 information, it can't think for itself. It is the job of a 105
12 computer programmer to supply the machine with step-by-step 117
13 instructions it will require to compute a problem.   127
14   These machines are becoming a way of life all over the   139
15 world. More and more companies are starting to computerize 151
16 all their paperwork--professional programmers, who are able 163
17 to translate such data into machine language, are very much 175
18 in demand. Since computers have a keyboard similar to your 187
19 typewriter, your knowing how to keyboard by touch is a step 199
20 ahead.   200
    | 1 | 2 | 3 | 4 | 5 | 6 | 7 | 8 | 9 | 10 | 11 | 12   SI 1.58

LAB CHECK

Type lines 21–28, providing the missing punctuation marks.

21 Julia keeps up to date records for our drive in restaurant.
22 Our next meeting is June 24 or is it June 25 at my home.
23 Please check the following tires battery and door lock.
24 An electronic computer is a time saver for vice presidents.

(Continued on next page)

JOB 104-1. LETTER

Block format (see page 172). Workbook 183–184. Body 66 words (plus 20 words for subject line).

(Today's date)/Shield Home Inspection ^Inc./1800 South Elm Street/Grand   19

Forks, ND 58201/Dear Mr. Shields:/Subject: Home Repairs Check   34

    A ^home buyer, [Mrs. Anne Shirek,] has asked that I contact you to arrange for an in-   51

spection ^of the foundation on a home that we repared [i] last March [year]. Please send all   101

charges for this inspection to my office.   110

    At the buyer's request, I will [would like you to inspect the basic   78

workmanship and materials used] in ~~renovating~~ [repairing] the foundation for the   91

house at 1210 South Elm (St.)/Sincerely yours,/Gordon H. ~~Hampton~~ [Hall]/   120

Building Contractor/(Your initials)/cc: Mr. & Mrs. Ralph M. Ernst   132

bcc: Kay West [P. S. Please let me know the exact day you plan to   146

make the inspection.]   150

LESSON 105

CLINIC

GOALS
- To review tabulator key and margin-release-key operations.
- To type 38/2'/2e.

FORMAT
- Single spacing   60-space line   Tabs every 8 spaces

KEYBOARDING SKILLS

Type lines 1–4 once. In line 5, use your tabulator key to advance from one word to the next through the entire line. Repeat lines 1–4, or take a series of 1-minute timings.

Speed	1	If an auditor signs the key amendment, I may work for them. 12
Accuracy	2	Have five more wax jugs been glazed quickly for two people? 12
Numbers	3	With 56 precincts tallied, Gray had 3,847; Green had 2,910. 12
Symbols	4	Interest on the $247 loan was 9 3/4%, which came to $24.08. 12
Technique	5	and nor the too den mop see for

  | 1 | 2 | 3 | 4 | 5 | 6 | 7 | 8 | 9 | 10 | 11 | 12

TAB AND MARGIN RELEASE REVIEW

Set your left margin at 20 and your right margin at 62. Set a tab every 10 spaces. Type lines 6–17 on page 177. Use the tabulator key to move from column to column. Use the margin release key to complete the typing of the last word in each line.

Heavy materials are not for television cloth- 385
ing they make a suit or dress look baggy and 394
bulky on camera. Women can enhance their 402
appearance by wearing a glossy blouse because 412
satins and sateen with high degree sheens 420
reflect a glow on a person's face. Women 429
should avoid patterns that are too busy and 437
too contrasting as well as stripes, polka dots, 447
or other closely spaced patterns. 454

Other Considerations 460

Television has the tendency to add a few 469
pounds on the person appearing on the screen. 479
Slim dresses and rather tight fitting suits are, 491
therefore, preferred. 493

Choose simple jewelry. Pearls photograph 503
well; sparkling jewelry should be avoided. 511
Men should not wear a tie clasp because it can 521
cause heavy flaring. 525

In general, choose colors for your on camera 535
clothes that are not too similar to your com- 544
plexion and the surrounding colors of the set. 554

If you will be standing behind a podium, 563
make certain that you stand erect. Good pos- 572
ture is very important and will add to your 581
overall appearance. If you are seated, assume 590
that your entire body will be on camera; so 599
make sure that your arms and legs are placed 608
attractively and naturally. 613

JOB 186-2. LETTER
Standard format. Workbook 395–396. Body 124 words
plus list.

[Today's date] / Mr. Edward T. Chin / The 13
Honolulu Post / 3200 Kapiolani Boulevard / 20
Honolulu, HI 96814 / Dear Ed: 27

I want to congratulate you for the splendid 37
series of articles you wrote for your newspaper, 47
The Honolulu Post. Luckily, our mutual 62
friend, Neil Kline, brought me the clippings— 71
otherwise I would have missed the series. 80

Your report, Ed, is the best coverage I have 90
ever read on the subject of educational im- 98
provement through the use of computers in 107
the classroom. 110

Be sure to read the recent articles based on 120

your research, which will appear in the (insert 129
the name of next month) issue of Classroom 137
Digest, especially the following: 146

F. M. Shada, pp. 16–22 162
Peggy Elliott, pp. 72–74 169
Louis Amodeo, pp. 110–114 176

Certainly you must send copies of The 187
Honolulu Post to Dr. Hightower. I know she 202
will be extremely pleased to learn of your 211
achievements. Sincerely, / Harold Zumerelli 227

JOB 186-3. RECEIPTS
Standard format. (If necessary, review page 298.)
Calculate the totals. Workbook 397 top.

1. [To] Clarke Hensell for 200 frisbee disks—for
   Station WXYZ's fund drive for Children's
   Hospital. [Unit price] $6.50.

2. [To] Vera Jane Sarel for 5,000 balloons—for
   Station WXYZ's fund drive for Children's
   Hospital. [Price] $8.25 per 1,000.

JOB 186-4. RULED TABLE
Standard format with leaders. Prepare as a handout
for women executives at a seminar on raising women's
self-esteem.

THE HALL OF FAME FOR GREAT AMERICANS

Year Elected	Female Members
1905	Mary Lyon
	Maria Mitchell
	Emma Willard
1910	Harriett Beecher Stowe
	Frances Elizabeth Willard
1915	Charlotte Saunders Cushman
1920	Alice Freeman Palmer
1950	Susan b. Anthony
1965	Jane Adams
1970	Lillian Wald
1976	Clara Barton

6	abide	bevel	crude	ditch	eaves
7	groan	hinge	igloo	judge	knock
8	meter	mourn	ounce	prowl	quart
9		slack	toast	until	venue
10		fixed	youth	zebra	adorn
11		clock	doubt	every	fable
12			heart	imply	joist
13			learn	music	north
14			phase	query	react
15				tempt	union
16				worry	exams
17				zings	again

PRETEST

Take a 2-minute Pretest on lines 18–26; then take a 2-minute Pretest on lines 27–34. Circle and count your errors on each Pretest. Double spacing; 5-space tab.

Speed

18	Have you ever wanted to record on a cassette tape some	12
19	of those favorite albums you like, so you could listen just	24
20	to those that please you? Many realize they can do it with	36
21	the right equipment; a tape recorder and record player will	48
22	do. Here are some reminders:	54
23	First, do not forget to use an extra-quiet area. Out-	66
24	side noises will often appear on the tape and cause distor-	78
25	tion in the quality of the taped songs. You would not want	90
26	such noises on your tape.	95

Accuracy

27	You must find a very good quality tape to give you the	12
28	very best possible sound for any taped recording. You must	24
29	be certain that any records from which you're taping are of	36
30	good quality. Tiny scratches will create skips in your re-	48
31	cording; warped records will likely distort the sound.	59
32	Finally, you must check the sound and recording levels	71
33	of the tape unit. You can adjust your sound from treble to	83
34	bass; then just set your recording level from soft to loud.	95

| 1 | 2 | 3 | 4 | 5 | 6 | 7 | 8 | 9 | 10 | 11 | 12 | SI 1.39

PRACTICE

In which Pretest did you make more errors? If in the speed lines (18–26), type the speed lines below six times and the accuracy lines three times. If in the accuracy lines (27–34), reverse the procedure.

Speed

35	awakened colorful catalog despite throat ratify upset rocky
36	facility keyboard forward handled pencil itself photo helps
37	pharmacy seaboard medical private embark charge fifth depth
38	steadily vitality solicit touched blouse always clips angry

Accuracy

39	price whole softly worked produce touched compiled brightly
40	grove liked kindly minute justice minimum happened employed
41	crude funny golden hungry enclose golfing medicine issuance
42	alone block filled deluxe ceiling delight shutdown peculiar

POSTTEST

Repeat the Pretests.

LESSON 186

GOALS
- To use dashes correctly while typing sentences.
- To review advanced formatting of various documents.

FORMAT
- Single spacing 60-space line 5-space tab

LAB 22

Type lines 1–4 once, providing the missing dashes and other punctuation. Edit your copy as your teacher reads the answers. Then retype lines 1–4 from your edited copy.

THE DASH

1 Bonnie Azen she used to live next to us works in Pontiac.

2 On June 12 or did he say July 12 we will move to Quincy.

3 The new drawings I can't wait to show you are in my room.

4 Those fireworks they were terrific lasted for two hours.

PUNCTUATION REVIEW

Type lines 5–7 once, providing the missing punctuation marks.

Colon

5 Check your lists of staples sugar salt flour and milk.

Hyphen

6 Our big dinner dance next month will be a black tie affair.

Dash

7 Call Mrs. Berger here's her number and check our account.

JOB 186-1. SPEECH

Standard format. (If necessary, review page 275.) To demonstrate your mastery of the LABs in Level 5, insert the needed punctuation: 1 colon, 1 dash, and 5 hyphens in compound nouns and adjectives.

Advice for Business People Who Are Invited   25
to Appear on Television   41

Speech Before Executive Council of Chicago   69
December 6, 19—   81

If you were invited to appear on television,   93
what would you wear? Would you worry about   101
your appearance? Are there certain things   110
you should do to improve how you will appear   119
on camera? Fortunately, there are some   127
things you can do about your makeup and   135
clothes when you are preparing for a television   145
appearance.   147

Makeup   151
Makeup for the camera is always used for   160
three basic reasons (1) to improve the appear-   169
ance of a person, (2) to correct the appearance   179
of a person, and (3) to change the appearance   188
of a person.   191

The camera picture tubes have a tendency   200
to pick up and darken certain shadow areas.   209
For example, dark shadows beneath the eyes,   218
nose, and chin quite often distort a person's   227
face unfavorably. A man may be as clean-   235
shaven as possible, but without makeup any   244
stubble may appear as dark blotches on the   253
television screen.   257

Correct makeup colors must be chosen to   267
offset the distortions. For instance, warm   274
colors (reds, brown, tans) appear slightly   283
washed out, whereas cool colors (blue reds,   292
blues, blue greens) photograph darker. Choose   301
makeup colors that are compatible.   308

Clothing   312
Naturally, the type of clothing worn by the   322
business person depends largely on his or her   331
taste. It also depends on the type of program   341
or occasion and the particular setting in which   351
the person will be televised. There are, how-   359
ever, certain types of clothing that look better   369
on television than others.   375

(Continued on next page)

LESSON 106

GOALS
- To use commas to set off appositives while typing sentences.
- To type credit memorandums.

FORMAT
- Single spacing   60-space line   5-space tab and as needed

LAB 11

Type lines 1–4 once, providing the missing commas for each line. Edit your copy as your teacher reads the answers. Then retype lines 1–4 from your edited copy.

COMMAS WITH APPOSITIVES

Workbook 185–186.

1 We thank you Ms. Gamble for all your help on our project.
2 Our employer the Quincey Corporation is moving to Boston.
3 Gregg Hanley's office the huge corner office was painted.
4 Ask our manager John Appezzatto to send five dozen boxes.

PRETEST

Take a 5-minute Pretest on lines 5–21. Then circle and count your errors. Use the chart on page 179 to determine which lines to type for practice.

5   The laws in this country permit us to drive an automo-   12
6 bile; many of us do so prior to finishing high school. The   24
7 majority of us today believe that we must own an automobile   36
8 to search for a new job, entertain ourselves, or visit good   48
9 friends. When we own an auto, we must be sure to check for   60
10 repairs frequently. Here are six quick suggestions that we   72
11 could certainly follow.   77
12   We must be certain to check for such things as the oil   89
13 level, the quantity of gas in the car, and the air pressure   101
14 in the tires. Obviously, we must clean the windshield with   113
15 care so that our view is not obstructed. We should observe   125
16 the condition of the windshield wipers so that if it should   137
17 drizzle or rain, our vision will not be reduced. The drive   149
18 belts should also be inspected for rips or tears. We could   161
19 possibly find ourselves waiting many hours for another per-   173
20 son to assist us if a belt tears, leaving us stranded while   185
21 we're on an extended trip.   190

| 1 | 2 | 3 | 4 | 5 | 6 | 7 | 8 | 9 | 10 | 11 | 12   SI 1.39

31 springs hotels appeal fancy large quite then cold but of to
32 clients summer during which round other good both the it is
33 outdoor income since sunny their began times food some most
34 include almost until rooms sound that open well many too as

POSTTEST

Repeat the Pretest, page 300, to see how much your skill has improved.

JOB 184/5-1. MEMO

Standard format. Workbook 389.

(To) Mr. Hamilton, General Manager — 6
(From) Kelly McGuire, Maintenance — 16
(Date) July 12, 19-- — 10
(Subject) No. 2 Ski Lift — 20

We have finished our regular inspection — 29
of No. 2 lift, and it appears to be in — 38
good working order. However, one of the — 47
the cables is beginning to show signs of — 55
wear and should be replaced. Although — 62
it would pass inspection by the state — 70
safety engineer, it could cause a problem when — 79
it is subjected to heavier use in the next — 88
next few months. I recommend that we — 95
order a new cable from Sta Co Products — 102
Company, Denver. Delivery takes 6 to — 110
8 weeks, and repairs to the lift can be — 119
completed in 1 day. — 126

JOB 184/5-2. MEMO

Standard format. Workbook 389.

(To) Kelly McGuire, Maintenance — 5
(From) Phillip Hamilton — 14
(Date) July 13, 19-- — 9
(Subject) Replacement Cable for No. 2 — 20
Ski Lift — 22

As you recommended, we will replace the — 32
cable on our No. 2 ski lift. Please pre- — 40
pare a purchase requisition for the — 47
cable *and any other parts you think* — 54
you will need. — 58
You suggested that we order the cable part — 66
from Sta Co Products, Denver. The last — 74
time we tried to order parts for our — 81
Skyway equipment, they wrote us that — 89
they no longer had the skyway dealership — 97
equipment. Will you please check into — 103
this matter and and locate a suitable — 110
supplier of the cable. — 117

FORMATTING CHECKS

Use the same format as for receipts (see page 298).

WESTERN RANCH   23-157
                                   1020
PAY
TO THE
ORDER OF Carmen Esposito--------------- $ 37.50

Thirty-seven and 50/100------------------ DOLLARS

Denver Trust
Plaza Branch

Memo _____   *Willa Horne*
                   AUTHORIZED SIGNATURE

⑈1020 01571⑈ ⑈08 5172321⑈

1. Carmen Esposito—10 hours   382-12-9622
2. Joe Wallace—8 hours   024-14-5872
3. Terry O'Connors—9 hours   781-01-2430
4. Chris Rubinski—7 hours   224-77-1101
5. Jane Klos—8½ hours   362-41-7430
6. Ernie L. Lum—18 hours   440-24-9871
7. Harold Van Eisen—6 hours   622-22-4387
8. Celeste Corey-Miller—11 hours 421-52-3472

JOB 184/5-3. CHECKS

Checks are to be made out to students who were temporaries at Western Ranch; they were paid $3.75 an hour; yours is the authorized signature. Format eight checks—no erasing on a check. Use the format shown in the illustration above. Compute the amount due. Date all checks July 5, 19—. Workbook 391, 393.

JOB 184/5-4. INCOMPLETE THREE-COLUMN TABLE

Format a three-column table from the information in Job 185-1: Type the student's name in column 1; amount earned in column 2; and social security number in column 3. Use standard format and an appropriate title. As a subtitle use July 6, 19—.

In the chart below, find the number of errors you made on the Pretest. Then type each of the designated drill lines four times.

Pretest errors	0–1	2–3	4–5	6+
Drill lines	25–29	24–28	23–27	22–26

Accuracy

22 clean vision quantity friends everyone finished suggestions
23 search school waiting repairs majority essential automobile
24 drive almost drizzle certain entertain ourselves windshield
25 time nation reduced pressure condition inspected obstructed

Speed

26 chance family could hours such tank care view help come not
27 owning course there tears when must here rain long trip gas
28 should wipers tires belts they have auto also many they six
29 visit check often quick items level alone ripe them has our

POSTTEST

Repeat the Pretest on page 178 to see how much your skill has improved.

FORMATTING CREDIT MEMORANDUMS
Workbook 187.

A credit memorandum is a form used to let a customer know that a credit (deduction) has been made to his or her account.

To format a credit memorandum:

1. Use the standard format for business invoices.

2. Type the words *Total amount credited* (instead of *Total amount due*) aligned with the *D* in *Description*.

3. Format any adjustments as follows:

Amount credited	75.15
5% Sales tax refund	3.76
Transportation refund	3.45
Total amount credited	82.36

JOB 106-1. CREDIT MEMORANDUM 756
Workbook 189.

[*To*] Alamosa Sports Equipment / 204 Main Street / Alamosa, CO 81101 / [*Credits:*]

10 Racquetball rackets, Model 75H
(handle wrapping defective)
[*Unit price*] 19.50 [*Amount*] 195.00

5 Racquetball gloves, right hand
(elastic torn)
[*Unit price*] 4.75 [*Amount*] 23.75

Amount credited	218.75
Transportation refund	17.50
Total amount credited	236.25

JOB 106-2. CREDIT MEMORANDUM 757
Workbook 189.

[*To*] C & R Sports Inc. / 378 Delaware Avenue, N.E. / St. Petersburg, FL 33703 / [*Credits:*]

3 Fastdart dart boards, 36″
(boards not ordered)
[*Unit price*] 15.65 [*Amount*] 46.95

12 Bullseye darts, #4560
(dart tips damaged)
[*Unit price*] 12.50 [*Amount*] 150.00

Amount credited	196.95
Transportation refund	8.76
Total amount credited	205.71

12-SECOND TIMINGS

Type each line four times, or take four 12-second timings on each line. For each line, type with no more than one error.

5 If the eight men do the work right, they may make a profit. 12
6 We hired six women—you did say six, didn't you?—to check. 12
7 I like to watch her zip through the job with lots of speed. 12

25	30	35	40	45	50	55	60

PRETEST

Take a 5-minute Pretest on lines 8–26. Then circle and count your errors. Use the chart below to determine which lines to type for practice.

8   Resorts have been popular since Colonial times, but it 12
9 was not until the spread of the railroads that the business 24
10 really expanded. Then Americans began to travel to seaside 36
11 resorts, hot springs, spas, and mountain resorts. 46
12   Traditionally, resorts were fancy hotels which offered 58
13 to their clients large rooms, good food, outdoor games, and 70
14 places of interest for both sight-seeing and shopping. The 82
15 resorts at that time were open only during the summertime— 94
16 September was included too—because travel was very hard in 106
17 the cold months. 109
18   Since then, the industry has grown to include not only 121
19 summer resorts but year-round resorts as well. Some of the 133
20 most popular are ski resorts—many of which now remain open 145
21 all year. Some Southern resorts have realized quite a jump 157
22 in popularity; and Hawaii, with its twelve-month season, is 169
23 magnificent with all of those sunny beaches and many scenic 181
24 islands, which appeal to almost everyone. 189
25   With income from other uses, such as conventions, most 201
26 resorts are sound and well-managed businesses. 210

| 1 | 2 | 3 | 4 | 5 | 6 | 7 | 8 | 9 | 10 | 11 | 12 | SI 1.58 |

PRACTICE

In the chart below, find the number of errors you made on the Pretest. Then type each of the designated drill lines four times.

Pretest errors	0–1	2–3	4–5	6+
Drill lines	30–34	29–33	28–32	27–31

Accuracy

27 spread twelve resorts managed business included conventions
28 really scenic popular beaches expanded Southern magnificent
29 places season offered mountain interest everyone popularity
30 Hawaii travel months seaside islands realized traditionally

(Continued on next page)

LESSON 107

GOALS
- To format and to type purchase requisitions and purchase orders.

FORMAT
- Single spacing   60-space line   Tabs as needed

KEYBOARDING SKILLS

Type lines 1–4 once. In line 5, backspace and underscore each underscored word immediately after typing it. Repeat lines 1–4, or take a series of 1-minute timings.

Speed 1 It is easy for them to type this short, brief line of type. 12
Accuracy 2 If we find the precise quiz, just give Bob an exam quickly. 12
Numbers 3 On 10/29/56 we drove 38 miles to Waco and 47 miles to Hico. 12
Symbols 4 Is #47 selling @ $.38 or $.56? It sold for 45¢ (20% less). 12
Technique 5 They _may_ soon _know_ how _good_ they are as _they_ type _the_ work.
| 1 | 2 | 3 | 4 | 5 | 6 | 7 | 8 | 9 | 10 | 11 | 12

12-SECOND TIMINGS

Type each line four times, or take four 12-second timings on each line. For each timing, type with no more than one error.

6 It is their wish to go to the city by auto when they do go. 12
7 Their goal is to do the work by the sixth or eighth of May. 12
8 Their firm is paid to paint half the signs for those towns. 12
   25   30   35   40   45   50   55   60

FORMATTING PURCHASE REQUISITIONS

Purchasing goods or services is a two-step procedure in most companies: First a *purchase requisition* is completed and sent to the purchasing department. Then the purchasing department completes an *official purchase order* and sends it to the supplier.

To format a purchase requisition:

1. Align the fill-ins in the heading with the guide words.
2. Begin typing the body a double space below the ruled line.
3. Visually center the quantity in the *Quantity* column.
4. Begin the description 2 spaces after the vertical rule. Single-space items that take more than one line. Double-space between items.
5. Insert the suggested supplier's name and address as an address block, 2 spaces after the vertical rule.

6. Do not fill in the bottom portion of the form. This will be completed by the purchasing department.

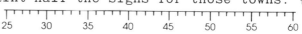

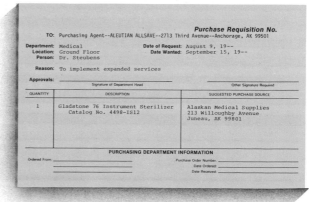

JOB 107-1. PURCHASE REQUISITION

Type and arrange the information below on a purchase requisition, using the illustration above as your guide. Workbook 191.

Purchase Requisition 1116. Mark Grove, Sales Manager, Room 710, needs the following items to renovate the conference room on May 12: 1 Green shag carpet, 14′ × 30′; 13 Baylor office chairs; 1 Parman executive chair; 1 Walnut conference table, 3′ × 20′. Order from Smythe Supplies, 250 Pine, Akron, OH 44302.

JOB 183-1. RECEIPTS

Use the format shown in the illustration on page 298. Receipts were all issued on September 20 to employees of the Paradise Hotel, Honolulu, Hawaii, to repay them from petty cash for expenses they incurred while on the job. Workbook 383.

① Alice Kolokowski — $9.20 for taxi fare for delivering papers to Mr. Kenneth at home.

② Toni Pizzari — $19.50 for

COD package at front desk
③ Alice Kolokowski — $8.60 for Mr. Kenneth's dry cleaning

④ Michael Fung — $26.00 Flowers for Lee banquet

⑤ Kim Mikoko — $19.50 for postage stamps and mailings for Mr. Kenneth.

Formatting Review: Alphabetic File Cards

1. Name on line 2, 4 spaces from left edge of the card.

2. Type the person's last name first, followed by the first name and middle initial or middle name (if any).

3. Type all titles (Ms., Mr., Dr., Mrs.) in parentheses after the name.

4. Tab-indent the other lines 3 spaces, a double space below name.

JOB 183-2. ALPHABETIC FILE CARDS

Format a card for each name listed below. All live in Detroit, MI; so only the ZIP Code is given. But you must be sure to include the city and state on each card. Standard format (see review in margin). Workbook 385, 387.

Mr. Lowell Cramer, 130 Glenville Street, 48215
Dr. Albert E. Etzell, 230 Jefferson Avenue, 48201
Mrs. Ellie Frontino, P.O. Box 2671, 48207
Dr. Janice S. Oshui, 225 Wood Street, 48226
Mr. McGrundy Barnes, 3000 Westchester Avenue, 48219
Ms. Pearl Ordway, 1474 Crescent Avenue, 48208
Mr. Hans Humperdinck, 14 Oswego Boulevard, 48215
Professor Lenora Trenton, 220 Haskell Road, 48213

LESSONS 184/185

GOALS
- To identify how dashes are used while typing sentences.
- To type 42/5'/4e.
- To format two memos, eight checks, and a three-column table from incomplete copy.

FORMAT
- Single spacing   60-space line   5-space tab and other tabs as needed

LAB 22

THE DASH

Type lines 1–4 once. Then repeat lines 1–4 or take a series of 1-minute timings.

1 Our new offices--do you have the address?--are just lovely.   12
2 Here is your assignment--do you recognize the major topics?   12
3 After the explosion--what a blast it was!--the police came.   12
4 She was born in Russia--Kiev, I think--but lives in Quebec.   12
  | 1 | 2 | 3 | 4 | 5 | 6 | 7 | 8 | 9 | 10 | 11 | 12

FORMATTING PURCHASE ORDERS

When a purchase requisition has been approved, the purchasing department completes a purchase order.

To format a purchase order:

1. Use the standard format for invoices.
2. Visually center the catalog number in the column marked "Catalog No."
3. Type the word *Total* aligned with the *D* in *Description*.

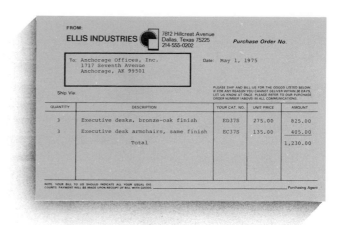

JOB 107-2. PURCHASE ORDER

Type and arrange the information below on a purchase order, using the illustration above as your guide. Workbook 191.

Purchase Order 345. Hanson Supplies Inc., 1248 Meridian Avenue, San Jose, CA 95125. 1 Carpet, Style 8962, 14′ × 30′ @ $6/sq. ft. = $2,520.00; 13 Office chairs, Model 498E @ $45 = $585.00; 1 Executive chair, Model 499EX @ $125 = $125.00; 1 Conference table, Model 50CT @ $454.00 = $454.00. Total = $3,684.00.

LESSON 108

GOALS
- To recognize how semicolons are used in compound sentences while typing.
- To format and to type a statement of account.

FORMAT
- Single spacing   60-space line   5-space tab and as needed

LAB 12

SEMICOLONS IN COMPOUND SENTENCES

Type lines 1–4 once. Then repeat lines 1–4 or take a series of 1-minute timings.

```
1  Ms. Wall is our personnel director; she is now on vacation.   12
2  Jeff must go to Zurich quickly; May is on her way to Zaire.    12
3  Alex's report is due next week; he has nearly completed it.    12
4  Bertha is in charge of this project; give her all my bills.    12
   |  1  |  2  |  3  |  4  |  5  |  6  |  7  |  8  |  9  | 10  | 11  | 12
```

In LAB 7 (page 132), you learned to use a comma before *and, but, or,* and *nor* in compound sentences. When no conjunction is used, place a semicolon between the two independent clauses.

Larry took a bus; Mary went by plane. (No conjunction joins the two independent clauses. A semicolon is needed.)

We have an office in New York; we will have one in Boston soon.

12-SECOND TIMINGS

Type each line four times, or take four 12-second timings on each line. For each timing, type with no more than one error.

```
5  Where in the world can we find an island on which to relax?   12
6  Once the rain began to pour, it just went on and on and on.   12
7  Now is the right time for you to sell the old black trucks.   12
```

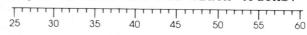

```
25   30   35   40   45   50   55   60
```

LESSON 183

GOALS
- To recognize how dashes are used while typing sentences.
- To format five receipts and eight alphabetic file cards.

FORMAT
- Single spacing   60-space line   Tabs as needed

LAB 22

THE DASH

Type lines 1–4 once. Then repeat lines 1–4 or take a series of 1-minute timings.

```
1  Here is Joan Zinn's paycheck--I signed it--for you to mail.  12
2  We finished all jobs under budget--and we did them quickly.  12
3  Give this to Allen--is he in Room 205?--no later than noon.  12
4  The announcement--he and I are excited!--will be made soon.  12
   |  1  |  2  |  3  |  4  |  5  |  6  |  7  |  8  |  9  | 10  | 11  | 12
```

A question mark or an exclamation point should be used at the end of a question or an exclamation that is set off by two dashes.

> Her proposal—is it really excellent?—will be reviewed today.
> Her proposal—it is really excellent!—will be reviewed today.

Do not capitalize the first word following a dash, even if that word begins a complete sentence. (Exceptions are the word *I*, proper nouns, and proper adjectives.)

5-MINUTE TIMINGS

Take two 5-minute timings on lines 7–25 on page 296.

FORMATTING RECEIPTS AND NEGOTIABLE INSTRUMENTS

To format receipts and negotiable instruments (such as checks and promissory notes):

1. The ruled line should be in the position of the underscore.
2. Backspace the month and date from the end of the ruled date line.
3. Begin all other lines as close to the start of the ruled line as possible.
4. After the name and the amount, fill in the rest of the line with hyphens. Do not space before or after the hyphens.
5. When spelling out amounts of money, capitalize the first word and express cents as a fraction.

```
                                    September 20, 19--
Received from Paradise Hotel----------------
Twelve and 00/100-------------------- Dollars
For taxi fare for delivering Lubetz papers
$12.00                   Alice Kolokowski
```

Take two 1-minute timings on each paragraph. Then take one 5-minute timing on the entire selection. Use single spacing for the 1-minute timings and double spacing for the 5-minute timing.

1'

8   Have you ever been on a fairly long trip by car simply to find   14

9 yourself bored because you did not have much to do? You, the   26

10 passenger, have many options available to minimize boredom.   38

11   One answer to the boredom is to read some books in the car. You   14

12 will find a paperback at the local bookstore; and as you read, you can   28

13 obtain many hours of entertainment and enjoyment.   38

14   But you, a passenger, can do much more than just read. There are   14

15 dozens of activities and games that can be played while you travel;   28

16 magnetic checkers and chessboards can be great fun.   38

17   There are also games where passengers count particular types of   14

18 signs or landmarks, or you might choose to partake in guessing games   27

19 with other passengers. And extra players add fun.   38

20   Therefore, if you are a person who does not quite like riding along   15

21 on an extended trip, plan ahead. Think of all the nice activities you   29

22 and others can participate in while traveling.   38

| 1 | 2 | 3 | 4 | 5 | 6 | 7 | 8 | 9 | 10 | 11 | 12 | 13 | 14   SI 1.42

FORMATTING STATEMENTS OF ACCOUNT

A statement of account summarizes a customer's trans-actions during a specific period (usually a month).

To format a statement of account:

1. Align fill-ins in the heading with guide words.
2. Begin typing the body a double space below the horizontal rule; single-space the body.
3. Visually center the date in the first column. Abbreviate long months. To align numbers on the right, space twice before typing one-digit numbers.
4. Begin items in the Reference column 2 spaces after the vertical rule.
5. Visually center amounts of money in the Charges, Credits, and Balance columns.

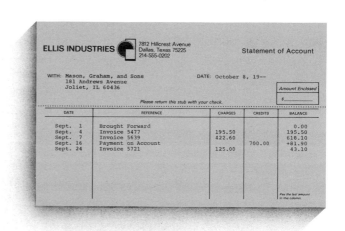

JOB 108-1. STATEMENT OF ACCOUNT
Workbook 193.

[*To*] Red's Sport Shop / West Acres Shopping Center / Fargo, ND 58102

May 1 Brought forward [*Balance*]72.00

    10 Payment [*Credit*]72.00
        [*Balance*]00.00

    15 Invoice 3559 [*Charges*]234.00
        [*Balance*]234.00

JOB 108-2. STATEMENT OF ACCOUNT
Set tabs as needed. Workbook 193.

[*To*] Clarks' Sports Center / South Washington Shopping Center / Grand Forks, ND 58201

July 1 Brought forward [*Balance*]135.50

    15 Invoice 3575 [*Charges*]89.25
        [*Balance*]224.75

    18 Payment [*Credits*]100.00
        [*Balance*]124.75

FORMATTING REVIEW

Business Forms

A. *Purchase Requisitions*

B. *Purchase Orders*

C. *Invoices*

1. Align fill-ins in heading 2 spaces after guide words.
2. Visually center information in number columns.
3. Begin information in description (or word) columns 2 spaces after the vertical rule.
4. Single-space entries; double-space between entries.
5. Align the word *Total* with *D* in *Description*.

JOB 181/2-1. PURCHASE REQUISITION

Standard format. Workbook 377.

Purchase Requisition 4862. To repair Skyway Ski Lift No. 2, Gregg Marshall, maintenance superintendent, needs the following items by January 2:

1   Transfer case gear, S&B #809297
3   Flexible tubing, 25-ft rolls
    Overhaul gasket set, S&B #37-4037W

JOB 181/2-2. PURCHASE ORDER

Standard format. Compute the total. Workbook 377.

Purchase Order 3576. Thor Manufacturing Co., 2041 Hawthorne Blvd., Torrance, CA 90503.

1   Transfer case gear, S&B #809297, for Model 776W @ $295.00 = $295.00
3   Plastic flexible tubing, 25-ft rolls, #33-674-11 @ $79.95 = $239.85
1   Overhaul gasket set, S&B #37-4037W, for Model 776W @ $22.50 = $22.50
    Total

JOB 181/2-3. INVOICE

Standard format. Compute the total amount due. Workbook 379.

[*To*] Skyway Ski Resort / [*Today's date*] / P.O. Box 7 / Vail, CO 81657 / [*Shipped via*] United Parcel Service

1   Transfer case gear, S&B #809297, for Model 776W
    [*Unit price*] $295.00   [*Amount*] $295.00
3   Plastic flexible tubing, 25-ft rolls, #33-674-11
    [*Unit price*] $79.95   [*Amount*] $239.85
1   Overhaul gasket set, S&B #37-4037W, for Model 776W
    [*Unit price*] $22.50   [*Amount*] $22.50
    Total amount due

JOB 181/2-4. PURCHASE REQUISITION

Standard format. Workbook 379.

Purchase Requisition 4869. To expand the Gift Shop at Skyway Ski, Madeline Strom, manager, needs the following items by January 15:

1   Showcase, 8′ × 2′ × 3′—all glass
3   Glass shelves, 8′ × 2′
2   Round display tables, 22″ diameter
4   Revolving display racks, 5′ tall

JOB 181/2-5. PURCHASE ORDER

Standard format. Compute the Amount column and total. Workbook 381.

Purchase Order 3577. Alpine Products, 4720 South Tacoma Way, Tacoma, WA 98409.

1   Decorative showcase, Style #6784, 8′ × 2′ × 3′, all glass with metal trim @ $867.50
3   Glass shelves with beveled edges, 8′ × 2′, @ $88.00
2   Round tables, Style #8407, 22″ diameter, plastic top with metal base, @ $72.60
4   Revolving display racks, aluminum, brown, Style #441R @ $102.50

JOB 181/2-6. INVOICE

Standard format. Compute the Amount column and total. Workbook 381.

[*To*] Skyway Ski Resort / [*Today's date*] / P.O. Box 7 / Vail, CO 81657 / [*Shipped via*] Greyhound Express

400   T-shirts, assorted colors and sizes, with Vail logo
    [*Unit price*] $8.95
250   Ski caps, assorted colors with Vail logo
    [*Unit price*] $10.75
  50   Pairs ski goggles, assorted colors and sizes
    [*Unit price*] $12.60
    Total amount due

LESSON 109

GOALS
- To identify how semicolons are used in compound sentences while typing.
- To format and to type alphabetic file cards.
- To format and to type business mailing labels.

FORMAT
- Single spacing   60-space line   Tabs as needed

LAB 12

SEMICOLONS IN COMPOUND SENTENCES

Type lines 1–4 once. Then repeat lines 1–4 or take a series of 1-minute timings.

```
 1   I may be able to help you with this; Vera may also be free.   12
 2   Yes, Joan types quickly; she is also an expert in spelling.   12
 3   Max Dubron prefers the new procedures; Ella Zeldon doesn't.   12
 4   Ken works in our Dallas office; he may be transferred soon.   12
     |  1  |  2  |  3  |  4  |  5  |  6  |  7  |  8  |  9  |  10  |  11  |  12
```

FORMATTING ALPHABETIC FILE CARDS

Workbook 188.

Names and addresses that are frequently referred to are often kept on 5 by 3 cards for quick reference. If the cards are arranged in alphabetic order by last name, they are called *alphabetic file cards*.

To format alphabetic file cards:

1. Start typing the person's name on line 2, 4 spaces from the left edge of the card.

2. Type the person's last name first, followed by the first name and middle initial or middle name (if any).

3. Type titles such as *Miss, Ms., Mr., Mrs., Dr.,* and *Prof.* in parentheses after the name.

4. Type the address a double space below the name, indented 3 spaces.

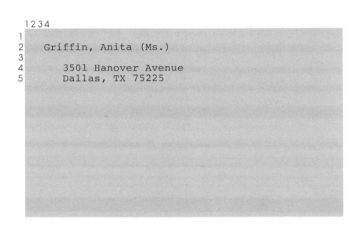

```
1234
1
2    Griffin, Anita (Ms.)
3
4       3501 Hanover Avenue
5       Dallas, TX 75225
```

JOB 109-1. ALPHABETIC FILE CARDS

Type a card for each name in the table below. Standard format. Workbook 195, 197.

INITIATES OF GAMMA EPSILON CHAPTER

November 14, 19--

Dr. Scott Harbison	7730 Idlewood Lane	Dallas, TX 75230
Miss Diane Goertzen	3433 Kaywood Drive	Dallas, TX 75209
Mr. Domingo Andrada	225 Shady Lane	Fort Worth, TX 76116
Ms. Louise Baum	2532 Eastridge Drive	Fort Worth, TX 76117
Dr. Margaret Dodson	7050 Arapaho Road	Garland, TX 75042
Mr. Joseph Yamata	5842 Live Oak Drive	Irving, TX 75061
Mr. Alvin Watson	2407 Greenhill Drive	Mesquite, TX 75150
Mrs. Gloria Tucker	1715 Langdon Road	Mesquite, TX 75149

JOB 109-2. THREE-COLUMN TABLE

Arrange the file cards you typed in Job 109-1 in alphabetic order (by last name). Then type the table above, arranging the names alphabetically. Standard format. Full sheet of paper.

GOALS
- To use dashes correctly while typing sentences.
- To type 42/5'/4e.
- To format two purchase requisitions, two purchase orders, and two invoices.

FORMAT
- Single spacing   60-space line   5-space tab and as needed

LAB 21

Type lines 1–4 once, providing the missing dashes. Edit your copy as your teacher reads the answers. Then retype lines 1–4 from your edited copy.

THE DASH

1 Success that's most important to Victor, Georgia, and Ken.
2 His one aim in life is to possess lots of one thing money.
3 Call Mrs. Max we have her number to adjust the quotation.
4 Dr. Mazzilli she is our physician explained it carefully.

PREVIEW PRACTICE

Type lines 5 and 6 twice as a preview to the 5-minute timings below.

Accuracy
5 each least decade create realize enjoyed started adventures
Speed
6 done golf make work into such land park been good high with

5-MINUTE TIMINGS

Take two 5-minute timings on lines 7–25.

7   There is an amazing wealth of hotel and motel services   12
8 available to the public today. For the thrifty people, the   24
9 budget motel is best. First started in the last decade and   36
10 aimed at quality, these motels have enjoyed a rapid growth.   48
11   Their success has been built upon good use of business   60
12 principles--every inch of space is used to realize the most   72
13 revenue. High occupancy levels and low investment per room   84
14 are combined. The sites chosen as locations are usually in   96
15 less expensive places. In addition, every operating method   108
16 is analyzed and applied so that the least amount of work is   120
17 done.   121
18   For the luxury-loving, there are grand hotels with all   133
19 sorts of recreational activities, such as golf, tennis, and   145
20 swimming. For the fun-loving, there are theme parks, which   157
21 were invented by Walt Disney. These parks create the make-   169
22 believe adventures that range from under the ocean to outer   181
23 space; others attract tourists into such divertissements as   193
24 a land of lions or a park-sized Polynesia--each one of them   205
25 a billion-dollar business.   210

| | 1 | 2 | 3 | 4 | 5 | 6 | 7 | 8 | 9 | 10 | 11 | 12 | SI 1.59 |

FORMATTING BUSINESS MAILING LABELS

When using sheets of labels, type the left-hand labels first; then move the margin stop and type the right-hand labels. Start each name and address 10P/12E from the left edge, and estimate the vertical center for each entry.

```
Ms. Anita Griffin
3501 Hanover Avenue
Dallas, TX 75225
```

JOB 109-3. BUSINESS MAILING LABELS

Type a mailing list for each person in Job 109-2; follow the illustration to the right. Standrd format. Workbook 199.

LESSON 110

GOALS
- To use semicolons correctly in compound sentences while typing.
- To type at least 38/5'/5e.
- To format postal card addresses.

FORMAT
- Single spacing   60-space line   5-space tab

LAB 12

Type lines 1–4 once, providing the missing comma *or* semicolon in each of the compound sentences. Edit your copy as your teacher reads the answers. Then retype lines 1–4 from your edited copy.

SEMICOLONS IN COMPOUND SENTENCES

1 Alex made copies for everyone he mailed them the next day.
2 Katie went to Brazil and she plans to stay there one week.
3 Call Ann quickly or write her a letter explaining my idea.
4 Just file these five or six copies discard all the others.

PRETEST

Take a 5-minute Pretest on lines 13–28 on page 185. Circle and total your errors. Use the chart below to find the number of errors you made on the Pretest. Then type each of the designated drill lines four times.

PRACTICE

Pretest errors	0–1	2–3	4–5	6+
Drill lines	8–12	7–11	6–10	5–9

Accuracy
5 can for security consider exciting different transportation
6 you many examined important needless apartments frustrating
7 well live looking furniture furnished occupancy perspective
8 see all listing following utilities facilities recreational

Speed
9 aspects search should public lease every large live pay you
10 deposit points making access lines kinds might rent how can
11 required proper travel place clear point; list sign pay all
12 points before during after order seems issue must line owns

POSTTEST

Repeat the Pretest (lines 13–28), page 185.

JOB 179-1. INCOMPLETE FIVE-COLUMN BOXED TABLE

Format Job 177-2 on page 292, but arrange the items in column 1 (Food Group) in alphabetic order. Full sheet of paper turned lengthwise. In the subtitle, use last Friday's date. Standard format.

LESSON 180

CLINIC

GOALS
- To improve keyboarding skills on some frequently used symbol keys.
- To type 42/5'/4e.

FORMAT
- Single spacing   60-space line   5-space tab

KEYBOARDING SKILLS

Type lines 1–4 once. Then practice using your shift key as you type line 5. Repeat lines 1–4, or take a series of 1-minute timings.

Speed	1	The six girls held a social to pay for a visit to the lake.	12
Accuracy	2	Paul reviewed the subject before giving Max and Kay a quiz.	12
Numbers	3	The total of 100, 290, 380, 470, and 560 is easy to figure.	12
Symbols	4	I typed receipts for #10, #29, #38, #47, and #56 on Monday.	12
Technique	5	Ruth Mary Zora Paul Rick Kate Dora Jean Ford Lena Alma Kent	

| 1 | 2 | 3 | 4 | 5 | 6 | 7 | 8 | 9 | 10 | 11 | 12

PRETEST

Take two 2-minute timings on lines 6–9, or type them twice to find out which symbol keys are the most difficult for you to type. Keep your eyes on your copy as you type. Circle each symbol in which an error is made.

6	Smith & Blake will lend us $500 at 6% interest if you wish.	12
7	Mr. Bilko wants 59# of sugar @ $1.76, which totals $103.84.	24
8	We got 6 orders @ 18¢, and each one now has a 10% discount.	36
9	Can you find #6887, which has a 6% discount for Reb & Neeb?	48

| 1 | 2 | 3 | 4 | 5 | 6 | 7 | 8 | 9 | 10 | 11 | 12

PRACTICE

Type lines 10–16 three times. Then repeat any of the lines that stress the symbol errors you circled in the Pretest.

¢ and @	10	Brett quoted us 400 @ 8¢, but we asked for 400 @ 5¢, right?
#	11	John claims Order #31 is for 31#, but Order #34 is for 32#.
$	12	Jane has $10; Bob has $29; Ida has $38; and Denny has $470.
% and &	13	Hart & Hill offers a 10% discount; H&H offers at least 15%.
% and &	14	Smith & Lerner offers a 2% discount, or is it Thomas & Roe?
¢ and @	15	Raymond finally closed the deal at 939 @ 7¢, plus 585 @ 6¢.
$	16	Take $1, $29, $38, $47, and $56; now total all the figures.

POSTTEST

Repeat the Pretest to see how much your skill has improved.

5-MINUTE TIMING

Repeat the Pretest/Practice/Posttest routine (lines 5–31) on page 294.

13   Looking for a place to live can be frustrating as well 12

14 as exciting; many different points must be examined before, 24

15 during, and after this search. In order to make what seems 36

16 to be a hazy issue clear, you should make a listing of pros 48

17 and cons for all apartments that you see. Needless to say, 60

18 you should consider important points when making this list; 72

19 you must put each point in proper perspective as well. 83

20   In making your list of pros and cons, quiz yourself on 95

21 the following aspects. How long will you have to travel to 107

22 get to work? If you don't own an auto, how near are public 119

23 transportation lines? Is your apartment furnished, or must 131

24 you provide the furniture? Will you have to pay all of the 143

25 utilities? What kinds of recreational facilities might you 155

26 have access to? Must you sign a lease, or can you just pay 167

27 rent every month? How large a security deposit is required 179

28 prior to your occupancy? How much rent will you pay? 190

| 1 | 2 | 3 | 4 | 5 | 6 | 7 | 8 | 9 | 10 | 11 | 12 | SI 1.39

What Increases Your Accuracy?

Sitting right and not moving.

Typing with fingers ONLY.

Keeping arms and wrists quiet.

Typing steadily, not speedily.

Thinking each letter to yourself.

Keeping your wits about you.

Keeping calm about your errors.

FORMATTING POSTAL CARD ADDRESSES

To format addresses on postal cards, follow the format for small envelopes:

1. Type a return address (if necessary) on line 3, 5 spaces from the left edge.
2. Begin the mailing address on line 12, 20 spaces from the left edge.

Remember to single-space all addresses. Type the city, state, and ZIP Code on one line; leave 1 space between the state name or abbreviation and the ZIP Code.

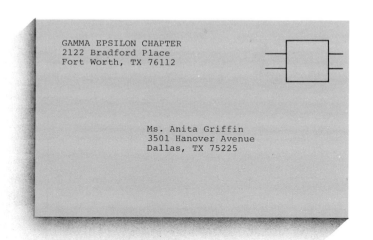

JOB 110-1. POSTAL CARDS

Using the alphabetic file cards you prepared in Job 109-1, send a postal card to each of the new initiates regarding the next meeting. The meeting will take place on February 21, 19--. The return address is Gamma Epsilon Chapter, 2122 Bradford Place, Fort Worth, TX 76112. Standard format. Workbook 201, 203.

Take a 5-minute Pretest on lines 5–23. Then circle and count your errors. Use the chart below to determine which lines to type for practice.

```
 5        Today, with more and more people traveling by airplane    12
 6    around the world, the airlines have become large companies,    24
 7    employing thousands of workers.  These corporations attempt    36
 8    at all times to ensure safety throughout the system.  A big    48
 9    part of this safety effort comes from the pilots.             58
10        Strict medical standards have been established to make    70
11    sure that pilots will have ample physical as well as mental    82
12    abilities.  A pilot must pass regular health exams to avoid    94
13    being grounded.  Since the cost of training jet pilots runs   106
14    around a half million dollars, grounding of a pilot implies   118
15    a loss of revenue for the airlines.                           125
16        Pilots work under a great deal of stress--and get very   137
17    little exercise.  Extreme fatigue can set in and then add a   149
18    lot to health problems.  Some airlines have started classes   161
19    to teach their employees the values of physical fitness.  A   173
20    few offer exercises to strengthen the mind and body against   185
21    the problems that result from jet lag, which does interfere   197
22    with quality performance.                                     202
23        Physical health is vital--prize it.                       210
      |  1  |  2  |  3  |  4  |  5  |  6  |  7  |  8  |  9  |  10  |  11  |  12   SI 1.55
```

In the chart below, find the number of errors you made on the Pretest. Then type each of the designated drill lines four times.

Pretest errors	0–1	2–3	4–5	6+
Drill lines	27–31	26–30	25–29	24–28

Accuracy

```
24  have exams safety result implies against exercise traveling
25  these values revenue extreme physical employees performance
26  pilots stress started million training interfere strengthen
27  great strict classes regular grounded standards established
```

Speed

```
28  mental people world today their with loss that well all the
29  around health since comes prize more work does will jet lag
30  abilities little being which ample pass have body for by it
31  companies ensure avoid vital times runs some half and to of
```

Repeat the Pretest to see how much your skill has improved.

GOALS
- To answer a series of technical questions with a minimum of 80 percent competency.
- To type a credit memo, a report, a letter, and a table.
- To type 38/5'/5e.

FORMAT
- Single spacing   60-space line   5-space tab

TECHNICAL QUESTIONS

Compose and type answers to the following questions. Your goal is to answer 16 or more questions correctly.

Reports

1. Are minutes of a meeting single- or double-spaced?

2. How do you type the page 2 heading of a magazine article?

3. What is the minimum acceptable bottom margin for all pages of a report?

4. What are the minimum acceptable side margins you may use on an unbound report?

5. How do you display a table in a report?

Tables

6. What vertical spacing is used before and after a ruled line in a table?

7. In tables containing figures, do you align the numbers on the left or on the right?

8. How many times do you space vertically between the last line of a table and the final horizontal ruling?

9. What are leaders?

Letters

10. How many pica or elite spaces are used in the line length of a standard business letter?

11. Does a *cc* notation precede or follow an enclosure notation when both are used in a letter?

12. What salutation do you use when using an attention line?

13. What does *bcc* mean?

14. Is a *cc* notation typed on the original copy of a letter so the addressee will see it?

15. In what order would you type the following notations at the bottom of a letter: postscript, reference initials, carbon copy notation, enclosure?

16. How do you type an attention line in letters? on envelopes?

Forms

17. How many spaces are left between the printed guide words and the ones typed on a memo?

18. What is a credit memorandum?

19. What is an invoice?

20. What is a statement of account?

JOB 111-1. REPORT

Standard format. Double-space on plain paper.

LEGAL TYPING   7
   Some Basic Differences in Format   29
   The typing of legal papers can present some   41
problems for the typist who has never before   50
had to prepare such documents. However, a   58
quick review of legal typing should clarify   67
most of the questions.   72

LINE LENGTH   76
   If legal paper is used, the line length is   86
established by the rules on both sides of the   96
paper. A typist should type within these lines,   105
which are placed at 15P/18E spaces from the   114
left edge and 5P/6E spaces from the right   122
edge.[1]   125

PARAGRAPHS AND MARGINS   132
   Paragraph Indentions. A 10-space para-   149
graph indention is used on legal papers.   157
   Top and Bottom Margins. On the first page   176
of the paper, the typist should use a top margin   186
of 12 lines. On other pages a 9-line top margin   196
is used. The bottom margin is always about   205
6 lines.[2]   209
                                                             215

   [1]Alan C. Lloyd et al., Typing 1, General   234
Course, Gregg Division, McGraw-Hill Book   245
Company, New York, 1982, p. 194.   251
   [2]Ibid.   257

3-MINUTE TIMINGS

Take two 3-minute timings on page 288.

FORMATTING REVIEW

Financial Statements

1. *Center vertically.*
2. *Use assigned line length (usually 60, 65, or 70 spaces).*
3. *Money columns 2 spaces apart.*
4. *Leaders between first and second columns.*

JOB 178-1. STATEMENT OF FINANCIAL HIGHLIGHTS

Use your best judgment to format an attractive copy, inserting the current year and last year where indicated.

all caps →

POWEREX CORPORATION
Summary of Financial Results
for the Year Ended December 31, 19-- *insert years*

Summary Items	This Year	Last Year
Operating Revenue	$491,230	$384,951
Income Before Taxes on Income and Minority Interests	57,809	46,252
Provision for Taxes on Income	28,579	23,194
Minority Interest in Earnings of Subsidiaries	5784	383
Net Income - - - - - - - - - - - - - - -	⟨ ⟩	⟨ ⟩	*add and insert totals*
Average number of Common Shares.	23,961	22,085
Earnings per Common Share	1.09	0.91

JOB 178-2. STATEMENT OF FINANCIAL HIGHLIGHTS

Retype Job 178-1; include figures for only the current year so that the financial statement will not be a comparison but simply a statement of the current year. Use your best judgment to format an attractive copy.

LESSON 179

GOALS
- To use dashes correctly while typing sentences.
- To type 42/5'/4e.
- To format one boxed table from incomplete copy.

FORMAT
- Single spacing   60-space line   5-space tab and other tabs as needed

LAB 21

THE DASH

Type lines 1–4 once, providing the missing dashes. Edit your copy as your teacher reads the answers. Then retype lines 1–4 from your edited copy.

1 Call Joe Quink he's with Zenith Axle and get his opinion.
2 Right now at this very minute we have never been happier.
3 Here is your roast beef dinner and for only a few pennies.
4 Are they going to San Francisco or did he say Los Angeles?

JOB 111-2. LETTER

Standard format. Body 63 words (plus 20 words for subject line). Workbook 205–206.

[*Today's date*] / Ms. Sarah Clem / 1183 Cecil {13}
Avenue / San Jose, CA 95128 / Dear Ms. {23}
Clem: / Subject: Banquet Speaker {29}

Thank you for agreeing to be our banquet {38}
speaker for the March 14 annual luncheon. {47}
We look forward to hearing your presentation, {56}
"Future Trends in the Office." {62}

Our luncheon will begin at 12 noon, and the {72}
program is now scheduled to begin at 1:30 {80}
p.m. Luncheon tickets are enclosed for your {89}
use. {90}

Once again, thank you for agreeing to speak {100}
to our group. / Yours truly, / Carl A. Spears / {115}
President / [*Your initials*] / Enclosure / cc: {123}
Andrew Thomas and Joyce Greene / PS: Please {132}
let me know if you have any special equipment {141}
needs for your talk. {145}

JOB 111-3. CREDIT MEMORANDUM

Standard format. Workbook 207 top.

[*To*] Custom Sporting Goods / [*Today's date*] / 290
Cheyenne Avenue, S. / Tulsa, OK 74103 /
[*Shipped*] Trailways Express

6	Ladies' bowling trophies, 18″		
	[*Unit price*] 12.50	[*Amount*]	75.00
2	League championship trophies, 24″		
	[*Unit price*] 18.00	[*Amount*]	36.00
	Amount credited		111.00
	Delivery charge refund		5.37
	Total amount credited		116.37

JOB 111-4. THREE-COLUMN TABLE

Standard format. Double-space on a full sheet of paper.

MAJOR RIVERS IN THE UNITED STATES

Name of River	Miles in Length	Source
Mississippi	2,350	Minnesota
Missouri	2,320	Montana
Yukon	1,770	Canada
Arkansas	1,460	Colorado
Red	1,270	Oklahoma
Columbia	1,240	Canada

LESSON 112

COMPETENCY CHECK

GOALS
- To type at least 38/5'/5e.
- To demonstrate competency in typing a letter, a ruled table, and a purchase order.

FORMAT
- Double spacing   60-space line   5-space tab

PREVIEW PRACTICE

Type each line twice as a preview to the timings on page 188.

Accuracy   1 priorities realistic decisions clothing saving dozens quite
Speed   2 you wage best about budget earner limited without judgments

FORMATTING BOXED TABLES

Use the standard format for ruled tables with this change: Vertical lines between columns are penned in after the table is completed. (Use a ruler to pen in the lines.)

Dollar signs in tables are shown only on the first line and on total lines. Percent signs are repeated on every line of a table if the heading does not clearly indicate that the data is a percentage.

JOB 177-2. FIVE-COLUMN BOXED TABLE

Standard format. Full sheet of paper turned lengthwise. In the subtitle, use last Friday's date.

center column heads

NATURAL FOODS STORES

Food Prices for the Week Ending (Insert date)

Food Group	Previous Week	Current Week	Percent change	Index Value*
Eggs and Dairy	$ 5.65	$ 5.66	+ .18	158%
Fats and Oils	8.37	7.90³	- 5.62 -5.16	180%
Sugar and Swets	4.78	4.99	+ 4.39	231%
Beverges	7.37	7.24	- 1.76	208%
Meats	18.04	17.68	- 2.00	136%
Dry and bakery	4.57	4.40⁸	- 3.72 -1.97	170%
Vegtables	8 7.76	8.56	+10.31 -2.28	186%
TOTAL	$57.54	$56.54	-1.74	183%

*The index value is the current price expressed as a percentage of the prices during the index period, September, 1975.

GOALS
- To identify how dashes are used while typing sentences.
- To format two copies of a Statement of Financial Highlights.

FORMAT
- Single spacing   60-space line   Tabs as needed

LAB 21

THE DASH

Type lines 1–4 once. Then repeat lines 1–4 or take a series of 1-minute timings.

1 Quota systems cost taxpayers double--and Jack can prove it.   12
2 Your costs--if you realize our overhead--are within reason.   12
3 This job should be done--moreover, it should be done right.   12
4 I'll need a few items--slides, slide projector, and screen.   12
| 1 | 2 | 3 | 4 | 5 | 6 | 7 | 8 | 9 | 10 | 11 | 12

30-SECOND TIMINGS

Take two 30-second timings on lines 5–7, or type each line twice.

5 Things seem to happen just right for some persons--when the   12
6 good chance comes along to be seized, they are quick to get   24
7 the exact vision of how the lucky moment can work for them.   36
| 1 | 2 | 3 | 4 | 5 | 6 | 7 | 8 | 9 | 10 | 11 | 12

Take two 5-minute timings on the paragraphs below.

```
3        Can you remember how easy it was when you were younger    12
4   and didn't have to worry about money?  In those years, your    24
5   parents paid for what you needed or what you couldn't quite    36
6   do without; you didn't even have to give a thought to where    48
7   the money had originated.  Now, however, you have dozens of    60
8   places where your limited amount of earnings must be spent.    72
9   Most of us know exactly how much money we can spend, and we    84
10  must make wise decisions and set realistic priorities about    96
11  spending.                                                      98
12       Because you must make these wise, realistic judgments,   110
13  it is best to plan a budget.  You, the wage earner, must be   122
14  careful enough to plan ahead.  Items such as food, housing,   134
15  transportation, and any other necessities must be taken out   146
16  first.  Only after all of these have been taken care of can   158
17  you afford to turn your attention to such items as clothing   170
18  and entertainment.  Then you should also think about saving   182
19  some of that money you worked to earn.                        190
    |  1  |  2  |  3  |  4  |  5  |  6  |  7  |  8  |  9  |  10  |  11  |  12    SI 1.44
```

JOB 112-1. LETTER

Standard format. Body 79 words (plus 20 words for subject line). Workbook 209–210.

[*Today's date*] / Mr. Roger Braum / 2476 Flora 13
Avenue / San Jose, CA 95130 / Dear Mr. 21
Braum: / Subject: July 14 Luncheon 29

It was a real pleasure to learn that you will 38
be our speaker for the July 14 luncheon meet- 49
ing. Your presentation, "The Office of the 57
80s," will be well received by all our members. 67

The enclosed luncheon tickets are for you 77
and your wife. The program will begin at 85
1 p.m., and you will have about 50 minutes in 94
which to give your talk. 99

Thank you again, Mr. Braum, for agreeing 108
to take part in our annual meeting. / Yours 118
very truly, / Ms. Jane R. Windom / President 131
/ [*Your initials*] / Enclosure / cc: Scott Webb / 138
cc: Brenda McDaniel / PS: The overhead pro- 148
jector and screen will be in the room for your 157
presentation. 160

JOB 112-2. THREE-COLUMN TABLE

Standard format. Double-space on a full sheet of paper. 10 spaces between columns.

MAJOR LAKES IN CANADA

Name of Lake	Square Miles	Location
Great Bear	12,275	N.W. Territories
Winnipeg	9,465	Manitoba
Athabasca	3,120	Saskatchewan
Nipigon	1,870	Ontario
Melville	1,133	Newfoundland

JOB 112-3. PURCHASE ORDER

Standard format. Workbook 207 bottom.

Purchase Order 350 / J. R. Company / 1201 Hite Street / Akron, OH 44307 / 4 Three-drawer filing cabinets, Model F330 @ $68.75 = $275.00; 2 boxes File folders, #31862 @ $8.25 = $16.50; 2 boxes Filing labels, #15562 @ $1.65 = $3.30; Total $294.80.

LESSON 177

GOALS
- To recognize how dashes are used while typing sentences.
- To format one 4-column ruled table and one 5-column boxed table from rough-draft copy.

FORMAT
- Single spacing   60-space line   Tabs as needed

LAB 21

THE DASH

Type lines 1–4 once. Then repeat lines 1–4 or take a series of 1-minute timings.

```
1  Our agents--as well as our justice officers--must be ready.   12
2  There is an error in this quiz question--the very last one.   12
3  Large appliances--ranges, washers, and dryers--are on sale.   12
4  That volcano exploded--with a force that rocked two states!   12
   |  1  |  2  |  3  |  4  |  5  |  6  |  7  |  8  |  9  |  10  |  11  |  12
```

As you read this text, note the difference between a typewritten dash (--) and a typeset dash (—).

Dashes share some of the same uses as commas, colons, semicolons, and parentheses. Dashes, however, provide a stronger, more emphatic break and, therefore, should not be overused.

> The Hale project—the one that was canceled—was handled by Al.
> Only one person should be named chairperson—Diana Quinten.

12-SECOND TIMINGS

Type each line four times, or take four 12-second timings on each line. For each timing, type with no more than one error.

```
5  Ida is going to show us the prize--we can't wait to see it.   12
6  Jack is working to make some money for his trip to see her.   12
7  Put your best effort into these tasks--then we can go home.   12
```
```
25    30    35    40    45    50    55    60
```

JOB 177-1. FOUR-COLUMN RULED TABLE

Standard format. Double spacing; full sheet of paper turned lengthwise in the typewriter. Center column headings.

Powerex Safety-Equipment Dealers

City or Town	Dealer	Street Address	ZIP
Hayward, CO CA	Haskells	21030 Mission Blvd.	94541
Buena Park, CA	Keystone	6401 Beach ~~Blvd.~~ Drive	90620
Sacremento, CA	Brody's	2735 Arden Way	95826
Colorado Springs, CO	Appollodorus	2558 Durango Drive	80910
Honolulu, HI	B & C	570 Auahi Street, No. 33	96813
Louisville, KY	Puloski	3718 Bardstown Road	40218
Northampton, ME MA	Ludwig & Sons	246 King Street	02060
Minneapolis, MN	Shaffer	1820 Quentin Avenue (South)	55146
Elmer, NJ	Downs	P.O. Box 51, Route 40	08328
Dallas, TE TX	Shingledecker	1900 ~~South~~ north Lamar	75215

LEVEL

BUSINESS FORMATTING

LESSON 176

GOAL
- To type three tables from handwritten copy in a format of your choice.

FORMAT
- Single spacing   60-space line   Tabs as needed

KEYBOARDING SKILLS

Type lines 1–4 once. Practice using the shift lock in line 5. Then repeat lines 1–4 or take a series of 1-minute timings.

Speed
1 The home row keys are easy to find as you type, type, type.   12

Accuracy
2 Joan saw six azure kites quickly drift by very huge maples.   12

Numbers
3 The party governed during 1910, 1929, 1938, 1947, and 1956.   12

Symbols
4 Los Angeles (California) and Chicago (Illinois) are cities.   12

Technique
5 He TYPES for BIG companies and EARNS a GREAT DEAL of MONEY.

| 1 | 2 | 3 | 4 | 5 | 6 | 7 | 8 | 9 | 10 | 11 | 12

12-SECOND TIMINGS

Type each line four times, or take four 12-second timings on each line. For each timing, type with no more than one error.

6 The man is to make six panels for them and then go to town.   12
7 Jan and Lena got them the right bowl and the six big forks.   12
8 If they handle the work right, the girls may make a profit.   12

25   30   35   40   45   50   55   60

3-MINUTE TIMINGS

Take two 3-minute timings on page 288.

Documents in this unit have been selected to challenge your ability to format tables according to your own judgment. In some jobs you will decide whether to use rules, to single- or double-space, to use leaders, or to use column headings.

JOB 176-1. TABLE
Half sheet of paper.

CALENDAR FOR MS. ORMSDORFF, SAFETY ENGINEER
Safety-Inspection Tour of Branch Plants

September 24	Denver	Great Western Airport Hotel
September 25	Salt Lake City	Hotel Utah
September 26	Los Angeles	Grand Palace Hotel
September 27	Los Angeles	Grand Palace Hotel
September 28	Chicago	Home

JOB 176-2. TABLE WITH FOOTNOTE
5 by 3 card.

MEDICAL DIRECTORS AT BRANCH PLANTS

Dr. Lee Kjelson, Colorado*	303-555-8200
Dr. Margaret Wenner, Utah	801-555-9393
Dr. Carl Zahn, California	213-555-3800

*On leave of absence. Dr. Margaret Tyhonas is Acting Medical Director.

JOB 176-3. TABLE
Half sheet of paper.

FLIGHT SCHEDULE FOR MS. ORMSDORFF
9/24 Flight TWA 68 departs 8:05 a.m., Chicago; arrives 9:28 a.m., Denver
9/25 Flight AA 335 departs 4:33 p.m., Denver; arrives 5:31 p.m., Salt Lake City
9/26 Flight AA 717 departs 5:12 p.m., Salt Lake City; arrives 6:22 p.m., Los Angeles
9/27 Flight TWA 52 departs 9:15 a.m., Los Angeles; arrives 3:10 p.m., Chicago

Level 4 of *Gregg Typing, Series Seven*, continues to focus on the formatting of business documents. In Level 4 you will:

1. Demonstrate keyboarding accuracy and speed on straight copy with a goal of 40 words a minute or more for 5 minutes with no more than 5 errors.

2. Correctly proofread copy for errors and edit copy for revision.

3. Apply production skills in keyboarding and formatting copy for four categories of business documents from six input modes.

4. Complete and compose documents required for a job application sequence.

5. Apply rules for correct use of punctuation, capitalization, and numbers in communications.

LESSONS 113/114

UNIT 19 FORMATTING REPORTS

UNIT GOAL
39/5'/5e

GOALS
- To use semicolons correctly in compound sentences while typing.
- To type a business report from handwritten copy.

FORMAT
- Single spacing   60-space line   5-space tab

LAB 12

SEMICOLONS IN COMPOUND SENTENCES

Workbook 211–212.

Type lines 1–4 once, providing the missing semicolon in each of the compound sentences. Edit your copy as your teacher reads the answers. Then retype lines 1–4 from your edited copy.

1 Jim Mazer is the new manager ask him for more information.
2 This quarter was very rewarding we made a million dollars.
3 Carole gave explicit instructions see her October 12 memo.
4 You and I will discuss this with Bart let's meet at 2 p.m.

"OK" TIMINGS

Type as many "OK" (errorless) timings as possible out of three attempts on lines 5–7. Then repeat the effort on lines 8–10.

5 Those folks who won big money prizes have vexed Jacqueline. 12
6 The four women in the jury box quickly spotted Dave dozing. 24
7 The judge may require the work to be typed with extra care. 36

8 Judy weaves quickly at large beaches for extra prize money. 12
9 Jack swung my ax quite rapidly, chopping five logs by size. 24
10 The next job was quietly sized up by that very good farmer. 36
   | 1 | 2 | 3 | 4 | 5 | 6 | 7 | 8 | 9 | 10 | 11 | 12

PREVIEW PRACTICE

Type lines 11 and 12 twice as a preview to the 5-minute timing on page 191.

Accuracy   11 job good apply future various critical appealing employment
Speed   12 most that have find like also they firm just know must very

1. *Center horizontally and vertically.*

2. *Type the ruled lines (underscores) the exact width of the table.*

3. *Single-space before and double-space after each ruled line.*

4. *End the table with a single line, typed from the left margin to the right margin.*

Leaders in Tables

1. *Use to spread a narrow table to a wider width.*

2. *Precede and follow the rows of periods by 1 blank space.*

3. *Backspace two spaces from the start of the second column to find the point on the scale where the final period will be typed.*

Footnotes in Open Tables

1. *Separate footnote from table by a 10P/12E line.*

2. *Single-space before line, double-space after.*

3. *Indent 5 spaces from left margin.*

4. *Single-space footnotes, double-space between footnotes.*

Footnotes in Ruled Tables

1. *Begin a double space below bottom line.*

2. *Follow Steps 3 and 4 above.*

JOB 175-1. RULED TABLE

Standard format. Full sheet of paper.

MEDIA LIBRARY

Video Tapes on Industrial-Safety Measures

Tape No.	Subject	Minutes
7624	Industrial Safety Is a Must	15
7629	Industrial Safety Means Better Wages	15
7630	Safety and Electric Lights	12
7631	Safety and Floors	12
7632	Safety and Housekeeping	12
7641	Working With Machines	9
7643	Working With Others	9
7657	Knowing About the Law	13

JOB 175-2. RULED TABLE WITH LEADERS

Standard format. Full sheet of paper.

Seminar for Safety Engineers
March 2, 19—

Topics	Speakers
Accident Investigations	W. Schuerle
Eye Protection	S. Cavallo
Fire Prevention	M. Dulac
Injuries	J. Volauski
Inspections	S. Tucci
Safe Job Procedures	K. Allerman
Safety Belts	S. Graham

JOB 175-3. RULED TABLE WITH LEADERS AND FOOTNOTE

Standard format. Half sheet of paper.

Expectation of Life in the U.S.*

Age	Number of Years
0–1	73.3
15	59.7
35	41.0
55	23.5
65	16.4

* 1980 estimates.

Take two 1-minute timings on each paragraph. Then take one 5-minute timing on the entire selection. Use single spacing for the 1-minute timings and double spacing for the 5-minute timing.

```
13      Locating a good job is one of the most critical things   12
14   you'll do in life.  There very well might be dozens of jobs   24
15   that will be appealing to you and for which you have suffi-   36
16   cient training.                                               39

17      A large number of people find good jobs through ads in    12
18   their local newspapers.  The ads may often quote the skills   24
19   and background you need for the positions for which you may   36
20   like to apply.                                                39

21      Friends might also prove to be a good source for hear-    12
22   ing about job openings that exist; they might learn about a   24
23   job that is going to be opening in the future for which you   36
24   could soon apply.                                             39

25      A fourth source for finding out about a new job may be    12
26   the firms that know just which jobs are vacant.  Employment   24
27   firms are excellent at finding out about positions that are  36
28   now in demand.                                                39

29      These are but a few of the various sources that you'll    12
30   use as you look for a job.  It's important to know that you   24
31   must use a number of options to be assured of the very best  36
32   job possible.                                                 39
```

| 1 | 2 | 3 | 4 | 5 | 6 | 7 | 8 | 9 | 10 | 11 | 12 | SI 1.30 |

JOB 113/4-1. BUSINESS REPORT

Standard format. Workbook 213–214.

THE ADVENT OF WORD PROCESSING

By Don Martin

HISTORY

The concept of word processing has been with us for quite a few years, back to the late 1800s when C.L. Sholes from Wisconsin invented the first typewriter for commercial production (1873). The touch system (1889) used on the typewriter was responsible for changing the outlook of the modern office in terms of the amount of work that could be done by a typist who used all the fingers working at the task instead of just two or four fingers. Dictating machines were also responsible for causing rapid changes in the office.

(Continued on next page)

PRACTICE 2

Type lines 20–23 four times.

20 Type page 10 or 29, page 38 or 47, and then page 56 or 100.
21 If you add 10, 29, 38, 47, and 56, the total should be 180.
22 I phoned Rooms 10, 29, 38, and 47 before he phoned Room 56.
23 He assigned us pages 10, 29, 38, 47, and 56 for our lesson.

POSTTEST

Repeat the Pretest on page 287 to see how much your skill has improved.

LESSON 175

UNIT 29 ADVANCED FORMATTING OF TABLES

UNIT GOAL
42/5'/4e

GOALS
- To hyphenate compound adjectives correctly while typing sentences.
- To format three tables from unarranged copy.

FORMAT
- Single spacing   60-space line   5-space tab and other tabs as needed

LAB 20

Type lines 1–4 once, providing the missing hyphens. Edit your copy as your teacher reads the answers. Then repeat lines 1–4 from your edited copy.

COMPOUND ADJECTIVES

Workbook 375–376.

1 Buy these water repellent jackets in finest quality fabric.
2 He likes a wide collar shirt made of high priced materials.
3 Now government owned land may be leased at an amazing cost.
4 Her up to date accounts are excellent low risk investments.

PREVIEW PRACTICE

Accuracy
Speed

Type lines 5 and 6 twice as a preview to the 3-minute timings below.

5 far fact race express advances services benefits technology
6 their with home many lazy they that pay for end own job the

3-MINUTE TIMINGS

Take two 3-minute timings. Circle your errors.

7 It is a well-known fact that progress in understanding 12
8 the human race has fallen far behind the quest for advances 24
9 in science and technology. Employees are taken for granted 36
10 in many offices and shops; and often these workers express, 48
11 in many ways, their frustrations by their behavior--staying 60
12 home from work, using drugs, or being lazy on the job. 71
13 Today many businesses will pay for counseling services 83
14 for workers as part of their health benefits. Employers in 95
15 the end will gain because, if their workers can solve their 107
16 own home problems, they will become more productive and get 119
17 along better with their co-workers. 126

| 1 | 2 | 3 | 4 | 5 | 6 | 7 | 8 | 9 | 10 | 11 | 12 | SI 1.54

Thus, like its predecessors, word processing systems have had great influence on the amount of work produced in the office of today. The completion of more work is made possible through the use of such equipment as the automatic typewriter and the cathode ray tube. Magnetic tape and magnetic card typewriters are able to capture on tape or card all that is placed into the machine and change or delete those words or sections that must be revised before the final copy is typed. The cathode ray tube shows on a screen above the keyboard what is being placed into the storage unit of the typewriter. The keyboard of this machine allows for changes to be made very easily in the text, and these changes are displayed on the screen.

DICTATION EQUIPMENT

Many different kinds of input dictation equipment for word processing are available. You can buy portable units that can be carried away from your desk, and these units are small enough to fit into your coat pocket. A desk-top unit can be purchased from many different suppliers. Many of these units operate with cartridges or cassette tapes; you can dictate, transcribe, or perform both functions on these machines.

Some offices have centralized systems that use private wire connections to all dictators. Sometimes, a telephone system can be used for a word processing dictation system. The number of people capable of using this system at one time is limited only by the number of telephone extensions in use in the office.

SELECTING EQUIPMENT

When choosing input equipment for your word processing center, you should weigh several factors. The cost factor, of course, is very important. Prices will vary greatly, depending on the options and special features you wish to have and the number of units you want. You must decide whether you want a service contract. You must be sure that service can be obtained on short notice and that the people who service your equipment are well trained.

You must set up a training session for all the people who are going to operate the equipment. Find out if the manufacturer will train operators free of

(Continued on next page)

JOBS 173-1 AND 173-2. LETTERS FROM INCOMPLETE COPY

Standard format with indented paragraphs. Use the programmed paragraphs on page 285. Change as many words as you can in the paragraphs so that you are composing some of the letters. If possible, add a paragraph that you compose. Complimentary closing: *Cordially yours*. Use your own name as writer. Title: *Assistant to the Editor*. Workbook 371–374.

1. Address a letter to Ms. Anna Marie Verdi / 745 Kendal / Dearborn, MI 48126. Use paragraphs 1, 6, and 9.

2. Address a letter to Mr. Pierre Dutou / Box 266 / Cornish, ME 04020. Use paragraphs 3, 4, and 7.

LESSON 174

CLINIC

GOAL
- To improve keyboarding skills on the number keys.

FORMAT
- Single spacing   60-space line

KEYBOARDING SKILLS

Type lines 1–4 once. In line 5, practice your space bar technique. Then repeat lines 1–4 or take a series of 1-minute timings.

Speed	1	Nan said she may go back to her job by the end of the week.	12
Accuracy	2	Max placed work before joy and had a zest for quiet living.	12
Numbers	3	Place 10 in group 29, 38 in group 47, but do not assign 56.	12
Symbols	4	An asterisk looks like a star (*); type two more asterisks.	12
Technique	5	Write again . . . and again . . . and again . . . and stop.

| 1 | 2 | 3 | 4 | 5 | 6 | 7 | 8 | 9 | 10 | 11 | 12

PRETEST

Take two 2-minute timings on lines 6–9, or type them twice to find out which number keys are the most difficult for you to type. Keep your eyes on your copy as you type. Circle each digit in which an error is made.

```
6   8123 6110 9102 8972 9019 4327 7286 9413 7283 6089 5369 2648   12
7   8968 9481 7068 9065 0914 2541 7395 7045 5923 8162 7951 5316   24
8   1431 7420 0543 7826 1283 4823 5263 7072 1357 9508 8917 5607   36
9   9065 7084 5603 8954 6250 5613 2364 6051 4378 8942 3145 4703   48
```

| 1 | 2 | 3 | 4 | 5 | 6 | 7 | 8 | 9 | 10 | 11 | 12

PRACTICE 1

* Omit line 10 if your machine does not have a 1 key in the top row.

Type lines 10–19 once. Then repeat any of the lines that stress the digit errors you circled in the Pretest.

```
1   10*  que 173 quo 179 qui 178 quip 1780 quit 1785 que 173 quo 179
2   11   wee 233 wit 285 wow 292 weep 2330 two 529 wet 235 writ 2485
3   12   tee 533 err 344 wee 233 ewe 323 eye 363 peep 0330 ewer 3234
4   13   rye 463 roe 493 rip 480 rot 495 rue 473 pert 0345 ripe 4803
5   14   tot 595 top 590 pot 095 pet 035 pit 085 trot 5495 trip 5480

6   15   yet 635 you 697 yep 630 eye 363 try 546 pity 0856 yore 6943
7   16   rue 473 pup 070 rut 475 out 975 our 974 true 5473 putt 0755
8   17   tie 583 rip 480 pit 085 ire 843 tip 580 pipe 0803 riot 4895
9   18   too 599 woo 299 woe 293 toe 593 top 590 toot 5995 your 6974
0   19   pep 030 pip 080 pup 070 pop 090 pot 095 poor 0994 poet 0935
```

JOB 113/4-1 (Continued)

charge or if you will have to 578
provide your own training. The 584
equipment you buy must be 590
easy to operate by both 594
the dictators and the transcribers. 602

And lastly, be sure that the 609
equipment you buy is flexible 615
and will be able to meet 620
the changes that will take 625
place in your business in the 631
years to come. 634

CENTER SURROUNDINGS 640
Once you know what kind 646
of equipment you are going 651
to buy, you must also decide 657
just where that equipment 662
is going to be placed. What- 668

ever space you choose, you 674
must control the air in the 679
office both for the protection 685
of the equipment and for the 691
comfort of the operator. Is 697
the air too cold or too warm? 703
Is it clean? And does it have 709
the right humidity level? 715

Because of all the typing, 721
reading, handwriting, and edit- 727
ing that are done in a word 733
processing center, it is impor- 739
tant to have the right lighting. 746

Sound must also be controlled 752
so that excessive noise does 757
not affect people's health and 763
performance on the job. 769

LESSON 115

GOALS
- To recognize when exclamation points are used while typing sentences.
- To format and type legal papers.

FORMAT
- Single spacing   60-space line   5-space tab and other tabs as needed

LAB 13

EXCLAMATION POINTS

Type lines 1–4 once. Then repeat lines 1–4 or take a series of 1-minute timings.

```
1  Wow!   Frank Klinger said that my raise will be retroactive!  12
2  It's just amazing!   None of us has ever heard such a story!  12
3  I can't believe it!   I scored six points more than Quentin!  12
4  Yes!   My manager said, "I will close at 2 p.m. on Fridays!"  12
   |  1  |  2  |  3  |  4  |  5  |  6  |  7  |  8  |  9  |  10  |  11  |  12
```

To indicate surprise, disbelief, or strong feeling, place an exclamation point at the end of a statement or sentence.

Congratulations! I wish you success in your new job.
Oh, no! I sent the check to the wrong address!
Hurry! We must be at the airport by 3 p.m.!

LESSON 173

GOALS
- To hyphenate compound adjectives correctly while typing sentences.
- To type 41/5'/4e.
- To format two letters from incomplete copy.

FORMAT
- Single spacing   60-space line   5-space tab

LAB 20

COMPOUND ADJECTIVES

Type lines 1–4 once, providing the missing hyphens. Edit your copy as your teacher reads the answers. Then retype lines 1–4 from your edited copy.

1 She wore an old fashioned dress to the late night jamboree.

2 We enjoy cross country skiing and some big league baseball.

3 Discuss tax free imports as well as up to date zoning laws.

4 It's a well known fact that Val quit working a 12 hour day.

1- AND 5-MINUTE TIMINGS

Take two 1-minute timings on each paragraph. Then take one 5-minute timing on the entire selection. Use single spacing for the 1-minute timings and double spacing for the 5-minute timing.

5   Most successful newspapers are large businesses with a   12

6 big staff and a lot of readers; there are now an increasing   24

7 number of smaller papers, however, whose aim is to focus on   36

8 one community or subject.   41

9   All the aspects of large-scale publishing are involved   12

10 in smaller papers and have the same ingredients: graphics,   24

11 words, and photos--elements that are reflected by the style   36

12 of the writing and layout.   41

13   Advertising is crucial to a newspaper of any size. It   12

14 is the money from advertisements, as well as from the sales   24

15 at the newsstands, that brings in the profits. All the ads   36

16 must be neatly formatted.   41

17   A small, well-produced paper that will serve its local   12

18 public is extremely challenging and rewarding for those who   24

19 are in the business. Newspapers, after all, give all of us   36

20 a vehicle for free speech.   41

21   With novel methods of typesetting and offset printing,   12

22 it is quite feasible for people to start up their own small   24

23 gazette. Even a small-scale venture would require a rather   36

24 large investment, though.   41

| 1 | 2 | 3 | 4 | 5 | 6 | 7 | 8 | 9 | 10 | 11 | 12 | SI 1.51

FORMATTING LEGAL PAPERS

Workbook 215–216.

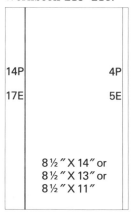

14P 4P
17E 5E

8½″ X 14″ or
8½″ X 13″ or
8½″ X 11″

Legal paper has a double vertical line ruled 14P/17E spaces from the left edge and a single vertical line 4P/5E spaces from the right edge. To format copy on legal paper:

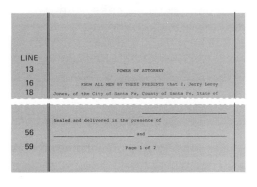

1. Set margin stops 2 spaces inside the vertical ruled lines.
2. Center the title of the document between the margins.
3. Indent paragraphs 10 spaces.
4. Double-space unless directed to do otherwise.
5. Maintain a top margin of 12 blank lines on the first page, 9 blank lines on others.
6. Center page numbers between the margins about 6 lines from the bottom of the page. The phrase to use is "Page 1 of 3," "Page 2 of 3," and so on. Omit the page number from a one-page document.

POWER OF ATTORNEY

A power of attorney gives one person the power to act as an agent, or proxy, for another.

JOB 115-1. POWER OF ATTORNEY

Standard format. Workbook 217.

POWER OF ATTORNEY ↓3 10
KNOW ALL MEN BY THESE PRESENTS 20
that the undersigned does hereby constitute 28
and appoint Jan R. Heinz, James R. Espinoza, 37
and Kyle R. Moen, and each of them, the true 46
and lawful attorneys and proxies of the un- 55
dersigned, with full power of substitution, and 64
revocation for and in the name, place, and 73
stead of the undersigned, to vote upon and act 82
with respect to all the shares of Common Stock 92
without par value of HENDERSON PROD- 99
UCTS, INC., standing in the name of the 107
undersigned on the books of the Company as 115
at the time of the meeting, at the Scheduled 125
Meeting of the Stockholders of the Company 134
to be held at the LeBaron Hotel in Dallas, 142
Texas, on Thursday, March 21, 19--, at 10:00 151
a.m. and at any and all adjournments thereof, 160
with all the powers the undersigned would 168
possess if personally present, hereby ratifying 178
and confirming all that said attorneys and 186
proxies or any of them shall do or cause to be 196
done by virtue hereof. 201
WITNESS the hand and seal of the under- 210
signed this   day of   , 19 219
↓3 227

BILL OF SALE

A bill of sale is an agreement by which one person agrees to sell a piece of personal property to another.

JOB 115-2. BILL OF SALE

Standard format. Workbook 219.

BILL OF SALE ↓3 7
KNOW ALL MEN BY THESE PRESENTS 16
That I, Grace Ann Roth, of 548 Blue Jay 24
Drive, Flint, Genesee County, State of Mich- 33
igan, party of the first part, for the sum of Six 43
Thousand Dollars ($6,000), to me in hand 51
paid, at or before the ensealing and delivery 61
of these presents by James Earl Grant, of 247 70
Cedar Street, Ingham County, State of Mich- 78
igan, party of the second part, do sell and grant 89
and convey unto the said party of the second 99
part my 1982 Buick Regal, serial number 106
KT1038-56-47-29S. 110
TO HAVE AND TO HOLD the same unto 118
the said party of the second part forever. And 128
I do covenant and agree to defend the sale of 137
the said automobile against all and every 145
person. 147
IN WITNESS WHEREOF, I have hereunto 155
set my hand and my seal on the sixth day of 164
June in the year of one thousand nine hundred 173
and 175
↓3
_____ 183
↓2 188
Sealed and Delivered
in the Presence of ↓3 191
_____ 197

12-SECOND TIMINGS

Type each line four times, or take four 12-second timings on each line. For each timing, type with no more than one error.

```
5  Sue said the five girls can swim across the lake with ease.  12
6  Please take two of these big boxes down to the post office.  12
7  May he go to the game with you, or do you have other plans?  12
```

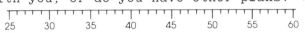

```
25    30    35    40    45    50    55    60
```

FORMATTING PROGRAMMED PARAGRAPHS FOR FORM LETTERS

To give form letters greater personalization and variety, and at the same time to prepare letters quickly, many companies develop a variety of opening, middle, and closing paragraphs for each type of form letter. The originator or writer merely chooses the appropriate paragraphs and gives this information to the typist along with the name and address of each person who is to receive that letter.

Lively Arts magazine, for example, receives many applications for jobs for staff writers. If no openings are available, the originator selects from the numbered paragraphs below the three paragraphs that will make up each response. In addition, the originator selects a complimentary closing. The paragraph numbers, the desired closing, and the applicant's name and address are all then sent to the typist.

JOBS 172-1 TO 172-4. FORM LETTERS

Prepare four form letters from standard paragraphs. Closing: *Sincerely, Amanda T. Brown, Personnel Director.* Workbook 363–370. Body varies.

1. Address a letter to Ms. Tina Parker / 721 Winebiddle Street / Baton Rouge, LA 70805. Use paragraphs #2, #6, and #8. (81 words)
2. Address a letter to Mr. Abraham C. Clark, 920 Main Street / Kansas City, MO 70805. Use paragraphs #1, #4, and #7. (103 words)
3. Address a letter to Ms. Doris Davella / 450 West Montrose Street / Meriden, CT 06450. Use paragraphs #3, #5, and #8. (73 words)
4. Address a letter to Dr. Marshall Oliver / U.S. 31 South / Berrien Springs, MI 49103. Use paragraphs #1, #6, and #9. (74 words)

Opening Paragraphs

1. Thank you for thinking of <u>Lively Arts</u> as a magazine for which you would be interested in working. There are many exciting careers in the publishing business for people with talent and ambition.
2. We have received your letter of application, and we thank you for thinking of <u>Lively Arts</u> as the magazine with which you would like to begin your publishing career.
3. Your letter of application has been reviewed by our editorial staff and by our graphic arts staff.

Middle Paragraphs

4. There are no openings for writers at the present time. However, we will keep your letter of application in our active files; if an opening occurs in the next few months, we will certainly contact you.
5. We do not have a need for new writers now. We hope, however, to expand our advertising department in a few months if our sales continue to grow.
6. At the present time, we have no openings for staff writers. We are, however, impressed with your résumé, and we hope that you will not be discouraged.

Closing Paragraphs

7. We hope that you will continue to pursue your ambition to be a magazine writer. You have excellent credentials, which will be a great asset to you as you search for a promising position.
8. Why not give us a call in three or four months if you are still interested in seeking employment in our advertising or creative arts departments?
9. Our best wishes to you for success in locating a job that meets your expectations.

LESSON 116

GOALS
- To identify when exclamation points are used while typing sentences.
- To format a last will and testament and a resolution.

FORMAT
- Single spacing   60-space line   10-space tab and center tab

LAB 13

EXCLAMATION POINTS

Type lines 1–4 once. Then repeat lines 1–4 or take a series of 1-minute timings.

```
1  Hurry!  To mail a dozen orders today, we must work quickly.   12
2  No!  Jo will not change her decision regarding this matter.   12
3  That was the most exciting basketball game Flo ever played!   12
4  Quick!  Look at that pretty rainbow across the eastern sky!   12
   |  1  |  2  |  3  |  4  |  5  |  6  |  7  |  8  |  9  |  10  |  11  |  12
```

LAST WILL AND TESTAMENT

A last will and testament is a document that enables people to ensure that their belongings are distributed as they wish after they die.

JOB 116-1. WILL
Standard format (see page 194). Workbook 221, 223.

```
                  LAST WILL AND TESTAMENT                    14
                          OF                                 17
                   Carolyn A. Johnson  ↓3                    30
        I, Carolyn Ann Johnson, residing in the City of Dayton,   45
   County of Hennepin, State of Minnesota, do hereby make and declare   58
   this to be my Will and Testament, hereby rescinding all former Wills   73
   and Codicils by me at any time made.                     80
        FIRST:  I hereby direct that all of my just debts and   92
   funeral expenses be paid out of my estate as soon as practicable after   106
   my death.  I further direct that my executor, hereinafter named,   119
   defend any claim against my estate.                       126
        SECOND:  I hereby appoint my Husband, Charles Duane   138
   Johnson, as sole executor of my estate; and I direct that no bond   150
   be required of him in performing these duties.            161
   THIRD:  I hereby give and bequeath to my beloved Husband,   173
   Charles Duane Johnson, all automobiles, books, china, clothing,   186
   fixtures, furniture, glass, household goods and supplies, jewelry, linen,   201
   ornaments, plaques, silverware, tapestries, and appliances that I   214
```
(Continued on next page)

JOB 171-1. (Continued)

Outdoor magazine is proud to award you this all-expenses-paid vacation, and we hope that you are looking forward to joining the other 71 highschool students across the country who were also winners. 61 / 68 / 76 / 83 / 91 / 94

no ¶ You have been assigned to attend during the week of [*allow 14 blank spaces here to insert the date*]. Later we will send you all the details concerning your travel plans, equipment, 100 / 107 / 109 / 116 / 124

and type of clothing you should bring. the group leaders at big Branch have planned for you an exciting shedule of mountain climbing, horse back riding, and white-water rafting. in the meantime, we hope you will read the articles about the camp, which will appear monthly in Outdoor Magazine. / Sincerely, Bruno T. Di Sibio / editor-in-chief / [*Your initials*] 130 / 138 / 146 / 149 / 153 / 160 / 168 / 179 / 200 / 207

FORMATTING INSERTS ON FORM LETTERS

To fill in the date, inside address, and salutation on a form letter, follow these steps:

1. Type the date at the center, using standard format.
2. Space down to the first line of text, and align the copy vertically and horizontally.
3. Count the total lines—usually 6—that you will need for the inside address (3 lines plus 1 blank) and the salutation (1 line plus 1 blank).
4. Roll the copy back the number of lines you counted in Step 3, and type the information. If you have a machine with vertical half-spacing, make sure you roll back 2 clicks for every line determined in Step 3.

JOB 171-2. FORM LETTER INSERTS

Address the letters you prepared in Job 171-1 to the people listed below. Add a personalized salutation to each letter, and insert the date in paragraph 3.

1. Harvey Cepekski, P.O. Box 1131, South Gate, CA 90280. [*Insert*] July 1–7.
2. Victoria Johnson, 7456 West Newberry Road, Wichita, KS 67213. [*Insert*] July 8–14.
3. Peter Schmitt-Matzen, 4201 Jacques Street, Richmond, VA 23230. [*Insert*] July 15–21.
4. Sally Ramando, 115 West Crawford Street, Dalton, GA 30720. [*Insert*] July 22–28.
5. Clifford Griffith, 102 Dominion Drive, Westlake, OH 44145. [*Insert*] July 22–28.

LESSON 172

GOALS
- To identify compound adjectives while typing sentences.
- To format form letters from programmed paragraphs.

FORMAT
- Single spacing   60-space line   5-space tab

LAB 20

COMPOUND ADJECTIVES

Type lines 1–4 once. Then repeat lines 1–4 or take a series of 1-minute timings.

1 Joan Mendez signed a two-year contract with Vickers Metals.   12
2 Al's municipal-bond investments give him a tax-free income.   12
3 Doctors use X-ray treatment to cure some kinds of sickness.   12
4 Fourth-quarter sales for many high-priced items have risen.   12
| 1 | 2 | 3 | 4 | 5 | 6 | 7 | 8 | 9 | 10 | 11 | 12

JOB 116-1 (Continued)

may posess at the time of my death, together with all my insurance 227

policies there on. All the rest of my estate, of whatever kind, I 240

bequeath and give to my beloved Husband, Charles Duane Johnson. 253

FOURTH: I direct that my Husband, Charles Duane 264

Johnson, shall not be required to furnish any security, unless 279

contrary to any law; nor shall he be liabel for loss, damage, or 292

destruction of said property. 298

IN WITNESS WHEREOF, I have here unto set my hand and 309

seal this fifteenth day of March, in the year one thousand nine 322

hundred and eighty-one. 327

_____ 337

THE ABOVE INSTRUMENT, consisting of two pages, was 352

subscribed by Carolyn Ann Johnson in our presence and was acnowl- 365

edged by her to each of us; and she at the same time declared the 378

above to be her Last Will and Testament; and we, at her request, 391

in her presence and in the presence of each other, have hereunto 404

signed our names as hereto witnesses. 412

_____ residing at _____ 427

_____ residing at _____ 442

_____ residing at _____ 457

Page 2 of 2

(Typist: Don't forget to add page number to first page.)

JOB 116-2. RESOLUTION

Standard format. Use plain paper. Copy is unedited and unarranged; make changes and corrections as you type.

R E S O L U T I O N

WHEREAS Ralph Marshall Thompson is retiring from her position as Chairman of the Business Department at Moore High School after having served this comunity for a total of twenty years; and

WHEREAS he devoted all his efforts to provide the students of Moor High High School with a highly credable and worthwhile start on careerrs of there onw, and all the while he has acted in a selfless and generos manner in his actions; and

Whereas he has given generously of himself in the encouragment and assistance of all those who were fortuntae enough too work with her personnally, to the end that all the teachers and all his peers have learned and gained much from this wise and gentel person; and

WHEREas he has proved himself a wise and discerning leader, and a men endowed as much with openess of heart and hand as with wisdom, so that his name is a legend in this school and that he is loved for what he is more then for what he has done; therefore be it

RESOLVED, that the faculty of the Business Department, the entire administrative staff at Moore High School, and the members of the School Board do, for his devotion to education and to this school system in which he has worked for the passed twenty years, commend

RALPH MARSHALL THOMAS

LESSON 171

GOALS
- To recognize compound adjectives while typing sentences.
- To format form letters with inserts.

FORMAT
- Single spacing   60-space line   5-space tab

LAB 20

COMPOUND ADJECTIVES

Type lines 1–4 once. Then repeat lines 1–4 or take a series of 1-minute timings.

1   Henry just sent various duty-free imports by quick express.   12
2   The board of directors held a high-level conference Friday.   12
3   Please prepare an up-to-date report for the talk in Zurich.   12
4   The owner said that she wants to erect a 50-story building.   12
    | 1 | 2 | 3 | 4 | 5 | 6 | 7 | 8 | 9 | 10 | 11 | 12

A compound adjective—two or more words joined to modify a noun—is usually hyphenated when it goes before a noun but not hyphenated when it follows a noun: a *well-known* actor (**but:** an actor who is *well known*), an *up-to-date* study (**but:** a study that is *up to date*). Exceptions are proper adjectives (a *New York* firm, the *United States* position) and very commonly used compounds (a *high school* teacher).

"OK" TIMINGS

Type as many 30-second "OK" (errorless) timings as possible out of three attempts on lines 5–7. Then repeat the effort on lines 8–10.

5   Paul reviewed the subject before giving Kay and Max a quiz.   12
6   Jasper quietly viewed the next game of checkers with Buzzy.   24
7   Ken promptly requested five dozen jugs of wax for the club.   36

8   Max had a zest for quiet living and placed work before joy.   12
9   With all kinds of gripes, Buz rejected every required exam.   24
10 Zeke quietly placed five new jumping beans in the gray box.   36
    | 1 | 2 | 3 | 4 | 5 | 6 | 7 | 8 | 9 | 10 | 11 | 12

FORMATTING FORM LETTERS

When one message is to be sent to many people, form letters are very effective. The form letter can be typed without the date, inside address, and salutation and copies can then be printed. The typist can then add the date, inside address, and salutation to each letter.

Word processing equipment, often called *text editing* or *automatic* typewriters, can be used for form letters.

The letter is recorded while it is keyboarded, and then the equipment "plays back" the recording at high speeds. Codes at key places allow the typist to include the date, inside address, salutation, and any other "personalized" information.

To format the form letter, allow space for the date, inside address, and salutation. Begin the body of the letter on line 26.

JOB 171-1. FORM LETTER

Standard format. Begin on line 26. Make four carbon copies for use in Job 171-2. Body 137 words. Workbook 353–362.

Congratulations! You are a winner   7

in the Bold journey contest sponsored   15

by Outdoor Magazine. As you know, you   29

have qualified for to attend the the   35

Outdoor Adventure camp this summer at   42

Big Branch, Uah.   46

(*Continued on next page*)

LESSON 117

GOALS
- To use exclamation points correctly while typing sentences.
- To type at least 39/5'/5e.
- To format a legal contract.

FORMAT
- Single spacing   60-space line   5-space tab and other tabs as needed

LAB 13

Type lines 1–4 once, providing the missing exclamation points. Edit your copy as your teacher reads the answers. Then retype lines 1–4 from your edited copy.

EXCLAMATION POINTS

1 Be careful. It is difficult to see very well in this haze.

2 Work quietly. Do not make noise. You will disturb others.

3 No. Daren cannot fix all these machines in just four days.

4 Great. Paul completed the project weeks ahead of schedule.

1-AND 5-MINUTE TIMINGS

Take two 1-minute timings on each paragraph. Then take one 5-minute timing on the entire selection. Use single spacing for the 1-minute timings and double spacing for the 5-minute timing.

1'

5   Today, a quick way to get from one place to another is   12

6 by plane. There are many airlines from which to select for   24

7 your flight. Airlines throughout the country provide daily   36

8 service to all.   39

9   If you are going to fly by airplane for the very first   12

10 time, you should contemplate arriving at the terminal about   24

11 an hour before your plane will depart so you can check your   36

12 extra baggage.   39

13   When flying on a large aircraft, you may choose to sit   12

14 in a smoking seat or nonsmoking seat. You can ask a ticket   24

15 agent for your preference when you are checking in for your   36

16 airline flight.   39

17   Would slight changes in air pressure affect your ears?   12

18 If increased pressure causes your ears to plug, chew gum or   24

19 some other substance so that your ears stay open during the   36

20 entire flight.   39

21   If you are flying across country or on some other long   12

22 trip, bring along something to read such as a magazine or a   24

23 new book. Or you might read some of the magazines that the   36

24 airline offers.   39

| 1 | 2 | 3 | 4 | 5 | 6 | 7 | 8 | 9 | 10 | 11 | 12   SI 1.33

FORMATTING LISTS IN LETTERS

To format a list in the body of a letter, follow these steps:

1. Block-center the list.

2. Double-space before and after the list.

3. Add 20 words to the body count for the special display.

JOB 170-1. LETTER WITH LIST

Standard format. Workbook 349–350. Body 103 words.

[Today's Date] / Mr. I. G. Skaff, Jr. / 373 West Shore Drive / Wantagh, NY 11793 / Dear Mr. Skaff, / For under $6 — less than an advertisement in your local newspaper — you can reach over 1 million readers in New York City and the surrounding areas to sell numerous items you no longer need or want, such as an automobile or electric appliance.

If you're trying to sell your house, you certainly will want to take advantage of the opportunity to reach as many prospective buyers as possible.

The Sunday New York Press has classified advertisements that get results. For a real time-saver, call one of these locations:

New York   212-555-9300
Nassau   516-555-5000
Suffolk   516-555-8100

Why not telephone us today while you are thinking about it? / Yours truly, / Suzanne Regina / Director of Advertising / [your initials]

JOB 170-2. LETTER WITH LIST

Standard format. Workbook 351–352. Type the letter in Job 170-1, and make the following changes.

Addressee: Mr. and Mrs. Francis Blackwood, 3535 Garden Drive, White Plains, NY 10604.

New Jersey   201-555-3090
Westchester   914-555-3600
Connecticut   203-555-7700

A legal contract is an agreement between two or more parties. It is usually in
typed format, and it is enforceable by law.

JOB 117-1. LEGAL CONTRACT
Standard format. Workbook 225, 227.

EMPLOYMENT C O N T R A C T   12

        THIS CONTRACT, ~~made and~~ signed on this (10th) day of June,   26

by and between ^the firm of^ Crane and Garth, of 7/01 Rome Street, Flushing, New   42

York, Party of the first part, and Ms. Erma Ostlund, 628 HighBluff   55

Road, Portland, Maine, party of the ~~first~~ ^second^ part.   65

        Article 1. The party of the second party covenants and   77

agrees to and with the party of the first party, to represent the   90

party ^of the first part^ as agent of the firm in the State of Maine for the period of 105

(1) year, or twelve (12) months, beginning on June 2/0 and ending (1)   119

year hence on June 19; and the (party)(said) of the second part does   132

agree to perform all the duties subject to this employment, to in-   145

clude, among others, attending District Sales Meetings heretofore   158

scheduled for the months of July, august, march, and may.   170

        ARTICLE 2. The said party of the first part covnants and   183

agrees to pay the ^said party of the^ second part for the performance of those duties   200

the sum of fifteen thousand three hundred dollars ($15,300), in   212

equal ^monthly^ installments of One Thousand Two Hundred Seventy-Five Dollars   228

($1,275), to be paid upon the ~~fifth~~ ^first^ day of each ^calendar^ month, starting   242

with ~~July~~ ^august^ 1; plus a comission of nine percent (9%) of the annual   255

sales in thta state over the average of the 3 three predcing ^ceding^ years.   269

        In Witness Thereof, the parties ^to this contract^ have, in the presents   284

of each other, hereunto set there ^ir^ hands and seals, the day and   297

year first written above.   302

Party of the First Part: Party of the second part: 314

_____   _____ 329
D. L. Wilde, Vice President   Erma Ostlund   339

_____   _____ 354
Witness to Signature   Witness to Signature   365

JOB 169-2. LETTER WITH INSERTS

Type the letter in Job 169-1, and address it to Addressee No. 2. At the places indicated, insert the name and station call letters of Addressees No. 1 and No. 3. Standard format. Workbook 345–346.

JOB 169-3. LETTER WITH INSERTS

Type the letter in Job 169-1, and address it to Addressee No. 3. At the places indicated, insert the name and station call letters of Addressees No. 1 and No. 2. Standard format. Workbook 347–348.

LESSON 170

GOAL
- To format from handwritten copy two business letters with special inserts.

FORMAT
- Single spacing   60-space line   5-space tab

KEYBOARDING SKILLS

Type lines 1–4 once. Then concentrate on your space bar technique in line 5. Repeat lines 1–4, or take a series of 1-minute timings.

Speed   1 Show her what a nice day it is so that she may take a walk. 12
Accuracy   2 The many jovial men expressed a quick welcome to big Fritz. 12
Numbers   3 Those five passengers are 10, 29, 38, 47, and 56 years old. 12
Symbols   4 Write to A/B/C Ltd., Rube & Dodd, and Hill's Inc. for bids. 12
Technique   5 q z p / w x o . e c i , r v u m t b y n a ; s l d k f j g h
                | 1 | 2 | 3 | 4 | 5 | 6 | 7 | 8 | 9 | 10 | 11 | 12

1- AND 5-MINUTE TIMINGS

Take two 1-minute timings on each paragraph. Then take one 5-minute timing on the entire selection. Use single spacing for the 1-minute timings and double spacing for the 5-minute timing.

6   Would you like to write for a magazine? The first and most   13
7   important requirement for staff writers is knowing how to type; most 27
8   successful journalists and other writers compose right at the machine. 41

9   Composing on the typewriter saves time. When a writer types his   14
10 or her first draft of an article, the writing can be corrected easier than 29
11 copy in script. Final copies of a manuscript must be typed.   41

12 Learning to use the typewriter as a tool requires some practice and 15
13 real desire. Begin first by expressing simply an idea or thought you 29
14 have about some topic. Try to write a short paragraph or two.   41

15 Once you have mastered typing your thoughts, you might decide   13
16 that you ought to pursue a career in writing. Today writers with   27
17 talent can be utilized and appreciated in many kinds of business   40
18 offices.   41

19 If you want magazine editors to read your writings, be sure to   14
20 format your copy in manuscript form. Also write an introductory   27
21 letter. Naturally, you will edit your work so that there are no errors. 41
    | 1 | 2 | 3 | 4 | 5 | 6 | 7 | 8 | 9 | 10 | 11 | 12 | 13 | 14 SI 1.50

LESSON 118

CLINIC

GOALS
- To practice using the number keys on which more drill is needed.
- To build skill in typing numbers.
- To type 39/5'/5e.

FORMAT
- Single spacing   60-space line   5-space tab

KEYBOARDING SKILLS

Type lines 1–4 once. Then do what line 5 tells you to do. Repeat lines 1–4, or take a series of 1-minute timings.

Speed   1 She paid Laurie to fix the ivory box that the visitor made.   12
Accuracy   2 A frozen bird squawked vigorously as Joseph coaxed him out.   12
Numbers   3 Players 29, 38, 47, and 56 all scored 10 points last night.   12
Symbols   4 On 1/31 we received a 9% raise, from $1,200/week to $1,308.   12
Technique   5 Strike your return key after typing each word in this line.
               | 1 | 2 | 3 | 4 | 5 | 6 | 7 | 8 | 9 | 10 | 11 | 12

PRETEST

Take a 2-minute timing on lines 6–9, or type them twice to find out which number keys are the most difficult for you to type. Keep your eyes on your copy as you type. Circle each digit where an error was made.

6 4703 6051 8954 5607 1283 7826 5316 0914 9065 7283 9413 8972   12
7 3145 2364 5603 8917 4823 0543 7951 2541 7068 6079 7286 9012   24
8 8942 5613 7084 9508 5263 7420 8162 7395 9481 5369 4327 6110   36
9 4378 6250 9064 1357 7072 1431 5923 7045 8968 2648 9019 8123   48
   | 1 | 2 | 3 | 4 | 5 | 6 | 7 | 8 | 9 | 10 | 11 | 12

PRACTICE

Type lines 10–19 once. Then repeat any of the lines that stress the errors you circled in the Pretest.

1   10 I have 1 tulip, 1 rose, 11 zinnias, 11 violets, and 1 iris.
2   11 We donated 2 quarters, 2 dimes, 22 nickels, and 22 pennies.
3   12 When multiplying 3 times 13, we get 39; 3 times 3 equals 9.
4   13 Study page 44 in Chapter 4 and read page 444 in Chapter 14.
5   14 The mileage between cities was 5, 45, 85, 95, 125, and 165.
6   15 On 6/6/76 and 6/16/76 we sold 66 units of Item 66 for $666.
7   16 Series 7 was used in 77 high schools in the area in 7/7/82.
8   17 On the 18th we bowled scores of 88, 118, 181, 188, and 208.
9   18 Their winning numbers are 9919, 9929, 9939, 9949, and 9959.
0   19 The metric system is founded on tens: 10, 20, 30, 40, etc.

POSTTEST

Repeat the Pretest to see how much your skill has improved.

GOALS
- To hyphenate compound nouns correctly while typing sentences.
- To format three business letters with inserts.

FORMAT
- Single spacing   60-space line   5-space tab

LAB 19

Type lines 1–4 once, providing the missing hyphens. Edit your copy as your teacher reads the answers. Then retype lines 1–4 from your edited copy.

COMPOUND NOUNS

1 Let's have one more run through before the final rehearsal.
2 Can they have a get together next week and discuss the job?
3 Ken's supper dance next evening may be quite an eye opener.
4 Jan Zorn, a senior vice president, gave a press conference.

FORMATTING INSERTS IN LETTERS

Sometimes the originator of a letter (the person sending the letter) can use the same copy for several letters simply by adding some information in the body of the letter and changing the inside address and salutation.

JOB 169-1. LETTER WITH INSERTS

Format the letter shown below to Addressee No. 1 and insert (at the points indicated in the letter) the name and station call letters of Addressees No. 2 and No. 3. Standard format (see page 265). Workbook 343–344. Body 154 words.

Addressee No. 1	**Addressee No. 2**	**Addressee No. 3**
Mr. Ramon Santiago	Ms. Georgia Boggs	Ms. Makiko Chun-Sun
Station Manager	News Director	Editorial Director
WTAM-TV	WKAN-TV	WFTL-TV
6100 Dodge Boulevard	920 Ocean Drive	700 Sunrise Boulevard
Hollywood, FL 33022	Miami, FL 33101	Ft. Lauderdale, FL 33305

[*Today's date*] / [*Use inside address of Addressee No. 1.*] / Dear [*Insert name*]:

I am writing to invite you to serve as a judge for a public speaking contest for students from Florida high schools. This meeting of the state finalists, called Florida Speak-Out, will be sponsored by the <u>Miami Daily</u> on Saturday, March 20. We are also inviting [*insert name and station call letters of Addressee No. 2*] and [*insert name and station call letters of Addressee No. 3*] to serve with you.

The contest will be held at Orlando College from 9 a.m. to 4 p.m., and the state winners will go on to the national competition in Washington, D.C., in April.

This activity has been one of the most successful educational projects we have ever sponsored. Last year more than one hundred young people from across the state competed for honors.

Since you have always been interested in public speaking and have a successful career in the field of television broadcasting, we know that you will be a most competent and well-qualified judge. We hope you will be able to accept our invitation. / Sincerely, / Alda Bitterman / Chairperson, Florida Speak-Out / [*Your initials*]

Take two 1-minute timings on each paragraph. Then take one 5-minute timing on the entire selection. Use single spacing for the 1-minute timings and double spacing for the 5-minute timing.

```
                                              1'
20     When you decide to redecorate a room, or move to a new      12
21  apartment, or help a friend getting settled in a new place,     24
22  you must make many decisions.  How could this place be made     36
23  more pleasant?                                                  39
24     After all the furniture is in place, you should decide       12
25  where to put wall hangings.  Would a picture look better on     24
26  one wall, or would it look better on another?  It must look     36
27  exactly right!                                                  39
28     Once these kinds of decisions have been made, you will       12
29  begin the hanging process.  First, you might want to locate     24
30  the horizontal center of the wall on which you have decided     36
31  to hang an item.                                                39
32     Then ask somebody to hold the picture steady while you       12
33  step back a little way and determine how high this painting     24
34  should be placed.  Many paintings and other items look best     36
35  at eye level.                                                   39
36     Once you have completed this procedure, you can use it       12
37  again and again to help you in placing pictures on the wall     24
38  quickly and easily.  All you have to do is just get started     36
39  and keep going!                                                 39
   |  1  |  2  |  3  |  4  |  5  |  6  |  7  |  8  |  9  |  10  |  11  |  12   SI 1.36
```

LESSON 119

UNIT 20 FORMATTING TABLES

UNIT GOAL
39/5'/5e

GOALS
- To use exclamation points correctly while typing sentences.
- To type three ruled tables.

FORMAT
- Single spacing   60-space line   5-space tab and other tabs as needed

LAB 13

Type lines 1–4 twice, providing the missing exclamation points. Edit your copy as your teacher reads the answers. Then retype lines 1–4 from your edited copy.

EXCLAMATION POINTS

1 Stop. We already have several dozen copies of these forms.
2 Congratulations. I'm happy that you've been promoted, Kay.
3 Wow. Our water taxes for last quarter have almost doubled.
4 Yes. Joan Kim has been awarded first prize for her design.

PRACTICE

Type lines 10–13 four times as a group. Then type lines 14–17 four times each.

```
10  er newer flower serious spotter reserves samplers reserving
11  ui build quilts builder require building quilting buildings
12  as basis assure glasses eastern casualty roasters canvasses
13  oi point choice boilers spoiler appoints adjoined appointed

14  visitor auditor bushel handle world panel then with got for
15  visible problem signal eighth amend turns rich body but aid
16  ancient suspend profit social signs ivory fish town icy ham
17  penalty signals formal turkey laugh eight busy such aid the
```

POSTTEST

Repeat the Pretest on page 278 to see how much your skill has improved.

5-MINUTE TIMINGS

Take a 5-minute timing on lines 18–35. Type six times each word on which you made an error, hesitated, or stopped during the 5-minute timing. Then take a 5-minute timing to see how much your skill has improved.

```
                      1                              2
18      Just why do expert typists use single spacing for most   12
                3                          4
19      Just why do expert typists use single spacing for most   24
        5                  6                          7
20      Just why do expert typists use single spacing for most   36
                          8                      9
21  of their reports?  A dozen answers can be given, but one is  48
            10                    11                  12
22  of their reports?  A dozen answers can be given, but one is  60
                          13                    14
23  of their reports?  A dozen answers can be given, but one is  72
                15                      16
24  that single spacing is convenient.  It conserves paper; and  84
        17                      18                  19
25  that single spacing is convenient.  It conserves paper; and  96
                20                      21
26  that single spacing is convenient.  It conserves paper; and  108
            22                      23                    24
27  when inflation is sweeping the country, businesses must cut  120
                    25                      26
28  when inflation is sweeping the country, businesses must cut  132
            27                      28
29  when inflation is sweeping the country, businesses must cut  144
        29                  30                      31
30  back expenses as much as possible in order to survive.  The  156
                    32                    33
31  back expenses as much as possible in order to survive.  The  168
            34                    35                      36
32  back expenses as much as possible in order to survive.  The  180
                        37
33  typist saves time by handling less paper.                    188
            38                    39
34  typist saves time by handling less paper.                    197
                40                          41
35  typist saves time by handling less paper.                    205
    |  1  |  2  |  3  |  4  |  5  |  6  |  7  |  8  |  9  |  10  |  11  |  12   SI 1.49
```

PRETEST

Take a 5-minute Pretest on lines 5–21. Then circle and count your errors. Use the chart below to determine which lines to type for practice.

5 Have you ever been [1]through an actual haunted[2] house? I 12
6 would really [3]enjoy going into one, but [4]I have never had the 24
7 [5]opportunity of doing so. [6]Actually, I am somewhat [7]afraid of 36
8 what may be in store[8] for me if such a wish [9]would come true! 48
9 I [10]visualize seeing ghosts or monsters[11] and having them chase[12] 60
10 me rapidly down the stairs[13] and out a window or door[14]! Worse 72
11 yet, I also view[15] being trapped in a dark[16] room with them and 84
12 not [17]being able to locate the exit[18]! 91
13 Exactly what [19]causes those fears to overcome[20] us? Where 103
14 do we [21]first begin to be afraid? [22]When thinking about it, we[23] 115
15 really have to laugh at [24]ourselves; then we quickly[25] see just 127
16 how foolish we[26] were to be scared. [27]Ghosts and monsters come 139
17 from[28] fantasy. In fact, many [29]of these fears probably [30]arose, 151
18 for the first time,[31] when our older brothers [32]or sisters were 163
19 trying [33]everything they could to [34]keep us out of their rooms.[35] 175
20 When we can look at it [36]in that light, there is no[37] longer an 187
21 unreasonable [38]fear. We laugh about it![39] 195
| 1 | 2 | 3 | 4 | 5 | 6 | 7 | 8 | 9 | 10 | 11 | 12 SI 1.37

PRACTICE

In the chart below, find the number of errors you made on the Pretest. Then type each of the designated drill lines four times.

Pretest errors	0–1	2–3	4–5	6+
Drill lines	25–29	24–28	23–27	22–26

Accuracy

22 been ever have actual foolish brothers somewhat opportunity
23 some what into fantasy quickly probably ourselves visualize
24 true come wish sisters trapped overcome actually everything
25 door down them really exactly rapidly monsters unreasonable

Speed

26 afraid trying house would enjoy going think about fear that
27 seeing scared never doing store chase laugh these look when
28 ghosts really stair worse being cause fears arose were just
29 stairs causes fears where first begin older could fact view

POSTTEST

Repeat the Pretest to see how much your skill has improved.

JOB 167-1. UNEDITED NEWSLETTER ARTICLE

Standard format for a magazine article (see page 271). No subtitles. Edit the copy as you type. (That is, correct spelling, capitalization, and punctuation errors.)

FOCUS ON OUR PEOPLE—MEET CYNTHIA BERANEK

Cynthia Beranek is blind, but that hasn't prevented her from becoming a whiz at the keyboard of her automatic typewriter. For the passed 6 years, Cynthia has been typing up a storm in the word processing group of the office services section at great falls steel corporation's headquarters offices in pittsburgh.

She types letters, memos, and other documents that are phoned in by enginers, buyers, lawyers, and other company employees. Because they dictate onto a tape cassette most of her "audio" bosses have never had the opportunity to meet or talk directly to her. If they could, they would discover a delightful young woman who is very profishent in her job.

Cynthia produces accurate, neat work on an automatic typewriter and a transcribng unit the same as those used by other typists in the group. She types by touch and has master her machine through training, determeration, and a fine sense of recall.

When she begins a job, Cynthia slips the tape casette into the transcribing unit, puts on her earpiece, listens to find out what format is desired, then types the job with speed and accuracy. Dictation requireing tabular work is handled by other typist.

Cynthias' timesaving machine permits her to mechanicaly correct conscieous typing errors on a line-by-line basis instead of having to retype the entire page. For fast character count-offs, she relyes on an abacus. The end result is a piece of final copy that is free of eraseres or any other type of correction marks. Although her work is checked by the group leader, it rarely needs addtional revision—a tribute to her fine typing skills.

LESSON 168

CLINIC

GOALS
- To build competency on selected keyboard reaches.
- To type 41/5'/4e.

FORMAT
- Single spacing   60-space line   5-space tab

KEYBOARDING SKILLS

Type lines 1–4 once. Then use the shift lock to capitalize the words in line 5. Repeat lines 1–4, or take a series of 1-minute timings.

Speed   1   I came to work for that firm and have been here since then.   12
Accuracy   2   When Zeth requested a bill, did Jack pay for fixing my van?   12
Numbers   3   Please clean Rooms 10, 29, and 38, but not Rooms 47 and 56.   12
Symbols   4   I will paint Rooms 10 and 29 (but not Ballroom # 38 or 56).   12
Technique   5   Do NOT type any CAPITAL in lowercase; always use UPPERCASE.

     | 1 | 2 | 3 | 4 | 5 | 6 | 7 | 8 | 9 | 10 | 11 | 12

PRETEST

Take four 1-minute timings on lines 6–9.

6   Asa has offered to trim several cherry trees within a week.   12
7   Louise saw the pier as she was walking over the sandy soil.   24
8   The eight men work when the firm lands a plane right by us.   36
9   Their wish is to make the men sit down or go to the fields.   48

     | 1 | 2 | 3 | 4 | 5 | 6 | 7 | 8 | 9 | 10 | 11 | 12

Numbers are usually aligned on the right. However, when numbers appear with other alphabetic data (such as with 4 reams *in the column to the right) in a table column, it is permissible to align the numbers at the left.*

JOB 119-1. THREE-COLUMN RULED TABLE
Standard format. Full sheet of paper.

SUPPLIES INVENTORY

Typewriting I, Room 142

Item	Number	Reorder
Paper	4 reams	No
Ribbons	5 boxes	Yes
Textbooks	38	No
Copyholders	35	Yes
Machine covers	30	Yes

JOB 119-2. THREE-COLUMN RULED TABLE
Standard format. Half sheet of paper.

TYPEWRITING SPEEDS
Beginning Typewriting

Student	Speed	Increase
Helen	45	8
Juan	41	5
Randy	35	4
Shelly	34	2
Stacy	45	4

JOB 119-3. THREE-COLUMN RULED TABLE
Standard format. Full sheet of paper.

AREA CODES/TIME ZONES

Selected Nebraska Cities

City	Time Zone	Area # Code
Alliance	Mountain	308
Lincoln	~~Mountain~~ Central	402
McCook	Central	308
North Platte	Central	308
Scottsbluff	Mountain	308
Wayne	Central	401 → 402

place this column last

LESSON 120

GOALS
- To format footnotes and decimal numbers in tables.
- To produce ruled tables.

FORMAT
- Single spacing   60-space line   Center tab and other tabs as needed

KEYBOARDING SKILLS

Type lines 1–4 once. In line 5, backspace and underscore each word containing double letters immediately after typing it. Repeat lines 1–4, or take a series of 1-minute timings.

Speed	1	The key to the problem with both their maps is their shape.	12
Accuracy	2	Jack bought five exquisite bronze bowls at Pam's yard sale.	12
Numbers	3	We set our tabs at 10, 29, 38, 47, and 56 for the problems.	12
Symbols	4	Only 9% of #47 and 8% of #56 were sold on the 1st (Monday).	12
Technique	5	They, too, shall give three good yells when the bell tolls.	

| 1 | 2 | 3 | 4 | 5 | 6 | 7 | 8 | 9 | 10 | 11 | 12

Take a 5-minute Pretest on lines 5–22. Then circle and count your errors. Use the chart below to determine which lines to type for practice.

```
 5       Editors of newspapers and magazines must read all copy    12
 6   for publication to be sure of the content; they select what   24
 7   will be final copy.  The typist is the person who must make    36
 8   sure that the copy is totally free of errors.                  45
 9       The proofreading techniques you use will be determined     57
10   by the kind of typing assignment you have completed.  Is it    69
11   a legal description of an estate or a brief memo to someone    81
12   down the hall?  Have you just typed a copy of a letter that    93
13   will be distributed at a conference to hundreds of persons?   105
14   Maybe you have just typed the corporate budget with columns   117
15   of million-dollar figures.  You must proofread the numbers,   129
16   as well as the alphabetic copy, for accuracy.                 138
17       Another concern of the typist must be how to make time    150
18   available for proofreading.  If your typing jobs are mostly   162
19   letters, pay attention to dates.  Check that the months are   174
20   spelled correctly and the years are exact.  Be sure to read   186
21   the name, address, subject, and signature lines.  Check the   198
22   format too.                                                   200
     |  1  |  2  |  3  |  4  |  5  |  6  |  7  |  8  |  9  | 10 | 11 | 12   SI 1.48
```

PRACTICE

In the chart below, find the number of errors you made on the Pretest. Then type each of the designated drill lines four times.

Pretest errors	0–1	2–3	4–5	6+
Drill lines	26–30	25–29	24–28	23–27

Accuracy
```
23   typist editors magazines newspapers publication description
24   someone hundreds corporate techniques determined assignment
25   columns concern attention signature alphabetic proofreading
26   brief accuracy available conference description distributed
```

Speed
```
27   must sure what that will kind have memo hall well name your
28   final error check lines down just make copy you pay and all
29   letters dollar typing person format legal who are the is it
30   spelled another million estate typed maybe too for an by or
```

POSTTEST

Repeat the Pretest to see how much your skill has improved.

FORMATTING ARTICLES FOR COMPANY NEWSLETTERS

Some companies publish in-house newsletters or magazines to keep their employees informed about business and company activities. Often these newsletters have feature articles focusing on a certain employee. Articles prepared for such in-house publications should be formatted as any other magazine article submitted for publication.

FORMATTING TABLES WITH FOOTNOTES

Workbook 229–230.

When a footnote appears in a table, it is typed much the same as a footnote in a report. To format footnotes in unruled and ruled tables:

Tables Without Rulings. (1) Separate the footnote from the body of the table with a 10P/12E underscore. (2) Single-space before typing the underscore; double-space after it. (3) Indent the footnote 5 spaces and type it the length of the table, with single spacing; double-space between footnotes.

(4) Type an asterisk or another symbol at the beginning of a footnote to indicate its use in the table.

Tables With Rulings. (1) Type the footnote a double space below the final rule. (2) Follow steps 3 and 4 under "Tables Without Rulings."

Note: The footnote reference in the body of a table should be counted as part of the key line if it follows the longest entry in the column.

JOB 120-1. THREE-COLUMN TABLE
Standard format. Full sheet of paper.

SEVEN WONDERS OF THE WORLD
By Sheila Thomas

Structure	Location	Date of Construction*
Colossus	Rhodes (Greece)	280 B.C.
Hanging Gardens	Babylon (Iraq)	600 B.C.
Mausoleum	Halicarnassus (Turkey)	350 B.C.
Pharos	Alexandria (Egypt)	270 B.C.
Pyramids	Giza (Egypt)	2800 B.C.
Statue of Zeus	Olympia (Greece)	500 B.C.
Temple of Artemis	Ephesus (Turkey)	350 B.C.

* Dates listed are approximate.

FORMATTING DECIMALS IN TABLES

Numbers usually align at the right; however, in decimal numbers, the decimals must be aligned when typed. The key line may be a combination of two lines, as illustrated in Job 120–2.

JOB 120-2. FIVE-COLUMN TABLE
Standard format. Full sheet of paper.

CHEMICAL ELEMENTS
(Noble Gases)

Name	Chemical Symbol	Atomic Number	Atomic Weight	Date of Discovery
Argon	Ar	18	39.948	1894
Helium	He	2	4.0026	1895
Krypton	Kr	36	83.80	1898
Neon	Ne	10	20.183	1898
Radon	Rn	86	122.00	1900
Xenon	Xe	54	131.30	1898

JOB 120-3. RULED TABLE, UNARRANGED COPY
Standard format. Half sheet of paper.

[Title] States Bordering Arkansas
[Subtitle] (Listed Alphabetically)
[Column headings] State, Position of Border, Length of Border*
[Body] Louisiana, South, 170 miles; Mississippi, East, 150 miles; Missouri, North, 325 miles; Oklahoma, West, 200 miles.
[Footnote] *In miles.

5 Mail addressed to occupants of multi unit buildings should include 236

the number of the apartment, room, suite or other unit. The unit 249

number should appear immediately after the street address on the 262

same line--never above, below, or in front of the street address. 275

Slide 3   The city, state, and ZIP Code should appear in that sequence 295

on the bottom line of the address block. This is where automatic 308

sorting equipment, for this information. Mail presorted by ZIP 325

is instructed to look

Codes by passes many processing steps in the post office and get gets 338

to it's destination quicker. 344

Slide 4   Window envelopes must be matched, If the insert slides around 370

with the address on the insert.

in the envelope, the envelope can not be delivered. Always check 383

the window envelope to be sure the address on the insert is fully 396

visible. 398

postal station   *Slide 5*

When a name is shown, it should be entered on the same line 420

as the box number. Correct spelling of street names is essential 433

postal

since some machines compare the address name to address names pro- 448

computer's

grammed in the memory. 455

One last reminder: You can increase the machine handling of 468

your mail by using two-letter abbreviations for state names. 480

Thank you for your attention, *and for coming, to this workshop.* 493

JOB 166-2. HANDOUT OF A SPEECH

Standard report format to prepare a handout of the speech in Job 166-1. Reword
paragraph three since no slide will appear in the handout. Double spacing. Add
the speaker's name in the subtitle: *Elizabeth Weingartz.*

LESSON 167

GOALS
- To hyphenate compound nouns correctly while typing sentences.
- To type 41/5'/4e.
- To format an article for a company newsletter.

FORMAT
- Single-spacing   60-space line   5-space tab

LAB 19

Type lines 1–4 once, providing the missing hyphens. Edit your copy as your
teacher reads the answers. Then retype lines 1–4 from your edited copy.

**COMPOUND
NOUNS**

1 This year our dinner dance will be at the big Jonquil Club.
2 The homeowners want the work done as a time saver for them.
3 We cannot expect the vice president to solve these puzzles.
4 Everything was at a standstill when the night light failed.

LESSONS 121/122

GOALS
- To recognize when question marks are used while typing sentences.
- To type leadered tables.
- To format "source" notes in tables.

FORMAT
- Single spacing   60-space line   5-space tab and other tabs as needed

LAB 14

Type lines 1–4 once. Then repeat lines 1–4 or take a series of 1-minute timings.

QUESTION MARKS

1 What is my expense budget for the last quarter of the year? 12
2 When did Maria decide to transfer to our office in Seattle? 12
3 Did John know why sixty or more members voted against this? 12
4 In your opinion, should we approve Mr. Adzick's loan? Why? 12
   | 1 | 2 | 3 | 4 | 5 | 6 | 7 | 8 | 9 | 10 | 11 | 12

Use a question mark (?) at the end of a question. Note that the question sometimes may not be a complete sentence:

Has the new contract been approved? When?
Who was named to head the committee? Shirley Anderson?

PRETEST

Take a 5-minute Pretest on lines 5–21. Then circle and count your errors. Use the chart on page 205 to determine which lines to type for practice.

5   When the snow begins to fall and the temperatures drop 12
6 to below freezing, sports fans in all those northern states 24
7 change their sports activities. Gone are the tennis, golf, 36
8 and swimming. To replace these sports are those quite well 48
9 suited to the cold, frigid days of winter. One of the most 60
10 popular winter sports for many who enjoy fishing is that of 72
11 ice fishing. It is a sport in which almost anyone can par- 84
12 ticipate, but did you know that it is inexpensive to enjoy? 96
13   Before going ice fishing, you must be certain that the 108
14 ice is strong enough to support you and all your equipment. 120
15 To be absolutely safe, don't go out on the ice unless there 132
16 is a minimum of six inches of ice covering the water. Also 144
17 watch for thin ice that could be lying over a concealed un- 156
18 derground spring. You should select an area that is not in 168
19 the direct path of the cold winds if you are going to stand 180
20 outdoors as you fish. For safety, try to take someone else 192
21 along with you. 195
   | 1 | 2 | 3 | 4 | 5 | 6 | 7 | 8 | 9 | 10 | 11 | 12   SI 1.37

LESSON 166

GOALS
- To identify compound nouns while typing sentences.
- To format a speech and a handout of the speech.

FORMAT
- Single spacing   60-space line   5-space tab and other tabs as needed

LAB 19

Type lines 1–4 once. Then repeat lines 1–4 or take a series of 1-minute timings.

COMPOUND NOUNS

1 The secretary-treasurer has the know-how to help us manage. 12
2 Their trade-in is of little value to the company right now. 12
3 We need to employ a clerk-typist to help us type the bills. 12
4 Jacqueline organized an exciting get-together for our club. 12

| 1 | 2 | 3 | 4 | 5 | 6 | 7 | 8 | 9 | 10 | 11 | 12

FORMATTING SPEECHES

A speech is formatted very much like a report, but with a few changes:

1. Margins: 50-space line. (Standard top and bottom margins for page 1 and for pages following page 1.)

2. Triple-space for easier reading.

3. If audiovisual materials such as slides are to be used, indicate in the copy where they occur by centering *Slide 1, Slide 2,* and so on.

JOB 166-1. SPEECH FROM ROUGH-DRAFT COPY
Standard format (see above).

SPEECH TO MAILROOM PERSONNEL

Mailroom Addressing for Automation   23

January 10, 19--   34

I am delighted to be with you today. It isn't often that mail room   49

personnel are given the opportunity to have a get-together and dis-   62

cuss the mail. So I ~~trust~~ hope that my brief review of how to ad-   74

dress the mail will make your jobs easier and keep you up to date.   88

(Slide 1)   188

Remember: You are doing essential work. You are the focal point of   103

a large part of your company's communications effort. how well   116

the mailroom functions has a major effect on how your company   128

looks in the eyes of its customers and how well it prospers. By   141

making sure that your mail is prepared for sorting by the Postal Ser-   155

vice's computerized sorting equipment, you promote better business,   169

improve communications, and enhance your own job performance.   182

Here is a correctly addressed envelope. Note that the address   202

area should be in blocked form--all lines begin at the left margin.   215

Slide 2   221

(Continued on next page)

PRACTICE

In the chart below, find the number of errors you made on the Pretest. Then type each of the designated drill lines four times.

Pretest errors	0–1	2–3	4–5	6+
Drill lines	25–29	24–28	23–27	22–26

Accuracy
22 below sports begins replace covering concealed temperatures
23 those change states outdoors freezing equipment participate
24 quite frigid suited popular northern activities inexpensive
25 which winter tennis fishing swimming absolutely underground

Speed
26 certain almost anyone safety these lying when snow fall are
27 support before unless strong enjoy areas fans gone golf all
28 minimum inches spring enough don't winds well days most who
29 someone select direct enjoys water going that must your ice

POSTTEST

Repeat the Pretest on page 204 to see how much your skill has improved.

JOB 121/2-1. DISPLAY WITH LEADERS

Standard format. Full sheet of paper and a 50-space line. Double-space the body.

N O T I C E

The following committee assignments are made for the Junior Class Prom:

Lisa Bender . . . . Refreshments

Yaki Husharu . . . . Invitations*

Fernando Lopez . . . . Theme

Mark Mitchell . . . . Cleanup

Bonnita Valdez . . . . Entertainment

*Also responsible for decorations.

JOB 121/2-3. TABLE WITH LEADERS

Standard format. Full sheet of paper and a 50-space line. Single-space the body.

JOB 121/2-2. TABLE WITH LEADERS

Standard format. Half sheet of paper, 40-space line.

AVERAGE MILES PER GALLON
(TOTAL DISTANCE TRAVELED: 9,000 MILES)

MONTH	MILES PER GALLON
JANUARY	25.6
FEBRUARY	27.3
MARCH	25.8
APRIL	26.9
MAY	24.7
JUNE	23.1

NORTH DAKOTA ZIP CODES

Cities in Walsh County

Cities	ZIP Code
Adams	58201
Fairdale	58229
Fordville	58231
Edinburg	58227
Grafton	58243
Hoople	58237
Minot	58261
Parkriver	58270

1. *Margins: 60P/ 70E.*

2. *Title and subtitle lines include the name of the group and the date. Begin the title on line 7.*

3. *Single-space. All-cap side headings; double-space before and after.*

4. *Closing lines begin at center; 3 blank lines for signature.*

JOBS 165-1 AND 165-2. MINUTES OF A MEETING

Standard format. Job 165-1, unbound; Job 165-2, bound in a three-ring binder—allow a wide left margin (15P/18E).

Downtowners Club
Minutes of the December Meeting
December 6, 19—

Attendance

The annual dinner meeting of the Downtowners Club was held at the Press Club on Friday, December 3, at 6 p.m. After dinner, President Solonchek called the meeting to order. All members were present, except Esther Falk and Ben Collard.

Unfinished Business

President Solonchek asked for ideas on ways to raise money to pay for the college scholarship fund that the Club voted in November to support. The fund is to be for a worthy student-writer who wants to major in communications. Several plans were put forth. President Solonchek asked for members to serve on an ad hoc committee to follow up on the suggestions, and four members volunteered: Susan Strauss, Nick Pappas, Rupert Nosel, and Ann Zogg.

New Business

Since this is the final meeting of the year, there was no new business. President Solonchek thanked all her officers who served with her during the past year: Mike Epson, First Vice President; Rachael Brewer, Second Vice President; Scott Carter, Secretary; and Jay Suggard, Treasurer.

The meeting adjourned at 8:30 p.m.
Respectfully submitted, Scott Carter, Secretary

10
31
44
47
55
62
69
76
82
89
96
101
111
118
126
135
143
151
159
167
174
180
186
194
197
207
216
224
232
240
247
255
257
267
277

FORMATTING SOURCE NOTES IN TABLES

A *source note*, which tells the source of information in a table, can be typed as a subtitle or as a footnote. If typed as a footnote:

1. Do not use an asterisk (*).
2. Type the word *Source* in all-capital letters, and use a colon after it.
3. Type the source note before footnotes (if any).

JOB 121/2-4. TABLE WITH LEADERS

Standard format. Full sheet of paper and a 50-space line. Double-space the body.

CLIMATIC Extremes

Measurement	Extreme
Highest Temperature	136 degrees
Lowest Temperature	-127 degrees
Greatest rainfall	74 inches *
Longest hotspell	162 days **
Greatest snowfall	76 inches *

Source: Information Please Almanac

* In 24 hours
** 100 degrees Fahrenheit or above

JOB 121/2-5. UNARRANGED TABLE WITH LEADERS

Standard format. Full sheet of paper and a 50-space line. Arrange in ascending order by page number; correct spelling errors.

THE COMPLETE DESK REFERENCE

Table of Contents*

Usage	210
Grammer	171
Numbers	87
Speling	132
Abreviations	105
Word Division	166
Compound Words	152
Capitolization	70
Plurels and Possesives	119
Punctuation: Other Marks	40
Punctuation: Majer Marks	1

*Part 1.

LESSON 123

GOALS
- To identify when question marks are used while typing sentences.
- To type at least 39/5'/5e.
- To type leadered displays.

FORMAT
- Single spacing   60-space line   5-space tab and tab at center

LAB 14

Type lines 1–4 once. Then repeat lines 1–4 or take a series of 1-minute timings.

QUESTION MARKS

1 Can you collate all these copies of the manuscript by noon? 12
2 Who requested a dozen extra copies of the January printout? 12
3 When did Marge and Karen schedule the meeting with Michael? 12
4 Have all invitations been printed? When will we mail them? 12

| 1 | 2 | 3 | 4 | 5 | 6 | 7 | 8 | 9 | 10 | 11 | 12

JOB 163/4-3. ANNOTATED BIBLIOGRAPHY
Standard format.

Burrell, M. R., <u>Are You an OK Boss?</u> Fabin 14
& Fabin, Inc., New York, 1979. 22

   Almost everyone is a boss at one time or 31
another. In this practical text, Muriel Bur- 41
rell takes a new look at "bossing," using 50
sound techniques for good communication. 60
You'll see how OK <u>you</u> are when it comes to 70
bossing and directing others. 78

Everett, John C., <u>Motivating People</u>, Newman 94
and Sons, Inc., Dallas, 1981. 101

A book to introduce you to the basic theories 112
of communication and to show you how to 121
apply them in your place of business. The 130
exercises provided are designed to expand 140
the text to fit any course of study. Each of 150
the 32 chapters includes case studies as well 160
as group activities. 165

Scarletti, Veronica, <u>Everybody Wants to Win</u>, 185
Arris House, Sacramento, 1981. 192

   The author brings together comments of and 201
programs for people throughout the country 211
and explains how certain people have 219
achieved good human relations by working 228
with people in groups. 234

LESSON 165

GOALS
- To recognize compound nouns while typing sentences.
- To format minutes of a meeting from handwritten copy.

FORMAT
- Single spacing   60-space line   5-space tab and other tabs as needed

LAB 19

COMPOUND NOUNS

Type lines 1–4 once. Then repeat lines 1–4 or take a series of 1-minute timings.

1 I hope to work as a clerk-typist for Joe Zwick next summer. 12
2 I will mail the invitations for our October 6 get-together. 12
3 The salesclerk said good-bye to the company vice president. 12
4 We do our banking at a drive-in quite close to Xenia, Ohio. 12
  | 1 | 2 | 3 | 4 | 5 | 6 | 7 | 8 | 9 | 10 | 11 | 12

Nouns such as *vice president, father-in-law,* and *paycheck* are compound nouns—two or more words joined into one noun. When the compound noun shows that one person or thing has two functions, as in *clerk-typist* and *dinner-dance,* the noun is hyphenated.

   For all other compound nouns, check your dictionary to see whether the noun is spelled as two words (*double entry*), is hyphenated (*get-together*), or is spelled as one word (*checkbook*).

30-SECOND TIMINGS

Take two 30-second timings on lines 5–7, or type the paragraph twice.

5 I should think that we might cut down our staff loss if you 12
6 could set up a pay scale by which each person would know if 24
7 he or she is being paid fairly for doing the work you want. 36
  | 1 | 2 | 3 | 4 | 5 | 6 | 7 | 8 | 9 | 10 | 11 | 12

TIMINGS

Repeat the 1- and 3-minute timings on page 271 (lines 8–19).

30-SECOND TIMINGS

Take two 30-second timings on lines 5–7, or type the paragraph twice.

5 You do not save very much time when you indent with the tab   12
6 key, but if the tab stop is set correctly, you do know that   24
7 each tab is quite uniform and each indention is just right.   36
   | 1 | 2 | 3 | 4 | 5 | 6 | 7 | 8 | 9 | 10 | 11 | 12

PRETEST

Take a 5-minute Pretest on lines 8–24. Then circle and count your errors. Use the chart below to determine which lines to type for practice.

8   Have you ever felt run down, tired, and fatigued? The   12
9 symptoms listed above are common to many of us today. They   24
10 affect our job performance, they limit the fun we have with   36
11 our family and friends, and they might even affect our good   48
12 health. Here are just a few ways that we can quickly mini-   60
13 mize the problems and become more active persons in all the   72
14 things we do daily.   76
15   It is essential that we get plenty of sleep so that we   88
16 are rested when we get up each morning. We must eat a good   100
17 breakfast so that we can build up energies for the day that   112
18 follows. Physical exercise is a necessity, and it might be   124
19 the one most important ingredient in building up our energy   136
20 reserves. We must take part in exercises that make us per-   148
21 spire, make our hearts beat faster, and cause our breathing   160
22 rate to increase appreciably. All these things can help us   172
23 increase our energies and make us healthier people. Can we   184
24 not enjoy life more if we concentrate on these items?   195
   | 1 | 2 | 3 | 4 | 5 | 6 | 7 | 8 | 9 | 10 | 11 | 12   SI 1.39

PRACTICE

In the chart below, find the number of errors you made on the Pretest. Then type each of the designated drill lines four times.

Pretest errors	0–1	2–3	4–5	6+
Drill lines	28–32	27–31	26–30	25–29

Accuracy
25 ever tired perspire problems fatigued breakfast performance
26 many above energies physical symptoms essential appreciably
27 might limit quickly exercise minimize important concentrate
28 heart sleep morning building healthier breathing ingredient

Speed
29 listed common family energy people today have ever felt you
30 friend health become hearts affect enjoy even many they our
31 active person things faster builds these have with beat and
32 plenty rested follow things causes items each that when all

POSTTEST

Repeat the Pretest to see how much your skill has improved.

JOB 163/4-1.
(Continued)

a home or place of business can self-activate the phone to signal the police 320
during a robbery. 323

    <u>Selective-Call Forwarding</u>. Instead of all your phone calls being transferred 350
to a place you plan to be, a computer system will select only the calls you want 366
to get through. Suppose you are a sales representative who is out of the office 382
a great deal, but you are expecting an extremely urgent call from an important 398
customer. You don't have to wait by your telephone. You can leave instructions 414
with the telephone company for calls to be forwarded to wherever you plan to 430
be. Only the call you were waiting for will get through; the others will be 445
answered by an automatic answering system. 454

    <u>Electronic Yellow Pages</u>. Linking the phone to the TV set opens up a wealth 479
of shopping-at-the-office or shopping-at-home services. Using a separate key- 495
board attached to the phone, the customer can turn on the TV set, ask to see 510
a certain catalog listing, and order by phone. 519

JOB 163/4-2. MAGAZINE ARTICLE
Standard format.

U.S. Firms Turn to Quality Circles 21
by M. L. Izumi 31

    Today 11 million workers in Japan belong 58
to Quality Circles. Quality Circles is an 68
American idea that helped Japan get back to 76
normal after World War II. Now it is aiding 85
companies in that country to boost worker 93
morale and open the lines of communication 102
between workers and their bosses. 109

    Workers in a Quality Circle meet in groups 118
of four to ten and hash over problems in their 128
departments. People in the group air their 137
feelings. Members of a Quality Circle try to 146
solve problems, and they make suggestions to 155
their bosses. 158

    The Circles deal not only with the quality 167
of a product or service but also with the quality 177
of working life. Projects and suggestions deal 187
with safety, work methods, worker morale, 195
and ways to cut costs. 200

    The approach of Quality Circles varies from 210
company to company. In some, meetings are 219
held on company time; in others, the groups 227
meet after work. Sometimes the unit leader 236
chairs the Circle; in others, the Circle elects 246
its own leaders. 249

    Suggestions that lead to savings often earn 259
cash rewards, but more important is the rec- 268
ognition given the members of the Circle. A 277
big part of the success in Quality Circles 286
results from the communication that occurs 294
when workers and employers sit down and 302
talk. 303

FORMATTING
ANNOTATED
BIBLIOGRAPHIES

An annotated bibliography lists not only some books on a certain subject but also a brief description of the contents of each book. To format an annotated bibliography, follow these instructions:

1. Use a full sheet of paper.
2. Margins: 50P/60E (or margins to match report).
3. On line 13, center the title
   ANNOTATED BIBLIOGRAPHY
   Triple-space after the heading.

4. Single-space each entry; double-space between entries.
5. Begin each entry at the left margin. Indent turnover lines 5 spaces.
6. Begin the description on a new line, a double space below the publication information. Indent all lines of the description 5 spaces.
7. List the entries alphabetically by author, last name first. Do not number the entries.

JOB 123-1. DISPLAY WITH LEADERS

Standard format. Full sheet of paper and a 50-space line. Single-space the body.

single-space {

SENIOR CLASS PLAY
"The Disappearance of J. J. Walker"
May 4, 19--
Central High School Auditorium

Player	Role
Kenny Loftsgard	J. J. Walker
Maria Sanchez	Mrs. Walker
Jane Zydlik	Carol Walker
Frank Startzel	Detective Ryan
Bernice Larson	Detective Urness
Bill Rodgers	Tom Wright
Paul Johnston	Sgt. LeRoy Foster
Annette Vango	Ms. Peterson
Pete Weingard	Mr. Benson
Beth Idluvani	Ticket Agent
Emily Rice	Dr. Swanson

LESSON 124

CLINIC

GOALS
- To type 39/5'/5e.
- To use question marks correctly while typing sentences.
- To strengthen typing accuracy via alphabetic drills.

FORMAT
- Single spacing 60-space line 5-space tab and tab for every fifth space thereafter

LAB 14

Type lines 1–4 once, providing the missing question marks. Edit your copy as your teacher reads the answers. Then retype lines 1–4 from your edited copy.

QUESTION MARKS

1 Has James Maxon submitted his estimates for this contract.
2 Does Jean agree that the azure cover is the brightest one.
3 Has Karen Boll rescheduled her meeting yet. For what date.
4 Has Pattie or Henry arrived yet. When should they be here.

PRETEST

Take a 5-minute Pretest on lines 5–10, repeating the paragraph until time is called. Circle each incorrect letter, and use the practice lines on page 209 to improve your skill. Use double spacing.

5   A typist might think that only his or her machine will   77 142
6 be found on a job, but typists frequently exchange machines 89 154
7 or elements to use what is most effective for the job. The 101 166
8 typist is free to zero in on what is best: one print style 113 178
9 or another, pica or elite, a correction key or other method 125 190
10 of correction, and so on.   130 195
   | 1 | 2 | 3 | 4 | 5 | 6 | 7 | 8 | 9 | 10 | 11 | 12   SI 1.39

1- AND 3-MINUTE TIMINGS

Take two 1-minute timings on each paragraph. Then take one 3-minute timing on the entire selection. Use single spacing for the 1-minute timings and double spacing for the 3-minute timing.

```
8        In the more than one hundred years since its invention   12
9    by Alexander Graham Bell, the telephone has changed the way   24
10   people all over the world communicate.  It has also spawned   36
11   an ever-growing business.                                     41
12        Today the major goal of this business is to serve with   12
13   efficiency our increasing demand for more service--although   24
14   we in this country already own about half of the telephones  36
15   used in the entire world.                                     41
16        Tomorrow telephones will be required to do more things   12
17   for you.  Technology is zeroing in on many new uses of your  24
18   telephone in the home and at work.  Phones are vital to all  36
19   parts of our daily lives.                                     41
     | 1  | 2  | 3  | 4  | 5  | 6  | 7  | 8  | 9  | 10 | 11 | 12   SI 1.50
```

FORMATTING REVIEW

Magazine Articles

1. *Double spacing.*

2. *Line length to match magazine.*

3. *Heading includes title, the author's name, and the number of lines and their length.*

4. *Top margins: 12 lines at the top of page 1; 6 lines on all other pages. Bottom margins: 6 to 9 lines.*

5. *Beginning with page 2, backspace the page number from the right margin on line 7; precede the page number with the author's name. Separate by a diagonal.*

When you finish typing the article, count the lines and insert the number in the heading.

JOB 163/4-1. MAGAZINE ARTICLE

Standard format (see review in margin). 5-space line. 5-space and center tabs. Read the problem before typing it.

YOUR PHONE CAN MAKE LIFE EASIER   13

by Adrienne Reifmueller   29

(lines of 50 spaces)   45

Teams of engineers, accountants, and marketing persons are working on new   63
services and equipment planned for telephone customers. When the company   77
will offer these new services and how much they will cost are not known; but   93
the company is planning to sell new phone and computer-based equipment that   108
will give their customers a variety of new ways to use their phones. Here are   124
some of the special uses.   129

Voice Storage. A computer will replace phone answering machines. Besides   150
taking messages, the new device will dial preselected phone numbers and   165
return a call with a recorded message. For example, suppose you put an ad in   180
your newspaper to sell your used car, and you get ten calls while you are outside   197
showing your car to a potential buyer. The computer will select the calls   212
related to your ad and return these calls with a recorded message, giving the   227
caller all the needed information about your auto, such as mileage and condition.   244

Meter Reading and Protection Service. Using sensors and more wiring tied   274
to your phone, the company can call your home or business and read your   288
meters: water, gas, and electricity. Also, sensors in doorways and windows of   304

(Continued on next page)

PRACTICE

Type lines 11–36 twice each. Then retype any lines featuring letters you made errors on in the Pretest. Use single spacing.

A 11 acreage adverse aboard acquit alias arena ajar auto art ask
B 12 boulder bouquet beware broken baker bumpy busy bias ban bet
C 13 chamber caption candid cavern cynic comet calm coat cat cry
D 14 deposit diagram domain during drive drift dust doze dim dry

E 15 elegant eternal emerge emblem elect enter even easy elk eye
F 16 feather forgive fiscal fabric fling field fuse form fix for
G 17 glisten gainful gasket govern gravy going goat gulf gun gym
H 18 housing harvest health height heart haste hint hand ham hem

I 19 iceberg impulse impede insect infer inept idle into ire imp
J 20 journal justice joyful jungle judge juice join joke jet jam
K 21 kitchen keynote kidney kindle knife knack kind kite kin kit
L 22 license lecture legion locker logic lemon late lawn lax lye

M 23 monthly morning method mishap might match mock mink mid mow
N 24 neither neglect napkin nation noted noisy nail next nag now
O 25 outlast outgrow origin oxygen ocean onion oath once oat oak
P 26 playful prairie pencil prefer pride poise paid past par pet

Q 27 quintet quarrel quarry quiver quote quilt quip quid quo qt.
R 28 reflect reptile result remark range ridge rack rail rye rig
S 29 soldier someone sample shower spoke split sway salt sew sap
T 30 thirsty tactful trance threat tease think tray town tax tar

U 31 unknown upright useful urgent urban upset ugly undo urn use
V 32 voucher vicious volume versus vault vague vice vest vow via
W 33 whoever wrinkle within winter wrist wound went wild wed web

X 34 exploit relaxed expect expand excel exile next axle six lax
Y 35 yardage yawning yearly yellow yucca yummy year yawn yam yet
Z 36 zippers zealous zigzag zither zippy zebra zing zest zoo zap

POSTTEST

Repeat the Pretest on page 208 to see how much your skill has improved.

LESSONS 125/126

UNIT 21 FORMATTING LETTERS

UNIT GOAL
40/5'/5e

GOALS
- To use question marks correctly while typing sentences.
- To type business letters with two special parts: a *cc* notation and an attention line.
- To format enumerations in letters.

FORMAT
- Single spacing   60-space line   5-space tab

LAB 14

Type lines 1–4 once, providing the missing question marks. Edit your copy as your teacher reads the answers. Then retype lines 1–4 from your edited copy.

QUESTION MARKS

Workbook 231–232.

1 When will Dr. Zukov and Mr. Kim arrive at the airport, Jim.
2 Does Sean have an exact transcript of the press conference.
3 Will you be able to carry all those boxes with you, George.
4 How many questions were asked at the end of Bill's meeting.

POSTTEST 1   Repeat Pretest 1 on page 269 to see how much your skill has improved.

PRETEST 2   Take two 2-minute timings on lines 20–23. Circle your errors.

20 Barbara called the clinic to get vitamins for Liza and Max. 12
21 Grace wants to buy nine boxes of memos and carbons at cost. 24
22 Cathy agreed to leave early to meet our staff at our place. 36
23 Daniel cannot remove those trunks for another month or two. 48
    | 1 | 2 | 3 | 4 | 5 | 6 | 7 | 8 | 9 | 10 | 11 | 12

PRACTICE 2   Type lines 24–27 four times.

24 fvf five viva very avid favor jmj jams many main mean major
25 dcd cede dice code dock occur sxs exit next taxi text taxes
26 aza maze haze hazy lazy azure jnj Jane June Joan Jean Janet
27 fbf beef fibs buff fobs fiber l.l Mr. Dr. Ms. Mrs. Sgt. Lt.

POSTTEST 2   Repeat Pretest 2 to see how much your skill has improved.

LESSONS 163/164

UNIT 27 ADVANCED FORMATTING OF REPORTS   UNIT GOAL 41/5'/4e

GOALS
- To use colons correctly while typing sentences.
- To format a magazine article and an annotated bibliography.

FORMAT
- Single spacing   60-space line   5-space tab

LAB 18   Type lines 1–4 once, providing the missing colons. Edit your copy as your teacher
                        reads the answers. Then retype lines 1–4 from your edited copy.

COLONS

Workbook 341–342.

1 Zoe can play several instruments piano, flute, and drums.
2 The group likes to wear vivid colors aqua, blue, and red.
3 Pack an extra basket with food fruit, bread, and cookies.
4 I bought this equipment skis, boots, gloves, and jackets.

**12-SECOND
TIMINGS**

Type each line four times, or take four 12-second timings on each line. For each
timing, type with no more than one error.

5 We have a lot of work to do before we will be able to vote. 12
6 A big red fox ran across the field and into the high grass. 12
7 If it does not rain, I hope to go to his house to get them. 12
                        25   30   35   40   45   50   55   60

Take a 5-minute timing on lines 5–22. Type six times each word on which you made an error, hesitated, or stopped during the 5-minute timing. Then take a 5-minute timing to see how much your skill has improved.

```
                                   1                        2
 5        The office of the future is going to see quite a large    12
                   3                        4
 6        The office of the future is going to see quite a large    24
             5                    6                        7
 7        The office of the future is going to see quite a large    36
                       8                          9
 8   change from today's office.  One of the amazing things that    48
              10                        11                      12
 9   change from today's office.  One of the amazing things that    60
                            13                        14
10   change from today's office.  One of the amazing things that    72
                    15                    16
11   will happen is that we may no longer see offices with fixed    84
          17                        18                      19
12   will happen is that we may no longer see offices with fixed    96
                      20                        21
13   will happen is that we may no longer see offices with fixed   108
               22                          23                      24
14   walls.  Instead, movable walls might be used so that a firm   120
                         25                        26
15   walls.  Instead, movable walls might be used so that a firm   132
                   27                        28
16   walls.  Instead, movable walls might be used so that a firm   144
           29                        30                      31
17   will be able to change the office layout when a new project   156
                         32                        33
18   will be able to change the office layout when a new project   168
                 34                        35                      36
19   will be able to change the office layout when a new project   180
                            37
20   team requires more room to work.                             186
                      38
21   team requires more room to work.                             193
                39                        40
22   team requires more room to work.                             200
     |   1   |   2   |   3   |   4   |   5   |   6   |   7   |   8   |   9   |  10   |  11   |  12    SI 1.32
```

In this unit, you will have to read the letters to see if you should add an enclosure notation. You will also have to remember to use the current date and your initials—no reminders are provided.

JOB 125/6-1. LETTER

Standard format (see page 168). Workbook 233–234. Body 98 words (plus 20 words for attention line).

Elementary Education Department, Mayville State College, Mayville, ND 58257, Attention: Chairperson, Ladies and Gentlemen:

The enclosed survey is being sent to all schools in the state to find out how you teach reading and writing skills in the lower level courses.

In addition to your answers to each of the questions on page 1 and page 2 of our survey, we would welcome your comments to the issues we have listed on page 3. If necessary, please feel free to use additional sheets for your comments.

We look forward to receiving your answers to our survey. A copy of the results of our survey will be mailed to you in a few weeks. Yours truly, Blanche Kile, Researcher, cc: Chris Van Vliet

LESSON 162

GOALS
- To type 40/2'/2e.
- To improve keyboarding skills by practicing right-hand words and down reaches.

FORMAT
- Single spacing   60-space line

KEYBOARDING SKILLS

Type lines 1–4 once. Then use your margin release to finish typing line 5. Repeat lines 1–4, or take a series of 1-minute timings.

Speed
Accuracy
Numbers
Symbols
Technique

1 Clair may wish to blame me for both of their big work jams. 12
2 Jeff quietly moved his dozen boxes with Angy's power truck. 12
3 Bob lost checks Nos. 10, 29, and 38; I lost Nos. 47 and 56. 12
4 Bring me #10, #29, #38, and #47, but leave #56 for Jeffrey. 12
5 The director of the panel may wish to amend the audit form
   slightly.

| 1 | 2 | 3 | 4 | 5 | 6 | 7 | 8 | 9 | 10 | 11 | 12

"OK" TIMINGS

This version of a 30-second timing is used to build your accuracy on alphabetic copy. Type as many "OK" (errorless) timings as possible out of three attempts on lines 6–8. Then repeat the attempt on lines 9–11.

6 Roxie picked off the yellow jonquils by the amazing cavern. 12
7 Jean gave my excited boy quite a prize for his clever work. 24
8 Holley acquired a prize for jumping backward over six feet. 36

9   Paul reviewed the subject before giving Max and Kay a quiz. 12
10 Vic quickly mixed grape juice with the frozen strawberries. 24
11 I quickly explained that few big jobs involve many hazards. 36

| 1 | 2 | 3 | 4 | 5 | 6 | 7 | 8 | 9 | 10 | 11 | 12

PRETEST 1

Take two 2-minute timings on lines 12–15. Circle your errors.

12 It is their opinion that Jimmy will join the union at noon. 12
13 Phyllis knows her pumpkins will soon look similar to yours. 24
14 Phillip enjoys looking at and collecting only common coins. 36
15 Jon gave all patrons pure stones from that pioneer village. 48

| 1 | 2 | 3 | 4 | 5 | 6 | 7 | 8 | 9 | 10 | 11 | 12

PRACTICE 1

Type lines 16–19 four times.

16 kink lily oily nook only pill upon yolk honk join limp kiln
17 hill pink hook pool moon join noon milk mill lion look junk
18 poppy hilly onion pupil pulpy nylon milky phony plump lumpy
19 jolly imply phylon minimum million homonym opinion nonunion

JOB 125/6-2. LETTER

Standard format with indented paragraphs. Workbook 235–236. Body 84 words (plus 20 words for attention line).

```
Dahl Dairy Products, 1145 Rock Street     16
Rockford, IL 61101, Attention:  Man-      24
ager, Ladies and Gentlemen:               30

     This morning we received your        38

letter awarding us the bid for design-    46

ing an office layout for your new         53

branch store in DeKalb. We are indeed     60

pleased that we were chosen to            67

work on this important project.           73

We have enclosed three designs            81
```

```
that incorporate an open office           88

concept such as the one we                93

looked at in your office last week.  I    101

will call next week to confirm the        108

desired layout.                           111

     We look forward to working with      120

you in designing the offices              126

of the DeKalb branch. Yours               134

very truly, Dwight R. Straight,           146

President cc: Ms. Fontaine and Mr. Parks  158
```

FORMATTING ENUMERATIONS IN LETTERS

When typing enumerations in a letter, use the following guidelines: (1) To display the enumeration, indent it 5 spaces from both margins. (2) Precede and follow each enumerated item with 1 blank line. (3) Single-space each turnover line. (4) Indent each turnover line 4 spaces. Add 20 words to the body count for the display.

JOB 125/6-3. LETTER

Standard format with indented paragraphs. Workbook 237–238. Body 102 words (plus 20 words for attention line).

```
L&S Office Supplies, 13980 Peach Grove, Van Nuys, CA 91423,        20

Attention:  Office Manager, Ladies and Gentlemen:                  32

¶ We are very pleased to send you a copy of the new catalog that shows our   48

line of office supplies.  In it you will find our complete line of products.  62

We think you will be interested in our following line of metric supplies:    78

     1.   A4 File Folders. These folders will hold both standard size        89
          and legal-size paper.                                              94

     2.   A3 to A8 Metric Paper for small poster boards and name tags.       109

     3.   C6/7 and DL envelopes (small and large envelopes).                 121

¶ We look forward to receiving your order from our catalog.  We in-          132

vite you to visit our Lane Street Store and view our complete line           145

of office supplies.  Yours truly, James P. Mason, Manager                    162
```

JOB 161-1. MEMORANDUM

Standard format (see review in margin). Workbook 337.

Memorandums:

1. *The guide words align on the colons, as follows:*

   TO:
   FROM:
   DATE:
   SUBJECT:

   Set left margin 2 spaces after the colon.

2. *Triple-space following the guide words.*

3. *Body: Single spacing; double spacing between paragraphs.*

[*To:*] Camera Crew / [*From:*] Herbert Schelling, Producer / [*Date: Today's date*] / [*Subject:*] Videotaping at South Park High School

Tomorrow we will videotape the students at South Park High School throughout the day in various classes, beginning at 8 a.m. We have volunteered to do this taping as part of our public service program, "Our Schools in Action."

Since many parents and community leaders will judge the school by what they see on television, I hope that you will be sure to involve as many teachers and students as possible in the planning of what will be taped in the classroom. We want to do an outstanding job so that the school will invite WXYR-TV again whenever they anticipate participating in a program of public interest.

The tape will be shown on Sunday, [*insert a Sunday date about two weeks from the date of the memo*], at 2 p.m. Students, teachers, and administrators will be invited to visit the studio at that time.

JOB 161-2. BUSINESS INVOICE

Standard format (see review in margin). Workbook 339.

Invoices:

Use printed forms, which have the guide words To, Date, *and* Invoice *printed at the top. Then:*

1. *Center number column entries within the ruled column areas.*

2. *Type descriptions 2 spaces after the vertical column rule. Indent turnovers 3 spaces.*

3. *Put a tab stop at the most frequently used digit in the Unit Price and Amount columns.*

4. *Double-space between each new entry line.*

5. *Align the word* Total *with the* D *in* Description.

[*Date: Today's date*] / [*To*] Station WXYR-TV / 3800 West Carson Street / Milwaukee, WI 53201

Quantity	Description	Unit Price	Amount
4	Plastic stackable file-cabinet boxes #1975—beige	24.95	99.80
3 boxes	File folders #6176 50 count	16.24	48.72
	Total		148.52
	Delivery		11.10
	Total amount due		159.62

JOB 161-3. BUSINESS INVOICE

Standard format (see review in margin). Workbook 339.

[*Date: Today's date*] / [*To*] South Park High School / Old Plank Highway / Milwaukee, WI 53209

The school has purchased 4 student terminals for a Mitronics Computer, LCS-90, Model II @ $3,967.50. There is no tax or delivery charge. Complete the Amount column by calculating the cost of the 4 stations.

JOB 125/6-4. LETTER

Retype Job 125/6-3, replacing the second paragraph with the material below. Standard format with indented paragraphs. Workbook 239–240. Body 99 words.

We think you will be <u>quite</u> interested in our ~~complete~~ <u>all new</u> line of office templates and office layout grids, <u>for your use.</u> We have all the latest supplies needed by the office ma*a*ngers who wish to re^design their offices by using the ~~modern~~ open ~~office~~ plans.

JOB 125/6-5. UNEDITED, UNARRANGED LETTER

Standard format. Make corrections in spelling, grammar, and punctuation as you type. Workbook 241–242. Body 126 words (plus 20 for attention line).

Metro Towers, 401 Beach Street, Fort Worth, TX 76111, Atention: Manager, Ladies and Gentlemen:

Fleet Window Cleaning are one of the newest high rise window cleaning company's in the Fort Worth area and we would like to tell you about our grand opening special. Just give us a few moments of your time to help you become aware of our fine service.

We will wash any and every window in your bilding, to include storm and screan windows. We have rates for weekly monthly or yearly contracts and will make bids on jobs you wish did on short notice. We are fully insured and give free estimites on any job requested this month.

Clean windows reflect your concern for good public relations. Wo'nt you let Fleet help you improve your image. Call us today and make arangements for our free estimate. Sincerly yours, Anne W. Shane, Managre, cc: Ken Wells and Chris Armstrong

JOB 125/6-6. UNEDITED, UNARRANGED LETTER

Standard format with indented paragraphs. Make corrections in spelling and punctuation, and provide other editing revisions as you type. Workbook 243–244. Body 147 words (plus 20 words for attention line).

Key Products Inc., 124 Second Street, Cleveland, OH 44131, Atention Purchasing Manager, <u>Ladies and</u> Gentlem*e*n:

In your <u>may</u> ten letter you asked that we arrange a time that we (both could) get together to discus the purchase of new dry copy machines and sup*p*lies fro your firm. As I will be in Cleveland, ~~Ohio,~~ next week Tusday miht be the best <u>time</u> for our meeting. Do you think it <u>would</u> ~~might~~ be a good idea to start ~~right~~ at 8 A.M. so that we coud discuss not only the purchase of new machines but also the other options of machine a*c*quisition that you might like to consider. You might like to trade <u>in</u> your ~~old~~ machines or rent some fo our new machines on a trial basis--with an option to buy the machines of course!

I will call you tomorow afternoon at 4:00 P.M. to finalize our plans for the meeting. I look forward to working with you and to showing you all our new dry copy machines. yours very truly, Edward <u>a.</u> Vincent, Sales Represenative [*Send copies to Sally Bolton, Mark Kaiser, and Theresa Santos.*]

JOB 160-3. FOUR-COLUMN TABLE

Standard format. (Notice that time is given on a 24-hour basis.) Half sheet of paper.

TELEVISION SPORTS THIS WEEK

September 9–15, 19—

Sport	Day	Time	Channel(s)
Baseball	Monday	20:00:00	2, 6
Boxing	Friday	21:00:00	4
Football	Saturday	13:00:00	11
Tennis	Saturday	14:30:00	7
Golf	Saturday	16:00:00	6

Reminder

Paper turned lengthwise has the following dimensions: Width—110 pica spaces 132 elite spaces Depth—51 lines

JOB 160-4. FIVE-COLUMN TABLE

Retype Job 160-3, adding the information below as the third column (between *Day* and *Time*). Standard format. Full sheet of paper turned lengthwise.

<u>Event</u>, Detroit at New York, Davis vs. Watts, Ohio State vs. Purdue, French Open, Kemper Open

LESSON 161

GOALS
- To use colons correctly while typing sentences.
- To type 40/5'/4e.
- To format memorandums and invoices.

FORMAT
- Single spacing   60-space line   5-space tab and other tabs as needed

LAB 18

Type lines 1–4 once, providing the missing colons. Edit your copy as your teacher reads the answers. Then retype lines 1–4 from your edited copy.

COLONS

1 Quintin likes many things animals, motorcycles, and jazz.
2 I enjoy many kinds of cooking Chinese, French, and Irish.
3 Check your list for staples sugar, salt, flour, and milk.
4 Remember Visit those local shops and that new wax museum.

12-SECOND TIMINGS

Type each line four times, or take four 12-second timings on each line. For each timing, type with no more than one error.

5 Nancy works well with their plants: iris, ivy, and laurel. 12
6 Ellen hopes to come back and assist her class with the job. 12
7 Les saw the ship as he was walking over the hill near here. 12

25	30	35	40	45	50	55	60

5-MINUTE TIMINGS

Take two 5-minute timings on lines 5–22, page 264.

LESSONS 127/128

GOALS
- To recognize when quotation marks are used while typing sentences.
- To type business letters with three special parts: *bcc* notation, subject line, and postscript.
- To format a table within a letter.

FORMAT
- Single spacing   60-space line   5-space tab and as needed

LAB 15

QUOTATION MARKS

Type lines 1–4 once. Then repeat lines 1–4 or take a series of 1-minute timings.

```
1  Gus said, "Send requisitions to Ms. Camp for her approval."   12
2  Mark these packages "Fragile," Jo; "they're very delicate."   12
3  "About two dozen boxes were damaged in the fire yesterday."    12
4  "Please ask Laura for a copy of the June inventory report."    12
   |  1  |  2  |  3  |  4  |  5  |  6  |  7  |  8  |  9  |  10  |  11  |  12
```

Use quotation marks around the *exact* words of a speaker or writer. Do not use quotations for *restatements* of someone's exact words. Also use quotation marks around words that need special emphasis, such as words following *so-called* and *marked*. **Note:** Always place commas and periods before the second quotation mark when they are used.

"The contract," said Mrs. Berry, "will help us to hold down costs for the next few years." (Exact words.)

This so-called "inexpensive" product could cost us a fortune! (Special emphasis.)

5-MINUTE TIMINGS

Take a 5-minute timing on lines 5–19. Type six times each word on which you made an error, hesitated, or stopped during the 5-minute timing. Then take a 5-minute timing to see how much your skill has improved.

```
5   Autumn in the "northlands" is very exciting.  You jump up in the       14
6   early morning; walk out under a clear, azure blue sky; and notice a     28
7   strong chill in the air.  The leaves have lost their brilliant green.  It   42
8   appears that they have been tinted by a so-called "passerby."  However,   57
9   during the late night hours a frost has painted the green to hues of    71
10  brown, yellow, red, and orange.  It is really a breathtaking panorama    85
11  in technicolor.  The leaves barely move in the quietly persistent        98
12  breeze.  Then, suddenly, a brisk puff lifts them from the limbs and     112
13  carries them gently like feathers to the ground below.  You watch as    126
14  legions of leaves jump free and float to the earth, covering it like a   140
15  quilted blanket that looks much like moss.                              148
16   As you glance down at the grass, you can no longer see any large      162
17  droplets of dew like those that had clung to each blade, bright in the  176
18  early morning summer sun.  Those drops of dew have been "crystal-       189
19  ized."  Now their appearance might possibly deceive you.                200
    |  1  |  2  |  3  |  4  |  5  |  6  |  7  |  8  |  9  |  10  |  11  |  12  |  13  |  14   SI 1.34
```

JOB 159-2. (Continued)

built this display to call attention to the fact that we attract more 95
than 13 million listeners a week! 102

Before you plan your advertising budget for next year, see this 116
presentation. It will convince you that radio advertising pays off—for 131
the price of one prime-time 30-second TV spot you can buy 14 network 144
radio spots. / Very truly yours, / Harvey S. Grimes / Station Manager 164
/ [*Your initials*] 165

LESSON 160

GOALS
- To identify how colons are used while typing sentences.
- To format tables.

FORMAT
- Single spacing   60-space line   Tabs as needed

LAB 18

COLONS

Type lines 1–4 once. Then repeat lines 1–4 or take a series of 1-minute timings.

1 I zealously play these sports: golf, tennis, and handball. 12
2 The box holds my tools: hammers, wrenches, and two drills. 12
3 Visit these buildings: dormitory, music studios, and gyms. 12
4 Hint: Joe and I like quiet places to ski, skate, and sled. 12

| 1 | 2 | 3 | 4 | 5 | 6 | 7 | 8 | 9 | 10 | 11 | 12

12-SECOND TIMINGS

Type each line four times, or take four 12-second timings on each line. For each timing, type with no more than one error.

5 They may wish to blame me for the fight to end the problem. 12
6 The plane took off with a gust of wind and a whine of jets. 12
7 A big fire is one in which the smoke curls high in the sky. 12

25   30   35   40   45   50   55   60

FORMATTING REVIEW

Tables:

1. *Center vertically and horizontally.*

2. *Double-spacing.*

3. *Titles: Centered, all caps. Subtitle(s): Centered; double-space before, triple-space after the entire subtitle.*

4. *Identify the key line—longest entry in each column, plus the spaces between columns (usually 6).*

5. *Backspace to center the key line; set the left margin.*

6. *Space across to the start of the next column; set a tab stop. Continue for as many columns as needed.*

7. *Column heads are typed in initial caps, underscored, centered over their column; double-space after.*

JOBS 160-1 AND 160-2. TWO-COLUMN TABLES

Standard format (see review in margin). Job 160-1, half sheet of paper; Job 160-2, full sheet of paper.

RADIO WXZR—FM

Your Fine Music Station

Schedule for Saturday, January 14, 19——

Time	Program
7–9 a.m.	A Morning of Music
9–Noon	Around the Town
Noon–4 p.m.	Absolutely Jazz
4–6 p.m.	For the Love of Music
6–9 p.m.	Symphony Hall
9–Midnight	Piano Personalities

JOB 127/8-1. LETTER WITH SUBJECT LINE, POSTSCRIPT, AND *BCC* NOTATION

Block format (see page 173). Workbook 245–246. Body 125 words (plus 20 words for subject line).

Ms. Rose T. Sands, Safety Life Insurance Company, 227 Chama Road, Clovis, NM 88101, Dear Ms. Sands:, Subject: New Product Line for CRT

As a user of our word processing equipment for the past ten years, we know you will be quite interested in the enclosed brochures on our new line of products.

Note on the brochure marked "Sample" that you will now be able to input data 20 percent faster on our new text-editing machines because we increased our line length, and we changed our format design for letters. Also note on page 5 of the same brochure that the visual display has been enhanced by providing an improved, softer contrast between print and background image.

Mr. James Lessard, our sales rep in Sante Fe, will be calling you by the end of next week to set up an appointment for demonstrating the new Editor 500. Sincerely yours, John W. Grace, Branch Manager, PS: Because of the immaculate condition of your 400-S, we will give you a fabulous deal on trade-in. bcc: T. R. Jordan

FORMATTING TABLES WITHIN LETTERS

When a table or display is typed in a letter or memo, follow these guidelines:

1. Precede and follow the table with at least 1 blank line.
2. Center the table within the margins and indent at least 5 spaces on each side. If the table is too wide, select intercolumnar spaces that will limit the table width to preserve the indention.
3. Single-space the body of the table.

Note: Add 20 words to the body count for the display.

JOB 127/8-2. LETTER WITH A TABLE

Block format. Workbook 247–248. Body 77 words.

Mrs. June R. Tijerina / Claims Department / Golden Insurance Company / 1846 Market Street / San Francisco, CA 94102 / Dear Mrs. Tijerina: /

Thank you for your call on Friday, June 25, requesting the loan of a Model 250 while your machine is in our shop for repairs. We do not have a Model 250 available at this time, but you may want to consider using one of the machines described in the table below. We currently have these machines in the shop, and you can use one of them at no charge while your Model 200 is being repaired.

(Continued on next page)

PRACTICE

In the chart below, find the number of errors you made on the Pretest. Then type each of the designated drill lines four times.

Pretest errors	0–1	2–3	4–5	6+
Drill lines	26–30	25–29	24–28	23–27

Accuracy

23 it's July quite depends comedies programs shutdown stations
24 operas there's outside outdoor revealed Thursdays homeowner
25 escape camping because hundred business companies broadcast
26 quiz enough license favorite majority Icelanders television

Speed

27 Iceland living which their makes down this work bit for all
28 persons during devote color when them that have big buy the
29 people enough time tell have used city pays soap zany of us
30 viewing watch money favor shuts shows never been less to go

POSTTEST

Repeat the Pretest on page 264 to see how much your skill has improved.

FORMATTING REVIEW

Workbook 327–328.
Letters: (Standard Format)

1. *Margins: 50P/ 60E.*
2. *Date: Line 15.*
3. *Inside address: 5 lines below date.*
4. *Salutation: Double-space before and after.*
5. *Subject line: Follows the salutation, with double space before and after.*
6. *Complimentary closing: Begin at the center, a double space below the body.*
7. *Writer's identification (writer's name and job title): 4 lines below complimentary closing.*
8. *Typist's initials: At left margin, double space below writer's identification. No. 10 envelope: Begin addressee's name and address on line 14, 40 spaces from left edge.*

JOB 159-1. LETTER
Standard format (see review in margin). Address a No. 10 envelope. Workbook 329, 331–332. Body 137 words.

[*Today's date*] / Mr. Gregory Cocagi / 7224 Lomar Drive / Geneva, NY   17
14456 / Dear Mr. Cocagi: 23

Now you can hear stereo music on AM radio. That's right—AM   36
stereo. Last week in Washington, stereo broadcasting by AM radio   50
stations was approved. This action will permit broadcasters to give   63
listeners like you the full range of stereo, which up to this time you   78
have been able to hear only on FM radio.   86

While your present car radio, for example, will be able to pick up   100
the music played on AM stereo, you will not be able to enjoy stereo   114
sound because a new radio receiver will be required.   125

As you know, Belm has been a leading maker of AM/FM radios for   138
many years. We are proud to inform you that all our new radios have   152
AM stereo capability.   157

Visit your Belm dealer today and select your new car radio so that   171
you will hear relaxing stereo on both AM and FM broadcasts. /   183
Sincerely yours, / Ms. Elizabeth McDowell / Advertising Director /   201
[*Your initials*]   203

JOB 159-2. LETTER WITH SUBJECT LINE
Standard format (see review in margin). Address a No. 10 envelope. Workbook 333–334. Body 84 words.

[*Today's date*] / Ms. Janet Velmar / Director of Advertising / Hector   18
Plastics / 200 West Wiley Avenue / Tinley Park, IL 60477 / Dear Ms.   31
Velmar: / Subject: The People Delivery System   41

Have you seen our new media program entitled "The People Delivery   55
System," which is being shown this week at Clear Beach Inn? Our   68
radio station, WPIT-AM/FM, together with the CBC Radio Network,   81

JOB 127/8-2. (Continued)

Manufacturer	Model	Storage
W.P. Systems	J43	Disk
Word Data Inc.	VIP	Diskette
Speed Terminal	PAC-II	Tape
First Typing	215	Card

Please call me if you would like to use one of the above machines while your Model 200 is being repaired. Very truly yours, Allen H. Jacobs, Manager P.S.: If your Model 200 is not repaired by the 6th, you may keep the machine you loaned until the Model 200 has been returned.

JOB 127/8-3. LETTER WITH *BCC* NOTATION
Block format. Workbook 249–250. Body 119 words (plus 20 words for subject line).

Dr. R. L. Stern, Chairperson, Business Education Department, Bronx   21

City College, 738 White Plains Road, Bronx, NY 10473, Dear Dr.   36

Stern: Subject: Keyboard Training   43

We would like you to share the enclosed brochures with your   56

students who might be interested in a business career.   Our key-   68

board training program is open to those who have a special desire   80

to work in the area of word processing.   88

We will provide key board training on four of the most popular text-   103

editing machines.   When the training has been completed, the   115

graduates will be assigned to an office where they will work as interns for at least eight weeks.   135

This Training Employment Program has proven to be a very   147

popular one, as we have already placed over 250 trainees in firms   159

throughout the state in the past 3 years.   We hope your students   173

will be added to our list too.   Sincerely, Claire V. Speel,   189

Training Director, bcc: Jayne Ross   198

LESSON 159

GOALS
- To recognize how colons are used while typing sentences.
- To format letters and envelopes.

FORMAT
- Single spacing   60-space line   5-space tab

LAB 18

Type lines 1–4 once. Then repeat lines 1–4 or take a series of 1-minute timings.

COLONS

1 Make this point clear: We need greater sales this quarter.   12
2 The car has several extras: clock, roof rack, and air bag.   12
3 We had three visitors: Mr. White, Ms. Zonn, and Ms. Yates.   12
4 Jan's set of silver is small: 6 forks, 6 knives, 6 spoons.   12

| 1 | 2 | 3 | 4 | 5 | 6 | 7 | 8 | 9 | 10 | 11 | 12

Use a colon even if the words *the following* or *as follows* are implied, not stated. Also, capitalize the first word after the colon if that word begins a complete sentence or is a proper noun.

She cited two examples: staff and budgets.
Remember: The deadline is May 28.

PRETEST

Take a 5-minute Pretest on lines 5–22. Then circle and count your errors. Use the chart on page 265 to determine which lines to type for practice.

5   Every July, Iceland shuts down its television stations   12
6   because all the people employed in this work want to escape   24
7   on their vacations. July is one month in Iceland when it's   36
8   never dark, which makes it the ideal time for Icelanders to   48
9   go outside and enjoy the extra sun.   55
10   The Icelanders devote July to outdoor living, camping,   67
11   and picnicking. The vast majority of them tell us that the   79
12   shutdown pleases them. A survey of several hundred persons   91
13   who live in one city revealed that most of them favor a bit   103
14   less television. Of course, these people have been used to   115
15   less viewing time because during the year the stations have   127
16   no programs on Thursdays. Although each homeowner pays for   139
17   a license for each color set, there's not enough money from   151
18   all sources to broadcast all week.   158
19   Television is quite a big business that relies on lots   170
20   of companies to buy time for their commercials. It relies,   182
21   too, on you to view your favorite shows: soap operas, zany   194
22   comedies, quiz and game shows.   200

| 1 | 2 | 3 | 4 | 5 | 6 | 7 | 8 | 9 | 10 | 11 | 12   SI 1.47

JOB 127/8-4. AMS LETTER WITH POSTSCRIPT AND *BCC* NOTATION

Standard format. Make corrections in spelling, grammar, and punctuation, and provide other editing revisions as you type. Workbook 251–252. Body 106 words (plus 20 words for subject line).

Mr. Ted Moore, Shield Products Inc., 582 College (Ave)., Des Moines, IA

59340, Subject: Dear Mr. Moore: Slides for Equipment Training

This year at Central ^state College we are expanding our information

procesing program.

No ¶ Although we do not have the funds to purchase a large volume of

word procesing equipment, we have been able to secure enough funds to

provide our students with two crt's for the comming year.

To acquaint our students with machines from other manufacturers,

we would like to develop a slide/tape program for there use. May we

have permission to tour your word processing department for the pur-

pose of developeing a portion of this Slide/Tape Program?

I would like to call you at 10 A.M. on Friday to discus our

visit. Yours truly, Jean R. Hall, Business Teacher, Ps: I will

bring some sample slides with me so that you can see how we are

going to use these materials.

GOALS
- To identify when quotation marks are used while typing sentences.
- To type at least 40/5'/5e.
- To format letters on baronial and monarch stationery.

FORMAT
- Single spacing   60-space line   5-space tab

LAB 15

QUOTATION MARKS

Type lines 1–4 once. Then repeat lines 1–4 or take a series of 1-minute timings.

1 June Mendez said, "Request more information on these forms."   12
2 Label this item "Caution" so that it gets extraspecial care.   12
3 "The issue," answered Vonda, "is whether you should cancel."   12
4 Verna insisted, "The best glue on the market is Stick-Glue."   12

| 1 | 2 | 3 | 4 | 5 | 6 | 7 | 8 | 9 | 10 | 11 | 12

Reports:

1. *Margins: 60P/ 70E.*
   Top margin:
   Page 1—12 blank lines (↓ 13)
   Page 2—6 blank lines (↓ 7)
   Bottom margin: 6 to 9 blank lines.

2. *Double spacing.*

3. *Title: Centered, caps, line 13.*

4. *Subtitle: Double-space before; triple-space after.*

5. *Side headings: All caps; triple-space before, double-space after.*

References and Footnotes:

1. *Text references: Type the appropriate superscript figure (raised, like this[1]) following the word, phrase, or sentence for which there is a footnote.*

2. *Separation line: At the left margin, 1 line below the last line of a full page of text, 20P/ 24E strokes long.*

3. *Double-space and indent 5 spaces. Type the superscript number followed by the reference.*

4. *Single-space; double-space between footnotes.*

JOBS 158-1 AND 158-2. UNBOUND REPORT WITH FOOTNOTES

Standard format (see review in margin). Job 158-1, double spacing; Job 158-2, single spacing. Workbook 325.

WORD PROCESSING   15

A concept known as word processing has lead the way toward making the   32
office worker more productive. Word processing can be defined in many ways,   47
but the main concept is to use people, procedures, and machines to speed   62
business communications.[1]   69

HISTORY   73

The first true word processing machine was placed on the market in 1965.   88
It was an automatic editing typewriter that could store typed copy and replay   104
it, error-free, at 150 words per minute.[2] Later, a newer model that recorded on   122
plastic cards was devised. Office workers began to see that word processing   138
had many benefits: easier revision of copy, mass production of form letters that   154
did not look like form letters, and faster handling of mailing lists.   168

VOCABULARY   172

Like any specialized industry, word processing has its own terms that can be   189
confusing to the untrained. For example, "floppy disks" are thin platters of   204
magnetic tape used for information storage. Printing is often done with a   219
"daisy wheel"—a typing element shaped like a wheel with a solid black center   235
and type on the outside edge—which can print at the rate of 55 characters per   250
second.   252

SHOPPING FOR EQUIPMENT   259

Office managers offer these pointers to those who are thinking of buying   274
word processing machines: 280

1. Consider the change fully. Word processing is not just fast typewriters;   296
   it is a change in the way the office operates.   308
2. Get expert help from the beginning, and test the equipment in your own   324
   office.   327
3. Be sure the type of machine you buy is simple to operate and easy to   343
   repair.   346

Footnotes: 353

[1]Michael Thoryn, "Office Equipment: Electronics Empties the Typing   372
Pool," Nation's Business, February 1979, p. 74.   388

[2]Christopher Byron, "Now the Office of Tomorrow," Time, November 17,   409
1980, pp. 81–82.   412

1-AND 5-MINUTE TIMINGS

Take two 1-minute timings on each paragraph. Then take one 5-minute timing on the entire selection. Use single spacing for the 1-minute timings and double spacing for the 5-minute timing.

```
 5        Animals are capable of defending themselves in various   12
 6   ways.  Defense to some means to run or fly away, to some it    24
 7   means to hide, to some it means to play dead, and to others    36
 8   it means to fight.                                             40

 9        The rabbits are very quick and can often run away from    12
10   their enemies.  They are also quite good at making a zigzag    24
11   jump as they bound off.  Birds, of course, will escape most    36
12   enemies by flight.                                             40

13        Some animals are very good at hiding as a means of de-    12
14   fense.  Some are hidden by their colors; others can use the    24
15   shape of their body to hide.  For example, a tiger can hide    36
16   well in the shadows.                                           40

17        An "expert" at playing dead, of course, is an opossum.    12
18   When it is threatened, the opossum closes its eyes and lets    24
19   its body go limp.  Even when it's bitten, it will remain in    36
20   this quiet position.                                           40

21        Many animals choose to fight as a defense.  Members of    12
22   the deer family might bite, kick, or use their antlers when    24
23   defending themselves.  Large members of the cat family will    36
24   use their sharp claws.                                         40

     |  1  |  2  |  3  |  4  |  5  |  6  |  7  |  8  |  9  | 10  | 11  | 12    SI 1.37
```

FORMATTING LETTERS ON BARONIAL AND MONARCH STATIONERY

Workbook 253–254.

Some firms have their short letters typed on either baronial stationery (5½″ by 8½″—metric A5: 148 by 210 mm) or monarch stationery (7¼″ by 10½″—about 181 by 263 mm). The more commonly used is baronial.

1. To format letters on baronial stationery:
   a. Date: line 12.
   b. Inside address: line 16 (↓4).
   c. Line length: 40P/50E.
2. To format letters on monarch stationery:
   a. Date: line 14.
   b. Inside address: line 19 (↓5).
   c. Line length: 40P/50E or 50P/60E.

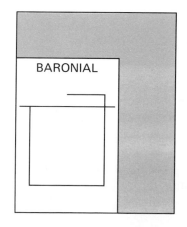

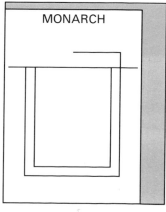

JOB 157-2. OUTLINE
Standard format (see review in margin). Full sheet of paper.

Outlines:

1. *Margins: Use judgment—center the longest line horizontally.*

2. *Title: Centered; triple-space after.*

3. *Roman-numeral lines in all caps— 2 blank lines before, 1 blank line after.*

4. *Single-space other lines.*

5. *Align the periods after the roman numerals.*

6. *Indent each subdivision 4 more spaces, thus:*
   I.
      A.
         1.
            a.

```
          YEAR-END SALES REPORT ON CLOCK RADIOS
            I.  RECORD SALES
            A.  New Models This Year
            1.  AM/FM Digital Clock Radio
            a.  Snooze Control
            b.  Earphone Jack
            2.  AM/FM Electronic Clock Radio
            a.  LED Readout Display
            b.  Alarm With Automatic Shutoff
            c.  Cassette Tape Recorder
            B.  New Outlets This Year
           II.  FORECAST FOR NEXT YEAR
            A.  Foreign Imports
            B.  Inflation
          III.  LONG-RANGE PLANNING
```

LESSON 158

GOAL
- To format reports and references.

FORMAT
- Single spacing   60-space line   5-space tab

KEYBOARDING SKILLS

Type lines 1–4 once. Then practice using your shift lock by typing line 5 twice. Repeat lines 1–4, or take a series of 1-minute timings.

Speed	1	The six forms she got from the firm may do for the problem.	12
Accuracy	2	Jacqueline was vexed by the folks who got the money prizes.	12
Numbers	3	She moved out of Rooms 10, 29, and 38 into Rooms 47 and 56.	12
Symbols	4	Recheck the invoices for Boxes #10, #29, #38, #47, and #56.	12
Technique	5	The SHIFT LOCK helps YOU to make ALL CAPS for DISPLAY work.

```
    |  1  |  2  |  3  |  4  |  5  |  6  |  7  |  8  |  9  |  10  |  11  |  12
```

12-SECOND TIMINGS

Type each line four times, or take four 12-second timings on each line. For each timing, type with no more than one error.

6 Holly typed three fewer lines than David thought she would. 12
7 The desk was moved over to the left and was not moved back. 12
8 We will go to the fair in the city for the rest of the day. 12

```
    25    30    35    40    45    50    55    60
```

JOB 129-1. LETTER ON BARONIAL STATIONERY

Standard format. Workbook 255–256. Body 66 words.

Ms. Roberta Kile, Office Administration De- 16
partment, Mayville State College, Mayville, 25
ND 58257, Dear Ms. Kile: 31

We are pleased to be able to take part in 41
your survey on reading and writing skills. I 50
have completed your survey and am returning 59
it as you requested in your letter. 66

My colleagues and I had some comments on 75
the issues you raised in your survey, and our 85
reactions appear on the enclosed sheet. 93

We look forward to receiving a copy of the 102
survey results. Yours truly, Frank S. James, 117
Chairperson 120

JOB 129-2. LETTER ON BARONIAL STATIONERY

Standard format. Workbook 255–256. Body 65 words.

Mr. James P. Hill, Manager, Lomax Sales 16
Associates, 20627 Hawthorne Boulevard, 24
South, Torrance, CA 90503, Dear Mr. Hill: 33

Thank you for the catalog showing your line 43
of office supplies. We were indeed interested 52
in looking at the volume of metric supplies 61
your store carries. 65

Next week Ms. Lang from our Long Beach 74
store will be in Torrance to view your line of 84
metric supplies. 87

You will be receiving our fall order by the 97
end of the week. Thank you again for the 105
catalog. Very truly yours, Karen T. Booker, 120
Office Manager 126

LESSON 130

CLINIC

GOALS
- To use quotation marks correctly while typing sentences.
- To type 40/5'/5e.
- To improve your typing speed on 12-second timings and 5-minute timings.

FORMAT
- Single spacing   60-space line   5-space tab and every fifth space thereafter

LAB 15

QUOTATION MARKS

Type lines 1–4 once, providing the missing quotation marks. Edit your copy as your teacher reads the answers. Then retype lines 1–4 from your edited copy.

1 David said, We will obviously need a quiet place to work.
2 The photo is fuzzy because of the poor lens, said Robert.
3 Joe and Vera know the combination of the safe, Will said.
4 Ask Xaveria for help on these projects, Marisa suggested.

12-SECOND TIMINGS

Type lines 5–7 four times, or take four 12-second timings on each line. For each timing, type with no more than one error. Repeat the procedure on lines 8–10.

5 A small tug pushed the liner into the quay and to the pier. 12
6 We would prefer to take a lot of quizzes, not one big exam. 12
7 If you put the sodas in the fridge, they will soon be cold. 12
8 All they want to do is to sit in the shade of the big oaks. 12
9 We had a kit of tools that we could use to fix the engines. 12
10 The two of them sat in the soft sand and soaked up the sun. 12

**PREVIEW
PRACTICE**

Accuracy
Speed

Type lines 5 and 6 twice as a preview to the 1- and 5-minute timings below.

5 only great serves cluster surveys viewers' overdue machines
6 produced making forms legal their turn dull with some by so

**1- AND
5-MINUTE
TIMINGS**

Take two 1-minute timings on each paragraph. Then take one 5-minute timing on the entire selection. Use single spacing for the 1-minute timings and double spacing for the 5-minute timing.   1'

7   In some companies, some departments need to have their   12
8 own centers, with just a few word processing machines––this 24
9 center is called a cluster, and the production done is only 36
10 for that department.   40

11   If the office belongs to the manager of the department   12
12 that has the surveys on viewers' likes and dislikes for the 24
13 local TV station, for example, the work of the cluster will 36
14 be tables or reports.   40

15   On the other hand, a department responsible for making   12
16 collections on overdue bills will have a great deal of mail 24
17 and just a few tables and reports to be produced by typists 36
18 within this cluster.   40

19   For one more example: A cluster that serves the legal   12
20 department will turn out a great many long documents, along 24
21 with the forms that require fill–ins, such as court papers, 36
22 contracts, and so on.   40

23   Thus the work of one cluster will differ from the work   12
24 of any other, but the work within a cluster is standardized 24
25 and repetitive. Although the work may seem dull, it really 36
26 is quite interesting.   40

| 1 | 2 | 3 | 4 | 5 | 6 | 7 | 8 | 9 | 10 | 11 | 12   SI 1.45

**FORMATTING
REVIEW**

Enumerations:

1. Margins: Block-center horizontally or 50P/60E.

2. Center vertically.

3. Title: Centered; triple-space after.

4. Single-space enumerated items with double-space between them.

5. Indent turnover lines.

JOB 157-1. ENUMERATION

Standard format (see review in margin). Full sheet of paper.

FORM LETTERS   7

In these days of mass mailings, form letters are especially   21
effective. Form letters have many excellent features, such   33
as the following: 37
1. Since the form letter is already written, it can be sent   49
    out immediately whenever it is needed.   60
2. One letter can be sent to hundreds of people by changing   74
    the inside address (and sometimes other variables).   86
3. A form letter can be stored on a machine, such as a word   100
    processor, and reproduced automatically at rapid rates.   113

Take a 5-minute timing on lines 11–28. Type six times each word on which you made an error, hesitated, or stopped during the 5-minute timing. Then take a 5-minute timing to see how much your skill has improved.

```
11        Do you realize that a more attractive office will most    12
                                                  2
12        Do you realize that a more attractive office will most    24
           3                             4
13        Do you realize that a more attractive office will most    36
           5                             6                 7
14   likely cause an office worker to produce at a higher level?    48
                    8                            9
15   likely cause an office worker to produce at a higher level?    60
            10                          11                      12
16   likely cause an office worker to produce at a higher level?    72
                            13                   14
17   More attractive color selections will be seen in offices of    84
          15                          16
18   More attractive color selections will be seen in offices of    96
          17                          18                      19
19   More attractive color selections will be seen in offices of   108
                    20                            21
20   the next decade.   Quite a few of the colors we select for a   120
              22                      23                          24
21   the next decade.   Quite a few of the colors we select for a   132
                              25                      26
22   the next decade.   Quite a few of the colors we select for a   144
              27                      28
23   new office will be those judged to best reflect light.   The   156
          29                30                    31
24   new office will be those judged to best reflect light.   The   168
                          32                    33
25   new office will be those judged to best reflect light.   The   180
              34                    35                          36
26   colors can help to diffuse light.                              187
                          37
27   colors can help to diffuse light.                              193
                    38
28   colors can help to diffuse light.                              200
              39                    40
     |  1  |  2  |  3  |  4  |  5  |  6  |  7  |  8  |  9  | 10  | 11  | 12    SI 1.38
```

LESSONS 131/ 132

UNIT 22 FORMATTING BUSINESS FORMS

UNIT GOAL
40/5'/5e

GOALS
- To use quotation marks correctly while typing sentences.
- To type three purchase requisitions and three purchase orders (from unarranged and incomplete copy).

FORMAT
- Single spacing   60-space line   5-space tab and other tabs as needed

LAB 15

QUOTATION MARKS

Type lines 1–4 once, providing the missing quotation marks. Edit your copy as your teacher reads the answers. Then retype lines 1–4 from your edited copy.

1 Now, Duane said, we will have accurate costs available.

2 Her so-called crazy idea, we think, is really quite sane.

3 I strongly recommend Dr. Joan Peterson, replied Jeremiah.

4 Send Kevin the exact schedule of each meeting, said Kent.

PRACTICE 1

Type lines 10–15 four times.

10 acts west cards drafts started greatest beverages afterward
11 read gates serve acreage created erasers rewarded decreased
12 tract state seats grave aware fever brave eager areas after
13 texts waste verbs tests saved great fewer stage weave wears
14 eats dear base acre rare text star ward grew verb fact safe
15 sad age bed ads dad wax tea war bet bar are ear cat tax wet

POSTTEST 1

Repeat Pretest 1 to see how much your skill has improved.

PRETEST 2

Take two 2-minute timings on lines 16–19. Circle your errors.

16 The surprised judge thanked her for getting the desk files. 12
17 Watch just to see who else puts anything on the two floors. 24
18 Thinking people have studied a multitude of needless words. 36
19 I hope the enclosed idea can keep the guests in the course. 48
   | 1 | 2 | 3 | 4 | 5 | 6 | 7 | 8 | 9 | 10 | 11 | 12

PRACTICE 2

Type lines 20–25 four times.

20 old used word think watch hidden studied thinking multitude
21 how need seem noted shown arises thanked needless surprised
22 dry just puts floor meant counts implied invested forwarded
23 use else grow files judge formed closest anything effective
24 kit loan step shown table plenty private journals scheduled
25 yes park very token total school program patients physician

POSTTEST 2

Repeat Pretest 2 to see how much your skill has improved.

5-MINUTE TIMING

Take one 5-minute timing on lines 5–19 on page 258.

LESSON 157

UNIT 26 BASIC FORMATTING REVIEW

UNIT GOAL
40/5'/4e

GOALS
- To use colons correctly while typing sentences.
- To format enumerations and outlines.

FORMAT
- Single spacing   60-space line   5-space tab and other tabs as needed

LAB 17

Type lines 1–4 once, providing the missing colons. Edit your copy as your teacher reads the answers. Then retype lines 1–4 from your edited copy.

COLONS

1 Walt quoted on these items forms, folders, and envelopes.
2 Choose one of these subjects management, finance, or tax.
3 I typed it thus single spacing, 50-space line, pica type.
4 Katy Venezia ordered these items inks, ribbons, and pens.

Type lines 5 and 6 twice as a preview to the 5-minute timings below.

Accuracy   5   search typing ability personal employer carefully emotional
Speed   6   always public mature touch adept loyal might work such when

5-MINUTE TIMINGS

Take two 5-minute timings on lines 7–23.

```
 7      When employers search for a new office worker, they do   12
 8   so by looking at many things.  Such a worker must have good  24
 9   skills that might be quite hard to find.  For instance, the  36
10   adept office worker must work quickly and carefully.  Also,  48
11   the valued office worker must be at ease while working with  60
12   other personnel as well as with the general public.  If you  72
13   wish to work in an office, you should touch up your skills.   84
14      The skills to work on are the professional skills such    96
15   as typing, shorthand, and math; the personal skills such as  108
16   need for initiative, being on time, and working with others  120
17   in the office; and, of course, the emotional skills such as  132
18   ability to work under stress, to be loyal to your employer,  144
19   and "to keep the business of an office in an office."  When   156
20   a mature person works in an office, these skills are always  168
21   easy to observe.  Just by being aware of the nature of work  180
22   in an office, you will be able to do the work with zeal and  192
23   become a winner; and that's important.                       200
     |  1  |  2  |  3  |  4  |  5  |  6  |  7  |  8  |  9  | 10  | 11  | 12   SI 1.39
```

JOBS 131/2-1 AND 131/2-2. PURCHASE REQUISITIONS

Type the information in Jobs 131/2-1 and 131/2-2 on two purchase requisition forms. Standard format. Workbook 257.

Purchase Requisition 1029

To expand the computer storage facilities, Virginia Hanes, Director / Computer Center, needs the following items: 3 Open tape-storage cabinets; 4 Double-door tape storage cabinets; 1 Sliding door cabinet; 20 10½″ tape canisters; 20 7″ Tape canisters. Obtain the supplies from Computer Supplies, 5078 Lakeshore Drive, New Orleans, LA 70146.

Purchase Requisition 1030

A new sales position has been added to Saratoga Enterprises, 413 Main Street East, Rochester, NY 14604. Charles Fuhrman, Facilities Manager, is ordering the following furniture from Harrison Business Furniture, 1698 Manitou Road, Rochester, NY 14626: 1 24″ × 54″ Desk; 1 Swivel desk chair; 1 Corner table; 1 Side chair with arms; 1 4-drawer 52″ File cabinet.

JOBS 131/2-3 AND 131/2-4. PURCHASE ORDERS

Type the information in Jobs 131/2-3 and 131/2-4 (page 221) on two purchase order forms. Standard format. Workbook 259.

PRACTICE

Type lines 20–23 twice, as a group, or take a series of 1-minute timings.

Accuracy
20 My fine ax just zipped through the black wood quite evenly. 12
21 Roxie picked off the amazing yellow jonquils by the cavern. 12
22 Jane gave my excited boy quite a prize for his clever work. 12
23 Kay bought five or six cans to award as equal major prizes. 12

Type each line twice, or take a series of 1-minute timings.

Speed
24 When she got to the lake, the girl paid for the oak panels. 12
25 I envy the six firms, for they fight for the right element. 12
26 Jane and the girl kept their title to the island cornfield. 12
27 The man got a snap of an authentic whale by the big island. 12
    | 1 | 2 | 3 | 4 | 5 | 6 | 7 | 8 | 9 | 10 | 11 | 12

12-SECOND TIMINGS

Type each line four times, or take four 12-second timings on each line. For each timing, type with no more than one error.

28 Mark can type fast on these words: the, for, but, can, go. 12
29 The four of them had to get to the bus by the time it left. 12
30 Sue says that she can fix the vase that fell from the desk. 12

    25   30   35   40   45   50   55   60

5-MINUTE TIMING

Repeat the 5-minute timing on lines 5–19 on page 258 to see how much your skill has improved.

LESSON 156

CLINIC

GOALS
- To type 40/5'/4e.
- To improve competency on selected key reaches.

FORMAT
- Single spacing   60-space line   5-space tab

KEYBOARDING SKILLS

Type lines 1–4 once. Then type each word in line 5 two times, returning your carriage or carrier before starting to type the next word. Repeat lines 1–4, or take a series of 1-minute timings.

Speed   1 Look. See how well his fingers are flying on the keys now. 12
Accuracy   2 Poor Jack was vexed about my long and quite hazy falsehood. 12
Numbers   3 Alice put markers at 10 km, 29 km, 38 km, 47 km, and 56 km. 12
Symbols   4 Some stores are offering 20% off; some are giving only 10%. 12
Technique   5 next pear lead yelp made near lame keep jade hard part open
               | 1 | 2 | 3 | 4 | 5 | 6 | 7 | 8 | 9 | 10 | 11 | 12

PRETEST 1

Take two 2-minute timings on lines 6–9. Circle your errors.

6 Stewart deserves to get a big reward after saving the girl. 12
7 Seven bears rested at the water's edge after the hard swim. 24
8 Barbara wore a dark red sweater to the fair in Texas today. 36
9 Edward said the test was extra hard and feared the results. 48
   | 1 | 2 | 3 | 4 | 5 | 6 | 7 | 8 | 9 | 10 | 11 | 12

Purchase Order 384

Computer Supplies, 5078 Lakeshore Drive, New Orleans, LA 70146. 3 Tape storage cabinets, Model TSC-8816 @ $171.65 = $514.95; 4 Tape storage cabinets, Model TSC-9816 @ $211.50 = $846; 1 Sliding door cabinet, Model TSC-7800 @ $141 = $141; 20 Tape canisters, Model TC-10 @ $14.50 = $290; 20 Tape canisters, Model TC-7 @ $9.70 = $194. Total = $1,985.95.

Purchase Order 385

Harrison Business Furniture, 1698 Manitou Road, Rochester, NY 14626. 1 Office desk, Model 2-DT-7703 @ $299.00 = $299; 1 Swivel desk chair, Model 2-DC-7702 @ $129.99 = $129.99; 1 Corner table, Model F2-AX-67 @ $134.50 = $134.50; 1

Side chair, Model DE-7750-N @ $135.00 = $135; 1 File cabinet, Model EFC-1613 @ $71.35 = $71.35. Total = $769.84.

JOBS 131/2-5 AND 131/2-6. PURCHASE REQUISITION 1031 AND PURCHASE ORDER 386

Prepare a purchase requisition and purchase order for May Clark in the Sales Department. Order from Harrison Business Furniture. Standard format. Workbook 261.

5 Standard staplers, Model OS-5647 @ $12.95 = $64.75; 2 3-hole Punches, Model OS-7413-38 @ $19.00 = $38; 5 Fluorescent swivel lamps, Model OS-8203-38 @ $72.99 = $364.95; 10 cans Spirit duplicator fluid, Catalog No. OS-9578 @ $7.99 = $79.90; 3 12" Electric clocks, Model OS-6285-38 @ $15.99 = $47.97. Total = $595.57.

LESSON 133

GOALS
- To recognize how quotation marks are used with other punctuation marks while typing sentences.
- To practice typing invoices and credit memorandums.

FORMAT
- Single spacing   60-space line   5-space tab and other tabs as needed

LAB 16

QUOTATION MARKS WITH OTHER PUNCTUATION

Type lines 1–4 once. Then repeat lines 1–4 or take a series of 1-minute timings.

```
1  Is the report titled "Study of Broadcast Media in Arizona"?   12
2  "No," said Ms. Quimby, "these statistics are not accurate!"   12
3  Hurry!  I must mark all the cartons "Biological Specimens"!   12
4  "Can we have five or six days to complete this?" she asked.   12
   |  1  |  2  |  3  |  4  |  5  |  6  |  7  |  8  |  9  |  10  |  11  |  12
```

Place a question mark *before* the second quotation mark when the words quoted form a question. In all other cases, place the question mark *after* the second quotation mark.

> "What is the date of the next stockholders' meeting?" asked Carole. (Because the quoted words form a question, the question mark is placed *before* the second quotation mark.)

> Does anyone know why these folders are stamped "Confidential"? (The word in quotations does *not* form a question.)

Likewise, place an exclamation point *before* the second quotation mark when the words quoted form an exclamation. In all other cases, place the exclamation point *after* the second quotation mark.

> Alicia said, "I can't believe that my design won first prize!" (The words in quotations are an exclamation.)

> I think it's ridiculous to say that this product is "overpriced"! (The word in quotations does *not* form an exclamation.)

26 ;p; ;p- ;p- ;-; ;-; -;- -;- ;-;- ;-;- -;-; -;-; ;-; p-p ;-;
27 Her phone is 412-555-4808. Her business phone is 555-8975.

28 ;/; ;/; ;/ /;/ ;/; 7/8 8/9 9/0 1/2 2/3 3/4 4/5 5/6 ;/; ;/;
29 Check these dates: 7/8/84, 8/19/85, 10/23/86, and 12/5/87.

POSTTEST

Repeat the Pretest, lines 5–9 on page 257, to see how much your skill has improved.

LESSON 155

GOALS
- To use colons correctly while typing sentences.
- To build keyboarding skills.
- To type 40/5'/4e.

FORMAT
- Single spacing   60-space line   5-space tab

LAB 17

Type lines 1–4 once, providing the missing colons. Edit your copy as your teacher reads the answers. Then retype lines 1–4 from your edited copy.

COLONS

1 Keep these items my bike, her typewriter, and his zither.
2 Jane has completed all of the following 38, 147, and 156.
3 Mark that quiz to fix these problems No. 6, No. 7, No. 8.
4 Virginia mentioned these two reasons costs and insurance.

**1- AND
5-MINUTE
TIMINGS**

Take two 1-minute timings on each paragraph. Then take one 5-minute timing on the entire selection. Use single spacing for the 1-minute timings and double spacing for the 5-minute timing.   1'

5   If you work in a word processing center, you will work with several   15
6 typists and a supervisor, which means that you will always have   27
7 someone willing and able to extend aid and assistance if needed.   40
                                                                           —
8   Most of the machines are assigned to the routine work, even though   14
9 they have the extra features needed for special projects. It is a relief 29
10 to know that someone can help you to use the features.   40
                                                                           —
11   Much of the work in a center consists of transcription from record-   14
12 ings. The writer of a letter, for example, will phone the center and   28
13 dictate a message. One of the typists then transcribes it.   40
                                                                           —
14   Because of the ease with which WP equipment can change or correct   14
15 information, it is widely used for mailing lists and price lists and   28
16 similar information that needs updating on a regular basis.   40
                                                                           —
17   There is a wide variety of work typed in a center, but every person   15
18 who works there will probably become an expert in just one type of   28
19 production and become recognized as one of the specialists.   40

| 1 | 2 | 3 | 4 | 5 | 6 | 7 | 8 | 9 | 10 | 11 | 12 | 13 | 14   SI 1.45

1-AND 5-MINUTE TIMINGS

Take two 1-minute timings on each paragraph. Then take one 5-minute timing on the entire selection. Use single spacing for the 1-minute timings and double spacing for the 5-minute timing.

```
 5      Each year when winter approaches, you might look up at    12
 6   the sky and view hundreds and maybe even thousands of birds   24
 7   flying toward warmer weather just to escape the severe days   36
 8   that come so soon.                                            40

 9      Have you ever wondered how birds know when to commence     12
10   their flight to another area, or how they always find their  24
11   way when their extensive journey has begun, or how they en—   36
12   dure their journeys?                                          40

13      In this country alone over 400 bird species travel the     12
14   flyways every year to a warm climate, and what is more sur—   24
15   prising is that they always seem to travel to the same area   36
16   as they did before.                                           40

17      Why do birds migrate?  Many experts hypothesize that a     12
18   bird migrates because it can't last in the harsh winters of   24
19   the cold north; others believe that a bird migrates to find   36
20   a better food source.                                         40

21      When the birds are traveling high in the sky, they use     12
22   directional signals to keep them on particular flight paths   24
23   in the flyways.  Birds have "built—in radar," a unique sys—   36
24   tem to guide them.                                            40
```

| 1 | 2 | 3 | 4 | 5 | 6 | 7 | 8 | 9 | 10 | 11 | 12 | SI 1.41

JOB 133-1. BUSINESS INVOICE 56102

Standard format (see page 113). Workbook 263.

[*To*] Safe Equipment Company / [*Today's date*] / 1457 Semple Avenue / St. Louis, MO 63112 / [*Shipped via*] Greyhound Express /

3	Insulated steel safes		
	[*Unit price*] 229.99	[*Amount*]	689.97
2	Computer media safes		
	[*Unit price*] 498.99	[*Amount*]	997.98
10	Chest files		
	[*Unit price*] 75.00	[*Amount*]	750.00
7	4-Drawer file cabinets		
	[*Unit price*] 74.99	[*Amount*]	524.93
	Total amount due		2,962.88

JOB 133-2. CREDIT MEMORANDUM 8259

Standard format (see page 179). Workbook 263.

[*To*] Data Systems, Inc. / 1216 Lee Street, S.E. / Portland, OR 97302 / [*Credits:*]

5	8″ Flexible disks (Containers cracked)		
	[*Unit price*] 5.95	[*Amount*]	29.75
3	Flexible disk hanging folders (hooks bent)		
	[*Unit price*] 4.40	[*Amount*]	13.20
10	Flexible disk markers (fluid evaporated)		
	[*Unit price*] 4.05	[*Amount*]	40.50
	Total		83.45
	Delivery charges paid		3.34
	Total charges paid		86.79

LESSON 154

GOALS
- To identify how colons are used while typing sentences.
- To build skill in keyboarding symbols.

FORMAT
- Single spacing   60-space line

LAB 17

COLONS

Type lines 1–4 once. Then repeat lines 1–4 or take a series of 1-minute timings.

1 Pack these car parts: valves, spark plugs, and fuel gauge.   12
2 Bring the following: two pencils, exam, and answer sheets.   12
3 Walk thus: east on Zion, left on 12th, right to City Hall.   12
4 Quote the job as follows: large type, a border, and color.   12

| 1 | 2 | 3 | 4 | 5 | 6 | 7 | 8 | 9 | 10 | 11 | 12

PRETEST

Your goal on symbol-filled copy is 30/2'/2e.

Take two 2-minute timings on lines 5–9, or take a series of 1-minute timings.

5 I am writing to ask you to check on an order for 6 machines   12
6 worth $8,000. I placed my order (#7799) with Wes & Benson,   24
7 a company that as of this date (9/26) sells office supplies   36
8 in a wide range of prices (the majority @ $5 to $10). Make   48
9 sure that I get the starred (*) 2% pay-as-you-can discount.   60

| 1 | 2 | 3 | 4 | 5 | 6 | 7 | 8 | 9 | 10 | 11 | 12

PRACTICE

Type lines 10–29 once. Then repeat any of the lines that stress the errors you circled in the Pretest.

@   10E sws sw2s s2s s2@s s@s s@s @s@ @s@ s@s @22 2@2 22@ @2@2 2@2@
@   10M ;@; ;@; ;@; @;@ @;@ @;@ ;@;@ ;@;@ ;@;@ @;@; @;@ ;@; @;@ ;@;
    11   She bought 10 @ 56, 29 @ 47, 38 @ 38, 47 @ 29, and 56 @ 10.

¢   12E juj ju6j j6j j6¢j j¢j¢ ¢j¢j j¢j j¢j ¢j¢ ¢j¢ j¢j 66¢ 77¢ 88¢
¢   12M ;¢; ;¢; ;¢; ¢;¢ ¢;¢ ¢;¢ ;¢;¢ ;¢;¢ ;¢;¢ ;¢; ¢;¢; ;¢; ;¢; ¢;¢
    13   Pretzels are 56¢, sweet rolls are 47¢, and cookies are 38¢.

*   14E kik ki8 k8k k8*k k*k* *k*k k*k k*k *k* *k* k*k 88* *88* 8*8
*   14M ;p; ;p- ;-; ;-*; ;*;* *;*; ;*; ;*; *;* *;* ;*; *__ _*-* _*-
    15   Nancy,* Henry,* Sarah,* and Gregory* were chosen to attend.

16   ded de3 d3d d3#d d#d# d#d# d#d 3#3 #4# #5# #6# #7# #8# d#d#
    17   Check my lists for #56, #47, #38, #29, #10, #7, #8, and #9.

$ 18   frf fr4 f4f f4$f f$f f$f f f f$f $44 4$4 $444 $555 $666
    19   Our game tickets should cost us $10, $29, $38, $47, or $56.

%   20   ftf ft% f%f f5%f f%f% %f%f f%f f%f 55% 55% 44% 33% 22% %f%f
    21   Let's hope to get a discount of 10%, 29%, 38%, 47%, or 56%.

&   22   juj ju7 j7j j7&j j&j& &j&j j&j j&j &8& &9& &1& &2& &3& &7&7
    23   Bennett & Shea, DeLuca & Nucci, and Brim & Todd sent gifts.

( ) 24   lol lo9 l9(l(l l l(l (l(;p; ;p) ;p) ;); ;););) (9) (0) (;)
    25   Donna (Adams), Gene (Ponti), and Helen (Yeo) came to visit.

(Continued on next page)

LESSON 134

GOALS
- To identify how quotation marks are used with other punctuation marks while typing sentences.
- To format and type ten geographic file cards.
- To type a three-column table.

FORMAT
- Single spacing   60-space line   Tabs as needed

LAB 16

QUOTATION MARKS WITH OTHER PUNCTUATION

Type lines 1–4 once. Then repeat lines 1–4 or take a series of 1-minute timings.

```
1  "Tomorrow," I said, "we will discuss the budget in detail!"  12
2  Andrew asked, "Does anyone know where Anne Rodriguez went?"  12
3  Gus said, "Send requisitions to Ms. Camp for her approval!"  12
4  Did you mark them "Fragile"?  Just mark each box "Caution!"  12
   |  1  |  2  |  3  |  4  |  5  |  6  |  7  |  8  |  9  | 10  | 11  | 12
```

FORMATTING GEOGRAPHIC FILE CARDS

Whenever it is easier to file names and addresses by location rather than by last names, create *geographic file cards*.

To format geographic file cards:

1. Type the state, city, and ZIP Code on line 2 beginning 4 spaces from the left edge of the card.
2. Type the name and address a double space below the state, indented 3 spaces.

```
1234
 |
 2    Louisiana, Baton Rouge 70802
 3
 4       Mr. Glen Vance
         489 Myrtle Avenue
         Baton Rouge, LA 70802
```

JOB 134-1. GEOGRAPHIC FILE CARDS

Type a card for each contractor listed below. Standard format. Workbook 265, 267.

LOIS MEREDITH, 528 CAPITOL STREET, HOUSTON, TX 77002
LAURA HOLMES, 1678 MADRID STREET, NEW ORLEANS, LA 70122
ETHEL THOMAS, 835 CRAWFORD STREET, JACKSON, MS 39203
LEON SANCHEZ, 5019 BOLM ROAD, AUSTIN, TX 78721
RITA EVERETT, 967 GREEN STREET, BIRMINGHAM, AL 35217
SHARON LEWIS, 938 PHILLIPS STREET, HUNTSVILLE, AL 35903
JOHN ORTEGA, 167 OSCEOLA STREET, TALLAHASSEE, FL 32301
RALPH EDWARDS, 226 ACADIA STREET, ATLANTA, GA 30344

JOB 134-2. RULED TABLE

Standard format except use 8 spaces between columns. Arrange items alphabetically by name of contractor. (Use the cards you prepared in Job 134-1.)

[*Title*] Southern Insulation Contractors
[*Subtitle*] Official Members List
[*Column headings*] (1) Name (2) Street Address (3) City/State/ZIP

When a clause contains a word or phrase such as *the following, as follows, thus,* or *these* and is followed by a series of words, phrases, or clauses, use a colon between the main clause and the series.

> Include the following: item number, description, and cost.
> Buy these items: rubber bands, paper clips, and markers.

12-SECOND TIMINGS

Type each line four times, or take four 12-second timings on each line. For each timing, type with no more than one error.

5　She said the four girls can swim across the lake with ease.　12
6　Please take one of these big boxes down to the post office.　12
7　May we go to the game with you, or do you have other plans?　12

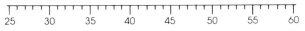

PRETEST

Your goal on number-filled copy is 30/2'/2e.

Take two 2-minute timings on lines 8–12, or take a series of 1-minute timings.

8　The class of 1980 will hold its spring reunion on August 16　12
9　with a dinner at the Quinton Hotel, 4422 West 66 Street, in　24
10　High Tor.　The cost is only $33 per couple; reserve a table　36
11　by calling one of these persons:　Zoe Strum (555-8416), Rex　48
12　Strength (555-7934), or Dr. Mary Jane Scholneck (555-8190).　60

| 1 | 2 | 3 | 4 | 5 | 6 | 7 | 8 | 9 | 10 | 11 | 12

PRACTICE

Can you keyboard the number keys while keeping your eyes on the copy?

13　tie 583 toe 593 toy 596 top 590 tip 580 wet 235 woe 293 293
14　pie 083 pet 035 pot 095 pow 092 row 492 rye 463 rue 473 473
15　rut 475 rot 495 roe 493 ire 843 ore 943 owe 923 ewe 323 323
16　eye 363 out 975 our 974 owe 923 per 034 pit 085 toe 593 593

17　your 6974 pour 0974 pout 0975 rout 4975 rope 4903 ripe 4803
18　wipe 2803 pipe 0803 were 2343 wore 2943 wire 2843 wiry 2846
19　pure 0743 pore 0943 port 0945 pert 0345 tore 5943 tire 5843
20　tier 5834 pier 0834 purr 0744 prow 0492 toot 5995 prop 0490

Clear your tabulator. Set seven tab stops, each one 8 spaces apart, beginning at the left margin. Type lines 21–28 twice—or more. Circle your errors, if any, as your teacher reads the copy.

21	235	236	237	238	239	240	241	242
22	599	598	597	596	595	594	593	592
23	632	633	634	635	636	637	638	639
24	480	479	478	477	476	475	474	473
25	788	789	790	791	792	793	794	795
26	334	333	332	331	330	329	328	327
27	993	992	991	990	989	988	987	986
28	878	879	880	881	882	883	884	885

POSTTEST

Repeat the Pretest, lines 8–12 on page 256, to see how much your skill has improved.

GOALS
- To use quotation marks correctly with other punctuation marks while typing sentences.
- To type 40/5'/5e.
- To format legal fill-in forms.

FORMAT
- Single spacing   60-space line   5-space tab

LAB 16

QUOTATION MARKS WITH OTHER PUNCTUATION

Type lines 1–4 once, providing the missing punctuation marks. Edit your copy as the teacher reads the answers. Then retype lines 1–4 from your edited copy.

1 My broker said, "The quoted price is very low, so buy now."
2 Has Gary found out why the envelope is marked "Top Secret".
3 Just say to him, "Ed, when will you complete this project."
4 Ex—mayor Schwartz said, "This proposed plan is ridiculous."

1-AND 5-MINUTE TIMINGS

Take two 1-minute timings on each paragraph. Then take one 5-minute timing on the entire selection. Use single spacing for the 1-minute timings and double spacing for the 5-minute timing.

1'

5   Stop to consider this question: "What is weather made   12
6   of?" Wind, sunshine, clouds, rain, snow, and sleet are all   24
7   brought to us by four elements: air pressure, temperature,   36
8   moisture, and wind.   40

9   Air pressure is just the weight of air pushing against   12
10 the surface of the earth. Warm air exerts less pressure on   24
11 the earth than cold air because it weighs less. Barometers   36
12 measure air pressure.   40

13   Rapid changes in temperature may create quite a severe   12
14 change in weather. If temperatures are above freezing, you   24
15 may get rain; and if they're at or below freezing, you will   36
16 have sleet or snow.   40

17   Moisture is known, of course, as precipitation. Mois-   12
18 ture reaches us from the sky as rain, snow, sleet, or hail.   24
19 However, it might possibly remain in the air as water vapor   36
20 and create clouds.   40

21   A weather pattern is drastically affected by winds. A   12
22 soft breeze may bring a very pleasant summer day, sea winds   24
23 transmit cool air over the land, and northern breezes might   36
24 provide us cool days.   40

| 1 | 2 | 3 | 4 | 5 | 6 | 7 | 8 | 9 | 10 | 11 | 12 | SI 1.41

PRACTICE

Study the errors you made on the 30-second timings and the timed writings on page 254. Identify the letters you are keyboarding incorrectly. Practice these letters by typing the appropriate drill lines twice. Then practice whichever letters have been causing you to slow down when you type.

A	26	art	amp	acts	aide	amen	asked	alive	about	again	amend	assert
B	27	bad	bat	bite	brag	brim	brand	bland	black	banks	blank	begins
C	28	cat	car	caps	crop	crew	check	could	claim	corps	chair	change
D	29	dad	dye	duet	drag	down	drums	digit	doing	dance	dread	disown
E	30	elm	eve	ears	etch	east	erase	eight	empty	exact	enter	effect
F	31	fir	fan	feud	fame	from	flown	favor	fruit	fancy	fable	female
G	32	gap	gag	gale	game	glow	glory	gauge	grain	green	gates	govern
H	33	hat	has	hope	have	hold	helps	hoist	hitch	hobby	heavy	hustle
I	34	its	imp	ills	into	ibex	ideal	inapt	issue	input	ivory	island
J	35	jar	joy	joke	jump	join	juice	judge	jokes	jeers	juror	jackal
K	36	key	kit	kids	kiln	kill	kings	keeps	knows	kayak	kicks	kindly
L	37	lob	lie	line	late	lake	laugh	labor	light	lucid	lumps	lagoon
M	38	mat	mad	maze	more	mist	music	month	money	minus	metal	mighty
N	39	nor	not	nags	norm	noon	nasty	night	noise	nutty	nymph	nickel
O	40	oak	old	odor	over	oath	olive	opens	ought	ounce	opera	occupy
P	41	pat	pay	paid	pour	past	proud	piano	plain	plane	plump	photos
Q	42	quo	que	quad	quip	quid	quick	quits	quire	quite	quote	quaint
R	43	row	rip	ride	reap	rake	right	ready	reach	roads	razor	record
S	44	sit	sky	sips	sing	stay	sting	sweet	scale	stone	state	savory
T	45	top	try	team	tame	task	throw	tests	teams	tense	tales	tactic
U	46	urn	use	ugly	upon	used	unite	under	usual	untie	upset	unique
V	47	vet	vex	vats	vote	vase	vague	verve	voice	vital	veins	vertex
W	48	was	wow	wage	when	what	white	water	wedge	weave	waves	wealth
X	49	tax	six	axes	oxen	axis	exact	exist	taxis	exits	vexes	exerts
Y	50	you	yet	yell	yard	year	young	yield	yours	youth	yacht	yellow
Z	51	zap	zig	zinc	zeal	zest	zooms	zebra	zones	zonal	zeros	zodiac

POSTTEST

Repeat the Pretest on page 254 by taking one 5-minute timing on lines 9–25 to see how much your skill has improved.

LESSON **153**

GOALS
- To recognize how colons are used while typing sentences.
- To build skill in keyboarding numbers.

FORMAT
- Single spacing   60-space line   Tabs every 8 spaces

LAB 17

Type lines 1–4 once. Then repeat lines 1–4 or take a series of 1-minute timings.

COLONS

Leave 2 spaces after a colon.

1 You need these personal traits: tact, quick wit, and zest. 12
2 He wants these ingredients: eggs, milk, and baking powder. 12
3 Please pack the following: visor, cosmetics, and six jars. 12
4 We trimmed all these: the grass, the edges, and the trees. 12

| 1 | 2 | 3 | 4 | 5 | 6 | 7 | 8 | 9 | 10 | 11 | 12

FORMATTING LEGAL FILL-IN FORMS

Workbook 216.

When typing legal documents on a form, you are required to insert the necessary information. Follow these guidelines and study the illustration to the right when typing on a preprinted legal form:

1. Align the insertions with the preprinted words.
2. Treat any blank areas on the form as follows:
   Ⓐ Fill in any blank spaces within individual lines of the form with *leaders* (a series of periods).
   Ⓑ Fill in any blank areas that occupy several blank lines with two horizontal underscores joined by a solid diagonal line. This is called a Z rule.
3. Leave 1 blank space between the preprinted word and the typed insertion.
4. Align margins with those of the form. **Note:** In some states erasing is not permitted on dates, addresses, amounts of money, and names.

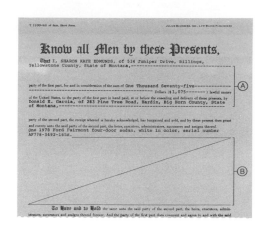

JOB 135-1. BILL OF SALE ON A FORM

Standard format. Workbook 269–270. Use the information in Job 115-2, page 194, to fill in the workbook form for a bill of sale.

LESSON 136

REVIEW

GOALS
- To answer a series of technical questions with a minimum of 80 percent competency.
- To type 40/5'/5e.
- To type a letter, a table, and a short report.

FORMAT
- Single spacing   60-space line   5-space tab and other tabs as needed

KEYBOARDING SKILLS

Type lines 1–4 once. Then do what line 5 tells you to do. Repeat lines 1–4, or take a series of 1-minute timings.

Speed	1	A whole kernel of corn was picked up by the hen last night.	12
Accuracy	2	Did Liz give Weldon your picturesque jukebox for Christmas?	12
Numbers	3	Fires raged all night at 1029 Pine, 3847 Oak, and 5610 Elm.	12
Symbols	4	We found out that 1/5 of $20 = $4 and that 10% of $40 = $4.	12
Technique	5	Use your return key after every word as you type this line.

| 1 | 2 | 3 | 4 | 5 | 6 | 7 | 8 | 9 | 10 | 11 | 12 |

5-MINUTE TIMING

Take a 5-minute timing on lines 5–24, page 224. Use double spacing.

TECHNICAL QUESTIONS

Compose on your typewriter answers to the following questions. Your goal is to answer 12 or more questions correctly.

Reports

1. How do the margins in a bound report differ from those in an unbound report?

2. What must be included in the heading of a magazine article?

3. What spacing is used for tables in reports?

Legal Documents

4. Where are page numbers positioned in a legal document, and what is the style for typing page numbers?

5. How wide are the margins in a legal document?

6. What is the paragraph indention for a legal document?

LESSON 152

GOALS
- To identify and practice the alphabetic keys on which more drill is needed.
- To build accuracy on the alphabetic keyboard using two practice routines.

FORMAT
- Single spacing   60-space line   5-space tab

KEYBOARDING SKILLS

Type lines 1–4 once. Then practice your space bar technique by typing line 5 twice. Repeat lines 1–4, or take a series of 1-minute timings.

Speed   1   The goal of the rich girls is to fix a bicycle for the man.   12
Accuracy   2   Jack would pay for fixing my novels if Elizabeth requested.   12
Numbers   3   Mark the chalkboards at 10, 29, 38, 47, and 56 centimeters.   12
Symbols   4   She bought 56 books @ $47; he bought only 38 records @ $29.   12
Technique   5   z y x w v u t s r q p o n m l k j i h g f e d c b a ; : , .

| 1 | 2 | 3 | 4 | 5 | 6 | 7 | 8 | 9 | 10 | 11 | 12 |

30-SECOND TIMINGS

Take two 30-second timings on lines 6–8, or type each line twice.

6   It is not the size, but just the quickness, of your fingers   12
7   that builds every extra word per minute in a timed writing.   24
8   Try to concentrate on keyboarding evenly and very smoothly.   36

| 1 | 2 | 3 | 4 | 5 | 6 | 7 | 8 | 9 | 10 | 11 | 12 |

PRETEST

Take two 5-minute timings on lines 9–25. Circle your errors on each.

9   In many firms, the text editing equipment has replaced   12
10   the typewriter and is used for all the normal typing tasks.   24
11   Since the machine is not part of a center or cluster, it is   36
12   called a standalone. It is an expensive typewriter, but it   48
13   is so efficient that in many offices it more than pays off.   60
14   The main value of word processing equipment is that it   72
15   makes correcting and retyping very easy. Surveys show that   84
16   more than half of the papers typed by a good typist will be   96
17   retyped for some reason. Any machine that can speed up the   108
18   process is, of course, extremely helpful in the office––and   120
19   just as much so for a standalone as for the other machines.   132
20   A modern WP unit can increase enormously the output of   144
21   any office worker, but one must realize that there can't be   156
22   an increase if there is not plenty of work to do. You need   168
23   the equipment to get more work done, not to make it pretty.   180
24   A standalone unit is cost–effective only when used by those   192
25   who cannot otherwise get their work done.   200

| 1 | 2 | 3 | 4 | 5 | 6 | 7 | 8 | 9 | 10 | 11 | 12 | SI 1.43

Tables

7. Describe step by step how to type a footnote in an open (unruled) table.

8. How many lines of spaces should there be before and after a rule in a ruled table?

9. What is a source note? How is it typed?

Letters

10. How is an enumeration in a letter typed?

11. What is a *bcc* notation and what is "special" about it. Where is it typed?

12. What line length is used on baronial stationery?

Forms

13. On an invoice, where is the word *TOTAL* typed?

14. What is the difference between a purchase requisition and a purchase order?

15. Why is a "Z" rule used on printed legal forms?

JOB 136-1. LETTER IN ROUGH DRAFT ON MONARCH STATIONERY

Standard format (see page 217). Workbook 271–272. Body 89 words (plus 20 words for subject line).

```
Ms. Blanche Kile, 2418 Camden Avenue,          15
Flint, MI 48570, Dear Ms. Kile:  Sub-          24
ject:  Writing Skills Survey                   30
    Enclosed is your survey on reading         38
and writing
skills courses.  You will note that in         48
addition to the questions we answered in       57
the survey, we have also attached 1 page       65
"interesting"
of comments to the issues you raised on        74
page 3 of your survey.  We think you           81
                           our
will be interested in in put on these          89
issues.                                        91
    We look forward to recieving a copy        99
of the results of your study.  We plan         107
to share the findings of your study with       115
the entire faculty, since your topic isa       124
relevant one for us.  Sincerely yours,         133
T. L. Harris, chairperson, Enclosure, cc:      148
Shirley A. Johnson, cc:  Carl B. White,        155
PS:  Could we have your permission to          164
duplicate the findings of your study?          171
```

JOB 136-2. FOUR-COLUMN RULED TABLE

Standard format (see page 159). Full sheet of paper.

Group	Boys	Girls	Totals
Freshman	237	268	505
Sophomore	295	281	576
Junior	284	277	561
Senior	301	329	630
Totals	1,117	1,155	2,272

CLASS ENROLLMENTS Fall Term

JOB 136-3. UNBOUND REPORT, PAGE 1

Standard format (see pages 117 and 118). Double-space the body.

ANIMALS AND WHERE THEY LIVE

March 10, 19--

By Paula R. West

Some animals spend their entire lives moving about from one home to another, but others stay in one place and have homes that last them a long time.

PERMANENT HOMES

Many animals, such as the ground squirrel and chipmunk, dig an underground burrow where they live "year after year after year." Bears and lions make their homes in caves or in dense thickets where they cannot be seen. Insects even make permanent homes by building hives or by digging tunnels in the ground.

TEMPORARY HOMES

Throughout the animal kingdom live animals that do not have permanent homes. They drift from place to place at certain times of the year. As an example, wild geese and other wild birds fly to warmer climates when the cold winter months arrive. Wild animals living on the African continent travel many hundreds of miles in search of water and food when the dry season approaches.

Take two 3-minute timings on lines 9–19.

```
9       Word processing happens in three office situations, so    12
10   when you try to define what word processing is, you must be   24
11   careful to explain all three of these versions and not just   36
12   one kind you know about.                                      41
13       In a big office several of the machines may be concen-    53
14   trated in one location, called a center.  The typists spend   65
15   most of their time on letter projects.  Some organizations,   77
16   to bring the equipment closer to the work, put the machines   89
17   in clusters where the typists turn out letters and reports.  101
18   The third version is the office that has one machine; it is  113
19   used to produce all kinds of work.                           120
     |  1  |  2  |  3  |  4  |  5  |  6  |  7  |  8  |  9  |  10  |  11  |  12   SI 1.40
```

Type lines 20–28 three times.

```
20   they lend duck coal wish pane form risk sign lens fish turn
21   dish lamb tidy jams when cork them name duty envy kept such
22   then tick maid keys firm gown both flay bush fuel goal work

23   their hairy angle endow right bugle gland chair laugh ivory
24   panel girls turns rotor fight world field shape eight forms
25   audit signs blame slept tithe shame visit gowns title burns

26   usual amend firms widow usury giant prism vigor whale vials
27   spend handy forks blend roams eight right field forms forks
28   profit enrich eighty handle theory island ambush enrich and
```

Type lines 29–36 three times.

```
29   robber beggar common arrive jobber bigger commas errors all
30   middle letter snooze supper fiddle little smooth puppet see
31   bubble gummed bottle happen effect agreed bullet middle zoo
32   dinner issues sizzle accord annoys puzzle keeper muffle off

33   breed flood class drill putty cliff offer witty hilly asset
34   goods green skill added seeks proof small radii guess dizzy
35   fluff abbey rummy ditto apple gummy petty upper sleep shall
36   issue floor speed essay gloss broom occur staff funny happy
```

Repeat the Pretest, lines 9–19, to see how much your skill has improved.

In Units 7 through 22, you completed 16 LABs (Language Arts Boosters) that presented modern rules of punctuation and style. In Unit 23 you will review all 16 LABs and will complete more exercises related to them. Learning activities will be introduced through (1) brief reviews of the rules, (2) examples of each rule, (3) sentence applications for each rule, and (4) production applications for each rule.

LESSON 137

UNIT 23 LANGUAGE ARTS REVIEW

UNIT GOAL
40/5'/5e

GOALS
- To use quotation marks correctly with other punctuation marks while typing sentences.
- To type a letter applying capitalization rules.

FORMAT
- Single spacing   60-space line   5-space tab

LAB 16

QUOTATION MARKS WITH OTHER PUNCTUATION

Workbook 273–274

Type lines 1–4 once, providing the missing exclamation points and question marks. Edit your copy as your teacher reads the answers. Then retype lines 1–4 from your edited copy.

1 We asked Greg, "What are the new sales quotas for January."
2 Mr. Axel ridiculed the idea that the price was a "bargain".
3 Jeffrey asked, "Did Karina Alzado approve all the designs."
4 Near the end of the commercial, two narrators yell "Hurry."

5-MINUTE TIMINGS

Take two 5-minute timings on lines 5–21.

```
 5        There are specific language arts skills which everyone     12
 6   should know.  Such skills will help us improve our speaking    24
 7   and writing skills, and they will permit us to express our-    36
 8   selves much better.  The language arts skills emphasized in    48
 9   our course have by now made us more cognizant of the unique    60
10   role they play in improving our methods of expression.         71
11        In previous lessons, we learned when to capitalize and    83
12   when not to capitalize.  We learned, for instance, that all    95
13   proper nouns are capitalized and that a specific place like   107
14   a city, township, county, or state is also capitalized.  We   119
15   learned that numbers from 1 through 10 are spelled out, but   131
16   figures are used for numbers above 10.  Several rules exist   143
17   on how and when to use the comma.  For instance, a comma is   155
18   used when three or more items appear in succession.  Commas   167
19   are also used at the end of an introductory clause which is   179
20   followed by a main clause.  Words such as if, as, when, and   191
21   because are used to introduce these clauses.                  200
    | 1 | 2 | 3 | 4 | 5 | 6 | 7 | 8 | 9 | 10 | 11 | 12    SI 1.41
```

Before you are introduced to advanced business formatting in Level 5, you will review your keyboarding skills and the basic techniques of formatting.

Thus in Level 5 you will:

1. Demonstrate keyboarding accuracy and speed on straight copy with a goal of 42 words a minute or more for 5 minutes with no more than 4 errors.

2. Correctly proofread copy for errors and edit copy for revision.

3. Apply production skills in keyboarding and formatting copy for four categories of business documents from six input modes related to these business subjects—communications (Lessons 157–174); employee health, safety, and fitness (Lessons 175–180), and recreational resorts and hotel/motel services (Lessons 181–185).

4. Demonstrate production skills on advanced formats for reports, letters, tables, and forms.

5. Apply rules for correct use of colons, hyphens, and dashes in communications.

LESSON 151

UNIT 25 KEYBOARDING SKILLS REVIEW

UNIT GOAL
40/5'/4e

GOAL
- To build speed on the alphabetic keyboard using two practice routines.

FORMAT
- Single spacing   60-space line   5-space tab

KEYBOARDING SKILLS

Type lines 1–4 once. Then practice using your shift lock by typing line 5 in all caps. Repeat lines 1–4, or take a series of 1-minute timings.

Speed   1 When did he go to the city and pay them for the world maps? 12
Accuracy   2 Max and Kay reviewed the subject before giving Phil a quiz. 12
Numbers   3 Read Chapters 10, 29, and 38; summarize Chapters 47 and 56. 12
Symbols   4 We bought 10 balls @ 56¢; he bought 29 @ 38¢ and 100 @ 47¢. 12
Technique   5 I WANT TO PRACTICE MY SHIFT-LOCK TECHNIQUE USING THIS LINE.
               | 1 | 2 | 3 | 4 | 5 | 6 | 7 | 8 | 9 | 10 | 11 | 12

12-SECOND TIMINGS

Type each line four times, or take four 12-second timings on each line. For each timing, type with no more than one error.

6 A sign of their blame is the half audit they did for Nancy. 12
7 A small dog and a girl ran down the long lane to the shore. 12
8 If that form is for the men, then the eight may sign today. 12
               25   30   35   40   45   50   55   60

CAPITALIZATION REVIEW

1. Capitalize proper nouns—the names of specific persons, places, or things. Capitalize common nouns when they are part of proper names.

Proper nouns:	Captain Ames	Kansas City	Chevrolet
Common nouns:	captain	city	car

Note: Capitalize adjectives formed from proper nouns—proper adjectives such as *American, European, French*, and *Freudian*. (One common exception is *french fries*.) Also capitalize the first word of a sentence and the word *I*.

> *She* and *I* worked for a *Greek* shipping firm.

Type lines 22–25 once. Then repeat lines 22–25 or take a series of 1-minute timings.

```
22  The Waco Paper Company is an excellent, dependable company.   12
23  Einz Plastics, a German manufacturer, supplies these pipes.   12
24  Rex Yount, a former colonel in the Marines, is our manager.   12
25  Subi, a Japanese import firm, makes high-quality materials.   12
    |  1  |  2  |  3  |  4  |  5  |  6  |  7  |  8  |  9  |  10  |  11  |  12
```

2. Capitalize *north, south, east*, and *west* when they refer to *specific* regions, are part of a proper noun, or are within an address.

> Wesley lived in the *North* until 1982. (Specific region.)
> He worked for the *West* End Realty Company. (Part of proper noun.)
> His new address is 121 *South* Grand Avenue. (Part of address.)
>
> You must travel *east* on Route 122. (General direction.)
> The office is on the *south* side of the city. (General location.)

Likewise, capitalize *northern, southern, eastern*, and *western* when they refer to *specific* people or regions, not when they refer to *general* locations or directions.

> Zambia was formerly known as *Northern* Rhodesia.
> That warehouse will be built in the *southern* part of the state.

3. Capitalize official titles that precede names. Do not capitalize titles that follow names.

> We asked *Mayor* Bradley to attend the reception.
> We asked James T. Bradley, *mayor* of Scranton, to attend the reception.
> A United States *senator* will be the main speaker.

Note: The titles of some officials of very high rank are capitalized even when they follow or replace a name—for example, *President, Pope, Governor, Secretary General*.

Type lines 26–31 once. Then repeat lines 26–31 or take a series of 1-minute timings.

```
26  Our warehouses in the East are inadequate for our purposes.   12
27  The new metals factory is in the western part of Kalamazoo.   12
28  Vera, Jacob, and Dan handle all accounts in South Carolina.   12
29  All six distributors are north of our Bogg Street terminus.   12
30  Turn east on the Western Expressway for about 3 or 4 miles.   12
31  Eleanor lived in the Midwest before she moved to the South.   12
    |  1  |  2  |  3  |  4  |  5  |  6  |  7  |  8  |  9  |  10  |  11  |  12
```

LEVEL 5

ADVANCED BUSINESS FORMATTING

JOB 137-1. LETTER
Standard format (see page 169). Workbook 275–276.
Body 29 words.

Mr. George Pera, Manager; Pera's Cam- 15
era Service, 105 Wilson Avenue, West; 23
Kingsford, MI 49801, Dear Mr. Pera: 31

    I am returning the Nobel Camera I 39
purchased from your store on Friday, 47
March 2. As stated in your warranty, 54
there will be no charge for the fol- 61
lowing repairs:↓2 65

5] 1. The film does not progress [73
    smoothly. It sticks when 78
    advancing from frame 6 to 83
    frame 7 on the film. 5 89
2. The shutter does not work. 96
3. The electronic F/stop does 103
    not work properly.↓2 107

    Please see that these repairs are 116
made within two weeks. My father will 124
call you at that time to pick up the 131
camera. Cordially yours, Jeffrey S. 145
Johnson, Photographer 152

LESSON 138

GOALS
- To practice using numbers rules.
- To type three letters in which these numbers rules are applied.

FORMAT
- Single spacing   60-space line   5-space tab

CAPITALIZATION REVIEW

Type lines 1–4 once, providing the missing capitals. Edit your copy as your teacher reads the answers. Then retype lines 1–4 from your edited copy.

1   the red river is nearby grand forks, wahpeton, and drayton.

2   i sent two letters to the president of the firm, earl jobe.

3   quinlan avenue is the site of our newest store in scranton.

4   al diaz, who imports spanish leather goods, is now in town.

NUMBERS REVIEW

1. Spell out numbers from 1 through 10; use figures for numbers above 10. Also spell out numbers that begin a sentence.

    We will need *three* or *four* more clerks.
    She estimates that the project will take *12* hours.
    Eleven committee members were invited.

When numbers above 10 *and* below 10 are mixed, use figures for numbers.

    Ellen surveyed *11* supervisors, *6* department heads, and *3* regional managers.

2. In technical copy, in dates, and for emphasis, use figures for all numbers.

    The next meeting is scheduled for May *3* at *2:30* p.m.
    The cost for *2* grams of this powder is only *$2*.

Type lines 5–10 once. Then repeat lines 5–10 or take a series of 1-minute timings.

5   Steve Beckley said to mix just 2 quarts of this new liquid. 12

6   We sent out 100 invitations and received just 90 responses. 12

7   Drive approximately 5.5 miles to route 122; then turn left. 12

8   Fifteen applicants were interviewed by Mrs. Mary Rodriguez. 12

9   Helen hired five clerks, two typists, and four secretaries. 12

10   Helen Greene hired 11 clerks, 2 typists, and 4 secretaries. 12

| 1 | 2 | 3 | 4 | 5 | 6 | 7 | 8 | 9 | 10 | 11 | 12

JOB 149/150-1. (Continued)

TABLE 1

MILES PER GALLON ESTIMATES

Miles per Gallon	Number of Drivers	Percentage
Less than 10	2	5.0
10 to 20	11	27.5
21 to 30	22	55.0
31 or more	5	12.5
Total	40	100.0

[1]Sheila Torrance, "Driving in the '80s," Car Report, May 1982, p. 27.

JOB 149/150-2. LETTER

Standard format (see page 92). Workbook 293–294. Body 59 words (plus 20 words for subject line).

Ms. Audrey L. Simms, Knight Insurance Company, 204 Pine Ridge Road, Boston, MA 02181 Dear Ms. Simms: Subject: Carpet Cleaning

As we discussed on the telephone today, we will be able to clean the carpeting on the fourth floor of your building on Saturday, March 3.

Our people will be at your office at 8 a.m. on that day to move out the furniture and vacuum the carpet before cleaning and shampooing.

Thank you for doing business with us. Yours sincerely, Archie T. Maisley, Manager

JOB 149/150-3. INTEROFFICE MEMO

Standard format (see page 107). Workbook 297.

[To:] Perry Davis, [From:] Helene Cotter, [Subject:] Room Reservations

Please reserve Room 3004 for me on Tuesday, April 4, from 8:30 a.m. to 12 noon. We will need a slide projector and screen for our meeting. Please make arrangements to have this equipment in the room by 9 a.m.

I would also like to reserve Room 3004 for April 10 from 1:30 p.m. to 3:30 p.m. I will send you my equipment requirements on the 6th.

HC

JOB 149/150-4. THREE-COLUMN RULED TABLE

Standard format. Full sheet of paper. Space the body.

MAJOR OIL-PRODUCING STATES*

By [Your name]

State	Capital City	Area in Sq. Miles
Texas	Austin	262,134
Louisiana	Baton Rouge	44,930
California	Sacramento	156,361
Oklahoma	Oklahoma City	68,782
Wyoming	Cheyenne	97,203

*Arranged from largest to smallest producer.

JOB 149/150-5. BUSINESS INVOICE 38644

Standard format. Workbook 299.

[To] Davidson Office Furniture / [Today's date] / 385 King Avenue / Dayton, OH 45420 / [Shipped via] United Parcel Service

		[Unit price]	[Amount]
10	Filing cabinets, #F780	62.50	625.00
2	Filing cabinets, #F880	72.50	145.00
6	Boxes of file folders	7.75	46.50
4	Boxes of file guides	2.50	10.00
	Total amount due		826.50

JOB 138-1. LETTER

Standard format. Workbook 277-278. Body 98 words
(plus 20 words for attention line).

Locksmith City Service, — 13
194 Lakeshore Drive, N.E., — 18
Atlanta, GA 30324, Attention: — 25
Chief Locksmith, Gentlemen: — 32

Last April 15 You — 36
installed the restricted — 41
access locks on all the — 46
doors for our new build- — 51
ing. Seven keys were — 55
stolen from one of our — 60
employees on July 7, and — 65
we would like to have — 69
new locks installed on — 74
the doors for which keys — 79
are missing. — 82

If I recall correctly, — 87
you said that each lock — 92
replacement would cost — 97
about seventeen dollars plus — 102
labor. Would the charge — 107
for replacing these seven — 113
locks be greater than $20 — 118
per lock? Please let me — 123
have your estimate by — 127
August 15 so that we can — 132
have our locks repaired — 137

as soon as possible. — 141
Cordially yours, R. T. Allen, — 153
Manager, cc: *Ruth Richards* — 161

JOB 138-2. LETTER

Standard format. Workbook 279-280. Body 80 words.

Mrs. R. T. Allen, Manager, Baird Insur- — 16
ance Company, 946 Pine Street, N.W., — 23
Atlanta, GA 30309, Dear Mrs. Allen: — 31
＃
Thank you for your letter informing — 40
me about the keys that were stolen from — 48
charge &
your company. The ~~price~~ quoted you for — 56
lock replacement was $17, and I will be — 64
July
able to replace your locks by ~~august~~ 15 — 72
or 16. — 72
Will you need ②, ③, or ④ dupli- — 81
cates of each key? On your ~~original~~ — 88
order you asked for three duplicates. — 96
The three duplicates for the locks that — 104
will be replaced should be returned to — 112
when the repairs are made.
you ~~to accompany the locks.~~ Yours truly, — 123
Edgar H. Hartchy, Chief locksmith, PS: — 139
I will be arriving at 10 a.m. to start — 147
replacing the locks. — 151

NUMBERS REVIEW

3. Spell out street names from *first* to *tenth*; use figures for street names above
tenth. Note that ordinal numbers (*11th, 21st, 42d, 53d,* and so on) are used
for street names.

They moved from *Fifth Avenue* to *19th Street.*

4. Use figures to express time with *minutes, a.m., p.m.,* and *o'clock.* (For greater
formality, numbers may be spelled out with *o'clock.*) Also use figures to
express years: *1981, 1983,* and so on.

The meeting should take only *15* or *20 minutes;* thus we should be able to leave by
3:45 p.m.

Take two 5-minute timings on lines 3–20. Circle your errors on each.

```
                         1                            2
3       Many people have often wondered what might possibly be      12
            3                          4
4   the greatest structure on earth.  The tallest buildings and     24
       5                      6                        7
5   the longest bridges and the mightiest dams might be closely     36
                          8                   9
6   examined in an attempt to identify an answer to this diffi-     48
        10                        11                    12
7   cult question.  In the minds of many people, though, one of     60
                            13                      14
8   the greatest structures ever built may be the Great Wall of     72
              15                        16
9   China.  It's well established that its features are so very     84
      17                     18                    19
10  overwhelming that astronauts could view the Wall from their     96
                     20
11  spaceship portholes.                                           100
                          21                       22
12      The structure was built primarily by mixing just earth     112
                 23                      24
13  and bricks.  It is wide enough at the top to permit several     124
         25                        26                    27
14  people to walk abreast on it.  It winds for miles through a     136
                     28                      29
15  large section of the country, over mountains and across the    148
             30                      31                      32
16  valleys.  It was built to keep out tribes from other lands.    160
                          33                      34
17  It is believed that building the wall required the labor of    172
                 35                      36
18  many, many thousands of persons for many dozens of decades.    184
         37                      38                      39
19  Actually, the wall was built during the reign of many vari-    196
                 40
20  ous tribal dynasties.                                          200
    |  1  |  2  |  3  |  4  |  5  |  6  |  7  |  8  |  9  |  10  |  11  |  12    SI 1.48
```

JOB 149/150-1. TWO-PAGE REPORT WITH TABLE AND FOOTNOTE
Double spacing. 5-space tab.

METHODS OF TRANSPORTATION

By James Rhoades

INTRODUCTION

The rising fuel costs in this country have had a profound effect on the driving habits and the means of transportation used by both young and old. The May issue of Car Report states that "student driving habits will change because of the rapidly rising fuel costs this nation is experiencing."[1] It appears that fuel costs will affect the methods by which students commute to their schools.

STATEMENT OF THE PROBLEM

The problem of this study is to reveal how students at Valley High School have changed their methods of transportation to and from school.

BACKGROUND OF THE PROBLEM

Valley High School is located between Green-ville, Loan Oak, and Sulphur Springs on a 20-acre tract of land. Because of this central location, many students commute to and from school. In the past, students have commuted by driving alone in their own cars, by driving with other students, or by riding the bus.

FINDINGS

A total of 96 seniors were surveyed in the study—25 of them drove alone, 15 car-pooled with other students, and 56 rode the school bus. Of the 40 students who drove cars (either alone or in a car pool), 35 percent drove mid-size cars, 46 percent drove small cars, and 19 percent drove large cars.

An additional finding of this study revealed the miles per gallon averages for all students' cars. Table 1 below reveals that 55 percent of the cars obtained an average of 21 to 30 miles per gallon. Only one-half that number (27 percent) were able to obtain from 10 to 20 miles per gallon. Five of the students indicated that their cars were getting over 30 miles per gallon.

(Continued on next page)

Type lines 11–14 once. Then repeat lines 11–14 or take a series of 1-minute timings.

```
11   The meeting has been rescheduled for 2:45 p.m. next Monday.   12
12   Meet Ms. Quimby at the corner of 25th Avenue and 47th Road.   12
13   Jack Mazer's law office is on First Street or on 12th Road.   12
14   Rebecca allowed 30 to 45 minutes for questions and answers.   12
     |  1  |  2  |  3  |  4  |  5  |  6  |  7  |  8  |  9  |  10  |  11  |  12
```

JOB 138-3. LETTER

Copy is unedited and unarranged; make changes and corrections as you type it. Standard format. Workbook 281–282. Body 67 words.

Mr. Matthew G. Mitchel, Hyde Department Stoer, 4579 Third Avenue, N.E., Saint Paul, MN 55422, Dear Mr. Mitchell:

You have been our best customer since we opened our store in '72. To celebrate *our tenth anniversary this month, we are offering to all our faithful customers a special price on all forms ordered during the month of ~~July~~ June.*

If you would like to place an order for your busness forms during the Month of june, please fill out and return the form by June 1. Yours truly, Mrs. Jean Sands, Manager, Enclosure

PS: I'll see you at approximately eight o'clock on Tuesday and will go with you to the auction at 11 a.m.

LESSON 139

GOALS
- To practice using two comma rules.
- To type two memorandums in which two comma rules are applied.

FORMAT
- Single spacing   60-space line   5-space tab

NUMBERS REVIEW

Type lines 1–6 once applying correct number style. Edit your copy as your teacher reads the answers. Then repeat lines 1–6 from your edited copy.

1 Add precisely four grams of potassium chloride to this liquid.
2 I typed just fourteen letters, twelve memos, and eight reports yesterday.
3 They asked for exactly one thousand dollars for a deposit on any machine.

(Continued on next page)

Commas (Continued)	39	I applied for the job but I have not yet been interviewed.
	40	Buy the new book at Sloan's Bookstore or order it by mail.
	41	Ann included a stamped addressed envelope with her letter.
	42	Ms. Judd wrote a short interesting letter to the engineer.
	43	We are very pleased therefore to hear about the discount.
	44	This new model will be in my opinion our most successful.
	45	For more information on this new policy call Andrea Smith.
	46	Our marketing director Rhonda Pierce developed this plan.
Semicolons	47	Order four dozen more boxes ask about a quantity discount.
	48	The television campaign begins on May 1 it ends on May 30.
	49	He may of course return the merchandise do it right now.
Question Marks	50	Gene Rand completed all the work before he left, didn't he.
	51	Arlene, where do we keep all the chronological file copies.
	52	Will the advertising copy be ready for Wednesday's meeting.
Exclamation Points	53	I cannot believe that Kyle rejected their tremendous offer.
	54	Congratulations on your promotion to director of marketing.
	55	It's true. Our firm was awarded a new government contract.
Quotation Marks	56	We must price this product under $100, said Ms. Holcroft.
	57	He replied, It is not economical to buy small quantities.
	58	Special orders should be stamped For Immediate Attention.
	59	Attach Handle With Care labels on each of the test tubes.

LESSONS 149/150

COMPETENCY CHECK

GOALS
- To type 40/5'/5e.
- To type a long report with footnotes, a letter, a memo, a ruled table, and an invoice.

FORMAT
- Single spacing   60-space line   5-space tab

PREVIEW PRACTICE

Type lines 1 and 2 twice as a preview to the 5-minute timings on page 249.

Accuracy 1 bridges wondered examined structure astronauts overwhelming

Speed 2 section several mixing answer built reign many ever was and

4   11 complaints were received about that defective motor.
5   Sarah bought 4 texts, and Jeffrey bought 5 magazines.
6   The 6 of them will meet at Twelfth Avenue and 8th Street.

x

5-MINUTE TIMINGS

Take two 5-minute timings on lines 7–23.

```
                        1                                        2
7        Commas might be used for more than a dozen purposes in      12
              3                              4
8    our language.  We use them to separate introductory clauses     24
         5                          6                        7
9    from main clauses, we use them to separate items in series,     36
                            8                        9
10   we also use them between clauses joined by conjunctions, we     48
             10                      11                       12
11   use them to show a special emphasis, and so on, and so on.       60
                        13                          14
12        The cousin of the comma is the semicolon.  A semicolon    72
             15                          16
13   can be used between two clauses that have no conjunction to     84
         17                  18                        19
14   join them.  For example:  "Janice left for Spain yesterday;     96
                    20                      21
15   Harold will leave Sunday."  A semicolon can also be used if    108
             22                      23                       24
16   one of the two clauses joined by a conjunction contains one     120
                            25                      26
17   or more commas and could be misread.  For example:  "George    132
                    27                      28
18   plans to attend the session on Monday, Thursday, or Friday;     144
         29                          30                       31
19   and Wednesday all of us will attend."  In addition, a semi-     156
                    32                      33
20   colon can be used just to show a stronger break between two     168
             34                      35                       36
21   clauses, even though a conjunction is used, as follows:  "I     180
                        37                          38
22   insist that we must change this schedule; but you must give     192
                39                      40
23   us newer costs when we meet next time."                         200
     |  1  |  2  |  3  |  4  |  5  |  6  |  7  |  8  |  9  | 10 | 11 | 12    SI 1.47
```

COMMA USAGE REVIEW

1. In a series of three or more words, numbers, phrases, or clauses, use a comma after each item in the series except the last item. In the following sentences, italics identify the items in a series:

    Our West Coast trip will take us to *Seattle*, *Eugene*, and *Helena*.
    She *quoted prices*, *checked bids*, and *prepared estimates*.

2. Use a comma after an introductory clause that begins with *if, as, when, although, since, because*, or a similar conjunction.

    Before Leroy and Carolyn arrive, let's review our agenda.
    Whenever you have time, please come to my office.

Type lines 24–27 once. Then repeat lines 24–27 or take a series of 1-minute timings.

```
24   When Mrs. Ulster arrives, we will discuss her tax problems.     12
25   Amy Zak, Paul Remy, and Bart Owens are the best applicants.     12
26   If the quality is poor, then you should retype these memos.     12
27   George drafted it, Jerry typed it, and Sharon proofread it.     12
     |  1  |  2  |  3  |  4  |  5  |  6  |  7  |  8  |  9  | 10 | 11 | 12
```

x

9   Jolly Flynn was very much puzzled by Alex's quick thinking.   12

10   Why did Professor Black give you a quiz on the major texts?   24

11   Jumping quickly from the taxi, Hazel brushed a woven chair.   36

| 1 | 2 | 3 | 4 | 5 | 6 | 7 | 8 | 9 | 10 | 11 | 12

5-MINUTE TIMING

Take a 5-minute timing on lines 12–28.

12   Hiking is one of the best ways to keep in top physical   12

13   condition.   Not only does it help your vital organs to keep   24

14   working well, it might also help improve your entire mental   36

15   attitude.   It is important that a beginning hiker recognize   48

16   the rules that make hiking more enjoyable.   First, one must   60

17   be comfortable while on the hike.   All the clothing and the   72

18   shoes must fit quite well.   A hiker should always wear good   84

19   shoes that are sturdy and well-fitting socks.   The clothing   96

20   should be very protective for use in rugged country.   Every   108

21   person should learn to keep both arms free while on a hike.   120

22   This means that each hiker must hoist all that equipment on   132

23   a backpack.   Carrying a backpack requires that every person   144

24   must use good posture; otherwise, many aches might develop.   156

25   The beginning hiker should start with short distances.   The   168

26   longer hike should be postponed until the person is in good   180

27   physical condition.   Hiking truly provides a way to explore   192

28   the country and become physically fit.   200

| 1 | 2 | 3 | 4 | 5 | 6 | 7 | 8 | 9 | 10 | 11 | 12   SI 1.48

LANGUAGE ARTS REVIEW

As you type the following groups of sentences, you will be applying a number of language arts rules. Do your best work as you apply the rules in these sentences. Workbook 291–292.

Capitalization

29   you must cross lee, alden, main, center, and grand streets.

30   an african lion, asian tiger, and american cougar are cats.

31   they visited the red river, the caspian sea, and rice lake.

32   dr. kramer, inspector carlisle, and sergeant stabor smiled.

33   your book on regional cooking sells very well in the south.

34   turn north at the intersection; then turn west immediately.

Commas

35   As both of you already know the seminar has been canceled.

36   If you want this to get there fast send it by parcel post.

37   The conference rooms are decorated in red green and blue.

38   The returns were 6.2 7.5 and 7.9 percent on each mailing.

(Continued on next page)

JOB 139-1. INTEROFFICE MEMORANDUM

Standard format (see pages 62 and 110). Workbook 283.

[*To*] All Department Heads, [*From*] Lisa L.   12
Davis, Office Manager, [*Subject*] New Office   20
Layout   21

   As you now know, we will be moving into   31
our new building next year. When the actual   40
move is made, office space will be assigned in   50
accordance with current office space standards   59
used in our company. If you think you will   68
need more space in the new building, please   77
let me know by the 20th.   82

   A copy of the new building blueprint is   91
enclosed so that you may study the aisle space,   100
office layout, and square footage that has been   110
planned.   115

JOB 139-2. INTEROFFICE MEMORANDUM

Standard format. Workbook 283.

TO: Lisa L. Davis, FROM: Rudy T. Barnes, SUBJECT: Office Layout

When I received the new office layout, I realized that the space allowed for my office is 50 square feet less than I now have. If our sales continue to expand as they have been expanding in the past three years, this space will not be sufficient for me. ¶ As you must realize, I cannot function with less than 175 square feet to accommodate files, furniture, and sales research area.

LESSON 140

GOALS
- To type sentences using comma and semicolon rules.
- To type two memorandums in which comma usage and semicolon rules are applied.

FORMAT
- Single spacing   60-space line   5-space tab

COMMA USAGE REVIEW

Type lines 1–4 once, providing the missing commas. Edit your copy as your teacher reads the answers. Then retype lines 1–4 from your edited copy.

1 Rodney Karen or Phil will be able to finish these orders.

2 When you land in Zurich call Jacques at our offices there.

3 We have more in the hall on the shelves and in my closet.

4 As soon as you mix all these ingredients cool this liquid.

COMMA USAGE REVIEW

3. A compound sentence is a sentence that has two independent clauses joined by the conjunction *and, but, or,* or *nor*. Place a comma before the conjunction in a compound sentence.

    Pamela recommended delaying delivery, *but* Angela objected.

4. Place a comma between adjectives that modify the same noun.

    Ms. Franco wrote a *clear, concise* summary.

5. Place a comma after most introductory words and phrases.

    No, she has not yet approved the contract. (Word.)
    Speaking distinctly, Marvin answered each question thoughtfully. (Phrase.)
    For the benefit of the audience, Lisa explained her reasons. (Phrase.)

6. Use commas to set off nonessential elements and nonessential appositives.

    Their offer is an excellent one, *in my opinion*.
    We asked our manager, *Sarah Wells,* for approval.

Paragraph 2

Objectives: Strengthen your qualifications. Express pleasure to be a candidate.

Example: You mentioned that three people were being considered seriously for this secretarial position. I'm very glad to be one of those people. My extensive secretarial experience would prove very beneficial for your company and would provide you with the administrative expertise you requested in the newspaper advertisement.

Practice: Compose and type the second paragraph for a follow-up letter. Use any one or more of the ideas suggested on page 245.

Paragraph 3

Objectives: Express greater interest in the job. Appear optimistic about the decision.

Example: My determination to become a valuable asset to your firm is greater than ever. I look forward to a favorable decision on my employment with your company.

Practice: Compose and type the final paragraph for a follow-up letter. Use any one or more of the ideas suggested on page 245.

JOB 7. FOLLOW-UP LETTER

Compose and type a complete follow-up letter using the three paragraphs you composed as Practice exercises. Add the following parts to complete the letter: (1) return address, (2) date line, (3) inside address, (4) salutation, (5) complimentary close, and (6) signature line.

LESSON 148

LANGUAGE ARTS REVIEW

GOALS
- To type 40/5'/5e.
- To type correctly a series of sentences requiring the application of various language arts rules.

FORMAT
- Single spacing   60-space line   5-space tab

KEYBOARDING SKILLS

Type lines 1–4 once. In line 5, use your tabulator key throughout the entire line to advance from numbers to dashes. Repeat lines 1–4, or take a series of 1-minute timings.

Speed	1 It is now time to take our last final look at all our work.	12
Accuracy	2 A lazy duck quacked before jumping next to a very wise hog.	12
Numbers	3 I typed at 10 and 29 and 38 and 47 and 56 words per minute.	12
Symbols	4 It was stored @ Dock #8, and it sold for $850 (10% profit).	12
Technique	5 10 -- 29 -- 38 -- 47 -- 56 -- 10 --	

| 1 | 2 | 3 | 4 | 5 | 6 | 7 | 8 | 9 | 10 | 11 | 12

"OK" TIMINGS

Type as many "OK" (errorless) timings as possible out of three attempts on lines 6–8. Then repeat the effort on lines 9–11, page 247.

6 Jinx gave back the prize money she won for her quaint doll. 12

7 Dave quickly filled a dozen mixtures in the deep brown jug. 24

8 On the way here, this quick fox jumped back over a gazelle. 36

| 1 | 2 | 3 | 4 | 5 | 6 | 7 | 8 | 9 | 10 | 11 | 12

(Continued on next page)

Type lines 5–9 once. Then repeat lines 5–9 or take a series of 1-minute timings.

```
5  Cora explained it very clearly, but Ann did not understand.   12
6  The tall, modern building on Fifth is now our headquarters.   12
7  At the end of the month–long trial, our attorneys appealed.   12
8  Jan prefers, as you know, working for a magazine publisher.   12
9  Our supervisor, Debra Kovacs, handles this account herself.   12
   |  1  |  2  |  3  |  4  |  5  |  6  |  7  |  8  |  9  |  10  |  11  |  12
```

JOB 140-1. INTEROFFICE MEMORANDUM
Single spacing. Use 50P/60E-space line. Workbook 285.

```
TO:         Nightshift Workers

FROM:       Training Director Jones

SUBJECT:    Writing Seminar
```

Last month we offered a seminar on planning meetings, and this month we will offer one to improve your writing skills. You may attend both sessions this month, but you must get approval from your shift supervisor. This new, exciting session will start on Monday, May 2. You may, if you wish, bring a recorder to the session.

SEMICOLON REVIEW

1. Two independent clauses can be joined by a comma plus *and, but, or,* or *nor.* When no conjunction is used, a semicolon is needed to join the clauses.

    Cora explained it very clearly, but Ann did not understand.
    Cora explained it very clearly; Ann did not understand.

2. If one of the clauses contains commas and a misreading is possible, use a semicolon even if a conjunction is used.

    On our way to San Francisco, we will visit our office in Chicago, Illinois; and Tucson, Arizona, may be added to our itinerary.

Type lines 10–13 once. Then repeat lines 10–13 or take a series of 1-minute timings.

```
10  Abe set the list price; Agnes Loo established the discount.   12
11  Joe wants to meet on May 12; and May 13 is Martha's choice.   12
12  Summer is the zenith of your sales season; winter is quiet.   12
13  Ask Vera for a copy of the agenda; if you prefer, call Tex.   12
    |  1  |  2  |  3  |  4  |  5  |  6  |  7  |  8  |  9  |  10  |  11  |  12
```

JOB 140-2. INTEROFFICE MEMORANDUM
Standard format. Workbook 285.

[*To*] Training Director, [*From*] Wade Reeves, [*Subject*] Writing Seminar

I would like to attend the seminar, but I have an out-of-town trip planned for that day. Could my associate, Gail Swane, attend the seminar in my place?

This seminar will be a unique, exciting one; of course, I want to be sure that one of our office employees will attend it. Ms. Swane, I am sure, will benefit much from the seminar.

COMPOSING FOLLOW-UP LETTERS

The final step in the job application process is writing a follow-up letter. After you have had your interview, you should send the company a written thank you for interviewing you. Note how each numbered paragraph of the letter shown at the right achieves the goals of a follow-up letter.

① In the **opening paragraph,** you should express appreciation for the interview and reaffirm your interest in the job.

② In the **second paragraph,** you may:
   a. Add new information that might be helpful in revealing your qualifications.
   b. Express pleasure at being considered a candidate for the job.
   c. Tell how you feel about the job now that the interview has been completed.

③ In the **final paragraph,** you may do one of the following:
   a. Express even greater interest in the job.
   b. Mention that you are looking forward to a favorable decision.
   c. Make yourself available for a second interview.

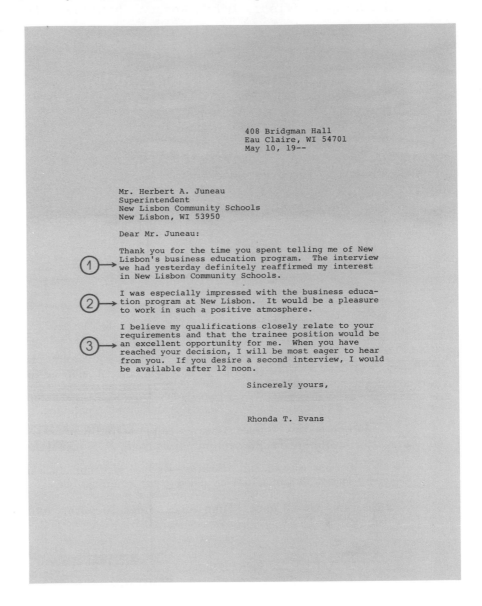

```
                        408 Bridgman Hall
                        Eau Claire, WI 54701
                        May 10, 19--


Mr. Herbert A. Juneau
Superintendent
New Lisbon Community Schools
New Lisbon, WI 53950

Dear Mr. Juneau:

Thank you for the time you spent telling me of New
Lisbon's business education program.  The interview
we had yesterday definitely reaffirmed my interest
in New Lisbon Community Schools.

I was especially impressed with the business educa-
tion program at New Lisbon.  It would be a pleasure
to work in such a positive atmosphere.

I believe my qualifications closely relate to your
requirements and that the trainee position would be
an excellent opportunity for me.  When you have
reached your decision, I will be most eager to hear
from you.  If you desire a second interview, I would
be available after 12 noon.

                        Sincerely yours,


                        Rhonda T. Evans
```

Before you compose and type your own follow-up letter, you will have the opportunity to work on each of the separate paragraphs necessary in a follow-up letter. Study the examples provided here and on the next page, and then compose your own paragraphs for a follow-up letter.

Paragraph 1

Objectives: Say thank you. Reaffirm interest.

Example: Thank you for the interesting time you spent with me this past Wednesday. My visit with you and the other members of your staff made me realize how very enjoyable it would be to work for your company.

Practice: Assume that the letter of application you wrote for Job 5 resulted in an interview. Compose and type the first paragraph of a follow-up letter to the job for which you applied.

LESSON 141

GOALS
- To type 40/5'/5e.
- To type sentences using the question mark, exclamation point, and quotation mark rules.
- To type a one-page report applying the above language arts rules.

FORMAT
- Single spacing   60-space line   5-space and center tabs

COMMA/ SEMICOLON REVIEW

Type lines 1–6 once, providing the missing commas and semicolons. Edit your copy as your teacher reads the answers. Then retype lines 1–6 from your edited copy.

1 When Agnes is absent Bert must approve cash disbursements.
2 Joyce as you know proofread all the statistics carefully.
3 Call Kroft Plumbing and Heating for fast reliable service.
4 This lacquer is highly flammable but that one is harmless.
5 Excell Products sells fertilizer seeds and bulbs by mail.
6 The list price is $17.50 quantity discounts are available.

5-MINUTE TIMINGS

Take two 5-minute timings on lines 7–24.

7 It's true for many of us that a very troublesome punc-   12
8 tuation placement rule is where we should put the quotation   24
9 marks when they're used with periods or commas. If we just   36
10 follow some very basic rules, we'll soon recognize that the   48
11 exact placement of a quotation mark is really quite an easy   60
12 thing for us all to remember.   66
13 The first general rule we should recall is that commas   78
14 and periods always go inside the closing quotation mark. A   90
15 good example would be to place in quotation marks the final   102
16 word in this sentence, such as "this." Notice that even if   114
17 the last word in the sentence is placed in quotation marks,   126
18 the period is typed before that final quotation mark. When   138
19 quotation marks appear in the middle of the typed line, the   150
20 comma at the end of that quotation would appear as follows: 162
21 The package was labeled "Pizza," so the delivery person was   174
22 very careful not to jar the package when it was moved. All   186
23 of us should have no problems in improving the placement of   198
24 the marks.   200

| 1 | 2 | 3 | 4 | 5 | 6 | 7 | 8 | 9 | 10 | 11 | 12   SI 1.47

Application forms vary from one company to another, but all ask for basically the same information. The illustrations at the right show two sides of an application form. This form, like most others, asks the applicant to provide information as follows (note that the numbers correspond to those included with the illustrations):

① **Date.** Include the month, day, and year.

② **Personal Data.** Be sure to provide your complete permanent address (and temporary address, if applicable)—your street address, city, state, and ZIP Code.

③ **Social Security Number.** Be prepared to fill in your social security number, because every person must have one when applying for a job.

④ **Type of Work.** A company will often inquire as to the type of position you are seeking. You may also be asked the salary you expect and the date you would be available for work. If you have special machine skills, you might be asked to identify your competencies on these machines.

⑤ **Education.** Many application forms ask for the name of your high school as well as any colleges or business schools, the dates you attended, and the courses you completed.

⑥ **Health.** Answer honestly all questions on health. The questions are essential for insurance purposes, as well as to find out who should be notified in case of medical emergency.

⑦ **Employment History.** Employers want to know about previous work experience. Past work experience may help you obtain a better entry-level position, so be as honest and as thorough as you can in completing this section.

⑧ **References.** To complete this section, use the list of references that you included in your résumé. References should be people such as past employers and former teachers, who can attest to your character, work habits, and work potential.

⑨ **Signature.** DO NOT FORGET TO SIGN THE APPLICATION FORM—and date it, too, if necessary.

JOB 6. APPLICATION FORMS

Apply for a job for which you are qualified. Workbook 287–290.

Application Form, Page 1

Application Form, Page 2

REVIEW OF EXCLAMATION POINT, QUESTION MARK, AND QUOTATION MARKS

1. Use an exclamation point (!) to show surprise, disbelief, or strong feeling.

   Good luck! I wish you success with your new business!

2. Use a question mark (?) at the end of a question. Note that an incomplete sentence may sometimes be used as a question.

   When will the announcement be official? Today?

3. Use quotation marks (") for someone's exact words and for words that require emphasis. Do not use quotations for short *restatements* of someone's exact words.

   He shouted, "Cancel this order!" (Exact words.)
   Is this the so-called "priceless masterpiece"? (Emphasis.)

Note: The exclamation point in the first example goes *before* the quotation mark because the entire quotation is an exclamation. In the second example, the question mark goes *after* the quotation mark because the words in quotations do *not* make up a question.

Type lines 25–28 once. Then repeat lines 25–28 or take a series of 1-minute timings.

```
25  Congratulations!  We are glad to hear about your promotion!  12
26  Have the reports about that merger been verified?  By whom?  12
27  Jan said, "That magazine is famous for excellent features!"  12
28  Do you think that Kent will have to "work another miracle"?  12
    |  1  |  2  |  3  |  4  |  5  |  6  |  7  |  8  |  9  |  10  |  11  |  12
```

JOB 141-1. BOUND REPORT

Standard format (see pages 76, 78, and 125).

TYPING I LANGUAGE ARTS SKILLS   18
By [your name]   34

Perhaps you have asked   41
yourself this question: "Why   47
is it important for me to learn   54
all these language arts rules?"   60
The answer is that the punctua-   66
tion and style rules that you are   73
learning in this book will help   79
you to communicate more clearly.   86
No, you do not have to become   94
an "expert" in grammar and   100
punctuation; you will have ref-   106
erences that you can use to check   112
rules. But you do have to master   119
the basics -- those rules which   125

you will use regularly as you type   132
letters, memos, and reports. Let's   139
review some of these rules.   145

PUNCTUATION RULES   151
We have studied the comma   157
(and a few of its uses), the semicolon,   165
the question mark, the exclamation point,   173
and quotation marks. We have seen   180
many of their most common uses.   187

OTHER RULES   191
In addition to the punctuation   199
rules, we have studied capitalization,   206
number usage, and spacing rules. All   214
these have helped us write more clearly.   222

JOB 5. LETTER OF APPLICATION COMPOSED FROM A CLASSIFIED AD

Compose a letter of application from the information provided in one of the two classified ads below. Select the ad that most closely resembles the type of position for which you would like to apply and for which you are better qualified.

SECRETARY

The Dallas Morning News has an opening in the Data Processing Department for a secretary.

All interested applicants must type 50 wam, take shorthand at 80 wam, use transcribing equipment, and have at least two years of secretarial training and/or experience. You must be a self-motivator and work with little or no supervision.

We offer excellent working conditions and company benefits.

Send a letter of application and résumé to:

**PERSONNEL OFFICE
THE DALLAS MORNING NEWS
400 WEST ABRAMS STREET
DALLAS, TX 75214**

An Equal Opportunity Employer

FILE CLERK

Southwest Oil & Gas Company has an opening for a file clerk.

This is an entry-level position within our accounting file room. Qualifications include dependability and willingness to learn. Applicant must have had some training in basic numeric and alphabetic filing procedures.

Excellent benefits include a comprehensive medical and dental program, disability income protection, and free parking.

If interested, send a letter of application and résumé to:

**PERSONNEL DEPARTMENT
SOUTHWEST OIL & GAS COMPANY
504 STATE STREET
TEMPE, AZ 85281**

SOGCO is an Equal Opportunity Employer

FILLING OUT APPLICATION FORMS

The third step in the job application process is the completion of an application form. Most business firms have the applicant fill out an application form either before or after the interview.

Before viewing a sample application form, you might find the following suggestions helpful when you are asked to complete such a form:

1. *Be neat and accurate.* Above all else, complete the application form neatly, and be sure to check for spelling and/or grammatical errors. Make any corrections carefully.

2. *Follow instructions.* Print neatly. If you are asked to type, then be sure to align all the typewritten responses on the lines provided for that purpose. Try to complete all the blanks; but if certain items do not apply to you, print or type "Not Applicable" or "N/A" in the space provided for your answer.

3. *Do not omit continuous dates.* If you are asked to supply the dates you attended high school, be sure to enter all dates—from the beginning school year to the ending school year. If you enter your years of employment, do not omit any years that you worked.

Note: There will be many differences on application forms from different companies. Many companies are in the process of revising their application blanks to comply with existing or pending regulations regarding nondiscriminatory questions. Employers are no longer permitted to ask for the specific age of a person (age ranges are permitted because employers need to know whether an applicant is under age and needs a work permit or is eligible for social security benefits). Other questions that may not be asked are those regarding marital status, religion, and nationality.

LESSON 142

GOALS
- To identify which of two motions is more difficult for you and to practice them proportionately.
- To type 40/5'/5e.

FORMAT
- Single spacing   60-space line

QUOTATION MARKS WITH OTHER PUNCTUATION

Type lines 1–4 once, providing the missing exclamation points and question marks. Edit your copy as your teacher reads the answers. Then retype lines 1–4 from your edited copy.

1 Why did Tom and Flo call this design sketch "too juvenile".
2 John asked, "Where is the new copy for the advertisements."
3 Mrs. Provenzano excitedly yelled, "Call the police--hurry."
4 How Bob quibbled over those requisitions marked "Rejected".

PRETEST

Take a 1-minute timing on lines 5–7. Then take a 1-minute timing on lines 8–10. Circle and count your errors on each timing.

5 Barbara was last seen at the new dress sale late last week. 12
6 Ada stated she had traded the car off after it was wrecked. 24
7 Gerald prefers trees that have very few leaves or branches. 36
   | 1 | 2 | 3 | 4 | 5 | 6 | 7 | 8 | 9 | 10 | 11 | 12
8 It is their opinion that Jimmy will join the union at noon. 12
9 Phyllis knows her pumpkins will soon look like they should. 24
10 Phillip enjoys looking at and collecting only common coins. 36

PRACTICE

In which Pretest did you make more errors? If in lines 5–7, type lines 11–15 below six times and lines 16–20 three times. If in lines 8–10, reverse the procedure.

11 treat severe dresses cabbage afterward addressee exaggerate
12 trade tweed wears agreed career starts assets awards better
13 cares carts darts deeds fares grade grass great reads staff
14 between pleases assure tassel passes tease refer meets wash
15 sixteen referee pretty letter masses meter sewer cases fast

16 jolly imply phylon minimum million homonym opinion nonunion
17 poppy hilly onion pupil pulpy nylon milky phony plump lumpy
18 hill pink hook pool moon noon join milk mill upon look junk
19 imp import impose imposes imports impress imposing imported
20 ill chills drills fulfill willing billing goodwill waybills

POSTTEST

Repeat the Pretest to see how much your skill has improved.

5-MINUTE TIMINGS

Take two 5-minute timings on lines 7–23, page 232.

2110 Ellen Court
Memphis, TN 38123
May 22, 19--

Mr. Samuel Davis
A to Z Contractors, Inc.
4701 Hanna Boulevard
Memphis, TN 38123

Dear Mr. Davis:

① One of your employees, Chris Corsi, mentioned that you have a secretarial position available at A to Z Contractors, Inc. I would like to be considered as an applicant for this position.

② My typing rate of 65 words a minute and my shorthand speed of 120 words a minute will enable me to serve your company as a competent office worker. In addition, I possess a knowledge of filing procedures and have received special training on telephone usage, as you will see in the enclosed resume.

③ In addition to these specific office skills, I have also been an active participant at several regional competitions for parliamentary procedure. These activities have provided me with valuable human relations and oral presentation skills.

④ I am definitely interested in working for A to Z Contractors. I will telephone your office on June 4 to arrange for an interview with you at your convenience. If you wish to speak with me before that date, please telephone me at 901-555-1212.

Sincerely,

Janice L. Dale

Enclosure

LETTER OF APPLICATION

UNIT 24 APPLYING FOR A JOB

GOAL
- To format and type papers needed when applying for a job.

FORMAT
- Margins and tabs as needed

Now that you are near the end of your first typing course, you may soon be looking for a part-time or full-time job. In applying for a job, you will need to use your typewriting skill (1) to prepare a résumé, (2) to compose a letter of application, (3) to complete an application form, and (4) to prepare a follow-up letter. Each of these tasks is discussed below and on the following pages.

FORMATTING RÉSUMÉS

Once you have identified a job you want to apply for, your first step is to prepare a *résumé*—a summary of your training, background, and qualifications for the job.

A résumé contains different sections, depending on what information you want to include about your education, experience, personal background, and so on. The résumé illustrated on the right and on page 239 shows the basic information to include. Read directions A through F below and on page 239 for formatting résumés. Follow the margin settings, spacing directions, and tab setting shown below the illustration on the right.

Ⓐ **Heading.** For easy identification, begin the résumé with your name, address, and telephone number. Include your area code.

Ⓑ **Education.** If you have little business experience, list your education after your name, address, and telephone number. The education section should begin with the highest level of education you have completed—that is, all items should be listed in *reverse* chronological order (the most recent first). For each entry, you should include the name and address of the school, any diplomas earned and the years in which you earned them, the year you graduated, and your major area of study.

Ⓒ **Experience.** If your experience is stronger than your education, include it after your name, address, and telephone number. If not, place the experience section after the education section. For each job you include, give the name, address, and telephone number of the company, the dates of employment, your job title(s), the name and title of your supervisor, and a brief description of the duties you performed.

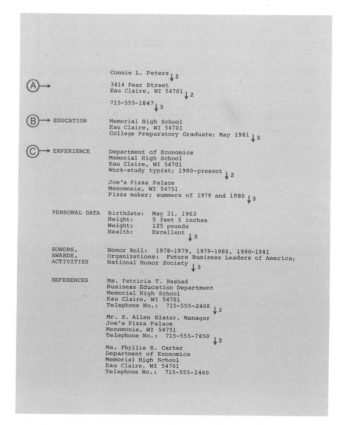

Top Margin: *On page 1, 9 lines; on continuation pages, 6 lines.*
Left/Right Margins: *10P/12E.*
Bottom Margin: *6 to 9 lines.*

Single-space within each entry; double-space and triple-space as indicated. Use 15-space tab.

FORMATTING LETTERS OF APPLICATION

The résumé is a summary of your skills and experiences. When you send your résumé to a prospective employer, you must, of course, send a covering letter—the *letter of application*. Together, the résumé and the letter of application are your introduction to the company.

Limit your letter of application to one page—about four paragraphs, as shown in the letter on page 242. Note the exact purpose of each paragraph:

① **Introduction:** Tell the reader the purpose of the letter, which job you are applying for, and how you learned of the job.

② **Second paragraph:** Give special consideration to the qualifications you have that make you especially valuable in this position and the skills you have that can help the employer and the company. Refer to the enclosed résumé.

③ **Third paragraph:** Mention special skills that set you apart from other applicants. (Are you exceptionally well organized?)

④ **Final paragraph:** Restate your interest in the job. Ask for an interview; give the date on which you will call to set up that interview. Include your home phone number so that the employer can reach you easily.

JOB 3. LETTER OF APPLICATION

Type the letter of application shown on page 242. Standard format (see page 87 for typing a personal business letter). Use plain paper. Line 50P/60E. Center tab.

COMPOSING A LETTER OF APPLICATION

Before you compose and type your own complete letter of application, you will have the opportunity to work on each of the separate paragraphs necessary in a letter of application. Read and study the examples provided in the following paragraphs, and then compose individual paragraphs for your own letter of application.

Paragraph 1

Objectives: Specify the job applied for and mention how you found out about it.

Example: I would like to apply for the position of clerk-typist for your company. My high school English teacher, Ms. Kathleen Hutchinson, informed me of this opening.

Practice: Compose and type the first paragraph for a letter of application in which you are applying for a position as clerk-typist. Add any information that you think is necessary.

Paragraph 2

Objective: List relevant skills.

Example: The experience I gained as a typist for my father's insurance agency qualifies me for the clerk-typist position in your company, as most of my duties involved daily use of typing, filing, and communications skills. These skills would be especially beneficial to your company.

Practice: Compose and type the second paragraph for a letter of application. Include specific clerk-typist skills you possess which would be beneficial to the company.

Paragraph 3

Objective: Convince the reader that you have special skills. Sell yourself!

Example: My secretarial skills and my English skills are well above average, and I feel that I could perform any of the jobs I would be called upon to do with a minimum of error and with a high degree of competence.

Practice: Compose and type the third paragraph for a letter of application. Identify in this paragraph any special skills that you have.

Paragraph 4

Objectives: Restate your interest. Arrange an interview. Give your telephone number.

Example: It would be a pleasure to work for your company as a clerk-typist. If you wish to interview me for this position, please telephone me at (301) 555-4774 any weekday after 3 p.m.

Practice: Compose and type the fourth paragraph for a letter of application. Review the illustration on page 241 to find out what information you should include in this paragraph.

JOB 4. LETTER OF APPLICATION

Compose and type a complete letter of application using the four paragraphs you just composed. Standard format. Add the following parts to complete the letter: (1) date line, (2) return address, (3) inside address, (4) salutation, (5) complimentary close, (6) signature line, and (7) enclosure notation.

FORMATTING RÉSUMÉS
(Continued)

(D) **Personal Data.** By law, employers cannot ask certain questions—for example, an applicant's age. Thus many applicants choose *not* to include a personal data section. If you do choose to include a personal data section, you might wish to have such items as your height, weight, social security number, health, birth date, and marital status. If used, this section should be placed after the Education and Experience sections.

(E) **Honors, Awards, and Activities.** Achievements mentioned in this section may give you an "edge" over other applicants. You should include your participation in clubs and organizations, any honors and awards you have received, and any special recognitions you have earned. You may also want to include your scholastic placement in your graduating class (such as "top 10 percent").

(F) **References.** The final section of a résumé lists the names, job titles, addresses, and telephone numbers of at least three persons who can tell a prospective employer what kind of worker you are. For this reason, most people use teachers, former supervisors, and former employers as references. Before you use anyone as a reference, you *must* get permission from each individual to use his or her name. Another option for the references section is to simply include this statement: "References will be furnished upon request."

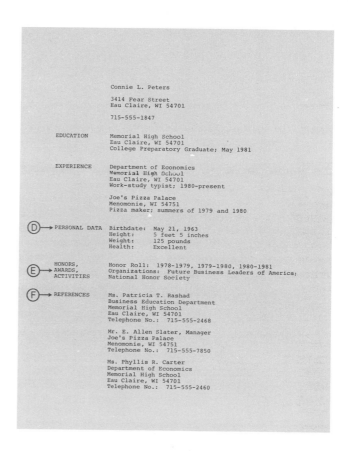

ALTERNATE FORMAT FOR RÉSUMÉS

The illustration on page 240 shows some alternate formats for the sections of a résumé. The standard format may be changed by using one or more of the alternate features.

(A) The name, address, and telephone number are centered between the left and right margins.

(B) Section headings are typed in initial capitals and are underscored.

(C) Pertinent business courses are identified in the educational background section.

(D) No references are given. Instead, a statement indicates that references will be provided upon request.

Note: No personal data section is included.

JOB 1. RÉSUMÉ

Type the résumé appearing on page 240, using the format described and illustrated on pages 238–239.

JOB 2. YOUR RÉSUMÉ

Prepare a résumé for yourself, using the guidelines introduced on pages 238 and 239. Include all sections that are pertinent and applicable to your background and experience. Do not include a section if you have no entries to place in that section. Use your typing teacher's name as one of your three references.

(A)

MARTINA VALDEZ
↓2

4101 Fuller Apartments
Clio, MI 48420
313-555-2714
↓3

(B) → Educational
Background

Clio High School; Clio, MI 48420. Graduated
June 1982.
↓2

Major: Clerical/Secretarial
↓2

Grade Point Average: 3.66
↓2

Business Subjects:
↓2

Accounting
Typing (75 wam)
Shorthand (120 wam)

(C) → Business Machines
Business English
Business Law
Steno/Clerical Lab
↓3

Employment
History

Rathjen Moving and Storage
471 Vienna Road
Flushing, MI 48477
Telephone No.: 313-555-5420
↓2

June 1982-Present
Position: General Office Clerk
Supervisor: Joyce Jones, Secretary
↓2

Duties: Composing and typing routine correspondence; filing customer records; placing and
answering telephone calls; preparing invoices
(part time employment)
↓3

(D) → References

A complete set of references will be furnished
upon request.

RÉSUMÉ